W9-ALT-593

The Management of Operations

Wiley Series in Management

The Management of Operations

JACK R. MEREDITH *University of Cincinnati*

THOMAS E. GIBBS *Potter and Company, CPA's*

JOHN WILEY & SONS *New York Chichester Brisbane Toronto*

Library of Congress Cataloging in Publication Data:

Meredith, Jack R
The management of operations.

(Wiley series in management)
Includes indexes.
1. Management. 2. Production management.
I. Gibbs, Thomas E., joint author. II. Title.

HD31.M3976 658.5′4 79-24512
ISBN 0-471-02574-7

Printed in the United States of America

10 9 8 7 6 5 4 3 2 1

TO CAROL AND JUDI

About the Authors

JACK MEREDITH received his undergraduate degrees in engineering and mathematics from Oregon State University. He obtained his MBA and his Ph.D. in business administration from the University of California, Berkeley, with a major in production management. He has held positions with Ampex, Hewlett-Packard, TRW, and Douglas Aircraft Company, and possesses extensive service sector experience through grants, consulting, research, and executive seminars.

Currently Associate Professor of Production/Operations Management and Director of Operations Management at the University of Cincinnati, he is also editor of *The Operations Management Newsletter,* associate editor of the new *Journal of Operations Management,* and reviewer for *Decision Sciences, Management Science, American Journal of Public Health,* and *Operations Research.* He has written articles for *Operations Research, Management Science, Computers and Industrial Engineering, Health Care Systems,* and *American Journal of Public Health* and is the author of *Fundamentals of Management Science* (with E. Turban) and *The Hospital Game.* Professor Meredith's research interests include service sector operations, scheduling applications in industry and services, and applications of computer technology to production. He is a member of TIMS, ORSA, AIDS, AIIE, AcM, APICS, and ASME.

THOMAS E. GIBBS is Principal and Functional Coordinator for Management Advisory Services with Potter & Company, CPA's. He has served as Assistant Professor of Accounting at the University of Kentucky, as Assistant Professor of Health Care Administration at Florida International University, and as Adjunct Professor of Public Administration in the NOVA University "Fly a Prof" Program.

He received his Ph.D. from the University of Cincinnati. He has consulted with numerous small businesses, governmental units, and health care organizations regarding information system development, computer selection, and software design. He is also Editor of *MAS Communication,* the newsletter of the Management Advisory Services Section of the American Accounting Association and Chairman Elect of the Section. He is the author of more than 30 articles, some of which have appeared in *The Journal of Systems Management, The Accounting Review,* and *The Internal Auditor.*

Preface

Crucial changes are currently taking place in the U.S. and world economies, and in the global society. These changes demand a new generation of managers. Clearly, considerations such as pollution, energy, occupational safety and health, and affirmative action pose significant managerial challenges. But beyond these challenges lie the explosion in technological ability, vast increases in knowledge, and the tremendous growth of services.

The greater levels of sophistication demanded of today's managers is indicated by the following quotation describing the skills a manager must now possess:

. . .communicating skills, leadership, persistence, tact, ability to learn—and yes, even hold a more encompassing view of the human condition. But what is not well understood, even by many counselors is that these things are not sufficient for successful industry careers in and of themselves. Technical knowledge relevant to industrial problem solving is paramount. *

It is not enough that a manager be able to direct people effectively, although this is certainly necessary to a manager's success. First and foremost the manager must know what it is that the people he or she supervises are supposed to do! The manager's responsibility is knowing *what* it takes to economically produce a product or a service and *how* to get it to the recipient when it is due—whether the recipient is a customer, a patient, a client, a passenger, or a pupil. This is the concern of operations management, the subject of this book.

Operations management, the management of an organization's operations to produce a product or a service, has had a long, and recently rather turbulent, history. Originally known as "manufacturing management," it was largely responsible for revolutionizing the production of goods in modern society and, thus, providing a standard of living that was undreamed of a few generations earlier. In the late 1950s and 1960s operations management came under the growing influence of the management science movement and was oriented toward the application of quantitative models to the operations of all kinds of product organizations. During this time the term "production management" emerged to signify the applicability of the field beyond the factories.

At the end of the 1960s the field expanded again to include operations in nonindustrial organizations: banks, public agencies, hospitals, stores, and schools. Al-

* Edwin A. Butenhof, Eastman Kodak Company, in *American Way,* November 1978, p. 75.

though "production" remains an integral part of the field—and of this text—the name has once again been changed to "operations management" to communicate this expanded area of concern.

Unfortunately, the manufacturing/production/operations management textbooks have had a difficult time keeping up with the changing pace. Many are strictly "manufacturing" texts (for which a great need still exists). Most, however, are "production" books, with some service examples added to illustrate the newest direction of the field. Very few provide a "generic" perspective for viewing the operations of every kind of organization in terms of an integrated, logical structure. It is this need for a generic orientation that motivated us to write this book.

Although our primary goal is to provide a generic view of the management of operations, we combine this goal with some additional objectives.

First, we present a unified structure of organizations, and the operations within them, that we believe to be clear and logical to the student. Every topic in the book, and every chapter, fits into this overall structure.

Second, we emphasize the relationship of operations to the other areas within modern organizations, and vice versa: marketing, personnel, finance, accounting, and the like. We are concerned throughout with the interrelationship of all areas of an organization and how the actions in each affect the others. This is in contrast to "departmentalized" textbooks where these areas are treated as self-contained and independent—thus unintentionally transmitting an erroneous view to the student.

Finally, we base the text discussion on the *functional operations* of management instead of on the *tools* for managers. We have noticed in our classes that even when quantitative tools are included with the functional concepts in a chapter, the students tend to focus on the tools rather than on the concepts. Hence, this book does not introduce a quantitative tool for its own sake, nor does it refrain from introducing a tool more than once where appropriate. In addition, every functional chapter is subdivided into a *Concepts* portion, where the important operations functions are communicated, and a *Tools and Applications* portion, where the concepts are further detailed and illustrated. This emphasis on a functional view is to give students a clear understanding of the situation and functions, as well as the problems, of the operations manager.

The main characteristics of this book are thus as follows.

1. *A Generic Framework.* We present a broad view of management through discussion, examples, and terminology. (For instance, in conceptual discussions, we use the terms "organization" instead of "company," "recipient" instead of "customer," and so on.) However, we also provide specificity through numerous examples: farms, fire departments, hospitals, funeral homes, libraries, manufacturers, typing services, hotels, schools, and insurance companies.

2. *A Design Approach.* In presenting the material we adopt a planning framework of the management function. Our view is thus from the perspective of how one would *design*:

The output itself.
The process to generate the output.
The systems to acquire the required resources.
The control systems to maintain the productive process.

These topics constitute the four parts into which the text is divided.

The direction of flow here is important. This is not the descriptive ("plant tour") orientation of "inputs-process-outputs" but is, instead, one that reflects a managerial viewpoint that leads logically step by step from goals to potential outputs to transformation process to inputs. In addition to helping the student understand *why* the operations are designed as they are, as well as *how* they are designed, we believe that this approach is superior to others in giving a more *integrated* view of the organization, and is thus inherently more generic.

3. *A Functional Orientation.* We focus on the operations functions under discussion and not on the quantitative techniques that are available to aid in addressing and analyzing those functions. Although we place the more complex tools such as linear prgramming and queuing theory in the *Tools and Applications* portion of each chapter, we do not avoid elementary quantitative ideas in the *Concepts* portion if they help to illustrate the concepts we are discussing.

4. *Interfaces.* To aid in relating other important areas of the organization to the operations function we include short "interface" chapters in the appropriate sections of the text, as dictated by the logical flow of the design framework. These chapters are *not* summaries of other courses that the student will be taking, but rather consist of selective information about those aspects of other areas that affect operations, and vice versa. Although in a very short course these chapters may be omitted without interfering with the flow of operations concepts, we recommend that they at least be assigned to the student for outside reading.

5. *An Introductory Level.* We stress practical, fundamental concepts in a clear fashion that will be relevant to students both during their current courses of study and later during their careers. In addition, the discussion should be easily understood by students from a variety of disciplines. Realistic examples, current news articles, short cases, marginal summaries and, on occasion, cartoons are included to convey the timeliness and significance of the operations management field.

Every chapter begins with a set of learning objectives and concludes with a self-review test and a number of problems concerning those objectives. This material facilitates the grasp of important concepts. Also included are discussion questions that probe into conceptual tangents and deeper issues raised by the chapter discussion.

A prerequisite to knowing a field is an understanding of its basic terminology. To aid the student in this task, a list of key terms is given at the end of each chapter for self-testing along with the page references where these terms are introduced and defined. A glossary of key terms is included in the appendix.

Finally, a case is included in every operations chapter to help the student understand the application of the concepts. Theory is one thing; application is often something else, as students typically learn on their first job. These brief cases are meant to ease that transition and to give a realistic perspective to students' learning.

We thank all those who were instrumental in guiding the development of this book. El Buffa's initial encouragement and continuing support was invaluable. Constructive criticism was given throughout the development of the manuscript by Sam Seward, Mike Maggard, Ed Heard, Steve Bolander, Jim Cox and, in particular, by Carol Meredith, an ever available critic and sounding board for our ideas.

Jack R. Meredith
Thomas E. Gibbs

Contents

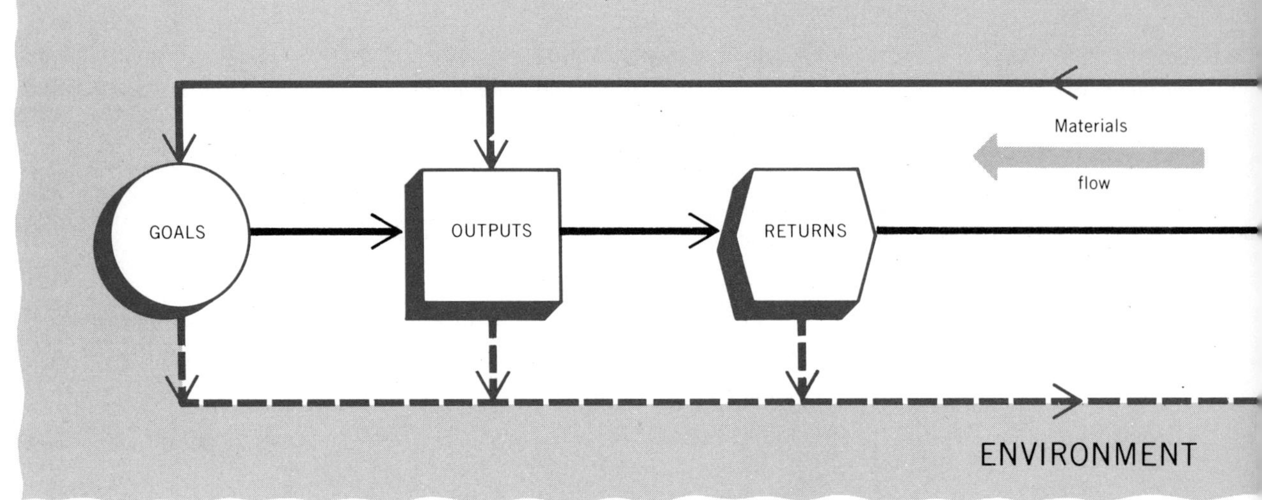

Chapter 1

Managing Organizational Operations

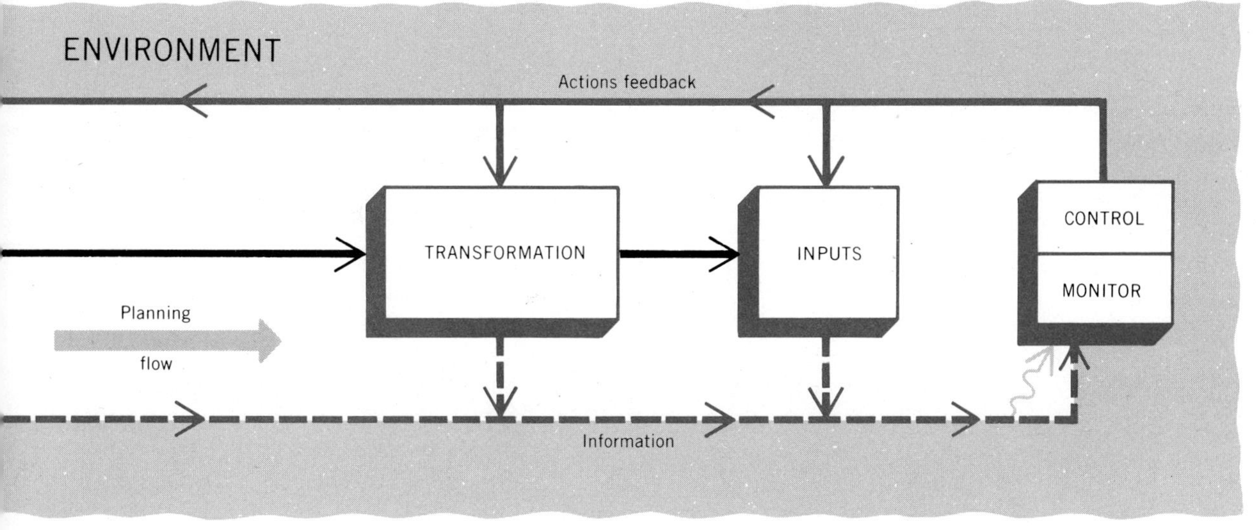

LEARNING OBJECTIVES

By the completion of this chapter the student should

1. Have an understanding of the nature of organizations and the basis for their formation.
2. Appreciate the importance and functions of management in organizations and be aware of the alternate views, or "schools," of management.
3. Know the historical development of operations management from early organizations through factories to modern service organizations.
4. Realize the importance of the recent emergence of the service sector in our economy and the role of productivity in this sector.
5. Understand how transformation operations are planned and the difference between the traditional descriptive approach and the design approach.
6. Have an appreciation for the breadth of operations functions and how they relate to other functional areas in the organization.

Man learned early in his evolution that cooperation with his fellow humans was the only way to achieve many important desires that he could not achieve by himself—desires for special foods, certain belongings, acceptance and fellowship, safety, and so on. The instruments for such cooperation to achieve these desires were *organizations* which, broadly defined, are groups of elements structured by policies, in greater or lesser complexity, to guide the members of a group in their activities. Typical productive organizations are easily envisioned, from Viking explorers to the Aztec Indian Nation to modern international businesses. But children's play groups and housewarming parties are also organizations for satisfying human desires, only the needs are slightly different.

This book is concerned with the *management of organizational* **operations**, that is, the management of the organizational *transformation processes*, or activities, which convert **inputs** to **outputs**. In particular, we are interested in the *goals* of the organization, the *design* of its operations (and policies), and the proper *management* of these operations to achieve the organization's goals.

Coordination is one function of management.

Any group endeavor requires *management* if it is to be effective in the attainment of its goals. Coordination of effort is the key to group success and management performs this function, among others. Even in ancient times management's role was noted occasionally, as illustrated by this biblical report of adept inventory management.

Let Pharaoh do this, and let him appoint officers over the land, and take up the fifth part of the land of Egypt in the seven plenteous years. And let them gather all the food of those good years that come, and lay up corn under the hand of Pharaoh, and let them keep food in the cities. And that food shall be for store to the land against the seven years of famine, which shall be in the land of Egypt; that the land perish not through the famine [Genesis, chapter 41, paragraphs 34, 35, and 36].

The new institution of management.

We also know [8, pp. 78–81] that the early Egyptian, Chinese, and Greek scholars conversed at length regarding management and administration. The need in early times for management becomes obvious when one considers such projects as the pyramids, the Great Wall of China, and the wars of Alexander. Nevertheless, the *function* of management received little recognition in these early times and reports of notable achievements in management were the exception rather than the rule. As the early handicraft* system evolved into craft guilds and then factories, however, the role of management as a necessary function gained new importance and recognition. Peter Drucker, an outstanding management scholar of today, has commented [5, pp. 3,4] that

The emergence of management as an essential, a distinct and a leading institution is a pivotal event in social history. Rarely, if ever, has a new basic institution, a new leading group, emerged as fast as has management since the turn of this century. Rarely in human history has a new institution proven indispensable so quickly; and even less often has a

* Made by hand, that is, before mass production.

new institution arrived with so little opposition, so little disturbance, so little controversy. . . . Management, which is the organ of society specifically charged with making resources productive, that is, with the responsibility for organized economic advance, therefore, reflects the basic spirit of the modern age. It is, in fact, indispensable—and this explains why, once begotten, it grew so fast and with so little opposition.

In this chapter we first investigate the nature of organizations and their management. We consider the organization as a system and describe its characteristics and forms. We next look at the need for management and the range of functions encompassed in managing. The historical development of operations management (OM) is then presented and the importance of the growth of services to the development of **generic** OM is noted. Finally, we sketch the process of designing and managing the organization's operations to form a general outline of the material to be covered in the remaining chapters of the text.

1.1 THE NATURE OF ORGANIZATIONS

Why humans form organizations.

Humans are social animals. We automatically form ourselves into social groups such as families, tribes, sororities, and clubs. It is no wonder then that faced with certain needs and desires, people learned to organize to satisfy them. But, humans are also rational beings and will only become members of organizations if doing so contributes, in some way, to their own personal goals. We join churches and civic organizations, become members of sailing clubs and baseball teams, and accept employment in businesses or other organizations because these activities aid in achieving our own needs and desires.

Development of an interdependent economy.

Throughout history people have formed organizations to satisfy individual or **collective goals**, and disbanded or left those organizations when they were no longer of use or when organizational goals conflicted with personal goals. As civilization advanced from a family-centered farming economy to a handicraft-trading economy, people began to recognize the advantages of specialization and trade. Rather than producing all of its own goods and services a family could often produce, with less total effort, an excess of a commodity for which it had a special advantage and trade the excess with others for desired commodities. Trade thus bound families closer together in cooperation since each family became more dependent on the others' commodities. As people making compatible commodities naturally began working with each other, the informal handicraft organizations evolved into the craft guilds of the Middle Ages and then into factories.

Classifying Organizational Systems

Organizational classification scheme.

Organizations can be classified according to three major characteristics.

Whether their outputs are **services** or physical products.

Whether they are privately owned and controlled or publicly (governmentally) controlled.

Whether they are operated for profit or are **not-for-profit**.*

Table 1.1 provides a three-way breakdown of some major organizations according to these characteristics. Note that some sections of this table are relatively sparse. Also note that some organizations (schools, hospitals) appear in a number of forms such as profit, not-for-profit, private, and public.

Public sector organizations are typically not-for-profit as compared to private sector organizations which are usually "for profit." However, there are many private organizations which are also not-for-profit, such as foundations, societies, churches, clubs, professional associations, and civic groups. These organizations, many of them corporations like their for-profit counterparts, may produce some goods but primarily provide services for their constituents. Let us now consider the management of these various types of organizations.

1.2 THE MANAGEMENT OF ORGANIZATIONS

Whether an organization is a church, grocery store, government agency, or baseball team, management must take place. Managers who operate in each of these organizations may face completely different environments, may require different technical skills or knowledge, may be confronted with different problems, and may have different scopes of authority, power, or influence, but each one of them will carry on similar basic managerial functions.

The generic nature of management.

In recognition of this universal, or **generic**, nature of management the bulletin *Program in the Graduate School of Administration* of the University of California, Irvine (1975), states

Three basic assumptions underlie the School's philosophy of graduate education. First, there are significant phenomena and problems common to business-industrial, educational, and governmental organizations; second, a common set of disciplines, concepts, techniques, and technologies can be found which are appropriate to a wide range of organizational or scholarly roles; third, many administrators in the future will work in more than one of the three arenas during their careers.

The brochure concludes

. . . future leaders will be able to communicate effectively and move easily from one kind of organizational unit to another . . .

Management Functions

The basic managerial functions listed below describe the continuing managerial process of attempting to create a working environment in which individuals can pursue

* We avoid the term "nonprofit" here because of its frequent association with private organizations. Thus a "not-for-profit" organization may be either public or private.

TABLE 1.1 THREE-WAY CLASSIFICATION OF ORGANIZATIONS

		Profit	Not-for-Profit
Private	Services	Ambulance Hospital School Janitorial Bank Legal office Transportation Airlines Insurance Realtor Mafia Waste disposal Casino Theater	Hospital School Union Charity Church Foundations Civic Social Health Professional society
Private	Products	Manufacturer Retailer Tailor Bakery Mining Drugstore Publisher Producer Farm Restaurant Utility	Blood bank Research foundation (research reports)
Public	Services	University executive seminar programs Federal reserve loans to member banks	Fire department Armed forces Library Hospital School Welfare/counseling Sanitation Legislature Waste disposal Justice Post office Ambulance
Public	Products	Police auctions State license plates	Corps of engineers Water works Public works TVA (electricity)

organizational goals in the most efficient and effective manner. Numerous management scholars, starting with Henri Fayol, a French industrialist of the late 1800s, have proposed various classifications of these basic "functions" of managers and this perspective is thus called the **Functional School** of management. While it is not always possible, in practice, to categorize a particular managerial activity into one or another managerial function, the set of *planning, acquiring resources, coordinating*, and *monitoring and controlling* is fairly descriptive of the managerial process. In a theoretical sense, management begins with planning, but no chronological order is im-

The functions of management.

plied in our list. All of the functions are continuous. That is, each of the functions depends on the others and all are constantly taking place.

Planning

Planning involves the selection of desired goals, the means for achieving the goal, and the policies, procedures, programs, and methods that will guide the organization. Organizational plans provide the general framework that motivates and integrates individual day-to-day operations within the organization. Plans specify what, where, when, who, and how the organization will operate.

"My program is to increase harvests, cure the economy and get some statues built."

(Punch cartoon reproduced with the permission of the Toronto Sun Syndicate)

Acquiring resources

An organization can have very clear goals and elaborately detailed programs and procedures, but unless it can acquire the necessary resources no transformation can take place. Decisions must be made and implemented regarding the best facilities, equipment, inventories, and supplies, as well as the personnel needed to staff the operations. These decisions are highly interdependent. For example, selecting a low priced machine may require more highly trained and costly personnel. Lower quality inventory may result in higher scrap rates and/or more rapid equipment deterioration. None of these acquisition decisions can be made in a vacuum, but must be made only after thorough consideration of the factors bearing on the overall benefits and costs to the organization.

Coordinating

It has been said that coordinating is the essence of management. Coordination is the integration and synchronization of individual actions in achieving group goals. Coordination requires actions throughout the organization. In larger organizations, coordination requires structure. That is, in order to synchronize efforts, some formal organizational structure is required so that individuals understand their own as well as others' roles in accomplishing the organizational purpose.

Monitoring and controlling

The best-laid plans often go awry. Without a system to monitor and control operations, chances are much greater that plans will not be carried out correctly. The organization must monitor and report information regarding both internal and external happenings. Feedback of information from within the organization allows management to recognize when deviations from the plan are taking place. External monitoring and reporting keeps management abreast of changes in the environment that may affect organizational plans.

Whenever activities deviate from plans or plans seem not to be achieving the intended goals, control must be exercised. When acts deviate from plans, the individual or component within the organization who is responsible for the deviation must be identified and their activities corrected to restore the process according to plan. When plans do not seem to be achieving the goals, the plans may have to be modified or possibly completely scrapped in favor of new proposals. In some instances the goals themselves may even have to be modified.

Inseparable interrelationships.

It should be obvious to the student that the entire management process is interrelated. Controls are based on goals and plans, actions cannot take place without resources, and all resources, which are the objects of monitoring and control, must be coordinated in order to avoid chaos. The manager is the person responsible for these functions and ultimately for the achievement, or lack of achievement, of the organization's goals.

Alternate Views of Management

Decision processing.

A newly emerging view of management is one of **decision processing**. This perspective maintains that the previously described functions of management should all focus on the decisions that must be made. (See the *B.C.* cartoon regarding the importance of decisions.) Thus, planning is decision making about the future, coordinating is deciding who will do what, and so on. Regardless of the particular function in which a manager is involved at the time, his or her activities must be either that of

The decision-processing view of management

1. *Identifying* a problem.
2. *Formulating* alternative solutions to the problem.
3. *Weighing* and analyzing the pros and cons of the various alternatives.
4. *Making* the decision choice.

5. *Implementing* the decision.
6. *Following up* on the implemented decision.
7. *Evaluating* the results of the decision.

These are the activities involved in decision processing.

B.C.

(Reprinted by permission of Johnny Hart and Field Enterprises, Inc.)

A considerable amount of effort has been directed toward the analysis-of-alternatives phase (3) of decision processing. In essence, this phase has been the primary focus of the **Quantitative School*** of management. The foundation for this school is **analysis**. Analysis is the process of breaking a system down into its basic parts and examining them. By careful analysis of the parts, a better understanding of the whole may then be obtained. However, Starr points out [14, p. vi] that

The analysis function.

Management is a synthesizing function. Therefore, mathematical analysis is used, not produced by the manager. He employs analysis for descriptive purposes so that he may better diagnose and prescribe for the system's performance.

The synthesis function.

Synthesis is the creative, insightful process that results in new products and inventions, new techniques, and many discoveries. The synthesizing function of management is thus the act of combining various parts to produce a complex whole, such as people, machines, and material to produce a table. Sasser even maintains [12] that our whole society has now passed from an age of analysis into a new age—one of synthesis. An elegant comparison of analysis and synthesis was made by Sir Arthur Eddington [7, p. 103], a physicist.

We often think that when we have completed our study of one *we know all about* two, *because "two" is "one and one." We forget that we still have to make a study of "and."*

Thus, the "decision-processing" perspective of management recognizes that the manager's task is composed of both analysis and synthesis. The former is used as a foundation that allows the manager to perform the latter, the creative aspect of management.

1.3 GENERIC OPERATIONS MANAGEMENT

The field of "operations management" has evolved in a very short span of time, historically speaking. Its roots, however, go back to the Industrial Revolution, which started in the 1770s with the following important developments.

The division of labor.

- The "division of labor" concept, espoused by Adam Smith.
- The steam engine, of James Watt.
- The "interchangeable parts" concept, developed by Eli Whitney.

Adam Smith.

Adam Smith is given much of the credit for the theoretical development of the economics of modern production. In his book, *The Wealth of Nations* (1776), he pointed out that where workers are organized to produce large quantities of an item

* The other major "school" of management is the **Behavioral School**; many of the insights of this school are included throughout this text, especially in Chapters 8 and 11I. For more discussion concerning the various schools of management see [16].

the labor required should be divided into discrete tasks. He believed that this "division of labor" would produce several benefits.

- Workers who continually performed the same task would acquire greater skill at that task.
- Time would be saved that is normally lost in switching from one task to another.
- A worker's increased concentration on the same task frequently would lead to the development of special tools and techniques for easier or faster accomplishment of that task.

The division-of-labor characteristic of factories described by Adam Smith over 200 years ago has continued its evolution and refinement all the way to the factories, hospitals, schools, governmental agencies, stores, libraries, restaurants, and other organizations of today.

Charles Babbage.

In 1832 a mathematician, Charles Babbage, extended Smith's work by recommending the use of the scientific method for analyzing factory problems. In particular, he suggested the use of time study, unit costing, research and development, economic location analysis, bonus payments, and pay on the basis of skill requirements. This latter recommendation was an outgrowth of Smith's observations regarding the specialization of labor. That is, with a division of labor, payment need be made only for the requisite amount of skill needed in a task and not for "craftsman" skills for all operations. Babbage is also known for his **Difference Engine** and his "Analytical Engine," the forerunners of today's computer. (However, the former was never completed due to a lack of tooling technology and financial backing was withdrawn for the latter by the Chancellor of the Exchequer because it was believed to be "indefinitely expensive.")

The first computer.

However, almost half a century passed after Babbage before anyone addressed the problem of managing the factories. In 1878, a U.S. national tennis champion turned his attention to the factories and began a movement that eventually earned him a reputation as "the father of scientific management." His name was Frederick Winslow Taylor. In that year, Taylor began working for the Midvale Steel Company whose president, William Sellers, was an advocate of experimentation in factory methods. Taylor adopted some of Sellers' ideas, and many other factory management ideas of common knowledge, and organized them to form a unique philosophy of management.

Taylor's philosophy.

Briefly, Taylor's philosophy was that successful management was not the result of applying individual management "techniques" to the job but rather of a systematic approach to business operations. He believed that improved efficiency in a business could be obtained by

1. Using managers as work *planners* by gathering traditional knowledge about the work and reducing it to standardized procedures for the workers.
2. Methodically *selecting, training*, and *developing* each worker on an individual basis.

3. Striving for *cooperation* between management and the worker to simultaneously obtain both maximum production and high worker's wages.
4. *Dividing* the work between management and the workers so each is working on what they are most proficient in doing.

Although Taylor added a number of his own contributions to the field, his most significant accomplishment was the massive amount of attention he focused on the field of management through his own determination and zeal. Taylor described his new management philosophy in a book, *Principles of Scientific Management*, published in 1911 [15]. This event, more than any other, can be considered as the beginning of the field of operations management.

The origin of operations management.

The colleagues, contemporaries, and followers of Taylor were many and included

1911: Frank Gilbreth

Therbligs.

Frank Gilbreth is considered by many to be the "father of motion study." He stressed the applications of principles of motion economy to the most minute details of tasks in an attempt to identify the "one best way" of performing a given task. He also developed the well-known motion study techniques involving the use of "therbligs" and *chronocyclegraphs*.

1911: Lillian Gilbreth

Psychology.

Lillian Gilbreth is known not only for her work with her husband but also for her human relations work in the field. Her book, *The Psychology of Management*, is one of the earliest works concerning the human factor in business organizations. From her studies dealing with worker fatigue and psychology she has gained the title of the "First Lady of Management."

1913: Henry Ford

The assembly line.

Henry Ford utilized Eli Whitney's idea of interchangeable parts and a continuous workflow concept he saw in Switzerland to bring "mass production" to large scale industry. He arranged the work stations into an assembly "line" with a moving belt for the parts, each worker performing a specialized task on the parts as they went by. Ford is also known for his concern for the human element in production with his early "Sociological Departments" being the framework for today's personnel departments.

1913: Henry Gantt

The Gantt chart.

Henry Gantt's most well-known contribution to management is the charting system he developed for scheduling production. However, he also developed some original incentive pay systems and emphasized the importance of worker psychology in areas such as morale.

1913: Harrington Emerson

Organization structure.

Harrington Emerson took Taylor's ideas and applied them to the organization *structure* with an emphasis on the firm's objectives. He emphasized, in a set of organizational "principles" he developed, the use of experts in organizations to improve organizational efficiency.

1931: H. F. Dodge, H. G. Romig, and W. Shewhart

Sampling inspection.

H. F. Dodge, H. G. Romig, and W. Shewhart were co-workers at Bell Telephone Laboratories. Together they developed the procedure of "sampling inspection" for the control of quality. To aid in this process they published statistical sampling tables, now in extensive use, which utilized statistical inference and probability theory.

1933: G. Elton Mayo

The Hawthorne studies.

G. Elton Mayo is best known for his studies at Western Electric's Hawthorne Plant where he emphasized the human and social factors in work. This study gave birth to the "behavioral school" of management thinking due to the resulting stress for so many years on human relations in management. Mayo felt that "scientific management" was often emphasizing technical skills at the expense of adaptive skills.

1935: L. H. C. Tippett

Work standards.

Tippett is known for his work in sampling theory. His studies, although not fully utilized until much later, provided industry with a method for determining standards for worktimes, idle times, and other such work activities.

Early names.

With so much attention being devoted to the management of factories, this special area of management came to be known by the 1950s as "manufacturing management" (other terms such as "industrial management" and "factory management" were used synonymously). The pace of development is illustrated graphically in Figure 1.1.

The importance of productivity.

Some disadvantages.

The central concern to many in manufacturing management was increased **productivity**, a measure of efficiency computed as output per manhour. And it was, rightly, of concern to our entire society. Increased productivity meant less human labor was required to produce a given product, which in turn increased the available quantity and decreased the cost of many products. In this country, factories and the "industrial machine" meant increases in the standard of living and availability of consumer goods unheard of in most parts of the world. However, in some instances it also meant pollution, dehumanization of the workplace, and boredom due to repetitive, meaningless tasks.

OM in the 1950s.

The systems view.

The 1950s saw the development of systems theory, operations research, and the computer, each of which furthered the cause of manufacturing management. Systems theory emphasized the interrelationships existing in the factory and pointed out the futility of considering problems in a vacuum. The **system**, a purposeful collection of people, resources, and procedures, is assumed to consist of **inputs** (such as raw materials or customers), a **transformation process** (such as educating, painting, or molding), and **outputs** (such as cured patients or automobiles) all operating within an **environment**. The environment is considered to lie outside the system because it affects the system but cannot be controlled from within the system. Not only does the environment include the physical, economic, legal, and other such conditions surrounding the system but the environment may itself be part of another system such as nature, the federal reserve system, or a national society. Thus we recognize

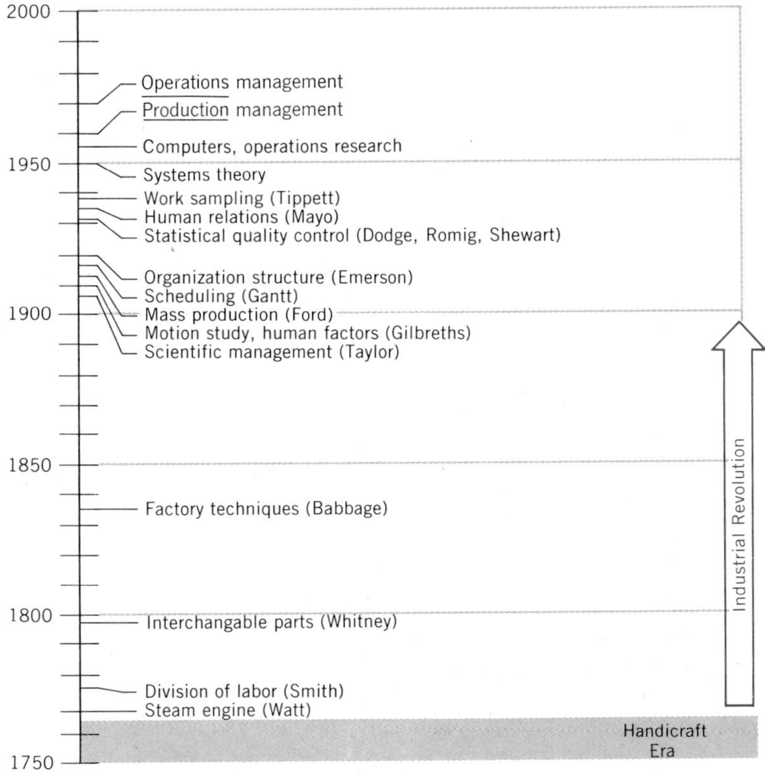

Figure 1.1. The history of operations management.

the idea of a set of *levels* of systems, each embedded within a larger system, to form a **hierarchy** of systems. The name given to this recognition of the interdependence of systems within organizations is the *systems approach*.

A system hierarchy.

Operations research.

Operations research provided mathematical models to help solve allocation, scheduling, planning, processing, inventory, layout, control, and location problems. And the computer allowed the fast and relatively inexpensive development of management information, expedited the solution of operations research models that were heretofore too large for manual solution, provided support for business functions (such as payroll, general and cost accounting, and customer billing), and formed a basis for automation.

Emergence of "production management."

In the late 1950s scholars and researchers in the field began to generalize the problems and techniques of manufacturing management to other productive organizations as well, such as petroleum and chemical processors, and wholesalers, and the name for the field evolved into "production management." The intent of this term was to stress the fact that the field had become a functional management discipline in itself and not just a set of manufacturing management techniques. In the late 1960s

"Operations management" to include services.

the field expanded even further, this time into the *service sector* of the economy. Since the word "production" seemed to connote "product" organizations, the more general term "operations" was substituted to emphasize the **generic** (or general) basis of the field. This transition from "production" to "operations" is still occurring today. Because it is likely to become an increasingly important area of management, the next section is devoted to a closer look at this continuing growth of services in our economy.

The Emergence and Growth of the Service Sector

The growth of services.

With the increased standard of living resulting from increased factory productivity came changes in the needs and demands of the population. A person could use just so many pairs of shoes, so many easy chairs, and so many cars. People found themselves working harder and harder to obtain goods that had less and less meaning for them. Rather than spending their income on more goods they decided to take in a movie, eat out more often, pay someone else to clean their house or cut their lawn, improve their education or health, and take advantage of many other types of **services**. As their standard of living continued to increase they found more and more interest in new and better services and in the **efficiency** and **effectiveness** of those services.

Services therefore began to catch up in importance to goods. Consider Figures 1.2 and 1.3. These figures dramatically illustrate that since 1950, services have been rapidly increasing as a proportion of both *expenditures* for personal consumption and *employers* of the workforce. In the last 15 years the service sector of the labor force increased 47 percent as opposed to 24 percent for the product sector. There are a number of implications inherent in such statistics. One of the most important is that

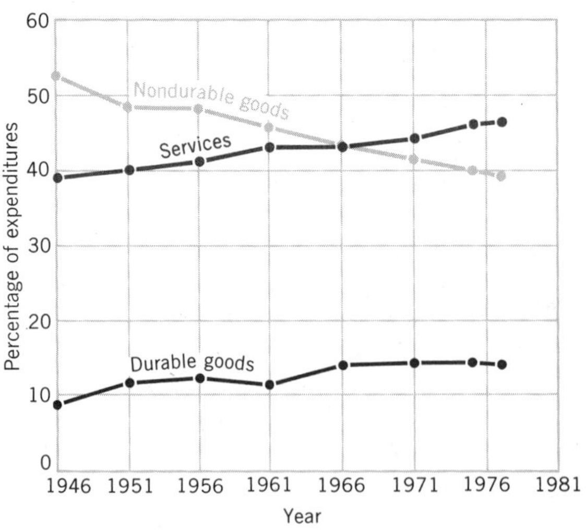

Figure 1.2 Percentage of personal consumption expenditures for goods and services. (*Source:* Economic Report of the President, 1978.)

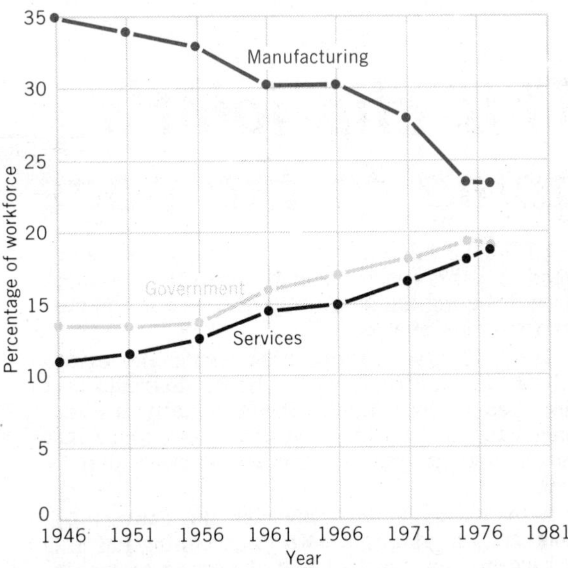

Figure 1.3 Percentage of workforce employed in manufacturing, services, and government. (*Source*: Economic Report of the President, 1978.)

service growth is providing greater employment opportunities for women, the self-employed, part-time workers, and so forth. This is because of the lesser amount of physical labor and greater personalization, skill, and education basic to services (see Figure 1.4, for example).

In addition to the growth in "private sector" services there has also been a significant increase in public (government) sector services such as fire protection, welfare, defense, and so forth, as indicated in Figure 1.3. In the last 15 years civilian public employment has increased 60 percent!

The growth of public services.

While there has clearly been a marked increase in the demand for services, one reason for the tremendous growth in service sector employment has been a negative one; namely, its lack of productivity growth. The inefficiency of services is evidenced by the constant and often bitter criticism of the post office, the railroads, the health care system, public schools, and many other such systems. Public concern usually stems from a focus on the productivity measure of cost per unit of service. As shown in Figure 1.5, the costs for services have increased much more rapidly than the costs for goods.

The lack of service productivity.

While there are many reasons which might help to explain the rapid increases in service sector costs, most experts would agree that a major contributing factor is the lack of substantial increases in productivity. Concern about this poor productivity led to the expansion of production management to include the service sector. Operations management thus includes both production and service organizations, regardless of whether they are public or private or whether they are for-profit or not-for-profit.

This clip joint's going to the dogs

BRYANT BEACH, N.J. (UPI) — Whoever heard of a barber making house calls? At least one is bringing her grooming business to the customers—dogs, that is.

Janet Morgan, 22, operates a specially equipped van to give the pooches baths, haircuts and other beauty treatments. Professionally trained, Janet has been working out of her van since last March, and grooms an average of 30-35 dogs a week.

A local van dealer converted the camper for about $13,000, adding a bath tub, running hot and cold water, two types of hair dryers, a hydraulic work table and air conditioning.

Figure 1.4 The growth of services. (*Source: The Cincinnati Post*, December 10, 1977. Reprinted by permission of United Press International.)

Productivity through management.

Productivity increases in the manufacturing sector of the economy in the last 70 years have been significant. As pointed out later in this text, much of this increase has been a direct result of improvements in the management of manufacturing operations. Among these improvements were:

1. Standardization of component parts.
2. Systematic production scheduling.
3. Control of inventories.
4. Quality, volume, and cost control of the output.
5. Plant layout techniques.
6. Use of computers and a systems approach in solving problems.

Redirecting attention.

Only in recent years have service sector organizations received the same attention from researchers as had been paid to manufacturers. Many of the concepts and ideas developed for the manufacturing sector can be modified and applied to service industries. For example, the problems of school bus routing, fire and rescue station facility location, and health center scheduling and layout have been addressed with modifications of manufacturing management methods with encouraging results. But we are only now viewing the tip of the iceberg. There are still numerous problems of design, improvement, and development of systems of welfare, health delivery, criminal justice, solid waste disposal, pollution control, urban renewal, and land use, which are ripe for the application of operations management methods.

The difficulty in the transfer of managerial know-how.

However, models and methods developed for manufacturers cannot be simply "transferred over" or "plugged in" to the service sector. Along with the obvious difference between the production of physical goods and the provision of a less tangible service, there are other important differences in the two sectors.

- The provision of services often involves dealing directly with the final recipient rather than with a wholesaler, retailer, or some other intermediary. The problems of producing physical goods, however, are usually removed from the complication of dealing directly with the customer, and even the intermediaries, by the marketing and distribution functions.
- The boundaries of operations, such as quality control and scheduling, in service organizations (e.g., orchestras, psychotherapists) are much less distinct than in manufacturing, primarily because of the lack of a physical product.
- Services pose unique scheduling difficulties because services not used today cannot be stored, as can unused products, typically, for use tomorrow; thus, the manager must use other techniques such as employing part-time help to balance supply and demand.

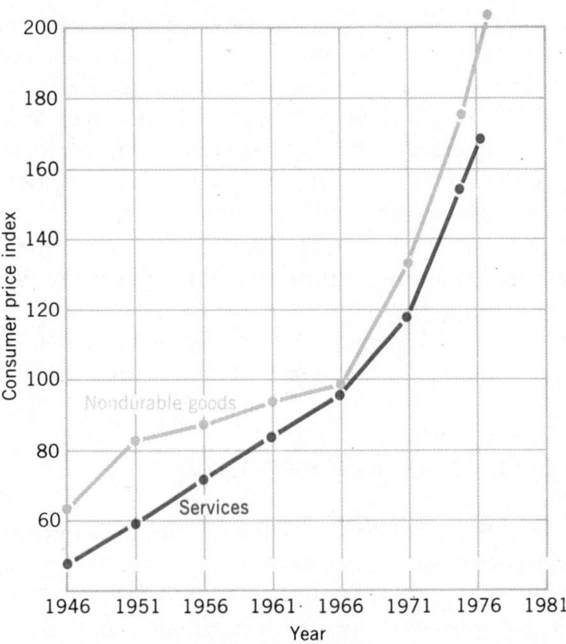

Figure 1.5. Consumer price indexes (1967 = 100) for nondurable goods (excluding food) and services (excluding rent). (*Source:* Economic Report of the President, 1978.)

TABLE 1.2 PRIORITY RANKINGS FOR OPERATIONS SUBSYSTEMS IN THREE TYPES OF NONMANUFACTURING ORGANIZATIONS

Subsystem	Hospital	Retail	University
Inventory	3	1	5
Work measurement	4	4	1
Scheduling	2	2	3
Quality control	1	3	4
Facilities planning	5	5	2

(Adapted by permission from Russell Morey, "Operations Management in Selected Non-Manufacturing Organizations," **Academy of Management Journal**, *19, 1976.)*

The differing importance of operations subsystems in different organizations.

Table 1.2 illustrates another important difference in organizations: the priority their managers are reported to place on common operations subsystems [11, p. 123]. Clearly, the health of a hospital's patients (its "quality control") will be of first priority, as will the capital investment a retailer has in inventory. But note that what is of first priority to each of these organizations is almost of last priority to the others. There is also little commonality on the importance of the remaining subsystems. Such substantial differences in even what is viewed as important organizational functions further hinder the transformation of manufacturing management know-how to service sector management.

The titles of the operations manager.

In summary, the field of operations management does not distinguish between managers in private or public, profit or not-for-profit, and service or product organizations. The operations function may be more difficult to recognize in nonmanufacturing organizations, but there is an operations manager nonetheless. He or she may be called the city manager, chief administrator, director, dean, or commissioner, depending upon the institution within which he or she functions, but the essential role of managing the operations is still the same.

Generic operations management.

While there are clearly notable differences between the various kinds of organizational systems, a common thread runs through each of them: management of the organization's operations. This common thread requires a *generic* approach to the problems of operations management, the approach to which this text is dedicated. The essence of this approach will be sketched in the remainder of this chapter.

1.4 MANAGING THE OPERATIONS FUNCTIONS

The design approach versus the descriptive approach.

We adopt in this text what we will term a **design approach** to operations management rather than the more commonly used *descriptive* approach illustrated in Figure 1.6. The difference is primarily one of direction or focus. The descriptive approach is similar to a plant tour. It starts with some *inputs*, such as people, lumber, hardware, and machines; proceeds through a number of *activities*, such as sawing, sanding, nailing, and painting; and ends with an output such as a table. However, the person

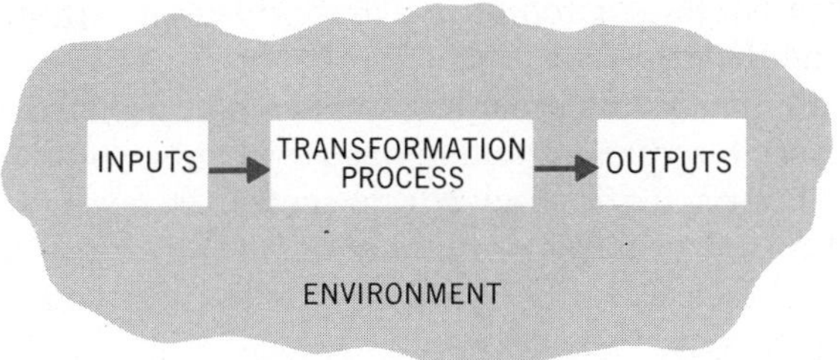

Figure 1.6 The traditional descriptive approach to operating systems.

on tour (you, the student) frequently does not see *why* the process performs as it does or what might happen if inputs or activities changed. Why is pine used instead of oak? Why is it not glued together instead of nailed? Although the descriptive perspective is easy to visualize, it is a **static** view of the organization's operations. If the organization's goals change or certain inputs are no longer available, this static approach to operations offers no insight into the required alterations in the operations to accommodate the change.

A static view

A dynamic view.

The design approach of Figure 1.7 presents a more **dynamic** view of operations and allows for the necessity of constant operations redesign due to changes in the environment and the organization itself. The design approach is, in essence, one of sequential planning, including the planning of change. It starts with the organization and its *goals*, identifies a number of potential organizational *outputs* that would gen-

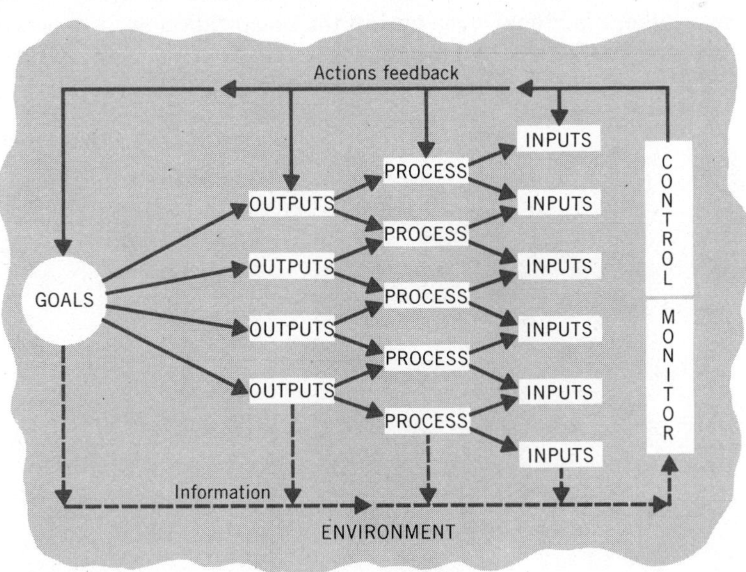

Figure 1.7 The design approach to operating systems.

erate returns from the *environment*, and considers all of the possible *transformation processes*, and then the *inputs*, which could produce those outputs. To ensure that operations are proceeding according to plan, operations and the environment are **monitored** and if significant differences are noted, control is exercised (known as **feedback**) to bring activities back within control. Hence, rather than a *single line* of operations being identified, a *complex* of many diverse possibilities is included. The design task is to select among these possibilities those which most effectively meet the organization's goals.

The inherently iterative nature of operations design.

The elimination and selection of the various possible outputs, processes, and so forth, is an **iterative** procedure. This means that the operations design is repetitive and cyclical in nature as illustrated in Figure 1.8 since the outputs depend upon the organization's goals and what input resources are available and the inputs depend upon the transformation process and what outputs are needed. Each stage of the operation must be repeated and improved in a repetitive manner. Furthermore, each stage must be designed with all the other stages in mind at the same time. This is an example of the *systems approach* that we described earlier.

The importance of environment.

But a one-time choice is not sufficient. Since both the internal and external environments of the organization are constantly changing (sales fall off, materials do not arrive, workers quit), continuous monitoring of these environments for control is necessary and these functions must also be designed from the start. The purpose of monitoring and control then is to sense changes in the subsystems and their environments, plus the external environment, and vary the selection of organizational operation possibilities to meet those changes.

The need for attention to the interfaces.

Because of the importance of these environments to the operation's function, it is crucial that the student be familiar with the **interfaces** between operations and other **functional areas** within the organization such as personnel, finance, accounting, marketing, and top management. For this reason we include in this text short "interface" chapters, identified as such (e.g., 2I), that relate operations management

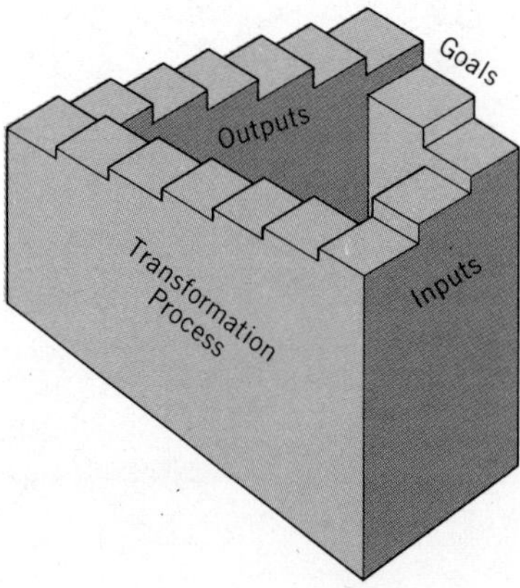

Figure 1.8 The iterative nature of operations design.

to the other major functions in the firm. If managers are only familiar with their own operations, and not with how they impact upon other areas, not only will they be unpromotable but they will also be constantly acting for the good of their own area (known as **suboptimizing**) rather than the organization as a whole.

1.5 OVERVIEW OF THE BOOK

Although it is important to bear in mind that the design of the operations are iterative in reality, for ease of discussion and comprehension we will follow each stage of the operations design sequentially in this text, as illustrated in Figure 1.9. To give perspective to these topics it is well to have some foreknowledge of the entire process so that the details of each topic can be integrated into the perception of the whole process. (This is referred to as a *holistic* view.) We thus conclude this chapter with a broad overview of each of the functions illustrated in the figure.

A holistic view.

Part I: The output decision

In this first part of the text we examine the goals of the organization and how they interface with operations planning in Chapter 2I, the marketing/R&D (research and development) interface in Chapter 3I, and how to forecast the environmental demand for the output in Chapter 4.

Part II: The transformation process

Chapter 5 addresses the issue of how much capacity will be needed to satisfy demand for the output and Chapter 6I considers the logistics function of getting the output to the recipients. Then in Chapter 7 the actual design of the transformation process is discussed. Placing the worker in this process is the topic of Chapter 8, Work Design. Lastly, "scheduling," the bringing together of all the resources to transform the inputs into outputs, is examined in Chapter 9.

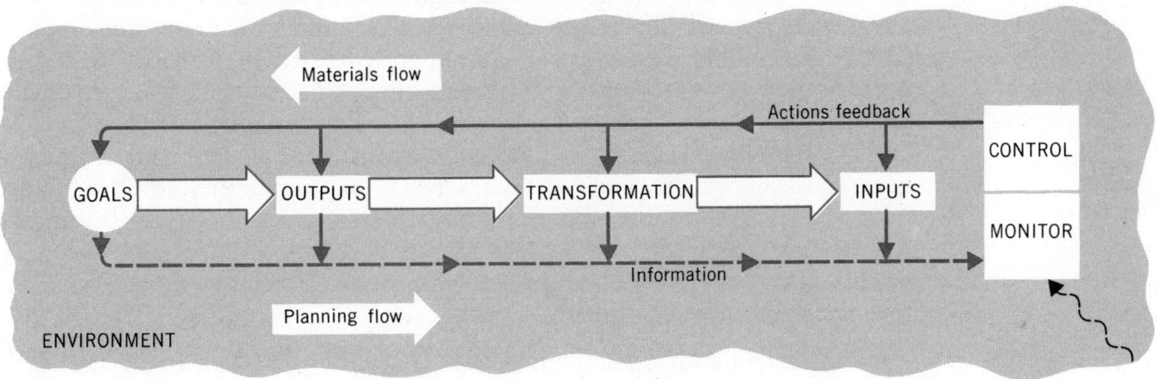

Figure 1.9 The basic flow of the design approach to organizational operations.

Part III: Acquiring the inputs

This part of the text examines three inputs of special importance to operations: capital, labor, and materials. Chapters 10I and 11I consider the first two of these, the financial and personnel interfaces. Materials acquisition is addressed in three chapters. Chapters 12 and 13 detail the materials management function and Chapter 14I discusses the purchasing interface.

Part IV: Controlling the system

The final part of the text addresses the control function of management. The general control process and techniques are discussed in Chapter 15 and then applied to quality in Chapter 16, cost (through the accounting interface) in Chapter 17I, and maintaining the proper functioning of the overall organizational system in Chapter 18. Concluding Part IV is a description of the information system required for adequate monitoring and control, given in Chapter 19I. An epilogue discussing the future of operations management then concludes the text.

1.6 SUMMARY

Organizations are the natural outcome of mankind's need to cooperate in order to obtain goods and services that would not otherwise be attainable. Fostering the creation and development of organizations has been the concept of the "division of labor" as noted by Adam Smith. Thus, the handicraft economy developed into the more specialized factory economy, which is now developing further into a product-service economy.

Once society progressed to the point that people were relatively satisfied with their *product* needs, they started seeking to improve the quality of their life with personalized *services*. Thus, the marketing demand shifted from that of maximizing the quantity of goods produced to maximizing variety. The main problem posed by this shift was one of productivity: the difficulty of mass producing personalized goods and services, which is almost a contradiction in terminology. In terms of any measure (dollars spent, GNP, number of workers), the growth of the service sector of the economy has been extremely rapid in the last few decades, now challenging the product sector in size.

The forms of organizations that have developed to satisfy the product/service needs of society can be classified three ways: first, whether they are a for-profit or not-for-profit organization; second, whether they are private or public (governmental); and last, whether they are product-oriented or service-oriented. Nevertheless, all organizations can be viewed as systems with the same common (generic) elements that require proper management:

- The inputs—such as information, capital, facilities, labor, and materials, which are then subject to:

- The transformation process—which entails capacity planning, activity scheduling, process design, and distributing:
- The outputs—either a product or a service (or both), in order to obtain from:
- The environment—including the political, legal, social, economic, physical, and technological:
- The desired returns—which, hopefully, will help achieve the organization's:
- Goals.—However, throughout this process:
- Monitoring and control—must be maintained in order to assure that results are consistent with plans. Both internal organizational operations and the external environment must be monitored with feedback for control so that organizational outputs will obtain the returns expected, which in turn will satisfy the goals.

The functions of management that are common to all organizations can be viewed from a number of perspectives. The classical view consists of the functions of planning, acquiring resources, coordinating, and monitoring/controlling. A more recent perspective that focuses on the analysis and synthesis tasks of management is that of "decision-processing."

1.7 READINGS

Branching Out

Major Retailers Offer Varied Services to Lure Customers, Lift Profits

Sears Schools Teach Driving To Auto-Law Violators; Cooking & Dental Clinics

Working Wives Spur Trend

BY BERNARD WYSOCKI JR.
STAFF REPORTER OF THE WALL STREET JOURNAL

For the beginning motorist, Sears, Roebuck & Co. offers a driver-training program. And now, for drivers needing remedial instruction, there are Sears schools for traffic violators.

. . .

If a department store looks like a strange place for such a school, look again. Retailers across the nation are adding to their basic business all kinds of services, ranging from steam baths and dental clinics to babysitting, educational seminars, income-tax help and even fashion shows catering to the deaf.

GROWING TREND

"The whole movement into services is really just beginning," says Thomas J. Noon of Management Horizons Inc., a Columbus, Ohio, marketing-consulting concern. "It's something that we see as being very strong in the future." The company estimates that as much as 20% of the department-store revenues may come from services by the end of the 1980s, up from 6% to 7% today.

Spurring the trend, experts say, is the growing number of working wives, who tend to be short on time and long on cash. Typically, these women want the convenience of a department store, need a lot of services and have the money to pay for them.

"When the working woman goes out in the evening to do a half-dozen chores, she doesn't want to go to a half-dozen places to find what she wants," says Patrick De Biase, national licensed-department manager at Montgomery Ward & Co., a Mobil Corp unit. "The more we can provide her, the better she likes us."

Some retailers have other reasons for loading up on services. "Often, it's to increase profit margins," says Bruce Walker, associate professor of marketing at Arizona State University. "Some department stores have found, for example, that they have more profit opportunities through a beauty salon than through expansion of their small-appliance department."

NOT A NEW IDEA

Services aren't entirely new to department stores, of course. Many stores have offered such things as travel bureaus and fur storage. Marshall Field & Co. in Chicago has even rewoven Oriental rugs and restored oil paintings for its customers. But nowadays the number and variety of services offered are rising rapidly, and some old-standby services are getting a complete overhaul.

Take restaurants, for example. Department-store food has typically been "tearoom kind of food—bland, uniform, nothing of interest—served in a big room where everything harked back to 20 or 25 years ago," says Kenneth Kolker, chairman of May Merchandising Co., a unit of May Department Stores Co., St. Louis. What's more, retailers have rarely considered the "tearooms" to be profit centers. "Most of them are lucky to break even," Mr. Kolker says.

But that's all changing. During the past three years, for example, five May Co. department stores in Los Angeles have opened Gilhooley's pub-type restaurants, featuring old-fashioned decor and elaborate menus. May's top brass believes that "food is just as much an attraction to customers as any merchandise category," Mr. Kolker says. "And these (restaurants) are geared to produce profitable revenue."

EXPANDING BEAUTY SALONS

Department-store beauty salons also are getting a new look. Many have added enough services to empty the mightiest pocketbook. A leader in the field is Seligman & Latz Inc., which operates leased beauty parlors in hundreds of department stores. In some of its shops, a customer can get a steam bath for \$5, a massage for \$15, "sculptured" fingernails (\$30 for normal length, \$40 for extra long), or a "day of beauty," including a champagne lunch, for \$100.

The fancy beauty shops cater to a young crowd. "The younger people spend more," says Margo Dworkin, salon manager at Saks Fifth Avenue's downtown-Chicago store, which installed a steam bath, shower and masseuse in its beauty salon in April. "The age group used to start at about 40. Now some of our customers are under 21, and they make weekly visits," she says.

Many retailers believe that in-store beauty shops pay an extra dividend. By making a woman look and feel her best, the store puts her in the mood to splurge at the sales counters. Even more basically, the beauty shops lure plenty of foot traffic into the store.

. . .

1.8 KEY TERMS*

hierarchy (p. 13)
system (p. 12)
services (p. 3)
operations (p. 2)
productivity (p. 12)
design approach (p. 18)
iterative (p. 20)
transformation process (p. 12)
feedback (p. 20)
inputs (p. 12)
outputs (p. 12)
Functional School (p. 5)
Quantitative School (p. 9)
collective goals (p. 3)
functional areas (p. 20)
dynamic (p. 19)
environment (p. 12)
difference engine (p. 10)
efficiency (p. 14)
effectiveness (p. 14)
interface (p. 20)
monitor (p. 20)
generic (p. 4)
synthesis (p. 9)
decision processing (p. 7)
not-for-profit (p. 4)
Behavioral School (p. 9)
analysis (p. 9)
static (p. 19)
suboptimizing (p. 21)
operations research (p. 13)

1.9 REVIEW TEST*

1. Public/private is one method of classifying organizations. (p. 3)
a. True b. False

2. Operations management emerged from an expansion of the field of production management. (p. 14)
a. True b. False

3. Decision-processing is an alternate view of the function of management. (p. 7)
a. True b. False

4. Most of the manager's time is spent making decisions. (p. 7)
a. True b. False

5. Synthesis is the finding of interrelationships between the elements of a system. (p. 9)
a. True b. False

6. A system may simply be described as a purposeful set of elements. (p. 12)
a. True b. False

7. The growth of the service sector can be attributed to its increasing productivity. (p. 15)
a. True b. False

8. The term "generic operations" is meant to include the activities of *all* types of organizations, regardless of their purpose. (p. 18)
a. True b. False

9. The transformation process is the heart of operations management. (p. 2)
a. True b. False

10. The Quantitative School of management has been an outgrowth of the synthesis phase of decision processing. (p. 9)
a. True b. False

11. Charles Babbage originated the very important concept of "the division of labor." (p. 10)
a. True b. False

12. A major part of Taylor's managerial philosophy was to obtain high worker's wages. (p. 11)
a. True b. False

13. Henry Ford invented the production line. (p. 11)
a. True b. False

14. The "environment" is defined to be that which is beyond the manager's control but does not affect the system. (p. 12)
a. True b. False

15. The most important operations subsystem in the university is quality control. (p. 18)
a. True b. False

16. An advantage of the "design approach" to operating systems is that it is a dynamic rather than static view. (p. 19)
a. True b. False

* Page numbers are indicated in parentheses following the terms and test questions where the relevant material is covered in the chapter.

Answers to Chapter Review tests are contained in Appendix C.

1.10 DISCUSSION QUESTIONS

1. Frequently, successful organizations lose sight of their original goals and strive to grow for growth's sake alone. What do you imagine might eventually happen to such an organization?
2. Since our high standard of living is largely due to the division and specialization of labor, might not trends toward job enrichment and enlargement threaten this standard?
3. Describe a football team in terms of an organization. Define all the system elements as well as the environment.
4. Relate society's current effectiveness orientation to the growth of services. Name some examples.
5. Identify some organizations that would fall in the sparse portions of Table 1.1.
6. Is the provision of electricity a product or a service? What of the telephone? Newspapers?
7. What are the reasons it is so hard to increase productivity in the service sector?
8. The classification of the functions of management frequently include staffing, directing, communicating, motivating, decision-making, organizing, and evaluating. How would these functions compare to those presented in this chapter?
9. Is the nature of management really universal?
10. Since management is frequently considered a decision-processing function, which elements of this function are analyzing and which are synthesizing?
11. Contrast the descriptive and design approaches to operations management.
12. Give some examples of the iterative nature of the design of operations.
13. What are the services embodied in the following products: piped-in water to your house, *Popular Science* magazine, a restaurant meal, a bank loan?
14. Why do you think the field of management took so long to develop?
15. Some people believe that America is experiencing a change in desire from ownership of goods to leasing or renting goods for a certain period of time. How would this trend affect the percentage of expenditures on durable goods, services, and nondurable goods?
16. What goals might a public welfare program have?
17. How can an organization such as a soft-drink bottler balance goals such as environmental cleanliness with convenient throwaway bottles?
18. How do you think a manufacturing firm would rank the operations subsystems in Table 1.2?
19. Should the federal government subsidize weak, profit oriented organizations such as railroads or let these companies fold when they cannot compete?
20. Why is it important for the operations manager to know about other functional areas such as finance, marketing, personnel, and so forth?

1.11 REFERENCES AND BIBLIOGRAPHY

1. Babbage, Charles, *On the Economy of Machinery and Manufacturers*, 4th ed., London: Charles Knight, 1835.
2. Burch, E. E., and Henry, W. R., "Production Management Is Alive and Well," *Academy of Management Journal*, 17:144–419 (1974).
3. Churchman, C. W., *The Systems Approach*, New York: Dell, 1968.
4. Drake, A. W., Keeney, R. L., and Morse, P. M., ed., *Analysis of Public Systems*, Cambridge, Mass.: MIT Press, 1972.
5. Drucker, Peter F., *The Practice of Management*, New York: Harper & Row, 1954.
6. Easton, A., *Complex Managerial Decisions Involving Multiple Objectives*, New York: Wiley, 1973.
7. Eddington, Sir Arthur, *The Nature of the Physical*

World, Ann Arbor, Michigan: University of Michigan Press, 1958.

8. Lepawsky, A., *Administration*, New York: Knopf, 1949.
9. Levitt, T., "Industrialization of Service," *Harvard Business Review*, 54:63–74 (1976).
10. Moran, William T., "Marketing-Production Interaction," in Starr, M. K., *Production Management*, 2nd ed., Englewood Cliffs, N.J.: Prentice-Hall, 1972.
11. Morey, Russell, "Operations Management in Selected Non-Manufacturing Organizations," *Academy of Management Journal*, 19:120–124 (1976).
12. Sasser, W. Earl, "Age of Synthesis," *Harvard Business Review*, 40:36–40 (1962).
13. Smith, Adam, *An Inquiry into the Nature and Causes of the Wealth of Nations*, London: A. Strahan and T. Cadell, 1976.
14. Starr, M. K., *Production Management*, 2nd ed., Englewood Cliffs, N.J.: Prentice-Hall, 1972.
15. Taylor, Frederick W., *The Principles of Scientific Management*, New York: Harper & Row, 1911.
16. Wren, Daniel A., *The Evolution of Management Thought*, revised ed., New York: Wiley, 1979.

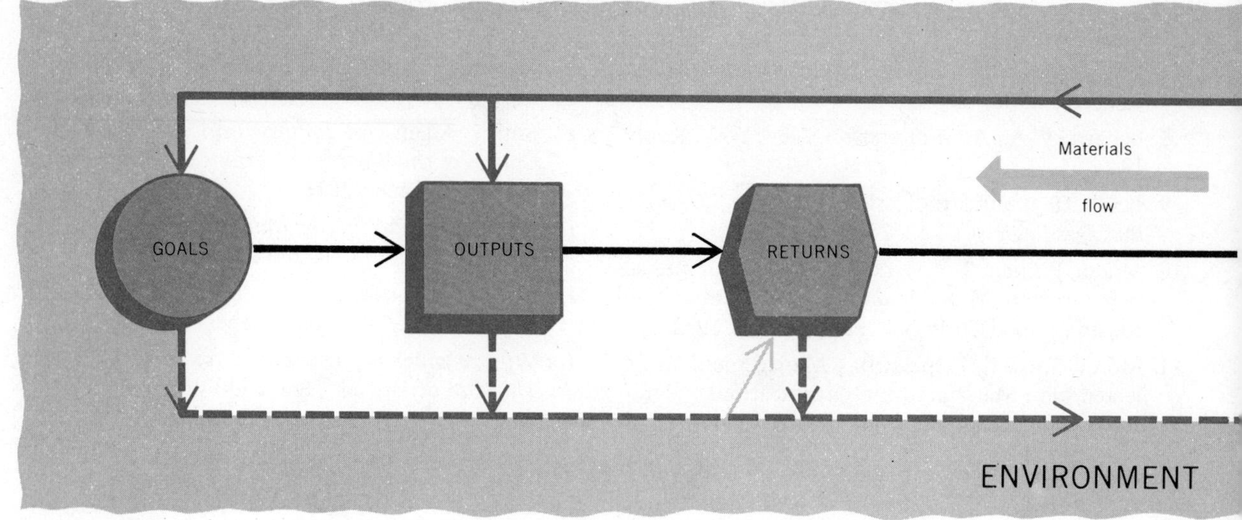

Part I

THE OUTPUT DECISION

"Would you tell me, please, which way I ought to go from here?"

"That depends a good deal on where you want to get to," said the Cat.

"I don't much care where—" said Alice.

"Then it doesn't matter which way you go," said the Cat.

"—so long as I get somewhere,*" Alice added as an explanation.*

"Oh, you're sure to do that," said the Cat, "if you only walk long enough."

— LEWIS CARROLL, *ALICE'S ADVENTURES IN WONDERLAND**

* *Lewis Carroll,* Alice's Adventures in Wonderland, *New Junior Classics, Mabel Williams and Marcia Dalphin, eds. (New York: P. F. Collier and Son Corporation, 1949), V, p. 51.*

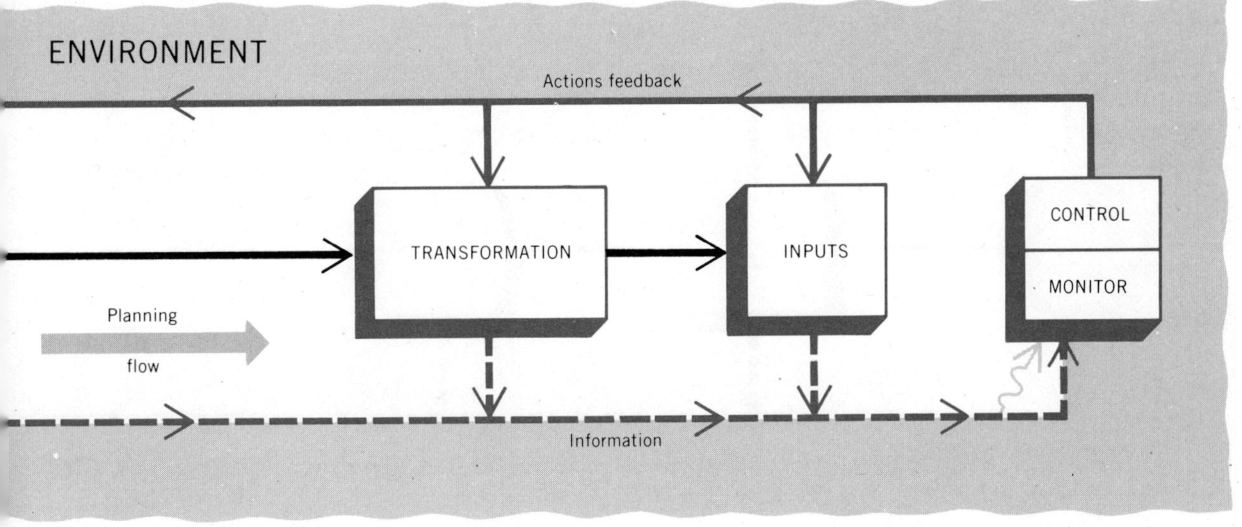

Clearly, if you do not know where you are going, any path will get you there. Goals are needed by organizations, as well as by individuals, to provide direction and purpose for their endeavors. In the limit, it is the organization's goals that dictate not only the returns required from the environment to satisfy its goals but also the outputs, and even the manner by which the outputs are produced.

This part of the text is about organizational goals and outputs, and the returns necessary from the environment to sustain the organization in its attempt to attain its goals. Chapter 2I describes the top management interface where *strategic* goals are usually set. However, the chapter also discusses their translation into multiple, and often conflicting, *tactical* goals for operating management and the necessity of establishing priorities and making tradeoffs to maximize the attainment of these goals. This chapter also introduces the concept of decision criteria by which the attainment of goals can be measured.

Chapter 3I, the marketing/R&D interface chapter, addresses the relationship of operations to the screening and selection of the organizational output(s). Discussion first centers on how candidate outputs are derived from a number of sources and the role of creativity in this process. Next, the organization's unique strengths and weaknesses are considered in the selection of the output, including the capabilities *and inabilities* of the operations area. Last, the design of the output and the requirements it places on operations is discussed.

An organization must obtain sufficient returns for its output to satisfy its goals if it is to remain viable. In Chapter 4 the returns that organizations obtain from their environment are discussed and typical returns, both desired and undesired, are described. In order to determine if sufficient returns for the output will be forthcoming, demand must be forecast. Different forecasting methods are therefore also described and illustrated.

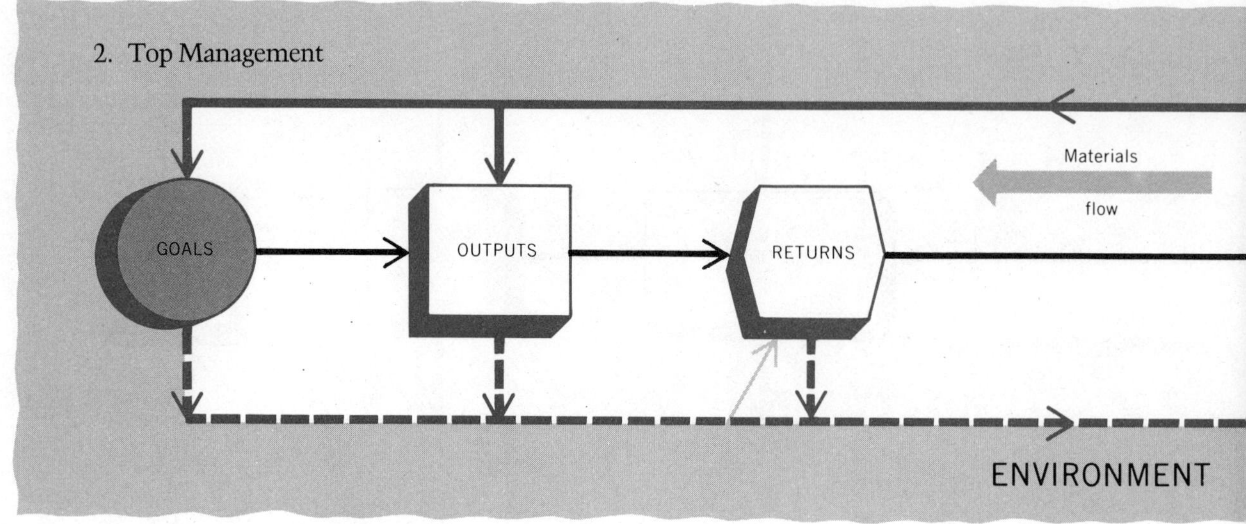

Chapter 2I

The Top Management Interface: Organizational Goals

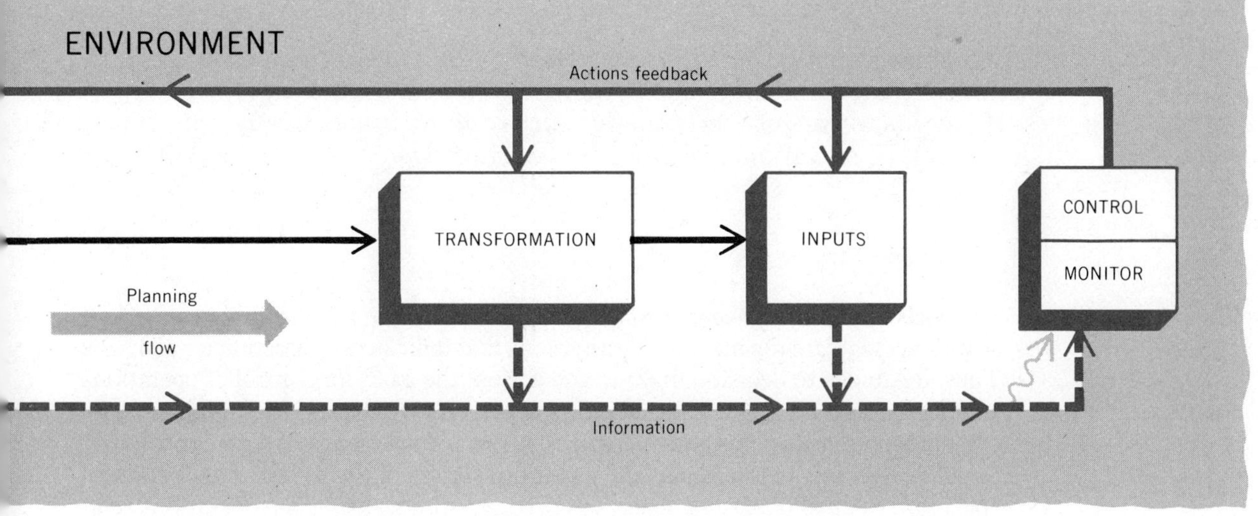

LEARNING OBJECTIVES

By the completion of this chapter the student should

1. Understand the origin of organizational goals.
2. Know why strategic goals are necessarily vague and tactical goals are specific.
3. Have a feel for how management deals with multiple and often conflicting goals.
4. Know how management "operationalizes" strategic goals.
5. Be familiar with some of the quantitative models used to make operating decisions regarding, and allocate resources between, the organization's tactical goals.

We the people of the United States, in order to form a more perfect union, establish justice, insure domestic tranquility, provide for the common defense, promote the general welfare, and secure the blessings of liberty to ourselves and our posterity, do ordain and establish this Constitution for the United States of America.

— PREAMBLE TO THE CONSTITUTION OF THE UNITED STATES

The uses for goals.

The **goals** of the U.S. government were clearly laid out in the Preamble to the Constitution. Goals are the intended destinations that indicate the direction for planning. They are guides to decision making and action, the basis for control of operations, and the logic for criteria when evaluating results. As we shall see in this chapter, the organization selects plans and operating programs on the basis of their contribution to the achievement of its goals. The direct translation of the organization's strategic goals into tactical operating objectives then sets the tasks for the operations managers.

2.1 ORGANIZATIONAL GOALS

The difficulty of goal specification.

For an organization's operations to be most effective they must be intimately tied to the organization's goals. Managers in public and not-for-profit organizations have often envied the manager in the profit sector because his or her goal was so clear. "You know each year how well you have done. All you have to do is look at the bottom line to assess your organization's performance. But, we cannot specify our objectives so clearly as profit maximization."

What priorities and commitments?

The goal of the manager in the public sector has been stated [6, p. 243] as "an unwavering commitment to the rule of efficiency: In every instance he chooses that alternative that optimizes the allocation of public resources." Of course, this goal presumes a knowledge of public wants and social welfare. It is simple to state that the public desires excellence in its public education system, a good system of streets, roads and highways, and the elimination of poverty. But, when it comes to the specification of priorities and resource commitments for these various general goals, there will be as many different opinions as there are individuals asked to specify one.

Multiple and conflicting goals.

The ease of goal specification for business is much more illusion than reality, however. For the businessman there is not only the obvious goal of profit maximization, but also the less clear-cut goals of providing meaningful employment for employees, continuing organizational growth, providing a fair return for investors, producing a good product or service, maintaining the company image, and generally, being the good corporate citizen. In addition to the problem of multiple organizational goals there is also the problem that some of the goals may be *conflicting* and thus greater achievement of one goal may only be possible by sacrificing other goals. That is, the manager, who, of course, has his own goals that may influence his decisions, must make goal tradeoffs when faced with conflicting goals.

2.2 STRATEGIC VERSUS TACTICAL GOALS

To help distinguish between the strategic and tactical levels in an organization refer back to the *B.C.* cartoon in Section 1.2. The tasks of picking, lugging, packaging, and delivering are all **tactical** activities—the realm of operations management. Deciding whether the organization is in the mushroom business or the toadstool business is a **strategic** activity that requires a decision from top management. Clearly these two levels are closely related. In this section we consider the very basis of that relationship—how the organization's goals are translated into operating policies.

Strategic goals.

An organization's goals are usually developed at the top level of the organization—the board of directors, the owner, the general, the trustees, the regents, and so forth. Such top level, or *strategic*, goals are often high sounding and admirable but purposely vague. This serves an important objective—giving general guidance to the organization's future leaders but, at the same time, allowing sufficient flexibility to respond appropriately to whatever new situations may arise. The risk inherent in being more specific in setting an organization's strategic goals is that the organization may be doomed to failure through following policies inappropriate to situations for which the policies were not designed.

As an example, reconsider the Preamble at the beginning of this chapter. The stated goals here are

1. Form a more perfect union.
2. Insure domestic tranquility.
3. Provide for the common defense.
4. Promote the general welfare.
5. Secure the blessings of liberty.

Abstractness of strategic goals.

Suppose that instead of stating number 3, for example, as it is, the founding fathers had been more specific and stated that a standing militia of three thousand men with muskets and 100 cannons would be maintained. The folly of such a specific goal in today's times of MIRV's, cruise missiles, and neutron bombs is clear. And it was clear to our founding fathers as well.

Explicitness of tactical goals.

Nevertheless, at some point more specific goals must be defined in order to give useful short-term direction to the organization. These lower level goals, called *tactical* goals, may also be developed by top management or may come from lower levels of management through interpretation of the strategic goals. In the case of the Preamble our founders provided the *Constitution* to more clearly articulate the tactical goals. In addition, they also provided a mechanism for modifying the Constitution, by amendments, as well as a continuing mechanism for providing even lower levels of tactical goals—the Supreme Court.

Operations focus as a key strategy.

When top managers translate the organizational goals into tactical goals for the operations area, the resulting strategy is known as the organization's operations **focus**. The operations strategy chosen by an organization is akin to, and should dovetail with, the organization's marketing and financial strategies, if the organization is to compete effectively in its environment. For example, it would be foolish for an organization to have a marketing strategy oriented toward a quality output while its operations were trying to produce the lowest possible cost output. Yet this is a frequent occurrence. This concept will be considered in more detail in Chapter 3 where marketing is discussed.

Goal hierarchy.

We see then that organizations typically form a **hierarchy** of goals. At the top are the strategic goals that serve as general guidance for long-term planning but are somewhat vague and nebulous (Figure 2.1). Examples are: to improve the condition of mankind, to serve a higher authority, to reduce pain and suffering, to enhance the organizational image, and so forth. Because of their lack of specific direction during particular periods of time such goals are often adopted as the organization's *permanent* goals and declared to be the official motto, creed, or whatever.

Rules as guidelines.

At the other extreme of the hierarchy are very explicit goals, sometimes called policies, procedures, or even rules, which, in terms of organizational desirability, are highly debatable, extremely specific, and typically only valid for a particular point in time. Examples here might be "every employee will begin work at 8 A.M.," "steel rods will not be moved without Foreman Smith's authorization," and so on. Even such specific goals (or rules) should still be subject to interpretation, however. Suppose the president needs to meet with the vice presidents at 7:45 A.M.? Or what if Foreman Smith is ill or unconscious at the local hospital? One of the most reliable methods employees have used to virtually halt production in organizations where they did not wish to officially strike has been to precisely follow the organization's rules and regulations. This has often been an eye-opener to managers who thought these goals were *orders* instead of general *guidelines*.

A nonstrike.

Between these two extremes of the *ultimate goals* of the organization and its set of *regulations* lie its tactical goals or "operating objectives." Such objectives might be

- Produce "zero defects" this month.
- Increase the serviced caseload 5 percent.
- Extend the number of accident-free days to 200.
- Save 10 percent on drug purchases.
- Increase on-time deliveries to 99 percent.

These are goals that operations managers are challenged with. Obviously, they are not organizational goals but rather *means* to those goals and thus constitute a portion of the operations strategy or **focus** of the organization.

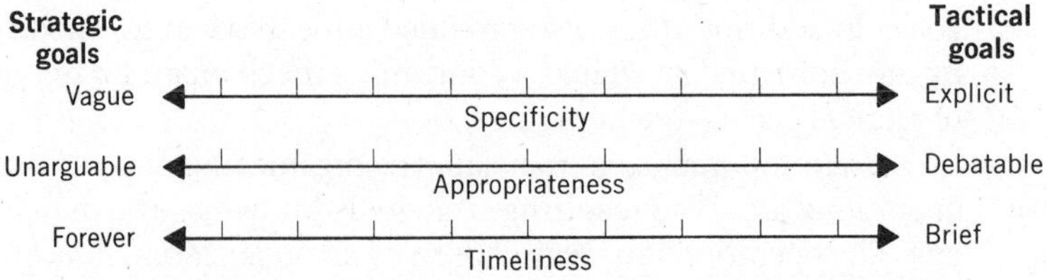

Figure 2.1 Strategic and tactical goals compared.

Management by objectives.

A fairly recent innovation on the management scene in the last decade or so has been the introduction of **MBO** (management by objectives) for operating managers. This concept formalizes the translation of strategic goals into measurable tactical goals. The interesting aspect of the concept is the stress put on not specifying *how* the tactical goals are to be achieved—only *what* goals are to be achieved, and then rewarding such achievement appropriately. For further details the interested reader should consult Reference 5.

2.3 THE EXISTENCE OF MULTIPLE GOALS

Multiple goals.

As the Preamble indicates, an organization typically has more than one goal. Even at the strategic level, multiple goals are common. In addition, organizations are made up of and represent many individuals and interests, each of whom has different motivations and goals. Employees want meaningful jobs with adequate and secure incomes. Stockholders desire a fair return on the money they have invested in the firm. And the managers themselves have their own personal goals and ambitions such as wealth, power, or prestige.

Environment imposed goals.

Beyond this, the environment also has some goals which it desires of organizations. Society, through the government and special interest groups, wants business firms to employ workers, pay taxes, and provide products and services but not pollute the environment, endanger the public health or safety, or prey on consumers. In addition, suppliers, competitors, customers, and others in the environment have an effect on the setting of an organization's goals.

Business goals.

Two major studies of top U.S. executives support the view that business firms subscribe to a large number of diverse organizational goals (see References 1 and 5). Table 2.1 lists those areas frequently mentioned as organizational goals. While profits were mentioned frequently in both studies, it is clear that profits are not the sole target of private enterprise. In several more recent studies it has been concluded that social responsibility is also gaining significantly as a major goal of business organizations (see Reference 2).

TABLE 2.1 SELECTED GOALS OF TOP CORPORATE MANAGERS

To grow
To contribute to the community
To provide a quality product
To progress technologically
To pay dividends to stockholders
To provide for the welfare of employees
To gain prestige
To produce a profit
To develop the organization
To produce efficiently and effectively
To meet consumer needs

Born Loser: © 1978 NEA, Inc.

Public goals.

Even more obviously than business firms, not-for-profit organizations (foundations, social clubs, charities) exhibit multiple goals. This is especially true for the largest category of not-for-profit organizations, the federal, state, and local government. There are few things in our lives that are not affected by some branch of government. In general, governments attempt to satisfy a multitude of public needs through various programs, but, in doing so, must tax individuals and organizations to generate the revenues to support those programs. Whereas business firms cannot force individuals to purchase their products and services, government can require all individuals to pay taxes, even if some of those individuals do not believe in one or more of the specific goals the government is attempting to achieve. Almost everyone is at least tacitly involved in the governmental goal-setting process of electing officials to run the government. Therefore, in theory, elected government officials have the same goals as the majority of the voting public. This process naturally results in government units, at the various levels, maintaining multiple, and often even conflicting, goals.

2.4 RECONCILING MULTIPLE GOALS

Conflict among goals.

The mere existence of multiple goals complicates the organization's activity planning. This is not only because resources must now be carefully allocated toward various objectives, a difficult enough problem in itself, but also because some of the goals will probably be in conflict: for example, hiring the handicapped and minimizing labor costs, reducing taxes and providing increased veteran's benefits, and so forth. In addition to conflicting strategic goals there clearly may be conflicts between organizational and personal goals (such as every manager wanting to be president).

Every organization must recognize and then meld these diverse interests and aspirations into a broader set of organization-wide goals. Whether goals conflict or

Resource restrictions on goal achievement.

not, an allocation of the available resources is necessary. Because resources are limited, it is seldom true that all organizational goals can be achieved simultaneously. The activities and operations required to achieve one goal consume the resources that could be used to move the organization closer to some of its other goals. Such limitations on resources have been clearly documented over the past few years with such examples as the "energy crisis" and the "capital crunch."

The limits on available resources place **constraints** or bounds on the level of achievement of the various organizational goals. For an organization operating with limits on the supply of money, labor, materials, energy, or equipment, the number of achievable goals can be quite limited. In fact, it is often the case that none of the organization's goals can be completely accomplished with the available resources.

Priorities

Setting priorities of the goals.

Even though they are faced with the problem of multiple goals and limited resources, organizations must still decide what new programs to initiate and which existing programs to increase or decrease. In order to make these decisions, organizations must establish **priorities** for each of the goals. Priorities are statements of the relative importance of the goals. That is, they indicate the *order* of importance to the organization (e.g., first priority) or the *weight* assigned to each goal. For example, President Kennedy placed a high priority on a moon landing before the end of the 1960s and thus the NASA budget was significantly increased. Likewise, President Johnson placed a great emphasis on social reform and hence a high priority was assigned to his "Great Society" programs. It should be noted that, like tactical goals, priorities also vary over time and between different individuals.

Tradeoffs

Establishing goal tradeoffs.

When resources are limited so that we cannot achieve all of our goals simultaneously, we are forced to make **tradeoffs**. A tradeoff is the substitution of achievement of one goal for another. We can, for example, trade the achievement of all of one goal for all or part of another. Or similarly, we can trade the achievement of one goal now for that of another goal later. The priorities are used to make the decisions regarding amounts of each goal to be traded or substituted for others. For example, during the economic slowdown of the early 1970s government economists had to trade off inflation with employment. Government goals were to simultaneously minimize the rate of inflation and maximize the rate of employment. Some inflation had to be accepted in order to achieve a higher level of employment. In our own personal selection of clothing, food, appliances, and automobiles we make tradeoffs between the goals of low price, high quality, and quantity. Also, we must trade purchases today for, perhaps, more important purchases later.

Reaching a goal concensus.

Together, the process of establishing priorities and trading off accomplishment of one goal for accomplishment of other goals allows the organization to reach a concensus of opinion regarding the most appropriate "direction" to take in its activities. Without this process it would be virtually impossible to allocate, in a rational manner, the scarce resources available to the organization.

2.5 CRITERIA FOR OPERATIONS MANAGEMENT

Establishing criteria to measure goal achievement.

Once we have established the goals that will guide the organization in planning its operations, management must decide what programs and activities will accomplish these goals. **Criteria** are the "yardsticks" or measures that we use to determine which activities will best achieve our goals. That is, criteria are practical, operational measures of goal achievement which can be used in the day-to-day management of operations.

For example, Table 2.1 lists "growth" as a major goal of top business executives. This goal itself cannot, however, be used in day-to-day decisions until it is **operationalized**; that is, translated into operating terms (criteria) that can be measured. Such criteria might be: share of the market, total assets, annual sales, size of the work force, plant size, number of plants, or any of a number of such measures.

Some profit criteria.

Similarly, in purchasing a new machine for the factory, the goal "to produce a profit" must be considered. It would be virtually impossible to analyze each investment decision so as to predict the impact on profit. Instead, we develop such decision criteria as *minimum payback period, maximum net present value*, and *maximum internal rate of return*. These are *operational* measures of impact on the profit goal which can be easily adopted and understood by the operations manager. Several of these methods will be discussed in Chapter 10I, The Financial Interface.

Need for multiple criteria.

Even with one goal, multiple criteria are often used because one criterion will rarely measure the direct achievement of a goal. For example, "response time to an alarm" is often used as a criterion in the provision of ambulance health service but this obviously does not, by itself, measure goal achievement (e.g., "protection of life and health," "reduction of mortality and morbidity"). Clearly, the proper administration of emergency care, transport time to a hospital, and other such measures must also be included.

Surrogate criteria.

However, some criteria themselves are difficult to measure and therefore many organizations use more easily measured "surrogate" criteria as a basis of goal achievement (e.g., professorial publications as a measure of contribution to knowledge, or even as a measure of professional competence; number of arrests as a measure of crime rate, and sometimes also, as a measure of the amount of *reduction* in crime).

Once priorities, tradeoffs, and operational criteria of goal achievement are specified there still exists the problem of determining the overall value of any alternative being considered. For example, in purchasing a new car, a buyer may establish riding comfort, mileage, and purchase cost as the three decision criteria. If a model exists that scores "best" on all three criteria, then that one is obviously the best buy. But such *dominant* alternatives seldom exist. How does the operations manager choose between alternatives where one does not dominate the others? There are a number

TABLE 2.2 OUTCOME OF TWO ALTERNATIVES

Criteria	Profit Increase	Sales Increase	Market Share Increase
Alternative 1	3%	$40,000	1¼%
Alternative 2	2%	$70,000	¾%

of methods (see [8, pp. 77–81]) available to the operations manager which make use of tradeoffs established by upper management to select the optimum alternative. Some of these are described below.

Express All Criteria in Terms of One Scale

Effective dollars criterion.

In some cases it is possible to express all the criteria in terms of one monetary unit. For example, a business firm may conclude that poor service to a customer "costs" the firm $500 per year in bad advertising and lost future profits, skimping on preventive maintenance costs $100 per machine, and so forth. That is, the dollar tradeoff for poor service is $500 and for skimping on preventive maintenance, $100 per machine.

In other situations, it may be feasible to express all of the criteria in terms of one of the other criteria; that is, to establish the tradeoffs between all criteria and one "baseline" criterion. For instance, a drug clinic may decide that each person counselled is equivalent to one drug-free person-week, each $100 of support is worth six drug-free person-weeks, and so on.

Translate all criteria into one.

An example using a weighted scale is given in Tables 2.2 and 2.3. Here the manager's problem is to choose between two alternatives with the expected results of following each alternative given in Table 2.2. Expressing all the criteria of Table 2.2 in terms of the baseline criterion "percentage of profit increase" with the tradeoffs listed gives the results shown in Table 2.3. There it is seen that alternative 2 is best since it achieves the greatest "percentage of profit increase."

TABLE 2.3 OUTCOME CONVERSION TO ONE SCALE

	Criteria	Profit Increase	Sales Increase	Market Share Increase	Total
	Tradeoffs:	—	1%/$10,000	1%/½%	
	Alternative 1	3%	$\frac{40,000}{10,000}=4\%$	$\frac{5/4}{1/2}=2.5\%$	9.5%
Best →	Alternative 2	2%	$\frac{70,000}{10,000}=7\%$	$\frac{3/4}{1/2}=1.5\%$	10.5%

Use of Indexes

Base scale criterion.

When the same criteria are measured over a long period of time it is often useful to construct a 100-point based scale with each criterion comprising a portion of the 100 points according to its importance weight. Evaluation of the same criteria in later periods can then be related back to this "base" period to determine progress in achieving goals.

EXAMPLE: Suppose the San Francisco BART (Bay Area Rapid Transit) uses two measures of service: "on-time" rate and annual number of passengers carried. BART authorities feel that the on-time rate is three times as important as the number of passengers carried. If, when they opened in 1972, the two measures were 61 percent and 10,000, respectively, and now the measures are 50 percent and 16,000, has service improved?

SOLUTION: Using a 100-point based scale, and since on-time rate is three times as important as the number carried, then

$$3x + x = 100 \text{ points for 1972}$$

$$x = 25 \text{ points for number carried}$$

$$3x = 75 \text{ points for on-time'' rate}$$

Currently the **index** for on-time rate is:

$$\frac{50}{61} \times 75 = 61.48$$

The index for number carried is $16000/10000 \times 25 = 40$. The current index value is therefore $61.48 + 40 = 101.48$ points, indicating a slight increase in service level since 1972.

An interesting application of this approach used by the Auto Club of Southern California is given in Readings, Section 2.7, of this chapter.

Mathematical Programming

Another common approach is to express one or more of the criteria as objectives in a mathematical **programming** framework. Mathematical programming models are used to optimize (maximize or minimize) an objective (goal) subject to the constraints or restrictions placed upon the problem. For example, mathematical programming could be used by a manufacturer to maximize the number of parts produced within one week subject to the constraints that no more than $2000 will be spent, only six employees will be used, and no more than 800 pounds of raw material will be used.

The use of linear programming.

When *one* criterion is being maximized or minimized subject to a number of restrictions, *linear programming* can often be used. The explanation and application of the linear programming concept will be discussed in detail in Chapter 5 so further discussion will be deferred until then.

Goal programming.

If *more than* one criterion is to be maximized or minimized the tool of *goal programming* may be used. This topic will not be discussed in this text; interested readers should consult References 4 or 8.

2.6 SUMMARY

We have seen how top management specifies abstract, strategic, and organizational goals which then must be operationalized by forming more specific tactical goals for operations managers. We have also discussed the fact that, in part due to a number of interested internal and external parties, some of the goals may be in conflict, thereby requiring management to set priorities and tradeoffs among them. But even having such tradeoffs may not give the operations manager sufficient direction in his/her work. In that case criteria must be specified so that progress toward goals may be measured and evaluated. Finally, some simple quantitative techniques were presented to aid the manager in choosing courses of action among competing goals.

In the next chapter we will look at how the organization chooses its output so as to maximize the likelihood of achieving its goals. We will see how this selection is constrained by the operations function and, in turn, significantly affects the entire operations system from purchasing all the way through distribution.

2.7 READINGS

The "Target Car"

U.S. car manufacturers are looking good these days, following some "catch up" years during which foreign cars did better than domestics in meeting current needs such as fuel conservation while still maintaining other desirable characteristics.

For the first time, a U.S.-built car topped the list in the Auto Club's Target Car program. This results from a new U.S. trend of zeroing in on smaller size and greater fuel economy.

The new champ is the recently introduced Oldsmobile Delta 88 Diesel (reviewed in the February *Auto Club News Pictorial*). It scored a record 84 points in the Club's 1978 Target Car Program . . . five more points than any other production vehicle has achieved in the four-year history of the program. Oldsmobile achieved this record by combining a high fuel economy diesel with a body that has a spacious interior. The Oldsmobile diesel gives good acceleration, has an acceptable noise level and should last as long as the gasoline engine.

Also in the first group, following in the wake of the Oldsmobile Diesel, are the Volkswagen Dasher with 79 points and the Volvo 244DL with 78 points (see table for a complete listing of the cars tested).

After this, the cars begin to bunch up. The second group consists of 10 cars that scored between 71 and 75 points. The last group of 11 cars scored between 64 and 68 points—still a significant improvement over previous years.

The American manufacturers are getting more and more competitive with the imports. Last year only one American car made it to the top group of seven cars that scored 71 or more points. This year *13* cars scored at least 71 points, and 5 are of American origin.

In 1978, because of the efforts of domestic manufacturers in down-sizing automobiles to meet current and future federal fuel economy regulations and because of the foreign manufacturers bringing out new models to be competitive, the number of cars from which selections were made was much larger than before. Out of 24 cars that made our list this year, 8 are entirely new models.

These include the top scorer—the Oldsmobile Delta 88 Diesel, and three new foreign cars that respond to the American demand for bigger cars—the Toyota Cressida, Audi 5000 and the BMW 733i. Other new American entries are the Dodge Omni, Lincoln Versailles, the Chrysler Le Baron and the Ford Fairmont.

Now, more about the nature of the program.

As stated in previous articles, the Target Car is an "ideal", or optimum, design which exists only on paper.

The 11 characteristics measured are listed in the table and represent, for the most part, the independent variables challenging modern auto manufacturers. In simpler language, that means most of the characteristics measured ride a see-saw with one or more of the others. Consider fuel economy, for example. Miles per gallon may easily go up while acceleration goes down. Or desirable small exterior dimensions can be bought at the price of some passenger discomfort, and, perhaps, less adequate protection in a collision. A prime activity of the Target Car program is to urge a reasonable balance among all these variables, together with technological advances, which will permit us to push forward in all areas at once.

Several ingredients go into developing Target Car values:

1. The results of scientifically conducted surveys about automobile characteristics using the opinions of the Club's Membership Advisory Group (MAG).
2. The subsequent identification of key trade-off characteristics.
3. The weighting of the 11 characteristics in terms of importance—see "points possible" in the table.
4. The use of test procedures, recognized in industry, or, as in some cases, established as a result of careful research and development. These procedures are designed to produce scores or ratings for each automobile characteristic.

Again, we caution readers concerning interpretation of results obtained in the Target Car program. First, let's consider limitations in connection with the testing performed. Where possible, generally recognized test procedures were used. In some cases, however, actual testing could not be performed. For example, crash testing was precluded because of cost. So a crashworthiness potential rating was substituted, using dimension data. Also, two characteristics, ease of entry/exit and ride quality, were evaluated subjectively.

The Target Car program was not designed to be a consumer guide to the purchase of a new car. However, the program can be used as one source of information for prospective buyers. To assist them, the cost of operating and owning various models can be compared to the Target Car score. Thus, the cost per Target Car point can be derived for various cars.

This and more detailed information about the 1978 Target Car program is contained in a full report which can be obtained by writing to the Automotive Engineering Department, Automobile Club of Southern California, 2601 South Figueroa Street, Los Angeles, Calif., 90007. Members interested in the test data and methodology are encouraged to ask for and review the full report. And, as always, all member comments are appreciated; they inform us of your concerns and are helpful in guiding the program.

1978 TARGET CAR RESULTS

	Points Possible	Olds Delta 88 Diesel	VW Dasher	Volvo 244DL	Mercedes 300D	SAAB 99 GLE	Chev Malibu 305	Datsun 810	Olds Cutlass 260/8	Toyota Cressida	Audi 5000	Ford 200/6 Fairmont	Peugeot** 504 Diesel*	Pontiac Le Mans 305	BMW 733i	Dodge** OMNI	Mercury Monarch 302	Plymouth Volare (318)	Lincoln Versailles 302	Mazda RX4*	Chrysler 318 Le Baron	Subaru DL 4 DR Sedan	Buick Electra 403	Cadillac 350 Seville	Jaguar* XJ6L
Fuel Economy City	12	12	12	12	12	12	6	11	11	12	9	12	12	6	3	12	8	6	8	12	6	12	5	3	3
	24																								
Fuel Economy Hwy	12	12	12	9	12	10	6	6	9	8	6	7	12	6	2	12	7	6	6	8	6	12	4	4	2
Interior front	5	5	4	4	5	4	5	4	5	4	4	4	5	4	4	2	4	5	4	5	5	4	5	5	5
	17																								
Interior Rear	12	11	6	10	6	8	10	9	6	5	5	8	9	8	9	2	8	10	5	4	10	2	9	10	9
Passing Ability 40-60	5	4	5	5	0	5	5	5	4	5	5	4	0	5	5	5	5	5	5	5	5	2	5	5	5
	10																								
Acceleration, 0-50	5	5	4	4	0	4	5	5	4	5	5	5	0	5	5	3	5	5	5	4	5	3	5	5	5
Crash Worthiness Potential	9	5	1	3	3	1	5	4	4	3	2	3	2	4	3	1	4	3	4	3	4	2	4	4	4
Noise @ 30 MPH	3	3	3	3	3	2	3	1	3	3	2	2	3	3	3	3	3	3	3	0	2	2	3	3	3
	9																								
Noise @ 55 MPH	3	3	3	1	3	3	3	1	3	3	2	2	3	3	3	2	3	3	3	1	2	2	3	3	3
Noise @ 60 MPH WOT	3	3	3	2	3	1	3	3	3	3	3	3	2	3	2	2	3	3	3	2	3	2	3	3	3
Luggage/Parcel Capacity	6	6	5	4	5	3	5	3	5	2	6	5	4	5	6	2	4	4	4	4	4	2	6	3	5
Entry and Exit	6	4	4	5	6	5	4	5	4	4	5	3	5	5	6	4	5	5	5	2	5	3	6	5	5
Slalom Handling	6	5	6	6	6	5	5	6	3	6	6	5	4	6	6	6	1	3	4	6	3	6	0	4	4
Small Exterior	5	1	5	3	3	5	3	4	3	3	3	3	4	2	3	5	2	2	2	5	2	5	0	2	2
Ride Quality	5	4	3	4	5	4	4	4	4	4	5	4	3	4	5	4	4	4	5	3	4	3	4	4	5
Small Turn Circle	3	1	3	3	3	3	2	3	2	3	3	1	3	2	3	3	2	1	1	3	0	3	2	1	1
TARGET CAR TOTAL	100	84	79	78	75	75	74	74	73	73	71	71	71	71	68	68	68	68	67	67	66	65	64	64	64

Source: Auto Club of Southern California, © 1978 by the Autombile Club of Southern California.

2.8 KEY TERMS

goals (p. 32)
constraints (p. 37)
criteria (p. 38)
priorities (p. 37)
focus (p. 33)
tradeoffs (p. 37)
programming (p. 40)
tactical (p. 33)
hierarchy (p. 34)
index (p. 40)
operationalize (p. 38)
strategic (p. 33)
MBO (p. 35)

2.9 REVIEW TEST

1. A priority identifies the amount of one goal an organization is willing to sacrifice to achieve some amount of another goal. (p. 37)
a. True b. False

2. Strategic goals include the strategy to operationalize them. (p. 33)
a. True b. False

3. Linear programming includes only one goal as an objective. (p. 40)
a. True b. False

4. Index evaluation of goals expresses all of the goals in terms of one "index" goal. (p. 40)
a. True b. False

5. A hierarchy of goals exists whenever top management formulates more than one strategic goal. (p. 34)
a. True b. False

6. An example of a tactical goal is to "develop a stronger competitive position." (p. 34)
a. True b. False

7. Resource allocation is required only when multiple conflicting goals exist. (p. 37)
a. True b. False

8. Organizational goals are typically very specific so as to allow flexibility. (p. 33)
a. True b. False

9. Profit is the only goal of business. (p. 35)
a. True b. False

10. An example of a business goal is "Employee Job Security." (p. 35)
a. True b. False

11. Multiple criteria are sometimes necessary even if an organization has only one goal. (p. 38)
a. True b. False

2.10 DISCUSSION QUESTIONS

1. What might the multiple strategic and tactical goals be for
a. A "lonely hearts" club (nonprofit).
b. A computer dating service.
c. A religious foundation.
d. A private charity.
e. A public sanitation department.
f. A drug manufacturer.

2. What priorities would you assign to the goals in Question 1? What tradeoffs would you as a manager entertain?

3. What criteria might be used for the organizations in Question 1?

4. What members of an organization should be consulted when goals are determined?

5. How can priorities in international affairs be decided when so many nations clamor for different actions?

6. Review the conditions under which each of the quantitative models in Section 2.5 would be appropriate.

7. Give two example criteria which might be used for the goal "provide for the common defense" as stated in the Preamble.

8. What problems do you feel that a governmental manager faces in determining tradeoffs?

9. If you do not know where you are going, any path will get you there. Discuss the importance of knowing where you are before deciding on a path to take.

10. Discuss the necessity of tradeoffs if resources are not constrained.

11. What primary difficulty do you envision in attempting to "express all criteria in terms of one scale"?

12. Consider your own personal income and some other personal goal. How or why would priorities regarding these two change over time?

13. How do individual employee goals relate to the "profit" goal of a business? Under what circumstances are they complementary and conflicting?

2.11 PROBLEMS

1. The city of Capital Beach is considering two new public works programs, a swimming pool and park, and an industrial park. The criteria which these alternatives are to be scored upon are (1) improving quality of life, (2) attractiveness to new business, (3) annual revenues generated per dollar of cost. Data for the two programs are contained in the following table.

	Improving Quality of Life	Attractiveness to New Businesses	Annual Revenue per Dollar of Cost
Pool and Park	3	6	0.10
Industrial Park	1	18	0.40

The city council has established the following tradeoffs between two of the criteria and the annual revenues/dollar of cost criterion:

Improving quality of life	1 point per dollar of revenue per dollar of cost
Attractiveness to new business	1.5 points per dollar of revenue per dollar of cost

Based upon this information, which alternative should be selected?

2. A small investment service, Onitswayup Associates, measures its analysts' value to the firm in terms of increase in market value of the portfolio and increase in average earnings per share of the portfolio. Increase in market value is twice as important as increase in average earnings per share. Last year, Merrill Lynch, a junior analyst, scored as follows.

Increase in market value	\$1,200,000.00
Increase in average EPS	\$0.98

This year, Merrill believes that his performance has significantly improved (and thus merits a substantial raise). He has posted the following results.

Increase in market value	\$1,050,000.00
Increase in average EPS	\$1.65

How much has Merrill's performance improved?

3. Tom DeMarce is currently in the market for a used car (\$300 purchase price). Tom establishes the following ground rules before going out to purchase a car.

1. Gas mileage is of primary importance.
2. Trunk size is half as important as mileage. (Tom carries his entire operations management library around with him at all times.)
3. Interior room is third in importance, being one-half as important as trunk size.

All other factors are irrelevant to Tom. Tom has located three cars and has scored each of the three criteria on a 10-point scale (10 being the best). Which of the cars should Tom purchase?

	Gas Mileage	Trunk Size	Interior Room
1951 Hudson Hornet	4	8	5
1964 Volkswagen "Beetle"	9	1	2
1962 Cadillac Sedan deVille	2	6	7

2.12 CASE METROPOLITAN UNIVERSITY

Metropolitan University was chartered as a secondary state university in 1971. The University opened its doors in 1975 and grew very rapidly for the first three years. Enrollment in 1978 was just over 9300 students. With this rapid growth came many problems. Faculty had to be hired quickly. There was no real organization. Curriculum was decided on a course by course basis. There was little standardization. The administration of the university was in a constant state of turmoil. Administrative offices were like "organizational musical chairs" with tenures being rather short. Perserverance and patience were the keys to organizational success.

The faculty of the Business School were typical of the confusion which gripped the entire university. The 26 faculty members were mostly recent graduates of major university Ph.D. programs. There were 21 assistant professors and instructors, 3 associate professors and 2 full professors. The Dean was an associate professor with five years teaching experience at a large northeastern university.

During an all-day faculty meeting devoted to "The Future of the Business School," many of the areas of confusion arose. Among the comments made were

> "Our student/teacher ratio is much greater than I was used to at my former university."
>
> "If we don't begin working on the MBA program the administration will never allow us to begin our feasibility study for a Ph.D. program."
>
> "Look, research is the primary purpose for our being here. Why don't we put our resources to work to produce top quality research."
>
> "The travel budget isn't sufficient to allow us to attend the meetings I'm interested in. How do you expect us to maintain visibility with the profession if we can't travel."
>
> "I've had these chapters of my new book with the secretary for six weeks now. How can we publish them if we don't have adequate secretarial support."
>
> "To hell with all the research and writing; we're here to teach and I haven't heard one comment about the poor classroom conditions."
>
> "I don't have the time for another committee. My consulting work simply keeps me too busy."

QUESTIONS FOR DISCUSSION

1. What goals do you see being voiced here?
2. Comment upon the interface between organizational goals and individual goals.
3. From the point of view of a student, what should the Business School's goals be? With what priorities?
4. Survey several faculty members to find out their personal goals and their posture relative to the school's goals.

2.13 REFERENCES AND BIBLIOGRAPHY

1. Dent, James K., "Organizational Correlates of the Goals of Business Management," *Personnel Psychology*, 12:365–393 (1959).
2. Estes, Ralph W., Distinguished Speaker Series, Lexington, Ky.: University of Kentucky, October 21, 1976.
3. Fleming, John E., "Study of a Business Decision," *California Management Review*, 8:51–56 (Winter 1966).
4. Lee, S. M., *Goal Programming for Decision Analysis*, Philadelphia: Ayerbach, 1972.
5. Raia, Anthony, *Management by Objectives*, Glenview, Ill.: Scott-Foresman, 1976.
6. Schick, A., "The Road to PPB: The Stages of Budget Reform," *Public Administration Review*, 26:243–258 (1966).
7. Schubik, Martin, "Approaches to the Study of Decision-Making Relevant to the Firm," in Gore, W. J., and Dyson, J. W., eds., *The Making of Decisions: A Reader in Administrative Behavior*, London: The Free Press of Glencoe, 1964.
8. Turban, E., and Meredith, Jack, *Fundamentals of Management Science*, Dallas: Business Publications, 1977.

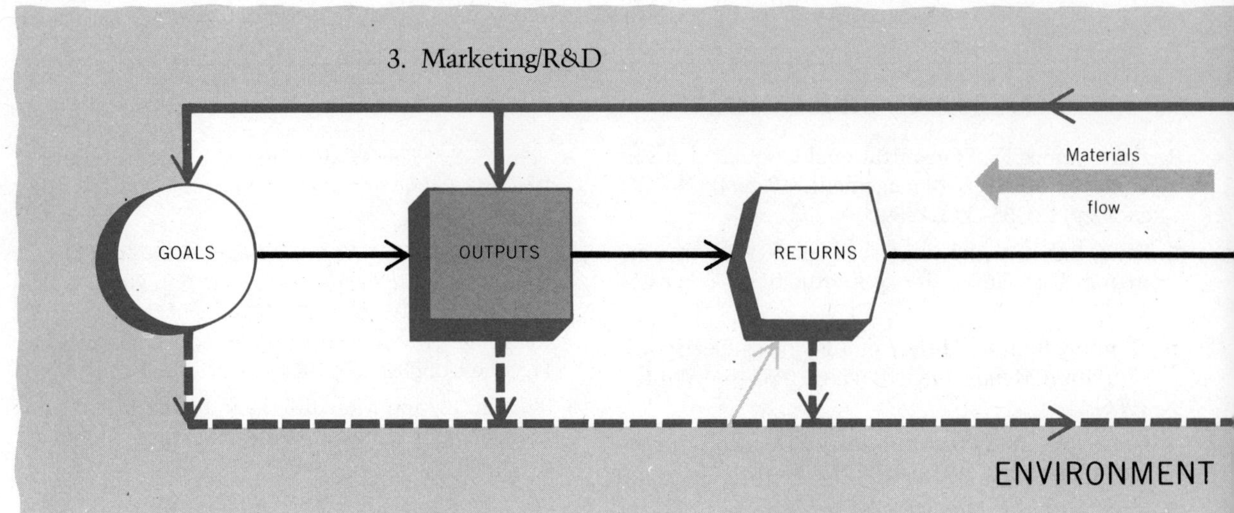

Chapter 3I

The Marketing / R&D Interface: Outputs

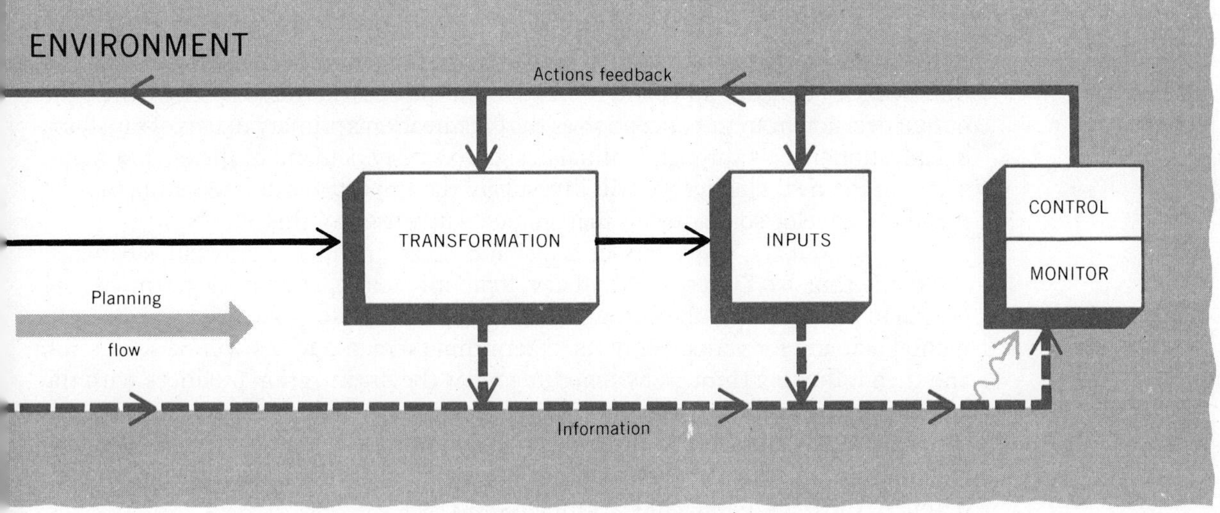

LEARNING OBJECTIVES

By the completion of this chapter the student should

1. Have developed a sense for the mortality history of new product/service ideas.
2. Be familiar with the basic elements of creativity and appreciate its complexity.
3. Understand the nature and roles of research in the organization and its inherent risks.
4. Appreciate the differences in selecting service, as opposed to product, outputs.
5. Know how the organization's strengths and character relate in the selection of the output.
6. Realize that "competition" also exists in the public sector.
7. Understand the use and purpose of a "fit" checklist.
8. Be aware of the economic tradeoffs that can exist with a new output or production process.
9. Know the important design characteristics of products and services and how they must be properly traded off to have a successful output.
10. Comprehend the history of output design, the stages in that history, and its relation to capacity.
11. Understand the differences and similarities between service design and product design.

In the previous chapter we studied how organizations formulate strategic goals and the necessary tradeoffs and compromises in this process. In this chapter we trace the output decision from its conception as the organization's primary means of satisfying organizational goals through its final design to satisfy demand in the environment. Then, in the next chapter we will investigate the importance of forecasting this demand and develop some models that are frequently used for this purpose.

Throughout the entire output decision process, the interrelationships between the marketing, **R&D** (research and development), and operations departments are crucial to the success of the output. Marketing plays the key role in judging environmental demand for various outputs, determining which outputs will be successful, and then following through by matching what the organization produces with the actual demand in the environment. These activities include suggesting new organizational product and service outputs (as well as new customers, new regions, and new technologies), market development and testing, and **commercialization** (getting the output to the right market and ensuring its success).

Role of marketing.

R&D is responsible for creating and developing (but not producing) the organizational outputs. On occasion, R&D also creates new processes by which outputs, either new or old, may be produced. *Research* itself is typically divided into two types: pure and applied. Pure research is simply working with basic technology to develop new knowledge. Applied research is attempting to develop new knowledge along particular lines—for example, a cure for the common cold. *Development* is the attempt to utilize the findings of research and expand the possible applications, typically along the line of interest of the sponsor (e.g., the development of new drugs).

R&D defined.

The operations considerations in the output decision process include the *variety* of outputs that can be produced, the *rate* at which they can be produced, and the *cost* of producing them. In some cases *no* process can produce the outputs—such as the wrist radio of Dick Tracy during the 1930s—because the technology is not available. Of course, wrist radios did finally become available but by then Dick Tracy was using a wrist *television*.

The operations manager must also be concerned with producing outputs that are *undesired* by society such as pollution. These negative outputs can also generate undesired returns for the organization—ill-will, lawsuits, and so forth.

The output selection process.

The selection and design of the product or service to be provided by the organization is a continually ongoing process. Various possible outputs are considered and general designs are developed to determine their approximate costs and performance characteristics. Of these, some are eliminated and others selected for further consideration through prototypes or redesign. This process continues until one or several outputs are finally selected for introduction.

New idea mortality curve.

Figure 3.1 illustrates the **mortality curve** (fallout rate) associated with the concurrent design/evaluation/selection process for a hypothetical group of fifty potential chemical products. The figure assumes that the 50 candidate products are available for consideration in year 3. (The first three years, on the average, are required for the necessary research preceding each candidate product.) Initial evaluation and selection reduces the 50 to about 17 and economic analysis further reduces the number to

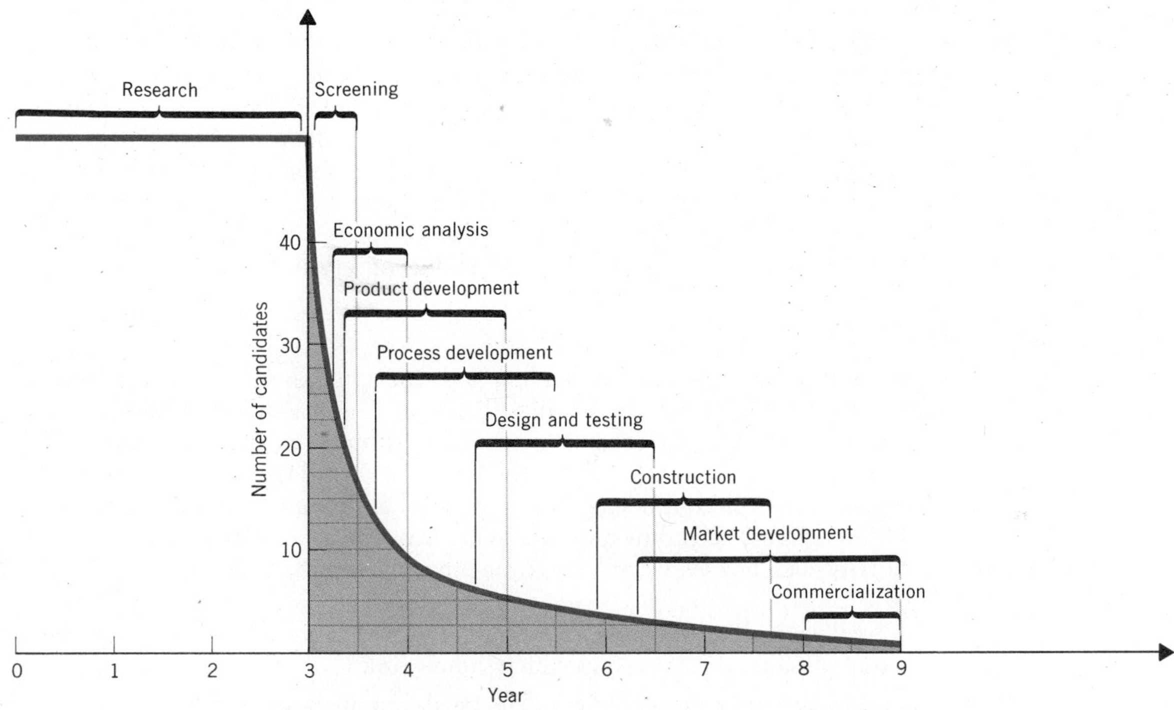

Figure 3.1 Mortality curve of chemical-product ideas from research to commercialization. *Source:* Adapted from *This is DuPont 30*, Wilmington, Del. by permission of E. I. DuPont de Nemours and Co., 1966.

about 9. Development reduces this number even more, to about 5, and design and testing to perhaps 3. By the time the construction for production, market development, and a year's **commercialization** are completed there is only one successful product left. (Sometimes there are none!)

In this chapter we will divide the continuous evaluation/selection/design process into several distinct stages so that each can be studied in turn. The student should keep in mind, however, that the stages are often continuous and occurring simultaneously. We will first consider the manner by which **candidate outputs** are generated. This includes sources of ideas, the role of R&D in organizations, and the need for **creativity** and ways to stimulate it. Next we will discuss the output selection process and the critical role of operations in that process. Lastly, design of the output and its effect on operations will be considered. (The construction and marketing stages will not be addressed.)

3.1 METHODS OF GENERATING CANDIDATE OUTPUTS

There are a number of sources for ideas from which the organization can obtain a set of potential outputs for consideration. In business firms these new output possibili-

Idea sources.

ties come from the marketing department, from company research laboratories, from competitors, customers, and employees, as well as from other sources. The marketing department, however, is responsible for the introduction of most new developments, and it is this department's responsibility to be on the lookout for new product or service ideas. Some of these are the result of recognizing a new or potential improvement through contact with customers who use existing products or services. Many are the direct result of, and response to, new introductions of competitors. Also, customers themselves will often directly request a special improvement that may evenutally be made standard for the product or service.

Creativity

Einstein has been credited with having said "Imagination is more important than knowledge." Both, though, are key ingredients to **creativity**—an essential element in the generation of new product and service ideas. Although creativity has been studied extensively [1, 4, 5, 6, 7, 8, 10, 11, 13, 16, 17] it is still not well understood. For example, Figure 3.2 contradicts the commonly held assumption that technological breakthroughs are becoming more and more frequent in our "future shock" society. Creativity does, however, appear to require the following basic elements.

The elements of creativity.

- **Intelligence:** To store and recall information and to understand and correctly conceptualize the manner in which things work.
- **Imagination:** To form unique and unusual combinations of elements and processes.
- **Motivation:** To be willing to concentrate on a problem for extended periods of time without becoming discouraged or fatigued.

Ways to increase creativity.

Apparently, creativity can be fostered, or stimulated, in individuals by education and training in creativity techniques and processes. A number of the procedures used by "creative" persons have been studied and reported on [4, 5, 6, 13, 17]. The general approaches such people use in being creative are summarized below.

- *Ongoing practice:* Stay informed and stimulated, develop an idea "library" or reserve, be alert to unusual events and thoughts, vary your routine, watch for problems, carry a pad and pencil, drill your mind regularly in idea generation.
- *Preparation:* Relax your mind ahead of time ("sleep on it"); identify your most creative time of day; be enthusiastic, alert, and confident; organize your approach; use a place where you will not be distracted.
- *Getting started:* State the "problem" carefully, do not evaluate as you go or worry about poor ideas, be ready for inspiration, do not limit yourself to the short-term—look ahead, be specific with ideas rather than vague or general.
- *The session:* Build on previous ideas, use a checklist, divide the problem into pieces, try other senses than sight, skip over a temporarily unsolvable aspect, change the words in the problem statement, state the old in new terms and the

TIMETABLE OF TECHNOLOGICAL BREAKTHROUGHS

Is the pace of technological innovation really accelerating? Major breakthroughs in the last quarter century were fewer than in the previous 25 years—and fewer than in the two preceding quarter centuries. And many of the breakthroughs that have had visible impact on our daily lives came more than a half century ago.

	Years Ago		Years Ago
Use of antiseptics in surgery	**100**	Rocket engine	**50**
Storage battery		Commercial fertilizers	**40**
Dynamite		Hybrid seed	
Use of petroleum for heating, cooking, lighting		Air conditioning	
Telephone		Xerography	
Steam turbine		Electron microscope	**35**
Use of steel in construction		Radar	
Internal combustion engine		Antibiotics	**30**
Synthetic chemicals		Artificial insemination	
Electric generator	**90**	Atomic bomb	
Elevator		Television	
Recording and reproduction of sound		Ballistic missile	
Electric light	**75**	Electronic computer	
Electric motor		Electronic transistor	
Machine gun		Gas turbines	**25**
Steel ships		Jet engines	
Aluminum		Stimulated emission of radiation (Maser)	
Submarine		Nuclear power	
Automobile		Practical use of space satellites	**10**
Synthetic drugs	**65**	Holography	**5**
Synthetic fibers and plastics		Brain scanner	**2**
Radio			
Airplane	**60**		

Figure 3.2 One hundred years of technological creativity. *Source:* IW and J. F. Kincaid. *Journal of the Assn. for the Advancement of Invention and Innovation*, July/Aug. 1976. Reprinted by permission of the Association for the Advancement of Invention and Innovation.

new in old terms, list the characteristics of the problem, work backward from the *ideal* solution.

- *Concluding:* Set a quota for new ideas, do not be satisfied with things as they are, do not worry about others' opinions, spot earlier mistakes, talk it over with someone else.

Brainstorming.

To facilitate the "imagination" phase of creativity a number of special group procedures have been utilized, the best known of which is **brainstorming** [2, 3, 5, 10, 11, 16]. A brainstorming session encourages group members to present unusual ideas and to build upon others' ideas, without evaluating the idea itself. A brainstorming session eliminates the "That's crazy!" or "It'll never work" responses that often result during group problem solving sessions. This stage of the process is designed to allow the subconscious mind to free associate without being inhibited by the conscious (evaluating) mind. The review and evaluation stage, which is an analytic rather than a creative process, can be conducted at a later time.

Research

Many organizations, both public and private, sponsor both pure and applied research in order to generate new ideas, processes, and products. Unfortunately, the returns from such research are frequently meager while the costs are great. For example,

SX-70 research.

Polaroid spent over $350 million on its new SX-70 camera in the early 1970s, anticipating large profits from the sale of *film* for the camera. Unfortunately, initial sales were much less than expected [14], and on July 2, 1975 Polaroid stock fell 11⅜ points, a drop of 32 percent (representing $360 million), apparently due to the announcement that SX-70 sales were only one-third of company projections. (Sales improved later after SX-70 price cuts.)

Two frequent alternatives to research used by organizations are *imitation* of a proven new idea or outright *purchase* of someone else's invention. Although the former approach does not put the organization first on the market with the new product or service, it does give them the opportunity to study any possible defects in the original product or service and rapidly develop a better design, frequently at a better price. The latter approach, that is, purchasing an invention or the inventing

Riskless innovation.

company itself, eliminates the risks inherent in research, but still requires that the company develop and market the product or service before it knows whether or not it will be successful. Either route spares the organization the risk and tremendous cost of conducting the actual research leading up to a new invention or improvement.

In addition to *product research* (as it is generally known) there is also **process research**. This involves the generation of new knowledge concerning how to produce outputs. Currently the production of so many familiar products out of plastic (toys, pipe, furniture, etc.) is an outstanding example of successful process research. Although not typically involved in the research side of such process innovation, the

Applying process research.

operations manager *is* intimately involved in *applying* these developments in the day-to-day production of the organization's outputs. The possible tradeoffs in such applications are many and complex. The new process may be more expensive but produce a higher quality output (and thus the repeat volume may be higher or the price can be increased). Or the new process may be more expensive and produce a *lower* quality output but be simpler and easier to maintain, resulting in a lower total cost and, ultimately, higher profits. It is clear that many considerations involving labor, maintenance, quality, materials, capital investment, and so on, are involved in the successful application of research to operations.

Patenting new ideas.

Important new R&D breakthroughs are usually *patented* in the U.S. Patent Office. This gives the patent holder the exclusive right to produce the new product or process, or license others to produce it, for 17 years. To obtain a patent, which now often takes over 3 years, the applicant must fully describe his/her invention and show that it is new, useful, tangible (i.e., not just an idea), and marketable. In a similar fashion, written, musical, and artistic creations can be *copyrighted* by sending two copies and an application fee to the U.S. Copyright Office in Washington, D.C. Lastly, trademarks can be *registered* at the U.S. Patent Office also (but, of course, have nothing to do with patenting or invention). The registering of a trademark, or brand name, prohibits others from using it without permission.

THE WALL STREET JOURNAL

"You rang, Sir?"

(*Source: The Wall Street Journal*, December 30, 1976. Reprinted by by permission of Cartoon Features Syndicate.)

3.2 SELECTING THE OUTPUTS

Selection of the best ideas.

Once the organization has enumerated a number of potential new product or service ideas, the task still remains to evaluate and select the "best" ones. In some situations the selection of the appropriate product or service is relatively straightforward once the goals of the organization have been established. For example, a municipal fire department that has established "minimization of life and property losses through fire" as its primary organizational goal will obviously select fire fighting and other fire prevention activities as a service. A restaurant on the other hand, which has established the primary goal of "earning a 15 percent profit on sales," has a broad range of service possibilities open to it. Decisions must still be made regarding the theme, the hours, the serving of alcohol, and many other such matters.

Services selection.

In general, the selection of a service is usually easier (but more subjective) than the selection of a product because of the following factors.

- The service organization's goal is usually directed to a generalized need on the part of the recipient or ability on the part of the organization (e.g., a recruiting firm, a podiatrist).
- Fewer elements are usually involved in the production of a service such as plant, equipment, supplies, materials, storage facilities, and so forth. (Exceptions exist where large amounts of equipment are concerned however: airlines, laundromats, laboratories.)
- If a change in the service is later found to be necessary, it can typically be accomplished with less difficulty and expense because services are typically labor, rather than equipment, intensive.
- Less **lead time** is involved in the development of a service since the product development and design stages, and much of the research stage, can be significantly shortened. The process design and production stages, however, are still required.

Whether the output is a product or a service, a number of guidelines exist for selecting among the candidate outputs. In general, these guidelines divide into the "screening" and "economic analysis" stages of Figure 3.1.

Screening and the Organizational Fit

In the **screening** stage each candidate output is subjected to several tests to determine which outputs are most likely to "succeed." Testing is based upon the **fit** of the output to the organization and its purpose. Any new output should capitalize on an organization's strengths and competitive advantage, complement the organization's existing outputs, and fit into the organization's structure, goals, and plans for the future.

The general areas of strength (and/or weakness) are

1. Experience with the particular output.
2. Experience with the production process required for the output.
3. Experience in providing an output to the same target recipients.
4. Experience with the distribution system for the output.

An organization must assess all its strengths and weaknesses, keeping in mind the goals of the organization, before a decision can be made to introduce a new product or service. A particular strength cannot necessarily be used as a justification for a new output if other major weaknesses exist. For example, an electronics company with the best professional staff and facilities for production of radio communications equipment may not find it advisable to enter the CB market if past sales have been exclusively military. The bidding and contract experience gained through government procurement will provide no help in marketing radios in the consumer market. The company would have to develop a complete distribution system for the retail level. This one major organizational weakness could be sufficient to convince management that entry into the consumer market is inadvisable, even though the technical capability exists.

Evaluate weaknesses as well as strengths.

Organizational strengths and weaknesses cannot be considered in a vacuum. In the private sector there typically exist other firms that produce similar products or services. Even if the output is a new one, the firm can expect competitors to enter the market quickly if its own introduction is successful. Even a public sector organization is not exempt from an analysis of the marketplace and the existing and potential "competitors." While we generally do not think of a state park being in *competition* with a county park, or a city hospital being in *competition* with a private religious hospital, these organizations do compete for limited demand in the community.

Public competition too.

The organization must consider the capabilities it possesses *relative* to the capabilities of other organizations in the marketplace and determine in which markets it might hold a **competitive advantage** due to such strengths as a particularly skilled labor force, a flexible set of facilities, an expensive and scarce piece of equipment, and so forth. In the great majority of organizations this competitive advantage must be reflected in the operations area, as illustrated above—it is the rare organization that can compete successfully with only a marketing, or financial, competitive advantage.

Competitive advantage.

In operations, the competitive advantage, when used as a top management *strategy*, is known as the operations *focus*, as defined in Chapter 2. (Needless to say, it is imperative that the marketing, financial, and operations strategies all dovetail and complement each other.) Three common operations strategies are:

Three operations strategies.

1. High volume, low cost (low variety, minimal quality)
2. High quality, high cost (high or low volume and variety)
3. High variety and quick response to demand, high cost

To illustrate the interrelationship of focus and output selection consider the following example. An organization with an operations focus oriented to high volume output rates should carefully consider whether a contemplated made-to-order output is compatible with the existing process. Similarly, an organization with a skilled labor force operating general purpose equipment to produce customized outputs should be wary of an output that requires high volume production to be profitable.

Operations compatibility.

Analyses similar to the above should be conducted for all the operations focus areas such as

- Capacity.
- Logistics.

- Location.
- Layout.
- Process design.
- Scheduling.
- Materials.
- Quality.
- Reliability/maintenance.

How operations can constrain the organization.

The organization may well find that its strategic goals are severely constrained by past, short-term (unfocused) decisions regarding the operations area and that to avoid being constrained in its strategy it will need to take an active hand in molding its productive operations toward a particular focus. For further discussion in this area refer to Reference 12.

Another aspect that the organization must address is the effect a new output will have on both the demand and the production methods used for existing outputs, a consideration of major importance to the operations manager. For example, introduction of color television sets reduced the demand for standard black and white T.V.'s. Clearly, a new output may very well change the "best" production methods to be used for existing outputs in terms of labor skills, type of equipment, and possibly even the operations focus of the organization. It will certainly change the scheduling, routing, and other production planning aspects of the operations area.

Effect on existing outputs.

Sometimes, of course, a new output totally changes the organization and its goals instead. On occasion, organizations do this on purpose to move into a new product or service area, especially if the old output is near the end of its life cycle.

The fit test.

One simple method for checking the organizational fit of the candidate outputs is by a **checklist**, such as that shown for *products* in Figure 3.3. Although such a list is not a substitute for analysis it does provide a starting point for analysis. We can begin by concentrating attention of the "Poor" fit areas and analyzing the impact of these and the tradeoffs available between areas checked as "Poor" and those checked as "Excellent."

Economic Analysis

The fit, in terms of economic costs and returns to the organization, must also be considered in this initial screening. Will the product or service result in an overall increase or decrease in returns to the organization? What will happen to demand for existing outputs? Will total costs stay the same? Generally speaking, the returns should exceed the costs—if not the monetary returns then at least the other returns, such as acquiring experience in a new output area. Because new outputs usually involve heavy advance investments with returns coming in over a long future horizon, the economic analysis should include the element of time since time effects the value of both cost and returns. Time is usually incorporated into economic analysis through the concepts of **present value** and **internal rate of return**, topics that will be deferred until Chapter 10I: The Financial Interface.

The time value of money.

Area of Fit	Poor	Fair	Good	Excellent
I. *General*				
1. Fits long-term organizational goals				
2. Capitalizes on organizational strengths				
3. Appealing to management				
4. Utilizes organizational experience				
II. *Market*				
5. Adequate demand				
6. Existing or potential competition				
7. In line with market trend				
8. Enhances existing line				
III. *Economics*				
9. Cost				
10. Price				
IV. *Production*				
11. Capacity availability				
12. Material supply and price				
13. Engineering know-how				

Figure 3.3 Typical organizational fit checklist.

Assuming that a preliminary output(s) has been selected we next focus on the design of the output and the critical role of operations in this process.

3.3 OUTPUT DESIGN

Types of design.

Once the outputs have been selected, the task of *design* can begin. Design is the determination of the particular specifications of an output so an organization can economically produce it. A **preliminary design** results in the gross specifications of the product or service such as size, color, energy requirements, lifetime, and so forth. Following this step, a more detailed design takes place. **Final design**, in reality, never really occurs because the output is always being improved or modified to meet new requirements. But, actually, a final design is needed, with its detailed specifications for components, tolerances, production processes, and so forth, to move the product or service from the "drawing board" (for example, Figure 3.4) to "production." However, once a design has been set and implemented in a production system it may be very difficult to change. For example, dozens of inventors have redesigned the standard, highly inefficient typing keyboard so that typing speeds could be significantly increased, even *doubled*. But too many people have already memorized the old keyboard and are not willing to relearn a new one.

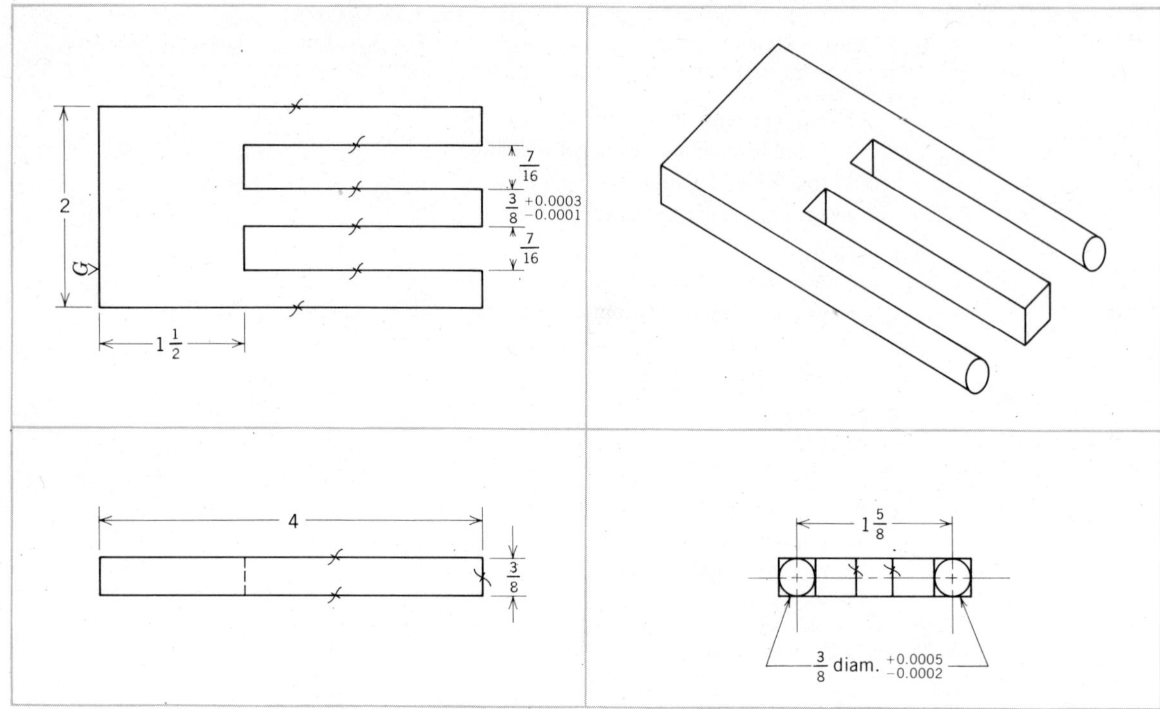

Figure 3.4 From the drawing board to production: standardization of fork plate for mass production.

History of Output Design

For some time the primary purpose of product design was only to facilitate the production process. Since demand for goods was plentiful as long as the price was low, companies desired to minimize the unit cost of items. One method of reducing unit cost was increasing capacity through *mass production* or assembly line manufacture. Thus, companies moved toward **standardization** and **interchangeability** of products and parts (Figure 3.4) to both minimize costs and assembly difficulty. Standardization had the following cost-related advantages.

Standardization to increase capacity.

1. It minimized the number of different parts to stock.
2. It minimized the number of production runs necessary.
3. It simplified processing procedures and thus reduced the need for certain controls.
4. It allowed larger purchases with quantity discounts.
5. It minimized repair and servicing problems.

On the other hand, standardization had several drawbacks. For example, using standard parts rather than specially made parts sometimes meant lower quality products. But the major disadvantage of standardization was the inflexibility of production; little variety was possible. The classic comment exemplifying this fact was that of Henry Ford who is reputed to have declared that his customers could have any color Model T they desired, as long as it was black!

The marketing phase

This standardization set the stage for the marketing phase of output design—designing for product characteristics other than cost, such as variety, quality, appearance, and so forth. Of course, cost could not be totally ignored. These other product characteristics had to be obtained while minimizing the increase in product cost. One method used to obtain variety, or at least the semblance of variety and still hold down costs, was **modularization**. This meant producing the product in "modules" or subassemblies that were interchangeable, thus giving the customer some choice in his product. For instance, the purchaser of a new car can specify the engine size, type of transmission, upholstery, color, and numerous other aspects of the product. Such variety is *not* achieved by producing some number of every possible model but rather by producing modules (e.g., engines, transmission, bodies with varying colors, upholstery, tires and wheels, etc.) and then joining the appropriate modules together in final assembly according to the customer's order.

Modularization allows variety.

As an example of modularization, an automobile with three possible engines, two possible transmissions, five different exterior colors and three different interiors available to the customer requires only 13 modules for the operations manager to keep track of. But these 13 modules can be combined to form $3 \times 2 \times 5 \times 3 = 90$ different versions of the same model automobile, a blessing for the marketing staff.

Shortages

A recent addition to the output design problem has been the recurring shortages of the factors of production and the resulting direct decreases in capacity. Recently we have seen, and are likely to continue to live with, "raw material scarcities," the "capital crunch," and the "energy crisis," all of which tend to restrict output capacity. There have been a number of responses to this dilemma. Some of the major responses have been

Recent shortages and some responses.

- *Reducing product lines.* Marginal products have been dropped and a general retrenchment has taken place. Some new lines have been postponed and existing lines combined.
- ***Simplification** programs.* Simplifying products means fewer parts (thereby saving materials and labor), easier service, and greater reliability. Simplification can also be applied to the production process with equally important benefits.
- ***Value analysis.*** Value analysis (or value engineering) examines the *function* of an output and attempts to achieve it with less cost (for example, replacing metal parts with plastic parts). It considers cheaper methods, materials, processes, designs, and so forth.

Regulation

Another recent set of restrictions concerning output design, with some of the same responses as above, has been federal laws and regulations concerning pollution, occupational safety and health (OSHA), consumer protection, and other, similar problems. Some of these regulations are directed toward the product or service itself such as labeling of ingredients, health warnings, statements of true interest rates, mandated automobile gasoline mileages, emission restrictions, drug and chemical prohibitions (red dye, freon, phosphates), and so on. These regulations directly affect the organization's output and hence the operations area that has the responsibility of producing the output.

Regulation affects capacity.

Other regulations, such as those regarding OSHA and pollution, concern the production process directly. Restrictions on the disposal of nuclear waste severely hamper electric generating capacity, for example. Similarly, safety restrictions in the workplace and the diversion of capital for pollution control tend to reduce productivity.

Service design

Designing services.

The current stage in the history of output design centers around the design of services. As mentioned in Chapter 1, services are usually considered to be labor intensive rather than capital (equipment, facilities) intensive and hence their design often centers around the skills of the person performing the service (e.g., physician, auto mechanic). As Levitt [9] points out, this may be a fatal perspective!

Focus on the recipient, not the output.

We have spent so many years in the mass production stage of output design that we now tend to erroneously focus on the output instead of the recipient, as illustrated below.

1. The design of services is labor intensive and typically includes personal attendance to the needs of the recipient. Improving the design of the service has been misdirected toward the *server* rather than the recipient.
2. The design of products is capital intensive. Improvements here have been misdirected toward improving the product itself or the capital equipment and facilities used to produce the product.

All outputs are services.

In actuality, all outputs can be viewed as services. A product, such as a wooden chair, is just the sum of a number of very specialized services. Some organization(s) located and purchased the wood, transported it, cut it, shaped and formed it, sanded it, painted it, stored it, sent it in the right quantity at the right time to a location where a customer could find it, informed him or her of its availability, kept its total cost low enough so that it could be purchased, and possibly even helped finance it, get it home, and repaired it when it broke. It is clear then that we use the word *product* to simply indicate a very special set of services and that we do not have to fragment our thinking about the output of operations into product outputs and service outputs unless it is helpful to do so. This "services" perspective should draw attention to the fact that it is the *recipient* who defines what services are in demand, not the *organization*.

Many organizations in the past who lost sight of this point found themselves in trouble; for example, many railroads saw themselves as being merely in the business of running trains instead of the business of providing efficient transportation. Today we see attempts to break out of such restrictive thinking in an effort to orient to what the customer wishes to buy rather than what the producer wishes to produce. For example, "Sell the sizzle, not the steak." And Revlon's: "In the factory we make cosmetics; in the store we sell hope." Today, we even find the gigantic oil companies quietly conducting research in solar and other forms of energy—they apparently see themselves as being in the "energy" business rather than the "petroleum" business.

Selling hope and sizzle.

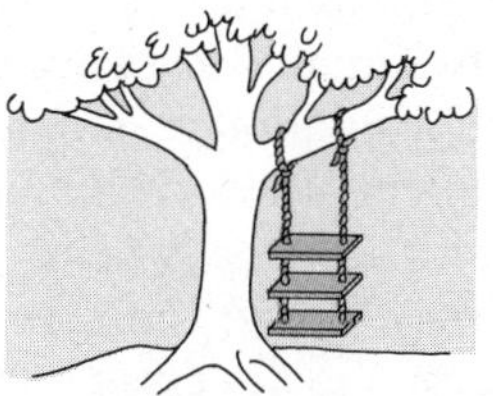

1. What Marketing suggested

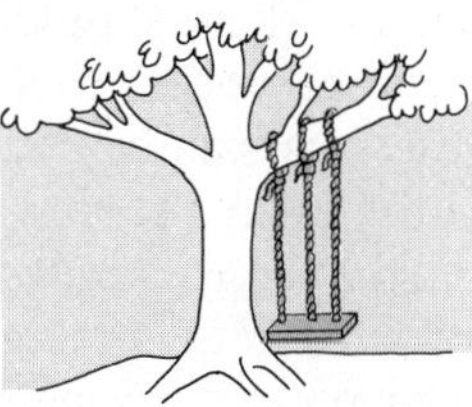

2. What Management approved

3. As designed by Engineering

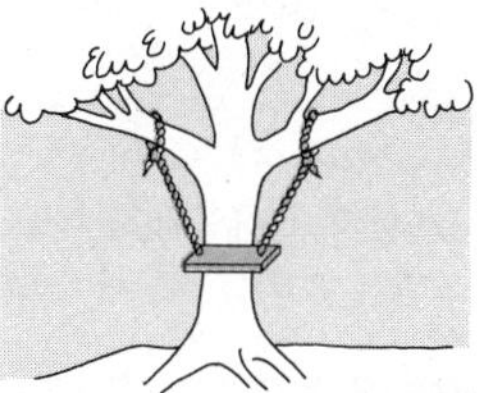

4. What was manufactured

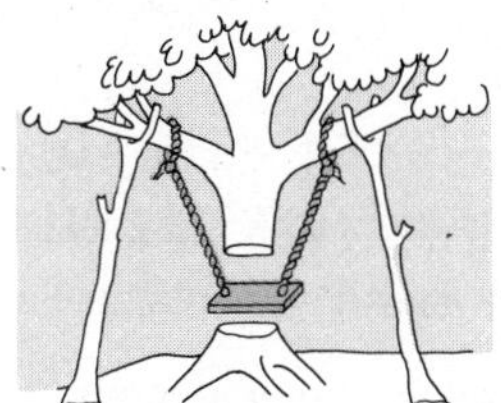

5. As Maintenance installed it

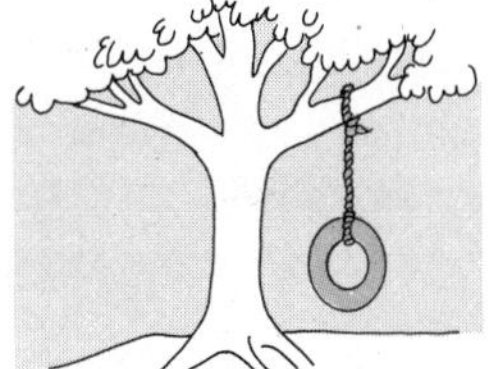

6. What the customer desired

Product services—something for nothing?

This perspective is important to operations managers because many product organizations still see the provision of customer service, financing, instruction, installation, promotion, and so forth, as a necessary evil in the process of producing their product. Some managers tend to consider it in the same category as giving trade stamps with every purchase—a wasteful cost allocated to overhead that the entire industry would rather dispose with but cannot because it is used as a competitive tool.

This attitude totally misses the truth. The demand is not only for the product but for the services as well. (In some instances the primary demand is not for the product *at all* but for the services.) In these instances redesign of the output would focus on the needs of the recipient. The provision of more services would probably be greatly increased, and promoted as well.

Product and service design the same.

In "service organizations" output design should also refocus on the recipient, rather than on the server. By considering what services the recipient is searching for, organizations can often design high efficiency approaches that minimize, or completely eliminate, the slow, highly variable result typically obtained through human labor. Levitt (Reference 9) gives as examples vending machines, packaged promotional displays, and modular servicing, all with the characteristics of complexity and attention to detail in their *concept and design* but simplicity in their *operation*. But these are the same characteristics as products!

Complex concept, simple operation.

Thus the current stage of services design is really not much different from what it has always been; we are simply more hampered by our attitudes and prejudices now than we used to be. There are, however, *some* differences between service and product design and these should be noted. Since the recipient is often directly involved in the output process, there may be output design limitations on the transformation *activities* that can be used (e.g., a limitation on strength), the *speed* of processing (to accommodate the slowest recipient), the *location* of the process (centrally accessible), and the service *storage* possibilities (usually none). If the skill of the recipient is also involved in the process this may further limit the output design. Nevertheless, the burden is still on the organization to design an output that

Design of services may differ due to involvement of the recipient in the process.

- May be complex in concept but is still simple in operation.
- Is directed to the recipients' needs.
- Can be produced at high volume and low cost.

Design Characteristics

Some typical design characteristics of outputs that organizations should consider in relation to demand and capacity are

- Function—the new design must properly perform the function for which it is required.
- Cost—the total cost (materials, labor, processing, etc.) cannot be excessive for the market under consideration.
- Size and shape—these must be compatible with the function and not distasteful or unacceptable to the market.
- Appearance—for some applications the appearance of the product or service is irrelevant; in other instances (e.g., art) the appearance is equivalent to the function.
- Quality—the quality should be compatible with the purpose. Excessive quality may increase cost unnecessarily; insufficient quality leads to complaints and decreased demand.
- Reliability—the output should function normally when used and last the

expected duration. Outputs with complex combinations of elements, all of which must work, will tend to have lower reliabilities unless this is allowed for in the design.

- Environmental impact—the output should not degrade the environment or pose a hazard to the recipient.
- Producibility—the output should be producible with ease and speed.
- Timing—the output should be available when expected. This characteristic is especially relevant to service outputs.
- Accessibility—the recipient should be able to obtain the output without difficulty.
- Recipient input requirements—the amount and type of input required of the recipient should be considered in the design. "Do-it-yourself" projects are an example of this for product outputs and "self-service" for service outputs.

Tradeoffs are the key in design.

The design task is to trade off the above characteristics in order to best meet the demands in the marketplace. For example, when Ford Motor Company introduced the Pinto, much of the initial advertising touted the "ease" of owner maintenance of the vehicle. Even the Owner's Manual contained specific instructions for undertaking the basic maintenance of the car. This improvement in maintainability was brought about by trading some aspects of size, function, and, to some minds, beauty. Another attribute of the new product that was greatly improved was cost, both initial purchase cost and operating cost. Recognition of a special need or desire in the marketplace is the first step, and a major one, in the design of a new product.

"Obviously, it'll have to inflate quicker than that."

(Reprinted with permission from *Changing Times*, © 1973, Kiplinger Washington Editors, Inc., November 1973.)

The rise of self-service.

In the service area, gasoline stations and fast food restaurants have become "self-service" to reduce the cost, as well as the service time, to the recipient. In return for the improvements in these two characteristics of the services, customers have had to give up such conveniences as battery, oil, and tire pressure checks, waiters and waitresses, full line menus, and individual attention. For those people who still desire these features, standard "full service" gas stations are available as are numerous dining alternatives.

Market "segmentation."

In both product and service design, many alternatives usually exist that will meet the basic function of the output. The key to good design is a recognition of the major characteristics of the demand and a detailed analysis of the tradeoffs available between and among the various attributes. Often, several different versions of the same output can be produced so that different market segments will find the output appealing. For example, Procter and Gamble offers a dazzling array of detergents, many of which undoubtedly even compete with each other to some extent. In the fast food business, the major companies have expanded their menus to broaden the appeal to new markets (e.g., McDonald's now offers chili, sundaes, and eggs and pancakes at many locations).

3.4 SUMMARY

The output selection and design process is characterized by a high mortality rate of new ideas, requiring in the neighborhood of 50 to 100 ideas (following, possibly, years of research) to produce, six years later, one successful output. These ideas come from a number of sources, such as marketing, customers, competitors, and R&D but all typically involve some amount of creativity, the basic elements of which are intelligence, imagination, and motivation. To some extent creativity can be stimulated and fostered by following certain procedures; group stimulation such as "brainstorming" can also be used.

Alternatives to research for new ideas that avoid some of the inherent risk are imitation of an existing successful output or process and outright purchase of an idea (or the organization owning the idea). The tradeoffs in applying process research to the organization's operations are many and complex including quality, simplicity, cost, investment, and so forth. Such complicated tradeoffs require a careful screening procedure, including economic analysis, for new ideas that will not overlook many hidden advantages and costs. Three main considerations in the initial screening of potential outputs are

1. How well the output capitalizes on the organization's strengths.
2. How well the output complements existing outputs.
3. How well the output "fits" the organization in terms of facilities, long-term goals, and so forth.

In designing the output, success often hinges upon how well the design characteristics (cost, appearance, etc.) are traded off to meet the needs of the recipients.

Originally, product design was primarily aimed at maximizing the output rate and minimizing the cost via standardization. Later, to increase the variety available to recipients, modularization became a design objective. More recently, with the energy, raw materials, and capital shortages, value analysis and simplification have entered the design picture. Output design is also affected by recent regulations concerning pollution and safety control.

In the design of services, special consideration should be made for the fact that the recipient often participates in (and therefore limits) the production process. Nevertheless, in the design of either services or products the design should center on the need of the recipient and not the server or the output.

3.5 READINGS

A Growing R&D Gap

BY PETER GWYNNE

American enterprise thrives on invention—the pursuit of an abstract formula in a lonely college lab, the fashioning of advanced computer hardware in a massive industrial complex. Yet, there are growing signs that this creative pulse is slowing down. Between 1971 and 1976, patents granted to Americans fell by 21 per cent. In the same period, the number of Japanese scientists and engineers performing nondefense research and development (R&D) climbed close to the U.S. total—even though Japan's population is less than half that of the United States. "The figures make it abundantly clear that our nation's position of R&D leadership is slipping," says Arthur Bueche of General Electric.

Such gloomy assessments have long been voiced by university researchers, miffed at what they regard as unrealistically low levels of government support. But now, the fears are spreading beyond the ivory towers. A fortnight ago, President Jimmy Carter wrote to all members of the Congressional committees that oversee basic research, pleading with them not to trim his budget for science. Equally worrying is the lag in industrial R&D. A report last week by the American Association for the Advancement of Science (AAAS) warned that industry is increasingly investing in short-term objectives and existing products.

Industry blames the trend on a variety of causes. For one thing, the current climate of economic uncertainty makes companies leery about making long-term commitments. For another, present patent law—which offers only seventeen years of protection—discourages industry from backing research on products that might not reach the marketplace until after the deadline. Last year, the DuPont Co. decided to devote about 75 percent of its research budget to existing products–a rise of 12 percent from the previous year.

Firms are also often hampered by a maze of government regulations designed to ensure the safety of workers and consumers. For example, an expanding proportion of the steel industry's R&D is devoted to finding better ways to reduce environmental pollution. Automobile companies are forced to put large sums into development of emission-control devices, while the pharmaceutical industry is pouring growing amounts into tests on the safety of its drugs.

BLEAK MOOD

On the campus, the mood is equally bleak. Even increases in research funds no longer draw outright applause. Thus, the scientific community's approval of the Carter Administration's proposed budget for fiscal 1979, which boosts grants for fundamental research by almost 5 percent beyond the rate of inflation, was tempered by awareness that the proportion of gross national product devoted to R&D has fallen by one-third in the past fourteen years.

Certainly, the additional funds are not enough to expand some highly visible research projects. The proposed budget reduces from five to four the number of orbiter vehicles that will be built for the first phase of the manned space-shuttle program, designed to provide a platform for scientific experiments in space. And the Federal budget for development of solar heating and cooling equipment has been cut by more than a third, from $60.5 million to $36 million.

OBSOLETE TOOLS

Most science administrators feel the extra cash will do little more than make up for past neglect. This was a major theme last week at a Washington, D.C., colloquium sponsored by the AAAS. "The fact is that after several years of stringent budgets, universities must now upgrade research equipment," said New York University president John Sawhill. His point: research tools quickly become obsolete and are more and more expensive. "Inflation has struck with a vengeance," added Frank Press, the Presidential science adviser, "with the price increases of some equipment taking quantum leaps." One recent survey among eight biomedical departments at the University of Iowa revealed an immediate need for $2 million worth of lab equipment simply to allow their scientists to keep up.

Can the situation be remedied? In May, a government panel was commissioned to work on a major study of the lag in industrial innovation. But the prospects for any quick turnaround are dim. The political response to the tax-cutting mood of California's Proposition 13 is likely to preclude any large influx of funds for science. Indeed, W. Bowman Cutter of the Office of Management and Budget warned the AAAS meeting last week that the fiscal 1980 budget is shaping up as the tightest in a decade—for scientists as much as for everyone else.

Source. Newsweek, July 3, 1978.

3.6 KEY TERMS

competitive advantage (p. 57)
candidate outputs (p. 51)
mortality curve (p. 50)
commercialization (p. 50)
R&D (p. 50)
creativity (p. 52)
brainstorming (p. 53)
lead time (p. 56)
interchangeability (p. 60)
screening (p. 56)
organizational fit (p. 59)
fit checklist (p. 58)
process research (p. 54)
intelligence (p. 52)
imagination (p. 52)
motivation (p. 52)
present value (p. 58)
internal rate of return (p. 58)
regulation (p. 62)
standardization (p. 60)
simplification (p. 61)
modularization (p. 61)
value analysis (p. 61)
preliminary design (p. 59)
final design (p. 59)

3.7 REVIEW TEST

1. Most new product ideas come from R&D. (p. 52)
   a. True b. False
2. It is not uncommon for new products to take almost a decade from lab to consumer to be successful. (p. 57)
   a. True b. False
3. Creativity is something people are born with and cannot effectively be altered or stimulated. (p. 52)
   a. True b. False
4. In a "brainstorming" session a group of people come up with ideas, many of which are based on the group's evaluation of preceding data. (p. 53)
   a. True b. False
5. Companies rarely imitate their competitor's products because of fear of a patent suit. (p. 54)
   a. True b. False
6. Motivation is an essential ingredient of creativity. (p. 52)
   a. True b. False
7. Due to the nebulous nature of services, the selection of a service output is more difficult than that of a product output. (p. 56)
   a. True b. False
8. The three important factors in screening potential outputs for selection are the organization's strengths, the organization's weaknesses, and the "fit" of the output with the organization's structure. (p. 56)
   a. True b. False
9. Competition is not a relevant issue in public sector output selection decisions. (p. 57)
   a. True b. False
10. The implementation of process research is fairly straightforward once the research problems are ironed out. (p. 54)
    a. True b. False
11. Laundromats and airlines illustrate the general rule that services are usually capital (equipment) intensive. (p. 56)
    a. True b. False
12. The drawback of standardization, loss of variety, was solved, in part, by modularization. (p. 61)
    a. True b. False
13. A product with three different tops, five middles, and two ends will supply ten totally different models. (p. 61)
    a. True b. False
14. In the design of services it is the server we must focus upon, just as we focus on the product in the design of new products. (p. 62)
    a. True b. False

3.8 DISCUSSION QUESTIONS

1. What kinds of organizations would have low new idea mortality rates? High rates?
2. Can creativity be learned?
3. What considerations are probably most important in the "fit" of an output to an organization?
4. Give examples of successful, and unsuccessful, attempts at tradeoffs in new products. In new services.
5. Is basic or applied research more profitable to society?
6. Was Kodak's new Instamatic camera the outgrowth of research or development?
7. Name some instances where the economic return to an organization did not justify the costs but the organization proceeded anyway. Why did it?
8. Has standardization hurt the service industry image in any way?
9. How should an organization go about balancing the design characteristics of a contemplated output?
10. What output mix considerations are there in addition to economic ones?

3.9 CASE CTS, INC.

CTS, Inc. was organized in 1977 by three engineers, Earl Tandreau, Don Wilson and Jack Wells. All three men had recently resigned from engineering positions in a large computer peripherals manufacturing company. Earl's education was in civil engineering, although his 20 years of experience was related principally to manufacturing engineering. Jack and Don were both electrical engineers. Jack spent the last 26 years working as a staff electrical engineer with the same company. Don had been chief of the research department for his previous employer. Don was the idea man. It was he who convinced the other two to quit their secure jobs and invest their life savings to pursue this new company.

CTS operations began in Don's basement. After six months these quarters became cramped and the three partners constructed a garage adjoining Don's house. They believed this space would be adequate until production got into full swing.

The product idea around which CTS was originally organized was a microcomputer-based printed circuit board testing device. The equipment that their previous employer had been using to test printed circuit boards required approximately 30 minutes per board and provided relatively poor diagnostics for any detected errors. Don had researched a method of using a microcomputer and computer programs specially written for each type of printed circuit board to test a board in a matter of seconds. After three months in operation, the three partners had produced a working prototype of testing equipment.

With this prototype, they made a sales call to their previous employer to demonstrate the equipment's capability. Not only could the microcomputer test a printed circuit (PC) board within 15 to 30 seconds, but it provided the exact location (pin number) for any PC board defect. The sales call was successful. Their previous employer gave them a purchase order for one of the systems plus computer programs written to test the highest production volume PC board. The order was for $50,000 and required delivery within six months. The three were elated. They now had a firm order, which made them (and their banker) much less concerned about the viability of their endeavor.

The new equipment was delivered in four and one-half months, and after two months of use a second order for an additional $50,000 unit was placed. Several other sales calls had been made to southern California and northeastern computer products companies and the three felt there were several hot leads. At this point, they were still doing all of the production work themselves including ordering parts and assembling and testing units. Don did all the computer programming.

Don was convinced that their new business was going to be a success. This conviction was so great that he began to turn his attention to other potential areas of business, even though there were still severe cash flow problems, which constrained their growth. Don had been approached by several local businessmen regarding the use of his microcomputer technology for business applications. After several discussions, he was convinced that a microcomputer with the appropriate business software and price tag under $15,000 would have a potentially great market. Don began the design of two different models of small business computers and also began to study the requirements for business application software. Several special cabinets were designed and after six months a working prototype of each of the two small business computer models were available. One model had a suggested price of $13,000 and the other a suggested price of just under $9000. CTS introduced their two new products at a two-day showing arranged at a local Holiday Inn. During the two days, approximately 45 local businessmen saw demonstrations of the new computer hardware.

While Don was pleased with the performance of his new business microcomputer line, CTS had reached its credit limit at the local bank. Also, they were currently three weeks late on the delivery of testing systems due principally to Don's involvement in the microcomputer introduction. Earl was very concerned over the cash flow problem and called on the company's accountant to see if he could not assist in acquiring the needed capital.

QUESTIONS FOR DISCUSSION

1. Discuss CTS's marketing philosophy.
2. What problems do you see in attempting to market the two product lines?
3. Suppose that the business microcomputers were just now being considered for development and production. What questions and answers would be provided by a formal screening method?
4. If you could advise CTS on a marketing course of action, what would be the major components of that marketing approach?

3.10 REFERENCES AND BIBLIOGRAPHY

1. Anderson, H. H. ed., *Creativity and Its Cultivation*, New York: Harper & Row, 1959.
2. Bennett, Keith W., "Tomorrow's New Products, Today, by the Hunch Bunch," *Iron Age* 209:49 (May 13, 1972).
3. Bouchard, T. J., "Whatever Happened to Brainstorming," *Industry Week* 170:26–27 (August 2, 1971).
4. Covington, C., et al., *the Productive Thinking Program: A Course in Learning to Think*, Columbus, Ohio: Merrill, 1974.
5. Crosby, A., *Creativity and Performance in Industrial Organization*, London: Travistock Publication, 1968.
6. deBoro, E., *Lateral Thinking: Creativity Step by Step*, New York: Harper & Row, 1970.
7. Drendahl, J. E., "Factors of Importance for Creativity," *Journal of Clinical Psychology*, 12:21–26 (1956).
8. Gordon, W. J. J., "Operational Approach to Creativity," *Harvard Business Review*, 34:41–51 (1956).
9. Levitt, Theodore, "Production Line Approach to Service" *Harvard Business Review* 50:41–52 (Sept.-Oct., 1972).
10. Oates, D., "The Boom in Creative Thinking," *International Management* 27:18 (Dec., 1972).
11. Osborn, A. F., *Applied Imagination*, New York: Scribner's, 1963.
12. Skinner, W., "Manufacturing—Missing Link in Corporate Strategy," *Harvard Business Review* 47:136–145 (May-June, 1969).
13. Summers, I., and White, D. E., "Creativity Techniques: Toward Improvement of the Decision Process," *Academy of Management Review*, 1:99–107 (1976).
14. "The SX-70 Camera Deglamorizes Polaroid," *Business Week*, p. 90 (Nov. 30, 1974).
15. Uman, D., *New Product Programs: Their Planning and Control*, New York: American Management Assn., 1969.
16. Whiting, C. S., *Creative Thinking*, New York: Reinhold, 1958.
17. Wilson, R. C., et al., "A Factor-Analytic Study of Creative-Thinking Abilities," Psychometrika, 19:297–311 (1954).

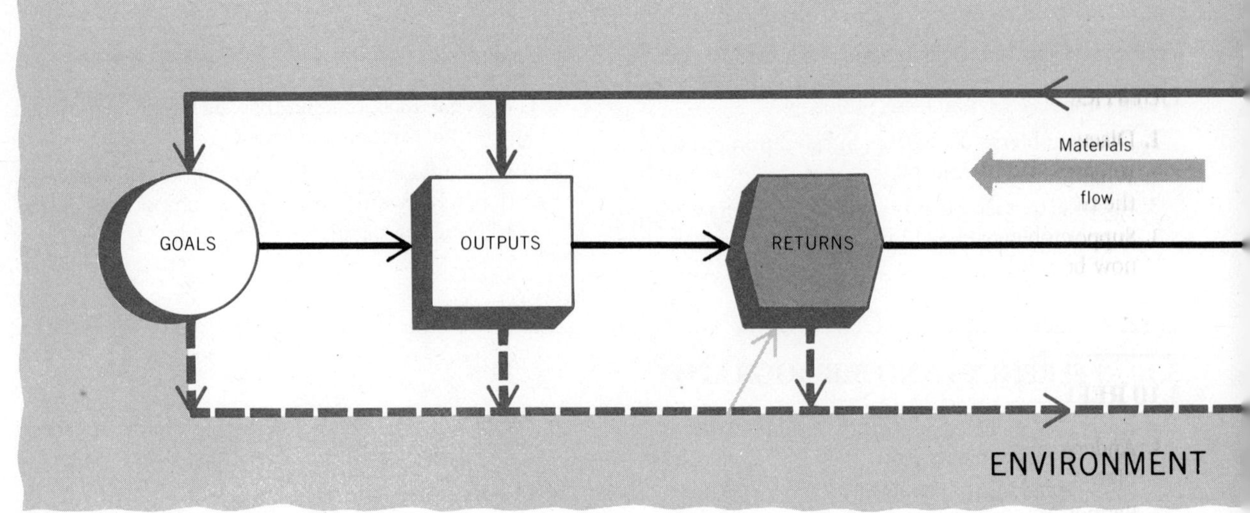

Chapter 4

Forecasting Environmental Returns

CONCEPTS

4.1 Returns to the Organization
- Money
- Recognition
- Information

4.2 Forecasting Environmental Demand
- Use of Forecasts
  - *The Historical Demand Data Available*
  - *The Money and Time Available*
  - *The Accuracy Required*

4.3 Qualitative Forecasting Methods
- The Market Survey
- Expert Opinion
  - *Delphi*
  - *Life Cycle Analysis*

4.4 Time Series Analysis
- The Trend
- The Seasonal
- The Cycle
- Random Variation

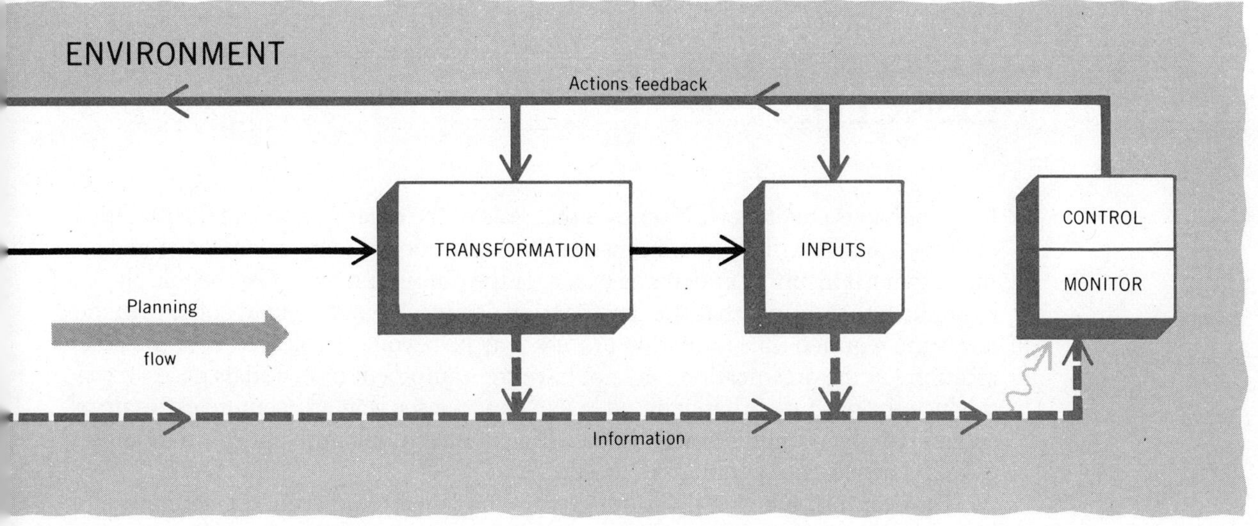

TOOLS AND APPLICATIONS

LEARNING OBJECTIVES

By the completion of the *Concepts* portion of this chapter the student should

1. Be familiar with the types of environmental returns organizations strive for.
2. Be aware that other, undesired returns also occur and should be planned for.
3. Understand the need for forecasts and their importance to operations.
4. Understand the nature of qualitative, time series, and causal forecasting methods and when each is used.
5. Be familiar with market survey and expert opinion methods of forecasting.
6. Comprehend the basis of time series analysis.

CONCEPTS

In the previous chapters we discussed the goals of the organization and the potential outputs available to it. Now we consider the prediction of environmental demand for the outputs. If insufficient demand exists for the output it may not be a viable choice to produce the returns that the organization desires. Beyond that, at some demand levels the required transformation process may be beyond the skill level of the organization. Or the organization may not have the equipment or materials necessary to produce the output at that demand level. Thus we see that an accurate estimate of demand for the output is crucial to the efficient operation of the transformation process, and hence, the operations manager.

For example, a hospital administrator who is contemplating the addition of a new emergency room must have a reasonable estimate of demand in order to determine the number of treating rooms, the size of the waiting area, and so forth, to specify in the plans. Once the facility is constructed, a more specific forecast will be needed of demand each day of the week on each shift. Only with this forecast will the administrator be able to schedule staff for efficient utilization. The same is true for capacity and scheduling/staffing decisions in a product organization. The size and capacity decisions regarding operations and the production/scheduling/staffing/materials decisions all require forecasting, whether it be a formal procedure or not.

The main topic of this chapter is forecasting. Also, some methods will be discussed that are often useful in producing forecasts of demand for the output.

4.1 RETURNS TO THE ORGANIZATION

Before proceeding to the available forecasting methods, let us dwell first on some of the returns frequently desired by organizations: money, recognition, and information relating to the organization's outputs.

Money

Money is an amazing invention. It is the *symbolic* equivalent of hard work, yet in a *physical* form that can be given (and stolen) from one person to another in only seconds. It is no wonder that money is thus the most common form of return to most organizations—it simply represents the hard work of people who value the organization's outputs. It can therefore be considered a measure of how well an organization is meeting the needs of its environment. Even nonprofit organizations can partially measure their success by the amount of monetary dues and donations they receive, as well as the budgets allocated to them by other organizations (e.g., the budget of a city parks department allocated by the elected city council).

Money represents hard work.

Recognition

Recognition important to both profit and not-for-profit organizations.

Recognition is a highly-sought-after return desired by most organizations. Even profit-oriented organizations desire recognition, in part to convey a positive image to their products. But especially for nonprofit organizations, recognition is usually a reflection of their continuing success in meeting the needs of their recipients. Such recognition is especially important to organizations that receive their monetary support through donations. Examples of high recognition organizations are the Red Cross, the Mayo Clinic, NAACP, and the National Geographic Society.

Information

Desire for feedback.

Even high recognition organizations usually desire and strive for another environmental return as well—information that their activities have been of service to the recipients. For example, anonymous donors to charities may wish *not* to be "recognized" because of the publicity but still desire to know that their donation has been put to good use. Information regarding the results of organizational activities may be obtained indirectly through hearsay and news accounts, or may be directly solicited by the organization itself, as in surveys.

Undesired returns.

In addition to the returns an organization desires from the environment, there will frequently be undesired, or at least unexpected, returns as well. Examples of such returns are complaints and lawsuits as well as the literal return of merchandise found by the recipient to be unacceptable. Experienced organizations anticipate and prepare for such undesired returns in order to further foster the achievement of their goals. Thus, one of the reasons that Sears' has become such a successful retailer has been its deliberately liberal policy regarding the return of unsatisfactory merchandise.

4.2 FORECASTING ENVIRONMENTAL DEMAND

To provide the organization with the returns it needs to satisfy its goals, the organization must usually interact with its environment. The organization provides products or services needed in the environment and receives certain returns in exchange.

Forecasting for efficiency.

In order to most efficiently conduct this process the organization needs to know not only *what* to produce but also *when, how much*, and at *what price*. To a certain extent these last two items are interrelated—generally, the lower the price the more that can be exchanged with the environment. It is therefore useful to have a *forecast* of environmental demand for the output.

Use of Forecasts

Forecasts are often used in organizations for three purposes.

Forecasting for new output introductions.

1. To decide whether environmental demand is sufficient to generate the returns desired by the organization. If demand exists but at too low a "price" to cover the "costs" the organization will incur in producing the output then the organization should reject the opportunity.

Forecasting for capacity needs.

2. To determine long-term capacity needs for facility design. An accurate projection of demand for a number of years in the future can save the organization great expense in expanding, or contracting, capacity to accommodate future environmental demands. Due to competitive forces in the environment, even in the not-for-profit sector, an organization that produces inefficiently, because of excess idle capacity, or insufficiently to meet demand, is courting disaster. This topic will be further discussed in Chapters 7 through 9.

Forecasting for production planning.

3. To ascertain short-term (1 week–3 month) fluctuation in demand for production planning, workforce scheduling, materials planning, and so forth. These forecasts are of special importance to operations management and crucially affect operational productivity (the "productivity crisis" currently of national interest), bottlenecks, master scheduling, meeting promised delivery dates, and other such issues of concern to top management and the organization as a whole. This area will be discussed in more depth in Chapter 9.

The method used to prepare a demand forecast depends upon a number of factors.

The historical demand data available

If such data are available one of the statistical forecasting methods described later can be used. Otherwise nonquantitative techniques are required.

The money and time available

The greater the limitations on time or money available for forecasting, the more likely it is that an unsophisticated method will have to be used. In general, management desires to use that forecasting method which minimizes not only the cost of making the forecast but also the cost of an *inaccurate* forecast; i.e., management's goal is to minimize *total* costs. Costs of forecasting inaccuracy include the costs of over or understocking or producing an item, the costs of under or overstaffing, and the intangible and opportunity costs associated with loss of customer/client goodwill because a demanded item was not available. This tradeoff situation is depicted in Figure 4.1. The best forecasting method is the one for which the combined costs are minimized but, since some of these costs are difficult if not impossible to measure, a "best" method is seldom absolutely determined.

Requirements for method of forecasting.

With the advent of computers and preprogrammed, off-the-shelf forecasting routines, the cost and time of statistical forecasts based on historical data has been reduced significantly. It therefore has become more cost effective for organizations to conduct more sophisticated forecasts and the optimum forecasting method has thus shifted to the right in Figure 4.1

The Accuracy Required

If, for whatever reasons, the forecast must be very accurate, highly sophisticated methods are usually called for. Typically, long range (3–10 year) forecasts require the

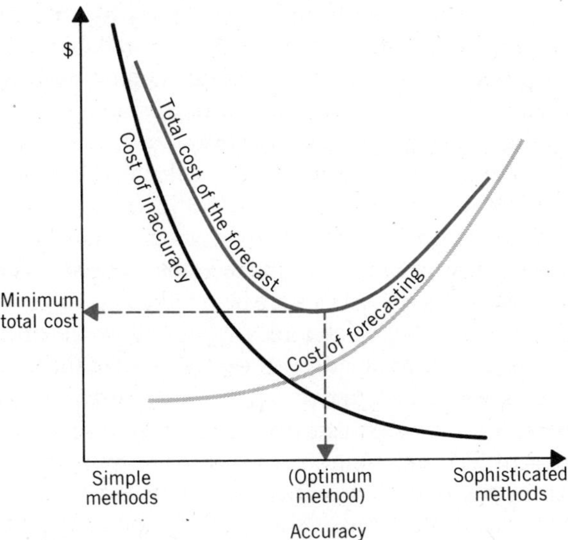

Figure 4.1 The costs of forecasting accuracy.

least accuracy and are only for general (or "aggregate") planning purposes, while short range (one week to several months) forecasts require great accuracy since detailed manpower and machine scheduling and materials planning are based upon these short range projections. Forecasting methods that can be used to make the demand forecast can be grouped into three broad categories.

- Qualitative techniques.
- Time series techniques.
- Causal techniques.

Three methods and their uses.

In general, qualitative forecasting methods are often used for long range forecasts and for new product/service introductions, time series techniques are typically most useful for short range forecasts, and **causal** methods (where cause-effect interactions have been identified) are widely used for short and intermediate range forecasting. Time series and causal forecasting methods are also used for ongoing operations planning. As we will see in subsequent sections of this chapter, both methods require historical data about the demand being forecast, and therefore cannot be used for introduction (go–no go) decisions when historical demand data is unavailable.

4.3 QUALITATIVE FORECASTING METHODS

Uses of qualitative forecasts.

Some of the most significant decisions made by organizations are made on the basis of **qualitative forecasts** These often concern either new product or service introductions or long range changes in the nature of the organization's outputs. In both cases, relevant historical demand data is typically not available. Qualitative demand forecasts for new product or service introductions will help operations managers decide the most efficient method of producing the output and whether the organization will gain or lose value ("profit") in the transaction.

Forecasts of long range output changes will allow the operations manager to plan for orderly replacement of facilities and modifications of the output production process. For example, a forecast of rapidly increasing demand for coal was used by many coal companies to justify changes in the technology used in coal mining. The process used to mine coal when 30 coal cars are being filled per day is neither economical nor feasible at 300 cars per day. Such forecasts also allow the operations manager to determine the cost of new production processes to meet these changes so top management can steer a wise course in maximizing the return to the organization.

Qualitative forecasts are made using information such as expert opinion, surveys of consumer attitudes and intentions about the output, or analyses of demand information for similar products or services which have been previously introduced and for which historical data are available. An example of the latter method, known as **historical analogy**, was the use of demand data for black-and-white television sets to predict the slope of the demand curve for color T.V. sets. Two qualitative forecasting methods are particularly common; these are the Market Survey and Expert Opinion.

Forecasting by historical analogy.

The Market Survey

New products and services are often subjected to extensive **market research** before a final decision is made regarding the introduction of this new output. Such devices as the telephone survey, the mail questionnaire, consumer panels, and test markets are used to ascertain estimates of demand. For example, both the Nielson T.V. ratings and the Gallup public opinion poll are based upon surveys of public attitude and behavior.

The various types of surveys.

Telephone and personal interview surveys as well as mail questionnaires can provide information about current attitudes and behavior, about past actions, and about intentions for the future. **Consumer panels**, which are made up of paid or volunteer participants, are provided with new and sometimes competing products and, after their use, requested to provide specific information to the market researchers. Also, consumer panels are often used to provide information about shopping and buying habits. Management can make use of a consumer panel over a long period of time to track changes in shopping and/or buying trends (called "longitudinal data").

Test marketing for consumer acceptance.

Test marketing can also provide longitudinal data about a new product or service. A test market is usually some specific geographical region that is selected because it represents some segment of the organization's overall market for the new output. The test market requires that the product or service actually be introduced into the limited test area; thus, the output must be in its final stages of development and production capacity must exist to supply the test market demand.

Test marketing provides management with information about actual consumer behavior rather than simply consumer attitudes, opinions, or intentions; and, there are often great differences between a consumer's attitudes and his/her actions. This last point is particularly important and raises some of the drawbacks of this type of forecasting. Attitude and opinion surveys can be very misleading. Subjects often try not to "disappoint" the pollster and thus tell him or her what they think he or she wants to hear, rather than what the subject really thinks. Also, a subject may honestly believe that a new soap, or deodorant, really is needed on the market and would be a very good product. However, as it turns out, they themselves do not personally happen to *need* that product. And even when a subject says that he or she *would* purchase a product, when the actual event presents itself the subject has often changed his or her mind.

Disadvantages of surveys.

In addition to these risks, market surveys are expensive due to packaging, mailing, analysis, and so forth. Current surveys sometimes even enclose $0.25 for the subject to fill out the questionnaire. Test marketing is also expensive in the sense that almost all development of the output must be completed, and production capacity must be available to supply the test market. Since the in-depth study of market research is beyond the scope of this text, the student is referred to References 4, 6, 7, and 8 at the end of this chapter.

Expert Opinion

Consider, for example, a company that has introduced, over the years, several dozen different consumer goods. It is conceivable that the experience of key managers, particularly those associated with the marketing of the products, could provide better forecasts of demand for another new product than any surveys of the potential market. In fact, this is often the case and methods have been developed to probe this expert knowledge. As "two heads are better than one," most expert judgment methods rely on the formation of a panel of experts who reach a concensus or compromise forecast based upon their individual experiences and judgment.

Using expert judgment.

But panel or committee solutions to the forecast problem are sometimes biased in favor of the opinion of one dominant member. Either that member is a better salesperson of his (her) own ideas, is more "expert" than fellow committee members (perhaps others on the panel simply believe this whether it is fact or not), or is simply more verbal than others on the panel. This bias may result in forecasts which are not good or as well thought out as predictions based upon *all* of the information available from the committee members.

The problems with committees.

Delphi

Using Delphi to improve expert forecasts.

One method for combining individual experts' forecast opinions is called **Delphi**. The Delphi method was developed by the RAND Corporation as a technique for group forecasting which would eliminate the undesirable effects of interaction between members of the group. The method generally begins by having each expert provide individual forecasts along with any supporting arguments and assumptions. These forecasts are submitted to the Delphi researcher who edits, clarifies, and summarizes

Rounds of questions are employed.

the data. This data is provided as feedback to the experts along with a *second round* of questions. Questions and feedback continue for several rounds, becoming increasingly more specific, until consensus among the panel members is reached. This method allows the benefits of multiple opinions and communciation between group members of diverse opinions and assumptions, but avoids the negative effects of dominant behavior and stubborness to change one's mind, which are often associated with committee solutions. For more details see References 4 and 5.

Life cycle analysis

Forecasting by life cycle analysis.

One device often used to aid in expert opinion forecasting is called **life cycle analysis**. Studies of successful new product introductions indicate that the **stretched S** growth curve provides a good pattern for the growth of demand for a new output. A typical growth curve is presented in Figure 4.2. The curve can be divided into three segments: introduction and early adoption, acceptance and growth of the market, and market saturation. After market saturation, demand may remain high or decline. Or the product or service may be improved and possibly start off on a new growth curve.

Experienced managers, who have introduced several new products, are often able to estimate the length of time that a product will remain in each of the stages of its life cycle. This forecast of the life cycle, coupled with other market information, can produce reasonably accurate estimates of demand in the intermediate to long range. This is useful to the organization in laying out long-range output plans. For operations management it indicates where periods of excess capacity might exist (and, thus, leasing out existing facilities or subcontracting might be required) or extra capacity might be required.

Operations management's use of life cycle forecasting.

The above described qualitative forecasting methods are typically one step removed from the operations manager. While they affect capacity, scheduling, labor, cost, and materials decisions, they are usually not conducted directly *for* the operations function. Operations, nevertheless, are often based on qualitative forecasts.

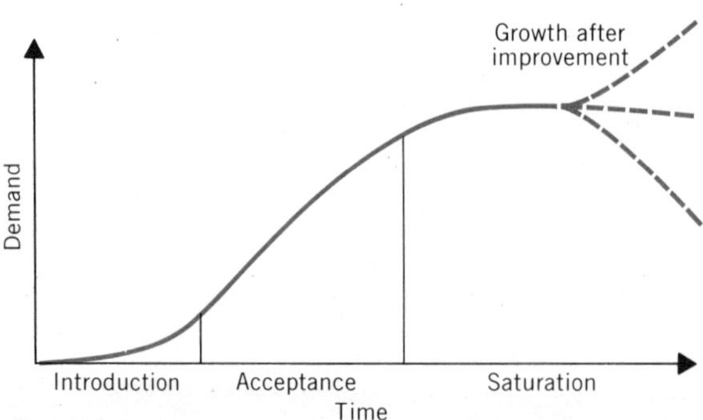

Figure 4.2 The life cycle curve.

4.4 TIME SERIES ANALYSIS

A **time series** is [1, p. 439] "an ordered group of values of a variable measured at successive points in time or for successive intervals of time." We measure the number of items in inventory at specific points in time and we measure the number of units sold over specific intervals of time. If, for example, we recorded the number of automobiles sold each month of 1979 by the Schroeder Oldsmobile Co. and kept those data points in the order in which they were recorded, the 12 numbers would constitute a *12 period time series*. We undertake *time series analysis* in operations planning because we believe that knowledge of *past behavior* of the time series might help our understanding of (and therefore our ability to predict) the behavior of the series in the future. In some instances, such as the stock market, this assumption may be unjustified but in operations planning we assume that (to some extent, at least) history will repeat itself and that past tendencies will continue. Time series analysis efforts conclude with the development of a *time series forecasting model* that can then be used to predict future demand. To begin our discussion of time series analysis let us consider the component parts of any time series.

Forecasting by time series analysis.

Components of time series.

Time series analysis assumes that the historical demand data is composed of four component parts.

1. The *trend, T*.
2. A *seasonal* variation, *S*.
3. A *cyclical* variation, *C*.
4. *Random* variation, *R*.

The Trend

The **trend** component is the long run direction of the series and includes any constant amount of demand in the data. Figure 4.3 illustrates three fairly common trend lines showing changes in the demand; a horizontal trend line would indicate a constant level of demand.

Straight-line trend.

A straight-line or "linear" trend (showing a constant amount of *change* as in Figure 4.3*a*) is most accurate over some limited range of time even though it might

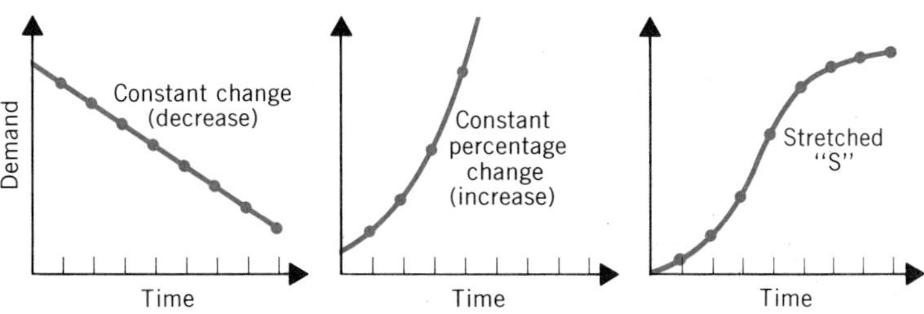

Figure 4.3 Three common trends.

provide a rather poor fit over an entire time series. For example, the curve in Figure 4.3*c* could be approximated by three separate straight trend lines as shown in Figure 4.4. Over each of these shorter ranges, a straight line provides a good approximation to the actual curve.

"Nonlinear" trends.

Figure 4.3*b* illustrates the situation of a constant *percentage* change. Here, change in demand depends on the current size of demand rather than being constant each period as in Figure 4.3*a*. Figure 4.3*c* indicates the trend line referred to earlier as the "stretched S" growth curve. Many new products follow this kind of growth pattern, which is characterized by a relatively slow start-up, a period of rapid product acceptance, and then a slowdown in the rate of adoption as the market becomes saturated.

The Seasonal

The bases for seasonal variation.

Seasonal fluctuations result primarily from nature but are also brought about by human behavior. Snow tires and antifreeze enjoy brisk demand during the winter months while sales of golf balls and bikinis peak in the spring and summer months. These are examples of seasonal variations induced by climatic conditions. Sales of "heart-shaped" boxes of candy and Christmas trees are brought about by events that are controlled by humans. The **seasonal** variation in events need not be related to the seasons of the year, however. For example, fire alarms in New York City reach a "seasonal" peak at 7 P.M. and a seasonal low at 7 A.M. every day. And restaurants reach three "seasonal" peaks every day at 7:30 A.M., 12:30 P.M., and about 8 P.M.

The Cycle

Long-term cycles.

The **cycle** or **cyclic** component is only obvious in time series that span several periods. A cycle can be defined as a *long-term oscillation* or swing of the data points about the trend line over a period of at least three complete seasonals. Figure 4.5 presents two complete cycles and the underlying straight-line trend of a time series where no yearly seasonal is assumed to exist. Note that the oscillations around the trend line are *not* symmetrical, as they seldom are in actual time series.

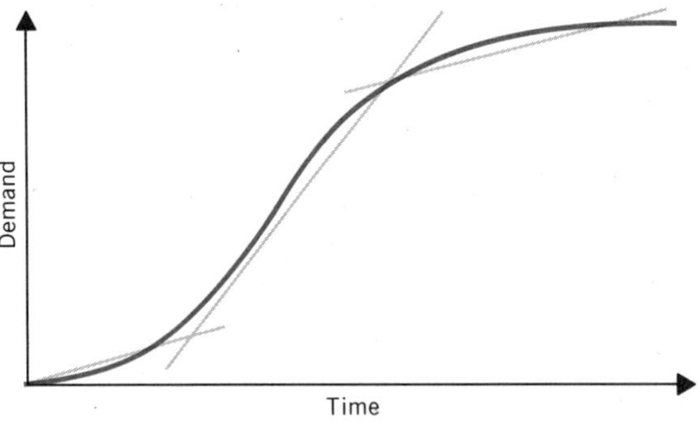

Figure 4.4 Straight trend approximation of stretched S growth curve.

Cycles, particularly business cycles, are often difficult to explain and economists have spent considerable effort in research and speculation about their causes. Identification of a cyclic pattern in a time series requires the analysis of a long set of data. For example, only two cycles were completed in nine years for the time series shown in Figure 4.5. For most operations forecasting the cyclic component is not considered since data are typically unavailable to determine the cycle. Also cycles are not likely to repeat in similar amplitude and duration; hence the assumption of repeating history does not hold.

Random Variation

Random variation is unpredictable.

Random variations are, as the name implies, without specific assignable cause and without pattern. Random fluctuations can sometimes be explained after the fact, such as the increase in energy consumption due to abnormally harsh weather conditions, but cannot be systematically predicted and, hence, are not included in forecasting models.

The objective of time series analysis models is to determine the magnitude of one or more of the time series components and to use that knowledge for the purpose of forecasting. Time series forecasts are more often found directly useful to the operations manager than are qualitative forecasts. For example, time series analysis is useful in planning annual production and inventory schedules based upon previous demand patterns.

In the *Tools and Applications* part of this text we will next consider three time series analysis models.

- Moving averages (trend component of the time series).
- Exponential smoothing (trend component of the time series).
- Linear trend multiplicative model (all three components).

Each of these models will be presented within the context of an example situation.

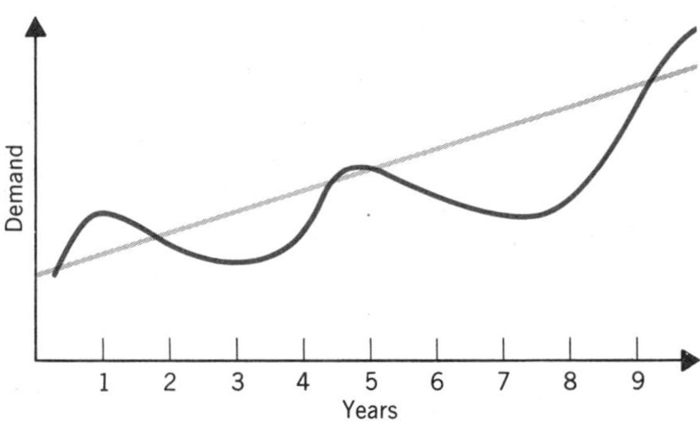

Figure 4.5 Typical cycles.

TOOLS AND APPLICATIONS

4.5 DEMAND FORECASTING FOR THE INNER CITY HEALTH CENTER

The Inner City situation.

Inner City Health Center is a federally funded health clinic which serves the needs of the inner city poor. The center is currently in its fourth year of operation and is presently preparing its staffing plan for the upcoming quarter. The federal government requires that the center prepare a budget request each quarter for the coming quarter. The request is based largely on the forecast of demand for specific services during the next quarter.

Attempts at forecasting.

Demand data are available for each of the four quarters of the preceding three years and for the first two quarters of the current year. The data presented in Table 4.1 and plotted in Figure 4.6 are for emergency services at the center. The health center administrator has in the past tried using the last period's demand and has also tried using the average of all past demand to predict the next period's demand for the center. Neither of these two techniques has proven satisfactory. The use of the last period's demand as a predictor of the next period's demand produced erratic forecasts. For example, using this method the administrator predicted (and staffed, scheduled, and purchased for) a demand of 3500 visits for the second quarter of 1971 when 8000 visits actually resulted (overtime and rush orders reached a peak during this quarter) and then predicted 8000 visits for the third quarter when only 5500 visits materialized. Clearly, this method could not sort out the fluctuations in the demand data and was therefore deemed unsatisfactory.

TABLE 4.1 EMERGENCY SERVICE DEMAND FOR THE INNER CITY HEALTH CENTER

Year	Quarter	Period Number	Number of Patient Visits
1971	1	1	3,500
	2	2	8,000
	3	3	5,500
	4	4	10,000
1972	1	5	4,500
	2	6	6,000
	3	7	3,000
	4	8	5,500
1973	1	9	5,000
	2	10	9,500
	3	11	7,500
	4	12	15,000
1974	1	13	13,500
	2	14	17,500

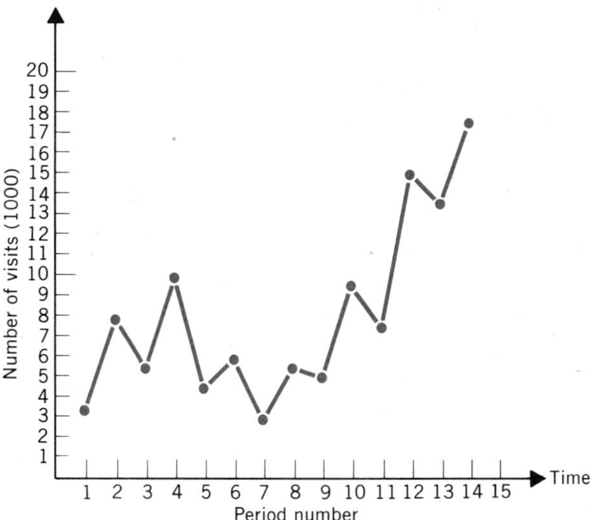

Figure 4.6 Plot of quarterly demand for emergency services—Inner City Health Center.

The administrator then turned to using the average of all demand data to predict the next period's demand. For the fourth quarter of 1971 the administrator predicted a demand of 5667 [i.e., (3500 + 8000 + 5000)/3] when 10,000 actually occurred and for the tenth period he forecast a demand of 5666 (i.e., the sum of the first nine periods' demand divided by 9) and 9500 occurred. The administrator recognized that this averaging method produced forecasts that *smoothed* out the fluctuations, but did not adequately respond to any growth or reduction in the demand trend. As a matter of fact, the averaging method performed progressively worse as the amount of data increased. This was because each new piece of demand data had to be averaged with *all* of the old data from period one to the present and therefore each new element of data had less overall impact on the average. In fact, if the administrator were to use the averaging method to forecast the third-quarter demand for 1974 the forecast would be 8143, clearly a poor forecast when compared to demand in the past few periods.

Smoothing the fluctuations.

After evaluating these two simple methods the administrator decided to consider the three time series forecasting methods mentioned earlier, each of which is capable of producing the needed forecasts. The remainder of this section will be devoted to an analysis of these three methods.

Moving Averages

To overcome the problem of using a simple average, the **moving average** technique generates the next period's forecast by averaging the actual demand for only the last n (n is often in the range of 4 to 7) time periods. The choice of the value for n is arbitrary, but should be based upon experimentation; that is, the value selected for n should be the one that works best for the available historical data.

Using only the last few periods to average.

Mathematically, the moving average is computed as

$$\overline{X}_{t+1} = \frac{1}{n} \sum_{i=t-n+1}^{t} X_i \tag{4.1}$$

where t = period number for the *current* period
$\overline{X}_{t+1}$ = forecast of demand for the next period
$\sum$ = mathematical notation meaning "sum up"*
X_i = actual demand in period i
n = number of periods of demand to be included (known as the "order" of the moving average)

For example, to forecast demand for the next quarter of this year (i.e., quarter 3 of 1974 or period 15 in Table 4.1) using a moving average of order four (that is, $n = 4$), the Inner City Health Center administrator would compute

$$\overline{X}_{14+1} = \frac{1}{4} \sum_{i=14-4+1}^{14} X_i$$

or

$$\overline{X}_{15} = \frac{1}{4} \sum_{i=11}^{14} X_i$$

$$\overline{X}_{15} = (X_{11} + X_{12} + X_{13} + X_{14})/4$$

$$\overline{X}_{15} = (7{,}500 + 15{,}000 + 13{,}500 + 17{,}500)/4$$

$$\overline{X}_{15} = 13{,}375$$

The forecast for the next quarter using a moving average forecast of order four would therefore be 13,375 emergency services.

The moving average as a compromise.

The moving average is a *compromise* between the last period's demand forecast and the simple average, both of which the administrator has rejected as being unsatisfactory. The number of periods to be averaged in the moving average is dependent upon the specific situation. If too few periods are included in the average, the forecast will be similar to the forecast obtained when only the last period's demand had been used as the forecast. Using too many periods in the moving average will result in a forecast similar to the forecast obtained when the simple average was used.

Forecasting objectives

Two objectives: accuracy versus change.

Two objectives in forecasting must be kept in mind and a compromise solution that satisfies both objectives must be sought. The first objective is to produce as good a forecast as is possible with the available data. Usually, this objective can be inter-

*The notation $\sum_{i=t-n+1}^{t}$ indicates a summation from $i = t - n + 1$ to $i = t$.

preted as using the most current data because those data are more representative of the present behavior of the time series. The second objective of forecasting is to "smooth" the random behavior of the data. That is, we do not want a forecasting system that forecasts increases in demand simply because the last period's demand has suddenly increased nor do we want a system that indicates a "downturn" just because demand in the last period decreased. All time series contain a certain amount of this erratic or random movement. It is impossible for a manager to predict this random movement of a time series, and it is folly to attempt it. The only reasonable conclusion is to avoid overreaction to a fluctuation that is simply random. The general interpretation of this objective is that several periods of data should be included in the forecast so as to "smooth" the random fluctuations that typically exist.

Clearly, methods to attain the two objectives will be somewhat contradictory. Using the most recent data results in only a few periods being included in the forecast but a desire for smoothed data results in large numbers of periods being included. The only approach to the problem of deciding upon the number of periods to include is to experiment with several different numbers of periods and evaluate each on the basis of its ability to produce good forecasts and to smooth out random fluctuations. The *mean absolute deviation* (**MAD**) is one measure of the "goodness" of a forecasting model. The MAD, which will be discussed in the upcoming section, is always the *lowest* for the best model.

Measuring the accuracy of a forecast with the MAD.

Exponential Smoothing

Achieving the two objectives by exponential smoothing.

We pointed out in our discussion of forecasting objectives that two objectives were relevant in choosing the amount of data to be included in a forecasting model. We generally want to use the most current data, and at the same time, use enough observations of the time series to smooth out random movement. One technique perfectly adapted to meeting these two objectives is **exponential smoothing**.

Exponential smoothing has an advantage over moving averages in that the computations required are much simpler and the data storage requirements are less, particularly in situations that require the use of data from a large number of past time periods.

The computation of a demand forecast using exponential smoothing is carried out with the following equation.

$$\text{new demand forecast} = (\alpha)\text{ current demand} + (1 - \alpha)\text{ previous demand forecast} \tag{4.2}$$

where α is a **smoothing constant** that must be greater than or equal to zero but less than or equal to one.

The smoothing constant as a weighting factor.

The smoothing constant α can be interpreted as the *weight* assigned to the last (i.e., the current) data point. The higher the weight assigned to this current demand the greater the influence this point has on the forecast. For example, if α is equal to 1, the demand forecast for the next period will be equal to the value of the current demand. The closer the value of α is to 0 the closer the forecast will be to the previous period's *forecast* for the current period.

Equal weights in a moving average.

In contrast, in a moving average all data is assigned equal weight in the determination of the next period's forecast. For example, in a four-period moving average, each of the four observations has a 25 percent weight in determining the forecast. In exponential smoothing, α determines the importance assigned to the most current data and automatically weights the historical data simply by using Equation 4.2 above.

Selecting the appropriate value of α

Our objective in exponential forecasting is to choose the value of α that results in the best forecasts. If forecasts are in error then operations costs will be unnecessarily high due to idle capacity for high forecasts and insufficient capacity (overtime, etc.) for low forecasts. The value of α is critical in producing good forecasts, and if a large value of α is selected, the forecast will be very sensitive to the current demand value. With a large α, exponential smoothing will produce forecasts that react quickly to fluctuations in demand. A small of value of α weights historical data more heavily than current demand and therefore will produce forecasts that do not react as quickly to changes in the data; that is, the forecasting model will be somewhat *insensitive* to fluctuations in the data.

Large values of α weight current demand the most.

Use large values of α if the data is smooth.

Generally speaking, larger values of α are used in situations in which the data can be plotted as a rather smooth curve, such as in Figure 4.7. The data in this figure are said to exhibit *low* **variability**. If, on the other hand, the data look more like Figure 4.8, a lower value of α should be used. These data are subject to a high degree of variability. Using a high value of α in a situation like the one depicted in Figure 4.8 would result in a forecast that constantly overreacted to changes in the most current demand.

Values of α usually between 0 and 0.3.

The appropriate value of α is, like n, usually determined through a trial-and-error process; values typically lie in the range of 0 to 0.3. One method of selecting the best α value is to try several values of α with the existing historical data (or a portion of it) and choose the value of α that minimizes the average forecast errors [i.e., the **absolute value** of the difference (**deviation**) between actual demands and exponentially smoothed forecasts]. This average is called the mean absolute deviation and is abbreviated MAD. A simple computer program can greatly speed the evaluation of potential smoothing constants and the determination of the best value of α.

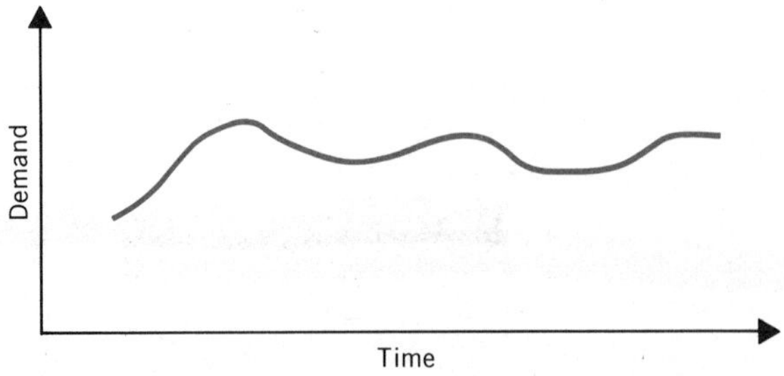

Figure 4.7 Data exhibiting low variability (use high α).

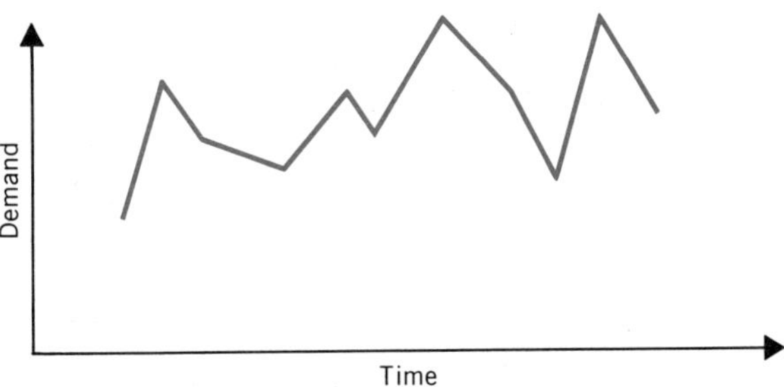

Figure 4.8 Data exhibiting high variability (use low α).

The MAD is also used as a "**tracking signal**" in certain **adaptive forecasting** models. Briefly, adaptive forecasting models *self-adjust* by increasing or decreasing the smoothing constant α when the MAD becomes too large. As long as the MAD remains within reasonable bounds the model is presumed to be doing well. But if the MAD increases beyond a set limit, the forecasting model increases α to "catch up" to whatever type of change has taken place. In the following example the MAD is incorporated as an evaluation criterion between two α factors in an exponential smoothing model.

Table 4.2 presents the actual historical data for emergency services provided by the Inner City Health Center and the exponentially smoothed forecasts for the corresponding periods using α values of 0.1 and 0.3. Since there was no data on which to

TABLE 4.2 ACTUAL AND EXPONENTIALLY FORECAST VALUES OF QUARTERLY DEMAND FOR THE INNER CITY HEALTH CENTER (DATA IN THOUSANDS)

Year	Quarter	Y Actual	$\overline{Y}$ Forecast ($\alpha = 0.1$)	$\overline{Y}$ Forecast ($\alpha = 0.3$)
1971	1	3.5		
	2	8.0	3.50	3.50
	3	5.5	3.95	4.85
	4	10.0	4.11	5.05
1972	1	4.5	4.69	6.53
	2	6.0	4.68	5.92
	3	3.0	4.81	5.95
	4	5.5	4.63	5.06
1973	1	5.0	4.71	5.19
	2	9.5	4.74	5.14
	3	7.5	5.22	6.44
	4	15.0	5.45	6.76
1974	1	13.5	6.40	9.23
	2	17.5	7.11	10.51
	3	?	8.15	12.61

base a forecast for period one, $\overline{Y}_1$ (the forecast that would have been made in period zero), some value must be selected. We let $\overline{Y}_1$ be equal to Y_1, the actual value of the series in period one. Then $\overline{Y}_2$ is computed (using $\alpha = 0.1$).

$$\begin{aligned}\overline{Y}_2 &= 0.1 \times 3.5 + (1 - 0.1) \times 3.5 \\ &\ 0.35 + 0.9\ (3.5) \\ &= 3.5\end{aligned}$$

In the same manner, we compute $\overline{Y}_3$ as

$$\begin{aligned}\overline{Y}_3 &= 0.1(8) + 0.9(3.5) \\ &= 3.95\end{aligned}$$

The computations for the exponentially smoothed forecasts continue for each period using the previous forecast and the value of the current observation. The current data is weighted by α and the historical data (all of which is embodied in the previous period's forecast) by $(1 - \alpha)$. As can be seen from Table 4.2, $\overline{Y}_{15}$, the forecasts for the next quarter using each of the two α values, are 8150 and 12,610 emergency services.

Table 4.3 presents the computation of the MAD for the forecasts prepared using the two α values. The MAD is computed as the sum of the absolute differences between actual and forecast demands divided by the number of forecast periods (in this case 13).

TABLE 4.3 CALCULATION OF THE FORECAST ERRORS, MAD

		Absolute Difference (|Actual - Forecast|)	
Year	Quarter	$\alpha = 0.1$	$\alpha = 0.3$
1971	1		
	2	4.5	4.5
	3	1.55	0.65
	4	5.89	4.95
1972	1	0.19	2.03
	2	1.32	0.08
	3	1.81	2.95
	4	0.87	0.44
1973	1	0.29	0.19
	2	4.76	4.36
	3	2.28	1.06
	4	9.55	8.24
1974	1	7.1	4.27
	2	10.39	6.99
	Sum of absolute differences $= \sum\|\,\|$	50.5	40.71
	Mean absolute deviation (MAD) $= \dfrac{\sum\|\,\|}{13}$	3.88	3.13

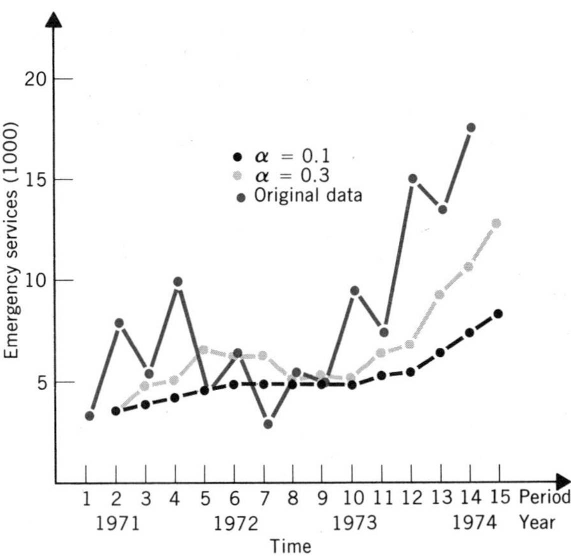

Figure 4.9 Plot of actual data and exponential forecasts.

Comparing values of α.

As indicated by the MAD computation, the forecasts prepared using $\alpha = 0.3$ are the better forecasts. This result is also seen in Figure 4.9, which shows the actual demand data and the forecast values using $\alpha = 0.1$ and $\alpha = 0.3$. Notice for example that the downturn after quarter 4 and the upturn after quarter 9 are detected more quickly by the $\alpha = 0.3$ model, as we have indicated should be the case. You may notice that both models lag behind the upward trend after quarter 9. A single smoothing model like the one presented in Equation 4.2 is best used in situations where demand fluctuates around an overall level trend. If the trend is increasing or decreasing a double smoothed model may be more appropriate. Also, exponential smoothing models can be developed to adapt to seasonal influences as well. These models are beyond the scope of this text, but the interested reader is referred to Reference 2 in the bibliography. In the next section we consider a time series model more sophisticated than those presented in this section.

Single and double smoothing models.

4.6 LINEAR TREND, MULTIPLICATIVE MODEL

The linear trend model for trend and seasonals.

In Figure 4.10 and Table 4.4 the quarterly ridership volume (in thousands) for the new Inner City Mass Transit is presented. Demand is seen to be generally increasing. To forecast future ridership, the city manager has decided to try the linear trend time series model which is based on a belief that demand follows both a fairly constant trend from quarter to quarter and a quarterly seasonal pattern. Just from observing the time series plot of the ridership demand data it is clear that demand is above

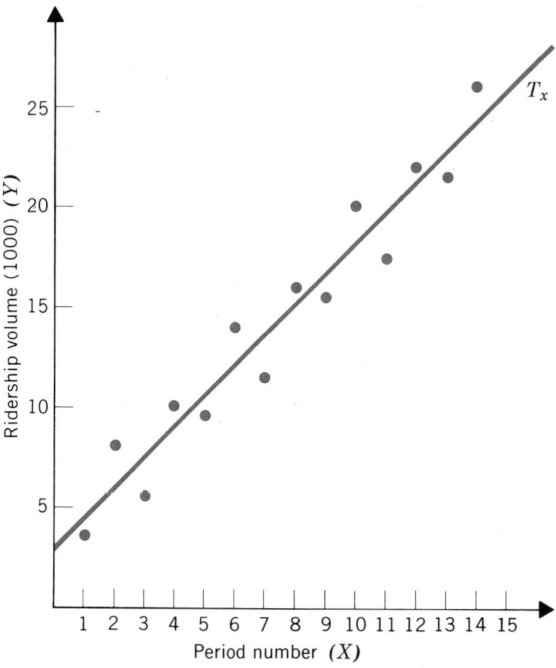

Figure 4.10 Quarterly ridership volume and trend line for the mass transit.

average during the second and fourth quarters and below average during the first and third quarters, probably due to weather.

Versions of the linear trend model.

There are several versions of the linear trend time series model (for example, there are additive and multiplicative versions) and also many different approaches to the determination of the components of these forecasting models. We will present one method for the determination of the two demand components of a simple multiplicative model. Conceptually, the model is presented as

$$\text{forecast} = \text{trend component (or } T) \times \text{seasonal component (or } S)$$

In order to develop this model we must first analyze the available historical data and attempt to break down the original data into its trend and seasonal components.

The Trend

As indicated earlier, the trend is the long run direction of the series of data. In our example the trend in demand appears to follow a straight line; that is, to be a **linear** trend with respect to time. In order to project this linear trend into the future, we must first be able to estimate the parameters of the trend line. Hence, we must locate

TABLE 4.4 QUARTERLY RIDERSHIP VOLUME AND LEAST SQUARES DATA FOR THE MASS TRANSIT

Quarter Number X	Ridership Volume (1000) Y	X^2	XY
1	3.5	1	3.5
2	8	4	16
3	5.5	9	16.5
4	10	16	40
5	9.5	25	47.5
6	14	36	84
7	11.5	49	80.5
8	16	64	128
9	15.5	81	139.5
10	20	100	200
11	17.5	121	192.5
12	22	144	264
13	21.5	169	279.5
14	26	196	364
$\sum X = 105$	$\sum Y = 200.5$	$\sum X^2 = 1015$	$\sum XY = 1855.5$

the line that best fits the observed data. The equation for linear (straight-line) demand is given by

$$Y_X = A + BX \tag{4.3}$$

where

Y_X = demand in quarter X
A = the Y axis intercept when $X = 0$
B = the slope of the demand line
X = the time variable (i.e., the quarter number)

The intercept and slope of the trend line equation.

The parameters of the straight line that must be estimated are the Y axis intercept (A) and the slope of the line (B). The *Y axis intercept* is the value of Y where the trend line crosses the Y axis. The *slope* is the amount of change in Y for a one period change in X.

Least squares regression most commonly used for trend determination.

We have already observed and collected the demand and time variables. There are several procedures for estimating the slope and intercept of a straight line from the observed values of X and Y_X, but a method known as **least squares regression** is the most widely used.* We will not attempt to derive the equations used in estimating the slope and the intercept, but will simply state and explain their use. The equa-

* The method derives its name from the way in which the parameters of the line are estimated. That is, the method minimizes the sum of the squares of the vertical deviations between the estimated trend line and the original data points.

tion that we will use to forecast the trend into the future is known as the *estimated regression equation* and is shown as

$$T_X = a + bX \tag{4.4}$$

where

T_X = the trend forecast value of demand for period number X
a = the estimate of A (the Y axis intercept)
b = the estimate of B (the slope of the demand line)
X = the period number

The two equations used to determine a and b are

$$b = \frac{\sum XY - n\overline{X}\,\overline{Y}}{\sum X^2 - n\overline{X}^2} \tag{4.5}$$

$$a = \overline{Y} - b\overline{X} \tag{4.6}$$

where

$\sum XY$ = X times Y for each period, summed over all of the periods
$\sum X^2$ = X squared for each period, summed over all of the periods
$\overline{X}$ = the average of the X values
$\overline{Y}$ = the average of the Y values
n = the number of periods of data used in the regression

Using least squares regression for the inner city mass transit

Using the data for the Inner City Mass Transit, we can estimate the slope and the intercept of the trend forecasting equation for the transit's quarterly ridership volume. To simplify the computations we will arrange the data into four columns as shown in Table 4.4. The numbers in column 3 are simply column 1 numbers squared and the numbers in column 4 are computed by multiplying the numbers in column 1 by the corresponding number from column 2. To compute the slope of the regression line (b) we need the average of column 1, which is

$$\overline{X} = \frac{\sum X}{n} = \frac{105}{14} = 7.5$$

and the average of column 2, which is

$$\overline{Y} = \frac{200.5}{14} = 14.32$$

In addition, we need the total of columns 3 and 4. In our alegebraic notation, $\sum X^2$ is the sum of column 3 and $\sum XY$ is the sum of column 4.

The slope can then be computed by using Equation 4.5.

$$b = \frac{1855.5 - 14(7.5)(14.32)}{1015 - 14(7.5)^2}$$
$$= \frac{351.9}{227.5}$$
$$= 1.55$$

The Y axis intercept is computed from Equation 4.6.

$$a = 14.32 - 1.55(7.5)$$
$$= 2.69$$

The forecasting equation for the trend in ridership volume is therefore

$$T_X = 2.69 + 1.55X$$

Figure 4.10 shows the regression trend line and the original data.

The Seasonal Component: Ratio-to-Trend Method

Calculating four seasonals.

As noted earlier, and made even clearer in Figure 4.10, the data is above the trend line for all of the second and fourth quarters and below the trend line for all of the first and third quarters. Recognizing this distinct seasonal pattern in the data should allow us to estimate the amount of seasonal variation around the trend line (i.e., the seasonal component, S).

The trend line is the long run direction of the data and does not include any seasonal variation. We can compute, for each available quarter of data, a measure of the "seasonality" in that quarter by *dividing the actual ridership volume by the computed value of the trend* for that quarter. This method is known as the **ratio-to-trend** method. Using the notation developed thus far for actual and forecast values we can write the seasonal component for any quarter X as

$$\frac{Y_X}{T_X} \tag{4.7}$$

Consider the second and third quarters of the first year. The computed trend value for each of these two quarters is

$$T_2 = 2.69 + 1.55(2)$$
$$= 5.79$$

and

$$T_3 = 2.69 + 1.55(3)$$
$$= 7.34$$

The actual ridership volume (in thousands) in quarters 2 and 3 were

$$Y_2 = 8.0$$
$$Y_3 = 5.5$$

Dividing Y_2 by T_2 and Y_3 by T_3 gives us an indication of the seasonal pattern in each of these quarters.

$$\frac{Y_2}{T_2} = \frac{8}{5.79} = 1.38$$
$$\frac{Y_3}{T_3} = \frac{5.5}{7.34} = 0.75$$

In quarter 2 the actual volume was 138 percent of the expected volume (i.e., the ridership volume predicted on the basis of a linear trend) and in quarter 3 the volume was only 75 percent of that expected. Note that over the 14 periods of available data we have four observations of ridership volume for first and second quarters and three observations of volume for third and fourth quarters. We can compute the average of each of these sets of quarterly data and use the averages as the seasonal components for our time series forcasting model.

Averaging the *Y/T* ratios to get the seasonals.

Table 4.5 will simplify our computation of the seasonal values for each of the 14 quarters. Once Table 4.5 is complete, the seasonal factors for each of the four seasons or quarters are averaged as in Table 4.6. The seasonal components for each of the four quarters are found in the bottom row of Table 4.6.

Using both the trend and seasonal components, the city manager now can forecast the ridership volumes for any quarter in the future. First, the trend value for the forecast quarter is computed and is, in turn, multiplied by the appropriate seasonal factor. For example, to forecast for the last quarter of the fourth year (quarter number 16) and the first quarter of the fifth year (quarter number 17) the city manager would first compute the trend values (in thousands).

$$T_{16} = 2.69 + 1.55(16) = 27.49$$
$$T_{17} = 2.69 + 1.55(17) = 29.04$$

TABLE 4.5 COMPUTATIONS OF QUARTERLY SEASONAL FACTORS

X	Quarter	Y	T	Y/T
1	1	3.5	4.24	0.83
2	2	8.0	5.79	1.38
3	3	5.5	7.34	0.75
4	4	10.0	8.89	1.12
5	1	9.5	10.44	0.91
6	2	14.0	11.99	1.17
7	3	11.5	13.54	0.85
8	4	16.0	15.09	1.06
9	1	15.5	16.64	0.93
10	2	20.0	18.19	1.10
11	3	17.5	19.74	0.89
12	4	22.0	21.29	1.03
13	1	21.5	22.84	0.94
14	2	26.0	24.39	1.07

TABLE 4.6 COMPUTATIONS OF SEASONAL COMPONENT (S) FOR QUARTERS 1 THROUGH 4

	Quarter Number			
Year	1	2	3	4
1	0.83	1.38	0.75	1.12
2	0.91	1.17	0.85	1.06
3	0.93	1.10	0.89	1.03
4	0.94	1.07		
Total	3.61	4.72	2.49	3.21
Average (S)	$S_1 = 0.90$	$S_2 = 1.18$	$S_3 = 0.83$	$S_4 = 1.07$

Next, she or he computes the forecast by multiplying the trend value by the appropriate seasonal factor. For the fourth quarter S_4 is 1.07, so the forecast, Y', is

$$Y_{16}' = 27{,}490 \times 1.07 = 29{,}410$$

The seasonal factor for the first quarter is 0.90; therefore, the forecast for quarter 17 is

$$Y_{17}' = 29{,}040 \times 0.90 = 26{,}140$$

These two forecasts correspond with the previous results for fourth and first quarters in that the fourth quarter forecast is above the trend and the first quarter forecast is below the trend.

This linear trend model can be useful to the operations planning and scheduling of Inner City Mass Transit. Procurement of new transit vehicles, scheduling maintenance and overhaul during slack seasons, and staff scheduling are all possible using this model. If data were available regarding ridership by route or area of the city, the operations staff could plan for new route additions or modifications and determine the number of buses to run on each route to produce acceptable wait times for riders.

Cautions

Inapplicability of linear models.

Although a simple linear trend model should be tried before more complex models, in many forecasting situations a linear trend model is simply not appropriate. The student is cautioned to recognize that a forecasting procedure produces useful results only if the input data conform to the assumptions of the model. Data that follow an obviously nonlinear pattern should not be subjected to a linear analysis. Also, models, for all their power in analyzing data, cannot think and reason intelligently about environmental changes that might affect demand.

External considerations may affect the forecast significantly.

For instance, in our earlier example of emergency services demand, there was a sudden upsurge after period 9, which the exponential forecasting models could only react to. But, suppose that the administrator knew that a local hospital was closing its evening clinic because it had not proved to be self-supporting. If the only medical services otherwise available in the community during the evening hours are those provided by the center's Emergency Services Division, the administrator could predict that demand would increase. This may in fact have been the cause for the noted increases.

To clarify the point of using a linear model to predict demand in an inherently nonlinear situation, consider again the demand data for emergency services (Figure 4.6). Demand first increases, then decreases, then appears to be increasing at an increasing rate. But, if the administrator were to use the least squares model on this data, the regression line computed would be

$$T_x = 2.62 + 0.736X$$

This line is shown superimposed on the plot of the original data in Figure 4.11. Note that a forecast for period 15 is well under that which would be expected if demand continues to grow as it has over the past five quarters. Use of a "nonlinear regression" model would be appropriate in this case whereas use of a linear model is not.

4.7 CAUSAL FORECASTING METHODS

Considering the factors that cause demand.

In the previous section we saw that demand for an organization's output could be related to time, that is, the demand changed as time changed. While a relationship existed, we could not say that time *caused* the demand. But, there are factors other than time which are often related to demand and, in fact, these factors often cause, or at least precede, the demand.

Marriages as a predictor of housing demand.

For example, increases in single-family housing demand during a given quarter might be highly related to the number of new marriages during the previous quarter. While marriages do not directly *cause* new houses to be purchased, it is logical to

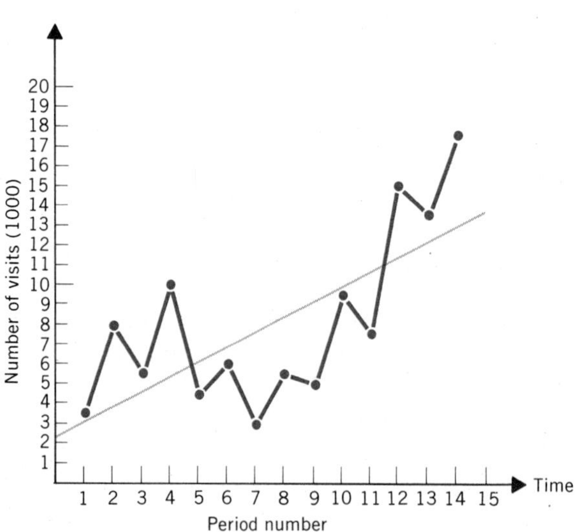

Figure 4.11 Plot of quarterly demand for emergency services—Inner City Health Center.

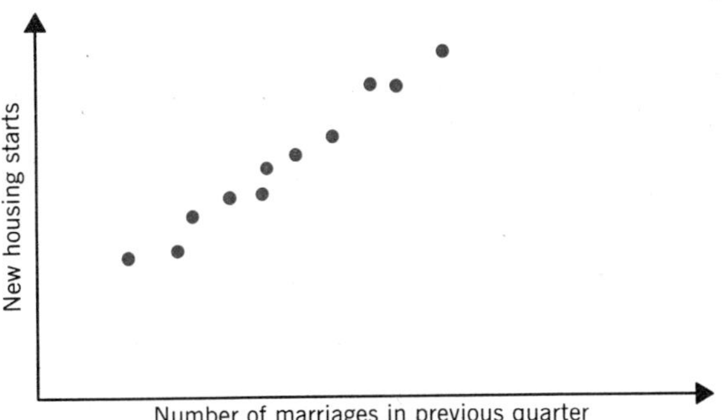

Figure 4.12. Plot of marriages vs housing starts showing the close relationship.

argue that marriages (which cause new households to form) are a major precondition to new housing starts. Figure 4.12 illustrates the likely relationship between new marriages (the independent variable) and single-family housing starts. This figure indicates a rather close relationship between the two variables. The variables are thus said to be highly **correlated**. The relationship between housing starts in one quarter and marriages in a previous quarter is an example of a *logical* relationship. Many causal models use such "leading indicators" to predict upcoming demand.

"At last! A leading indicator I can understand!"

(Reprinted with permission from *Changing Times*, © 1975, the Kiplinger Washington Editors, Inc.)

Predictor variables.

The least squares regression method used in the preceding section to determine the linear time series trend can also be used to estimate a **predicting equation** for new housing starts. The linear equation:

$$Y_X' = a + bX \tag{4.8}$$

would be interpreted as

Y_X' = the predicted number of new housing starts
a = the Y axis intercept
b = the slope
X = the number of new marriages in the previous quarter

and the two parameters a and b are estimated in the same manner as before, that is

$$b = \frac{\sum XY - n\overline{X}\,\overline{Y}}{\sum X^2 - n\overline{X}^2}$$

$$a = \overline{Y} - b\overline{X}$$

Including many causative factors through multiple regression.

This linear regression methodology can be extended to situations in which more than one variable is used, called **multiple regression**, to explain the behavior of the dependent variable Y. For example, in addition to the number of marriages, the employment rate in the previous quarter might also explain a great deal of the change in housing starts. The regression equation would be of the form

$$Y'_{X_1X_2} = a + b_1X_1 + b_2X_2 \tag{4.9}$$

where

$Y'_{X_1X_2}$ = the predicted number of housing starts based upon new marriages *and* the employment rate
a = the Y axis intercept
b_1 and b_2 = the slopes (rates of change in Y') with respect to X_1 and X_2
X_1 and X_2 = the number of marriages and the employment rate, respectively, in the previous quarter

Generally, a computer is used to solve multiple regression models.

Econometric forecasting for interdependent variables.

Another extension of regression methodology is the **econometric model**. In many cases the dependent and independent variables used in forecasting models are **interdependent**. That is, demand may be a function of personal income and personal income a function of demand. Econometric models take these interrelationships into consideration by formulating, not one regression equation, but a series of simultaneous regression equations which relate the demand data to all of the interdependent factors, many of which are also predicted by the model.

The operations manager can use causal forecasting methods to help predict the impact on production costs of increases or decreases in volume, and changes in the product mix. In addition, production time can be estimated on the basis of a number of independent factors. For example, the time required to design, program, and implement a new computer system has been estimated on the basis of such factors as the number of files required, the number of reports produced, the number of individual programs, and subjective factors relating to the level of complexity of various portions of the system.

4.8 SUMMARY

The returns from the environment must satisfy, at least in part, the organization's goals. Typical returns desired by organizations are money, recognition, and information regarding the results of organizational activities. Other, undesired, returns also frequently occur such as returned merchandise, complaints, and even lawsuits.

For the organization to decide if it can "profitably" supply a product or service to the environment, it must *forecast* the demand in the environment. Higher demand rates allow the use of expensive, high volume equipment and facilities that can be charged off against a larger output to give a lower unit cost. Forecasts are also needed to determine long-term capacity needs for facility design as well as short-term demand for production planning and scheduling. The long-term forecasts need not be as accurate as the short-term forecasts.

Three general forecasting methods are in common use.

1. *Qualitative methods*—such as market surveys, expert opinion, Delphi, and life cycle analysis.
2. *Time series analysis*—such as moving averages, exponential smoothing, and the linear trend multiplicative model which are based on historical data.
3. *Causal techniques*—such as multiple regression and econometric models.

The choice of the most appropriate method depends on whether historical demand data are available, and the money and time are available for conducting the forecast study. The accuracy required also affects the choice.

4.9 KEY TERMS

Concepts

qualitative forecasts (p. 77)
causal forecasts (p. 77)
trend (p. 81)
historical analogy (p. 78)
cycle, cyclic (p. 82)
seasonal (p. 82)
random (p. 83)
market survey (p. 78)
time series (p. 81)
test market (p. 78)
life cycle analysis, stretched S (p. 80)
Delphi (p. 79)
consumer panel (p. 78)

Tools and Applications

interdependent (p. 100)
least squares regression (p. 93)
linear (p. 91)
exponential smoothing (p. 87)
moving average (p. 85)
smoothing constant (p. 87)
deviation (p. 89)
MAD (p. 87)
variability (p. 88)
absolute value (p. 89)
ratio-to-trend (p. 95)
tracking signal (p. 89)
adaptive forecasting (p. 89)
econometric models (p. 100)
multiple regression (p. 100)
correlation (p. 99)

4.10 REVIEW TEST

Concepts

1. Information is a typical environmental return to the organization for its output. (p. 75)
   a. True b. False
2. Forecasts are typically just used for long-term capacity planning and short-term production planning. (p. 75)
   a. True b. False
3. If little time is available to make a forecast, a causal model is probably most appropriate. (p. 77)
   a. True b. False
4. A test market provides an improvement in information over an opinion or attitude market survey. (p. 78)
   a. True b. False
5. Historical analogy is forecasting on the basis of past, similar products. (p. 78)
   a. True b. False
6. Delphi is a probability model for combining a number of forecasts into one. (p. 79)
   a. True b. False
7. Delphi is designed to minimize forecast bias in a group. (p. 79)
   a. True b. False
8. Which of these is *not* a time series forecasting method? (p. 83)
   a. Exponential smoothing b. Moving averages c. Delphi method
9. One component of a time series forecasting model is random variation. (p. 83)
   a. True b. False

Tools and Applications

10. The seasonal component, once computed, is assumed to remain relatively fixed. (p. 95)
    a. True b. False
11. Econometric forecasting is a type of multiple regression. (p. 100)
    a. True b. False
12. Econometric forecasting is a causal type of forecasting. (p. 100)
    a. True b. False
13. Under what condition does exponential smoothing give the same forecast as the last period demand method? (p. 87)
    a. $\alpha = 0$ b. $\alpha = 1$
14. A linear trend model should always be the first forecasting method used before more complex models are tried. (p. 97)
    a. True b. False

4.11 DISCUSSION QUESTIONS

1. Name some other types of undesired returns organizations may get.
2. Why do you think values of smoothing constants above 0.3 are rarely used?
3. If Delphi is so good why do we not see more of it?
4. Test marketing provides data regarding the monetary returns people really will provide as opposed to what they *say* they will. Why is there such a difference?
5. For many years it was believed that group forecasts were much more conservative than any individual's forecast in the group. Now it is known that just the opposite is true, a phenomenon known as the "risky shift." Why is this so?
6. In what situation might you have historical data but choose to use a qualitative forecasting method instead, ignoring the data?
7. What forecasting methods might be able to predict "turning points" in future demand? (That is, effects that had not happened in the past history of demand.)
8. A linear trend *additive* forecasting model is of the form $Y = T + S$. How might forecasts with such a model differ from the mutliplicative model?
9. What returns from the environment do regulatory agencies such as the SEC and the FTC desire?
10. Why do you think that technical analysts of securities, who as a group use time series analysis, have come to be called "mystics" by many investors?

11. How accurate do you think government forecasts need to be when business and labor often depend upon such estimates as cost of living statistics and inflation indicators?

12. What techniques could you devise for forecasting what a competitor's price might be next year or what amount she or he will bid on a project?

13. How can such events as strikes and disasters be integrated into a forecasting process to account for significant data shifts?

4.12 PROBLEMS

Tools and Applications

1. Data are available for the first six months of operations. Using least squares regression, develop a trend line and use it to predict demand for the next three months.

X	Y
1	3600
2	3683
3	3740
4	3812
5	3898
6	4100

2. Using the data in Problem 1 forecast month 7 using a three-period moving average.

3. Using the data from Problem 1 and letting $\overline{Y}_1 = 3600$, find exponentially smoothed forecasts for month 7 using $\alpha = 0.05$ and $\alpha = 0.25$. Which smoothing constant do you prefer and why?

4. The Harlan County Lemon Store and Used Car Lot has maintained auto sales data for the past three years on a quarter-by-quarter basis as follows:

Year	Quarter	Time	Auto Sales
1	1	1	10
	2	2	13
	3	3	14
	4	4	12
2	1	5	12
	2	6	14
	3	7	15
	4	8	13
3	1	9	13
	2	10	15
	3	11	18
	4	12	14

Compute the trend and seasonal components and forecast sales for the upcoming year.

5. Using the data in Problem 4 forecast year 4, quarter 1 using an exponential forecast with $\alpha = 0.2$ and compare to the results of Problem 4.

6. Demand for snow tire sets in Madison, Wisconsin is expected to depend on the amount of snowfall (in inches) in the previous winter season. Data for snow tire demand (Y) and snowfall (X) have been collected for the past 10 seasons.

Y (demand)	X (snowfall in previous season)
972	12.5
1125	13.8
850	11.2
921	12.0
1202	14.1
878	11.1
890	11.7
1072	12.6
931	11.9
986	12.3

Determine the trend using least squares regression. If snowfall this season was 13.1 inches, what demand would you predict for next winter?

7. Newstore Inc. is a recently opened clothing store in a new shopping center. Newstore's sales for the first eight weeks are as follows.

1	750	5	3530
2	1200	6	4410
3	1800	7	4850
4	2520	8	5140

a. Plot the data on graph paper.
b. Compute the least squares regression line to predict sales.
c. Advise the owner of Newstore on the desirability of using this forecasting method for the above situation.

4.13 CASE BARDSTOWN BOX COMPANY

Bardstown Box Company is a small, closely held corporation located in Bardstown, Kentucky. The stock of the company is divided among three brothers with the principal shareholder being the founding brother, Bob Wilson. Bob formed the company 20 years ago when he resigned as a salesman for a large corrugated box manufacturer.

Bob attributes his success to the fact that he can better serve the five-state area which he considers "his territory" than can any of his large competitors. Bardstown Box supplies corrugated cartons to many regional distilleries and to several breweries. Also, standard size boxes are printed to order for many small manufacturing firms in the region. Bob feels that the large box manufacturers cannot economically provide this personal level of service to his accounts.

Bob recognizes the danger of becoming too dependent upon any one client and has enforced the policy that no single customer can account for over 20 percent of sales. Two of the distilleries account for 20 percent of sales each, and hence are limited in their purchases. Bob has convinced the purchasing agents of these two companies to add other suppliers since this alternative supply protects them against problems Bardstown might have in shipping, paper shortages, or labor problems.

Bardstown currently has over 600 customers with orders ranging in size from a low of 100 boxes to blanket orders for 50,000 boxes per year. Boxes are produced in 16 standard sizes with special printing to customers' specifications. Bardstown's printing equipment limits their print to two colors. The standardization and limited printing allows Bardstown to be price competitive with the big producers but they also provide the service for small and "emergency" orders that large box manufacturers cannot provide.

Such personal service, however, requires tight inventory control and close production scheduling. So far, Bob Wilson has always forecast demand and prepared production schedules through experience but because of the ever-growing number of accounts and changes in personnel in customer purchasing departments, the accuracy of his forecasting has been rapidly declining. The number of backorders is on the increase, late orders are more common and inventory levels of finished boxes is on the increase. A second warehouse has recently been leased due to the overcrowded conditions in the main warehouse. Plans are to move some of the slower moving boxes to the leased space.

There has always been an increase in demand for boxes prior to the Christmas holiday season when customers begin stocking for holiday promotional demand. Such seasonality in demand has always substantially increased the difficulty of making a reliable forecast.

Bob Wilson feels that it is now important to develop an improved forecasting method. It should take both customer growth and seasonality into consideration. Bob believes that if such a method can be applied to forecasting total demand, it can also be used to forecast demand for the larger customers; the requirements of the smaller customers could then be integrated to smooth production and warehousing volume.

Bob has compiled the following demand data.

	Sales (in number of boxes)				
Month	1974	1975	1976	1977	1978
January	12,000	8,000	12,000	15,000	15,000
February	8,000	14,000	8,000	12,000	22,000
March	10,000	18,000	18,000	14,000	18,000
April	18,000	15,000	13,000	18,000	18,000
May	14,000	16,000	14,000	15,000	16,000
June	10,000	18,000	18,000	18,000	20,000
July	16,000	14,000	17,000	20,000	28,000
August	18,000	28,000	20,000	22,000	28,000
September	20,000	22,000	25,000	26,000	20,000
October	27,000	27,000	28,000	28,000	30,000
November	24,000	26,000	18,000	20,000	22,000
December	18,000	10,000	18,000	22,000	28,000
	195,000	216,000	209,000	230,000	265,000

QUESTIONS FOR DISCUSSION

1. Develop a forecasting method for Bardstown and forecast total demand for 1979.
2. How might Bob improve the accuracy of the forecast?
3. Should Bob's experience with the market be factored into the forecast? How?

4.14 REFERENCES AND BIBLIOGRAPHY

1. Boot, J. C. G., and E. B. Cox, *Statistical Analysis for Managerial Decisions*, 2nd ed., New York: McGraw-Hill, 1974.
2. Brown, R. G., *Smoothing, Forecasting and Prediction of Discrete Time Series*, Englewood Cliffs, N.J.: Prentice-Hall, 1963.
3. Green, Paul E., and Donald S. Tull, *Research for Marketing Decisions*, 2nd ed., Englewood Cliffs, N.J.: Prentice-Hall, 1970.
4. Linstone, H. A., and M. Turoff, *The Delphi Method: Techniques and Applications*, Reading, Mass.: Addison-Wesley, 1975.
5. Ramond, Charles, *The Art of Using Science in Marketing*, New York: Harper & Row, 1974.
6. Wasson, Chester, and David H. McConaughy, *Buying Behavior and Marketing Decisions*, Englewood Cliffs, N.J.: Prentice-Hall, 1968.
7. Wentz, Walter, *Marketing Research: Management and Methods*, New York: Harper & Row, 1972.

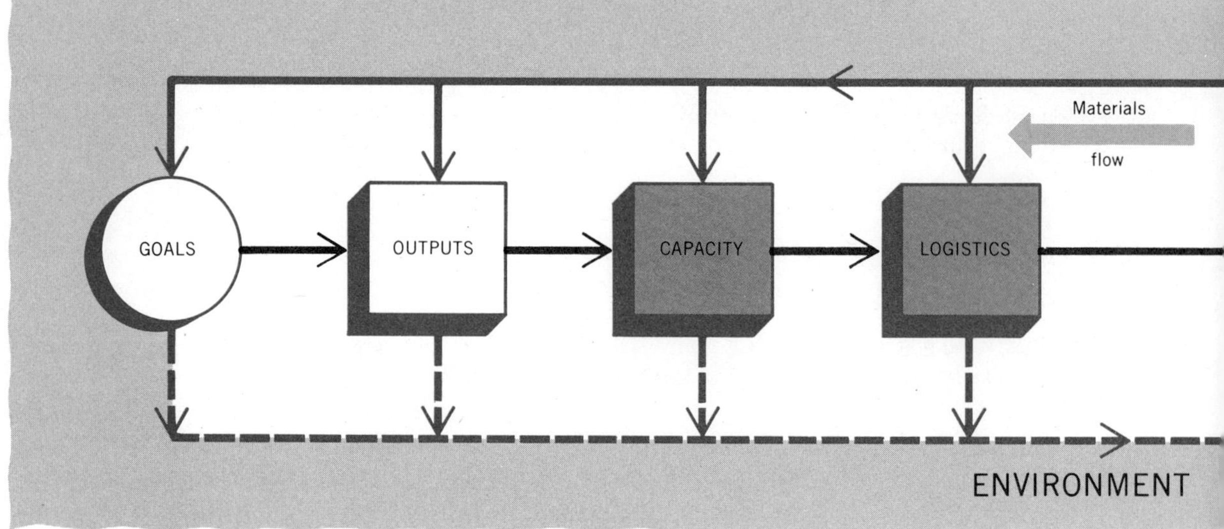

Part II

THE TRANSFORMATION PROCESS

At this point in the design of the organization's operations, the outputs have been selected and designed and demand forecasts have been made. Based on these two factors, we may now establish preliminary capacity plans, select the method of distributing the outputs to the recipients, and design and schedule the transformation operations. This part of the text is devoted to these subjects, the heart of the operations function.

In Chapter 5, Capacity Planning, we relate the forecasted output demand to the transformation process. Different levels of demand dictate different distribution techniques and transformation procedures. In the chapter, short- and long-term capacity alternatives are contrasted in terms of costs, benefits, and risk.

In Chapter 6I we consider the distribution process in two stages. First we look at the logistical function of transporting goods between locations and the advantages and disadvantages of various modes of transportation. Then we analyze the facility location decision, the second major element in the distribution process. Important national, regional, and local considerations are enumerated and the location of multiple and branch facilities is

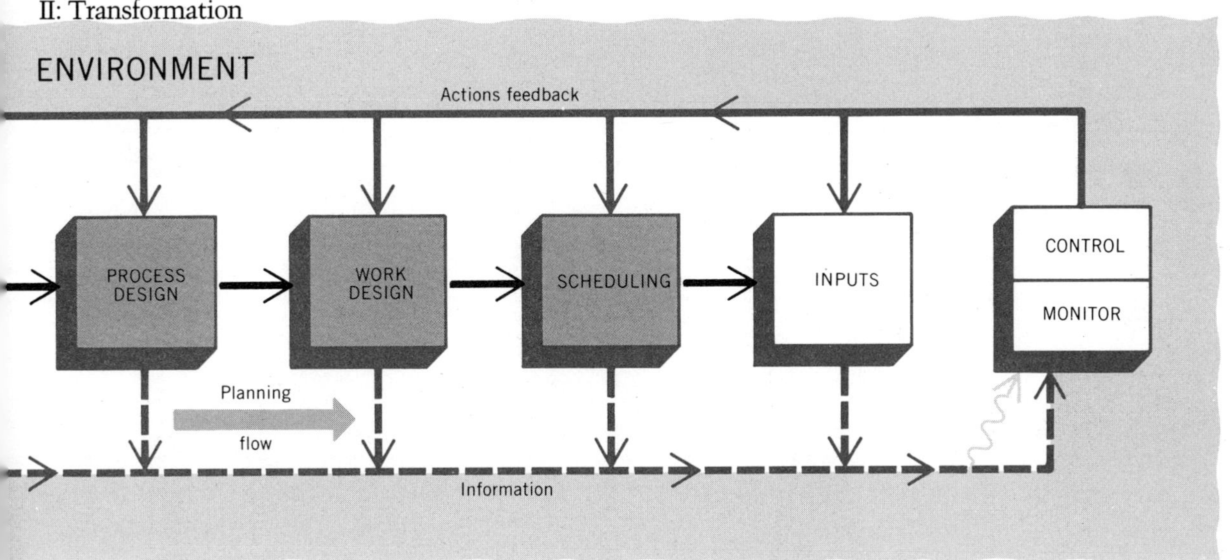

discussed. Finally, studies and models of distribution in the product and service sectors are detailed.

In Chapter 7, Designing the Transformation Process, we focus on designing the transformation process itself. Here we discuss the nature of some standard transformation processes and compare their advantages and disadvantages. We consider layout techniques, equipment/labor tradeoffs, service processes, fabrication techniques, and so forth.

In Chapter 8, Work Design, we consider the worker in the transformation process—a subject variously known as "ergonomics" and "sociotechnical" analysis. This includes physical, physiological, psychological, and social considerations such as motion study, occupational safety and health, job enrichment, and so forth.

Then, Chapter 9, Scheduling the Transformation Activities, we will cover the scheduling problem ranging from what is termed "aggregate scheduling," a gross-cut, preliminary scheduling process, through "expediting" to rush a delayed job out to a waiting recipient. These activities are then described in detail, and techniques that managers have found to be useful are illustrated. Although the above scheduling activities apply equally to services there are some special considerations concerning the scheduling of services that are also discussed. Lastly, some specialized project scheduling concepts are explained and illustrated.

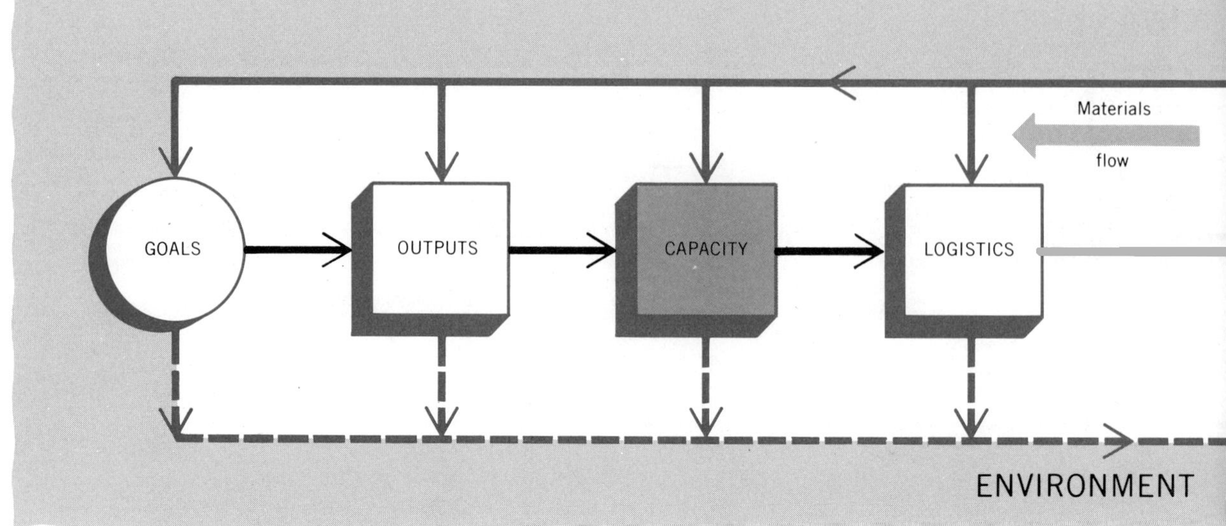

Chapter 5

Capacity Planning

CONCEPTS

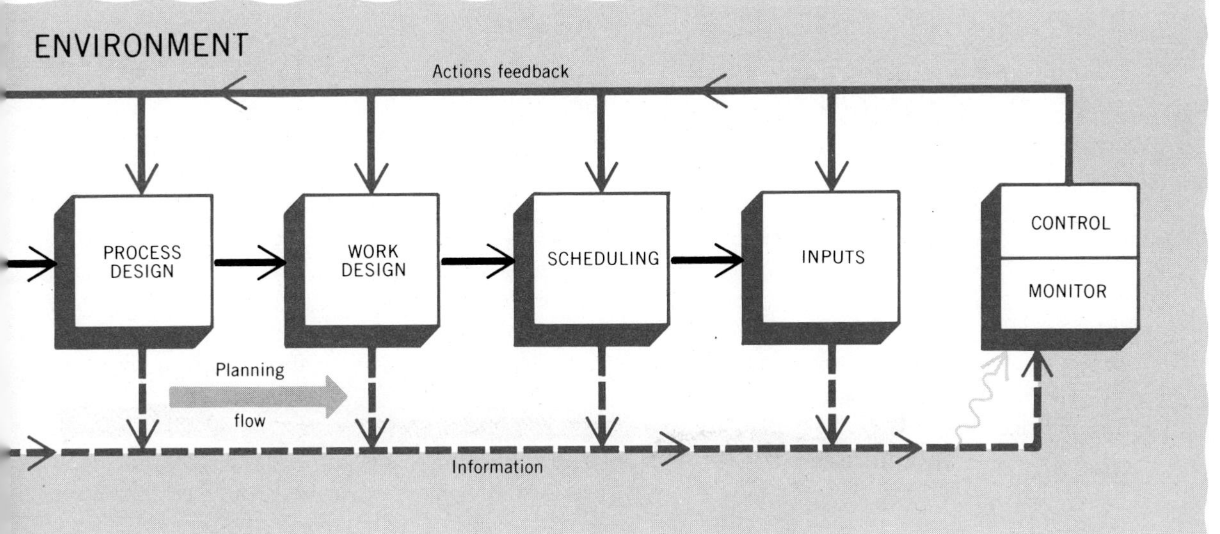

TOOLS AND APPLICATIONS

LEARNING OBJECTIVES

By the completion of the *Concepts* portion of this chapter the student should

1. Know how to use the breakeven model for economic analysis of both for-profit and not-for-profit organizational outputs.
2. Know when an organization needs "anticyclic" outputs.
3. Be familiar with the standard managerial alternatives for changing short-term capacity.
4. Realize that scheduling of operations to meet due dates may not be possible with supposedly ample capacity due to "bottlenecks."
5. Know how and when to use the learning curve in determining capacity.
6. Be able to determine required capacity investment for various levels of demand and compute the utilization efficiency of that investment.

CONCEPTS

In the last chapter we talked about determining the demand for the output that exists in the environment and the importance to the operations function of forecasting this demand. In this chapter we investigate the alternative methods available to obtain the *capacity* for economically supplying that demand. We treat the short and long run capacity problem separately because good short run methods of increasing capacity, such as the use of overtime, may be less desirable for long run or permanent capacity increases.

Capacity defined.

"Capacity" may be considered to mean the amount of output of an operation over some specified duration. For instance, airlines measure their capacity in "available seat miles" (ASM's) over a year. One ASM is one seat available for a passenger for one mile. Clearly, the number of planes an airline has, their size, how often they are flown, and the route structure of the airline all affect its ASM's, or capacity. An elementary measure of a hospital's capacity is often stated simply in terms of the number of beds in the hospital. Thus, a 50-bed hospital is a "small" one and a 1000-bed hospital is a "large" one.

Capacity complicated by multiple outputs.

Notice that the above measures of capacity do not recognize the multiple types of outputs an organization may, in reality, be concerned with. ASM's say nothing about the freight capacity of an airline but freight may be a major contributor to profits. Similarly, number of beds says nothing about outpatient treatments, ambulance rescues, and other services provided by a hospital. Thus, capacity planning must often consider the capacity to produce multiple outputs. Unfortunately, this is frequently complicated by the fact that some of the outputs may be able to use the same resources but require some specialized resources as well. We will consider this issue again later in the chapter.

Handling peaks in demand.

The capacity planning problem facing the operations manager is to have the "most economic" amount of capacity available to meet demand. The manager should not necessarily always be able to meet the peak demands because this may simply be too expensive. For example, to meet peak demand in a service is sometimes extremely difficult because of the tendency for service demands to peak at various intervals (doctor's offices at 9 A.M. and 1 P.M., university classes at 10 A.M., and fire alarms at 5 P.M.—see Figure 5.1). One way of handling this problem so as to not have to continuously staff for maximum demand is to schedule appointments, if possible, and spread out the demand. Another way is to overlap shifts during the peak demand periods. In a similar manner, part-time help can sometimes be called upon for peak periods. Other ways of handling short-term overloads in service capacity are illustrated by the typical 1940s lunchroom during the noon rush hour (based on Reference 9):

As the customers started filling all the tables, a receptionist came on duty and attended to the parties queuing for a table. More waitresses, bus boys, and an extra cook also showed up

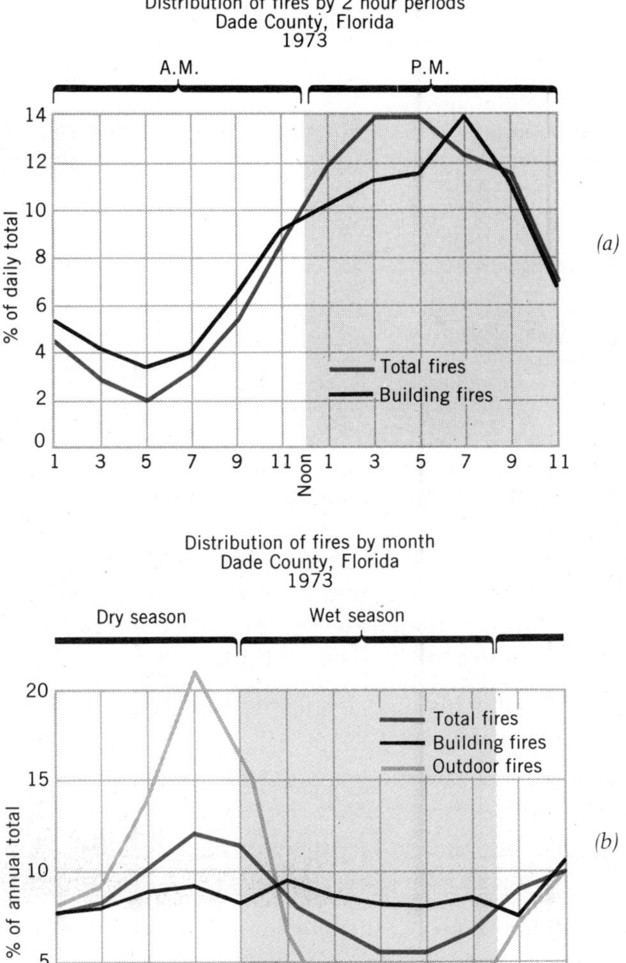

Figure 5.1. Fire alarm histories. (*a*) Hourly. (*b*) Monthly.

and started working. As customers got to a table and opened the menu they noticed the statement "No substitutions between 11 A.M. and 2 P.M." Waitresses were a long time in coming to take orders and service in general seemed slow. Hamburgers and other sandwiches were served plain with lettuce and tomato on the side, regardless of how they were ordered. Pre-prepared relish cups were included on every plate whether ordered or not. At the conclusion of the meal, signs on the table implored the customer to do his/her part to leave the table clean.

TABLE 5.1 TECHNIQUES TO INCREASE SERVICE CAPACITY

1. Add more servers.
2. Form a queue.
3. Standardize the menu.
4. Pre-prepare elements of the meal.
5. Eliminate custom treatment.
6. Decrease service time.
7. Let the customer perform part of the work.

Other alternatives are:

8. Schedule appointments.
9. Do not supply all demand.
10. Overlap shifts.
11. Lower prices for off-peak periods and vice versa.

From this brief description we can see a number of special techniques designed into the system for increasing service output capacity. They are listed more specifically in Table 5.1.

In queuing for tables, we are more sophisticated in this regard these days, of course. The receptionist takes our name and party size and tells us there will be a 20-minute wait (they must never tell a customer the wait will be longer than 20 minutes) and then motions us to a bar. This serves three purposes.

1. It gets us out of his/her hair and into more comfortable surroundings where we are less likely to leave.
2. It makes money for the restaurant whose greatest profits come from drinks, not food.
3. It deadens our senses so when we do finally receive our meal it does not really taste too bad and the service does not seem as terrible as it really is.

We will now consider this problem of meeting short-term capacity needs more fully in the next section. We will defer the topic of long run capacity changes until the following section.

5.1 SHORT-TERM CONSIDERATIONS

The short-term capacity problem is economically handling unexpected actual demand, either less than or more than expected. It is known, of course, that the forecast will not be perfect and, thus, the operations manager must plan what short-term capacity alternatives to use in either case. Such considerations are usually limited to, at most, the next six months, and usually much less.

Capacity versus scheduling.

Capacity planning is very closely related to the scheduling function, a topic to be discussed in Chapter 9. The difference is that capacity involves the *acquisition* of productive resources whereas **scheduling** concerns the *timing* of their use. However,

TABLE 5.2 SEQUENTIAL OPERATIONS REQUIRED FOR TWO JOBS

Job	Operational Resource Needed	Time Required (hr)
1	A	10
	C	10
	A	30
	B	20
	C	5
2	B	15
	A	10
	C	10
	A	10
	B	10

where human resources are involved, such as the use of overtime or the overlapping of shifts, it is difficult to separate the two. And in actual practice, scheduling and short-term capacity planning are often conducted simultaneously.

Bottlenecks.

For example, suppose an organization has the two jobs shown in Table 5.2 to complete within two weeks. The table shows the sequential processing operations still to be completed and the times required. (The operational resources may be of any form—a facility, piece of equipment, or specially skilled worker.) In total, 60 hours of resource A are needed, 45 hours of B, and 25 hours of C. It would appear that two weeks (80 hours) of capacity on each of these three resources would be sufficient and additional capacity would, therefore, be unnecessary.

Infinite loading on a Gantt chart

Figure 5.2 is a sketch showing the resource requirements of the two jobs plotted along a time scale. Such a chart is called a **Gantt** chart and can be used to show time schedules and capacities of facilities, workers, jobs, activities, machines, and so forth. In this case each job was "scheduled" on the required resource as soon as it finished on the previous resource, whether or not the new resource was occupied with the other job. This is called **infinite loading** because work is scheduled on the resource as

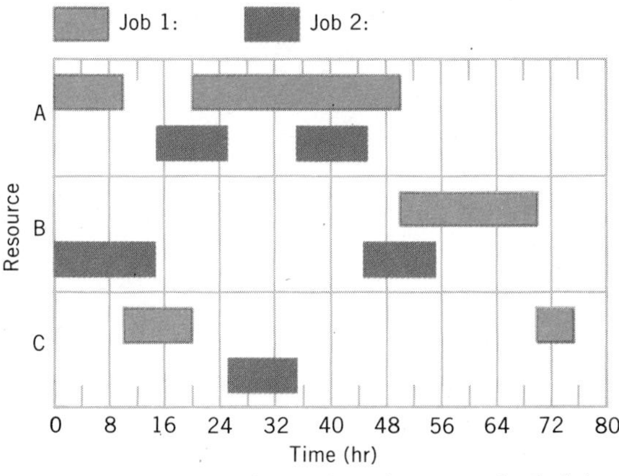

Figure 5.2. Gantt Chart for capacity planning and scheduling.

if it had infinite capacity to handle any and all jobs. Note that in this way, capacity conflicts and possible resolutions can be easily visualized.

Short-term resource conflicts.

The first resource conflict in Figure 5.2 occurs at 20 hours when job 1 finishes on resource C and next requires resource A, which is still working on job 2. The second conflict, again at A, occurs at 35 hours, and the third, on B, at 50 hours. It is quickly seen that deferring one job over the other has drastic consequences on resource conflicts later on, as well as job completion times. Another consideration, not specified here, is whether an operation can be partially completed in stages or, once started, must be completely finished or else restarted from scratch.

Capacity Alternatives for the Short Run

We will investigate some scheduling approaches to the above problem in Chapter 9. In terms of short-run capacity, however, management has a number of possible alternatives (other than permanent expansion) available to meet the problem of actual demand differing from the forecast although some are more expensive than others or have certain restrictions on them. The major ones, as exemplified earlier, are

1. Overtime.
2. Additional shifts.
3. Hiring or laying off staff (including part-time workers).
4. Subcontracting.
5. Leasing facilities and/or staff.
6. Backlogging demand.
7. Marketing promotions or price changes.
8. Undersupply.

Problems with each alternative.

Each of these has advantages and disadvantages. The use of overtime is expensive (time and a half) and efficiency after eight hours of work is typically poor. It is a simple and easily invoked process, however, that does not require additional investment. The use of extra shifts requires permanent hiring but no extra facilities or higher labor costs. However, due to idle time it is not feasible for handling much less than an outright doubling of demand. Permanent hiring and laying off entail training or termination benefits, are often subject to union regulations, and can be demoralizing to the staff. Part-time hiring can be expensive and is usually only feasible for low or unskilled work. Subcontracting typically requires a long lead time, is considerable trouble to implement, and may leave little, if any, profit.

Leasing facilities and staff is often a good approach but the extra cost reduces the profit, and these external resources may not be available during the high demand periods when they are usually necessary. If recipients are willing, the backlogging of demand to be met with production during later, normally slack periods, is an excellent strategy; no forecast is needed and finished goods investment is nil. However, such a situation is usually an open invitation to competition. Running promotions and/or price differentials for slack periods is an excellent method for leveling out demand, especially in utilities, telephone, and similar services. Prices are not easily increased above normal in high demand periods, however. Lastly, the manager may simply decide not to meet the market demand, again, however, at the cost of inviting competition.

Few viable alternatives.

In actuality, many of these alternatives are not feasible except in certain types of organizations or in particular circumstances. Typically, when demand is high, subcontractors are full, outside facilities and staff are already overbooked, second shift workers are employed elsewhere, and marketing promotions are already low-key. Thus, of the eight strategies, only 1, 6, and 8 are typically available to the manager and 6 and 8 are default alternatives (nothing else can be done).

The Learning Curve

Effect of learning on capacity.

It was pointed out earlier that hiring additional workers was one managerial alternative for increasing capacity. Initially, however, this approach may *lower* capacity because these workers need to be trained in their jobs, often by other workers. It is important to capacity planning then to know what the learning rate of new workers will be. This improvement in productivity, generally called the **learning curve** effect, is not necessarily due to learning alone, however. Better tools, improvements in work methods, upgraded output designs, and other such factors also help increase productivity, and hence such curves are also known as *improvement curves, production progress functions, performance curves,* and *experience curves*.

Based on airplane production.

The derivation of the learning curve is an outgrowth of the airframe manufacturing industry of the 1930s where it was found that the manhours to build each successive airplane decreased relatively smoothly. In particular, each time the output *doubled*, the manhours per plane decreased to a fixed percentage of their previous value—in this particular case, 80 percent. Thus, when the first plane of a series required 100,000 manhours (mh) to produce, the *second* one took 80,000 mh, the *fourth* one took 80,000 × 0.80 = 64,000, the *eighth* one took 64,000 × 0.80 = 51,200 mh, and so on. This type of mathematical relationship is described by the **negative exponential function.**

$$M = mN^{-r}$$

where

M = the manhours for the Nth unit*
m = the manhours required to produce the very *first* unit
N = the number of units produced
r = the exponent of the curve corresponding to the learning rate

The plot of this function for the airplane example is shown in Figure 5.3.

* Two forms of the learning curve relationship are used in the literature. In one form M corresponds to the cumulative *average* manhours of all N units and in the other form M corresponds to the *actual* manhours to produce the Nth unit. The second interpretation is more useful for operations management and will be the interpretation used here. For example, then, a learning rate of 90 percent would mean that each time production doubled from, say, N_1 to N_2, unit N_2 will require 90 percent of the manhours that N_1 required.

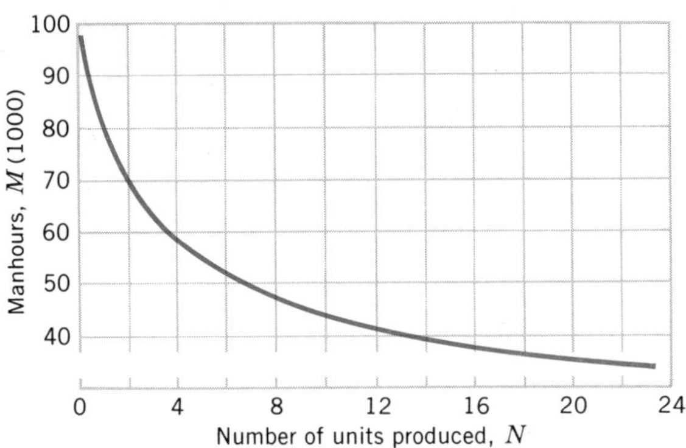

Figure 5.3. Eighty percent learning curve for airplane production.

Amount of human input is the key.

A number of factors affect the learning curve rate but the most important is the percentage of human, compared to mechanical, input in the task and the complexity of the task. Greatest learning, sometimes with as much as a 60 percent rate, occurs for highly complex tasks consisting primarily of human inputs. A task that is highly machine automated clearly leaves little opportunity for learning to occur (only the human can "learn," the machine generally cannot). In airframe manufacturing the proportion of human effort is about 75 percent and an 80 percent learning rate applies. For similar work of the same complexity and ratio of human to machine input, approximately the same rate will apply.

Applicable to groups and systems too.

But learning curves are not limited to manufacturing, or even product-oriented organizations. These curves apply just as well to beauty shops, selling, finding a parking space, and preparing pizza. As indicated, they also apply to *groups* of individuals, and *systems* that include people, as well as to individuals.

The primary question, of course, is what learning rate to apply. If previous experience is available this may give some indication; if not, a close watch of the time it takes to produce the first few units should give a good indication. Let us illustrate the use of the learning curve, and some learning curve tables, with a simple example.

Biocontrol, Inc.

Biocontrol has just entered the growing brainwave feedback market with a contract from a semireligious organization to teach biocontrol techniques to the organization's 10 elders for alpha and gamma brainwave rhythm control (which would hopefully enhance the elders' meditation abilities). The lessons for the last elder have just finished and the organization, considering the lessons highly successful, has engaged Biocontrol to give the same lessons to their congregation of 150 members. The lessons for the first elder were highly experimental, requiring 100 hours in all, but careful analysis and refinement of the techniques have gradually decreased this time to the point where the average time for *all* of the lessons was just under half that value, 49 hours each. To properly staff, schedule, plan, and cost out the work for the 150 lessons, Biocontrol needs to know how many hours of lessons will be required.

Analysis

Biocontrol will use Tables 5.3 and 5.4 to solve their dilemma. These tables provide the fraction of time the *N*th unit will require of what the first unit required (Table 5.3) and the cumulative fraction of time that the first *N* units will take of what the first unit took (Table 5.4). Returning to our 80 percent learning curve airplane example for a moment, Table 5.3 shows that unit 2 (left-hand column) under the "80%" column will require 0.8 of what unit 1 required (100,000 mh), that unit 4 will require 0.64, unit 8 will take 0.512, and so forth. In addition, we also see that unit 3 will take 0.7021 and unit 6, for example, 0.5617 (i.e., 0.5617 × 100,000 or 56,170 mh). The *total* manhours to produce two, four, or eight planes can be found by adding the necessary values above together, or by looking at Table 5.4 where this is already done. Again reading under the "80%" column for two, four, and eight units we get 1.8, 3.142, and 5.346 times 100,000, respectively, for 180,000, 314,200, and 534,600 manhours, cumulative.

To now consider Biocontrol's situation, the average of 49 hours each, times 10 elders, gives 490 hours, cumulative. This is 4.9 times what the first elder required (100 hours). Finding the value 4.9 in Table 5.4 for 10 units will then give the learning curve rate applying to these complex lessons. Reading across the 10 unit row we find 4.931 under the "70%" column (on occasion, interpolation between columns may be necessary).

Assuming the lessons are continuous and the teaching techniques are not forgotten (an important assumption), we can look further down the "70%" column of Table 5.4 to find the value corresponding to the *total* number of lessons to be given: 10 + 150 = 160. This value, 22.72, is then multiplied by the amount of time required for the first lesson (100 hours) to give a grand total of 2272 hours for the 160 lessons. Since the initial 10 elders required a total of 490 hours by themselves then the second group, consisting solely of the congregation, will require 2272 − 490 = 1782 hours. The time phasing of this 1782 hours is also available, if desired, from Table 5.3.

Plateaus, forgetting, relearning and natural variability.

The learning curve is only a theoretical construct, of course, and it therefore only approximates actual learning. A more realistic learning pattern is illustrated in Figure 5.4. Initially, actual manhours per unit vary about the theoretical curve until a "learning plateau" is reached at, perhaps, the tenth unit. At this plateau no significant learning appears to occur, until a breakthrough materializes. Learning typically involves a number of such plateaus and breakthroughs. At about 30 units, production is halted for a period of time and **forgetting** occurs, rapidly at first but then tailing off. When production is later reinitiated, relearning occurs very quickly (as when relearning to ride a bicycle after 40 years) until the original efficiency is reached (at about 33 units). If the conditions are the same at this time as for the initial part of the curve, the original learning curve rate will then hold. After sufficient time passes, the improvement due to learning becomes trivial in comparison to natural variability in efficiency and at that point we say that "learning has ceased."

TABLE 5.3 UNIT VALUES OF THE LEARNING CURVE

Units	Improvement ratios 60%	65%	70%	75%	80%	85%	90%	95%
1	1.0000	1.0000	1.0000	1.0000	1.0000	1.0000	1.0000	1.0000
2	0.6000	0.6500	0.7000	0.7500	0.8000	0.8500	0.9000	0.9500
3	0.4450	0.5052	0.5682	0.6338	0.7021	0.7729	0.8462	0.9219
4	0.3600	0.4225	0.4900	0.5625	0.6400	0.7225	0.8100	0.9025
5	0.3054	0.3678	0.4368	0.5127	0.5956	0.6857	0.7830	0.8877
6	0.2670	0.3284	0.3977	0.4754	0.5617	0.6570	0.7616	0.8758
7	0.2383	0.2984	0.3674	0.4459	0.5345	0.6337	0.7439	0.8659
8	0.2160	0.2746	0.3430	0.4219	0.5120	0.6141	0.7290	0.8574
9	0.1980	0.2552	0.3228	0.4017	0.4930	0.5974	0.7161	0.8499
10	0.1832	0.2391	0.3058	0.3846	0.4765	0.5828	0.7047	0.8433
12	0.1602	0.2135	0.2784	0.3565	0.4493	0.5584	0.6854	0.8320
14	0.1430	0.1940	0.2572	0.3344	0.4276	0.5386	0.6696	0.8226
16	0.1296	0.1785	0.2401	0.3164	0.4096	0.5220	0.6561	0.8145
18	0.1188	0.1659	0.2260	0.3013	0.3944	0.5078	0.6445	0.8074
20	0.1099	0.1554	0.2141	0.2884	0.3812	0.4954	0.6342	0.8012
22	0.1025	0.1465	0.2038	0.2772	0.3697	0.4844	0.6251	0.7955
24	0.0961	0.1387	0.1949	0.2674	0.3595	0.4747	0.6169	0.7904
25	0.0933	0.1353	0.1908	0.2629	0.3548	0.4701	0.6131	0.7880
30	0.0815	0.1208	0.1737	0.2437	0.3346	0.4505	0.5963	0.7775
35	0.0728	0.1097	0.1605	0.2286	0.3184	0.4345	0.5825	0.7687
40	0.0660	0.1010	0.1498	0.2163	0.3050	0.4211	0.5708	0.7611
45	0.0605	0.0939	0.1410	0.2060	0.2936	0.4096	0.5607	0.7545
50	0.0560	0.0879	0.1336	0.1972	0.2838	0.3996	0.5518	0.7486
60	0.0489	0.0785	0.1216	0.1828	0.2676	0.3829	0.5367	0.7386
70	0.0437	0.0713	0.1123	0.1715	0.2547	0.3693	0.5243	0.7302
80	0.0396	0.0657	0.1049	0.1622	0.2440	0.3579	0.5137	0.7231
90	0.0363	0.0610	0.0987	0.1545	0.2349	0.3482	0.5046	0.7168
100	0.0336	0.0572	0.0935	0.1479	0.2271	0.3397	0.4966	0.7112
120	0.0294	0.0510	0.0851	0.1371	0.2141	0.3255	0.4830	0.7017
140	0.0262	0.0464	0.0786	0.1287	0.2038	0.3139	0.4718	0.6937
160	0.0237	0.0427	0.0734	0.1217	0.1952	0.3042	0.4623	0.6869
180	0.0218	0.0397	0.0691	0.1159	0.1879	0.2959	0.4541	0.6809
200	0.0201	0.0371	0.0655	0.1109	0.1816	0.2887	0.4469	0.6757
250	0.0171	0.0323	0.0584	0.1011	0.1691	0.2740	0.4320	0.6646
300	0.0149	0.0289	0.0531	0.0937	0.1594	0.2625	0.4202	0.6557
350	0.0133	0.0262	0.0491	0.0879	0.1517	0.2532	0.4105	0.6482
400	0.0121	0.0241	0.0458	0.0832	0.1453	0.2454	0.4022	0.6419
450	0.0111	0.0224	0.0431	0.0792	0.1399	0.2387	0.3951	0.6363
500	0.0103	0.0210	0.0408	0.0758	0.1352	0.2329	0.3888	0.6314
600	0.0090	0.0188	0.0372	0.0703	0.1275	0.2232	0.3782	0.6229
700	0.0080	0.0171	0.0344	0.0659	0.1214	0.2152	0.3694	0.6158
800	0.0073	0.0157	0.0321	0.0624	0.1163	0.2086	0.3620	0.6098
900	0.0067	0.0146	0.0302	0.0594	0.1119	0.2029	0.3556	0.6045
1000	0.0062	0.0137	0.0286	0.0569	0.1082	0.1980	0.3499	0.5998
1200	0.0054	0.0122	0.0260	0.0527	0.1020	0.1897	0.3404	0.5918
1400	0.0048	0.0111	0.0240	0.0495	0.0971	0.1830	0.3325	0.5850
1600	0.0044	0.0102	0.0225	0.0468	0.0930	0.1773	0.3258	0.5793
1800	0.0040	0.0095	0.0211	0.0446	0.0895	0.1725	0.3200	0.5743
2000	0.0037	0.0089	0.0200	0.0427	0.0866	0.1683	0.3149	0.5698
2500	0.0031	0.0077	0.0178	0.0389	0.0806	0.1597	0.3044	0.5605
3000	0.0027	0.0069	0.0162	0.0360	0.0760	0.1530	0.2961	0.5530

Source: Albert N. Schrieber, Richard A. Johnson, Robert C. Meier, William T. Newell, Henry C. Fischer, *Cases in Manufacturing Management* (New York: McGraw-Hill Book Company, © 1965), p. 464. Reprinted by permission of McGraw-Hill.

TABLE 5.4 CUMULATIVE VALUES OF THE LEARNING CURVE

Units	Improvement ratios 60%	65%	70%	75%	80%	85%	90%	95%
1	1.000	1.000	1.000	1.000	1.000	1.000	1.000	1.000
2	1.600	1.650	1.700	1.750	1.800	1.850	1.900	1.950
3	2.045	2.155	2.268	2.384	2.502	2.623	2.746	2.872
4	2.405	2.578	2.758	2.946	3.142	3.345	3.556	3.774
5	2.710	2.946	3.195	3.459	3.738	4.031	4.339	4.662
6	2.977	3.274	3.593	3.934	4.299	4.688	5.101	5.538
7	3.216	3.572	3.960	4.380	4.834	5.322	5.845	6.404
8	3.432	3.847	4.303	4.802	5.346	5.936	6.574	7.261
9	3.630	4.102	4.626	5.204	5.839	6.533	7.290	8.111
10	3.813	4.341	4.931	5.589	6.315	7.116	7.994	8.955
12	4.144	4.780	5.501	6.315	7.227	8.244	9.374	10.62
14	4.438	5.177	6.026	6.994	8.092	9.331	10.72	12.27
16	4.704	5.541	6.514	7.635	8.920	10.38	12.04	13.91
18	4.946	5.879	6.972	8.245	9.716	11.41	13.33	15.52
20	5.171	6.195	7.407	8.828	10.48	12.40	14.61	17.13
22	5.379	6.492	7.819	9.388	11.23	13.38	15.86	18.72
24	5.574	6.773	8.213	9.928	11.95	14.33	17.10	20.31
25	5.668	6.909	8.404	10.19	12.31	14.80	17.71	21.10
30	6.097	7.540	9.305	11.45	14.02	17.09	20.73	25.00
35	6.478	8.109	10.13	12.72	15.64	19.29	23.67	28.86
40	6.821	8.631	10.90	13.72	17.19	21.43	26.54	32.68
45	7.134	9.114	11.62	14.77	18.68	23.50	29.37	36.47
50	7.422	9.565	12.31	15.78	20.12	25.51	32.14	40.22
60	7.941	10.39	13.57	17.67	22.87	29.41	37.57	47.65
70	8.401	11.13	14.74	19.43	25.47	33.17	42.87	54.99
80	8.814	11.82	15.82	21.09	27.96	36.80	48.05	62.25
90	9.191	12.45	16.83	22.67	30.35	40.32	53.14	69.45
100	9.539	13.03	17.79	24.18	32.65	43.75	58.14	76.59
120	10.16	14.11	19.57	27.02	37.05	50.39	67.93	90.71
140	10.72	15.08	21.20	29.67	41.22	56.78	77.46	104.7
160	11.21	15.97	22.72	32.17	45.20	62.95	86.80	118.5
180	11.67	16.79	24.14	34.54	49.03	68.95	95.96	132.1
200	12.09	17.55	25.48	36.80	52.72	74.79	105.0	145.7
250	13.01	19.28	28.56	42.08	61.47	88.83	126.9	179.2
300	13.81	20.81	31.34	46.94	69.66	102.2	148.2	212.2
350	14.51	22.18	33.89	51.48	77.43	115.1	169.0	244.8
400	15.14	23.44	36.26	55.75	84.85	127.6	189.3	277.0
450	15.72	24.60	38.48	59.80	91.97	139.7	209.2	309.0
500	16.26	25.68	40.58	63.68	98.85	151.5	228.8	340.6
600	17.21	27.67	44.47	70.97	112.0	174.2	267.1	403.3
700	18.06	29.45	48.04	77.77	124.4	196.1	304.5	465.3
800	18.82	31.09	51.36	84.18	136.3	217.3	341.0	526.5
900	19.51	32.60	54.46	90.26	147.7	237.9	376.9	587.2
1000	20.15	34.01	57.40	96.07	158.7	257.9	412.2	647.4
1200	21.30	36.59	62.85	107.0	179.7	296.6	481.2	766.6
1400	22.32	38.92	67.85	117.2	199.6	333.9	548.4	884.2
1600	23.23	41.04	72.49	126.8	218.6	369.9	614.2	1001
1800	24.06	43.00	76.85	135.9	236.8	404.9	678.8	1116
2000	24.83	44.84	80.96	144.7	254.4	438.9	742.3	1230
2500	26.53	48.97	90.39	165.0	296.1	520.8	897.0	1513
3000	27.99	52.62	98.90	183.7	335.2	598.9	1047	1791

Source: Albert N. Schrieber, Richard A. Johnson, Robert C. Meier, William T. Newell, Henry C. Fischer, *Cases in Manufacturing Management* (New York: McGraw-Hill Book Company, © 1965), p. 465. Reprinted by permission of McGraw-Hill.

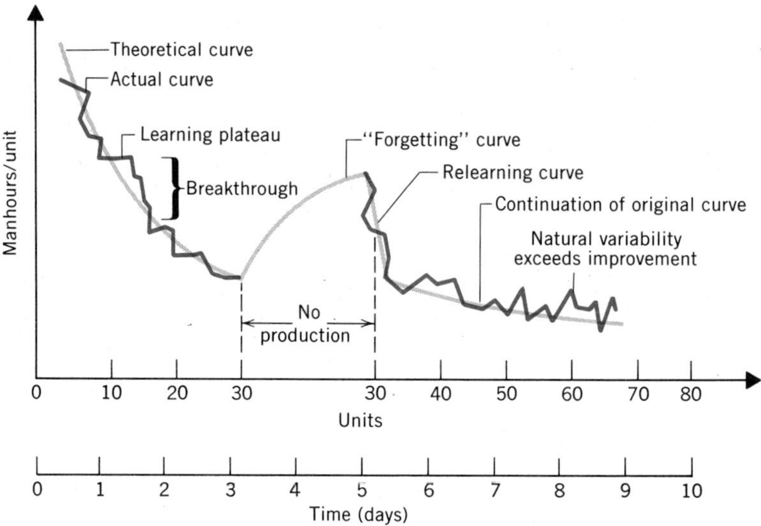

Figure 5.4. Typical learning-forgetting pattern.

5.2 LONG-TERM CONSIDERATIONS

Capacity planning issues over the long run relate primarily to the expansion and contraction of major facilities used in producing the organization's output. Realistically speaking, organizations are not always expanding their capacity. We usually focus on this issue because we are studying firms in the process of growth, but even successful organizations often reduce their capacity.

Capacity contraction.

Adding on outputs instead.

Major ways of contracting capacity are to divest operations, layoff workers, and sell or lease equipment and facilities. Most organizations, however, only try to contract capacity that is inefficient or inappropriate for their circumstances. If it appears that organizational resources are going to be excessively idle in the future, organizations often attempt to add new outputs to their current output mix rather than contracting capacity (the latter frequently being done at a loss). This entails an analysis of the output's life and seasonal demand cycles.

Demand and Life Cycles for Multiple Outputs

Many organizations are oriented to a demand that is "seasonal" and hence find themselves in a frenzy at certain times and idly bored at other times. Figure 5.1 illustrates how this is true in two ways for fire departments. In Figure 5.1*a*, we see that 5–7 P.M. is the peak buildings fire period and that at 5 A.M. fire outbreaks are almost nonexistent. In Figure 5.1*b* we see that, for Dade County, Florida, April is the peak demand month (primarily due to grass fires following a long, dry winter) and September is the slack month (following the summer tropical rainy season).

Demand seasonality

Adding an anticyclic output.

It is traditional in fire departments to use the slack months for building inspections, fire prevention programs, safety talks, and other such activities. The large investment in labor and equipment is thus more effectively utilized throughout the year by the organization's adoption of an *anticyclic* (counter to the fire cycle) output—fire prevention. For much the same reasons, many fire departments have been given the responsibility for the city or county's medical rescue service (although rescue alarms are not entirely anticyclic to fire alarms).

Furnaces and air conditioners.

Clearly, many organizations face this cyclic difficulty, such as the makers of Christmas ornaments, fur coats, swimming pool equipment, fireworks, and so forth. A classic case, however, has been that of furnace dealers. For the last 100 years their business typically was all in the late autumn and winter months of the year, as illustrated in Figure 5.5. With the rapid acceptance of air conditioning in the 1950s and 1960s many furnace dealers eagerly added this product to their output mix. Not only was it conceptually along the same lines (environmental comfort) and often interconnected with the home furnace but, most importantly, it was almost completely anticyclic to the seasonal heating cycle. As shown in Figure 5.5 the addition of air conditioning considerably leveled dealers' sales throughout the year in comparison with furnace sales alone.

Output life cycles

Multiple life cycles to even out capacity utilization.

In a similar manner, and for much the same reasons, organizations add outputs to their mix that are anticyclic to existing output **life cycles**. Figure 5.6 illustrates, in solid lines, the expected life cycles of an organization's current and projected outputs. Total required capacity is given by the heavy solid line, found by adding together the separate capacities of each of the required outputs. Note the projected dip in required

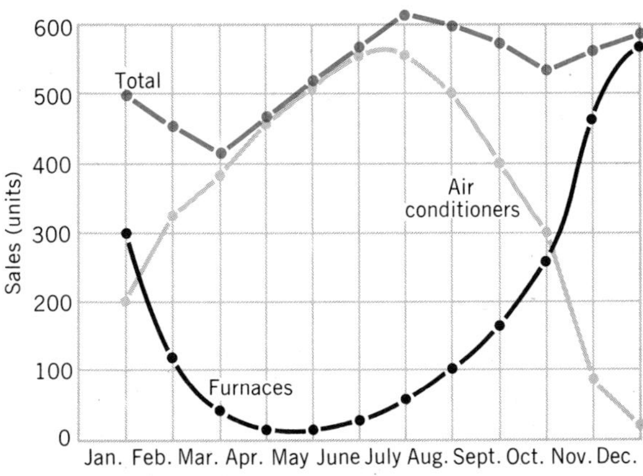

Figure 5.5. Anticyclic product sales.

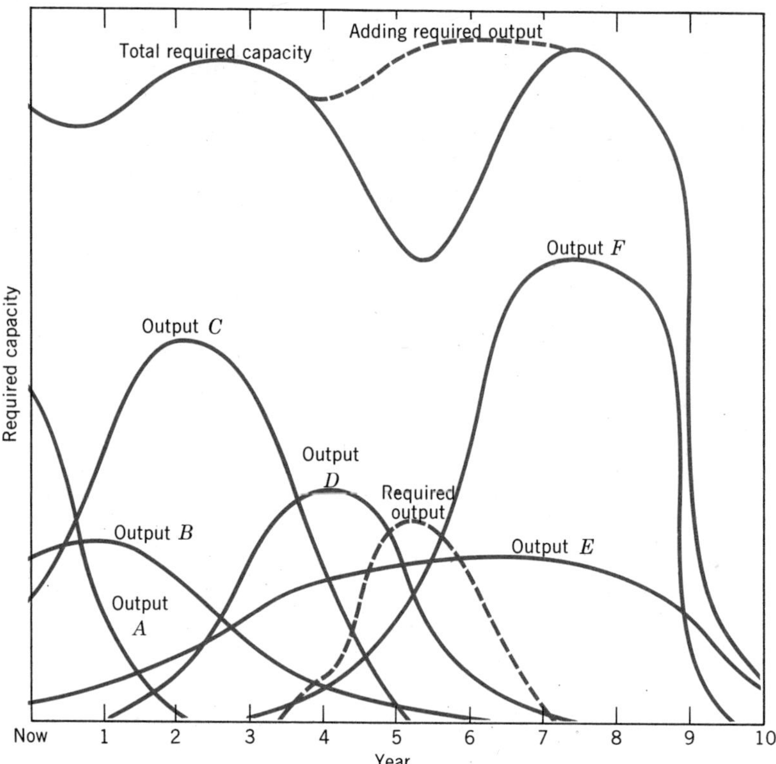

Figure 5.6. Forecast of required organizational capacity from multiple life cycles.

capacity five years in the future, and, of course, beyond the eight-year planning horizon.

The message of Figure 5.6 should be clear to the organization—an output with a three-year life cycle (appearing similar to the dashed line) is needed between years 4 and 7 in order to maintain efficient utilization of the organization's available capacity. A priority output development program will have to be instituted immediately along the lines illustrated in Chapter 3I. At this point it is probably too late to develop something through R&D; a more effective strategy, especially in light of the relatively low volume and short life cycle, might be an extension of an existing output.

Breakeven Analysis

Breakeven analysis for new outputs.

The introduction of a new output into the organization's existing output mix should only be implemented if a complete economic analysis has been conducted beforehand as discussed in Chapter 3I. This analysis would consider the fixed cost of existing capacity, the variable costs of the output, the return from the output, and the effect of different volumes of demand. Such an evaluation is called a **breakeven** analysis (also known as "cost-volume-profit" analysis). It was originally developed as an accounting technique used in the preparation of a profit budget for the firm. The analysis is based upon a simplified income or "profit and loss" statement which can be written as

	revenue (price × units sold)
less	variable costs (variable cost per unit × units sold)
equals	contribution margin
less	fixed costs
equals	net profit

Simplifications of the breakeven concept.

Clearly, there are many simplifications in the quantities above that will rarely hold in practice over a large range in output volume. For example, variable cost per unit may decrease, or increase, with larger output volumes. And small volumes of products are usually higher priced than if large volumes are sold. And in terms of our primary topic, capacity, fixed costs will certainly jump if additional facilities are necessary to increase output capacity.

Nevertheless, within small ranges of volumes the basic income statement relationship depicted above aids the operations manager in deciding whether or not a new product/service should be produced. Consider, for example, a sporting goods manufacturer who is faced with the decision of whether or not to produce a new fiberglass tennis racket.

Whataracket, Inc.

Revenue determination.

Sharon Rigg, operations manager for Whataracket, has determined a sales forecast for their new fiberglass tennis racket using one of the methods described in Chapter 4. The selling price assumed in preparing the forecast was \$18. Sharon reasons that this price puts the racket somewhere in the medium price range for similar quality rackets. To determine total revenue she simply multiplies the selling price (\$18) times the number of units (rackets) expected to be sold.

Variable costs from a number of sources.

Variable costs are the "per racket" costs of manufacturing and selling. The costs that would vary with the number of rackets sold are the fiberglass and bonding materials used in the racket, the nylon used to string the racket, the leather grip, and the labor and energy used to mold, string, assemble, and package the racket. Since the company has been in the sporting goods field for some time, and is familiar with the production methods required, a good estimate of variable costs can be made. Sharon estimates that the variable cost per racket will be \$11.

Elements of fixed costs.

Fixed costs are costs that do not vary with the volume of production or the number of rackets sold. In this case, the costs that would remain constant as production increased and decreased are building rent, insurance, property taxes, depreciation on equipment, administrative salaries, and interest on borrowed capital. Fixed costs are substantially determined through the selection of manufacturing equipment and the plant facility itself. We will postpone discussion of equipment and facility selection until Chapter 10I but assume, for now, that the annual fixed costs associated with this new product have already been determined to be $140,000. That is, the annual depreciation costs of the new molding equipment, the space rental, and other non-variable costs total to $140,000.

A graphical approach

We can visually show each of the three factors bearing on net profit in a breakeven graph. Volume of sales is shown on the horizontal axis and dollars (of revenue or cost) are measured on the vertical axis. Figure 5.7 shows the breakeven graph for the sporting goods manufacturer. We can first plot the fixed costs, recognizing that this line will be horizontal at $140,000 because fixed costs do not increase or decrease with volume of sales. The variable costs per unit of sales are $11. Therefore, the variable cost line will cross the point (0, 0) since at zero sales volume the variable costs are zero and will have a slope of 11. We can select any sales volume (e.g., 20,000 × $11 = $220,000) and then draw the straight line connecting the points (0, 0) and (20,000; 220,000). Likewise, the total revenue line is found in the same manner; it will cross the (0, 0) point since selling zero units will produce zero revenue, and will have a slope of 18. Finally, the variable cost and fixed cost lines are added together to form the *total cost* line. Note that the total cost line is parallel to the variable cost line and $140,000 (the amount of the fixed costs) higher than the variable cost line.

Graphing the data for revenue, variable costs, and fixed costs.

The point at which the total revenue line and the total cost line intersect is called the *breakeven point*. It is given this name because the sales volume at this point is just enough to cover the fixed plus variable costs of operation without either earning a profit or suffering a loss. The firm just breaks even. For our sporting goods manufacturer we can see from the figure that the new tennis racket will break even if sales are

Breakeven point at the intersection of the revenue and cost lines.

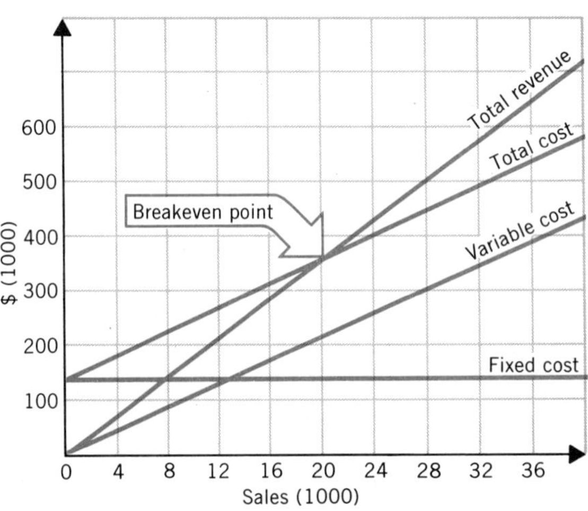

Figure 5.7. Breakeven graph for a tennis racket.

20,000 units. We can check this figure using the income statement format presented earlier with the sporting goods manufacturer data.

	revenue ($18/unit × 20,000 units)	$360,000
less	variable costs ($11/unit × 20,000 units) =	220,000
	contribution margin	140,000
less	fixed costs	140,000
	net profit	-0-

Any sales volume greater than the breakeven volume will result in a net profit for the firm and any volume less than the breakeven volume will result in a net loss for the firm. This can be seen by the fact that the total cost line is above the total revenue line to the left of the breakeven volume and is below the total revenue line to the right of the breakeven volume.

For example, if Sharon has forecast that annual sales will be 32,000 units then profits for the year can be estimated from the graph as the difference between total revenue and total costs at the volume of 32,000. Total revenue at 32,000 units equals $576,000 and total costs equal $492,000. Therefore, net income would be estimated to be $84,000 for the period.

An algebraic approach

Since graphical analysis is sometimes inconvenient, we can produce the same results through an algebraic analysis of the problem. We can write the income statement equation algebraically as follows.

$$\text{Revenue} - \text{variable costs} - \text{fixed costs} = \text{net profit}$$

and we can note that

$$\begin{aligned} \text{revenue} &= \text{selling price} \times \text{units sold} \\ \text{variable costs} &= \text{variable cost/unit} \times \text{units sold} \end{aligned}$$

If we let

SP = selling price
U = volume in units sold
VC = variable cost/unit
FC = fixed cost
NP = net profit

then the income statement equation can be written as

$$SP \times U - VC \times U - FC = NP$$

or

$$U \times (SP - VC) - FC = NP$$

or

$$U \times (SP - VC) = NP + FC$$

and finally

$$U = \frac{NP + FC}{SP - VC}$$

For example, to break even and therefore earn a zero net profit the number of units that must be manufactured and sold is

$$U = \frac{0 + 140{,}000}{18 - 11} = \frac{140{,}000}{7} = 20{,}000 \text{ units}$$

to earn a net profit of $10,000

$$U = \frac{10{,}000 + 140{,}000}{18 - 11} \approx 21{,}429 \text{ units}$$

If the best estimate for sales in units for the next period is less than 21,429 units then the company will not earn the desired profit and should decide not to produce the product. If the sales forecast is for less than 20,000 units then introduction of the new racket will result in a net loss for the firm.

Use of breakeven for rules of thumb.

One of the most useful aspects of the breakeven model for operations managers is its ability to clearly illustrate the overall effect of different managerial and environmental actions. For example, if inflation increases the variable costs by 10 percent what will the new breakeven volume be? Or, what volume must be sold to maintain our current profit? Or, at current volumes what price increase will maintain current profits?

Simplicity as a virtue.

Suppose, on the other hand, that, due to increased demand, management is planning on increasing capacity at a significant increase in fixed costs. Then what additional sales volume must occur to maintain current profits? Although the breakeven model is somewhat oversimplified it is just this simplicity that makes it an ideal tool for operations managers. It allows quick, relatively accurate rules of thumb for small, day-to-day changes in production.

Comparing capacity alternatives

Comparing alternatives via breakeven.

Another important application of the breakeven concept for operations managers is the comparison of alternate methods of achieving capacity. For example, Figure 5.8 shows three different methods of producing a product. (Only the total cost functions are depicted.) Method A is an almost all-labor approach (VC = $160) with very little equipment (FC = $20,000) and hence is good for small volumes but very expensive for large volumes. On the other hand, method C is a mass production automated factory with high fixed costs ($400,000) but low variable costs ($10) and hence is best for large output volumes. Method B (FC = $160,000; VC = $85) is a compromise between A and C.

Depending upon the forecast of demand capacity required, now and in the not too distant future, either method A, B, or C may be the wisest capacity choice. For

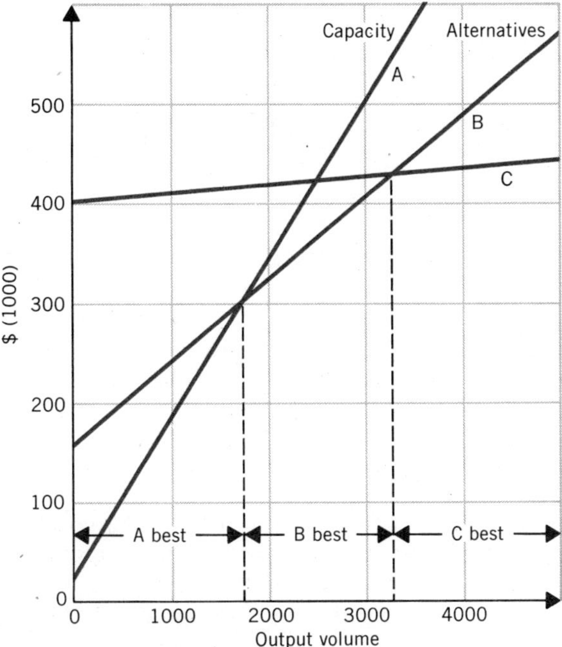

Figure 5.8. Capacity alternatives comparison.

example, for volumes in excess of 3200 units, method C is best. This value can be determined by equating the costs of methods B and C to find the intersection: 160,000 + $85U$ = 400,000 + $10U$ or U = 3200. Clearly, other considerations such as resale value and alternative uses will also affect the capacity alternative decision but the breakeven model gives an important economic comparison between the alternatives.

Application in the public sector

Because public sector organizations are not profit oriented, breakeven analysis is not directly applicable. But minor modification of the approach again makes the technique a useful aid for the public operations manager.

Public sector breakeven.

While there are no "profits" involved in the operation of a public organization (e.g., a police department), there are revenues that are often fixed by the annual budget. This situation is shown in Figure 5.9. As with the traditional breakeven analysis, the breakeven point is the point at which the total cost line and the revenue line intersect. But, the interpretation here is somewhat different. To the right of the breakeven volume the organization exceeds its budgeted revenue—a situation analogous to a "loss" for a profit oriented firm. To the left of the breakeven volume the organization is not "using up" all of its budget and therefore is not producing the level of service for which it was budgeted. The *ideal volume*, for the *public sector* organization, is the *breakeven volume*.

Ideal volume is the breakeven volume.

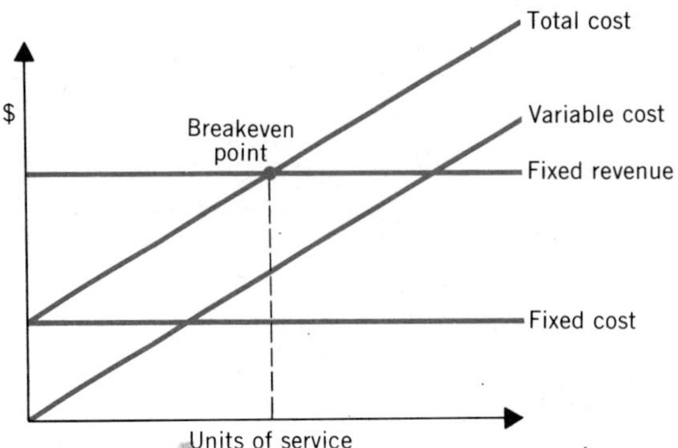

Figure 5.9. Fixed annual budget chart for public sector operations.

Resource Investment to Gain Capacity

Capacity versus investment.

Up to this point we have considered the volume of productive capacity and the necessary resource investment to gain that capacity as proportional. In the case of one worker, or one machine, this is generally true but when many workers and/or machines are required to produce the output (as is usually the case) there is not a simple correspondence. That is, if rubber balls are molded in a machine run by one full-time worker at the rate of 100 per hour and a capacity of 1000 per hour is required then the resource investment translates directly—10 workers and machines will be needed. For outputs involving more complex production operations the resource investment does not translate so directly with the required capacity, as illustrated in the example below.

Assume Whataracket produces a variety of rackets sequentially on four machines and the cycle time required for the fiberglass racket is as follows:

Machine 1	4 min
Machine 2	3 min
Machine 3	10 min
Machine 4	2 min

Cycle time based on the slowest machine.

To minimize the equipment cost, Sharon could use one of each machine and have a resulting output rate (based on the slowest machine cycle of 10 minutes) of six units per hour. In doing so, however, the first, second, and fourth machines would be idle 6, 7, and 8 minutes out of every 10-minute cycle for a utilization efficiency of only

$$\text{Efficiency} = \frac{\text{output}}{\text{input}} = \frac{4 + 3 + 10 + 2}{4(10)} = 47.5\%$$

If Whataracket was willing to invest in a fifth machine of the same type as machine 3, Sharon could run machines 3 and 5 concurrently and put out *two* units every

TABLE 5.5 RETURN TO WHATARACKET FOR RISKING USE OF MORE MACHINES

Number of Machines	Type Number of Next Machine	Machine Times (min) No. 1	No. 2	No. 3	No. 4	Total Cycle Time	Hourly Output	Utilization Efficiency (%)
4	—	4	3	10	2	10	6	47.5
5	3	4	3	5	2	5	12	76.0
6	3	4	3	3.33	2	4	15	79.2
7	1	2	3	3.33	2	3.33	18	81.4
8	3	2	3	2.5	2	3	20	79.2
9	2	2	1.5	2.5	2	2.5	24	84.4
10	3	2	1.5	2	2	2	30	95.0
11	4	2	1.5	2	1	2	30	86.0
12	1	1.33	1.5	2	1	2	30	79.2
13	3	1.33	1.5	1.67	1	1.67	36	87.5
14	3	1.33	1.5	1.43	1	1.43	42	94.9

10 minutes, obtaining an average cycle time of 5 minutes. The effect of this single investment would be to *double* her output rate to 12 units per hour and increase her efficiency to

$$\frac{4 + 3 + 5 + 2 + 5}{5(5)} = \frac{19}{25} = 76\%$$

Continuing in this manner results in the data shown in Table 5.5 and sketched in Figure 5.10.

Efficiency and output do not change at the same rate.

Note from the table and figure that efficiency of production does not always increase when machines are added, although the general trend is upward. This is because some systems are fairly well "balanced" to begin with (e.g., with 7 machines, the cycles are quite even, 2, 3, 3.33, 2; more so at 10 machines; and the addition of only one extra machine at such points does not pay for itself). If points of high effi-

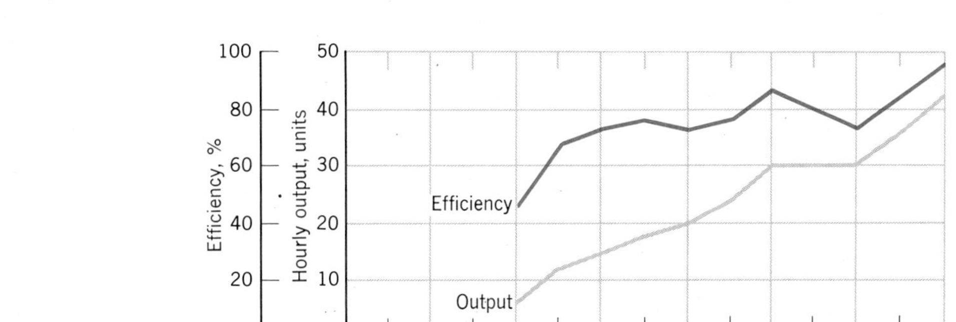

Figure 5.10 Efficiency and output increases from adding machines.

ciency are reached "early" (as machines are added), these points will tend to be natural operating solutions for Sharon's problem. For example, a tremendous gain in efficiency (and in output percentage) is reaped by adding a fifth machine to the system. Further additions do not gain much. The next largest gain is when the tenth machine is added to the system.

Natural operating points.

Although the above analysis describes the general tradeoffs of the system, no mention has been made of demand. Suppose demand was 15 units per hour. Then, to minimize risk but still keep an efficient system, Sharon might use five machines and either work overtime, undersupply the market, or use a number of other strategies as will be discussed later. Similarly, for a demand of 25–35 per hour, the use of 10 machines would be appropriate.

This completes our discussion of the basic concepts of capacity planning. The next three sections of the *Tools and Applications* portion of the chapter illustrate the use of linear programming and decision trees to resolve more complex capacity planning situations. First we investigate the difficulty that producing multiple outputs poses for capacity planning and illustrate the application of linear programming to this difficulty. Then we consider the effect of uncertainty on capacity planning and how decision trees (a valuable tool that we will use again in later chapters) can aid the operations manager in handling this problem.

TOOLS AND APPLICATIONS

5.3 THE MULTIPLE OUTPUTS PROBLEM AND LINEAR PROGRAMMING

Throughout our discussion of capacity planning we have referred to the complication that multiple outputs place on both capacity planning and scheduling. The objective, of course, is to maximize the returns to the organization by selecting the "best" mix of outputs which do not exceed the organization's resource capacity limitations. This problem is known as the **output mix problem**. To determine this best mix of outputs requires simultaneously considering three factors:

The best output mix.

1. The forecast demand for each output.
2. The resource requirements for each output.
3. The relative return of each output.

Three factors.

The expected demand for each output provides an upper limit on the number of each that will be provided. There is no reason why an organization would want to produce more of a product or service than can be expected to be consumed. The organizational resource requirements for each output determine the maximum number of each type of output that can be produced. For example, if a social worker can make only five visits per day and the Municipal Social Services Department employs seven social workers, then we cannot expect to "produce" more than 35 visits per day.

The return to the organization from the production of each type of output does not limit or constrain the organization in the amounts that can be produced or sold but rather guides management in maximizing the returns to the organization. The contribution of each of the different outputs toward the objective of maximizing the total return to the organization is measured by the **contribution margin**, as it is called, which tells management the increase in return for providing one more unit of a given output.

Some products and services have higher marginal returns than others. For example, in a restaurant, the marginal profit on wines and liquors is higher than the return on the same dollar amount of food. And auto dealers earn a higher contribution for each dollar in sales from accessory items than they do from basic automobiles.

Limited resources.

If demand and resources were both unlimited, then the obvious conclusion regarding optimal output mix would be to make and sell *"everything;"* that is, everything that has a positive contribution margin. But demand is *seldom* unlimited, even though it may appear to be for short time periods, and resources are *never* unlimited. The question then becomes: How do we simultaneously consider all three sets of factors to arrive at the best combination of outputs? One answer to this question is provided by **linear programming**, a mathematical tool demonstrated in the following example.

Addemup, Inc.

Addemup, Inc. is a relatively small firm in the fast growing pocket calculator market. Addemup entered the business with the production of an inexpensive four-function hand-held calculator, the A-1000, which sells for $15. It has recently added a more powerful version of the A-1000 (it has square, square root, and percent functions) named the A-2000. The A-2000 sells for $25.

The variable costs of producing an A-1000 and an A-2000 are given in Table 5.6.

TABLE 5.6 VARIABLE COSTS OF CALCULATOR PRODUCTION

	A-1000	A-2000
Labor	$ 3.00	$ 5.00
Material	6.00	12.00
Factory overhead	2.00	2.00
Total	$11.00	$19.00

Addemup produces its own integrated circuits (the internal logic of the calculator) and purchases all other materials from other firms. Manufacturing of integrated circuits is a complex operation which requires precision equipment. Addemup has the capacity to produce, at most, 61,000 four-function circuit boards per month. One of these circuit boards is used in each A-1000 calculator produced. It takes three times as long on this precision equipment to manufacture the seven-function circuit board for the A-2000 calculator (i.e., add, subtract, multiply, divide, square, square root, percent) as it does for the A-1000. Therefore, if they made no four-function circuits at all, they could produce no more than 20,333 (i.e., 61,000/3) of the A-2000 boards. Addemup can manufacture any combination of A-1000 and A-2000 circuit boards, as long as the combined production time does not exceed the available capacity.

Assembly time on the two calculators is

A-1000	0.2 hr
A-2000	0.25 hr

If the company maintains its current two shift operation it has available 8000 hours of assembly time per month.

The marketing manager has undertaken a detailed study of the calculator market and foresees a monthly demand of 40,000 units for the A-1000 calculator and 18,000 units for the A-2000.

If we assume that Addemup is interested in maximizing its monthly profit we can begin to structure this problem in a way that will lead to a relatively simple solution procedure. Total monthly profit for next year will be equal to the marginal profit of each calculator times the number of each produced and sold.

If we let

$A1$ = number of A-1000's produced and sold
$A2$ = number of A-2000's produced and sold

then we can write an equation for the monthly profit as follows:

$$\text{profit} = (15\text{-}11)A1 + (25\text{-}19)A2$$
$$= 4A1 + 6A2$$

If the capacity were available and if the marketing manager's demand forecasts are correct, the company could expect to earn

$$\text{monthly profit} = 4(40{,}000) + 6(18{,}000)$$
$$= \$268{,}000$$

But there is only limited circuit manufacturing capacity so even though they may be able to *sell* 40,000 A-1000's and 18,000 A-2000's, the capacity is not available to produce these quantities. The capacity to produce circuit boards thus limits the number of calculators that can be manufactured and sold. Using the same notation as before, we can algebraically express this capacity limitation as

$$1(A1) + 3(A2) \leq 61{,}000$$

This inequality states that Addemup can produce either 61,000 A-1000's and no A-2000's, or 20,333 A-2000's and no A-1000's, or any combination of A-1000's and A-2000's that does not exceed the 61,000 equivalent circuit capacity.

But circuit manufacturing capacity is not the only limited resource. Assembly time is limited to 8000 hours per month. This capacity restriction can be written as

$$0.2(A1) + 0.25(A2) \leq 8000$$

This inequality states that the hours used to assemble A-1000's (0.2 hours/unit × number of units) plus the hours to assemble A-2000's (0.25 hours/unit × number of units) must not exceed the available assembly time (8000 hours).

Finally, the restrictions on demand for the two models must be considered. The marketing manager expects to be able to sell 40,000 A-1000's and 18,000 A-2000's. Since we do not want to produce any more than we can sell, the following two **constraints** must also be included.

$$A1 \leq 40{,}000$$
$$A2 \leq 18{,}000$$

The first constraint states that the number of A-1000's produced cannot exceed 40,000 units and the second constraint states that the number of A-2000's cannot exceed 18,000.

Bringing together all of the previous equations and inequalities we have the following mathematical formulation of the problem.

maximize: profit $= 4A1 + 6A2$ (objective)
subject to the following limitations:

$$A1 + 3A2 \leq 61{,}000 \quad \text{(circuit manufacturing capacity)}$$
$$0.2A1 + 0.25A2 \leq 8{,}000 \quad \text{(assembly time capacity)}$$
$$A1 \leq 40{,}000 \quad \text{(maximum demand for A-1000's)}$$
$$A2 \leq 18{,}000 \quad \text{(maximum demand for A-2000's)}$$

Again, our objective is to find the combination of A-1000's and A-2000's that can be produced and sold, within the limitations of capacity and demand, to maximize profit.

This output mix problem is in a form that can be solved by *linear programming*.

Linear programming.

Linear programming is a mathematical technique that can solve management problems characterized by

1. A single **objective** (e.g., maximize profit) that can be stated algebraically as a linear equation.
2. A set of constraints (e.g., capacities) that can be stated algebraically as linear equalities or inequalities.
3. One or more management decision variables (e.g., how much to produce of each output) that can assume only non-negative values.

In this highly simplified example only two products and a few limited organizational resources were considered but linear programming can and has been used to solve much larger, more realistic product mix problems. In the lumber and petroleum refining industries it is not uncommon to see computer solutions to linear programs with hundreds of constraints and thousands of variables. **Canned** (preprogrammed) computer packages are available from a number of computer manufacturers, research organizations, and universities (Reference 2) to solve linear programming problems.

Computer packages.

Although it is beyond the scope of this text to teach linear programming solution techniques, in the next section we present a simple graphical solution procedure for linear programming problems and demonstrate it with the Addemup example. (For other linear programming solution methods and further discussion see References 1 and 7.) The solution to Addemup's output mix problem is to produce 25,000 A-1000's and 12,000 A-2000's for a total profit of $172,000. This solution uses all the assembly time capacity

$$0.2(25{,}000) + 0.25(12{,}000) = 8000 \text{ hr}$$

and all the circuit manufacturing capacity

$$1(25{,}000) + 3(12{,}000) = 61{,}000 \text{ equivalent boards}$$

5.4 GRAPHICAL SOLUTION TO A LINEAR PROGRAM

If a linear program has only two decision variables, as does the Addemup example, a simple solution procedure is the graphical method. The method begins by developing a graph that can be used to display the possible solutions (values of $A1$ and $A2$). We will show the solution to our linear program to be the most profitable number of A-1000's and A-2000's.

Plotting the Constraints

By using a graph to plot the constraints and objective we can begin to limit the set of solution points to only those that satisfy the constraints in the problem. But remember that only non-negative values of $A1$ and $A2$ are possible. Consider first the constraint on circuit manufacturing capacity, which was of the form

$$A1 + 3A2 \leq 61{,}000$$

We want to locate all of the solution points that satisfy this relationship and therefore we start by plotting the line corresponding to the equation

$$A1 + 3A2 = 61{,}000$$

Plotting the constraints.

To plot this line we need only find two points on the line and then draw a straight line through the points. The simplest way of finding two points on the line is to first set $A1$ equal to zero and solve for $A2$ and then set $A2$ equal to zero and solve for $A1$.

$$\text{If } A1 = 0, \qquad \text{then } 3A2 = 61{,}000 \text{ or } A2 = 20{,}333$$

Therefore, (0;20,333) is on the line.

$$\text{If } A2 = 0, \qquad \text{then } A1 = 61{,}000$$

Therefore, (61,000;0) is on the line. With these two points we can plot the equation

$$A1 + 3A2 = 61{,}000$$

which is called the circuit capacity constraint. The line is shown in Figure 5.11. We know that for any $\leq$ constraints the solution points that satisfy the constraint are

1. All points on the constraint line itself.
2. All points "below" the constraint line.

All points that satisfy the circuit capacity constraint are shown by the shaded area in Figure 5.11.

Next we can identify all points satisfying the assembly time capacity constraint

$$0.2A1 + 0.25A2 \leq 8000$$

Again, we draw the line corresponding to the equation

$$0.2A1 + 0.25A2 = 8000$$

as shown in Figure 5.12.

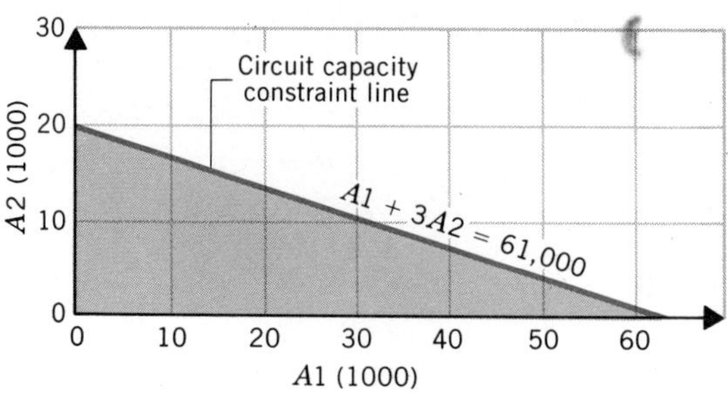

Figure 5.11. Circuit capacity constraint.

Our third constraint, the maximum demand for A-1000's, is given by $A1 \leq 40000$. The feasible region for this constraint corresponds to all points to the left of the vertical linc $A1 = 40{,}000$ in Figure 5.12.

The final constraint is the limitation on demand for A-2000's, which is $A2 \leq 18{,}000$ and is also shown in Figure 5.12.

Since our original intention was to determine all of the points that satisfied the four constraints we must locate all of the points that satisfy the four constraints simultaneously. These points are shown in Figure 5.12 by the shaded area. Any point on the border of this area or within the area is a *feasible solution* to the linear program. The whole set of points is called the *feasible region*. Any one of these points is a potential solution point, but only *one* of them (in this case) will be the *optimal solution point*.

Finding the feasible region.

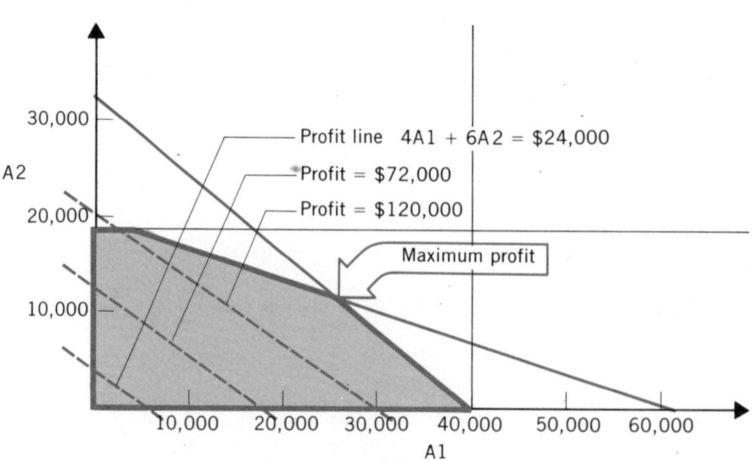

Figure 5.12. Feasible region with isoprofit lines.

Finding the Maximum Profit Solution Point

Because there are such a great number of feasible solution points it is virtually impossible to determine the solution point that maximizes profit by trial and error. A less time-consuming method than this is to continue with our graphical analysis of the problem. The objective that we want to maximize is given by the equation

$$\text{profit} = 4A1 + 6A2$$

Plotting the profit line.

If we arbitrarily select some value of profit we can then plot a profit line just as we plotted the constraint lines. For example, the set of points that yield a profit of $24,000 is given by

$$4A1 + 6A2 = 24{,}000$$

This profit line is superimposed on the feasible region in Figure 5.12.

Clearly, there are an infinite number of points that will yield a profit of $24,000; that is, all of the points on the profit = $24,000 line that are in the feasible region. Since our objective is to maximize profit we select larger and larger values for profit and plot the lines as shown in Figure 5.12.

What you should recognize by now is that

1. The profit lines are parallel to one another.
2. The further the line moves to the right, the higher the profit.

Moving the profit line to maximize profits.

Realizing this, a logical solution procedure is to simply move the profit line *parallel* to the lines already determined and to the *upper right*. As we do this, we are moving in the direction of higher and higher profits, but eventually we will not be able to move the profit line any farther without moving outside the feasible region. The point at which the profit line is farthest to the upper right and just touches the feasible region is the point of maximum profit.

Reading from the graph this point is (25,000; 12,000). That is, to maximize profit Addemup should produce and sell 25,000 A-1000 calculators and 12,000 A-2000 calculators, resulting in a net profit of $172,000 [4(25,000) + 6(12,000)].

5.5 ANALYZING RISK: THE DECISION TREE

Considering uncertainty in the capacity decision.

In previous examples we assumed that the operations manager, in trying to estimate future capacity needs, could reliably estimate the values of the factors that affect the profitability of a new output. Those factors were the selling price, the variable cost, the fixed cost, and the demand for which capacity would have to be available. If any one of these factors is uncertain (and generally all will be) then the analysis becomes more complicated. Consider, for example, the following situation.

Whataracket is considering the introduction of one of two low-priced rackets: a standard wooden racket that would sell for the going rate, about $20, and a fiberglass racket that could sell either at the low end of the fiberglass range for $18 or in the middle of the range for $25. (It is not a "high quality" racket.) Sales for the wooden racket can be reliably predicted to be about 25,000 units. However, sales of the fiberglass racket are more difficult to predict. Sharon estimates that at the lower price there is a 50-50 chance that sales will either be slightly below expectations, averaging 30,000 units, or slightly above, averaging 40,000 units. At the higher price of $25 she feels there is a wider possible range of demand. She estimates there is a 20 percent chance sales will be as high as 25,000 units, a 50 percent chance they will be about 20,000 units, and a 30 percent chance they will be as low as 10,000 units.

The wooden racket requires only a minimal amount of additional production equipment since the manufacturer has some excess capacity for wood forming in the current plant. The annual fixed cost of this additional capacity will be $30,000. The variable cost per wooden racket is known to be $15. The annual fixed costs to add the capacity to produce the fiberglass racket are much higher, $140,000, but the variable cost is only $11.

All of the above data is summarized in Table 5.7. Understandably, given this mass of information, Sharon wonders how to determine which racket to select and, if she selects the fiberglass racket, at what price it should be sold. A modeling procedure developed primarily for sequential decisions, called a **decision tree**, will help Sharon analyze this data.

The decision tree construction.

The decision tree is formed, sequentially, from the left to the right, as **decision points** and **chance points**, both known as **nodes**, are encountered in time. Decision nodes are indicated by squares and chance nodes by circles. Connecting the nodes are **branches**.

- Branches emanating to the right of decision nodes indicate all the possible management decision alternatives available at that point. If a cost or return accompanies any of the decisions that fact is indicated in parentheses along the decision branch.
- Branches emanating to the right of chance points indicate all the possible results that may occur. Each branch is labeled with its probability of occurrence and if a cost or return is involved, it is so indicated in parentheses.

TABLE 5.7 WHATARACKET, INC. RACKET DATA

	Alternatives			
Factors	$20 Wooden	$18 Fiberglass	$25 Fiberglass	Nothing
$ new fixed cost	30,000	140,000	140,000	0
$ variable cost	15	11	11	0
$ margin	5	7	14	0
Demand/probability:	25,000/1.0	30,000/.5 40,000/.5	25,000/.20 20,000/.50 10,000/.30	0

The decision tree for the sporting goods manufacturer is illustrated in Figure 5.13. At the left, the decision node indicates three possible decision alternatives: wooden (with an investment of $30,000), fiberglass ($140,000 investment), or neither (investment of 0). If the wooden alternative is chosen, only one result is expected: sales of 25,000 units. If neither racket is developed there will be no sales (but no loss either). If the fiberglass alternative is chosen then another decision must be made, to price the racket at $18 for a contribution margin of $7 ($18-$11 variable cost) or to price it at $25 with a contribution margin of $14. Following the $18 branch, two results may occur, each with a 50 percent chance: sales of 30,000 units and sales of 40,000 units. Along the $25 branch, three outcomes are possible: sales of 10, 20, or 25,000 units with probabilities of .3, .5, and .2, respectively.

At this point the problem is now formulated in the decision tree format. Next it must be solved. To solve the tree we start at the far *right* and work backward to the beginning of the problem at the left, the first decision node. To evaluate the branches of the tree we employ the expected value concept, as illustrated below.

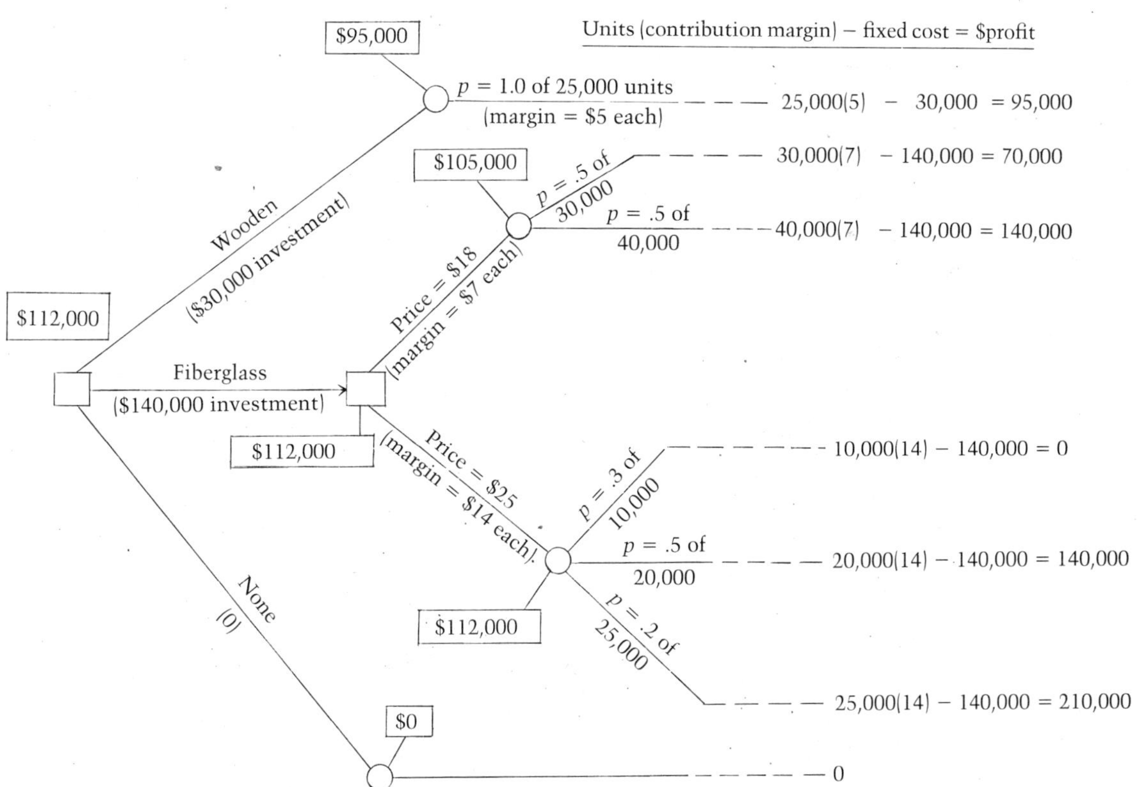

Figure 5.13. Whataracket, Inc. decision tree.

If the *wooden* racket is introduced the net profit will be [25,000 units × ($20 price – $15 variable cost)] – $30,000 fixed cost = $95,000. This value is indicated in the rectangle attached to the result node at the top of the diagram. Similarly, "$0" is indicated for the "*none*" alternative and is shown in the rectangle attached to its result node. The "price = $18" decision branch of the fiberglass alternative is evaluated as

expected net profit = .5[30,000 units × ($18 price – $11 variable cost) – $140,000 fixed cost] + .5[40,000 units × ($18 price – $11 variable cost) – $140,000 fixed cost]
= $105,000

which is shown in the rectangle attached to the "$18 price" result node. Similarly, the "price = $25" decision branch is evaluated as

expected net profit = .3($0) + .5($140,000) + .2($210,000)
= $112,000

which is shown attached to the "price = $25" result node.

At this point the manufacturer must decide between the $18 racket and the $25 racket. With the former the net profit is expected to be $105,000 and with the latter, $112,000. Since the expected net profit from the introduction of the $25 racket is greater than the expected profit for the $18 racket, the $25 price should be chosen. An arrow is drawn on the "price = $25" branch to indicate the decision. The value $112,000 is then indicated in a rectangle attached to the price decision node.

Lastly, we must decide whether to choose the wooden or fiberglass racket or to introduce no new rackets at all. Just as we did previously in deciding between the two prices for the fiberglass racket, we select the alternative with the *largest expected net profit*. The fiberglass racket with an expected net profit of $112,000 is the "best" alternative; it has the highest **expected value**.

Other decision criteria may also exist.

Note that in the above analysis, the criterion of choice was the *expected value*. This may not, however, always be the best criterion. For example, the fiberglass, $25 price decision has a 30 percent chance of selling only 10,000 rackets resulting in a net profit of $0. Thirty percent is a rather high chance of just breaking even. By choosing the wooden racket alternative the manufacturer would be "guaranteed" (assuming that the sales estimate is accurate and reliable) of receiving $95,000 profit. Thus, the question the manufacturer must answer is: Is an additional $17,000 of *expected* profit worth the 30 percent risk of making nothing? This is a subjective decision based on personal values that only the manufacturer can make; the role of the decision tree is to *pose* these types of questions.

5.6 SUMMARY

A number of alternatives are available to the manager in meeting short run changes in capacity. Often, however, overtime is the most viable alternative. For estimating the capacity increase of adding workers to the production process the learning curve has been found to be quite helpful.

In estimating the short run capacity requirements of multiple, complex outputs, the scheduling problem of "bottlenecks" may invalidate normal common sense estimates. Multiple outputs create another short run capacity problem for the operations manager—finding the best output mix for the organization. Linear programming can help considerably here.

Long-term capacity problems relate to the life cycles of the organization's current and contemplated mix of outputs. On occasion, a capacity analysis will indicate the need for a stopgap output at some point in the future to efficiently utilize existing capacity and a breakeven analysis will indicate the economic feasibility of introducing such an output. Breakeven analysis is also useful for selecting the best alternatives for increasing capacity. For decisions involving high risk, the decision tree concept is a simple and valuable aid to the operations manager.

In many situations the addition of new facilities not only increases the organization's capacity but increases demand for the output as well (e.g., branch libraries). In fact, the location of an organization's facilities itself often has an important effect on capacity, either directly or indirectly. The next chapter on the distribution function will investigate some of these issues.

5.7 READINGS

Grounded Hopes

Air-Cargo Firms, Hit by Lack of Capacity And by Red Ink, Still Strive to Take Off

BY JOHN D. WILLIAMS
STAFF REPORTER OF THE WALL STREET JOURNAL

The air-cargo industry is still struggling to get off the ground.

Back in the mid-1960s, the industry had ordered more than $1 billion of cargo planes, and its leaders were widely predicting that in the 1970s mighty boxcars in the sky would haul a fat share of the nation's freight. Moreover, a leading transportation analyst recalls, "Operators of trucks, railroads and steamships were worried about the advent of jumbo jets." Truckers, particularly, envisioned trailerloads of everything from orchids to auto parts being whisked overhead on high-speed, scheduled-run jets.

"But their fears were overblown, and they aren't worried anymore," the analyst adds.

Air-cargo ton miles (a ton mile is a ton of cargo hauled one mile) have been increasing, but only a bit. Last year ton miles totaled 5.93 billion, little changed from the 5.89 billion in 1975 and behind the record 6.1 billion in 1974, the Air Transport Assocation of America says. That's appreciably higher than the 4.98 billion ton miles in 1970, but it's far short of the 15 billion that the ATA in 1966 was predicting for the mid-1970s.

SURGE IN REVENUES

Helped by inflation, air-cargo revenues of U.S. airlines have climbed more sharply. Last year they totaled a record $1.5 billion, up from $1.3 billion in

1975 and more than double the $713 million in 1970, the ATA says.

The profit-and-loss picture, however, is cloudy. Although the ATA could fill a 747 with its air-cargo statistics, it avoids profitability figures like a fogged-in airport. Much domestic air cargo probably isn't profitable, experts say, adding that international cargo earns money only eastbound from the Far East to the U.S.

What has caused all the disappointment? Industry experts blame many factors: soaring fuel costs since the Arab oil boycott in late 1973, higher wages and inflation's impact on all costs, recessions, delays in winning rate rises, and new equipment that didn't fulfill expectations.

. . .

CAPACITY INADEQUATE

The upshot of all these problems is that much freight doesn't travel by plane because the airlift capacity is no longer there.

Faced with shortages of cargo space on airlines, the generally profitable airfreight forwarders are reluctantly resorting to chartering their own planes. A few months ago Emery, the nation's largest airfreight forwarder, began chartering 15 planes for a system linking 21 of its markets. At a Dayton, Ohio, airport at 3 o'clock on a cold morning, one can get nostalgic looking at 10 World War II-vintage DC3s being loaded and unloaded of Emery's freight.

Mr. Emery, however, seems to get more nostalgic about the money that the chartering costs—some $40 million over the next three years. He also estimates that if current trends continue, by 1980 airlines will move only half of Emery's freight, compared with slightly less than 75% today and about 95% six years ago.

. . .

MURKY PROFIT FIGURES

Most airlines are reticent about discussing airfreight profits or losses, and in any event such calculations hinge significantly on how costs of handling cargo in the bellies of passenger jets are allocated. But some domestic lines say they make money on airfreight; among them is American Airlines.

A CAB official says airfreight from the Far East to the U.S. generally is profitable because of the large volume of flyable imports from such countries as Japan, Taiwan and South Korea. Westbound, the volume is smaller, and U.S. exports to the Far East lean heavily toward nonflyable bulk commodities such as coal, grain and lumber. Transatlantic airfreight, although 2½ times bigger in volume than the U.S.-Far East trade, also is unprofitable, the official says, largely because too many airlines compete for the business.

In the transpacific service, Flying Tiger Line, the all-cargo subsidiary of Tiger International Inc., is consistently more profitable than Northwest Airlines and Pan American World Airways. The CAB official explains that Flying Tiger, by closely gearing its schedules to demand, tends to operate with larger loads. "Air cargo is our business," a Flying Tiger spokesman says. "We have to pay close attention to the types of planes we use, our rates and our markets."

Among the airlines that haven't made money on air cargo in recent years, Trans World Airlines is widely rumored to be considering dropping the service within a year. But TWA flatly denies the rumor. It says it plans aggressive efforts to make its air-cargo business profitable this year.

5.8 KEY TERMS

Concepts

Gantt chart (p. 113)
breakeven (p. 122)
learning curve (p. 115)
negative exponential function (p. 115)
forgetting curve (p. 117)
life cycle (p. 121)
scheduling (p. 112)
infinite loading (p. 113)

Tools and Applications

decision tree (p. 138)
nodes (p. 138)
branches (p. 138)
decision points (p. 138)
chance points (p. 138)
expected value (p. 140)
output mix problem (p. 131)
linear programming (p. 132)
canned programs (p. 134)
objective function (p. 134)
constraints (p. 133)
contribution margin (p. 131)

5.9 REVIEW TEST

Concepts

1. In public sector organizations, as in private sector organizations, we wish to operate as far above the breakeven point as possible. (p. 127)
a. True b. False

2. The learning curve only applies to humans and can not be used in man-machine systems (p. 116)
a. True b. False

3. The exponent r in the learning curve formula is the learning rate. (p. 115)
a. True b. False

4. The purpose of an anticyclic output is to reduce the peak demand of the original output (p. 121)
a. True b. False

5. The only viable short run capacity alternatives open to management without running short, are often just overtime and inventory stockpiling. (p. 115)
a. True b. False

6. Sometimes adding capacity to obtain higher output rates *reduces* efficiency instead. (p. 129)
a. True b. False

7. Even with "plenty of capacity," it may not be sufficient due to scheduling difficulties. (p. 113)
a. True b. False

Tools and Applications

8. A decision tree can handle both decision and chance events and is especially helpful for sequential decisions. (p. 138)
a. True b. False

9. We solve a decision tree by starting at the end and working backward. (p. 139)
a. True b. False

10. Using a decision tree removes the uncertainty involved in a new product or service introduction. (p. 140)
a. True b. False

11. The output mix problem involves the simultaneous consideration of each output's demand, resource requirements, and profitability. (p. 131)
a. True b. False

12. Unfortunately, noneconomic constraints cannot be handled by linear programming. (p. 133)
a. True b. False

5.10 DISCUSSION QUESTIONS

1. Suppose per unit variable costs decrease as volume increases. Draw the breakeven chart. What happens to per unit profit above and below the breakeven point?
2. Frequently, simple models such as "breakeven" are much more appealing to management than more sophisticated ones (such as linear programming). Why might this be so?
3. What are the dangers for a not-for-profit organization in operating *below* the breakeven point? *Above* the breakeven point?
4. The decision tree example in the chapter alluded to the fact that a manager may decide *not* to follow the solution of the tree. For what conditions might such a strategy be appropriate?
5. How does the existence of multiple outputs complicate capacity planning?
6. Does the learning curve continue downward forever?
7. What marketing approaches are useful in capacity planning?
8. How do operations managers estimate what capacity will be needed with multiple, complex outputs?

5.11 PROBLEMS

Concepts

1. River City operates a Senior Services Department providing specialized services to senior citizens. One program, the Meals on Wheels program, is partially funded by the federal government and partially funded by collections from recipients who can afford to pay. The fixed cost of operating the program is $60,000 per year and the variable cost is $0.80 per meal. The Federal contribution to the program is $140,000. If, on the average, $0.35 of the cost of each meal is covered by recipient contributions, how many meals can be served annually?
2. I provide a personal service with a weekly fixed cost of $1000 for equipment and a variable cost of $90 per customer. I charge each customer $100 for this service. I have $100 per week available to invest in my business to improve my profit. If I invest the $100 in advertising I can increase my customer volume 15 percent and if I purchase more equipment I can decrease my variable cost by 10 percent. If my customer volume is currently 120, what should I do?
3. Sardine Properties, Inc. operates a large apartment complex and is contemplating opening a second. Management estimates that fixed costs of operation for this new 100-unit complex will be $85,000 per year and that variable costs (including heat, light, maintenance, trash collection, etc.) will be $85 per month per unit rented. If the apartments will rent for $175 per month, how many units must be occupied to just break even?
4. Parking took you a full hour for Monday's classes. But you have been doing better since then. You just parked your car today, Thursday, and so far this week you have only spent 2 hours, 45 minutes finding parking spaces in the morning. How long will it take you to find a space tomorrow, Friday?
5. All of the reports you wrote for one class had three sections: Introduction, Analysis, Conclusions. The times required to complete these sections (includes typing, etc.) are shown below in hours.

Report	Introduction	Analysis	Conclusion
1	1.5	6	2
2	————	(lost data)	————
3	1	3	0.8

You are now starting report 4 and can only afford to spend 1 hour a day on these reports. Report 5 is due in one week (7 days). Will you be done in time?

$$\# \text{ Workstations} = \frac{20 \text{ min.}}{5 \text{ min.}} = 4$$

Station	Tasks				
1	a				
2	b				
3	c		c,d		c,e
4	d,e	or	e	or	d
5	f				

$$\text{Efficiency} = \frac{20}{25} = 80\%$$

√11. a. Cycle time = $\frac{60}{6}$ = 10 min.

Station	Tasks
1	b, h, g
2	a, c, e
3	d, f
4	i

b) Efficiency = $\frac{39}{40}$ = 97.5%

99

3.

	Office A	Office B	Office C
Dean	3 x 35 = 105	150	45
Xerox	15 x 50 = 750	600	150
Library	5 x 25 = 125	50	150
Elevator	4 x 15 = 60	200	100
Total	1040	1000	445 (min)

locate in C

* If Oven 2 is prepared here instead, an extra cycle can be squeezed in.

10.

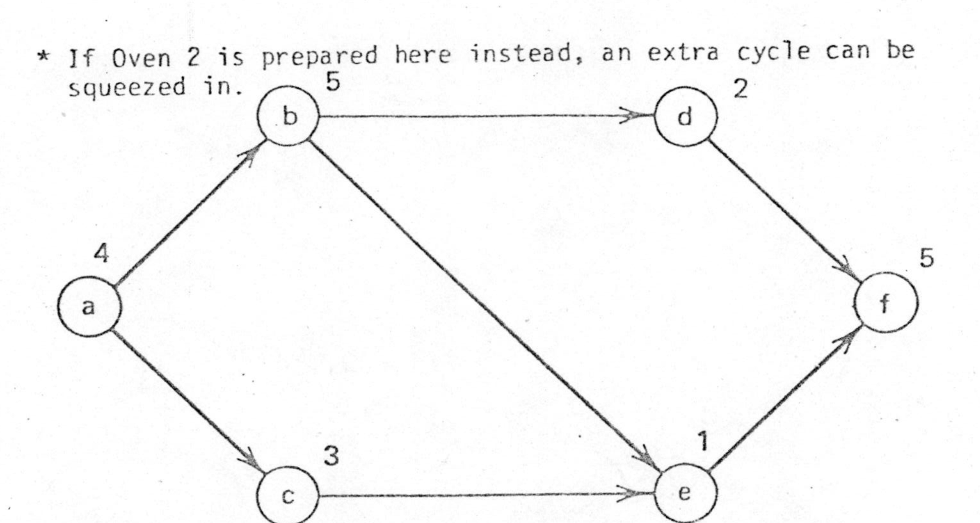

Σ times = 20 min.

Cycle time = $\frac{60 \text{ min.}}{96} \times 8$ = 5 min.

6. Tom's Tom-Toms produces toy drums sequentially on three machines A, B, and C with cycle times of 3, 4, and 6 minutes, respectively. Determine the optimum utilization efficiency and output rates for adding 1, 2, . . ., 6 more machines.

Tools and Applications

7. Sportshoo sells men's and ladies' tennis shoes. It makes a profit of $1 each on the men's shoes and $1.20 each on the ladies'. It takes two minutes of a salesperson's time and two minutes of a cashier's time to sell a pair of men's shoes, and three and one minute, respectively, to sell a pair of women's shoes. The store is open eight hours per day, during which time there are two salespersons and one cashier on duty. Formulate a linear program to determine how much of the salesperson's and cashier's time should be allocated to the men's and ladies' shoes and how many shoes of each type should be sold to maximize daily profits.

8. The N. Berry Company has just received an order to produce 1000 Mark I valves. Two production lines are available. Line 1 can produce the valves at 15 minutes per valve and is available for 300 hours at $8 per hour. Line 2 can produce the valves at the rate of five valves per hour but is only available for 170 hours at $5 per hour. Formulate a linear program to find the best production plan. Determine a logical solution and compare it to the program statement.

9. The owner of Black Angus Ranch is trying to determine the correct mix of two types of chicken feed. (This is a chicken ranch, actually.) Feed A costs 50 cents a pound and B costs 75 cents a pound. Five essential ingredients are contained in the feed, as shown in the table below, which also indicates the minimum daily requirements of each ingredient.

Ingredient	Percent per Ounce of Feed: Feed A	Feed B	Minimum Daily Requirement (ounces)
1	20	25	3
2	30	10	5
3	0	30	2
4	40	15	6
5	10	20	4

Formulate a linear program to find the least-cost daily blend for the ranch; that is, how many ounces of A and B will be included in the mix.

10. Sherwood Acres, a central Kentucky farm, grows tobacco and soybeans on its 350 acres of land. An acre of soybeans brings a $150 profit and an acre of tobacco brings a $500 profit. Because of state agricultural regulations, no more than 150 acres can be planted in tobacco. Each acre of tobacco requires 100 manhours of labor over the growing season and each acre of soybeans requires 20 manhours. There are 16,000 manhours of labor available during the growing season. How many acres should be planted in tobacco and how many in soybeans to maximize profit?

11. A machine breaks down either zero, one, or two times a day with probabilities ½, ⅜, and ⅛, respectively. The amount of time it takes to repair the machine is either 1 hour or 2 hours with probabilities of ⅔ and ⅓, respectively. Use a decision tree to find the machine's expected downtime per day.

12. ABC's growth rate in past years has been slower than the average for the industry. The company is considering two alternatives to rectify the situation: (1) expand the number of product lines and (2) increase inventories for better service.

There is a 70 percent chance that the economy will go into a growth stage, in which case there is an 80 percent chance for increased demand. If demand increases and the produce line is expanded, a profit of $1,000,000 is expected; however if demand does not increase, only an $800,000 profit is anticipated from the expansion. If inventories are increased, a profit of $900,000 is anticipated in case of high demand; otherwise, $600,000 will be realized.

In the event the economy does not grow, a mild recession is anticipated. In this case, there is a 50–50 percent chance for either high or low demand. The profits are then estimated to be

Expansion and high demand	$750,000
Expansion and low demand	600,000
Inventories and high demand	550,000
Inventories and low demand	400,000

Profit figures are forecast for one year of operation.

A product expansion policy requires $100,000 in cash now. Keeping inventories will cost $12,000 for the year, payable at year-end. Should the company expand its products or work with inventories?

13. An oil explorer, commonly called a wildcatter, must decide whether to drill a well or sell his rights to a particular exploration site. The desirability of drilling depends upon whether there is oil beneath the surface. Before drilling, the wildcatter has the option of taking seismographic readings that will give him further geological and geophysical information. This information will enable him to deduce whether subsurface structures usually associated with oil fields exist in this particular location. However, some uncertainty about the presence of oil will still exist after seismic testing because oil is sometimes found where no subsurface structure is detected and vice versa.

The wildcatter estimates that the cost of drilling a well would be $250,000 (in net present value terms, after making allowance for all taxes). The yield that would be expected from a typical oil well is estimated to be $1,200,000 (in net present value terms, net of all taxes and operating costs but excluding drilling costs). Seismic tests would cost $50,000 per test.

The wildcatter could sell his rights for $230,000 before either drilling or testing. However, if he should decide to carry out seismographic readings and no subsurface structure is indicated, the site will be considered almost worthless by other wildcatters, in which case he will barely be able to sell the rights for $10,000. If substructure is indicated by the test, he can sell his rights for $300,000. If no oil is found, the value of the exploration site is considered to be zero.

The probability of getting oil from the site without any test is 30 percent. If he carries out the seismic test, he feels that the test will indicate subsurface structure with a 40 percent probability. In case of structure, he can drill with a 65 percent chance of finding oil. In the case of no structure, he can drill with a 75 percent chance of finding the well dry.

What should the wildcatter do? Draw a decision tree to solve the problem.

14. Robin, Inc. produces two different concrete products with the following price and input data.

	Selling Price	Input Requirements		
		Material	Power Consumed	Labor
Construction blocks	$0.75	4 lb	0.1 kWh	0.04 hr
Decorative blocks	$1.75	3 lb	0.2 kWh	0.10 hr

Labor cost is $5 per hour, materials cost $0.05 per pound and power costs $1.00 per kWh.
If the company is limited to

100,000 lb of material
9,000 kWh of power
1200 hr of labor

and if demand for Decorative Blocks is at most 3500, what quantity of each block should be produced to maximize profit?

15. Cheap-Way Gas Company operates a chain of discount gas stations in a large midwestern city. Cheap-Way profits have been slipping and management is considering several different plans which they believe might revitalize the company's performance. The plans are

1. Increase service offered to gas buying customers (wash windows, check oil and battery, etc.).
2. Decrease service offered to gas buying customers, turning the stations into self-service stations.
3. Offer premiums for gas purchases (trading stamps, small gift items, etc.).

The current gas price is $0.60 per gallon and management believes that this price is a minimum, and can only be continued if option 2 is selected. The price could conceivably be increased to $0.63 per gallon with the following expected impact on demand:

Effect of Price Increase to $0.63 with Various Options

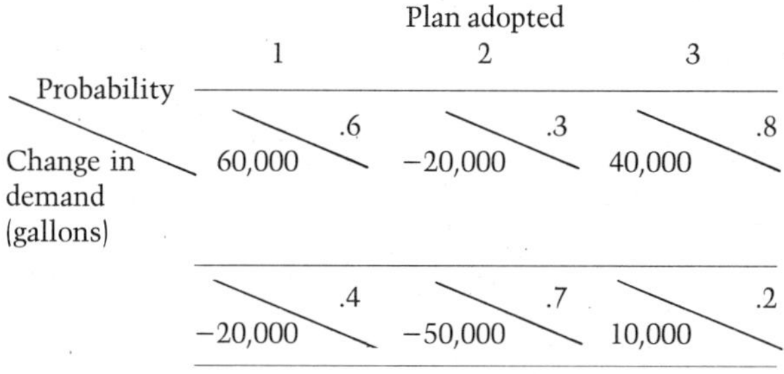

Change in demand (gallons) / Probability	Plan adopted 1		Plan adopted 2		Plan adopted 3	
	60,000	.6	−20,000	.3	40,000	.8
	−20,000	.4	−50,000	.7	10,000	.2

If Plan 2 is adopted with no change in price, the gallon change is expected to be

30,000 with probability 0.4, and
15,000 with probability 0.6.

All three viable options (i.e., Plans 1 and 3 with price increase and Plan 2 without increase) produce identical per gallon profits.

Which option should management select? Should price be increased? Draw and label a decision tree for this problem.

5.12 CASE EXIT MANUFACTURING COMPANY

The planning committee of Exit Manufacturing Company (made up of the vice presidents of marketing, finance, and production) was discussing the plans for a new factory to be located outside of Atlanta, Georgia. The factory would produce prehung-metal-over-Styrofoam insulated exterior doors. The doors would be made in a standard format with 15 different insert panels which could be added after manufacture by a retail organization. The standardization of construction is expected to create numerous production efficiencies over competitor factories that produce multidimensional doors. Atlanta was felt to be an ideal site because of its location in the heart of the sun belt with its growing construction industry. By locating close to these growing states, distribution costs would be minimized also.

The capital cost for the factory was expected to be $14,000,000. Annual maintenance expenses were projected to total 5 percent of capital. Fuel and utility costs were expected to be $500,000 per year. An analysis of the area's labor market indicated that a wage rate of $7.50 per hour could be expected. The new facility was estimated to require 1.5 man-hours of operating labor per door. Fringe benefits paid to the operating labor were expected to equal 15 percent of direct labor costs. Supervisory, clerical, technical, and managerial salaries were forecast to total $350,000 per year. Taxes and insurance would cost $200,000 per year. Other miscellaneous expenses were expected to total $250,000 per year. Depreciation was based on a 30-year life with use of the straight-line method and a $4,000,000 salvage value. Sheet metal, Styrofoam, adhesive for the doors, and frames were projected to cost $8.00 per door. Paint, hinges, door knobs and accessories were estimated to total $4.80 per door. The crating and shipping supplies were expected to cost $1.50 per door. Production labor has been estimated to be 1.5 hours per door produced.

Exit's marketing manager prepared the following price-demand chart for the distribution area of the new plant. Through analysis of this data the committee felt they could verify their belief of an increase from 15 to 25 percent in the current market share due to the cost advantage of standardization.

Average Sales Price ($/door)	Area Sales (in units)
$ 80	40,000
93	38,000
105	31,000
125	22,000

QUESTIONS FOR DISCUSSION

Develop a breakeven capacity analysis for Exit's new door and determine

a. The best price, production rate, and profit.

b. The breakeven production rate and cost with the price in a.

c. The breakeven price with the production rate in a.

d. The sensitivity of profit to variable cost, price, and production rate.

5.13 REFERENCES AND BIBLIOGRAPHY

1. Anderson, D. R., D. Sweeney, and T. A. Williams, *Linear Programming for Decision Making*, St. Paul, Minn.: West Publishing, 1974.
2. Harris, R. D., and M. J. Maggard, *Computer Models in Operations Management: A Computer Augmented System*, 2nd Ed., San Francisco: Harper & Row, 1977.
3. Hinomoto, H., "Capacity Expansion with Facilities Under Technological Improvement," *Management Science* 11:581–592 (1965).
4. Levitt, Theodore, "Production Line Approach to Service," *Harvard Business Review*, 50:41–52 (Sept.-Oct., 1972).
5. Magee, J. F., "Decision Trees for Decision Making," *Harvard Business Review*, 42:126 (1964).
6. Monroe, A. S., ed., *Investments for Capacity Expansion*, Cambridge, Mass.: The M.I.T. Press, 1967.
7. Turban, E., and Meredith, J. R., *Fundamentals of Management Science*, Dallas, Texas: Business Publications, 1977.
8. Schultz, R. S., "Profits, Prices, and Excess Capacity," *Harvard Business Review*, 41:68–81 (July-Aug., 1963).
9. Whyte, William F., *Human Relations in the Restaurant Industry*, New York: McGraw-Hill, 1948.

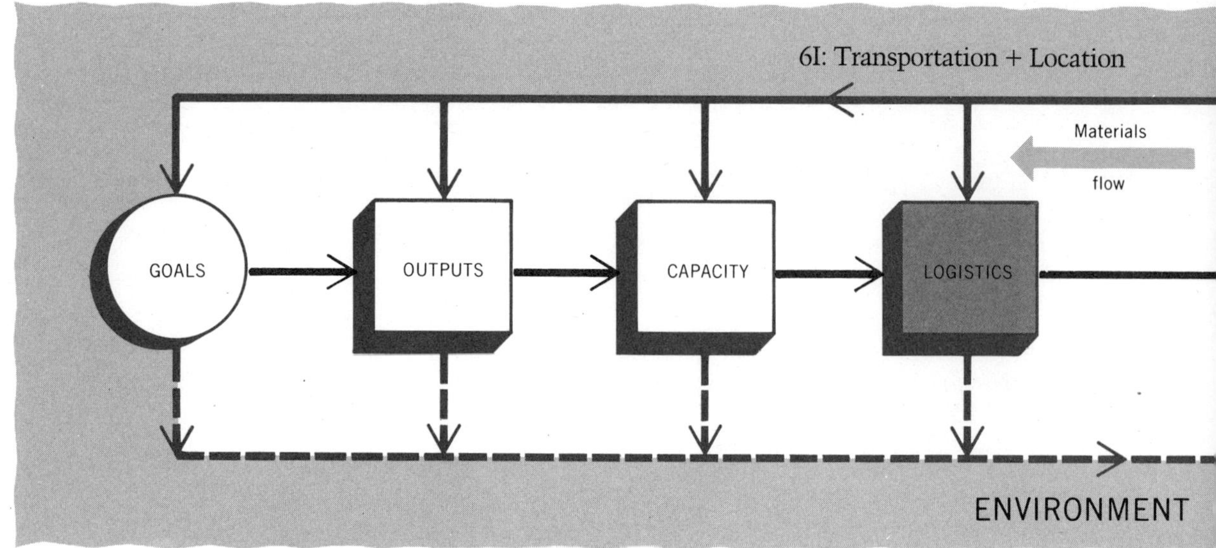

Chapter 6I

The Logistics Interface: Transportation and Location

CONCEPTS

6.1 The Distribution System
- Natural Resources
- Immobile Products
- Minimal Transportation Costs
- All Factors Relevant

6.2 Distribution by Transportation
- Water
- Pipeline
- Rail
- Truck
- Air
- The Routing Problem

6.3 Distribution by Location
- National/International
- Community
- Site Selection

6.4 Evaluating Transportation Location Tradeoffs
- The Single-Facility Problem: Comparing All Factors
- Venereal Disease Center

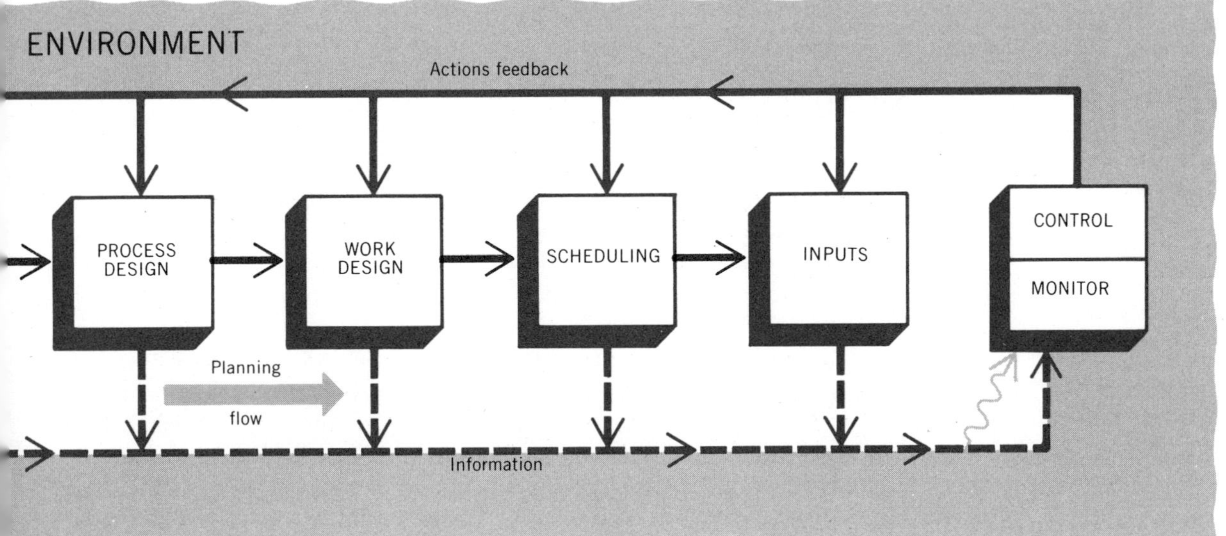

TOOLS AND APPLICATIONS

LEARNING OBJECTIVES

By the completion of the *Concepts* portion of this chapter the student should

1. Understand how transportation and location trade off in distribution logistics.
2. Be aware that the special characteristics of some organizations dictate their location and hence their distribution system.
3. Know the five major modes of transportation and their characteristics.
4. Be familiar with the concept of pipelining slurries.
5. Understand the complexities of the "routing" and "traveling salesman" problems in distribution.
6. Know the three stages involved in the location decision and the considerations involved in each stage.
7. Have a feel for the various levels of difficulty of distribution problems, ranging from single to multiple facilities, criteria, outputs, and distribution levels.
8. Understand and be able to use a "weighted score" model to compare multiple distribution criteria.

CONCEPTS

Up to this point in the design of the operations function we have selected the output, forecasted the demand in the environment, and sized our production facility for sufficient capacity to economically meet the demand. The next step is to decide how to best get the output to the recipients. This decision must be made next because it will determine where we *place* the production facility and how much *transportation* of the output will be necessary. This function involves what is known as **logistics**.

The breadth of logistics management.

The term *logistics management* as currently used in organizations often includes the supply and movement of materials, personnel, equipment, and finished goods within the organization and between it and its environment. Such an all-encompassing interpretation would thus include the functions of purchasing, materials management, **distribution**, personnel, maintenance, and a number of others. In this chapter, however, we will primarily consider only the distribution aspect of logistics. The other functions will be addressed later in separate chapters.

Impact on the operations manager.

The manner in which the output is distributed to the recipients is of special concern to the operations manager. First, the location of the production facility will affect the quality of the supply of labor, the shipment cost of materials, the timeliness of repair services, and numerous other aspects of the production process. Secondly, the transportation of the output will place certain additional constraints on the production process regarding weight, throughput time, sturdiness, and so forth. In addition, intermediate distribution points will impact the functions of inventory control, materials handling, warehousing, routing, and so on.

In this chapter we will first address the general subject of distribution and then focus in turn on transportation and location. Following this we will look at tradeoffs between the two distribution methods. In the *Tools and Applications* portion of the chapter we will look at some models useful, first, in locating a single facility by itself and second, in locating and allocating resources between multiple facilities.

6.1 THE DISTRIBUTION SYSTEM

The distribution system.

A major aspect of transportation logistics occurs in the *distribution system*. The manner in which the organization's input is distributed is important because of its impact on the total cost of the output, the number of recipients that can be reached, and even the location of the organization itself. For example, the cost of *physical distribution*, that is, getting the product or service to the consumer, ranges from about 10 percent of sales in the mechanical equipment industry to 30 percent in the food industries.

Distribution improvements.

A good distribution system will generally reduce distribution costs and provide better customer service (faster deliveries, fewer **stockouts**, and greater variety) at the same time. For example, the move by many companies such as the Borden Company and Whirlpool Corporation in the early 1960s from multiple warehouses to only a few general-purpose distribution centers reduced the costs of order preparation, warehousing, materials handling, inventory control, and record-keeping while simultaneously providing faster customer service, fewer stockouts, and greater variety of selection. This was accomplished primarily by utilizing the new technologies of **automated data processing** for credit checking, record-keeping and inventory control, and **unit load** principles ("containerization," "palletization") in materials handling.

Transporting-versus-locating tradeoffs.

The determination of the "best" distribution system depends upon the type of output being considered and the relative costs in dollars, time, and trouble of *transporting to* versus *locating near*. That is, the best choice depends on the costs of moving the output to the recipients from a centralized location as compared to *locating* the transformation activities in close proximity to the recipients. Since service outputs are generally difficult, expensive, or even impossible to transport, service organizations have typically distributed their output by means of locating in the vicinity of their recipients. Examples of this approach are medical clinics, churches, parks and playgrounds, dry cleaners, and beauty shops. Of course, there are exceptions to this general practice when the recipients transport themselves to the service location. These situations usually occur where the service is of exceptional quality, scarce, or famous, such as the Mayo Clinic, to which people come from all over the world, or Yosemite National Park, which delights thousands of visitors every year.

Transporting services.

Some service organizations, however, do attempt to transport their services, although frequently at a great deal of trouble. These instances occur when the nature of the service makes it impractical to remain in one fixed location for an extended duration (traveling carnivals, home shows), or, more commonly, when the service is deemed to be very important to the public but may otherwise be inaccessible (mobile x ray, blood donor vehicles, bookmobiles).

Locational categories of product organizations.

Product organizations, on the other hand, can generally trade transportation costs for location costs with more ease and, therefore, usually locate in an economically advantageous spot. Product organizations often fall into one of four categories which dictate their distribution patterns as well as their most economic location.

Natural Resources

Those organizations that process natural resources as raw materials to obtain their final product will locate near their raw material source if one of the following conditions hold.

1. There is a large loss in size or weight during processing.
2. High **economies of scale** exist for the product. That is, the operating costs of one large plant with the same total capacity as two smaller plants is significantly less than the combined operating costs of the two small plants.
3. The raw material is perishable (fish processing, canning) and cannot be shipped long distances before being processed.

Examples of these types of industries are mining, canning, and lumber. In these cases the natural inputs (raw materials) are either voluminous or perishable and the final product is much reduced in size, thus greatly reducing the cost of transportation to the recipients (either final users or further processors).

Immobile Product

The products of some organizations may be relatively immobile such as dams, roads, buildings, and bridges. In these cases (referred to as "projects") the organization locates itself at the construction spot and transports all required inputs to that location. The "home office" is frequently little more than one room with a phone, secretary, file, and billing and recordkeeping facilities.

Minimal Transportation Costs

A few product organizations, such as electronics firms, have both relatively minor raw material *and* finished product transportation costs so that the location decision is based on other considerations such as access to suppliers, or community amenities. For example, Hewlett-Packard's choice of Corvallis, Oregon for its calculator plant was based, in part, on the fact that Oregon State University with its engineering research facilities, especially important in electronics, is located there (see Readings, Section 6.10).

All Factors Relevant

The majority of product organizations do not have one single overriding transportation cost factor with which to contend. They must consider the costs of land, labor, capital, equipment, and transportation as well as other nonquantitative factors such as local zoning regulations or the supply of labor in choosing their pattern of distribution. These organizations have particular difficulty in selecting the best pattern of distribution since no one factor predominates.

6.2 DISTRIBUTION BY TRANSPORTATION

There are five basic modes of physical transportation.

- Water.
- Pipeline.
- Rail.
- Truck.
- Air.

Traffic shares by mode.

Table 6.1 lists the traffic shares held by these modes (excepting pipeline) and their relative costs per ton-mile (a railroad box car moving 90 miles with a load of 40 tons generates 3600 ton-miles). As indicated by the values in the table, trucks (and then railroads) carry the great majority of tonnage whereas water, and then rail, have the majority of ton-miles. This implies that rail and water are the major transportation

TABLE 6.1 TRAFFIC SHARES AND COSTS FOR MAJOR TRANSPORTATION MODES

Mode	Tons (%)	Ton-Miles (%)	Average Cost/Ton-Mile
Water	26.3	43.7	$0.006
Rail	32.9	36.8	0.01
Truck	40.5	19.0	0.04
Air	—	0.1	0.10
Miscellaneous	0.3	0.4	—

Source: Adapted by permission from E. W. Smykay, *Physical Distribution Management*, Third Edition, Macmillan, 1973.

Long-haul versus short-haul.

modes in the high-tonnage, *long-haul* (over 800 miles) market whereas truck and rail are the major modes in the short-haul market.

Water

Water is cheap but slow.

The least expensive **mode of transportation** is water but this mode also has major drawbacks. It is slow, very limited in accessibility, and generally is used for bulky, nonperishable items of low unit value such as petroleum, coal, scrap iron, salt, and mineral ores.

Pipeline

Pipelines are cheap but specialized and inaccessible.

Pipelines are also frequently used for petroleum products and natural gas, but their use has recently been extended to other products such as coal and sawdust, which can be formed into water based mixtures called **slurries** and pumped through the line without damage to the pumps or the basic product. The disadvantage of using pipelines is their limited accessibility, slow rate of travel (about 15 miles per hour), and the requirement that the product be in a liquid or gaseous form.

Rail

Rail is inexpensive and accessible.

Railroads handle a vast range of products such as cereals, coal, nonferrous metals, lumber, and food products. Rail offers a number of advantages as a form of transportation. It can transport large items as well as small, has good accessibility, offers services for specialized products [refrigeration, dock-to-dock **piggy-back** (see Figure 6.1), trilevel auto hauling, petroleum tank cars, etc.], and is relatively inexpensive.

Truck

Trucking offers accessibility and service.

However, truck transport has grown considerably, at the expense of rail, because of the following factors that either reduced the cost of trucking or improved service to the recipients:

- Liberalized trucking regulations (speed, size).
- Improved national highway system.

Myth:

Truck traffic can move only on the highways.

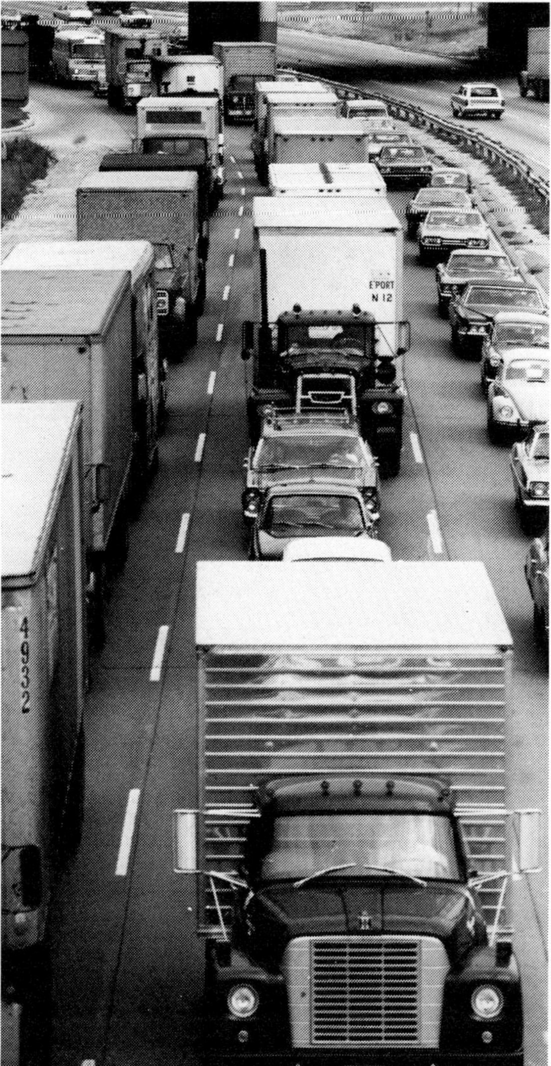

Fact:

More than two million truckloads moved by railway last year.

Piggybacking—the movement of truck trailers or containers by rail—is the fastest-growing part of the railroad business. It set a new record in 1977 and it's now our second-largest source of traffic—next to coal.

The piggyback concept has come of age. Better yet, it has generated a wealth of innovations and improvements. Containerized cargo destined for foreign countries now moves across America by rail. New designs in flatcars are saving fuel and increasing loads. Truck trailers that actually ride either roads or rails with two separate sets of wheels are being tested.

This is good news for the railroads, but it's better news for the consumer and the nation. Many piggyback trains move their cargo with about half the fuel that would be required by trucks to move the same goods.

Usually there's a cost saving in piggyback shipments, too, with the advantage of fast, long-distance travel and expedited door-to-door delivery service.

Because these truckloads travel on the railroads, not the highways, the motoring public enjoys a greater degree of safety and less congestion, while damage to the highway system is reduced.

Not all trucks can move by train, but thousands more are doing so every year. And the ones that do aren't leaving potholes in your favorite road.

Association of American Railroads,
American Railroads Building,
Washington, D.C. 20036

Surprise:

We've been working on the railroad.

Figure 6.1. Piggybacking truck trailers by rail. (Reprinted by permission of the Association of American Railroads.)

- Better trucking equipment.
- New, improved materials handling equipment.
- Speed, flexibility of service.
- Dock-to-dock availability.

Like rail, trucking is used for a vast array of products: office machinery, livestock, petroleum products, automobiles, and nonferrous metals.

Air

Air is fast but expensive.

Air transport is typically used for items that are small or fragile but have high value such as optical instruments, electrical recording instruments, solid-state electronic components, or are highly perishable such as live Maine lobster for a Chicago restaurant or tropical fish from a Key West aquarium fish company. Speed of delivery is the major characteristic of air transport and for small, high-valued, or perishable products the use of air freight can significantly reduce inventory and warehousing costs with a corresponding improvement in customer service.

The Routing Problem

The routing difficulties of transport.

Independent of the specific mode of transport there are additional transportation problems involving such considerations as the *number* of transporting vehicles, their *capacities*, and the *routes* that each vehicle will take. In general, these interrelated problems are frequently included under the heading of the **routing problem**.

Solving the routing problem involves finding the best number of vehicles and their routes to deliver the organization's output to a group of geographically dispersed recipients. When only one vehicle is serving all the recipients, the problem is known as the **traveling salesman problem**. In this problem a number of possible routes exist between the organization and all of the recipients but only a few, or perhaps just one of these routes minimizes the total cost of delivery to all the recipients.

The traveling salesman problem.

Although there are certain procedures available to minimize either the distance traveled or the cost in the routing and traveling salesman problems, quite often there are other considerations such as balancing the workloads among the vehicles or minimizing the idle or delay time. For approaches to such routing problems see Reference 15.

6.3 DISTRIBUTION BY LOCATION

Advantages of proximity.

Organizations that supply a product to a recipient may locate close to their "market," not necessarily to minimize transportation costs of distribution, but to improve customer service. Being in close proximity to the market makes it easier for the recipient to contact the organization and, also, allows the organization to respond to changes in demand (both in quantity and variety) from current and new recipients. As in war, the people on the front line are closest to the action and are able to respond to changing situations faster than those far away simply because information about changes is available on a more timely basis and is generally more accurate.

For organizations that supply a service to recipients, there is usually little choice—they generally locate near their market because services are not easily transported. Frequently, the service is received directly by the recipient (surgery, hair cuts, counseling) but not always. That is, some intermediary may exist in the provision of the service. For example: the counseling/entertainment service "Dear Abby" uses newspapers as a communication medium and therefore Abby can "counsel" from a central location. College extension courses use both educational television and the U.S. Postal Servicc as intermediaries, patient symptoms and test results can be sent over telephone lines to a centralized health computer service for diagnosis and interpretation, and in-home shopping and bill paying can be conducted by telephone.

Intermediaries in services.

In each of these cases, the primary service facility can be considerably removed from the recipient but some form of intermediary must be in contact with him or her. This allows the organization to then locate the primary facility according to other requirements. For instance, "Abby" can reside in an attractive, quiet area conducive to creative counseling; the college can locate in a big city or at a teaching and research hospital with large capacity computer equipment and top medical specialists.

On occasion, the distribution function is handled by multiple, "branch" facilities which may or may not perform the actual processing themselves. The problem of determining the best locations for the multiple facilities is known as the *multifacility location problem*. Franchises are a specialized form of branch facilities, as are warehouses, branch banks, and adult evening classes offered at local high schools and colleges.

Branch facilities.

Innovation in service distribution.

Recently, several examples of innovation in service distribution have appeared. The "bookmobile," a mobile branch library, has been around for a number of years, of course, providing a service to local communities, schools, and churches, which were physically distant from central or branch libraries. The "Meals on Wheels" program, originally developed under an Office of Economic Opportunity grant program, is widely used to provide prepared food for the elderly and handicapped who otherwise would find it difficult to provide or prepare their own meals. Other offshoots of this kind of program are the home health care ("visiting nurse") programs, providing health services without going to the doctor's office, and the homemaker services, which provide assistance for the elderly and handicapped, thereby allowing them to maintain their own residences rather than moving into nursing homes. And finally, a mobile automotive tune-up service is also now being offered. A fully equipped van with an inventory of tune-up parts and electronic testing devices offers tune-ups and minor repairs at the customer's home or office. The result is a "low overhead" operation which offers both convenience and price advantages to the client.

Three stages in the location decision.

In general, the location decision is divided into three stages: national/international, community, and site selection. Sources of information for these stages, as they are discussed below, are chambers of commerce, realtors, utilities, banks, suppliers, transportation companies, savings and loan associations, government agencies, and management consultants who specialize in relocation decisions.

National/International

The four major considerations in the selection of a national or overseas region in which to locate are

1. The proximity of the region to the organization's recipients and raw materials, if any are used.
2. The type and quantity of labor available in the region.
3. The availability of other inputs such as land, supplies, transportation, and utilities.
4. The acceptability of the "environment" (climate, tax rates, regulations, political situation).

Proximity

To minimize transportation costs and provide acceptable service to customers it is desirable that the facility be located in a region of close proximity to the customers and suppliers. Although methods of finding the location with the minimum transportation cost will be presented later in the chapter, a common rule of thumb within the United States is that the facility should be within 200 miles of major industrial and commercial customers and suppliers. Beyond this range, transportation costs begin to rise quickly.

Labor supply

The region should have the proper supply of labor available and in the correct proportions of required skills. One important reason for the expansion, during the 1960s, of American firms abroad was the availability of labor at wage rates much lower than U.S. rates. Currently, this disparity has been reduced significantly due to increased wages abroad; however, the real consideration should not be wage rates but the productivity of domestic labor as compared to productivity abroad. This comparison would thus involve skill level, equipment use, and wage rates combined to determine the most favorable labor region in terms of output per dollar of wages and capital investment.

In addition to regional wage rates, consideration should also be given to the organization of the labor pool; that is, whether all the skills are unionized or an open shop situation exists. Some states have passed **right-to-work laws** (see Figure 6.2) which forbid any requirement that all employees join the union in order to work in an organization. Often, these laws result in significantly lower wage rates in these states.

Availability of inputs

The region selected for location of the facility should have the necessary inputs available. For example, those supplies that are difficult, expensive, or time-consuming to ship and those which are necessary (i.e., no reasonable substitutes exist) to the organization should be readily available. The proper type (rail, water, highway, air) and

In Louisiana, Government and Industry Work Side by Side.

Louisiana has always offered industrial benefits: abundant energy and raw materials, available and efficient workers, effective transportation and delivery networks. We also have the philosophy that business and industry are the keys to the prosperity and economic welfare of our citizens.

That's why Louisiana can offer your next plant free training programs, tax incentives, financing, a right-to-work law, one of the lowest tax loads on business in the nation and a minimum of red tape. In Louisiana, you'll find government at all levels working with people and industry to make life better for all. Consider Louisiana for your next plant site . . . you'll be in good company.

For further information on Louisiana's industrial advantages, write to:

Andrew F. Flores, Executive Director
Office of Commerce & Industry
625 North 4th St. Suite 1-S
Baton Rouge, Louisiana 70804
or telephone: 504/389-5371

LOUISIANA

Figure 6.2. Location factors. (Reprinted by permission of Louisiana Office of Commerce and Industry.)

supply of transportation; sufficient quantities of basic resources such as water, electricity, gas, coal, and oil; and appropriate communication facilities should also be available. Obviously, many American industries are located abroad to use the raw materials (oil, copper, etc.) available there.

Environment

The regional environment should be conducive to the nature of the organization. Not only should the regional weather patterns be appropriate but the political, legal, and social "climates" should also be favorable. Several matters that should be considered are

1. State taxes.
2. Regional regulations on operating matters (pollution, hiring, etc.).
3. Import/export barriers.
4. Political stability (nationalization policies, kidnappings).
5. Cultural and economic peculiarities (e.g., restrictions on working women) of the region.

Community

Many of the considerations made at the regional level should be reconsidered here. For example, the availability of acceptable sites, local government attitudes, regulations, zoning, taxes, labor supply, market size and characteristics, and weather would again be considered. In addition, the pollution peculiar to the community, the availability of local financing, monetary inducements (such as tax incentives) for establishing operations in the community, and the community's attitude (Figure 6.2) toward the organization itself would be additional factors of interest to the organization.

Lastly, the preferences of the organization's staff should play a role in community selection. These would probably be influenced by the amenities available in the community such as homes, churches, shopping centers, schools and universities, medical care, fire and police protection, and entertainment as well as local taxes and other costs. Upper level educational institutions may also be of interest to the organization in terms of opportunity for relevant research and development. For example, it is no coincidence that major IBM plants are located in Lexington, Kentucky; Denver, Colorado; and Austin, Texas, which are also sites of major state universities.

Site Selection

Lastly, the *site*, the actual location of the facility, should be appropriate to the nature of the operation. Such matters as size; adjoining land; zoning; community attitudes; drainage; soil; the availability of water, sewers, and utilities; waste disposal; transportation accessibility; local market size; and development costs are typically considered in the site selection process. The analysis of customer market characteristics is, of course, a major factor in retail location studies, a science almost in itself. For further

"We can be proud, gentlemen. Before we came, this was just desert!"

Cartoon by Chris Jensen. (Reprinted with permission from *Changing Times*, © 1973, Kiplinger Washington Editors, Inc., August 1973.)

details the reader is referred to References 3 and 16. The development of industrial parks in some communities has alleviated many of the site selection difficulties of organizations since most of these matters are automatically taken care of by the developer.

6.4 EVALUATING TRANSPORTATION-LOCATION TRADEOFFS

Combining transportation and location approaches.

Up to this point in our discussion of output distribution we have considered the costs and characteristics of the major types of transportation as well as the various factors affecting location. It is now necessary to combine these two approaches to obtain the best overall method of distributing the outputs to the recipients. The problem for the operations manager is complex, frequently involving subjective and nonquantifiable factors as well as extremely involved quantifiable factors. Fortunately, the availability of computers has eliminated some of the difficulty of transportation/location decisions through the ability to keep track of voluminous data and through the computational power to perform sophisticated quantitative analyses upon the data. Some of these analytical techniques are discussed in the *Tools and Applications* portion of this chapter.

The single facility location problem.

The least complicated of the location problems involves *one* facility that distributes a product or service to a group of *geographically dispersed* recipients, as illustrated in Figure 6.3. A "best" location for this *single-source, multirecipient* problem is found by determining the location that best meets some **decision criterion**. The

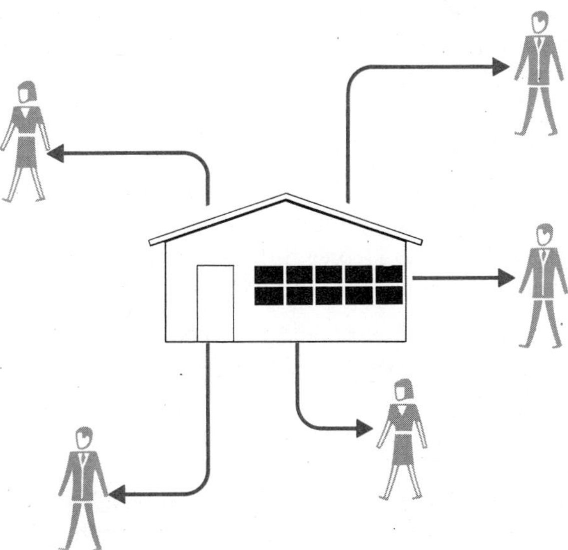

Figure 6.3. The single-source, multirecipient location problem.

problem could take into consideration only one decision criterion or several criteria. For example, locating a fire station in a small "one station" town might be based simply on the criterion of *response time*, the average time to travel from the station to the scene of the fire once a call has been placed. It could also be based upon any *one* of other criteria such as minimizing expected annual monetary fire losses, or minimizing expected lives lost, each of which might produce different "best" locations.

Complication of multiple criteria.

The location decision is complicated by the use of multiple criteria such as minimizing the frequency of stockouts, maximizing use of the facility's capacity, and minimizing inventory levels or personnel requirements. These additional criteria may be very difficult to quantify, or even measure qualitatively; yet if they are important to the decision, they must be included in the location analysis. A simple model that addresses this issue is discussed below.

The Single-Facility Problem: Comparing All Factors

The weighted score model for multiple factors.

There are a number of ways (see, for example, Reference 5) of handling the comparison of location criteria. The most common is probably just managerial intuition: which location is best on the important criteria? A simple formalization of this intuitive process for the problem of locating a single facility is the **weighted score** model. In this model a "weight" is assigned to each factor (*criterion*) depending upon its importance to the manager. The most important factors receive proportionately higher weights. Then a "score" is assigned to each of the location alternatives on each factor, again with higher scores representing better results. The product of the factor weights and the location scores then gives a set of "weighted scores," which are added up for each location alternative. That location with the largest weighted score is considered "best." This process is illustrated in the example below.

Venereal Disease Center

A county health department is investigating three possible locations for a specialized venereal disease (VD) control clinic that will monitor the new incurable and highly communicable viral VD, Herpes Simplex Type 2. The county director of public health is particularly concerned with four location factors.

1. The most important consideration in the treatment of VD is ease of access for infectives. Since they are generally disinclined to recognize and seek treatment for their health problem, it is foolish to locate a clinic where it is not easily accessible to as many patients as possible. This aspect of location is probably as much as 50 percent more important than the lease cost of the building.
2. The annual cost of the lease is not a minor consideration. The health department, unfortunately, is limited to a very tight budget and any extra cost for the lease will result in less equipment and staff being available to the clinic.
3. For some infectives it is of the utmost importance that confidentiality be maintained. Thus, although the clinic must be easily accessible, it must also be relatively inconspicuous. This factor is probably just as important as the cost of the lease.
4. Also, the director wants to consider the locational convenience of the clinic for its staff since many of the physicians will be donating their time to the clinic. This consideration is the least important of all, perhaps only half as important as the cost of the lease.

The three locations being considered are: a relatively accessible building on Adam's Avenue, an inconspicuous office complex near the downtown bus terminal, and a group of public offices in the Civic Center, which would be almost rent-free.

The director has decided to evaluate (score) each of these alternative locations on each of the above four factors. He has decided to use a four-point scale on which 1 represents "poor" and 4 represents "excellent." His scores and the factor importance weights (derived from the relative importance of the four factors) are shown in Table 6.2. The problem now is to somehow use this information to determine the best location for the clinic.

To determine the weighted score for each location requires the multiplication of each location score by the importance weight for that factor and then the summation over all factors for each location as illustrated in Table 6.3. Since larger scores indicate better ratings, the location with the largest score, B, the office near the bus terminal, is best, followed by C, the Civic Center.

More complicated location problems involve the distribution of the output from more than one facility. The problem becomes complex because the best distribution

TABLE 6.2 POTENTIAL VD CLINIC SITES

		Potential Locations		
W: Importance Weight	*F*: Factor[a]	A: Adam's Ave.	B: Bus Terminal Complex	C: Civic Center
2	1. Annual lease cost	1	3	4
3	2. Accessibility for infectives	3	3	2
2	3. Inconspicuousness	2	4	2
1	4. Accessibility for health personnel	4	1	2

[a] Factor scoring scale: 1, poor; 2, acceptable; 3, good; 4, excellent.

Complication of multiple facilities.

Multiple outputs.

pattern for each facility depends on the distribution patterns of *all* the other facilities. Hence, the problem cannot be solved by locating each facility one at a time. Rather, they must all be located "at once" since changing the distribution patten of any one facility will change the distribution pattens of some or all of the other facilities as well. In addition to the above complications is the fact that most organizations produce more than one output and thus the distribution problem must be solved with many products or services in mind. We will next address some of the simpler distribution problems in the *Tools and Applications* portion of the chapter. First we consider the effect of uncertainty in the location parameters and next focus on the transportation costs when only one central facility is involved. Lastly, we consider the complications of the multifacility problem and illustrate the application of linear programming for resource allocation among multiple facilities.

TABLE 6.3 FACTOR COMPARISON BY THE "WEIGHTED SCORE" METHOD

Factor	Weight	Sites:	A	B	C
1	2		$2 \times 1 = 2$	$2 \times 3 = 6$	$2 \times 4 = 8$
2	3		$3 \times 3 = 9$	$3 \times 3 = 9$	$3 \times 2 = 6$
3	2		$2 \times 2 = 4$	$2 \times 4 = 8$	$2 \times 2 = 4$
4	1		$1 \times 4 = 4$	$1 \times 1 = 1$	$1 \times 2 = 2$
Total			19	24	20

TOOLS AND APPLICATIONS

6.5 THE SINGLE-FACILITY PROBLEM: HANDLING UNCERTAINTY

Even when methods for comparing the different factors among locations are known and understood, the operations manager still might not know for certain the values of the factors. That is, any number of the factors may be subject to some form of uncertainty: material costs depend on output rate, labor availability depends on regional employment patterns, and demand depends on the national economy.

Breakeven model for uncertainty.

A useful technique for handling some types of uncertainty is the "breakeven" technique for cost comparison of different alternatives (presented in Chapter 5). For example, suppose the uncertain variable is the *level of demand for the output* and the decision criterion is the *total annual operating cost* for the facility. Various location/distribution alternatives may be compared by graphing each alternative's total operating costs for the different demand levels as in Figure 6.4.

This is accomplished by dividing the total operating cost into two components: fixed costs that do not vary with the demand for the output (e.g., land, buildings, equipment, property taxes, insurance) and variable costs such as labor, materials, and transportation, and plotting them on the axes of a graph. At the demand point E (the

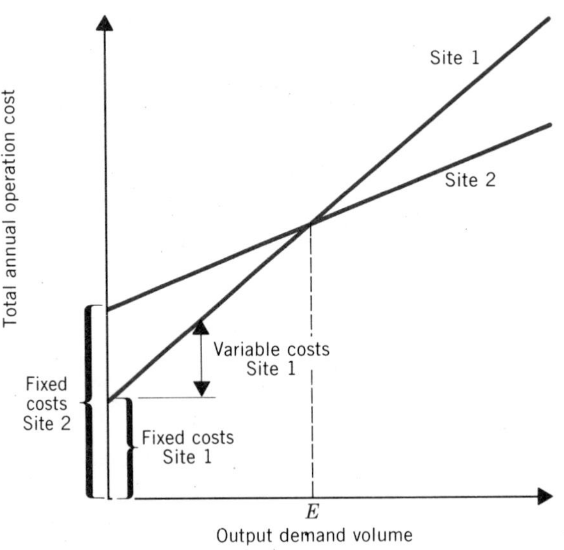

Figure 6.4. Breakeven location model.

intersection of the two lines) the costs for the two alternatives are the same; for demand levels in excess of *E*, site 2 is best, and for levels less than *E*, site 1 is best. Thus, if the range of uncertainty concerning the output volume is entirely *above* point *E* the manager need not be concerned about which site to choose—site 2 is best. Similar reasoning holds for any uncertainty existing entirely *below* point *E*—site 1 is best. If the uncertainty encompasses point *E* then two additional situations must be considered.

1. If the range of uncertainty is closely restricted to point *E*, then either site may be selected because the costs will be approximately the same in either case.
2. If the range of uncertainty is broad and varies considerably from point *E* in both directions, then the breakeven chart will indicate to the manager the extra costs she or he will incur by choosing the wrong site. The manager should probably try to gather more information to reduce the range of uncertainty in demand before selecting either site.

We will demonstrate with the following example.

Upp and Adam Elevators, Ltd.

Figure 6.5 depicts the total costs for four candidate locations for the Upp and Adam organization. Note from the figure that sites 1, 2, and 3 all have approximately the

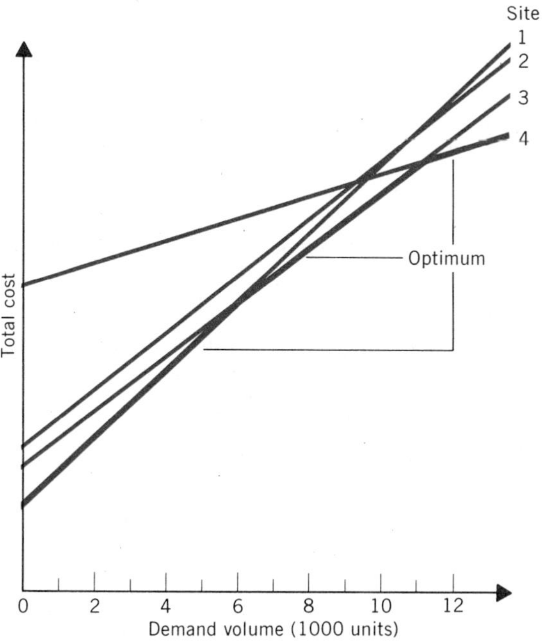

Figure 6.5. Cost comparison for four potential sites.

same fixed costs and the same variable costs compared to site 4, which has a very high fixed cost but low variable cost—beyond a demand volume of 11 (thousand units) site 4 is clearly the best. Also note from the figure that site 2 should never be considered because site 3 is *always* better than site 2; its fixed costs and its variable cost are *both* lower. Site 3 appears to be optimal between volumes (in thousands) of 6.5 and 11; below 6.5 site 1 is best and above 11 site 4 is best.

Suppose uncertainty in demand volume for Upp and Adam is relatively high because the product is a new one and may catch on quickly or, just as likely, languish along for years at fairly low sales before any significant growth. Ms. Down N. Out, the operations manager, believes, under these circumstances, that the demand could range anywhere between 4 and 12 thousand units.

For such a situation can the breakeven chart be helpful? Most certainly! For the majority of this range, site 3 is best. At demand volumes of 4, although site 1 is best, site 3 is only slightly worse whereas site 4 is very poor. And at volumes of 12, although site 4 is best, site 3 is not much worse. Thus, site 3, assuming other factors are acceptable, appears to be a safe bet. Of course, for considerably higher volumes only site 4 would be economically acceptable but, according to Ms. Out's estimate, such volumes are not expected to occur.

6.6 THE SINGLE-FACILITY PROBLEM: MINIMIZING TRANSPORTATION COSTS

Having dealt with multiple decision criteria and uncertainty in demand as it affects location choice, we may now focus on the transportation cost aspects of the problem. First, we will consider the simplest case: the single-facility, multirecipient distribution problem.

Minimum transportation cost.

The approach to the problem of locating the single facility is relatively straightforward. Total transportation cost is used as the location decision criterion. We assume that the amounts and locations of demand by recipients are known and that the transportation cost to ship output to each demand location is known (or can easily be found) for any given facility location. We start by selecting a "promising" initial site for the facility and calculate the total transportation cost to supply all the geographically dispersed demands. This initial site may be chosen either at random or from a list of available, or potential, locations. In the latter case, the facility is then relocated at each of the potential sites, new transportation costs are calculated, and the location with the lowest total transportation cost is deemed "best."

Incremental analysis.

In the former case (that is, where no list of potential sites is available) the facility is moved slightly north, east, south, and then west of the initial site and the total transportation cost calculated for each of these changes, in turn. This is a simple variant of a technique known as **incremental analysis.** If all four changes result in higher costs, then the initial site is best* and the problem is solved. However, if some

* At least among sites in that region. Although it does not frequently happen, there is occasionally a somewhat better site much farther away.

movement results in a lower cost, the facility should be moved in that direction and the entire process repeated until a final location is found where none of the directional changes produce an improvement.

The method of calculating the total transportation cost is as follows. We use the following symbols.

T = the cost for the type of transportation needed, in dollars per unit volume (or weight) per unit distance [e.g., \$/(lb · mile)]
V = the volume (or weight) being transported.
D = the distance from the facility to the recipients' demand locations.
C = the total cost
$1,2,3, \ldots, n$ = subscripts denoting the first, second, third, through the nth recipients

Then we compute

$$C = T_1V_1D_1 + T_2V_2D_2 + T_3V_3D_3 + \cdot \cdot \cdot + T_nV_nD_n$$

which is the total cost of shipping the desired quantities to all n recipients. This procedure is illustrated in the example below.

BRANDEX Medical Supplies

A new firm, BRANDEX, is entering the acetaminophen (aspirin substitute) market and plans to compete directly with Tylenol, the major acetaminophen supplier, by offering retailers a generic drug that could be sold as a "house brand" at a reduced price. BRANDEX has made contact with two large wholesalers in the Dallas (D) and Seattle (S) areas and has established two manufacturing representatives in Los Angeles (L) and Chicago (C) who would then further distribute the product on a house brand basis (Figure 6.6).

Denver, Colorado has been suggested as a possible site at which to locate the production facilities. Trucking rates, T, for the product to the four demand cities and the mileages, D, from Denver (obtained from a truck routing map) are given in Table 6.4. Included in the table are the levels, V, of demand (in cartons) expected in the first year and the product of T times V which (we assume here) is independent of the facility location.

At the bottom of Table 6.4 the total annual transportation cost is shown. The first figure, \$13,064, represents the cost from Denver. The next figure \$13,074, is the cost due to changing the distances involved simply by moving the facility 10 miles north. As can be seen in the table, the effect of this move is to *increase* the distance, and thus costs, to Los Angeles (L), an expensive, high-demand area, and Dallas (D) for a cost increase of 4133 − 4109 = 29 for L and 690 − 683 = 7 for D, thus totaling 36. But this move also *decreases* the cost for Seattle (S) and Chicago (C) for a decrease of 21 + 5 or 26. The net effect of this location shift is thus a total *increase* in cost of 36 − 26 or \$10.

Comparing the total costs of next moving the facility 10 miles east, then south,

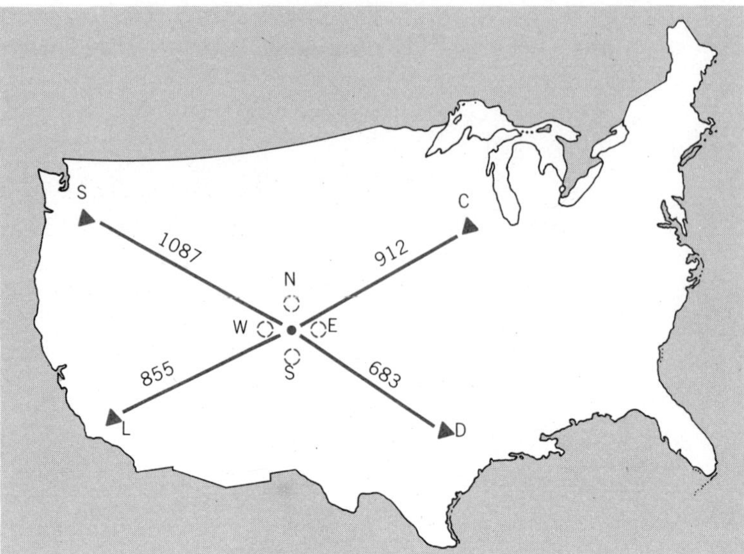

Figure 6.6. Nationwide distribution map.

and then west it is seen that the lowest cost results by moving south. Moving west also reduces the cost somewhat, though not nearly as much as moving south, so the next step is to look for an acceptable location somewhat south of Denver and perhaps a bit west and then repeat the entire process. A natural question, for which there is no single answer, is "How far should the facility be moved for the next test?" Clearly, we would not move farther south than Dallas because then the facility would be farther away from *all* the demand points. It is best to be conservative in this process and locate a city, or site, that is generally acceptable on other factors and is not very far from the previously tested location. In this case, Colorado Springs would be a logical next choice for BRANDEX and is only 75 miles away.

6.7 THE MULTIFACILITY PROBLEM

Solving allocation problems with the transportation model.

The next level of complexity in distribution situations is the **multifacility** location problem. Again, the potential locations may or may not be given. In addition, the *number* of facilities may not even be specified. However, even when the number of facilities is specified *and* their sites are given, the transportation cost is not immediately obtainable because it is still necessary to decide *which* facility, or more commonly facilit*ies*, will supply *which* recipient. This is known as an *allocation* problem. This problem of allocating output from specific facilities to specific demand locations has been given a special name, the "transportation problem," and is illustrated in the example below.

TABLE 6.4 DATA AND CALCULATIONS FOR DENVER LOCATION

Destination	*T* [($/carton · mile)]	*V* (car-tons)	*TV* ($/mile)	*D* (miles)	*C* = *TVD* ($)	*D*(N) (miles)	*C*(N) ($)	*C*(E) ($)	*C*(S) ($)	*C*(W) ($)
S	0.0015	2000	3	1087	3261	1080	3240	3282	3282	3240
L	0.0012	4000	4.8	855	4104	861	4133	4142	4075	4066
D	0.0010	1000	1	683	683	690	690	676	676	690
C	0.0011	5000	5.5	912	5016	911	5011	4967	5022	5066
			Total costs:		$13,064		13,074	13,067	13,055	13,062

The Green Tomato Company

Tom, Green Tomato's operations manager, was having trouble trying to decide which processing plants should supply Green Tomato's new warehouse in Los Angeles. Green Tomato had opened their new warehouse in Los Angeles to serve the growing population in that region. But now management wondered which of their processing plants should supply the new warehouse, and to what extent, to minimize shipping costs.

Green Tomato has two processing plants for their Mexican tomatoes, one in Tijuana, Mexico (A), with a supply capacity of 100 tons per day, and one in Mexicali, Mexico (B), with a supply capacity of 110 tons a day. Green Tomato also has three warehouses: R in Calexico, California; S in Yuma, Arizona and the newly added T in Los Angeles. The warehouses could use, if available, 80, 120, and 60 tons of tomatoes each week, respectively, to meet demands.

The shipping costs from each plant to each warehouse are given in Table 6.5 below.

Characteristics and Assumptions of the Transportation Problem

Green Tomato's distribution problem exhibits some typical characteristics.

1. A limited supply of a commodity is available at specific locations.
2. There is a specific demand for the commodity at other locations.

TABLE 6.5 GREEN TOMATO'S SHIPPING COSTS

From	To	Cost per Ton
A (Tijuana)	R (Calexico)	1
A (Tijuana)	S (Yuma)	2
A (Tijuana)	T (Los Angeles)	3
B (Mexicali)	R (Calexico)	4
B (Mexicali)	S (Yuma)	1
B (Mexicali)	T (Los Angeles)	5

3. The *cost* of transporting the commodity from each supply point to each demand location is constant.
4. The *problem* is to minimize the total shipping cost by finding how many units each supply point should ship to each demand location.

Transportation problems often have a very large number of solutions. Although **linear programming** can solve such allocation problems, an especially simple variant of linear programming called "the **transportation method**" was developed specifically to solve this type of problem. The concept behind the transportation method is to keep improving on *any* beginning, feasible solution. To determine whether a solution can be improved, one unit is shipped between every supply and demand route, one at a time, that does not have a flow in the current solution. This unit is allocated by "borrowing" units back and forth between other current shipping routes until all supplies and demands are again in balance. If any of these one unit shipping possibilities *decreases* the cost of distribution then as many units as possible are diverted to that route.

The details of this procedure are presented in the next section of this chapter (see also References 2 and 19) and illustrated using the Green Tomato Company problem. The optimal solution of Tom's problem is

80 units from A to R	cost of $80 \times 1 =$	80
10 units from A to S	$10 \times 2 =$	20
10 units from A to T	$10 \times 3 =$	30
110 units from B to S	$110 \times 1 =$	110
		240

Note that the demand at T, the most expensive shipping point, is not completely filled due to limited supply.

6.8 THE TRANSPORTATION METHOD*

The transportation method is a search and evaluation process involving five steps, as shown in Figure 6.7.

STEP **1. Arrange the Problem in Tabular Form.** Transportation problems are presented in tabular form because it is a convenient form for applying special solution procedures. Table 6.6 shows Green Tomato's distribution problem. This table is explained below.

Left side: The sources of supply (plants) are listed on the left. Each source is represented by a row.

Top: The destination points (warehouses) are listed at the top. Each destination is represented by a column.

* Section 6.8 is adapted by permission from Efraim Turban and Jack R. Meredith, *Fundamentals of Management Science* (Dallas, Tex.: Business Publications, 1977) pp. 193–205. © 1977 by Business Publications, Inc.

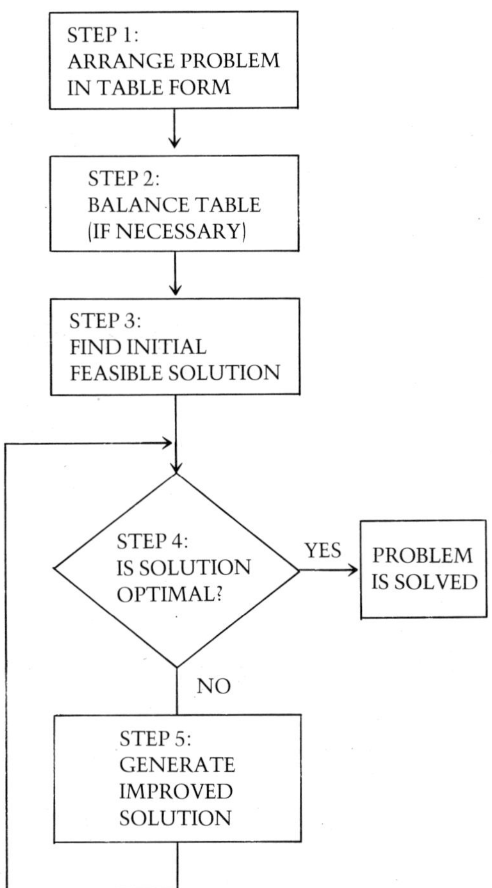

Figure 6.7. Steps in solving the transportation problem.

Right side: This column designates the capacity (supply) at the sources.

Bottom: The requirements (demand) of each destination are listed here.

Center: The center of the table is composed of "cells." In this case there are six. Each is designated by the letter of its row and column; for example, cell AR is in row A and column R. The corresponding shipping costs (per ton) are in the upper right-hand corner of each cell. For example, the shipping cost from plant A to warehouse S is 2. For each cell there is to be determined the quantity to be shipped from the plant in that row to the warehouse in that column.

STEP 2. **Balance the Table.** The use of the transportation solution technique requires that the problem be balanced; that is, the total supply must equal the total demand. If the matrix is not balanced, this must first be done. Two causes of imbalance are excess supply or excess demand. As an example, consider excess supply.

TABLE 6.6 MATRIX PRESENTATION OF GREEN TOMATO'S PROBLEM

From Plant \ To Warehouse	R	S	T	Supply
A	1	2	3	100
B	4	1	5	110
Demand	80	120	60	260 \ 210

Table 6.7 shows an example of an unbalanced matrix where the total supply of 300 exceeds the total demand of 260. In this case there will be 40 unshipped units.

This matrix is balanced by adding a column for excess supply (sometimes labeled a "dummy" destination). The amount in this column equals the excess supply as shown in Table 6.8. The cost of "shipments" to the dummy is usually set at zero: this ensures that all excess capacity will be absorbed by the dummy. For excess demands a dummy source is added in the same manner, as demonstrated further below.

STEP 3. **The Initial Feasible Solution.** An initial solution can be found by any of several available procedures. One of these is demonstrated next; initial assignment by the northwest corner rule.

a. Starting with the northwest corner (left, uppermost in the table), allocate the smaller amount of either the row supply or the column demand.

b. Subtract from the row supply and from the column demand the amount allocated.

TABLE 6.7 UNBALANCED MATRIX (Excess Supply)

Source \ Destination	R	S	T	Supply
A	1	2	3	200
B	4	1	5	100
Demand	80	120	60	260 \ 300

TABLE 6.8 BALANCED MATRIX

Source \ Destination	R	S	T	D (dummy)	Supply
A	1	2	3	0	200
B	4	1	5	0	100
Demand	80	120	60	40 (excess supply)	300 / 300

c. If the column demand is now zero, move to the cell next on the right; if the row demand is zero, move down to the cell in the next row.

d. Once a cell is identified as per step c, allocate to it an amount as per step a.

e. Repeat the above a–d until all supply and demand are zero.

The advantage of this rule is that it is a simple mechanical process. The problem presented in Table 6.6 is balanced in Table 6.9 and serves as an example to illustrate an assignment by the northwest corner rule.

Initially, an amount of 80 tons is allocated to cell AR, out of the 100 available in source A, meeting all the demand of destination R. The remaining supply of 20 tons at source A is then allocated to cell AS, since that is the closest in the A row to AR. The capacity of row A has now been exhausted, but the demand of S has not yet been fully satisfied. Therefore, 100 tons of the 110-ton supply of source B is allocated to

TABLE 6.9 INITIAL SOLUTION BY THE NORTHWEST CORNER RULE

Source \ Destination	R	S	T	Supply	Remaining Supply
A	[1] 80	[2] 20	[3]	100	0
B	[4]	[1] 100	[5] 10	110	0
D (dummy)	[0]	[0]	[0] 50	50	0
Demand	80	120	60	260	
Remaining Demand	0	0	0		

cell BS in order to meet the entire demand of destination S. Then, moving to the right in row B, the remaining supply of B (10 tons) is allocated to cell BT. This exhausts the supply in row B, but the destination T still needs 50 units. Moving down column T the remainder (50 tons) is allocated to cell DT. In this fashion, the entire supply has been used and the entire demand has been satisfied. Cells that receive allocations are called "occupied" to distinguish them from the remaining empty or unoccupied ones.

The initial solution shown in Table 6.9 calls for shipments of

80 tons from A to R at a cost of 80 × 1	= $ 80
20 tons from A to S at a cost of 20 × 2	= 40
100 tons from B to S at a cost of 100 × 1	= 100
10 tons from B to T at a cost of 10 × 5	= 50
50 tons from D to T at no cost	= 0
Total	$270

Note that warehouse T supposedly obtains 50 tons from D (dummy); that is, there is a shortage (unsatisfied demand) of 50 tons at warehouse T.

Once an initial solution is achieved a test for optimality can be conducted.

STEP **4. Testing for Optimality.** The purpose of the optimality test is to test if the proposed solution, just generated, is optimal or not. For each empty cell, the effect of changing it to an occupied cell is examined. If any of these changes are favorable, the solution is not optimal and a new solution must be designed. A general method for calculating the effect of such a change is called "the stepping stone method."

Note: The solution to be checked for optimality must be "nondegenerate"; that is, the number of occupied cells must be $m + n - 1$ (where m = number of sources and n = number of destinations). A method to handle degeneracy is given in Reference 19.

The stepping stone method. The stepping stone method executes the final two steps of the transportation algorithm combined.

Step 4: Testing for optimality. This is done by calculating the "cell evaluators" for all the empty cells.

Step 5: Improving a nonoptimal solution. This is done by the following:

1. Identify the incoming cell.
2. Design an improved solution.

Details of step 4: start with building a closed loop. A "cell evaluator" for an empty cell is a number designating the cost change that results from occupying that cell rather than one of the currently occupied cells. In order to fill an empty cell, a transfer has to be made from a currently occupied cell. Such a transfer, subject to the supply and demand constraints, will affect a total of four or more cells. The evaluator is calculated by determining the overall effect on the total cost of shifting one unit to that empty cell. The signs of the cell evaluators enable us to test for optimality.

In Table 6.10 a demonstration is given of how to calculate the cell evaluator for the empty cell AT (based on the Northwest Corner initial solution, Table 6.9). One unit is moved from the occupied cell AS to AT (following the top double arrow). Cell AT is called the *gaining cell* and a "+" sign is placed there; cell AS is labeled the *losing cell* and a "−" sign is placed there. However, since one unit is moved to cell AT, column T will now have 1 + 10 + 50 = 61, which is more than the 60 required. Therefore, in order to maintain the demand requirement, one unit is moved from the occupied cell, BT, to occupied cell BS (follow bottom double arrow). The new number of units in each cell is now circled.

As a result of this transaction, the row supply requirements are maintained.

For row A: 80 + 19 + 1 = 100
For row B: 101 + 9 = 110

So are the column demands.

For column S: 19 + 101 = 120
For column T: 1 + 9 + 50 = 60

The entire movement process is indicated by a *closed loop* of arrows. Such a closed loop will involve at least four, and sometimes more, cells.

Rule for drawing each closed loop. When tracing a closed loop, start with the empty cell to be evaluated and draw an arrow from it to an occupied cell in the same row (or column). Only occupied cells are used; otherwise it would not be clear which unoccupied cell the evaluator corresponded to. Next, move vertically or horizontally, but never diagonally, to another occupied cell. Follow the same procedure to other occupied cells until returning to the original empty cell. At each turn of the loop (the loop may cross over itself at times), plus and minus signs are alternately placed in the cells, starting with a + sign in the empty cell. One further important restriction is that there must be exactly one positive cell and exactly one negative cell in any row or column through which the loop happens to turn. This restriction is imposed to

TABLE 6.10 EVALUATION OF CELL AT

Source \ Destination	R	S	T	Supply
A	[1] 80	[2] (19) ~~20~~ −	[3] (1) +	100
B	[4]	[1] (101) ~~100~~ +	[5] (9) 10 −	110
D (dummy)	[0]	[0]	[0] 50	50
Demand	80	120	60	260

ensure that the requirements of supply and demand will not be violated when the units are shifted. Note that an even number of at least four cells must participate in a loop and the occupied cells can be visited once and only once.

Evaluation of cell AT. Let us calculate the cost effect of the changes arising from the decision to ship one unit to the empty cell AT. In cells AT and BS, one unit is added so the additional cost is $(3 + 1) = 4$. In cells BT and AS, one unit is deleted and the cost is reduced by $(5 + 2) = 7$. Thus, by executing this exchange we simultaneously *increase* the total cost by 4 and *reduce* the total cost by 7; that is, alter the total cost by $4 - 7 = -3$.

This value of -3 is then the *cell evaluator* of cell AT. The minus sign indicates a cost reduction; that is, the transaction in this case is favorable.

> *Definition.* The cell evaluator is the sum of the costs of all cells that gained one unit minus the sum of the costs of all cells that lost one unit.

This evaluation process must now be extended to *all* unoccupied cells.

Cost analysis. By drawing these closed loops, *all* the empty cells of Table 6.9 can be evaluated. The results are

Empty Cell	Cell Evaluator
AT	−3
BR	+4
DR	+5
DS	+4

Test of optimality. Once the cell evaluators for *all* the empty cells have been computed, their signs are examined.

Test for a minimization (cost) problem. If one or more of the cell evaluators is negative,* the existing solution is not optimal.

The logic for this test is that an empty cell (not presently part of the solution) with a negative sign will reduce the total cost if it becomes occupied. The proposed solution is thus *improvable* and therefore not optimal.

In the example just presented, cell AT has a negative evaluator. Thus, the initial solution of Table 6.9 is not optimal.

STEP **5. Improving a Nonoptimal Solution.** Having discovered that a solution is not optimal, the next step in the transportation algorithm is to find a better solution. The operations in this step are

1. Identify the "incoming" cell (empty cell to be occupied). In a minimization case the "incoming" cell is located by identifying the *most negative* cell evaluator.† In the example, the incoming cell is AT (since only one cell is negative).
2. *Design an improved solution.* Once the "incoming" cell has been identified, an improvement is made by shifting *as many units as possible* along the "closed

* A cell evaluator of 0 indicates the existence of another solution just as good as the current solution. Thus, in the final solution, if cell evaluators of 0 exist, this indicates the existence of multiple optimal solutions.

† If two or more cells have the same value, then either may be selected.

loop" into that empty cell. The quantity limit to this shifting process is reached when one of the two "losing" cells becomes empty.‡ In our case, of the two "losing" cells in Table 6.10, AS and BT, cell BT becomes empty first, when 10 units are shifted around the closed loop (10 from BT to BS, 10 from AS to AT). The improved solution is shown in Table 6.11. Once an improved solution is generated, the optimality test (step 4) is repeated.

Optimality test. The evaluators of all the empty cells are computed. The results are

Empty Cell	Cell Evaluator
BR	+4
BT	+3
DR	+2
DS	+1

Since *all* the empty cells have nonnegative cell evaluators, an optimal solution has been obtained. This optimal solution calls for a shipment of

80 units from A to R at a cost of $1/ton, total	$ 80
10 units from A to S at a cost of $2/ton, total	20
10 units from A to T at a cost of $3/ton, total	30
110 units from B to S at a cost of $1/ton, total	110
50 units from dummy to T at no cost	0
Total cost	$240

TABLE 6.11 IMPROVED SOLUTION

Source \ Destination	R	S	T	Supply
A	80 [1]	10 [2]	10 [3]	100
B	[4]	110 [1]	[5]	110
D (dummy)	[0]	[0]	50 [0]	50
Demand	80	120	60	260

‡ If two or more of the "losing" cells contain the same number of units, both will become empty simultaneously and a "degenerate" solution will result (see Reference 19 for solution approaches).

This, compared with the original Northwest Corner solution, represents a reduction in cost of $30. Notice that the demand requirements of destination T have, in reality, not been completely satisfied since 50 units are shipped out of the dummy source D.

6.9 SUMMARY

The distribution function of logistics is dependent on the two operations activities of facility location and goods transportation. Depending on the economics of the situation and the nature of the output (some services and products are not highly transportable) the distribution function will be composed of varying combinations of location and transportation.

Organizations that process voluminous, or highly perishable, natural resources to obtain a much smaller output will locate near the source of their raw materials and transport the output. On the other hand, organizations that produce relatively immobile outputs such as dams and roads will locate at the final site itself. Some organizations have relatively minor transportation costs and thus will locate on the basis of other factors such as available labor. But most organizations will have to consider all factors together and trade them off to determine the best location-transportation mix for distributing their outputs.

The five basic modes of transport are water, pipeline, rail, truck, and air. Water and pipelining are the lest expensive but are slow and often inaccessible. In addition, pipelines are limited to slurry forms of products. Water and rail are the major transport modes in the long-haul, high-tonnage market. Rail is quite accessible, inexpensive for large volumes, and can handle a variety of products.

Trucking is the major transport mode in the short-haul market, especially since the addition of a number of trucking services. Air transport is most appropriate for low-weight, low-volume, high-value products, or highly perishable products, where speed of delivery is essential for customer service.

The determination of the number of transporting vehicles, their capacities, and the best routes for each is known as the routing problem. When only one vehicle is considered the problem is called "the traveling salesman problem."

The location decision for an organization is usually broken into three stages:

- **National/International** The issues of concern are proximity to the raw materials and recipients; type and supply of labor; availability of land, supplies, transportation, and utilities; and acceptability of the overall "environment."
- **Community** Issues here duplicate those above but also include community receptiveness, financing, and staff preferences.
- **Site** Size, zoning, utilities, transportation, and development costs are the major concerns here.

For either product or service organizations there may exist a number of complexities regarding the distribution system.

- There may be more than one distribution criterion to satisfy.
- Output demand levels may be unknown.
- There may be multiple products.
- There may be an unspecified number of multiple facilities.
- The potential locations of the facilities may be unspecified.
- There may be intermediate distribution levels.

Some techniques for handling these complexities are available. Multiple criteria may be handled by a "weighted score" type of model and uncertainty by a breakeven model. Incremental analysis is an important approach for both the single and multi-facility problems. Also for multiple facilities, when the potential sites are known, the transportation variant of linear programming can be usefully applied to allocate the output.

6.10 READINGS

Hewlett-Packard After One Year

by ROBERT GOLDSTEIN

When Hewlett-Packard Company (HP) announced it was moving its lucrative Advanced Products Division (maker of HP pocket calculators) from Cupertino, California to Corvallis, it caused quite a stir in the university town of 40,000.

Local businessmen were elated, administrators at Oregon State University envisioned growth in their School of Engineering graduate programs and some city council members welcomed the prospect of a solid industrial tax base.

But not all residents saw HP's arrival as a blessing. A vocal minority argued that HP would start an avalanche of industries descending on Corvallis, ruining the city's livability and swelling its population to unmanageable proportions.

That was about three years ago.

Now the first phase of HP's four phase $37 million facility is in operation. The effects when noticed are difficult to separate from the city's regular growth pattern.

"There's no way of segregating out what effect HP people and HP has had on the waste water plant," says Alton Andrews, Corvallis utilities engineer. In fact, adds Andrews, the city's sewage decreased by 150,000 million gallons between 1976 and 1977 "in spite of any growth."

The economic impacts, so far as they can be measured, have ranged from nothing to mildly positive.

"I can definitely notice a difference in sales due to HP people," says Eric Blackledge, owner of Blackledge Furniture and president of the Downtown Businessmen's Association. "We notice this because we ask about employment on credit applications."

He says business in general is up in town, but he isn't sure how much of this can be credited to HP.

OSU with its 16,000 students, 1,200 faculty members and an army of classified workers, is the city's largest industry. University growth has leveled off recently, but the corresponding slack in business has not occurred this year, says Blackledge. He adds that HP people seem to be compensating for this lag.

Roy Cop, a J. C. Penney's employee is still bemoaning the closure of a local cannery that provided many jobs.

"That hurt," he says, "but little by little something has made the difference."

Cop says he cannot determine whether to attribute that "something" to HP.

Carmen West, an HP marketing engineer who transferred from Cupertino, says she and her husband do most of their "small item" shopping in Corvallis. But for the big ticket items like furniture, she says they "hunted around in Salem and Eugene."

Another transferee, David Curtis and his wife have adopted the same shopping habits of the West's. Curtis says he recently bought a truck in Eugene.

PREDICTED IMPACTS

To assure wary residents that it indeed was a clean industry and would not ruin Corvallis, HP contacted Parametrix Inc. a Eugene counsulting firm to do a study on the impacts of that proposed plant. The study was a prerequisite for HP's approval by the city council.

The study, completed in September 1974, predicted that phase 1 would employ 500 persons with a total disposable income of $4 million. When all four phases are completed sometime around 1992, HP will employ 4,900 persons with a disposable income of about $39.2 million.

The study also notes that most of the local employees would come from the unemployed in Corvallis (Benton County) and neighboring Albany (Linn County) and that no supporting electronics industries were expected to move in. HP calculator components, it explains, were to be shipped in from other HP divisions.

Parametrix wasn't far off its original estimates (the differences can be attributed largely to a change in siting plans made after the study was completed).

Parmelee Brooks, an HP personnel employee, says slightly more than 600 persons are now working at the plant. Of this total about 250 transferred from Cupertino with the remaining employees coming almost exclusively from Benton and Linn Counties.

HP's penchant for hiring, however, caused some concern at OSU.

Wil Post, administrative assistant to OSU's President Robert MacVicar, says at one time the university feared HP would hire away the school's best secretaries.

Because many employees would be commuting via cars the study also took special note of the roads leading to and from the plant. According to the study the roads "had sufficient capacity at full plant development."

However, Jack Barrow, Corvallis traffic engineer, says there has been an increase in city traffic on the streets near HP and he thinks much of it is a result of the new plant.

A survey comparing traffic flow from 1975 to 1976 shows a significant increase in cars per day on these roads.

REAL ESTATE PRICES CLIMB

Perhaps the most dramatic economic effect is on property values.

"Homes which sold for $17,000 before (HP's arrival) are now selling for $30,000," says a realtor at O'Hare and Associates. He adds that most homes sold to HP people were in the $50,000 to $90,000 range.

A Dee Jay Realty spokesman also says his big increase in business has been greatest for homes selling for more than $50,000.

Increased property values means a higher assessed valuation which translates into more money for the city and county. The assessed valuation of property purchased by HP personnel to date should bring in about $152,000 in additional property taxes, says the study.

But the biggest contributor to property taxes will be HP itself.

"This is the first time we've had an industry move in that will help reduce the tax rate," says Lloyd Anderson, Benton County tax assessor.

Anderson and members of the city council have good reason to be happy with HP. Since much of the city's property is occupied by OSU and federal agencies (the Environmental Protection Agency and the U.S. Forest Service both have regional offices in Corvallis), which are immune from paying property taxes, Corvallis must rely on small businesses and property owners to finance city services and School District 509J. Lately residents have grown increasingly hostile to property tax increases regularly rejecting city and school district budgets on the first ballot.

Anderson says HP will pay about $138,000 in property taxes this year. That, however, is peanuts compared to the $1.6 million the company is expected to contribute to city and county coffers by 1991.

The Parametrix study shows that the school district will also benefit greatly from the increased valuation. By 1991 about 314 new students from HP families are expected to be enrolled in district schools, but these students will bring with them about a $1.2 million surplus over the cost of their education.

Anderson says the surplus could be used by the district to offset property tax increases in the future.

One HP criteria for selecting a site for its Advanced Products Division was location near a "major" university, preferably one with a school of engineering, says HP's Curtis. He says the reasons for this were the company's desire to give its employees an opportunity to pursue post-graduate studies on a part-time basis and to be near a technically orientated student labor force.

Curtis notes that the division, when operating in Cupertino, had significant interaction with Santa Clara University and Stanford University.

OSU administrators also see HP's arrival as an advantage.

"Our understanding is that at full development HP will employ 500 (persons) in research and development," says Fred Burgess, dean of the School of Engineering. "We feel our students will be part of this 500."

HP's close proximity will help the engineering faculty keep up with what's happening in industry, he says.

Ron Mohler, head of the electrical engineering department, says there has been "a lot of discussion" with HP about various programs, but it was "too early to be specific."

Mohler says his department has received many promises of good things to come from HP.

Source. Engineering Focus, School of Engineering, Oregon State University, June 1977, p. 3. Reprinted by permission of Oregon State University, School of Engineering.

6.11 KEY TERMS

Concepts

logistics (p. 152)
distribution function (p. 152)
stockouts (p. 152)
unit load (p. 153)
automated data processing (p. 153)
economies of scale (p. 153)
pipelining (p. 155)
slurry (p. 155)
routing problem (p. 157)
traveling salesman problem (p. 157)
mode of transport (p. 155)
piggyback (p. 155)
weighted score (p. 163)
right-to-work laws (p. 159)
decision criterion (p. 162)

Tools and Applications

transportation method (p. 172)
linear programming (p. 172)
incremental analysis (p. 168)
multifacility (p. 170)

6.12 REVIEW TEST

Concepts

1. Transportation is a major distribution method for service organizations. (p. 153)
   a. True b. False
2. Which of the following is *not* a major mode of product transport? (p. 154)
   a. Rail b. Pipeline c. Auto d. Ship
   e. Plane
3. Since finished lumber is so heavy, most lumbermills locate near their customers. (p. 153)
   a. True b. False
4. If the transportation cost is immaterial then organizations will locate according to other criteria. (p. 154)
   a. True b. False
5. Rail is a major transport mode in both the short-haul and long-haul markets. (p. 155)
   a. True b. False
6. Pipelines can only transport products whose natural state is liquid or gaseous. (p. 155)
   a. True b. False
7. After solving the distribution-transportation-location problem there is often still a routing problem to be solved. (p. 157)
   a. True b. False
8. Zoning is an important location factor at the community stage of the location decision. (p. 161)
   a. True b. False
9. Magazines are forms of distribution intermediaries. (p. 158)
   a. True b. False
10. There is no distribution problem when the facilities are mobile. (p. 158)
    a. True b. False
11. The manner of weighting factors in a weighted score model may be subjective. (p. 163)
    a. True b. False

Tools and Applications

12. Breakeven type models always plot dollars against volume. (p. 166)
    a. True b. False
13. Incremental analysis is useful for both single and multiple facility problems. (p. 168)
    a. True b. False
14. The transportation method is useful for handling multiple, unspecified sites. (p. 170)
    a. True b. False

6.13 DISCUSSION QUESTIONS

1. When would an organization *not* use the three-stage location decision approach discussed in the chapter?
2. Describe other methods for handling multiple criteria. For handling uncertainty or risk.
3. What factors would be considered in locating an airport in a metropolitan area?
4. How much financial inducement should governments be allowed to offer companies to locate in their area?
5. For what service organizations is transportation a viable method of distribution?
6. How have the "piggyback," and now "fishyback," concepts improved the transportation of goods?
7. Contrast the terms logistics, materials management, procurement, purchasing, distribution, and materiel.
8. Are there any other special categories of organizations than the four given whose characteristics might determine where they locate?
9. Interpret the meaning of the data in Table 6.1; in particular, trucking has 40.5% of the tonnage but water 43.7% of the ton-miles.
10. What other products might be suitable for slurrying for pipelines?
11. What transport modes does the U.S. Post Office use?
12. Interpret the routing problem for garbage trucks. For U-Haul trucks. For prescription deliveries out of a drug store.

6.14 PROBLEMS

Concepts

1. Nina Lewis is trying to decide in which of four shopping centers to locate her new boutique. Some cater to a higher class of clientele than others, some are in an indoor mall, some have a much greater volume than others, and, of course, rent varies considerably. Because of the nature of her store she has decided that the class of clientele is the most important consideration. Following this, however, she *must* pay attention to her expenses and rent is a major item, probably 90 percent as important as clientele. An indoor, temperature-controlled mall is a big help, however, for stores such as hers where 70 percent of sales are from passersby slowly strolling and window shopping. Thus, she rates this as about 95 percent as important as rent. Lastly, a higher volume of shoppers means more potential sales and she thus rates this factor as 80 percent as important as rent.

To aid her in visualizing her location alternatives she has constructed the following table. A *Good* is scored as 3, *Fair* as 2, and *Poor* as 1. Use a weighted score model to help Nina come to a decision.

	Location			
	1	2	3	4
Class of clientele	*Fair*	*Good*	*Poor*	*Good*
Rent	*Good*	*Fair*	*Poor*	*Good*
Indoor mall	*Good*	*Poor*	*Good*	*Poor*
Volume	*Good*	*Fair*	*Good*	*Poor*

Tools and Applications

2. The location subcommittee's final report to the board has focused on three acceptable communities. Table 15b in the appendix to the report indicates the cost of locating in communities 1, 2, and 3 to be approximately \$400,000, \$500,000 and \$600,000 per year amortized over 30 years. Paragraph two on page 39 of the report indicates the variable cost per unit of product will increase 15 percent in community 1 but decrease 15 percent in community 3 due to labor rate differences. As plant operations manager you know that variable costs to date have averaged about \$3.05 per unit and sales for the next decade are expected to average 20 percent more than the last 10 years, which saw annual sales vary between 40,000 and 80,000 units. Which location would you recommend?

3. Father Sarratt must decide which site to choose for the new parish emerging in the northern suburb of the city. Most of the important factors such as land and building costs, priest selection, and so on have already been considered by the appropriate committees. Father Sarratt's concern, however, is with a potential future shortage of nuns for the accompanying school. Having considered the other factors mentioned above, the final choice is now between a lower-middle (LM) class region and an upper-middle (UM) class region. In the former region the initial number of nuns needed would only be 10 but would increase at the rate of one extra nun per 1000 increase in city population because of the low percentage of community volunteers in such regions. The upper-middle class region would originally require 15 nuns but due to the higher community awareness and volunteer rate, would only require one extra nun per 3000 increase in city population.

Father Sarratt then remembers his conversation with the city manager last Sunday after Mass regarding how much things had changed in the community in the last 15 years. He recalled the city manager saying that the entire city had grown considerably and would probably continue increasing in population at about 2000 per year for the next few years.

Use the breakeven model to help Father Sarratt reach a decision.

4. Use a map of the United States to optimally decide between Chicago and St. Louis to locate a single facility to serve the following cities.

a. Portland, Oregon—5 carloads per week.
b. Des Moines, Iowa—2 carloads per week.
c. New York, N.Y.—1 carload per week.
d. St. Louis, Missouri—7 carloads per week.
e. Chicago, Illinois—10 carloads per week.
f. New Orleans, Louisiana—5 carloads per week.

Assume the same transportation rate per carload to all destinations and a zero cost for same city delivery (e.g., Chicago to Chicago). Use straight-line distances measured by a ruler.

5. You are an ant on a window screen at $x = 3, y = 4$. There are three deadly spiders which you fear at ($x = 4, y = 2$), (1,5), and (6,6) with deadlinesses 2, 3, and 5, respectively. Develop an index of fear based on the spiders' distance (along the wires) and deadliness and determine if there exists a path to get away from your uncomfortable situation without getting more uncomfortable in the process. (Assume the spiders do not move and you and the spiders can only travel along the screen's wires.) See figure below.

6. Consider Problem 4 again, assuming two small warehouses can be built and operated for 50% more than a single ($175,000/yr) warehouse. What per mile cost results in the same expense as the best answer in Problem 4 if the two warehouses are located in Chicago and St. Louis?

7. Given below are three potential warehouse locations to serve four customer regions. In which location should a warehouse be built and what regions should it serve?

Potential Warehouse Location	Warehouse Annual Fixed Cost ($)	Annual Variable Cost to Serve Each Customer Region ($)			
		Northeast	Southeast	Central	South
1	100,000	80,000	115,000	200,000	210,000
2	120,000	100,000	220,000	190,000	200,000
3	125,000	150,000	110,000	210,000	100,000

8. A firm owns facilities at five geographically remote locations. It has manufacturing plants at points A and B with daily production capacities of 60 and 40 units, respectively. At points C, D, and E it has warehouses with daily demands of 20, 30, and 50 units, respectively. Shipping costs between these points are exactly proportional to the distances between them, which are indicated in miles below.

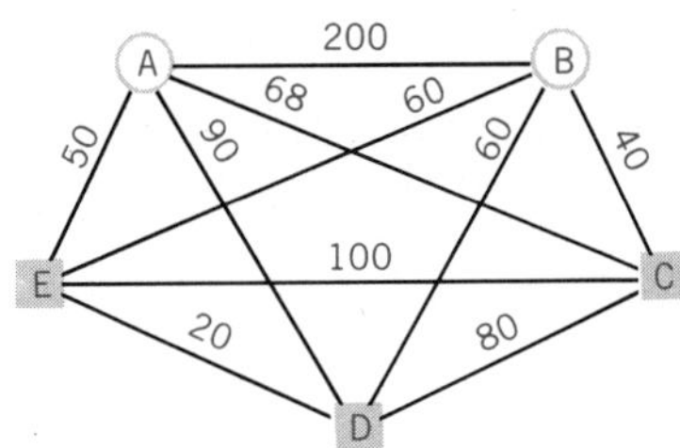

a. Given that the firm wishes to minimize its total transportation costs, formulate as a transportation problem.
b. Solve using the transportation method.

9. The Pollution Control Board of Alligator County has 100 employees: 20 live in city A, 35 in city B, and 45 in city C. The employees have interchangeable skills and are to be assigned to various laboratories. The Water Laboratory requires 40 employees, the Air Lab requires 30 employees, the Solid Waste Lab requires 20 employees, and the Central Lab requires 10 employees. The distance between the cities and the labs is shown on the map below (in miles along the available streets).

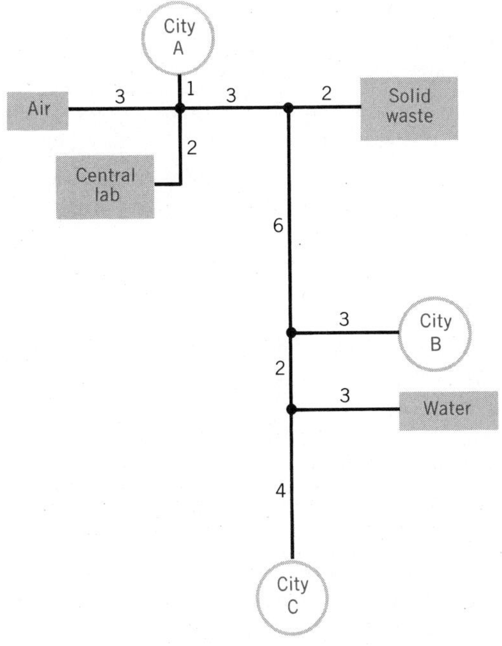

Workers travel by the shortest available route along the streets shown. What worker to lab arrangement minimizes the total distances traveled by all the employees?

a. Formulate as a transportation problem.

b. Solve.

c. What assumptions are necessary in this case?

10. The service man for Bells & Whistles Computer Corp. is located in Cincinnati, Ohio. Bells & Whistles has two installations in Lexington, Kentucky, one in Huntington, West Virginia, three in Louisville, Kentucky, and three in Cincinnati. Travel distances to the cities are shown on the following map.

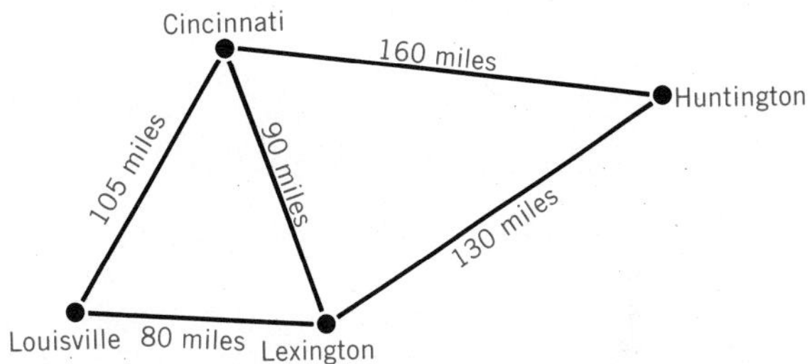

Bells & Whistles is considering the transfer of the service man to Lexington, Kentucky. Based upon a $20 per mile trip cost, which of the two cities would be the best location, assuming that each installation is visited once each week and that only two calls can be made each day and no more than 400 miles can be driven in a day? The service man returns home each night since motel costs would exceed the travel cost.

6.15 CASE RED RIVER BLOOD CENTER

Red River is a community of 65,000 people in which there are three hospitals with a total of 287 beds. The Red River Blood Center was formed four years ago to provide the needed whole blood and plasma for emergency and surgical use within the three hospitals. The blood center is also part of a statewide network that shares blood resources. The Center is located downtown next to the largest of the three hospitals. It is on the fourth floor of a doctors' office building.

Given the size of the Red River community, the blood center does relatively poorly in attracting a sufficient number of blood donors. The administrator of the Red River Blood Center is constantly calling on other members of the network to provide blood needed in emergency cases. On the other hand, Red River is very seldom able to help other members of the network in their emergencies. During the initial two years of operations, the administration believed that newness of the center was the cause for "substandard" donor performance. But, now that the center has been operating for four years, that "excuse" will no longer hold up. Donors have often complained of the horrible traffic conditions downtown and the fact that parking is so scarce.

One of the lab technicians who recently moved from

a larger community commented about the use of a mobile blood unit and setting up temporary clinics in meeting halls and other public facilities. She indicated that numerous civic and religious organizations had helped in organizing blood drives through their memberships. The new assistant administrator even commented about the possibility of moving from the downtown location to an outlying shopping center. The administrator argued that the blood center was located where it was to be close to the hospitals.

QUESTIONS FOR DISCUSSION

1. What location/transportation tradeoffs have been made here?
2. Comment on the "demand(s)" made by the blood center's constituents.
3. What factors should be considered in comparing the benefits and costs of mobile or temporary units with a shopping center-based unit?

6.16 REFERENCES AND BIBLIOGRAPHY

1. Ammer, D. S., *Materials Management*, Homewood, Ill.: Irwin, 1962.
2. Anderson, D. R., D. J. Sweeney, and T. A. Williams, *Linear Programming for Decision Making: An Applications Approach*, St. Paul, Minn.: West Publishing, 1974.
3. Beckman, M., *Location Theory*, New York: Random House, 1968.
4. Brown, P. A., and D. F. Gibson, "A Quantified Model for Facility Site Selection—Application to a Multiplant Location Problem," *AIIE Transactions*, 4:1–10 (1972).
5. Easton, A., *Complex Managerial Decisions Involving Multiple Objectives*, New York: Wiley, 1973.
6. Geoffrion, A. M., and G. W. Graves, "Multicommodity Distribution Systems Design by Benders Decomposition," *Management Science*, 20:822–844 (1974).
7. Hoover, E. M., "Some Programmed Models of Industry Location," *Land Economics*, 18:303–311 (1967).
8. Karasaka, G. J., and D. F. Browball, *Location Analysis for Manufacturing*, Cambridge, Mass.: The MIT Press, 1969.
9. Khumawala, B. M., and D. C. Whybark, "A Comparison of Some Recent Warehouse Location Techniques," *The Logistics Review*, 7:63 (1971).
10. McGarrah, R. E., *Production and Logistics Management*, New York: Wiley, 1963.
11. Magee, J. F., *Industrial Logistics*, New York: McGraw-Hill, 1968.
12. ———, *Physical Distribution Systems*, New York: McGraw-Hill, 1967.
13. Markland, R. E., "Analyzing Geographically Discrete Warehousing Networks by Computer Simulation," *Decision Sciences*, 4:216–236 (1973).
14. Meredith, J. R., and A. Shershin, "Locating Emergency Medical Rescue Vehicles Under Conditions of Urgency," *Computers and Industrial Engineering*, 2:31–39 (1978).
15. O'Neil, B . F., and D. C. Whybark, "Vehicle Routing from Central Facilities," *The International Journal of Physical Distribution*, February, 1972.
16. ReVelle, C., P. Marks, and J. D. C. Liebman, "An Analysis of Private and Public Sector Location Models," *Management Science*, 16:692–707 (1970).
17. Smykay, E. W., *Physical Distribution Management*, 3rd ed., New York: Macmillan, 1973.
18. Tertz, M. B., "Toward a Theory of Urban Public Facility Location," *Papers of the Regional Science Assocation*, 21:35–51 (1968).
19. Turban, E., and J. R. Meredith, *Fundamentals of Management Science*, Dallas, Texas: Business Publications, 1977.

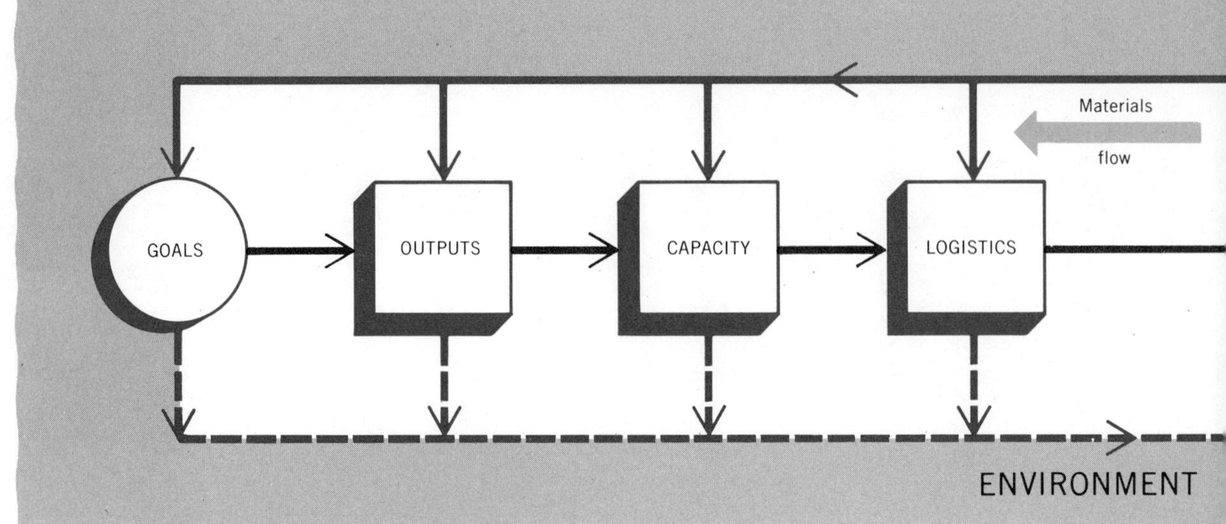

Chapter 7

Designing the Transformation Process

CONCEPTS

7.1 Forms of Transformation Processes
- Intermittent
- Continuous
- Batch
- Project

7.2 Process Design for Intermittent Operations
- Advantages of the Intermittent Form
- Disadvantages of the Intermittent Form
- Process Layout for Intermittent Operations
  - *The Department Chairman's Office*
  - *CRAFT*

7.3 Process Design for Continuous Operations
- Advantages of the Continuous Form
- Disadvantages of the Continuous Form
- Process Layout for Continuous Operations

7.4 Processing Industries

7.5 Project Processes
- Choosing the Project Form of Process Design
- Project Process Design
- The Project Operations Manager

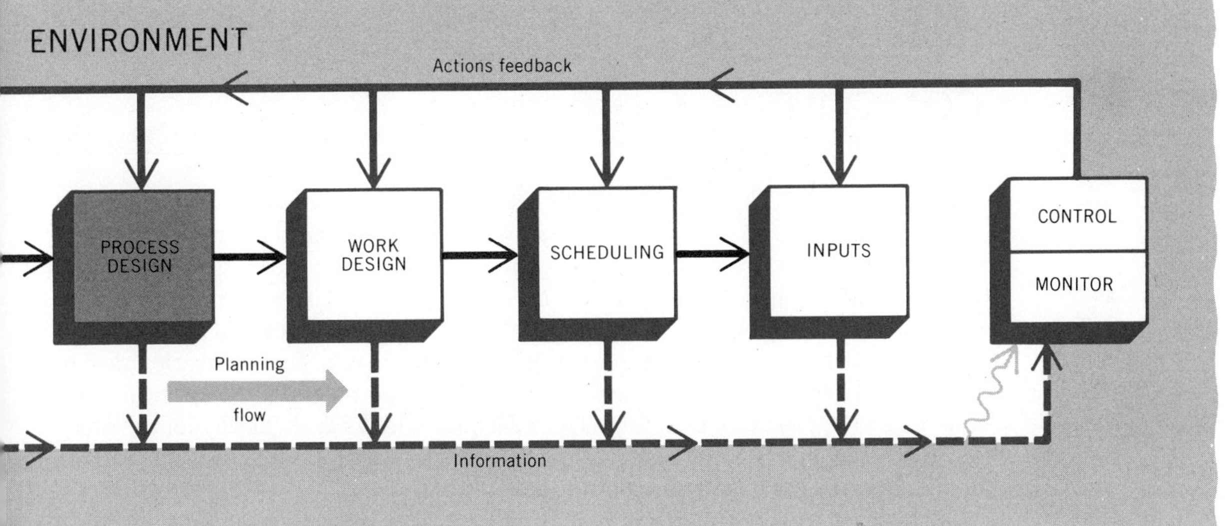

TOOLS AND APPLICATIONS

LEARNING OBJECTIVES

By the conclusion of the *Concepts* portion of this chapter the student should

1. Appreciate the complexity of transformation process design and the tradeoffs involved.
2. Realize that process design is a continuing process rather than a one-time task.
3. Understand the differences between intermittent, continuous, batch, and project process forms.
4. Be familiar with the advantages and disadvantages of intermittent processes.
5. Know the basis for laying out intermittent process operations and the available computer routines.
6. Be familiar with the characteristics of the continuous process design form and its advantages and disadvantages.
7. Understand the procedure for designing continuous process operations.
8. Comprehend the differences between and similarities of the "processing" industries and continuous (unit) process organizations.

CONCEPTS

Chapter 7 focuses directly on the central issue of operations management, designing the transformation process. This is where we decide whether to use mostly labor or mostly machines, whether to employ pushcarts or conveyer belts, whether to hire primarily physicians or nurses, and so on. Up to this point in our progress we have determined how much capacity we will need and how the output will be distributed to the recipients. Now, we will devote two chapters to the transformation design process. Chapter 7 deals with the "form" of the process and how the operations are laid out in the production facility. Then Chapter 8 looks at the design of the work itself in considerably more detail—the work environment, how individual workers do their job, the organization structure, and so forth.

This chapter concerns the design of the central element in the operations function: the transformation activities. The general procedure in designing the transformation process is to consider all available transformation alternatives in combination with all potential inputs to devise the best strategy for obtaining the desired outputs.

The major considerations in process design.

The major considerations in this design are **efficiency, effectiveness, capacity,** and **flexibility**. Unfortunately, these considerations are so interdependent that changing the process to alter one will change the others as well.

Suppose, for example, that you decide to go into business for yourself by producing skateboards. There are many options open to you. In terms of the product, you could produce wooden skateboards, plastic boards, or even metal boards. The wheels, too, could be steel or high impact plastic, perhaps tinted or bright translucent red.

Wooden, plastic, or metal skateboards.

Now a wooden board would be simple to make—you could even work out of your own garage. On the other hand, each board would take quite a while to saw, plane, sand, and so on. Much faster would be injection molding a plastic board. You could produce them by the thousands, and at very low cost. But the molding dies will cost you about $30,000. ("How much money did you say you had?") And you would have to subcontract the work because injection molding machines are way beyond your league.

So far we have been talking about efficiency, capacity, and flexibility. That is, garage produced wooden boards would be a low capacity, high flexibility operation efficient for low volumes at high prices. But is there a market for wooden boards at high prices? If not, such an operation will not be very *effective*—at least in terms of making a profit. Perhaps a more effective process would be to invest in some semiautomatic equipment to produce a higher volume at a lower unit price.

As you can see from this simple example, the design of the transformation process is a rather complex, but important, procedure. Numerous tradeoffs are available between different materials, labor and equipment, quality and volume, efficiency and flexibility; and every tradeoff will affect the success of your business.

But the transformation design problem is one that never has a final answer; there are only answers given the present circumstances, and circumstances are always changing. Although successful organizations such as Ford Motor Co., the Red Cross, and Sears, Roebuck and Co. may appear to be common, they in fact are exceptions in the world of organizations. Their key to continued success is that they have constantly redesigned their transformation process as the environment and demand changed—that is, they have *adapted*. Many organizations chose, or continued to use, a transformation process that was not viable for the environment or demand; in some cases *no* transformation process would have been viable because the market was insufficient, or the technology was unavailable.

Process design is an unending problem: Adaptation is the key.

In an environment of constant change the transformation process may have to be constantly redesigned to cope with changing demands, new products and services, government regulations, and constant technological advances. Automation, materials scarcities, integrated circuitry, and energy shortages are only a few examples of the changes in the past decade which have forced organizations to recognize the necessity of adaptation in their operations.

Constant environmental change.

7.1 FORMS OF TRANSFORMATION PROCESSES

A general schematic of the transformation process design is illustrated in Figure 7.1. Initially, the desired output is specified in terms of function (form, quality, etc.) and quantity for a given time horizon (e.g., 100 wooden skateboards a month for the first year). The output is then subdivided into a set of natural or logical components (wheels, boards, screws), each of which can be separately studied. This procedure may be repeated with subcomponents (ballbearings) and sub-subcomponents until some elemental component is reached. Each component is then analyzed to determine how it can be (1) obtained (make or buy), and (2) combined with other components (screws, glue). Consideration is given to equipment, staffing, leasing, subcontracting, workplace design, tooling, and so forth. Continuous specification and respecification of both the output (fiberglass boards?), and the process (100 percent hand made?), is required to remain competitive, simplify the process, make it more efficient, improve output quality, increase flexibility or output rate, eliminate bottlenecks, and so on.

The general design procedure.

Historically, process designs have tended to evolve along one of the following four lines.

Intermittent

In this design each output is processed differently and therefore the flow of work through the facility tends to be of an **intermittent** nature. The general characteristics of this form are a grouping of staff and equipment according to function (all sawing in one area); a large variety of inputs; a considerable amount of transport of either staff, materials, or recipients; and large variations in system throughput times. In general, each output takes a different route through the organization, requires different operations, uses different inputs, and takes a different amount of time.

Intermittent design for one-of-a-kind outputs.

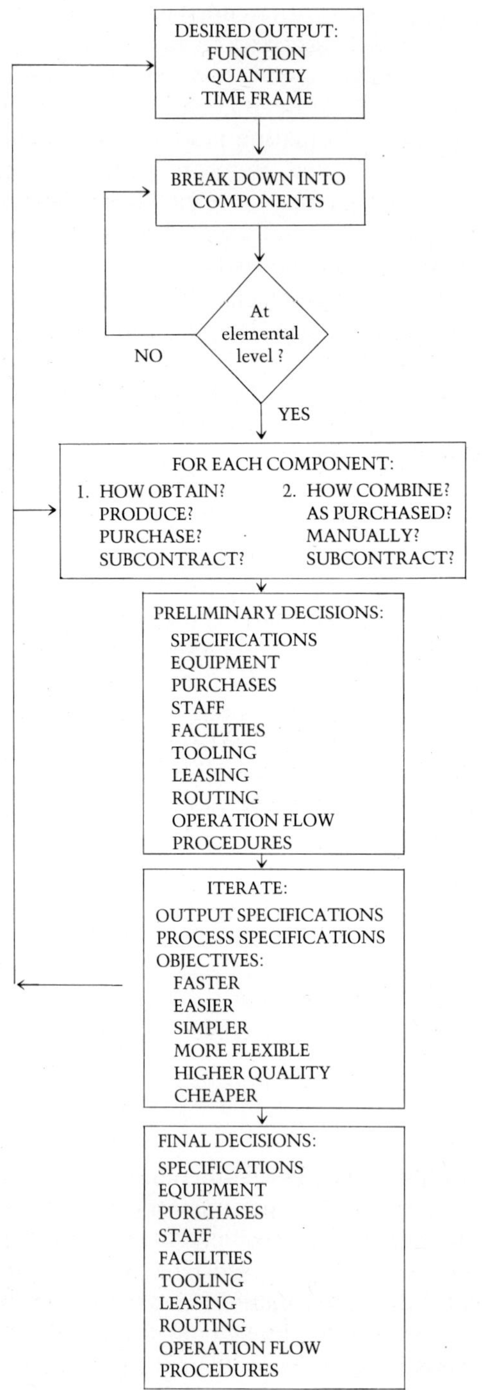

Figure 7.1. The general transformation process.

This type of process design is common when the outputs differ significantly in their form, structure, materials, or their required processing. For example, an organization with a wide variety of outputs or one that does custom work (e.g., custom skateboards) would probably use an intermittent process form.

The job shop.

Product organizations of this type are known as **job shops**. Specific examples of both product and service organizations of this form are tailor shops, general offices, machine shops, public parks, physician's offices, supermarkets, libraries, automobile repair shops, criminal justice systems, department stores, and wholesalers. Note that, by and large, the intermittent process is especially appropriate to service organizations. This is because services are often customized and hence each service (e.g., serving a department store customer) requires different operations. Process design for intermittent operations will be discussed in detail in Section 7.2.

Continuous

Continuous design form for identical outputs.

In this design form all of the outputs are, basically, treated the same and work flow is thus relatively **continuous**. Product organizations of this form are called **flow shops** and often are heavily automated. The characteristics of this process design are relatively fixed inputs, operations, throughput times, and outputs. Only one route usually exists which is generally known as the "line." If the operation is the physical *assembly* of a product (e.g., one type of skateboard), then the line is called an **assembly line**. A special type of continuous design is the **processing plant** such as is used in the production of drugs, chemicals, and petroleum products.

Other examples of the continuous form are food processors, steel mills, automobile manufacturers, multiphasic medical screening, the automatic car wash, and life insurance application processing. Process design for continuous operations will be specificaly addressed in Sections 7.3 and 7.4.

Batch

Batch form for limited inputs.

This process is characterized by a short run of one particular output and then a run of another, different output (different models of skateboards). If the output is a product, the **batch** may be produced to fill a customer's order or to restock inventories. Between runs the process is usually modified (called **setup**). During a run the process may either appear in continuous or intermittent form. Examples of the former are theaters, clothing manufacturers, and touring agencies. Examples of the latter are roving carnivals and furniture manufacturing.

Most processes are batch.

Batch processing usually occurs when there is a fixed amount of a particular input such as one fabric design, one color of paint, one "brochure-full" of information, and so forth. Since, in reality, almost all outputs are run in batches due to fixed sizes of groups of inputs, the distinction between intermittent, batch, and continuous processing is somewhat artificial. Theoretically, in intermittent operations every output is different and in continuous operations every output is identical. However, in actual use these strict limits are rarely considered and the concepts of intermittent and continuous are "stretched" to also cover small batches and large batches, respectively, as illustrated in Figure 7.2.

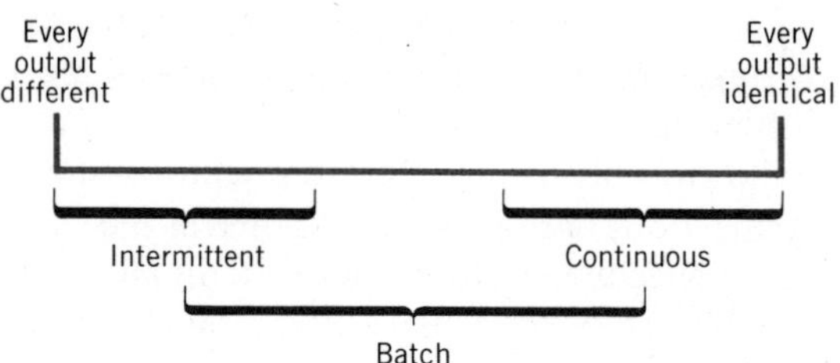

Figure 7.2. The overlap in intermittent, batch and continuous processes.

For example, machine shops typically make up batches of machine castings and automobile manufacturers produce batches of different sized engines for their cars. Services are often available in batches also; airline flights, rock concerts, and church services are typical examples.

Project

Project form for fixed-position assemblies.

The primary characteristics of the **project** form of process design are that the operations are of limited duration and, if the output is a physical product, are immobile during processing (referred to as **fixed position** assembly). Examples of projects are firefighting, political campaigns, corporate audits, landscaping, some forms of mining, and the construction of roads, pipelines, airplanes, buildings, ships, dams, tunnels, and large machine tools.

Limited lives.

Generally, the staff, materials, and equipment are brought to the output and located in a nearby **staging area** until needed. Projects have particularly limited "lives." Resources are brought together for the duration of the project, some are consumed and others, such as equipment and personnel, are deployed to other uses at the conclusion of the project.

Frequently, the output is unique (dam, fire) but need not be (airplanes, buildings). Furthermore, once at the staging area, the process may even appear to be more continuous in nature than intermittent. For example, housing reconstruction in Europe following World War II utilized mammoth equipment that would dig entire basements at once or pour complete foundations and then roll over to the next homesite and do the same thing.

Most operations are combined forms.

From the above discussion it should be noted that these four processing forms are somewhat simplified extremes of what is likely to be observed in practice. Few organizations use one of the above four transformation processes in a pure sense; most combine two or more forms together. For example, in manufacturing typewriters, some subassemblies are produced in *intermittent* form but then feed into a *continuous* final assembly line where a *batch* of one model is produced and then the line is modified to produce a batch of another model.

Mass producing services.

Although services are typically of intermittent form, the emphasis has recently been on trying to "mass produce" (i.e., continuous form) them so as to increase the volume and reduce their unit cost [Reference 18]. Some examples are fast-food outlets, multiphasic medical screening, and group life insurance. Even with services we often find combined forms of process design: McDonald's prepares *batches* of Big Mac's but will accept individual custom orders. Burger King uses a conveyorized *assembly line* for its Whoppers but advertises its ability to customize its burgers to suit any taste.

Some examples of the process designs selected by various organizations are listed in Table 7.1. A few of these deserve special mention. The social and character-building goals of the girl scouts dictate a complex of activities such as trips and camp-outs (projects), regular troop meetings (batch), training and counseling (intermittent), and cookie production (continuous). Similarly, the family has family *projects*, regular *batch* activities such as laundry and shopping, relatively *continuous* activities such as meal production and television viewing (assuming children are present), and *intermittent* activities such as baths, music lessons, and naps.

The problem for the operations manager is to decide what processing form is most appropriate for the organization, considering long run efficiency, effectiveness, capacity, and flexibility. The selection task may be even more difficult due to the possibility, as mentioned above, of combining processing forms to attain efficiency in some portions of the production process and flexibility or capacity in other portions. It is clear that the tradeoffs must be well understood by the manager and the expected benefits and costs well known. Unfortunately, such accurate knowledge frequently is *not* known beforehand and many organizations design processing activities that are not viable. To better understand these forms we will now discuss them in greater detail.

7.2 PROCESS DESIGN FOR INTERMITTENT OPERATIONS

Suppose you have decided to open up a local day-care service for neighborhood mothers (or fathers). As young couples tend to find out after awhile, every child is different.

TABLE 7.1 COMMON ORGANIZATIONAL DESIGN FORMS

	Process Design Form			
Organization	Intermittent	Continuous	Batch	Project
Hospital	X			
Railroad			X	
Farm		X	X	X
Supermarket	X			
University			X	
The family	X	X	X	X
Construction				X
Girl scouts	X	X	X	X
Church			X	
Charity				X
Distributor	X			
Chemical processor		X	X	

This means that your "care" for such children will probably also have to be different. Some like to be read to, others like to be left alone, some like toys, others like television, still others like children like themselves to play with, and almost all like to eat (but different things). As you can imagine, this makes for quite a mess.

You will need "general purpose" equipment (television, play yards, bicycles, juice and crackers) that appeals to general interests and varied ages. You cannot *afford* to buy equipment that only an 18-month old is interested in—you may not even *get* an 18-month old. Similarly, your staff should be broadly skilled—equally at home keeping records and forms, playing the piano, and making mud pies. Again, you cannot afford someone who can only keep books and hates mud.

What you have started is an organization designed along the *intermittent* transformation process form. An organization that desires to produce a wide variety of individualized outputs (reading, eating, playing) will probably utilize an intermittent production process to gain *flexibility*. To gain the flexibility required to produce the large variety of outputs, general purpose equipment and broadly skilled staff are necessary. Also, due to the variety of outputs there is usually a need for a variety of input materials.

The flexibility of intermittent processes.

Since only small volumes of any one output are produced, it is not worthwhile to form "production lines" for the outputs. (In a production line each child, one at a time, would first eat, then play with toys, then go to the restroom, then to the playground, then music, etc.) Instead of organizing around standard *outputs* the most efficient procedure for intermittent production is to organize around standard *operations functions*. In intermittent production, then, all similar types of operations are grouped together. For example, all the children have juice and crackers in one spot, sandbox play at another spot, and so on. Or in a hospital, all x-ray functions are grouped together, all pharmaceuticals together, and all obstetric patients together.

Organizing around standard operations.

The result of such a process design is that each output, or small group of outputs, follows a different processing "route" through the facility, from one location to another. This type of process design, as a result, usually requires a considerable amount of transportation equipment: fork lifts, pallet trucks, little legs, dumbwaiters, wheelchairs, and so forth. It also typically results in large variations in production times for different outputs to be processed (called **throughput time**) through the facility. (Many children are ready to go home by 10 A.M.; others want to stay forever.) Each output may require different operations or sequences, thereby using different paths through the process. In some instances, all the outputs require one common operation (such as use of the restroom or, in manufacturing, inspection) and hence bottlenecks may occur.

Characteristics of the intermittent process.

The difficulty of management.

Clearly, the efficient management of an intermittent process is a difficult task since every output must be treated differently. Also, the resources available to process them are limited. Furthermore, not only is it management's task to assure the performance of the proper functions of each output, where the outputs may have varying quality and deadline considerations, but management must also be sure that the available resources (staff, equipment, materials, supplies, capital) are being efficiently utilized. Some of the techniques available to operations managers to aid them in these tasks will be illustrated later.

Figure 7.3 pictorially represents the flow through an intermittent process operation. This facility may be a library, an auto repair shop, or an office. Each particular "job" travels from one operations area to another, and so on, according to its unique routing, until it is fully processed. Temporary in-process storage may occur between various operations while jobs are waiting for subsequent processing (standing in line for the coffee machine).

Product organizations that organize on an intermittent basis, such as machine shops, supermarkets, warehouses, and department stores, are known as "job-shops." But this form is also very common to service organizations such as physicians' offices, libraries, repair shops, and general offices. The widespread use of the job-shop process design form is due to its many advantages.

Job-shops for services too.

Advantages of the Intermittent Form

The intermittent design form is usually selected to provide the organization with the flexibility needed to respond to individual, small volume (or even custom) demands in the environment. The ability to produce a wide variety of outputs at reasonable cost is thus the primary advantage of this design form. Since general purpose rather than special purpose equipment is used, it is in greater demand and is usually available from more suppliers at a lower price than special purpose equipment. In addition, used equipment is more likely to be available, further reducing the necessary investment. There is a larger base of experience with general purpose equipment and therefore maintenance and setup problems are more predictable and replacement parts more widely available. Lastly, since general purpose equipment is easier to modify or use elsewhere and disposal is much easier, obsolecence expense is minimized.

Variety at low cost.

Because of the functional arrangement of the intermittent process design form, other advantages accrue to the organization as well. Functions requiring special staff, materials, or facilities (e.g., painting or audio-visual equipment) may centralize the location of these resources at that function and save through high utilization rates.

Facility advantages.

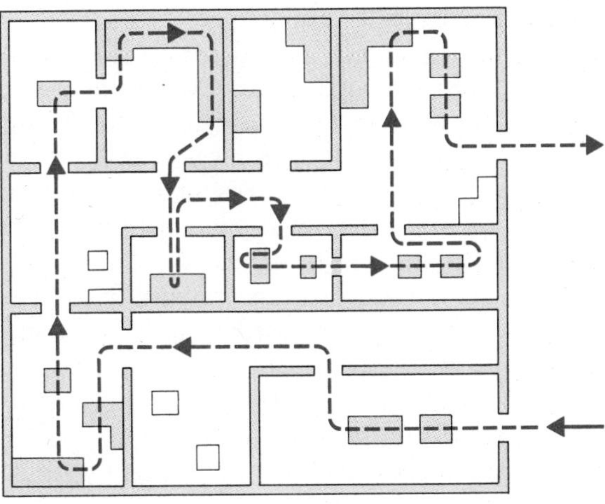

Figure 7.3. A generalized intermittent process design operation.

Distracting, or dangerous, equipment, supplies, or activities may also be segregated from other operations in soundproof, airtight, explosion proof, and so forth, facilities.

Staff advantages.

An advantage to the staff of a functional arrangement is the increased responsibility, pride of workmanship, and reduced boredom that accompanies more highly skilled work involving constantly varying jobs. Other advantages to the staff are the concentrations of experience and expertise available and the increase in morale when similarly skilled staff work together in the centralized locations (all music teachers together). And because the pace of the work is not dictated by a moving "line," incentive pay arrangements may be set up to further benefit the staff. Lastly, because no "line" exists that must forever keep moving, the entire set of organizational operations do not halt whenever any one part of the operation stops working; other functional areas can continue operating, at least until in-process inventory is depleted. And commonly, other general purpose resources can substitute for the nonfunctioning resource: one machine for another, one staff member for another, one material for another.

Disadvantages of the Intermittent Form

The general purpose equipment of intermittent processes is usually slower than special purpose equipment, resulting in higher variable (per unit) costs. In addition, the cost of direct labor for the experienced staff necessary to operate general purpose equipment further increases unit costs of production above what semi- or unskilled staff would require. The result, in terms of costs for the outputs, is that the variable costs of production for the general purpose equipment, facilities, and staff are higher than for special purpose, but the initial cost of the equipment and facilities is significantly less. For small output volumes the intermittent-process design alternative results in a lower total cost. As output volumes increase, however, the high variable costs begin to outweigh the savings in initial investment. The result is that, for high production volumes, the intermittent process design form is not the most economic (although its use may still be dictated by other considerations such as when particular equipment threatens workers' health or safety).

Poor for high volumes.

Inventories are also frequently a disadvantage in the intermittent form of operations, especially in product organizations. Not only do many types of raw materials, parts, and supplies have to be kept for the wide variety of outputs anticipated, but **in-process inventories**, that is, jobs waiting for processing, typically become very large and thereby represent a sizable capital investment for the organization. Because there are so many inventory items that must travel between operations areas to be processed, the materials handling costs are also typically high. Since the job routings between operations are not identical, inexpensive fixed materials handling mechanisms like conveyor belts cannot be used. Instead, larger and more costly materials handling equipment is used and therefore corridors and aisles must be large enough to accommodate them. This necessitates allocating even more facility space beyond the extra needed to store additional inventories.

Large inprocess inventory.

Lastly, management control of the intermittent form is extremely difficult, as mentioned earlier. Because of the output variety in function, processing, quality, and timing, the management tasks of routing, scheduling, cost accounting, and such become nearly impossible when the output demand is high. "Expeditors" must track down lost jobs and reorder priorities. And, in addition to watching the progress of individual jobs, management must continually strive to achieve the proper balance of materials, staff, and equipment; otherwise, highly expensive resources will sit idle while bottlenecks occur elsewhere. (In Chapter 9 we discuss some of the available scheduling techniques to help manage such problems.)

Need for expeditors.

Process Layout for Intermittent Operations

Due to its relative permanency, the layout of the processing operations is probably one of the most crucial elements affecting the efficiency of an intermittent operation. In general, the problem of layout design for intermittent operations is quite complex. The difficulty stems from the variety of outputs and the constant change in outputs that is characteristic of organizations with an intermittent process design. The optimal layout for the *existing* set of outputs may be relatively inefficient for the outputs to be produced *six months from now*. This is particularly true of job shops where there is no proprietary product and only outside customers are served. One week such a shop may produce 1000 ash trays and the next week an 8000-gallon vat. Therefore, a process layout is typically based upon the historically stable output pattern of the organization, and expected changes in that pattern, rather than upon current operations or outputs.

The layout problem.

The main purpose of layout, or relayout, analysis is generally to maximize the efficiency of operations. But other purposes also frequently exist such as minimizing safety or health hazards, facilitating crucial staff interaction, freeing up bottleneck operations, and minimizing interference, noise, or distractions between different operational areas. Eilon [Reference 10] points out that most operations layouts are originally designed efficiently but as the organization grows and changes to accommodate a changing environment, the operations layout becomes less efficient, until eventually a relayout is necessary. Some operations problems that might indicate the need for relayout are

Purposes of relayout.

- Congestion.
- Poor utilization of space.
- Excessive amounts of materials in processing.
- Excessive work flow distances.
- Bottlenecks occurring in one location simultaneously with idleness in another.
- Skilled workers doing excessive unskilled work.
- Long operation cycles and delivery delays.
- Worker anxiety and strain.
- Difficulty in maintaining operational control of work or staff.

When such special reasons exist for a relayout analysis then, of course, the layout criterion is based on the resolution of the particular difficulty. Two- and three-dimensional scale models of the operation, such as an interior decorator might use with model furniture, are often used to aid in resolving such problems. In general, however, the primary criterion for layout analyses is the "efficiency" of operations. Assuming every potential layout satisfies any *required* constraints (location of loading or shipping docks and restrooms, shape of certain departments, etc.), the efficiency criterion usually reduces to a concern for the *interrelations* between operations. Examples of such interrelations are the cost of materials handling when the main flows between operations are materials, staff time when the major flows are of people, or costs of lost or delayed information when the main flows are of paperwork.

The criterion of efficiency of interrelation.

The objective is then to minimize the costs of these interrelations between operations by locating those operations that interrelate close to one another. If we label one of the operations "i" and another operation "j" then the cost of i relating with j typically depends upon the distance between i and j, D_{ij}, as measured by the route of the flow from i to j. If this is the case and the cost of the flow from i to j is C_{ij} per unit distance (e.g., feet, floors) then the total cost from i to j is C_{ij} times D_{ij}. Note that C and D will have different values for different types of flows and that they need not have the same values from j to i as from i to j since the flow in this opposite direction may be of an entirely different nature. For example, information may be flowing from i to j, following a certain paperwork path (e.g., by pneumatic tube) but sheet steel may flow from j to i following a lift truck or conveyor belt path. Similarly, a fluid might be pumped up a pipe to a tank but flow down another path by gravity.

Adding the flows from i to every one of N possible operations, the total cost of interrelations with operation i is then

$$\sum_{j=1}^{N} C_{ij}D_{ij} \tag{7.1}$$

(It is normally assumed that $C_{ii}D_{ii} = 0$ since the distance from i to itself is zero.) Adding together the costs for all the other i operations relating to each of the j operations results in the total cost.

$$TC = \sum_{i=1}^{N}\sum_{j=1}^{N} C_{ij}D_{ij} \tag{7.2}$$

Our goal is to find the layout that minimizes this total cost. This may be done by evaluating the cost of promising layouts or, as in the example below, by evaluating *all possible* layouts.

The department chairman's office

The section of the business school containing the Operations Management Division's administrative offices is illustrated in Figure 7.4. Each office is approximately 10 by 10 feet so the walking distance (D) between adjacent offices is 10 feet whereas

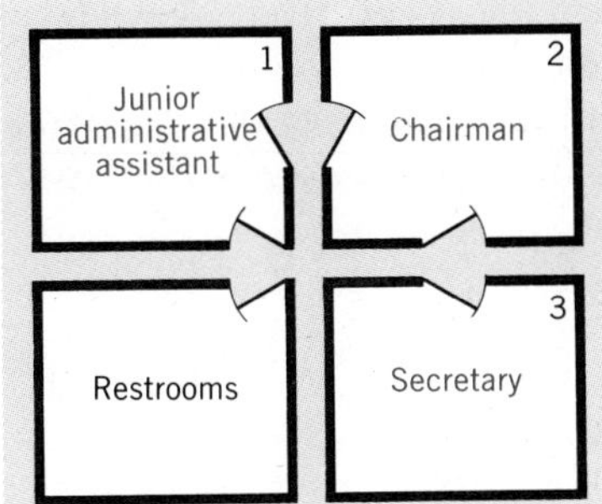

Figure 7.4. Office layout.

The load matrix for travel.

between diagonal offices is 15 feet. The average number of interpersonal trips made each day is given in the travel or **load matrix** of Table 7.2.

Assuming the chairman is paid approximately twice as much as the secretary and the junior administrative assistant, determine if the present arrangement is best (i.e., least costly) in terms of transit time and if not, what arrangement would be better.

Analysis. For convenience in notation, the offices are numbered in the illustration. Before calculating total costs of all possible arrangements, some preliminary analysis is usually worthwhile. First, because of special utility connections, restrooms are usually not considered relocatable. In addition, the relocation of the restrooms in this example would not achieve any result that could not be achieved by moving the other offices instead.

Secondly, many arrangements are mirror images of other arrangements and thus need not be evaluated since their cost will be the same. For example, interchanging offices 1 and 3 will result in the same costs as the current layout. The essence of the problem then is to "determine which office should be located diagonally across from the restrooms." There are three alternatives: chairman, assistant, or secretary.

Lastly, the number of trips times the relative earnings of each person constitute the effective cost per unit distance in this case (the distances must still be determined

TABLE 7.2 LOAD MATRIX, T_{ij} (TRIPS)

		To		
	From	1 Assistant	2 Chairman	3 Secretary
1	Assistant	—	5	17
2	Chairman	10	—	5
3	Secretary	13	25	—

from the locations). Thus, *relative* cost-effectiveness will be a sufficient criterion here and *actual* costs need not be determined.

Letting T_{ij} represent "number of trips from i to j" and evaluating each alternative layout, that is, in terms of who is diagonally across from the restrooms, results in

$$\text{Total Cost} = C_{12}T_{12}D_{12} + C_{13}T_{13}D_{13} + C_{21}T_{21}D_{21} + C_{23}T_{23}D_{23} + C_{31}T_{31}D_{31} + C_{32}T_{32}D_{32}$$

Diagonal office

1. *Chairman TC* $= 1(5)\,10 + 1(17)15 + 2(10)10 + 2(5)10 + 1(13)15 + 1(25)10 = 1050$
2. *Assistant TC* $= 1(5)10 + 1(17)10 + 2(10)10 + 2(5)15 + 1(13)10 + 1(25)15 = 1075$
3. *Secretary TC* $= 1(5)15 + 1(17)\,10 + 2(10)15 + 2(5)10 + 1(13)10 + 1(25)10 = 1025$

The "best" arrangement is therefore to put the secretary in the office diagonal to the restrooms for a cost of $1025.

One difficulty with the method above is that the number of calculations for larger problems quickly becomes unmanageable. Because of the symmetry in this example, we were able to reduce the number of calculations from 6 to 3. In general, however, the number of calculations required to locate N facilities in N different areas is $N!$ ($3! = 3 \times 2 \times 1 = 6$ in our example). Thus, for an organization with just 10 different operational areas, the number of calculations would be $10! = 3{,}628{,}800$. It is, therefore, usually necessary to use a computer to analyze realistic layout problems. However, even with the speed and power of a computer many problems are still too large to be economically evaluated and **heuristic*** routines, as discussed below, must be employed.

CRAFT

Three inputs for CRAFT.

Typical of such computer approaches to the layout problem is **CRAFT**, *Computerized Relative Allocation of Facilities Technique* [Reference 5]. This program assumes that the cost of interrelations between operations is the product of a "rate" matrix (such as cost per unit volume per unit distance) and a "load" matrix (such as volume or trips), both of which are inputs to the CRAFT program. Interoperation distances are obtained from an initial floor plan layout (existing or preliminary) which is read into the program; the computer routine itself then calculates distances between operational areas from the floor plan.

Interchanging two areas at a time to reduce costs.

The program's relayout heuristic is to interchange two areas at a time (more recent versions of CRAFT use three), recompute the total costs, and save the identity of the best switch. After all possible interchanges are evaluated, the best switch is

* Heuristics are logically or experimentally derived rules of thumb. See Reference 27 for details.

then substituted for the original layout (if less costly) and the entire process repeated. Common results with CRAFT are 20 percent savings over initial layout costs. To analyze a 20-operation area takes about half a minute of computer time although CRAFT can handle up to 40 separate departments.

Limitations of CRAFT.

Even though CRAFT does not guarantee a least cost layout, the nature of the layout problem is such that usually only trivially better solutions may exist. Although limited to single-story buildings, CRAFT does have the flexibility of allowing certain areas to be specified as fixed. A minor drawback of CRAFT is that the solution found is not allowed to alter the shape of the building, which is appropriate when the building is already in existence but perhaps inappropriate if a new building is being designed. Lastly, the realities of a particular situation may violate the CRAFT assumptions. For example, straight line distances between operations areas may be inaccurate when only limited access exists to some areas (such as by fork lift), CRAFT designed shapes may not be appropriate for areas needing specialized shapes (such as L or T patterns), and certain areas may require other specific areas to locate (or not locate) near to them (e.g., inspection near shipping; painting away from sanding). Nevertheless, these difficulties can usually be resolved with slight manual modifications to the final CRAFT solution, quick relayouts on CRAFT with higher costs between areas to bring them closer together (or lower costs to space them farther apart), or by relayouts with fixed locations for certain areas.

Other computerized layout routines.

Other computerized layout routines also exist such as **ALDEP** (*Automated Layout Design Program*) [Reference 24] and **CORELAP** (*Computerized Relationship Layout Planning*) [Reference 17]. In these programs, department closeness preferences are specified directly (e.g., very important to be close to department A) and used as the criterion variable, which may or may not be more appropriate than interoperation cost. Also, as opposed to CRAFT, buildings of more than one-story may be analyzed.

7.3 PROCESS DESIGN FOR CONTINUOUS OPERATIONS

Continuous operations for high volume, standardized outputs.

An organization that produces, or plans to produce, a high volume of a small variety of outputs such as pencils or car washes will probably organize the operations on a continuous process basis. In doing so, the organization will take advantage of the simplicity and variable cost savings that accrue from such a process. Since outputs and operations are standardized, specialized equipment can be used to perform the necessary operations at low per unit costs while the relatively large fixed costs of the equipment are distributed over a large volume of outputs.

Standard routes—standard operations.

Continuous types of materials handling equipment, such as pipelines and conveyors, again operating at low per-unit costs, can be used because the operations are standardized and, typically, all outputs follow the same path from one operation to the next. Also, this standardization of treatment provides for a fixed, known throughput time, giving operations managers easier control of the process, and marketing more reliable delivery dates. The continuous process is easier to manage for other reasons as well: routing, scheduling, and control are all facilitated by the fact that each output does not have to be individually monitored and controlled. Standardization of operations means that lower worker skill levels can be used and each manager's span of control can increase.

The famous assembly line.

The general form of the continuous process is illustrated in Figure 7.5. Shown here is a *production line*; if only assembly operations were being performed, as in many automotive plants, the line would be called an *assembly line*. This production line could represent patients at a multiphasic health testing facility, new military inductees taking their physical exams, small appliances being assembled, or double-deck hamburgers being prepared.

Advantages of the Continuous Form

Main advantage—low unit cost.

The primary advantage of continuous process operations is the low per unit cost that is attainable due to specialized, high volume equipment, bulk purchasing, lower labor rates, efficient facility utilization, low in-process inventories, and simplified managerial problems. Due to the high rate of output, materials can often be bought in large quantities at significant savings. Also, because operations are standardized, processing times remain relatively constant so that large in-process inventories are not required to wait in queue for processing. This keeps in-process inventory investment and queue (buffer) space at minimal levels.

Low labor costs.

Because the machines are specialized, operator skills can be lower and, therefore, lower wages can be paid. Also, fewer foremen and supervisors are needed, further saving costs. Since the layout is continuous, with materials handling often built into the system itself, the operations can be designed to perform compactly and efficiently with narrow aisles, thereby making maximum use of facility space.

Simpler managerial control.

The simplification in managerial control of a well-designed continuous process operation should not be overlooked. Constant operations problems requiring unend-

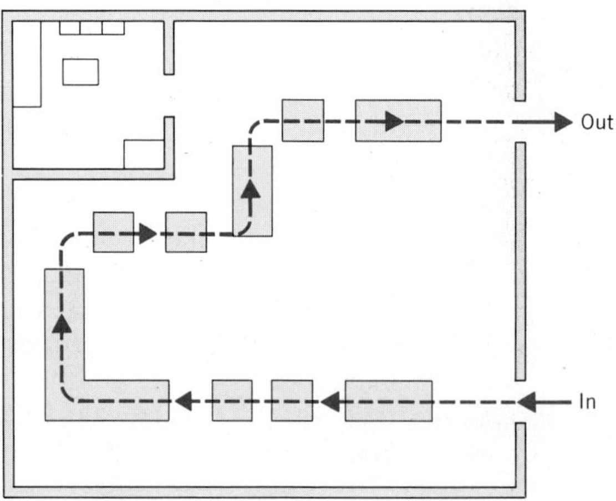

Figure 7.5. A generalized continuous process design operation.

ing managerial attention penalize the organization by distracting management from their normal planning and decision-making duties.

Disadvantages of the Continuous Form

Difficult to change the process or output.

In spite of the very important cost advantage of the continuous form of process design there are some serious drawbacks. Not only is variety of output difficult to obtain; even changes in the *rate* of output are hard to make. Because of this, important product design changes are frequently not made, thereby weakening the marketing position of the organization.

Many worker problems.

A well-known problem in continuous manufacturing organizations is the boredom and absenteeism of the labor force. Since the equipment performs the skilled tasks there is no challenge for the workers. And, of course, the constant, unending pace of the manufacturing line dehumanizes the workers with its repetitiveness. (Current attempts to combat this effect are discussed in Chapter 8.) Since the work generally *is* paced, incentive pay and other output based motivation devices are not possible.

If the line ever stops . . .

The continuous production line form has another important drawback. If the line should stop for any reason, a breakdown of a machine or conveyor, a shortage of supplies, and so forth, *all* production (depending on the type of line) comes to an immediate halt. (The workers often cheer wildly.) Such occurrences are prohibitively expensive.

Other problems exist too.

Other requirements of continuous processes also add cost and problems. For example, parts must be standardized so they will easily and quickly fit together on the assembly line. And, since all machines and labor must work at the same repetitive pace in order to coordinate operations, the entire line is generally **balanced** to the pace of the slowest element on the line. In so doing, work loads may be unequal and a sore point among workers. And to keep the line running smoothly, a large support staff is required, as well as large stocks and large **safety stocks**, of raw materials, all of which further add to the expense.

High initial cost for low unit costs.

Lastly, in the continuous process design form, simplicity in *ongoing operation* is achieved at the cost of complexity in the initial *setup*. Also, the planning, design, and installation of the typically complicated, special purpose, high volume equipment is a mammoth task. Not only is the equipment costly to set up originally, but also to maintain and service. Furthermore, such special purpose equipment is very susceptible to obsolescence and is difficult to dispose of or modify for other purposes.

Process Layout for Continuous Operations

Explosion, assembly, and flow process charts.

The appropriate layout for a continuous product or service operation is based on an analysis of the basic elements, or parts, of the output. This analysis will result in an *explosion* chart of the various parts of the output (and, perhaps, subparts as well), an *assembly* chart to show how the parts and subassemblies go together and in what order, an *operations* (or *flow*) *process* chart, which includes subassembly and part specifications, and detailed production and assembly requirements and times. In combination with the operations process chart there may also be a *route sheet* describing each operation, the department, the equipment needed, and setup and running times. At this point, make versus buy decisions are made and tooling costs estimated. Clearly, considerable knowledge concerning technical processes and machine capabilities is needed at this stage.

The route sheet for detailed information.

Based on this information, further detailing of the operations may then be made such as constructing *activity* (or *man-machine*) *charts*, that list the activities of operators and their equipment side by side with a time scale, *simo* (*simultaneous motion*) *charts*, which show, alongside a time scale, what the right and left hands of an operator are doing, and a preliminary *layout diagram* illustrating the location of workers, equipment, workplaces, materials handling equipment, and so on. These diagrams and charts are illustrated in Section 7.9.

Activity and simo charts for efficiency.

The preliminary layout.

The crux of the problem of attaining the advantages of the continuous process form is whether the work flow determined above can be subdivided sufficiently so that labor and equipment are utilized smoothly throughout the processing operations. If, for example, one operation takes longer than all the others then this will become a "bottleneck" operation, delaying all of the operations following it and restricting the overall output rate to *its* low value.

Dividing the work flow to smooth processing.

This is especially a problem where machines play a major production role as in the fabrication of parts. In these cases the utilization of machines waiting for a bottleneck operation to finish will be unprofitably low unless the machines are used for alternate purposes during slack times. But alternate uses will require special materials handling, storage space, and so forth, and will thus reduce the efficiency of both the alternate process as well as the original process.

Bottleneck operations.

The result in most organizations is that fabrication of basic parts and subassemblies occurs off the main production line either in intermittent process flow or on a subassembly line. When completed, these components are brought to the main assembly line as in Figure 7.6. This procedure is also advantageous in that most subassembly lines can produce considerably more parts per period than the main assembly line. This is often required because multiples of some parts are used in each final output (e.g., every roller skate requires four wheels), and also because the organization must produce spares for its output or perhaps subcontract parts for sale to other companies. For example, a Chevrolet engine plant might produce engines for other cars (such as Oldsmobiles) or for other uses.

The majority of production is off the main line.

Final assembly operations usually have more labor input and less fixed equipment cycles and can, therefore, be subdivided easier for smooth flow. Either one of two types of lines can then be used. A **paced line** typically uses some sort of conveyor and moves the output along at a continuous rate while operators do their work as the output passes by them. For longer operations the worker may walk or ride alongside the conveyor and then have to walk back to his or her starting work station. Many disadvantages, such as boredom and monotony, are of course well known. An automobile assembly line is a common example of the paced line. Workers actually install doors, engines, hoods, and such as the conveyor moves past them.

Conveyors for paced lines.

In unpaced lines, such as that used in IBM typewriter assembly plants, the workers build up queues between the work stations and can then vary their pace to meet

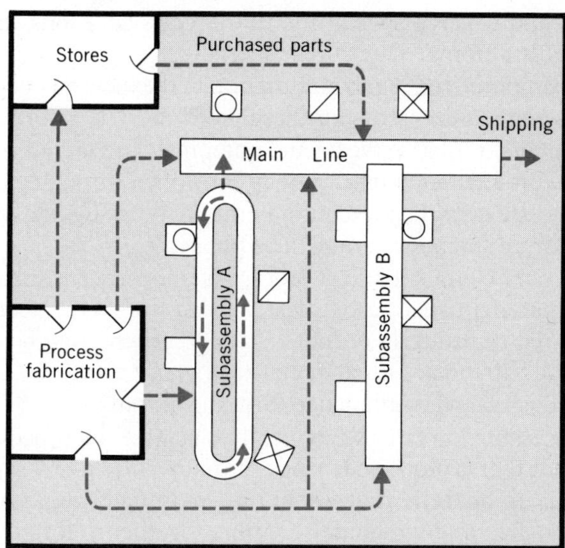

Figure 7.6. Typical configuration of off-line processing and subassembly.

Between-station storage of unpaced lines.

the needs of the job or their personal desires; however, average daily output must remain the same. The advantage of an unpaced line is that a worker can spend longer on the more difficult outputs and balance this with the easier outputs. Similarly, a worker can vary his or her workpace to add variety to a boring task. For example, he or she may work fast to get ahead of the pace and then rest for a few seconds before returning to the task.

There are some disadvantages to unpaced lines also, though. For one thing, they can not be used with large bulky products because of the excessive in-process storage space requirements. But more importantly, minimum output rates are difficult to maintain because short duration times in one operation usually do not dovetail with long durations in the next operation. And when long duration times coincide, operators downstream from these operations may run out of in-process inventory to work on and thus be forced to sit idle.

Choosing an output rate and "balancing" the line.

For operations that can be smoothed to obtain the benefits of a production line there are two main elements in designing the most efficient line. The first is deciding upon the necessary output rate and the second is subdividing and grouping job elements into balanced tasks. The approach to this task is discussed in Section 7.10.

7.4 PROCESSING INDUSTRIES

Although the processing industries such as water, gases, chemicals, ores, foods, rubber, flour, spirits, cements, petroleum, paints, milk, and drugs use continuous processing, they are, in many ways, different from both discrete product and service or-

The automated processing industries.

ganizations and deserve special mention. The operations in these industries are typically highly automated with very specialized equipment and controls, often electronic and computerized. Such automation and expense is necessary because of the strict processing requirements for these products. The facility is typically a maze of pipes, conveyors, tanks, valves, vats, and bins. The layout follows the processing *stages* of the product and output rate is controlled through equipment capacity and flow and mixture rates. Labor requirements are typically low and are devoted primarily to monitoring and maintaining the equipment.

A single, fluid input.

The primary characteristic of processing industries is that one primary, "fluid"-type input material usually exists (gas, wheat, milk, etc.). Commonly, this input is then converted to multiple outputs, although there may be only one output (e.g., water). In (unit) manufacturing, in contrast, *many* types of materials are commonly made or purchased and combined to form the output.

Analytic versus synthetic processes.

In a processing industry we typically visualize the process as having a singular material input that is processed (hence the name) into many separate outputs. This is referred to as an **analytic process**. In *unit* manufacturing , on the other hand, we typically visualize many materials coming together to form a singular unit output, known as a **synthetic process**. ("Synthetic fabrics" require joining many inputs to make a single fiber, such as nylon.)

These concepts, as with job shops and flow shops, are not definitive but are merely aids in visualizing and understanding the differences between organizations. No organization probably uses a pure synthetic or analytic transformation process but rather many combinations of the two. And our definition of "fluid" inputs is itself rather fluid, including granulated plastics, crushed ores, powdered foods, and so forth.

The basic similarity of continuous processes.

Although more highly automated, the process design for processing organizations must follow the same steps laid out in this chapter for unit continuous processes. Specifications must include the order of adding, and tapping off, various materials, the operations (including temperatures, times, etc.) to be conducted on the materials, where storage is to be held, what operations must be conducted simultaneously, and so on. And, like line balancing, materials must come together in the proper amounts at the right time. Rates must be strictly regulated and operations carefully "balanced" to achieve perfect control over the process.

Very high initial costs to reduce unit costs.

Although human variation in processing firms does not usually make for the problems it does in unit manufacturing, the demands of processing are usually more critical. Chemical reactions must be accurately timed in their duration. The result is that initial setup of equipment and procedures is even more complex and critical than for continuous unit processing. Fixed costs are extremely high and the major variable cost is that of materials. Variable labor (excluding distribution) is usually insignificant.

7.5 PROJECT PROCESSES

As discussed earlier, project operations are typically large-scale, finite duration, nonrepetitive tasks consisting of multiple, and often simultaneous, activities that are highly interdependent. Project operations include

Typical projects.

Highways, bridges, tunnels, dams.

Ships, planes, rockets.

Skyscrapers, steel mills, homes, processing plants.

Amusement parks, camping grounds, refuges.

Conferences, banquets, conventions.

R&D projects such as the Manhattan Project (atomic bomb).

Political campaigns, war operations, advertising campaigns.

Ad hoc task forces, government agency planning, corporate audits.

The growth of project processes.

As can be seen from the above list, the number of project operations is growing in our economy, probably at about the same rate as services (which many of them are). Some of the reasons for this growth in project operations are

1. *More sophisticated technology*—an outgrowth of our space age, and its technology, has been an increased public awareness of project operations (e.g., Project Apollo) and interest in using the project form to achieve society's goals (Operation Headstart).
2. *Better educated citizens*—people themselves are more aware of the world around them and techniques (such as project management) for achieving their objectives.
3. *More leisure time*—people have the time available to follow, and even participate in, projects.
4. *Increased accountability*—society as a whole has increased its emphasis on the attainment of objectives (affirmative action, environmental protection, increased gasoline mileage) and the evaluation of activities leading toward those objectives.
5. *Higher productivity*—people and organizations are involved in more activities, and more productive in those activities, than ever before.

Choosing the Project Form of Process Design

Projects for high output diversity or differing technologies.

In designing a processing system there are a number of considerations that may indicate the appropriateness of the project design form. One of these is the diversity in the mix of outputs. If the technology for one output differs significantly from that of another (e.g., bridges, tunnels) then separate projects for the two outputs are appropriate. Another, similar consideration is the rate of change in the organization's outputs. If one department must keep current on a number of outputs (e.g., satellites, rockets, planes) that are rapidly changing, the organization will soon be falling behind its competition. The project form offers extremely short reaction times to environmental or internal changes; thus, separate project operations would again be called for. Lastly, if the tasks are for only a limited duration, the project form is indicated.

One of the advantages of the project form of process design is its ability to perform under crucial time and cost constraints. Therefore, if the performance time or cost are crucial factors for the output being considered, the project form is most appropriate. However, the project form, having a mixed personnel complement of different functional specialists (engineers, scientists, theoreticians, technicians, etc.) may be less capable of advancing high technology areas than some process designs (such as batch) in which operations are organized by specialty areas. In these latter designs, a number of specialists can be brought together to solve a problem. In addition, specialized resources (such as staff and equipment) often cannot be justified because of their low utilization; hence, generalized resources must be used instead.

Not of value in advancing technology.

Lastly, the project design form is typically chosen when the output is of a very large scale with multiple, interdependent activities requiring close coordination. During the project, coordination is achieved through frequent meetings of the representatives of the various functional areas.

Projects for coordinating multiple activities.

For more extensive discussion of these topics refer to References 9, 19, or 22.

Project Process Design

The short life cycle of projects.

Since one of the main advantages of project processes is the ability to perform under time constraints, most projects are designed for a limited lifetime. The usual life cycle is characterized by an early buildup of resources and activities, a leveling off as work nears completion, and a cutting back as project termination approaches. This aspect of the design presents two problems.

Two personnel problems.

1. To quickly increase the staff, many of the personnel are "borrowed" from other ongoing areas in the organization. They therefore often have limited experience with the special duties of the project, short-lived interest, and limited loyalty.
2. Since everyone knows the project is of limited duration, as the end of the project draws near, the staff begin spending more time getting prepared for the next job, typically leaving the project to drag out beyond its due date.

The choice of the project form usually indicates the importance of the project objective to the organization. Thus, top grade resources, including staff, are often made available for the project operations. The result is that project organizations typically become very "professionalized" and are often managed on that basis. That is, minimal supervision is exercised, administrative routine is minimized, and "management by objectives" (MBO) is the rule. In this adaptation of the MBO approach, the professional is given the problem and the performance (results, cost, time deadline) that is required. She or he is then given the privacy, comfort, and freedom to decide *how* to solve her or his portion of the problem.

Managing professionals. The use of MBO.

A great many projects require varying emphases during their life cycle. For example, technical performance may be crucial at the beginning, cost overruns in the middle, and on-time completion at the end. The flexibility of making such spur-of-the-moment changes in emphasis by trading off one criterion for another is basic to the project design form. This ability results from the close contact of the project manager with the technical staff—there are few, if any, "middle managers."

Sudden changes requiring tradeoffs.

In physical project operations, such as bridge construction, most of the *produc-*

tion, per se, is completed elsewhere and brought to the project area at the proper time. As a result, a great many project activities are *assembly* operations. The project design form concentrates resources on the achievement of specific objectives primarily through proper *scheduling* and *control* of activities, many of which are simultaneous. Some of the considerations in project management are knowing what activities must be completed and in what order, how long they will take, when to increase, and decrease, the labor force, when to order materials so they will not arrive too early (thus requiring storage and being in the way) or too late (thus delaying the project), what can, and might, go wrong, what resources can be shifted among activities to keep the project on schedule, and so forth. In Chapter 9 we discuss some useful approaches to aid operations management in planning and scheduling project operations and in Chapter 15 we consider the control of project operations.

Importance of scheduling and control.

With so many project activities occurring, many of them simultaneously, one of the most important design aspects is *coordination* of effort. Particular attention is devoted, through regular meetings and special liaison, to three interfaces.

Primacy of coordination.

1. Those areas that have a significant number of communications between them in the performance of their activities.
2. Those areas that depend on another area for input required in the completion of their tasks.
3. Those areas that must interface but are at significantly different status levels in the organization.

Since the responsibility for effective coordination rests with the project operations manager we will next discuss the most important characteristics of a person holding this position.

The Project Operations Manager

Characteristics of importance in the project manager.

One of the most important aspects of the design of project processes is probably the selection of the project operations manager. The following managerial characteristics are especially important to the effective performance of the project.

- A working knowledge of the many technical fields involved in the project and specialized knowledge in one of them (for professional respect).
- A wealth of experience to draw upon since early project operations are at high risk until much later feedback comes in.
- A good comprehension of the functions of management such as financial, purchasing, personnel, marketing, legal, and operations management.
- The tenacity and ability to keep fighting all types of obstacles that invariably seem to arise during projects, from spur-of-the-moment front office progress presentations to high technology laboratory roadblocks.

In short, all that is needed is a "Six Million Dollar Manager."

The subject of general management will be discussed further in Chapter 8.

TOOLS AND APPLICATIONS

Our procedure in this portion of the chapter will continue to follow the design approach. We first present two background sections on the types of manufacturing processes and principles of materials handling for those with interests in manufacturing and general product organizations. Next we present simulation as a methodology for analyzing the general transformation process and then we consider a complete example of process design. Lastly, the procedure of "balancing" a set of operations to maximize efficiency is illustrated.

7.6 MANUFACTURING PROCESSES

Six types of manufacturing operations.

To examine the general manufacturing processes, the following six very general groupings may be made: extraction, forming, machining, change of properties, joining, and finishing. These groupings apply more directly to metallic materials, but can also be used for nonmetallics and organics as well.

Extraction

Materials, regardless of their classification, are rarely used in their natural form. For example, wood must be cut and stripped, natural rubber must be tapped and refined, and a tremendous amount of petrochemical processing has been developed to produce the vast array of plastics so commonplace in everyday life.

Smelting and alloying.

Of the metallic materials, some are easily **extracted** from their ores (known as **smelting**) while others are not. For example, iron is melted from iron ore in a **blast furnace** but aluminum is typically produced by converting **bauxite** to an oxide by a caustic solution and then **electrolytically** reducing the oxide into oxygen and molten aluminum though the use of intense electrical heat. Of all the metal produced in the world, iron and steel account for 95 percent due to their excellent physical properties, especially when **alloyed** with other metals, and their low cost.

Forming

Molding and working.

Most **forming** processes create the rough shape of the desired product, leaving final shaping to machining or further processing. However, in some cases (e.g., some plastics) the final shape is directly attained in the forming stage. The general forming processes are *molding* and hot and cold *working*.

Molding

There are various types of **molding** processes but the great majority consist of "casting," where a fluid material such as cement, clay, iron, rubber, or plastic is poured or pressure-fed into a mold. The casting of plastics is in many ways similar to the casting of metals. **Thermoplastics** undergo no chemical change in molding and remain soft at high temperatures. They may be continuously remelted and only become hard upon cooling. The other primary type of plastic, **thermosetting** may only be melted once. Upon cooling it becomes permanently hard.

Working

Cold and hot working.

Forming of materials by **working** is usually categorized as either "hot working" or "cold working." Although it is easier to hot work glass, plastic, and metal because of their increased pliability, it is often desirable to cold work metals such as steel because the metal tends to form a scale at elevated temperatures which must constantly be removed. In addition, cold working can significantly improve the physical properties (such as strength) of some metals. Some of the principle methods of working are **forging** (as blacksmiths did) and **rolling** (see Figure 7.7).

Machining

Removing material by machining.

Once a product is nearly in final shape by molding and/or forming processes, the excess material is frequently removed by **machining**. This category includes the sanding of wood, for example, as well as the numerous forms of metallic machining, some of which are illustrated in Figure 7.8. Many common household objects, such as table legs and picture frames, are machined to achieve their final shape.

Change of Properties

There are many purposes for attempting to **change the properties** of materials: to make them soft for machining or hard to resist abrasion, to make them pliable for working or tough for strength, to reduce grain size, relieve internal stresses, or produce a hard surface. Most of the change-of-properties effects have been directed toward steel: **case hardening, tempering** (to make the metal less brittle), **annealing** (to soften the steel for machining).

Joining

Many varied processes exist for **joining** materials together. For nonmetallic materials we are generally familiar with adhesives, nails, tape, thread, banding, screws, pegs,

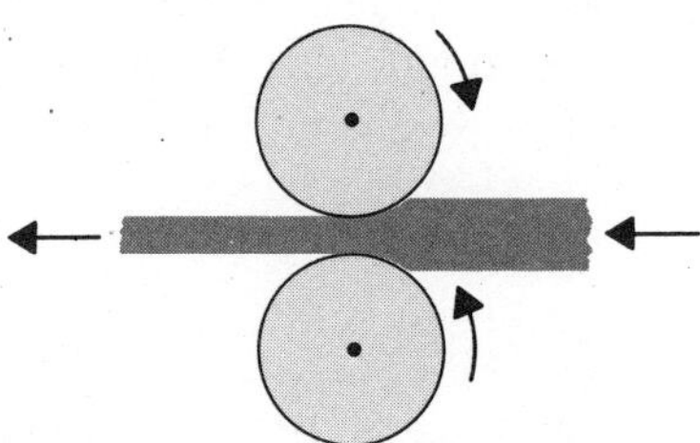

Figure 7.7. Reducing plate thickness by rolling.

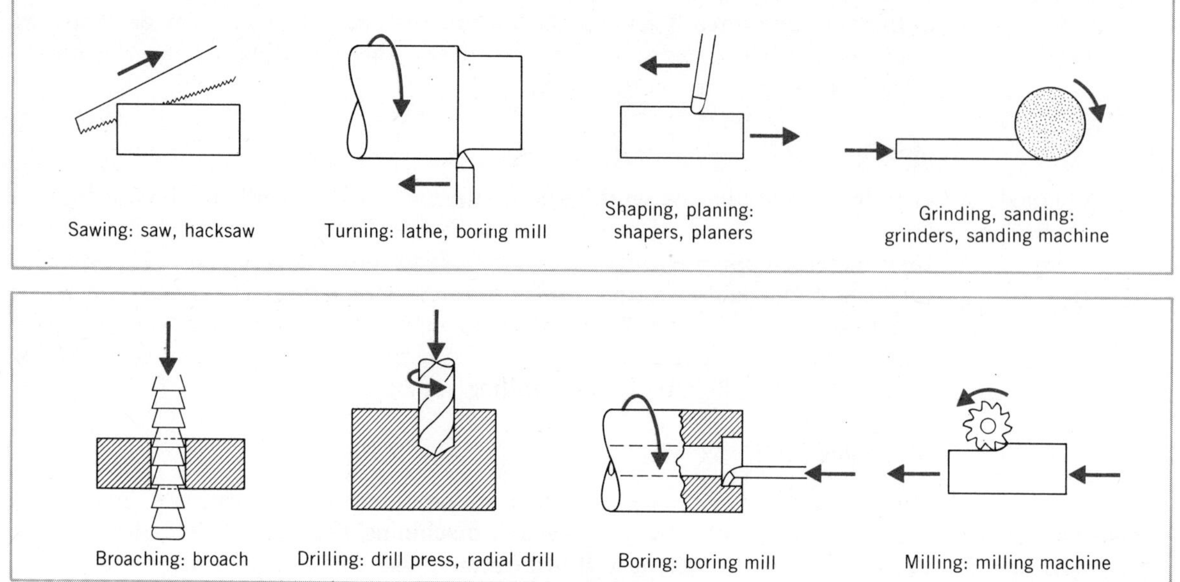

Figure 7.8. Various types of machining processes.

staples, clips, cotter pins, retaining rings, carriage bolts, and so on. For metallic materials many of these are also used as well as *riveting, soldering, brazing*, and *welding*. The common bicycle is an example of many of these processes with its welded frame, bolted handlebars, pinned chain, riveted fenders, and so forth.

Finishing

The purposes of surface **finishing** operations are to improve the dimensional accuracy of the material, ensure a smooth surface, improve the appearance, or provide a protective coating. In the nonmetallic areas we are familiar with buffing, painting, polishing, cleaning, sanding, rubbing, porcelain enameling, and washing. For metallic materials there is also **honing**, in which abrasive sticks correct the trueness of bored holes, and **lapping**, which corrects the flatness of a workpiece.

In addition, there are various forms of plating processes such as **galvanizing** and **electroplating**. In galvanizing, steel is coated with zinc, often by hot-dipping, to protect it from rusting. Nickel, tin, chrome, and silver plating are deposited electrolytically for the protection of food in containers, wear resistance in metals, and general corrosion resistance.

7.7 MATERIALS HANDLING

As mentioned earlier, a major disadvantage of the intermittent process design is the amount of movement required between operations. In the case of product organiza-

A generic problem.

tions this becomes a serious materials handling problem. But the problem is a generic one and applies to all types of organizations whether it is "people handling" in libraries, "paper handling" in home offices, "food handling" in restaurants, or "money handling" in banks.

For example, think back a couple of months ago when you stood in line to register for your classes, or sent your registration material in through the U.S. Post Office, another intermittent process design. Or, remember that time when you had classes on opposite sides of the campus and 10 minutes to make the trip? And the extra difficulty of the trip in the rain or snow?

The importance of materials handling.

Depending on the organization, these costs of "materials" handling can be as high as 75 percent of total expenses. In the manufacturing industry these costs run about 25 percent of factory payroll. Therefore, the subject of materials handling deserves special consideration in the design of the organization's operations.

Principles of materials handling.

Before discussing the types and costs of various materials handling systems it will be useful to examine some of the basic "principles" of materials handling. These principles are grouped under two general approaches to materials handling: (1) minimizing the amount of handling, and (2) improving the efficiency of the handling that must be done.

Minimize Handling

The principles here are as follows:

1. *If possible, do not handle the material at all.* Sometimes this is possible when the operations are arranged so that the output of one is the input to the next (as in continuous processes). Closer analysis of sequential operations, or perhaps output redesign, may allow the combining of separate operations and thus eliminate a handling step.

2. *Minimizing handling by shortening travel distances.* Layout (and relayout) analysis focusing on travel distances and costs of materials handling equipment can save a significant proportion of materials handling costs. And rearrangement of aisles, doorways, and impediments can often allow the use of nearly straight-line distances between locations.

3. *Use gravity to move materials whenever possible.* The creative use of chutes, roller conveyors, pipelines, ramps, and other such gravity-based equipment can save significant costs over equivalent power equipment. In addition, it is fast, reliable, and typically maintenance-free.

Improve Efficiency

There are five general principles used in improving the efficiency of materials handling.

1. *Clearly identify materials.* Incorrect, unknown, and misplaced materials critically hamper operations and add considerably to the costs of materials handling. Not only must the materials be located and/or identified, a costly process in itself, but the materials handling cycle must be repeated again for twice the cost.

2. *Avoid partial loads.* Using high capacity equipment on small loads is an expensive policy. Operations should be scheduled and coordinated so that full or nearly full loads can always be carried. In addition, full loads should be carried in *both* directions to maximize the utilization of expensive labor and equipment.

3. *Minimize pickup and delivery delays.* To increase the utilization of expensive equipment, its idle time while waiting to receive and deliver materials should be minimized. It is this concept that has been used in rail transit for years where carloads of materials are dropped off on sidings for unloading at the recipient's convenience while the main train continues on its way. Also in rail transit, the piggyback railroad car is an example of the application of this principle. In trucking, the classic dump truck best illustrates the principle.

4. *Use unit loads when feasible.* The objective of **unitization** is to standardize the weight and form of materials in order to systematize not only their handling but their storage as well. There are three main types of unitization—*palletization, containerization*, and general packaging.

Palletization

The use of **pallets**, or platforms, (see Figure 7.9), upon which materials are stacked is the most common form of unitization. Typically, the pallets are constructed of wood, 4 by 4 feet, and are carried around by fork lift trucks whose blades enter between the pallet boards to lift the entire load. The load is attached to the pallet either by straps, metal bands, chains, nets, or **shrink-wrap**, a plastic film that, when heated, shrinks around the load and pallet and seals it tight. This then keeps the load from falling off the pallet during transport as well as protecting it from contamination, weather, and theft.

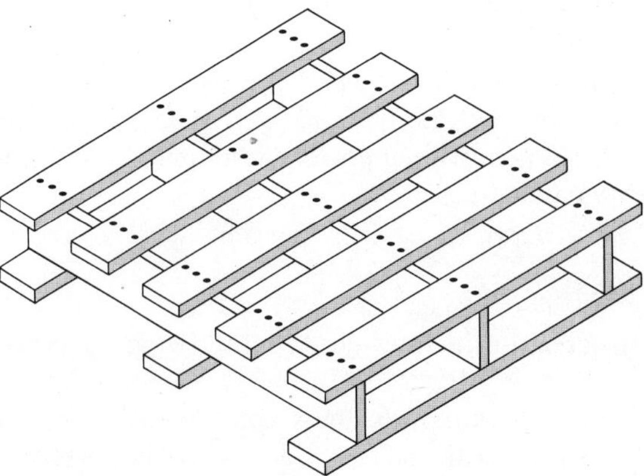

Figure 7.9 Typical wooden pallet.

Containerization

This unitization method encloses the material being transported and thus offers environmental protection and security, as well as unit handling efficiency and economy. Containers vary from tote boxes, cushioned mailing bags (for books and small parts), bins, and drums, to large rectangular metal shipping containers (called "rigid containers"). These are designed to load conveniently on railroad flatcars (called **piggyback**, Figure 7.10), airplane cargo compartments (**birdyback**), and the holds of ships (**fishyback**) but require specialized handling equipment.

General packaging

Used for both commerical and industrial purposes, general packaging serves the objectives of standard quantity dispensing (three different sized boxes of cereal), product identification and differentiation, protection, and, sometimes, advertising. Through the use of unitization, often by means of shrink-wrap, products can be made available which were not previously possible, such as packaged sets of nails in supermarkets. One important innovation in general packaging is the use of the *Universal Product Code* (**UPC**, see Figure 7.11) to permit more efficient handling of supermarket items. This set of bars of varying widths was selected as a standard code by industry after years of study. An optical scanning device can "read" the code, which identifies the company and product only, and can communicate the information to a computer which then can be used to ring up the product price, keep track of any reorders and the shelf inventory, and maintain cash sales information.

Figure 7.10 Piggyback containerization. (Santa Fe Railway photo, July 10, 1978.)

Universal Product Code (UPC)

The series of dark lines and white spaces set over numbers is the symbol for the Universal Produce Code (UPC), an industry-developed way of identifying food producers and products.

Each participating manufacturer is permanently assigned the first five digits as its own number—this allows identification of about 100,000 companies. The firm uses the second set of five digits to designate each of its products.

For instance, Hunt's tomato paste in the 6-oz. size is 27000 (the company number) 38815 (the product number); Kellogg's Special K cereal in the 15-oz. box is 38000 01620, and a 2-lb. can of Maxwell House regular grind coffee is 43000 70297.

The widths of the dark bars and the white spaces between them are different for each product. Each of the numbers and its version of the symbol is printed on the product's label.

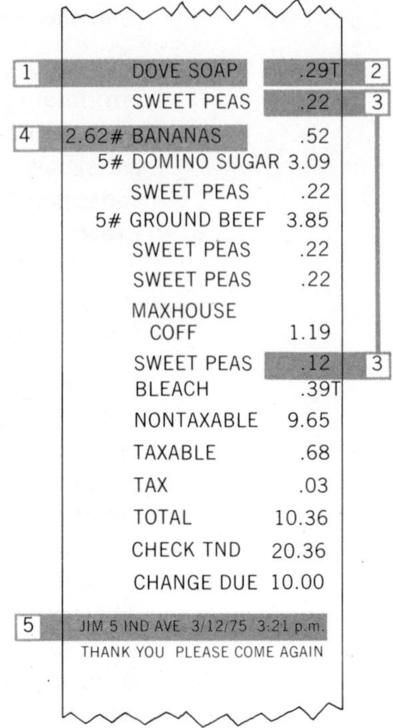

1
DOVE SOAP .29T
2
SWEET PEAS .22
3
4
2.62# BANANAS .52
5# DOMINO SUGAR 3.09
SWEET PEAS .22
5# GROUND BEEF 3.85
SWEET PEAS .22
SWEET PEAS .22
MAXHOUSE COFF 1.19
SWEET PEAS .12
3
BLEACH .39T
NONTAXABLE 9.65
TAXABLE .68
TAX .03
TOTAL 10.36
CHECK TND 20.36
CHANGE DUE 10.00
5
JIM 5 IND AVE 3/12/75 3:21 p.m.
THANK YOU PLEASE COME AGAIN

What the grocery receipt might look like

1. You'll be told what you are buying either by brand name or product type. The receipt you now get usually uses cryptic abbreviations, such as "gro" for canned and packaged groceries, "pro" for fresh produce, "mt" for fresh meat.

2. "T" indicates taxable item.

3. Sweet peas were programed at 22 cents a can or five cans for $1. The system allows the items to go through the checkout counter in a random order but still gives you a price break when you buy the appropriate number of items to get the savings.

4. The system weighs and correctly prices the produce after the proper code numbers have been manually keyed into the computer.

5. At the bottom of the receipt you are told the name of the checker, the number of the checkout lane, the store name or location, the date and the time.

Figure 7.11. A UPC label. (Reprinted with permission from *Changing Times*, © 1975, Kiplinger Washington Editors, Inc., February 1975.)

5. *Mechanize handling tasks whenever cost-effective.* In these days of ever-higher labor rates and extensive development of mechanical methods of materials handling there are relatively few tasks for which manual handling is most economical. Mechanical materials handling equipment is generally classified as either variable-path or fixed-path equipment. Thus, we will consider the various general equipment forms under these two categories.

Variable-path equipment

Equipment for materials handling.

This type of equipment is generally self- or labor-powered and quite flexible in its routing. It handles materials in separate batches, or lots, such as cartons, and therefore is especially suited to intermittent process operations. It generally consists of some form of truck.

Trucks. The two common types of materials handling trucks are the interterminal trucks, seen on the road, and intraplant trucks. The former type range from pickup trucks to garbage trucks, cement trucks, and tank trucks. Of the intraplant trucks the **fork lift** (Figure 7.12) is without doubt the most universal. It generally has two forks (or **tines**) in front but can be specially rigged to handle barrels, drums, bales, rolls, and so forth.

Tractors. The advantage of tractors is that terminal pickup and delivery time can be minimized by loading and unloading the trailers without the tractor, and remaining trailers, standing idle. We see this concept in "semi's" and tractor-trailers on the road and intraplant trailer trains such as is commonly used for baggage handling at airports.

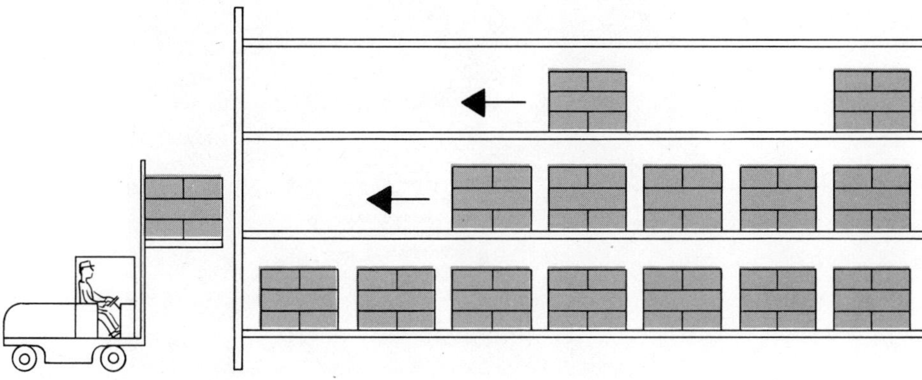

Figure 7.12. Fork lift trucks.

Manual vehicles. Dozens of varieties fall in this inexpensive category, which includes supermarket carts, wagons, hand trucks, and dollies.

Fixed-path equipment

This equipment usually handles materials continuously without need for separate identification of the materials. In initial cost it is usually more expensive than variable-path equipment but for large volumes it is more cost-effective. It is usually driven by a central power unit between fixed locations and therefore is best for continuous process operations. A vast amount of this type of equipment is used in automobile assembly.

Conveyors. The countless varieties of conveyors (roller, screw, overhead, work level, floor height) constitute the main type of fixed-path materials handling equipment. One example is illustrated in Figure 7.13. The advantages of conveyors are many: they operate independently of workers; they can position, transfer, and hold the work (as with **automatic transfer machines**); they can be used for temporary in-process storage; they can pace a production line; and they can buffer operations by, for example, allowing the proper time for cooling, drying, filling, heating, and so forth. Although typically used for continuous horizontal motion as in supermarket check-

Figure 7.13. A typical conveyor. (Reprinted by permission of American Chain and Cable Company, Inc., Acco.)

(Reprinted from *Changing Times*, © 1975, Kiplinger Washington Editors, Inc., February 1975.)

out counters and moving sidewalks at airports, they can also move up and down inclines or stop and go. Turntables constitute another specialized form of conveyor.

Elevators. Closely related to conveyors are the various forms of vertical lifting equipment such as grain elevators, hydraulic lifts (e.g., truck tailgates), dumbwaiters, and man lifts (a vertical belt conveyor with regularly spaced platforms and handles).

Cranes. There are typically three types of cranes. One is the large overhead indoor type running on tracks near the ceiling, controlled by an operator in a suspended cage, and using hooks, buckets, or magnets to raise and lower materials. The outdoor equivalents of this are the mobile and fixed cranes used for building construction, loading and unloading of ships, and earth-moving. The third type is the small, self-powered crane, or hoist, with suspended controls used by workers on the floor to move heavy equipment and parts.

Pipelines. These types of equipment can be either powered or gravity-fed and include pipes, chutes, ducts, and tubes. The powered type are either hydraulic, air-pressure, or vacuum, and transport oils, slurries, water, effluents, gases, fumes, dust, and other common bulk materials. Pneumatic tubes and gravity-assisted chutes are used to move rigid materials.

General Considerations

The primary consideration in choosing a materials handling system is, of course, the nature of the material and the operations; for example, liquids can not be moved by hand cart alone. Next in line are the comparative costs. The breakeven chart is of use here. As shown in Figure 7.14 each type of equipment will have its own fixed and variable (per unit) costs that also depend on the distance the materials must be moved. The number of possible alternatives can be limited by knowledge of the amount of volume that must be moved. For high volumes more mechanized and specialized equipment can be used than for low volumes.

Other considerations include equipment lifetime, salvage, resale value, operating costs, maintenance, ease of use, safety, and reliability. Also, the rate of technology development for the equipment should be considered since new and better equipment may be available in the near future. Lastly, the rate of change and growth in the organization itself should be considered since the organization's operating needs may change significantly in a short time.

7.8 PROCESS DESIGN ANALYSIS BY SIMULATION

In actual operation, as mentioned earlier, very few organizations utilize a purely intermittent or purely continuous process. Even in "custom" work, jobs are often done in groups of generally common items throughout most of their processing, leaving minor finishing details such as the fabric on a couch or the facade of a house to give the impression of customizing.

And even processing industries such as sausage manufacturing typically run "batches" of their product corresponding to one full vat of mixture, or one tank car of product. After completing one batch of output the facilities are usually cleaned and set up to run a batch of another output. This continues until all the organization's mix of outputs are completed and the cycle then starts over again.

Therefore, process designs in practice represent points on a continuum ranging from intermittent to continuous processes. Organizations choose to operate at partic-

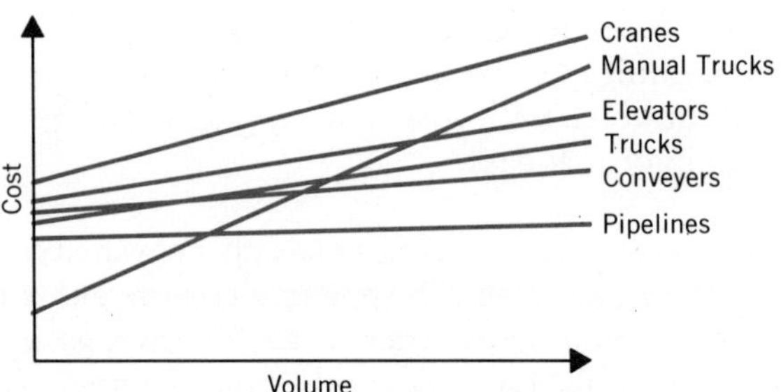

Figure 7.14. An illustration of typical cost tradeoffs in materials handling.

A continuum of process forms.

ular points along this continuum in order to trade off certain advantages, such as the flexibility of the intermittent form with some of the economies of the continuous form.

Simulation for process design analysis.

The complexity of the process design problem necessitates a flexible approach that a manager can easily modify and experiment with. Given such an approach, each transformation design could be evaluated through experimentation. Different criteria for viability could be checked and the best overall design selected. One approach for doing this would be to physically construct the process designs and experiment with them. But this is much too expensive. A better approach is *simulation*.

Simulation

Simulation by mathematical/logical model.

Simulation is a technique for experimenting with a real situation through an artificial model that represents that situation. The three-dimensional models that architects and car designers frequently employ are forms of simulation. In these cases, the models are physical and small scale versions of the real object. However, the simulations we are concerned with here are *mathematical/logical* models, which are usually programmed on a computer. The purpose of the simulation is to discover the "characteristics" of a particular processing design.

Simulation has a number of inherent advantages that other evaluation methods frequently do not.

- The simulation can begin very simply and grow with the addition of more and more realistic processing complexity as the operations manager gradually understands the dynamics of what is happening in the system.
- The mathematics and logic of simulation are relatively simple.
- There are no "generalized" parts to the model; every component in the model corresponds to some real-life element.
- A considerable amount of "what if" type experimentation can be conducted on the model to test new and creative designs, without altering an existing actual design.
- Considerable time compression is possible, especially if the simulation is computerized. Years of experience can be obtained in seconds of model operation.
- Simulation can handle an extremely large variety of situations and problems.

The primary disadvantage of simulation is that it takes time and money to construct the model, especially if a complex system is being simulated. Also, it will not *find* an optimal design—it will only describe the results of those designs identified by the manager.

Monte Carlo simulation.

The type of mathematical simulation we will consider here is called **Monte Carlo**, after the famous gambling kingdom. The procedure is used where events follow patterns that can be described by probability distributions. The steps for building a Monte Carlo simulation are

→Step 1. Describe the process design in mathematical and logical terms and any relevant probability distributions such as processing times or servicing times.

↓

Step 2. Decide what the appropriate performance measures are for the processing system.

↓

Step 3. Construct cumulative probability distributions for the process design and assign representative numbers to correspond to them.

↓

→Step 4. Generate "random numbers" for each of the distributions and determine the corresponding system variables.

↓

Step 5. Compute the measures of performance.

↓

Step 6. Repeat steps 4 and 5 until the measure of performance "stabilizes."

↓

Step 7. Repeat steps 1–6 for alternate processing designs and select the best one.

Let us demonstrate the procedure with a simple processing design example. (For further discussion of simulation, see References 21 or 27.)

Oriental Rugs Worldwide

Oriental rugs are enjoying a new popularity after being out of style for decades. Originally made out of natural fibers, many of today's synthetic fibers are now also being used. One of the problems of mass manufacture of rugs with synthetic fibers, however, is maintaining color consistency from one dye lot to the next. As a result of this inconsistency, the production volume of the batch dyeing operations (multiple lots of one color) is never known with certainty. This is because a significant portion of the day's production is involved in obtaining exactly the right color (called **setup time**) and only a limited amount of time is therefore available for actual dyeing.

The problem for the operations manager is to decide how to guarantee stable dyeing output rates without excessive capacity. Clearly, a much larger volume than required could be scheduled and then, if things went well, the extra production could be cancelled. However, this results in low efficiency and high costs due to excessive capacity in the form of idle labor, unutilized plant and equipment, and high inventories of raw materials.

One partial solution to this problem is to provide finished goods storage space as a buffer between dyeing and later operations (weaving, etc.). The amount of space that is "best" depends upon a number of factors, however: the cost of the space, the variation in dye lot output, the cost of a shortage, management's willingness to accept various probabilities of shortages, and so on.

Oriental Rugs Worldwide (ORW) is a small manufacturer in the rug business. ORW has managed to build up its sales to the point that demand now runs about 15 lots per day, the absolute limit of its current manufacturing capacity. Existing dye lot capacity is 16 per day and the dye lot operations manager, based on experience, has been consistently scheduling the limit of 16 lots input to dyeing.

Based on the last six months of operation, ORW has found that daily dye lot output was two lots below input 20 percent of the time, one lot below input 50 percent of the time, and "as input" 30 percent of the time. The average output has therefore been

$$0.2(2 \text{ below}) + 0.5(1 \text{ below}) + 0.3(0 \text{ below}) = 0.9 \text{ below input}$$

It would seem that sufficient dye lot capacity exists (16 – 0.9 = 15.1 lots) to supply manufacturing. Yet dye lot output has frequently been unable to supply manufacturing with the required 15 lots a day. Management desires that no more than one day in 20 (5 percent) should dye lot output be less than 15.

Let us simulate this situation and see if adding storage to the process will alleviate ORW's problem. We start with step 1.

STEP **1.** The description of ORW's transformation process is specified in the paragraphs above. We assume that, on those occasions when 16 lots would come out of dyeing, the last lot is cancelled since insufficient manufacturing capacity exists to process 16 lots and no storage space currently exists to store the last lot until the next day.

STEP **2.** There is only one **measure of performance** in this case—the percent of time dye lot input to manufacturing is less than 15.

STEP **3.**

	Dye Lot Output		
Level	Probability	Cumulative Probability	Representative No.
2 below	.2	.2	1–2
1 below	.5	.7	3–7
0 below	.3	1.0	8–0

For the simulation it is important that 20 percent of the **representative numbers** indicate an output level of 2 below, 50 percent 1 below, and 30 percent 0 below. One simple way of doing this is by letting the cumulative probabilities specify the *highest* representative number for that category (e.g., 7 for the cumulative probability .7). The next category then begins with the next highest representative number. If the cumulative probabilities above had been .199, .699, and 1.0 then the representative numbers would have been 001 – 199, 200 – 699, and 700 – 000. (This last category includes 700 – 999 plus 000.)

STEP **4.** This step is the basis of the Monte Carlo process. **Random numbers** are values, typically taken from a table, where every digit 0–9 has the same chance of being selected. The table is entered at some arbitrary point within the body of the table and the digits read in *any* direction: up, diagonally, whatever. If single digit random numbers are needed, as in the case here, then the digits are used one at a time. If three-digit random numbers are needed then they are read three at a time.

As an example, consider the random number table in the appendix. To simulate 20 days of operation will require 20 random numbers. Reading *backward* from the bottom-right number in the table we get the values shown in Table 7.3. Using the table in step 3 then gives the dye output, in "amount below." Following each of these values is the actual daily dye output assuming 15 lots is the maximum input to manufacturing. The last column gives the running measure of performance, the percentage of time output is less than 15.

STEP **5.** The measure of performance, the percentage of time dye lot input was less than 15 was 4/20, or 20 percent, in the above simulation. Note that this is four times greater than management desires (5 percent).

STEP **6.** The above simulation was only for 20 cycles of the process. Yet the variation in the measure of performance has reduced to only six percentage points (23–17) by the thirteenth cycle. Figure 7.15 shows the **stabilizing** of the simulation toward its theoretical mean of 20 percent (see step 3). In some cases many, many more cycles are necessary for a measure to stabilize, particularly if the measure only occurs infrequently in the simulation.

STEP **7.** Let us now test the effect of adding storage space in the transformation process. We will first consider adding enough space to hold *one* dye lot following the dyeing operation. This would then save some of the cancellations of those sixteenth lots which currently occurs 30 percent of the time.

TABLE 7.3 ORW DYE PROCESS SIMULATION

Day	Random No.	Amount Below	Output[a]	Percentage of Time <15	Day	Random No.	Amount Below	Output[a]	Percentage of Time <15
1	7	1	15	0	11	8	0	15[a]	18
2	4	1	15	0	12	3	1	15	17
3	9	0	15[a]	0	13	2	2	14	23
4	8	0	15[a]	0	14	7	1	15	21
5	4	1	15	0	15	3	1	15	20
6	8	0	15[a]	0	16	7	1	15	19
7	8	0	15[a]	0	17	9	0	15[a]	18
8	2	2	14	12	18	2	2	14	22
9	1	2	14	22	19	7	1	15	21
10	5	1	15	20	20	0	0	15[a]	20

[a] If 0 amount below, the sixteenth lot is cancelled.

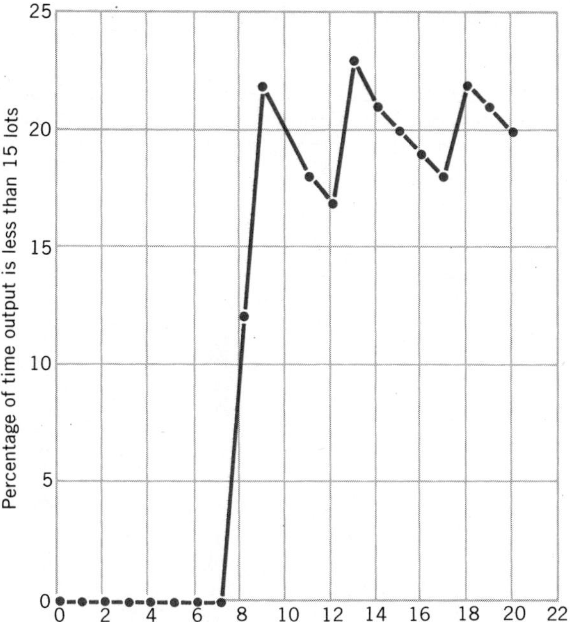

Figure 7.15. Stabilization of the measure of performance.

So that the comparison to Table 7.3 is a fair one and effects under the new process design are not due to different random numbers, we will use the same random numbers as given there. The results are calculated in Table 7.4.

In the 20-day simulation there was only one day when manufacturing input slipped below 15 lots. Although this is the level specified by management (5 percent) the last column of the table clearly indicates that the measure of performance has not yet stabilized and many more cycles must be run before it can be stated that providing storage space for one lot will achieve management's goal. With a larger simulation it would also be of interest to see what effect storage space for two lots would have on the measure of performance.

This example has illustrated the use of simulation in analyzing batch process design alternatives. Although the example was highly simplified, simulation can also handle exceedingly complex processes. Simulation is particularly appropriate for problems that do not satisfy the assumptions of some of the optimizing models of management science, or where human behavior is concerned. Of course, simulation is not limited to process design analysis but has been used throughout the field of operations management for logistics analysis, quality control, maintenance, layout, scheduling, and so on. And, of course, simulation is so general and powerful that it is used in physics (to study atomic interactions), chemistry (for analyzing molecular behavior), biology (to study metabolism), and many other fields as well.

TABLE 7.4 SIMULATION WITH STORAGE INCLUDED

Day	Random No.	Amount Below	Dye Lot Output[a]	Lots in Storage[b]	Manufacturing Input	Percentage of Time <15
1	7	1	15	0	15	0
2	4	1	15	0	15	0
3	9	0	16	1	15	0
4	8	0	15[a]	1	15	0
5	4	1	15	1	15	0
6	8	0	15[a]	1	15	0
7	8	0	15[a]	1	15	0
8	2	2	14	0	15	0
9	1	2	14	0	14	11
10	5	1	15	0	15	10
11	8	0	16	1	15	9
12	3	1	15	1	15	8
13	2	2	14	0	15	8
14	7	1	15	0	15	7
15	3	1	15	0	15	7
16	7	1	15	0	15	6
17	9	0	16	1	15	6
18	2	2	14	0	15	6
19	7	1	15	0	15	5
20	0	0	16	1	15	5

[a] If 0 amount below when one lot in storage, the sixteenth lot is cancelled.

[b] Assumes nothing in storage to start.

7.9 TRANSFORMATION PROCESS DESIGN EXAMPLE

To illustrate the procedures involved in process design, consider the manufacture of the commonplace push-button ballpoint pen. The **explosion chart** of the pen, and a

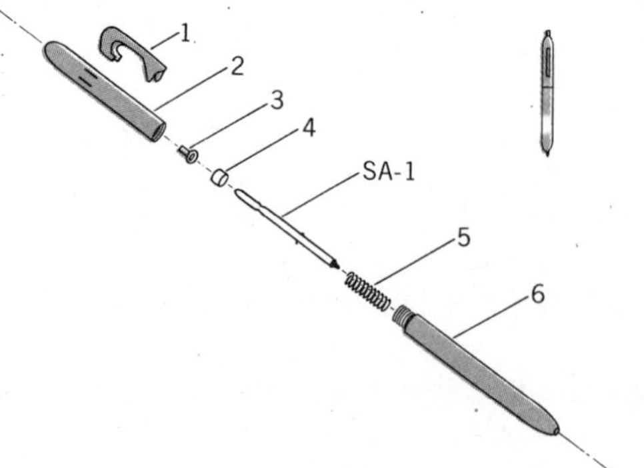

Figure 7.16. Ballpoint pen explosion chart.

completed view, is shown in Figure 7.16 and the **assembly** and **operations process charts** in Figures 7.17 and 7.18. Note that we have only illustrated final assemblies—subassemblies such as SA-1 would typically be included in separate charts. The explosion diagram separates each of the parts as if they had been "blown apart" in exact order of their assembly. A centerline (—-—) is usually included to indicate how the parts fit together. In complicated explosions where it is impossible to fit all the parts in a straight line on the same piece of paper the centerlines may be bent (⁻⁻⁻/___) so as to draw the parts in an empty corner of the paper. Such explosion charts are crucial to the proper assembly of even slightly complex parts.

The importance of the explosion chart for proper assembly.

Main and subassemblies on the assembly chart.

The assembly chart of Figure 7.17 gives more detailed assembly instructions than the explosion chart and includes subassemblies as well (such as SA-1 in the figure). Note, however, that the assembly chart does not tell what the raw materials are, or how to construct the parts—it is simply for assembly operations. The construction information is given in the operations process chart (Figure 7.18) and includes the standard time for each operation.

The symbols used in the assembly chart of Figure 7.17 and operations process chart of Figure 7.18 are as follows.

O: *Operation* being performed.

⇩ *Transportation* of item takes place.

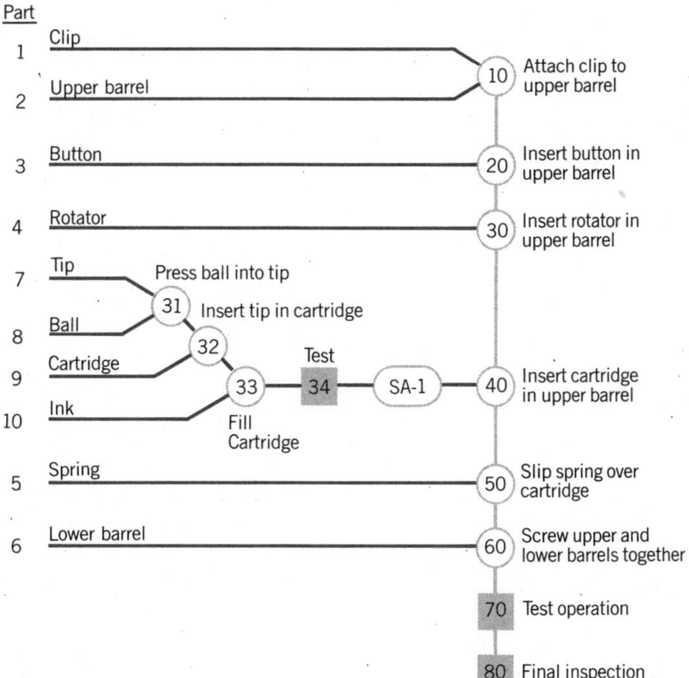

Figure 7.17. Assembly chart for ballpoint pen.

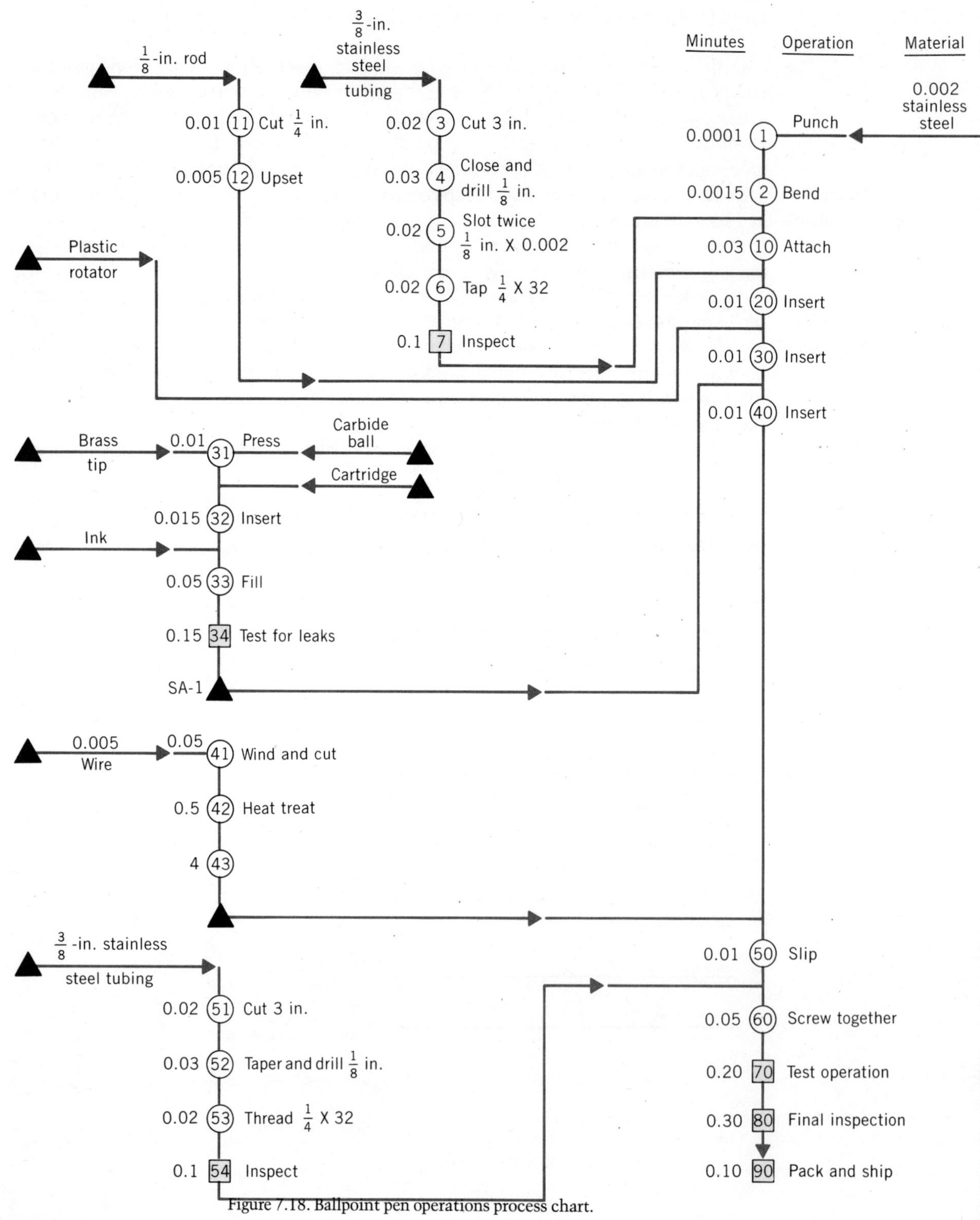

Figure 7.18. Ballpoint pen operations process chart.

△: *Storage* of some item occurs.

▽: *Delay* for further processing. Paperwork not required.

□: *Inspection* of an item occurs.

The **route sheet** for the cartridge **subassembly**, SA-1, is shown in Figure 7.19. Four departments (inventory, press, paint, and inspection) are involved in the production of this subassembly. As can be seen, the operations start at the inventory department where a batch of raw materials are requested. The operations finish at a later date, with the batch of subassemblies being stored back in inventory. The required equipment is also indicated, along with setup and run times.

Activity charts for maximizing utilization.

Since one operator performs all of the press operations, we may analyze the operator's **activities** by a **man-machine chart** as in Figure 7.20. This kind of chart shows what the operator and each machine are doing at every point in time and thus facilitates obtaining the maximum use out of both the operator and the machines. As can be seen, once they are started, both machines are fully utilized but the operator is idle $2 + 0.5 + 1.5 + 1 = 5$ out of the first 12.5 minutes for a **utilization** rate of only

$$\frac{(12.5 - 5.0)}{12.5} = 60 \text{ percent.}$$

Differing cycles limit utilization.

Furthermore, there is no regularity in the activity. All of the idle times are of different durations and the machines "cycle" at different intervals. As seen in the chart, on the first cycle the operator loads the Sheridan and then immediately loads the Cummings. On the second cycle he must wait 0.5 minutes between loadings because the Cummings run is not completed when he finishes loading the Sheridan. On the third cycle he must wait 1.0 minute. Clearly, there will soon come a cycle when both machines complete their runs at the same time and then one machine must sit idle while the other is being loaded, as occurred in the first cycle. This is an inefficient use of equipment, as well as of labor (60 percent idle). Better "balancing" of the machine cycles by varying the run loads and perhaps adding other tasks to the

Part name Cartridge subassembly — Date issued ______ — Job ______

No. SA-1 — Date completed ______ — Issued by ______

Date	Oper. no.	Operation	Dept.	Set up min	Rate/min	Equipment
	—	Tip and ball	Inventory	—	—	—
	31	Press ball into tip, 100 psi	Press	30	100	Sheridan press
	—	Cartridge	Inventory	—	—	—
	32	Insert tip into cartridge, 43 psi	Press	30	75	Low volume Cummings press
	33	Fill cartridge, 0.15 each	Paint	45	20	Simms high viscosity pump
	34	Test	Inspection	—	4	#1538 pressure tester, Fields Bros.
	—	Subassembly transport	Inventory	—	—	—

Figure 7.19. Route sheet for cartridge subassembly.

Part name	Cartridge subassembly	Dept. Press	Operator ______
No.	SA-1	Date ______	

Time (min)	Operator	1: Machine Sheridan	2: Machine L.V. Cummings
–0 – –1	Load and start Sheridan	Load	Idle
–2	Load and start Cummings		Load
–3 – –4	Idle	Run 300 units	
–5 –	Load and start Sheridan	Load	Run 300 units
–6	Idle		
–7	Load and start Cummings		Load
–8 – –9	Idle	Run 300 units	
– –10	Load and start Sheridan	Load	Run 300 units
–11	Idle		
–12	Load and start Cummings	Run 300 units	Load

Figure 7.20. Press operator activity chart.

operator's duties would significantly improve the utilization of all these resources.

Hand motion shown on the **simo chart**.

Figure 7.21 illustrates the right- and left-hand operations required to perform the cartridge subassembly leakage test by the inspector. Note that, as much as possible, use is made of both hands simultaneously. Principles such as this involving the efficient use of human labor will be discussed in more detail in Chapter 8.

Lastly, a preliminary **layout** can now be designed based on the previous analyses. For the ballpoint pen, this layout is depicted in Figure 7.22. In actual practice there are miniature two-dimensional cutouts and three-dimensional blocks representing machines, and so forth, available from firms specializing in layout to help visualize what a proposed layout would actually look like, its problems, and its advantages. The operation analysts (typically, industrial engineers) would then shift the pieces in

PartName Cartridge subassembly Dept. Insp. Operator ____ No. SA-1 Date ____ Operation Leakage test		
Left	Time (min)	Right
Reach for cartridge	.01	Reach for pressure probe
Pick up cartridge	.02	Pick up probe
Carry to probe	.03	Carry to cartridge
Position	.04 .05	Insert probe in cartridge
Hold probe-cartridge assembly	.06 .07	Reach for pressure switch
	.08 .09	Actuate switch
	.10	Reach for probe
Hold cartridge	.11	Replace probe
Check for leaks	.12	Idle
Scribble	.13	
Check for blotches	.14	
Place into accept or reject bin	.15 .16	

Figure 7.21. Simo chart for leakage test.

this scale model around to check for safety problems, bottlenecks, materials flow, in-process storage, and other such complex, interrelated aspects of designing a continuous flow process. Alternative layouts would be considered and shown to operations managers and supervisors for their evaluation until, finally, a "best" layout would be selected for actual implementation.

Trial layouts with scale models.

7.10 BALANCING A CONTINUOUS PROCESS PRODUCTION LINE

In this section we will focus on the problem of "smoothing" the productive operations in a continuous process so that all operations work at approximately the same speed. If this were not done then the transformation process would be relatively inefficient with all operations working at the slowest rate of the most lengthy operation. For example, if a process consisted of three machines, A, B, and C, with individual output rates of 98, 50, and 100 units per day, respectively, then the resuling output of the entire system would be 50 units a day. The obvious solution is to use another machine B and increase the output to 98 units per day, assuming this volume is

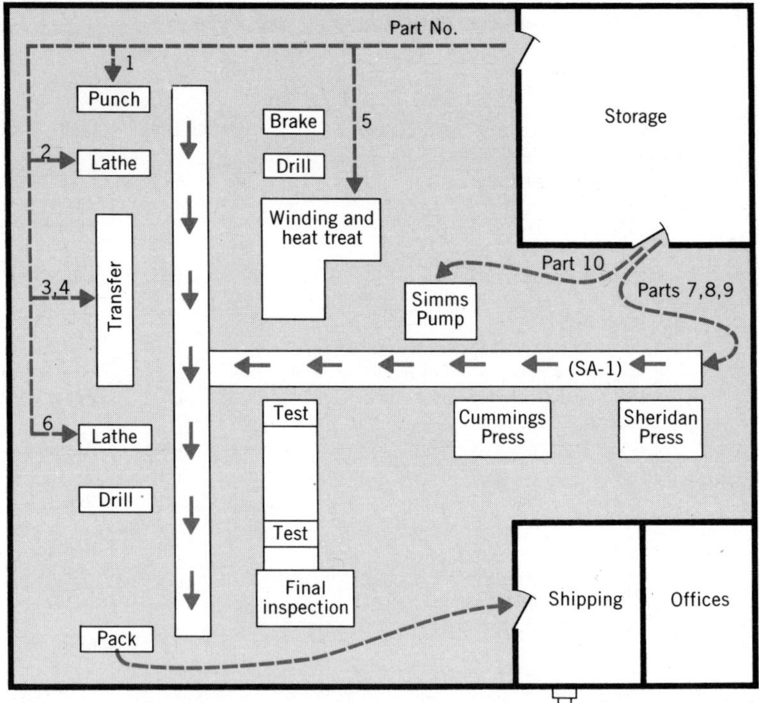

Figure 7.22. Preliminary operations layout diagram.

usable. The following example illustrates the general *line balancing* methodology of smoothing production operations.

Longform Credit, Inc., receives 1200 credit applications a day, on the average. Their advertising touts Longform's efficiency in responding to all applications within a matter of hours. The daily application processing tasks, standard times, and required preceding tasks (those tasks that must be completed before other tasks) are listed in Table 7.5.

A precedence graph for order of assembly.

The **precedence graph** for these tasks is depicted in Figure 7.23 and is constructed directly from Table 7.5. This graph is simply a picture of the operations (a circle) with arrows indicating which tasks must precede each other task. The number, or letter, of the operation is shown inside the circle with the time directly above it.

Analysis

A common cycle time for all stations.

In *balancing* a line the intent is to find a **cycle time** in which each work station can complete its tasks. Conceptually, at the end of this time each work station passes its part on to the next station. Task elements are thus grouped for each work station so as to utilize as much of this cycle time as possible but not to exceed it. Typically, each work station will have a slightly different **idle time** within the cycle time.

Cycle time is based on the output rate.

The cycle time is determined from the required output rate. In this case, the average daily output rate must equal the average daily input rate, 1200. If it is less

TABLE 7.5 CREDIT APPLICATION PROCESSING TASKS

Task	Average Time (min)	Immediately Preceding Tasks
a. Open and stack applications	0.20	none
b. Process enclosed letter; make note of and handle any special requirements	0.37	a
c. Check off form 1 for page 1 of application	0.21	a
d. Check off form 2 for page 2 of application; file original copy of application	0.18	a
e. Calculate credit limit from standardized tables according to forms 1 and 2.	0.19	c,d
f. Supervisor checks quotation in light of special processing of letter, notes type of form letter, address, and credit limit to return to applicant	0.39	b,e
g. Secretary types in details on form letter and mails	0.36	f
Total	1.90	

than this figure, a backlog of applications will accumulate. If it is more than this, unnecessary idle time will result. Assuming an 8-hour day, 1200 applications per 8 hours means completing 150 every hour (2½ every minute) or *one* every *0.4 minutes*—this is then the cycle time.

$$\text{cycle time} = \text{available work time/demand} = \frac{(8 \times 60)}{1200} = 0.4 \text{ min} \qquad (7.3)$$

Finding the number of work stations.

Adding up the task times in Table 7.5 it can be seen that the total is 1.9 minutes. Since every work station will do no more than 0.4 minutes worth of work during each cycle, it is clear that a minimum of 1.9/0.4 = 4.75 work stations are needed or, always rounding *up*, 5.

$$\begin{aligned}\text{number of work stations, } N &= \textstyle\sum \text{task times/cycle time} \\ &= \frac{1.9}{0.4} = 4.75 \text{ (i.e.,5)}\end{aligned} \qquad (7.4)$$

Calculating the efficiency and balance delay of the line.

It may be, however, that the work cannot be divided and balanced in 5 stations and 6, or even 7 may be needed. If this is the case, the production line will be less efficient. The **efficiency** of the line with N stations may be computed from

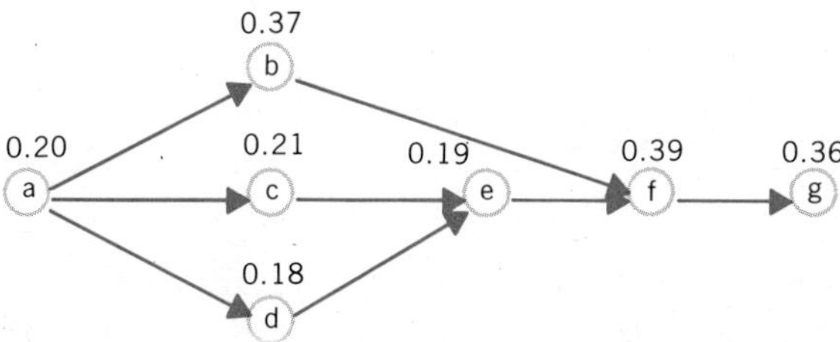

Figure 7.23. Credit application precedence graph.

$$\text{efficiency} = \frac{\text{output}}{\text{input}} = \frac{\text{total task time}}{(N \text{ stations}) \times \text{cycle time}}$$
$$= \frac{1.9}{5 \times 0.4} = 95\% \text{ if the line can be balanced with 5 stations} \quad (7.5)$$
$$= \frac{1.9}{6 \times 0.4} = 79\% \text{ if 6 stations are required}$$

On occasion, the *inefficiency* of the line is calculated instead; this is called the **balance delay**

$$\text{balance delay} = 1.0 - \text{efficiency} = 1.0 - 0.95 = 5\% \text{ with 5 stations} \quad (7.6)$$

The balancing process.

At this point we may now attempt to balance the line by assigning tasks to stations. We begin by assuming all workers can do any of the tasks and check the result later. The first tasks to consider are those with no preceding tasks. Thus, task a, taking 0.2 of the 0.4 minute available, is put into station 1. This then makes tasks b (0.37 minute), c (0.21 minute) and d (0.18 minute) available for assignment. Of the three, only d can be assigned to station 1 without exceeding the 0.4 minute cycle time; thus, station 1 will include tasks a and d. Since only 0.02 minute remain unassigned in station 1 and no task in the job is that short, we next consider assignments to station 2.

Only b and c are available for assignment (since e requires that c be completed first) and b (0.37 minute) will clearly require a station by itself; b is, therefore, assigned to station 2. Only c is now available for assignment since f requires that both e and b be completed and e is not yet completed. But by assigning c (0.21 minute) to station 3, task e (0.19 minute) becomes available and can also be just accommodated in station 3. Task f (0.39 minute) is the next available task and clearly requires its own station, 4, leaving g (0.36 minute) to station 5. These assignments are illustrated in Figure 7.24.

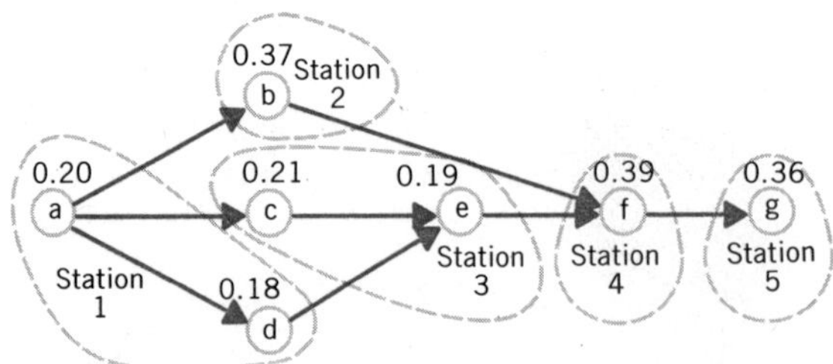

Figure 7.24. Station assignments.

We now check the feasibility of these assignments. In many cases a number of aspects must be considered in this check (as discussed further below) but here our only concern is that the clerk or the secretary does not do task f and that the supervisor does not do task g (or, hopefully, very much of a–e). As it happens, task f is a station by itself so there is no problem.

Some realistic complications.

The above example is, of course, highly simplified. In realistic situations many other difficulties and considerations are present, which complicate the problem even more. Some of these complications are listed below.

- Many, many more tasks are involved with considerably more interactions and precedence relationships. Considerable research has been done on this problem and numerous heuristic techniques (e.g., choose as the next task the one with the longest operation time) are available to aid in obtaining a solution (see References 6, 15, and 20 for details). Worthy of special mention are the computerized techniques **COMSOAL** [3] and **MALB** [6], which can handle hundreds of tasks in only a few minutes.
- Some sets of tasks require the same skills, tools, parts, equipment, worker positioning, or facilities and might be more efficiently grouped together than is indicated from the pure line balancing solution. Thus, it is always worthwhile to inspect the time-oriented solution for further possible efficiencies.
- In the spirit of job enrichment (discussed further in Chapter 8) it may be worthwhile to group some tasks together that normally would not be, simply to ward off boredom and allow some variety, or even pride of workmanship.
- Potential task interference should be considered. For example, noisy, dangerous, or polluting tasks should be grouped and confined in facilities designed for them.
- Frequently, some tasks exceed the cycle time by themselves. The best approach in this case is to assign such tasks to two (or more) stations, each completing their task *every other* cycle. An approach to the opposite situation where one uncombinable task has a *low* cycle time is to utilize two (or more) complete parallel lines with the one, short cycle task in common.

7.11 SUMMARY

Transformation process design is a complex task involving many tradeoffs between cost, quality, output rate, risk, investment, and so on. Also, the decision is a never ending one due to constant technological and environmental change.

The four most common forms of process design are intermittent (or job shop) where each output is unique, continuous (or flow shop) where each output is identical, batch where one group of outputs is produced and then another group, and project where the output is large, often immobile, complex, and frequently unique.

The intermittent process design form is typically used when the organization's outputs are expected to be relatively individualized or exhibit considerable variety. The main advantage of this form is the low investment cost and the flexibility in processing small volumes. Some disadvantages, however, are the complexity in managing the operations, the variation in throughput times, and the amount of materials handling equipment needed.

The layout of the intermittent process form is usually based on minimizing the difficulty of interoperations relationships such as materials handling. Computer programs such as CRAFT, ALDEP, and CORELAP are available to aid in this task.

A number of helpful "principles" of materials handling can aid in intermittent process design through minimizing handling and improving the efficiency of handling. A host of materials handling equipment is available to aid in the task also.

The continuous process design form is most advantageous for high volume production of standardized outputs. The main advantages are the low unit cost of outputs and the ease of ongoing management control of the operations. Disadvantages are the inability to change the output and the boredom of the labor force.

In the continuous form, the difficulty of process design is in the initial setup. There are a number of charts and figures to aid in this process of analyzing the output, the equipment, the workers, and the worker-equipment interface.

One of the major aspects of setting up the initial operations is balancing the line. There are both paced and unpaced lines, each having its own advantages and disadvantages. The demand rate and available work time set the cycle time for the line and then the length of the tasks in combination with the cycle time determines the minimum number of work stations. The actual balancing of the tasks among stations is often simply based on experience, taking special restrictions and considerations into account. For extremely large problems, computer based heuristic approaches have proven useful and a number of such programs exist.

The processing industries are a special form of continuous process design, typically based on a single, fluid-type material input. However, the same manner of analysis of the output and the processing operations must be conducted and the timing and flow rates of processes must be balanced.

Simulation is a powerful, all-purpose technique of great value in process design, as well as in other areas of operations management. Through the use of simulation, alternate processing forms can be tested and analyzed, new ideas checked out, and a final form selected that appears to best meet management's objectives.

7.12 READINGS

Furniture Craftsman Shuns Production-Line Methods

BY ELLEN ESHBACK, CHICAGO TRIBUNE

He simply calls himself a woodworker, but that describes only one facet of George Nakashima. Yes, he produces what the Smithsonian magazine describes as "some of the best hand-built furniture in America." Yes, about 100 pieces of that furniture fill the Tarrytown, N.Y., home of former Vice President and Mrs. Nelson Rockefeller.

And yes he has won worldwide recognition for his ability to find richness and beauty in wood that other craftsmen might discard.

Educated in forestry and architecture, he has more than a knowledge of wood, a trained eye, and skilled hands. He has the strength to an antisocial, antistyle, antimodern—all words he uses to describe his philosophy that has evolved from and shaped the 72 years of his life.

It was his philosophy that brought him to Chicago recently from New Hope, Pa., where he has 35 acres of wooded land and nine buildings, including his home, workshops, and showrooms. Invited to give three lectures sponsored by the Illinois Institute of Technology's College of Architecture, Planning and Design, he delighted in the chance to "offer a contrast" to audiences in a steel-and-glass building set in the heart of a concrete city.

The contrast he offers is that of a contemporary man who has succeeded financially and esthetically in producing furniture without using production-line techniques or bowing to merchandising demands for twice-yearly style changes.

His furniture is crafted from the mountainous inventory he has built over the years, including trees from the forest where Iran, Turkey, and Russia meet; burry English oaks, some close to five feet wide, from the reforestation plantings of Elizabeth I; root ends of great English walnut trees; and odd and extraordinary American walnut. Only solid wood—no veneers—is used for the variety of tables, chairs, benches, cabinets, chests, desks, and lamps Nakashima makes.

He is just as particular about construction. Corners customarily are dovetailed, and butterfly inlays often connect planks for table tops. Joints are mortised and tenoned, often with the tenons showing, and leaving a board's natural edge is characteristic.

The styles (though Nakashima wouldn't use that word because "styles don't exist for me") are timeless, and prices are reasonable—$225 for a rocking chair, $80 for a 36-inch-diameter table, $620 for a double-pedestal desk, $270 for a floor lamp.

Though Nakashima asserts that what he is doing is antisocial because "it doesn't really fit into our economy or our lives," he does take some satisfaction in seeing the returning and growing interest in natural and real things, including antiques. He notes that "the basis of our business is this appreciation."

A designer and businessman, Nakashima also is an environmentalist who has been a Hindu monk, and neither his success nor his furniture can be fully appreciated without knowing this.

He walks his acreage daily, communing with nature as he clears the forest. "The trees are all my friends, and when I clean their surroundings, even the wildlife seem to enjoy it better. The deer romp more easily, and the birds fly more freely."

If Nakashima's success is due to his sensitivity, it also has been a question of stubbornness, he says.

"In the beginning, I was stubborn enough to do without money, and when I didn't have, I improvised," he says.

A Japanese-American born in Spokane, Nakashima learned some of that stubbornness when he was graduated from Massachusetts Institute of Technology into the Depression job market and decided to leave for Europe. Working variously as a house painter, printer in a music publishing house, and cook, he financed travels that eventually landed him in Japan. There, American architect Antonin Raymond, who had offices in Tokyo, put him to work as the architect he was schooled to be.

Working for Raymond, Nakashima went to Pondicherry, India, to design a dormitory for a Hindu monastery. He ended up creating furniture for the entire monastery and remained two years, taking a Hindu name and living the life of a monk.

His family ties pulled him back to the United States, however, and he settled in Seattle with his Japanese-American wife, whom he had met in Japan on the way home. When World War II started shortly after that, they and their infant daughter were sent to an internment camp in Idaho, a miserable experience that ended only when Raymond, who by this time had moved to Pennsylvania, arranged for Nakashima to come work for him again.

In May, 1945, Nakashima and his family moved onto their own three acres nearby, and George Nakashima, woodworker, set up his own business.

At first he created furniture for local restaurants and friends and also designed for Hans Knoll, whom he met through the Raymonds, and later for Widdicomb-Mueller. The local papers began to give him publicity, primarily, he said, as a human interest story illustrated with photographs of him and his wife and their young daughter carving their niche in the wilderness. They were true pioneers, Nakashima remembers, noting that they lived in a tent from May to Thanksgiving.

Source. "Your Home," *The Cincinnati Enquirer*, November 20, 1977. Reprinted by courtesy of *The Cincinnati Enquirer*.

7.13 KEY TERMS

Concepts

efficiency (p. 192)
effectiveness (p. 192)
capacity (p. 192)
flexibility (p. 192)
intermittent process (p. 193)
continuous process (p. 195)
batch process (p. 195)
project process (p. 196)
assembly line (p. 195)
processing plant (p. 195)
job shop (p. 195)
flow shop (p. 195)
throughput time (p. 198)
fixed position (p. 196)
staging areas (p. 196)
assembly line (p. 195)
balanced line (p. 207)
safety stock (p. 207)
setup (p. 195)
in-process inventory (p. 200)
synthetic process (p. 210)
analytic process (p. 210)
load matrix (p. 203)
CRAFT (p. 204)
heuristics (p. 204)
ALDEP (p. 205)
CORELAP (p. 205)
paced line (p. 208)

Tools and Applications

pallets (p. 218)
shrink-wrap (p. 218)
unitization (p. 218)
containerization (p. 219)
piggyback (p. 219)
birdyback (p. 219)
fishyback (p. 219)
UPC (p. 219)
variable-path (p. 221)
fixed-path (p. 222)
tines (p. 221)
fork lift (p. 221)
automatic transfer machines (p. 222)
explosion chart (p. 230)
assembly chart (p. 230)
operations process chart (p. 230)
route sheet (p. 233)
activity chart (p. 233)
man-machine chart (p. 233)
simo chart (p. 234)
layout diagram (p. 234)
subassemblies (p. 233)
utilization (p. 233)
precedence graph (p. 236)
cycle time (p. 236)
idle time (p. 236)
balance delay (p. 239)
efficiency (p. 237)
COMSOAL (p. 239)
MALB (p. 239)
extraction (p. 214)
forming (p. 214)
machining (p. 215)
joining (p. 215)
finishing (p. 216)
change of properties (p. 215)
smelting (p. 214)
blast furnace (p. 214)
bauxite (p. 214)
electrolytically (p. 214)
alloy (p. 214)
molding (p. 214)
working (p. 215)
thermoplastic (p. 215)
thermosetting (p. 215)
forging (p. 215)
rolling (p. 215)
boring (p. 216)
shaping (p. 216)
planing (p. 216)
broach (p. 216)
milling (p. 216)
lathe (p. 216)
turning (p. 216)
tempering (p. 215)
case hardening (p. 215)
annealing (p. 215)
honing (p. 216)
lapping (p. 216)
galvanizing (p. 216)
electroplating (p. 216)
simulation (p. 225)
representative number (p. 227)
random number (p. 228)
Monte Carlo (p. 225)
setup time (p. 226)
measure of performance (p. 227)
stabilizes (p. 228)

7.14 REVIEW TEST

Concepts

1. Process design involves trying to find that design which gives the best tradeoffs among efficiency, effectiveness, flexibility, and capacity. (p. 192)
   a. True b. False
2. The successful organization in our society today found the best process design for their own objectives and stayed with it. (p. 193)
   a. True b. False
3. Intermittent processes are typically used where there is great variety in the outputs. (p. 193)
   a. True b. False
4. A disadvantage of the job shop is the investment cost of its general-purpose equipment. (p. 200)
   a. True b. False
5. The investment in in-process inventory for the low volume job shop is minimal. (p. 200)
   a. True b. False
6. The CORELAP computer program lays out a facility according to input measures of the amount of traffic between sets of operations. (p. 205)
   a. True b. False
7. Processing plants such as refineries are classified as continuous processes. (p. 209)
   a. True b. False
8. The primary process design activities for projects are those concerned with scheduling. (p. 213)
   a. True b. False
9. Organizations rarely try to combine different process forms because their management requirements are so different. (p. 196)
   a. True b. False
10. The difficulty of managing the high volume, specialized equipment, continuous process operations is one disadvantage of this form. (p. 205)
    a. True b. False
11. It is difficult to economically change the rate of output of continuous process operations. (p. 207)
    a. True b. False
12. An unpaced line uses inventory between workers to buffer their operations. (p. 208)
    a. True b. False
13. Most of the production work is typically done on the main production line. (p. 208)
    a. True b. False

Tools and Applications

14. Materials handling is a big problem in product organizations but not as much in service organizations where no physical product exists. (p. 217)
    a. True b. False
15. Palletization is reducing bulk products into small lumps to ease its handling and transport. (p. 218)
    a. True b. False
16. One important principle of materials handling is to clearly identify materials. (p. 217)
    a. True b. False
17. One of the main purposes of the UPC label on packages is to speed up checkouts by having the optical scanner quickly read and register the price. (p. 219)
    a. True b. False
18. Organization charts and maps are forms of simulation. (p. 225)
    a. True b. False
19. A disadvantage of simulation is that it will not find an optimal solution. (p. 225)
    a. True b. False
20. The representative number identifies the level of a process variable corresponding to a selected random number. (p. 227)
    a. True b. False
21. The simulation should be terminated when all the relevant system variables have very small changes between cycles. (p. 228)
    a. True b. False
22. The assembly chart describes each operation, the required equipment, and operation times. (p. 231)
    a. True b. False
23. An activity chart is also called a man-machine chart. (p. 233)
    a. True b. False

24. The symbol □ is used in assembly charts to denote the inspection of an item. (p. 233)
    a. True b. False
25. Little model buildings and machines are often used by industrial engineers to aid in layout design. (p. 234)
    a. True b. False
26. In line balancing, the cycle time for an operation is the time it takes the machine to return to its starting position. (p. 236)
    a. True b. False
27. The balance delay refers to the efficiency of the line. (p. 238)
    a. True b. False
28. In line balancing we assume all the workers are identical to start with. (p. 237)
    a. True b. False

7.15 DISCUSSION QUESTIONS

1. Why is managing a high volume, continuous operation easier than, for example, a low volume job shop?
2. Are there more or less inventories with a continuous process compared to an intermittent process?
3. Why is the special purpose equipment for continuous processes especially susceptible to obsolescence?
4. How are explosion charts drawn for overlapping, interconnected, and hidden assemblies?
5. Why are irregular cycles in activity charts considered undesirable instead of desired for their change of pace and elimination of boredom?
6. What other considerations might an operations analyst have to consider in a layout other than those mentioned?
7. How would a task that takes longer than the cycle time be handled if it can be broken into smaller subtasks? If it cannot?
8. Can you think of any logical heuristics to aid in balancing a line?
9. Where might the term "balance delay" have come from?
10. In calculating the number of stations in line balancing, why must we always round up?
11. Could tasks be taken out of precedence if it were easy to route them back to earlier stations, in order to achieve better balance?
12. Is a logging mill an analytic processing operation or a synthetic continuous operation?
13. The equipment of a job shop is less specialized than a flow shop. Is the labor also?
14. How would a relayout be conducted if the objective was to minimize congestion?
15. What might the advantages of CORELAP's criterion of closeness be compared to CRAFT's?
16. Interpret the principles of materials handling for a library.
17. Why does the UPC not include the price of the product?
18. What are the advantages of shrink-wrap?
19. Contemporary approaches to the solution of skyrocketing labor costs have been aimed at increasing corporate operating leverage by utilizing automated machinery wherever feasible. What are the advantages and disadvantages of such a strategy?
20. Consider a typical grocery store operation. What type of process design would be best? How might this operation be analyzed for layout and facilities requirements?
21. What operations setup would be best suited for processing college registration changes under deadline conditions?

22. Project processes such as building construction often focus upon scheduling techniques to aid in planning the project. How do such techniques help improve the production process?

23. Why is it important for batch processing industries (such as fashionable clothes and cement production) to have reliable forecasts of customer demand and production time?

24. How could a simulation process help a doctor plan his office staff and facilities requirements?

25. In simulation, how would an operations manager decide if the simulation was *sufficiently* stable to terminate the analysis?

26. If the large majority of organizations really operate in a batch processing mode, why do we consider intermittent and continuous process forms?

7.16 PROBLEMS

Concepts

1. Five departments, located in two separate buildings, as shown in the following figure, all use the same fork lift truck. The fork lift can be located in one of two locations as indicated by points A and B in the figure.

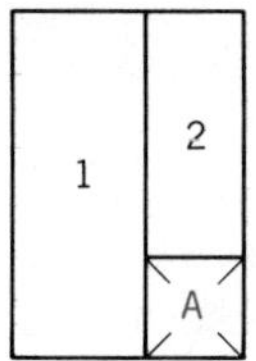

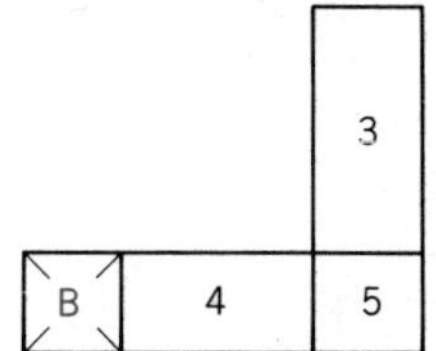

The departments make use of the fork lift with the following approximate weekly frequences.

Dept.	Weekly Frequency
1	30
2	15
3	10
4	25
5	35

The time (in minutes) to travel to and from each of the departments to the two possible locations is given below.

	Location	
Dept.	A	B
1	10	15
2	5	12
3	15	10
4	12	5
5	20	10

Which location would result in the least total travel time?

2. In Problem 1, suppose travel time for an operator and the equipment is worth $0.50 per minute. What weekly rental cost for a second fork lift would be justified on the basis of travel time eliminated?

3. Dr. Duncan Dickinson, a new member of the Business School faculty, is considering three vacant offices from which he can choose a "home." The offices are located on the sketch he has made along with the various other offices which Dr. Dickinson will frequently visit.

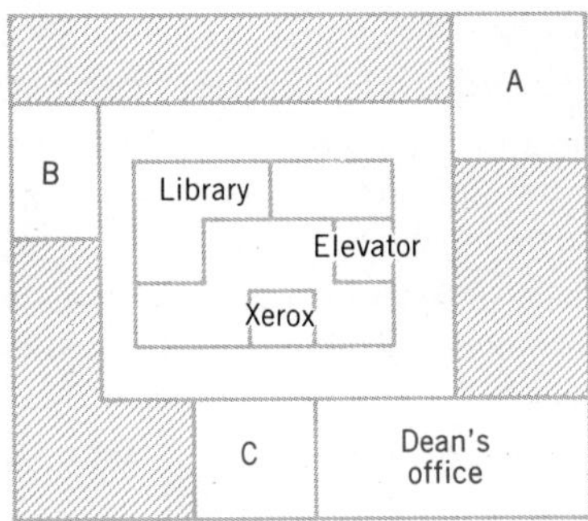

Dr. Dickinson has calculated the walking distances from each potential office (A, B, C) to each potential destination as follows.

	A	B	C
Dean's office	35	50	15
Xerox room	50	40	10
Library	25	10	30
Elevator	15	50	25

He also estimates the following number of trips each day to and from each location.

Dean's office	3
Xerox room	15
Library	5
Elevator	4

Which potential office minimizes his total distance?

Tools and Applications

4. The Duke County Police Department receives calls according to the following probability distribution.

Calls per Hour	Probability
0	.2
1	.5
2	.3

Thirty percent of the calls are "2 hour" calls, requiring a patrol car to be out for a 2-hour time block. Other calls are expected to consume one full hour of a patrol car's time. Cars are staffed on a 24-hour basis. If the county decides to attempt operation with four cars, what will the number of idle hours be in a day? What will be the number of calls for which an immediate response can be made? Assume that calls are placed in a queue and that response is made on a first-in-first-out basis. For simplicity, simulate for a single 8-hour period.

5. Rowan and Martin are the inspector and packager at the end of a long production process. Rowan receives a large batch of items each morning to be inspected and packaged during the day. Since no buffer inventory is available, Rowan inspects, stamps, and then passes each item to Martin. Martin cannot package until Rowan has inspected and Rowan must hold an uninspected item until Martin has packaged the preceding item. The operation time distribution for the two are as follows.

Rowan		Martin	
Inspection Time (hr)	Probability	Packaging Time (hr)	Probability
0.1	.3	0.1	.4
0.2	.5	0.2	.4
0.3	.2	0.3	.2

Simulate the process for 10 items. What percentage of time is Rowan waiting? What percentage is Martin waiting?

6. Suppose that the industrial engineer recognizes the amount of time being spent in waiting by Rowan and Martin in Problem 5. Rowan suggests to him that a conveyer that would hold two inspected items be placed between he and Martin. Martin counters with the suggestion that a new inspection gauge be purchased which would shift Rowan's inspection time distribution as follows.

Inspection Time	Probability
0.1	.5
0.2	.3
0.3	.2

Presuming the waiting time is equally costly for each man, which idea will reduce total waiting cost the most?

7. Mouce, Inc. is preparing to modify its order entry procedures on the basis of a consultant's report. The tasks necessary are as follows.

a. Open envelope, remove customer purchase order (PO), make two copies.
b. Run credit check on copy A, note, and send to next station for use in preparation of picking ticket.
c. Price and total copy B after credit check is approved; send to shipping ticket preparer and notify of credit results.
d. Prepare and send picking ticket to warehouse after credit check, send copy to file clerk.
e. Prepare shipping order for shipping department from copy B, send copy of shipping order and copy B to file clerk.
f. File PO copies A and B, picking ticket, and shipping order copies in customer file.

Prepare a precedence graph for this process. The following performance times have been estimated.

a	3 min
b	10 min
c	5 min
d	2 min
e	3 min
f	1 min

If Mouce processes 40 orders per 8-hour day, how many people will be needed to complete the above tasks? What is the cycle time required? How efficient will the system be?

8. Suppose that the order entry rate must increase to 50 per day and that tasks cannot be divided between two workers. Will the system developed in Problem 7 still work? If not, why not? What could be done to remedy the situation?

9. I.M. Sweltering, a laborer in the heat treating department of a large machine tool manufacturer, operates three heat treating ovens. Load times, cycle times, and unload times on the three ovens are as follows.

	Load Time (min)	Cycle Time (min)	Unload (min)
Oven 1	20	80	20
Oven 2	10	60	20
Oven 3	30	70	15

I.M. loads and starts the three ovens in 1, 2, 3 order each morning and cannot leave at night until the last load is removed. The shift is 8 hours with a half-hour lunch break coming after the first 4 hours. No job is started which cannot be completed within a half-hour after the end of the shift. Prepare an operator activity chart for this job. How efficient is the utilization of this operator?

10. Demand for a certain subassembly in a toy manufacturing facility is 96 items per 8 hour shift. The following six tasks are required to produce one subassembly.

Task	Time Required (min)	Predecessor Tasks
a	4	—
b	5	a
c	3	a
d	2	b
e	1	b,c
f	5	d,e

What is the required cycle time? Theoretically, how many work stations will be required? Balance the line. What is the line's efficiency?

11. An assembly line has the following tasks (times shown in minutes).

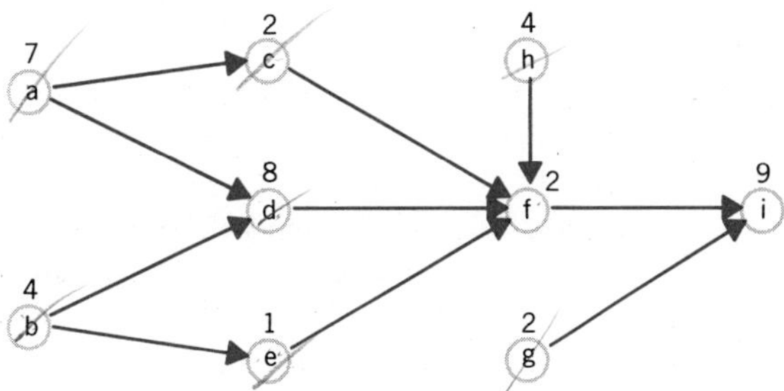

a. Six assemblies are required per hour. Balance the line.
b. What is the efficiency of the line?

7.17 CASE BLUE GRASS TOBACCO

The Blue Grass Tobacco Warehouse is making plans for a new tobacco warehouse in Paris, Kentucky. Presently, Blue Grass owns and operates three warehouses in Lexington, Kentucky. The warehouses are owned by John Abel and Bob Crane, whose fathers had owned the business before them. John and Bob took over the management of the warehouse in 1972 when Bob's father, the younger of the original owners, retired.

The Blue Grass area is the world's largest burley tobacco market with several million pounds being auctioned through the warehouse system each year. Farmers bring tobacco to market each day and buyers transport it from the warehouse after the auction is complete. An important planning factor is thus determining the number of docking platforms the new warehouse should have. Knowing the frequency of arrival of trucks and the time required to service them will determine the number of docking platforms and crews that will be required.

Based upon the size of the area and the history of the other three warehouses, the following distribution of time between truck arrivals has been estimated.

Time (min)	Probability
10	.1
20	.3
30	.5
40	.1

The average service time for a truck is 40 minutes. Service time is approximately normally distributed with a standard deviation of 10 minutes. The warehouse opens at 7 A.M. and turns away new arrivals at 4 P.M. With this information, Blue Grass believes that it can make docking and servicing plans.

QUESTIONS FOR DISCUSSION

1. Describe the method you would use to determine the number of docking platforms and crews which Blue Grass should have.
2. What assumptions will be necessary to obtain this answer?
3. Are there any important qualitative factors?

7.18 REFERENCES AND BIBLIOGRAPHY

1. Amstead, B. H., Ostwald, P. F., and Begeman, M. L., *Manufacturing Processes*, 7th ed., New York: Wiley, 1977.
2. Apple, J. M., *Materials Handling Systems Design*, New York: Ronald Press, 1973.
3. Arcus, A. L., "Comsoal: A Computer Method of Sequencing Operations for Assembly Lines," in Buffa, E. S., ed., *Readings in Production and Operations Management*, New York: Wiley, 1966.
4. Bolz, H. A., *Materials Handling Handbook*, New York: Ronald Press, 1963.
5. Buffa, E. S., Armour, G. C., and Vollman, T. E., "Allocating Facilities with CRAFT," *Harvard Business Review*, 42:136–150 (Mar.–April 1964).
6. Buffa, E. S., and Miller, J., *Production-Inventory Systems: Planning and Control*, 3rd ed., Homewood, Ill.: Irwin, 1979.
7. Buxey, G. M., Slack, N. P., and Wild, R., "Production Flow System Design—A Review," *AIIE Transactions*, 5:37–48 (March, 1973).
8. Chase, R. B. "Survey of Paced Assembly Lines," *Industrial Engineering*, 6:14–18 (Feb., 1974).
9. Davis, E. W., ed., *Project Management: Techniques, Applications, and Managerial Issues*, Norcross, Ga.: American Institute of Industrial Engineers, 1976.
10. Eilon, S., *Elements of Production Planning and Control*, New York: Macmillan, 1962.
11. Elmaghraby, S. E., *The Design of Production Systems*, New York: Reinhold, 1966.
12. Foster, D., *Automation in Practice*, London: McGraw-Hill, 1968.
13. Francis, R. L., and White, J. A., *Facility Layout and Location: An Analytic Approach*, Englewood Cliffs, N.J.: Prentice-Hall, 1974.

14. Helgeson, W. B., and Birnie, D. P., "Assembly Line Balancing Using the Ranked Positional Weight Technique," *Journal of Industrial Engineering*, 12:394–398 (1961).

15. Ignall, E. J., "A Review of Assembly Line-Balancing," *Journal of Industrial Engineering*, 16:244–254 (1965).

16. Kilbridge, M.D., and Wester, L., "A Heuristic Model of Assembly Line Balancing," *Journal of Industrial Engineering*, 12:292–298 (1961).

17. Lee, R. S., and Moore, J. M., "CORELAP—Computerized Relationship Layout Planning," *Journal of Industrial Engineering*, 18:195–200, (1967).

18. Levitt, T., "Production Line Approach to Service," *Harvard Business Review*, 50:41–52 (Sept.–Oct., 1972).

19. Lock, D., *Project Management*, London: Gower Press, 1969.

20. Mastor, A. A., "An Experimental Investigation and Comparative Evaluation of Production Line Balancing Techniques," *Management Science*, 16:728–746 (1970).

21. Meier, R. C., Newell, W. T., and Pazer, H. L., *Simulation in Business and Economics*, Englewood Cliffs, N.J.: Prentice-Hall, 1969.

22. Middleton, C. J., "How to Set Up a Project Organization," *Harvard Business Review*, 45:73–82 (Mar.–April 1967).

23. Moore, J. M., *Plant Layout and Design*, New York: Macmillan, 1962.

24. Seehof, J. M., and Evans, W. O., "Automated Layout Design Program," *Journal of Industrial Engineering*, 18:690–695 (1967).

25. Starr, M. K., ed., *Management of Production*, Middlesex, England: Penguin, 1970.

26. Tonge, F. M. "Assembly Line Balancing Using Probabilistic Combinations of Heuristics," *Management Science*, 11:727–735 (1965).

27. Turban, E. and Meredith, J. R. *Fundamentals of Management Science*, Dallas: Business Publications, 1977.

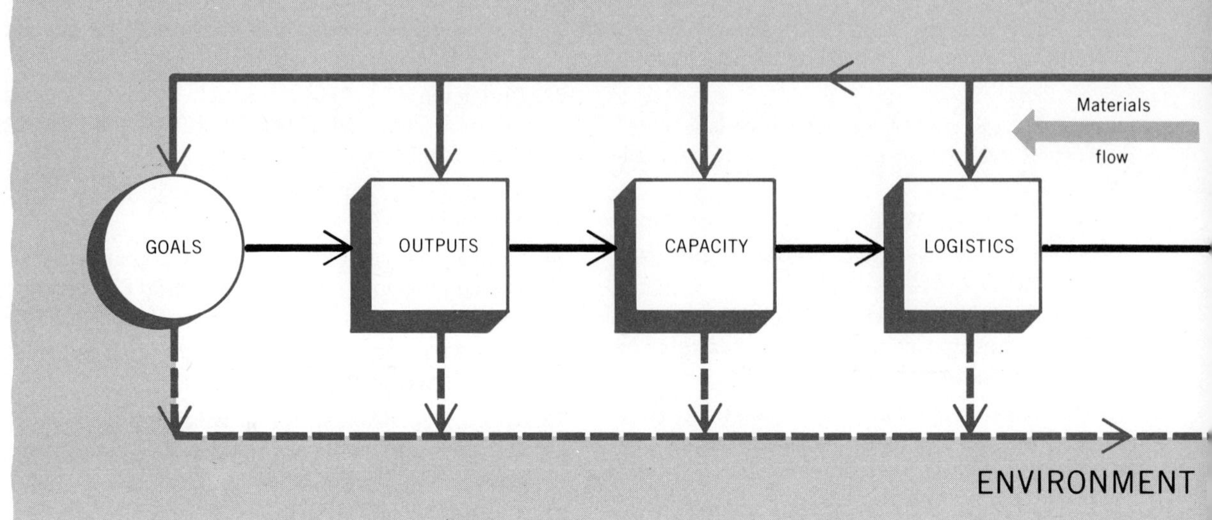

Chapter 8

Work Design

CONCEPTS

8.1 Labor and Productivity
The Effects of Automation
Productivity
8.2 Physical Elements of Work Design and Measurement
Motion Study
Therblig Analysis
Micromotion Study
Memomotion Study
Chronocyclegraph Study
Work Measurement
Time Study
Work Sampling
Predetermined Standards
8.3 The Physiological Environment of the Workplace
Anthropometric Factors
Neurological Factors
Muscular Factors
Temperature and Humidity
Illumination
Noise
Safety and Health

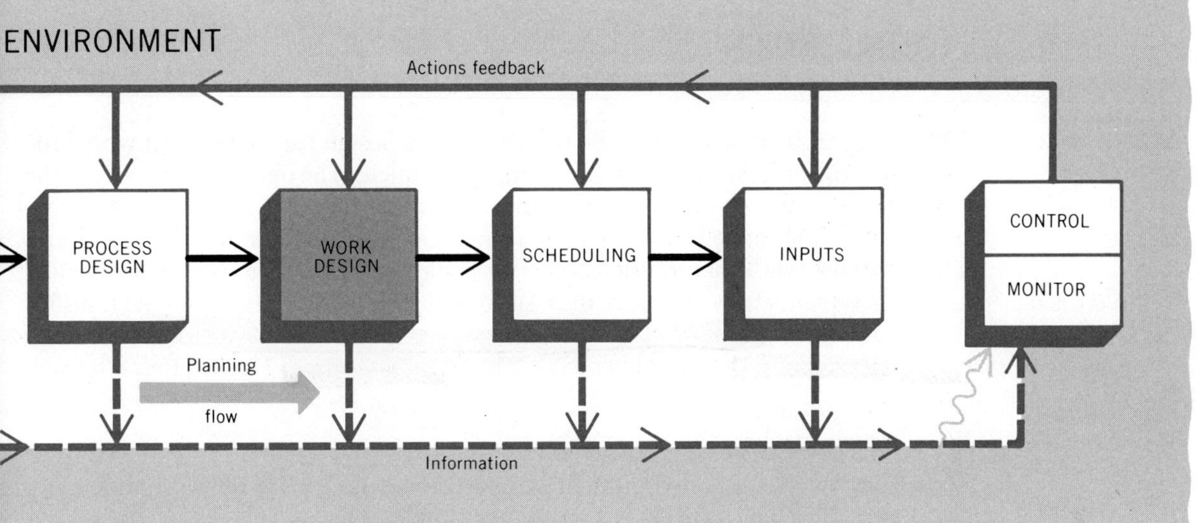

TOOLS AND APPLICATIONS

LEARNING OBJECTIVES

By the completion of the *Concepts* portion of this chapter the student should:

1. Be familiar with the nature of productivity and the main techniques for improving it.
2. Know the difference between time study and motion study, how to conduct each one, and some of the standard methods of each.
3. Understand the important physiological elements of the workplace environment and know the OSHA standards for them.
4. Be aware of the concept of feedback and its use in numerically controlled machines.
5. Realize the importance of organizational structure to work design and the role that the informal organization plays in work patterns.
6. Be conversant with the standard theories of management and motivation.
7. Understand the role of standards in designing the transformation process and the concepts of performance rating and allowance.

CONCEPTS

We have reached the point in the transformation design part of this text where the design of the processing operations is largely complete. The only thing missing is the worker. But have we taken into account the fact that humans get bored with repetitive tasks? And that physically strenuous tasks require more rest than less strenuous tasks? And all the other multiple facets of people that affect their work performance?

Work design to maximize productivity.

This chapter now addresses the issue of integrating the *worker* into the transformation process. Our goal is to design the work environment so the long run organizational **productivity** (output per worker hour) is maximized. This requires attention to

- The *physical* design of the workplace.
- The *physiological* environment (temperature, noise, etc.) of the workplace.
- The *social* aspects of the organizational environment in which the work is being done.
- The *psychological/behavioral* tenets of good management of the workforce.

We begin the chapter with a review of the role of the worker in operations and the historical importance of productivity. Next, we consider how productivity is actually measured. Lastly, we turn to the matter of how to increase the productivity of workers. We focus on two elements in particular.

1. Designing the optimum workplace environment (*Concepts* section).
2. Designing the optimum organizational and managerial environment (*Tools and Applications* section).

8.1 LABOR AND PRODUCTIVITY

Goods available due to specialization.

In Chapter 1 we described how the division of labor increased specialization, thereby increasing productivity and reducing costs. This enabled the public to obtain the products of the Industrial Revolution by both decreasing the *cost* of the products and, simultaneously, increasing the general public's ability to pay for the products through wages earned in the factories.

People supplied factories with physical labor and were often considered by managers to be relatively interchangeable commodities that could be bought or sold at will. Quite naturally, management was interested in producing the organization's output at minimal cost, and human labor was most cost-effective. They were generally not concerned with an employee's satisfaction with the job, except as it affected job performance. As human labor became more expensive, either directly in terms of wages, or indirectly in terms of requiring special consideration (such as managerial

Machines replace labor.

attention and "fringe benefits"), machines became relatively more cost-effective and began to substitute for human labor. Where this substitution was less feasible, such as in service operations, costs rose relative to product costs because the same substitution advantages could not be used.

The Effects of Automation

Automation changes the skill levels.

The increasing technological sophistication since the Industrial Revolution has had major effects. The substitution of machines for labor, in addition to significantly improving productivity, has resulted in both increased *and* decreased skill levels being required of the humans working with these systems. For example, a high degree of skill is necessary to set up a large, numerically controlled machine center. But, on the other hand, the skill levels required in a large auto assembly plant have, on the whole, declined. Automation results in challenging jobs for some, those designing the sophisticated equipment, but tedious and boring jobs for others, those being paced by the equipment.

Mechanization led to automation.

The overall result has been to substitute mechanical power for human physical labor (called **mechanization**) and, in the process, to create needs for both higher and lower levels of human skills. This trend is continuing even today where electronic equipment is replacing human sensing skills (called **automation**). It is not hard to imagine complex equipment doing much of the work occupying humans in their jobs today.

Machine sensing for automation.

Automation is not universally defined in the same way. To some, automation is simply the substitution of mechanical for human energy. However, it is becoming more common for people to also expect some form of control to exist in the form of substituting machine sensing for human sensing. This implies that *feedback* must occur in the process of automation.

Feedback and control.

The role of the comparator and effector.

The most widely used example of a feedback and control system is the common thermostat. Figure 8.1 illustrates graphically the design of a heater's thermostat. Note that there is a measuring device that senses the actual temperature, a system for reporting the termperature to the *comparator*, which compares the actual temperature with the predetermined desired temperature, a decision maker with a decision rule, and an *effector* for control. The decision maker considers the information submitted by the comparator, and, using the decision rule, adjusts the effector (heater). A typical decision rule for a thermostat might be of the following form.

If (actual temperature–desired) exceeds 3 degrees, turn heat off.

If (desired temperature–actual) exceeds 2 degrees, turn heat on.

Labeling machines.

One example of a mechanized, *nonfeedback* process involves food packaging. Many supermarket meat counters use label applying machines to weigh, print, and affix price labels on packaged meats. Anyone watching this machine at work would notice that it continues "applying" labels even after the packages of meat are all labeled—thus feedback does not occur and this would not be considered automation.

The most frequent form of feedback in automation is provided by electronics. Indeed, the extension and adoption of dedicated minicomputers to organizational

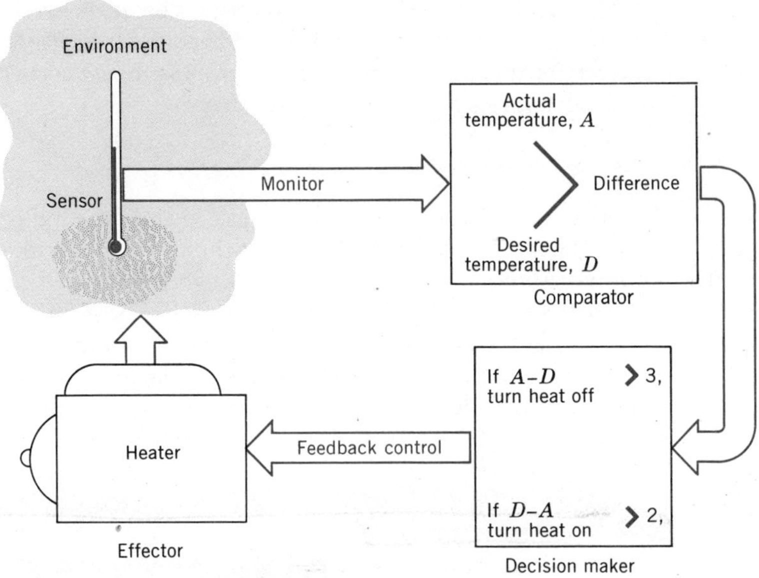

Figure 8.1 Thermostat monitor/control system.

operations, especially manufacturing, is a current technological revolution. This process has been an outgrowth of the contemporary transformation to **numerically controlled (NC)** manufacturing processes.

Numerical control allows a machine to operate automatically through the use of coded numerical instructions. Until recently, these instructions were on punched paper tape which directed the machine's operations in the same way that an operator would (e.g., a player piano). Numerical control of machines is considerably more flexible than automation since it can handle various operations, materials, speeds, and so forth.

Advantages of numerical control.

The advantages of NC are many: better utilization of the machine, fewer setups, fewer manual operations, fewer fixtures, less machining time, optimal machining speeds and feeds, automatic tool selection, potential for development of a **machining center** that has multiple tools, fewer rejects, less scrap, consistent quality, easy modification of processes, reduced inspection costs, and so on. Some disadvantages are the initial cost ($20,000 to $500,000), higher maintenance costs, expensive programming costs, and time.

Point-to-point versus continuous path programming.

NC programming is of two types. For machining to be done at one *point*, such as drilling,* *point-to-point* programming is used. For machining over a *surface*, such as milling* or planing,* *continuous path* programming is used to keep the tool in constant contact with the workpiece. Two types of NC control can be used with either

* Refer to Section 7.6 for definitions.

Open-loop versus closed-loop control.

type of programming: *open-loop* (without feedback) and *closed-loop* (with feedback). The meat labeling machine discussed earlier would be an example of the former and illustrates the dangers in such control mechanisms. An example of a single-axis, closed-loop control system is illustrated in Figure 8.2.

Automation and NC certainly appear promising for our productivity crisis. We have, however, noted in Chapter 1 the trend in our economy toward services and many of these service occupations appear somewhat more difficult to replace mechanically or electronically: the teacher, the waiter, the masseur, the doctor. Nevertheless, someone will only too quickly point out the computerized teaching machine; the vending machine; the vibrating beds and recliners, roller massage chairs, and pulsating showers; and computerized diagnosis and multiphasic screening. There is even a computer game called "Psychiatrist" whose "patients," communicating through a terminal connected to the computer, swear there is a real person on the other end and have even felt significant psychological improvement following "sessions" with the computer.

Computerized psychiatry.

Are humans superior to computers?

The question that often arises is: What can machines, like the computer, *not* do? Some researchers (e.g., McCormick [13]) have attempted to answer this question. To summarize their views, human abilities surpass machines in terms of

- *Organizing* patterns and information, using *judgment*, reasoning *inductively*.
- Responding *flexibly* to situations, *selecting* appropriately.
- Being *innovative* and *creative, synthesizing* elements of a situation or problem.

In a way, all of these abilities seem to relate to each other; for example, an important element of creativity is the ability to organize information and respond flexibly. And one aspect of reasoning inductively is selecting and synthesizing. It might be noted also that humans have a considerable amount of **redundancy** in their makeup

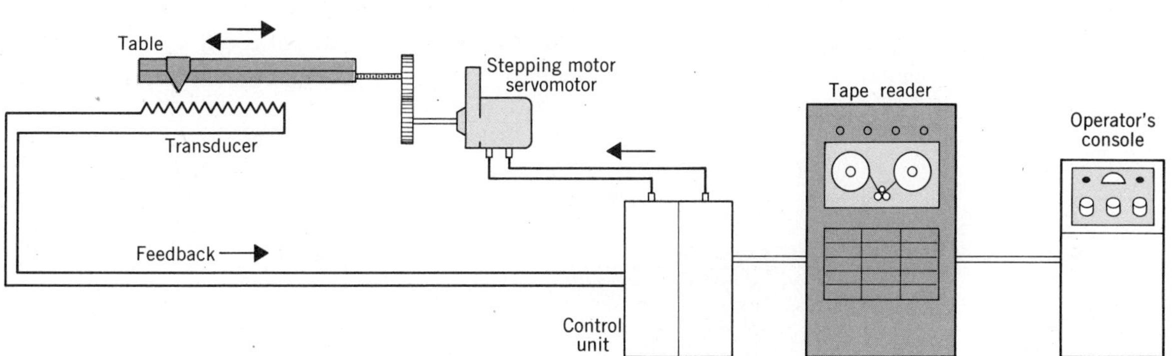

Figure 8.2. One-axis, closed-loop numerical control system. (*Source*: B. H. Amstead, P. F. Ostwald, and M. L. Begeman, *Manufacturing Processes*, Seventh Edition, John Wiley and Sons, Inc., 1977. Reprinted by permission.)

and this too might contribute to the abilities above, as well as to increased **reliability** (as will be discussed in Chapter 18).

The human use of human beings.

Ideally, workers would only be used for their highest abilities as mentioned above: creativity, synthesis, organization, judgment, flexibility, and so forth. Although society is clearly advancing in this direction, the achievement of this goal is still a long way off. In the meantime, there is work to be done, much of it menial, and to the extent that this work can be made more palatable to the indispensable human worker, productivity will be improved.

The sociotechnical approach to high productivity.

In spite of the tremendous potential of machines to replace human endeavor in organizations, virtually all of today's productive systems are still combinations of facilities, equipment, materials, and *humans*. These organizations are frequently referred to as **sociotechnical systems** because they intimately combine people and technology in complex forms to produce outputs. To the extent that the worker is considered to be simply a cheaper substitute for a machine, there will be managerial problems. The sociotechnical approach to work design is illustrated in Figure 8.3. Although there are clearly certain *technical* requirements for each job there are also certain human (*social*) factors that must be considered (comfort, interest, etc.). Work designed to lie in the region of overlap of these factors then is expected to have continuing high productivity.

Productivity

The major benefit of increased automation and mechanization, productivity, has in recent years become a major national issue. We have come to expect that our sociotechnical systems can become more and more advanced and that productivity can and should continue to grow in all areas of operations. In simple terms, productivity is defined as "output (units, gallons, visits, etc.) per worker hour." As noted in Chapter 1, organizations must be particularly sensitive to the output per unit input of *all* resources and not just worker hours. However, in this section we will limit our discussion to the issue of *worker* productivity.

Figure 8.4 illustrates the trend in labor productivity in the United States since 1890. Note that up to 1945, productivity gains increased at about 2 percent per year and then at about 3 percent per year thereafter. In the early 1960s annual productivity

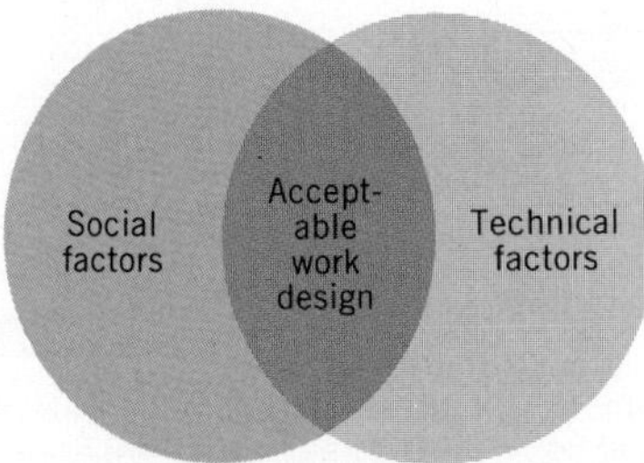

Figure 8.3 The sociotechnical approach to work design.

Decreasing productivity gains since mid 1960s.

increases hit a peak of almost 4 percent a year but since that time productivity increases have been declining. Whether this decrease is due to the marked rise in the services sector of the economy with its accompanying low rate of productivity or to some other factor is not known. One reason for the importance of this drop in productivity is its devastating effect on our competitive position in world markets and the U.S. balance of payments.

A number of things can affect "productivity" when simply measured as output per workhour. Most of the increase in manufacturing productivity has resulted from

Figure 8.4 History of productivity in the United States. (*Source:* J. L. Riggs, *Production Systems: Planning, Analysis and Control,* Second Edition, John Wiley and Sons, Inc., 1976. Reprinted by permission.

capital investments in more efficient facilities and equipment such as basic oxygen furnaces in steel making, numerically controlled machining, automated assembly lines, conveyor systems, and so forth. However, there have also been some productivity gains directly from workers due to better work organization, output standardization, higher motivation, profit sharing, better working conditions, longer training periods, zero-defects programs, and so on.

Productivity gains from both workers and equipment.

GOOD NEWS • BAD NEWS

"Mr. Bruckner would like a word with you in his office."
(Reprinted by permission of the Chicago Tribune–New York News Syndicate, Inc.)

The difficulty of measuring productivity.

One of the problems in measuring productivity is that the output being counted is not always constant. It is easy enough to increase productivity by letting quality decrease. Rapidly changing technology has made output comparisons almost meaningless in many areas, such as electronics. And in the service sector the definitions are even more difficult: if arrests per police officer go down in one year compared to the year before, has police protection improved because of prevention, or worsened because, perhaps, of a slackening in apprehension efforts?

In both the the product and service areas there appear to be three primary ways of increasing productivity: through equipment, methods, and the workers.

Equipment

Advanced technological methods have been referred to above. Mechanization, automation, and computerization are commonplace and expected in our society's organizations. In fact, as consumers we get irritated and indignant on the few occasions when the computer mis-bills us for merchandise or loses our reservation, when the vending machine dispenses cold coffee, or when the traffic signal gets stuck on red. We forget the savings in cost, increase in speed, and enlarged service capacity this equipment has also provided.

Methods

A number of changes in work methods often help in improving productivity such as

- Suggestion plans.
- Parts interchangeability.
- Unitization and containerization.
- Standardization.
- Better work design.
- Cost reduction programs.
- Improved workplace organization.
- Waste reduction programs.
- Zero-defects programs (Chapter 16).
- Value analysis programs.
- Using managerial aids such as control charts (Chapter 15), computer models such as CRAFT, and so on.

We will consider some of these approaches to improving productivity, and equipment-based approaches as well, in Sections 8.2 and 8.3.

Workers

A considerable amount of attention has been focused on directly improving the staff's performance through good management as well as by such specialized techniques as four-day workweeks, profit-sharing, absentee and turnover programs, "sensitivity training," "job enlargement" (a direct response to increasing specialization and boredom), and so on. This approach to productivity is considered in the *Tools and Applications* portion of this chapter.

8.2 PHYSICAL ELEMENTS OF WORK DESIGN AND MEASUREMENT

Designing the workplace.

The first aspect of physical work design should perhaps concern the design of the workplace within which the work will be conducted. This is a continuation of the layout analyses of Chapter 7 but now in relation to the human worker's place in the system. The objectives of the work to be done should, in large measure, dictate the basic workplace design. If customer service is the task, then a work arrangement that optimizes customer contact should be used. Entry and exit should be easy, waiting should be minimal, and so on. If committee work is the task, then the workplace should allow for the easy, interpersonal communication that is necessary. The area should be quiet, comfortable, and segregated from distractions such as phones and the comings and goings of others.

Work simplification questions.

But in considering the various aspects of work design, the analysis seems to backtrack without end. *Is this the best way to serve a customer? Should a tool be employed? Can a machine do the work instead? Could this task be more efficiently combined with an earlier or later one? Is this task necessary? Could redesigning the output eliminate the task?* These are all fruitful questions for simplifying work, and cutting costs as well, and should precede the purely physical aspects of work design. Some other useful questions to aid in simplifying work are

1. Is this task necessary?
2. Can the task be shortened?
3. Can the task be more efficiently combined with an earlier or later one?
4. Is there a better way to do the task?
5. Can a machine be used more effectively?
6. Would tools or equipment help in this task?
7. Can handling be minimized?
8. Are the working conditions best for this task?
9. Is necessary idle time usefully employed elsewhere?
10. Is fatigue minimized?
11. Are worker skill levels appropriate to the task?

One classical area of physical workplace design has been known as "time and motion study," popularized in the media of the 1950s by the concept of the "efficiency expert." The reason that time and motion study is important to the operations manager is that these studies set the *capacity* of the productive process and thus determine the output rate of the operation. Without a "standard" no planning can be done, nor for that matter can anyone tell if work is taking longer or shorter than it should. Actually, these are two separate areas of study–**motion study** is oriented toward *improving* productivity and **time study** toward *measuring* productivity. We will consider each of them separately.

Time study versus motion study.

Motion Study

Principles of economy of motion.

As with the task analysis process above, the purpose of motion study is to increase the worker's efficiency of movement and decrease fatigue. There are also a number of accepted "principles" of economy of motion, primarily based on Barnes [1]. These principles can be divided into worker and workplace guidelines as follows.

Worker

1. Minimize all movements (including eye movements) by eliminating unnecessary ones, combining movements, and shortening them.
2. Make all movements smooth, continuous, curved, and rhythmic instead of zig-zagged, angular, stop and go, and so forth.
3. Balance motions by using both hands with symmetry, simultaneity, and equality of effort.
4. Do work with the smallest muscle group necessary; use gravity if possible.
5. Provide variety with foot controls, intermittent muscle use for tension relief, perceptual variety (shape, color) for control.

Workplace

6. Use holding fixtures, guideways, and stops to minimize the muscular forces required.
7. Optimally locate tools and equipment to suit the task.
8. Use equipment that can be easily operated in the proper manner.
9. Workplace conditions such as lighting, temperature, seat height, and so forth, should be appropriate to the task and the worker.

Therblig analysis

Therblig analysis for basic elemental motions.

One of the techniques for describing task motions has come to be called **therblig analysis**. Frank and Lillian Gilbreth, who developed the technique, needed a term to describe the most basic elemental motions of which all tasks are composed. Since any name was sufficient, they simply chose a reverse spelling of their own, with the t and h transposed. (If the authors had invented the technique we probably would have called the motions "Sbbigs" or "Thiderems," clearly much better terms.)

The analytic technique consists of breaking any task down into its elemental component movements, therbligs, and analyzing these to eliminate wasted motion and improve the overall task. Typical therbligs, represented in the analysis by letters, are reach (R), move (M), and grasp (G). Such studies are relatively rare these days because they are expensive and are only useful when a task is repeated many, many times. Today, many such tasks are typically automated instead.

Micromotion study

Micromotions through a high speed camera.

The determination of the exact sequence of therbligs is rather difficult since they are all "micromotions" (very small motions) and occur quickly. To aid the analysis, a high speed motion picture camera is often used in what is called a **micromotion study**. The task is filmed at high speed and then replayed in the laboratory over and over, both forward and backward, and in slow motion, until a full analysis can be made to obtain the time durations for each motion. Either a high speed clock, called a **microchronometer**, is included in the background of the film or else the basic frame speed of the camera itself is used to time the worker's movements.

Memomotion study

Slow speed memomotion.

A similar type of study, but for very *long* duration tasks, is **memomotion study** where a *slow speed* camera is used in a fashion similar to "time lapse" photography. The film is then run at a higher rate of speed to visualize the continuous motions.

Chronocyclegraph study

Light streak chronocyclegraphs.

Another variation of these studies is called a **chronocyclegraph study**. In this study, small flashing lights are attached to the worker's hands and a single time-exposure photograph is taken of the work. The resulting single picture shows the worker's hand motions as streaks of light, which may then be analyzed for balance, symmetry of motion, speed, and so forth.

In all the above cases, the same procedure is employed of analyzing basic movements in an attempt to improve the efficiency of the task. In the process, many of the worker and workplace principles of motion economy stated earlier are drawn upon.

Work Measurement

The need to measure work.

When human labor is used as part of the productive operations, it is necessary to know the productivity of that labor for capacity planning, process design, and scheduling considerations. Thus, there is a strong need for work measurement to establish standards for output rates. Three general methods of determining output rates are available: time study, work sampling, and predetermined standards. However, all three of these methods only relate to physically observable work done by humans. Machine-paced work and mental activity, for example, would not fall in these categories.

Time study

Continuous versus snapback timing.

The basic tool used in time study is a stopwatch, typically one that measures in hundredths of a minute. Two timing methods are common. One is to start the watch at the beginning of the study and let it run *continuously*, observing and recording the times at the end of each task element in sequential fashion. The other method, called **snapback timing**, is to read the time at the end of each task element and then reset the time to zero by depressing the crown for the next task element. (This procedure has occasionally been criticized as being less accurate.)

Time study is a sensitive subject.

In preparing a time study, considerable care must be taken. Time study, and motion study as well, has had especially bad press and workers often view the process with at least suspicion, if not irritation; in some unionized organizations time study is not even allowed.

Changing pace under observation.

Beyond this basic consideration, the operations analyst will want to make sure the worker has been properly trained for the job and is aware of what the analyst is doing. Frequently, a worker will change his or her pattern of work while being observed, sometimes to try to increase the allowed time for the task or in an attempt to perform well (fast) under a test situation. The well-trained analyst can detect and compensate for these changes, however, by methods we will discuss later.

MOTLEY'S CREW

(Reprinted by permission of the Chicago Tribune–New York News Syndicate, Inc.)

Time the job elements.

The analyst should be thoroughly familiar with the job being timed. This is necessary in order to divide the job into meaningful, timeable elements. It is desirable to time elements of a job rather than complete job *cycles* for a number of reasons.

- Performance speeds may vary among elements.
- Standards for *similar* jobs involving the same elements can later be set without repeating the study.
- The job is better described in terms of its elements. Some elements may be of relatively consistent duration whereas other elements may vary widely. This can then give considerable insight into ways to improve the productivity of operations.
- Timing errors or performance aberrations (dropping a tiny screw in a hole) can more easily be spotted when timing by elements.
- Different multiples of elements (e.g., assembling wheels onto carts) may exist in one cycle of the job.

Number of cycles to time.

Lastly, the analyst should know about how many cycles must be timed to give a reliable time standard. To be 95 percent confident that the observed times will be within 5 percent of the actual required times refer to Table 8.1.

TABLE 8.1 NUMBER OF CYCLES FOR TIME STUDY

	If Annual Number of Cycles	
Cycle Time (min)	<10,000	>10,000
0.25	40	80
0.50	30	60
1	20	40
5	10	20
10	7	13
20	5	9
50	3	6
100	2	4
400	1	2
1000	1	2

(*Note:* 95% confidence of being within ± 5% of actual time)

To illustrate the various aspects of time study, let us consider the following simple office paperwork example.

The insurance form

In a mail order insurance company, applicants apply for insurance by filling out a multiple copy form. The daily mail of forms is delivered to Ms. "Trip" L'Cutt who handles them according to a special procedure. She cuts open each envelope, lays any enclosed letters in one stack, locates the *second* page of the application and pulls out the snap-apart original and carbon copy, separates them on her desk, snaps out the original and carbon copy of the first page, lays them on top of the second page, staples the originals together and sets them in a stack, and staples the copies together and sets them in a separate stack.

The time study form for two cycles (abbreviated here for simplicity) is shown in Figure 8.5 filled in with continuous time readings in hundredths of minutes. Note the stapler problem indicated on the form by an asterisk; such "aberrations" are ignored in determining standard times. Alongside the continuous times are listed the **elemental times**, Δt, obtained by subtraction of the continuous time from the preceding continuous time. The average of these element times is then listed to the right. (Again, the average element times of *all* cycles would be used but here only two cycles are shown, for simplicity.)

A performance rating for normalization.

The next column lists a **performance rating**, a subjective estimate based upon the experience of the operations analyst of how fast Ms. L'Cutt is working on each element compared to an "average" worker doing this task day in and day out. A rating such as 0.90 means that she is only 90 percent as fast as expected of an average worker, perhaps due to a lack of manual dexterity or such. When these ratings are multiplied by the average elemental times, the results are the **normal times** for each job element;

that is, the time it would take the normal worker. Again, using the 0.90 rating, the effect would be to *decrease* the amount of time a normal worker would take for this element, which is indeed the proper correction. (This multiplying, instead of dividing, should have confused you for a second. If it did not, reread the last paragraph until it does.)

Allowance for fatigue, and so forth.

Adding up the elemental normal times then results in the total normal time for this job, 17.5 hundredths of a minute. On top of this, an **allowance** is given for such unavoidable delays as a jammed stapler, conferring with a supervisor, visits to the restroom, fatigue, and so forth. Typically, about 5 percent is allowed for personal needs; fatigue allowances depend on the strenuousness of the task but usually only apply to those task elements that *are* strenuous, not the entire task. For highly strenuous task elements (ditch digging, tapping molten steel from a furnace), allowances of up to 30 percent are sometimes used. Appropriate allowances can often be developed by work sampling, a technique discussed later, but in many cases allowances are determined as part of a labor-management bargaining agreement.

Standard time from normal time.

In Figure 8.5 and quite commonly, 15 percent is used as an average allowance. Adding the 15 percent of normal time for unavoidable delay to the 17.5 then results in the **standard time** of 20.1 hundredths of a minute (12 seconds). This is now the time that can be used to verify the number of cycles times in the study (about 40 from Table 8.1) and to design the insurance form processing operation for the organization. For example, the *hourly rate* for this job would be

$$\frac{60 \text{ min/hr}}{0.201 \text{ min/job}} = 300 \text{ jobs/hr.}$$

Worker	Ms. L'Cutt	Date	Feb. 20, 1979	Times	Cont. 0.01 min.
Task	Insurance Form	Analyst	R.P.G.	Allowance	15%

Element	Cycle 1	Δt	Cycle 2	Δt	Average Δt		Performance Rating		Normal Times
Open envelope	05	5	47	3	4	×	0.90	=	3.6
Papers out, envelope trash	07	2	49	2	2	×	1.10	=	2.2
Letter stacked	09	2	51	2	2	×	1.00	=	2.0
Locate page 2	10	1	54	3	2	×	0.90	=	1.8
Snapout, separate page 2	13	3	55	1	2	×	1.20	=	2.4
Snapout, separte page 1	15	2	57	2	2	×	1.20	=	2.4
Staple, stack original	16	1	58	1	1	×	1.10	=	1.1
Staple, stack copy	44*	X	60	2	2	×	1.00	=	2.0
							Total	=	17.5

Comments: *Stapler jammed

Normal time: 17.5

Allowance: 2.6

Standard time: 20.1

Figure 8.5. Time study of insurance form.

At a pay scale of \$4.50 per hour this then results in a *piece rate* of

$$\frac{\$4.50/\text{hr}}{300 \text{ jobs/hr}} = \$0.015/\text{job}.$$

One of the reasons that time study has come under fire is due to the necessity of making a *subjective* performance rating of the worker being timed. Considerable effort has been expended by organizations to assure that time study analysts have been properly trained by using training films, certified by time study organizations, and so forth.

One way of avoiding the interpersonal problems associated with time study is through **work sampling** where the worker is not directly timed and often is not even aware that she or he is being studied.

Work sampling

The advantages of work sampling.

Another way of acquiring information similar to that obtained in work measurement is through *work sampling*. In work sampling a large number of random observations are made of a worker, and in each case, a note jotted down regarding what the worker is doing. A number of advantages accrue to this procedure: it is simple, no stopwatch is needed, less training is required, the worker is often not even aware he or she is being observed, and true work performance is more likely to be observed.

Large number of observations required.

On the negative side, work sampling may involve a considerable number of observations in order to obtain 95 percent confidence. The required number of observations, N, is given by the formula

$$N = \frac{4p(1-p)}{e^2} \tag{8.1}$$

where p is the percent of time the worker spends on the activity being observed and e is the allowable error in percentage points, expressed as a decimal. That is, the observed percentage should be within $\pm$ 0.01 if 1 percent accuracy is desired. To demonstrate the use of the formula, suppose an activity is to be timed that is expected to represent 20 percent of the working day and an accuracy of $\pm$ 3 percent with 95 percent confidence is deemed sufficient (that is, from 17 to 23 percent or, if the initial estimate was wrong, from, say, 22 to 28 percent, of the working day). The required number of observations is then

$$N = \frac{4(0.2)(1 - 0.2)}{(0.03)^2} = \frac{0.64}{0.0009} = 711$$

A common and valuable use of work sampling is the establishment of allowances. If a worker is observed a sufficient number of times and in 5 percent of the observations is idle for personal reasons and 7 percent for unavoidable reasons then a total allowance of 12 percent may be used for this task.

The full use of work sampling is to establish standards for a job as a whole or even subelements of a job. To illustrate, reconsider the insurance form example and assume we are interested in setting a standard for the overall job. Since the standard allowance is 15 percent we will assume p, the proportion of time spent on the mail, is 0.85. If the allowable error is four percentage points then the number of observations required is

$$N = \frac{4(0.85)(0.15)}{(0.04)^2} = 319$$

If these 319 random observations are collected over a week's duration this will require an observation about every 8 minutes, on the average.

Suppose the results of the week's study were that 80 percent of the time Ms. L'Cutt was working (with an average rating of 110 percent), 3 percent she was avoidably idle, and 17 percent of the time she was unavoidably idle for both personal and work-related reasons. During the week of observation (40 hr × 60 min/hr = 2400 min) she processed 12,000 applications.

The standard time would be determined as follows.

$$\text{normal time} = \frac{\text{actual work time} \times \text{performance rating}}{\text{number of applications processed}} \tag{8.2}$$

$$= \frac{(2400 \text{ min} \times 80\%) \times 1.10}{12{,}000}$$

$$= 0.176 \text{ min}$$

$$\text{standard time} = \text{normal time} + \text{allowance} \tag{8.3}$$

$$= 0.176 + (0.176)\,0.15$$

$$= 0.202 \text{ min}$$

Note in this example that the 15 percent allowance is not in agreement with Ms. L'Cutt's 20 percent total idle time. However, when she was working Ms. L'Cutt worked 10 percent faster than normal to produce more than the standard number of applications per week.

$$\frac{2400 \text{ min}}{0.202 \text{ min/application}} = 11{,}881 \text{ applications}$$

Predetermined standards

Another way to determine output rates is to use **predetermined** data (e.g., from a previous time study) concerning the movements involved in a task. A knowledge of the movements then allows the synthesis (adding together) of known normal times to arrive at a total normal time for the task.

The MTM system for constructing a synthetic time study.

One of the most popular sets of such standard time elements is that used in the *methods-time-measurement* (**MTM**) system, a sample of which is shown in Figure 8.6. This system uses predetemined times called time measurement units (**TMU's**)

METHODS-TIME MEASUREMENT
MTM-I APPLICATION DATA

1 TMU	= .00001 hour	1 hour	= 100,000.0 TMU
	= .0006 minute	1 minute	= 1,666.7 TMU
	= .036 seconds	1 second	= 27.8 TMU

Do not attempt to use this chart or apply Methods-Time Measurement in any way unless you understand the proper application of the data. This statement is included as a word of caution to prevent difficulties resulting from misapplication of the data.

MTM ASSOCIATION FOR STANDARDS AND RESEARCH

16-01 Broadway
Fair Lawn, N.J. 07410

TABLE I – REACH – R

Distance Moved Inches	Time TMU A	Time TMU B	Time TMU C or D	Time TMU E	Hand In Motion A	Hand In Motion B	CASE AND DESCRIPTION
3/4 or less	2.0	2.0	2.0	2.0	1.6	1.6	A Reach to object in fixed location, or to object in other hand or on which other hand rests.
1	2.5	2.5	3.6	2.4	2.3	2.3	
2	4.0	4.0	5.9	3.8	3.5	2.7	
3	5.3	5.3	7.3	5.3	4.5	3.6	B Reach to single object in location which may vary slightly from cycle to cycle.
4	6.1	6.4	8.4	6.8	4.9	4.3	
5	6.5	7.8	9.4	7.4	5.3	5.0	
6	7.0	8.6	10.1	8.0	5.7	5.7	
7	7.4	9.3	10.8	8.7	6.1	6.5	C Reach to object jumbled with other objects in a group so that search and select occur.
8	7.9	10.1	11.5	9.3	6.5	7.2	
9	8.3	10.8	12.2	9.9	6.9	7.9	
10	8.7	11.5	12.9	10.5	7.3	8.6	
12	9.6	12.9	14.2	11.8	8.1	10.1	
14	10.5	14.4	15.6	13.0	8.9	11.5	D Reach to a very small object or where accurate grasp is required.
16	11.4	15.8	17.0	14.2	9.7	12.9	
18	12.3	17.2	18.4	15.5	10.5	14.4	
20	13.1	18.6	19.8	16.7	11.3	15.8	
22	14.0	20.1	21.2	18.0	12.1	17.3	E Reach to indefinite location to get hand in position for body balance or next motion or out of way.
24	14.9	21.5	22.5	19.2	12.9	18.8	
26	15.8	22.9	23.9	20.4	13.7	20.2	
28	16.7	24.4	25.3	21.7	14.5	21.7	
30	17.5	25.8	26.7	22.9	15.3	23.2	
Additional	0.4	0.7	0.7	0.6			TMU per inch over 30 inches

TABLE II – MOVE – M

Distance Moved Inches	Time TMU A	Time TMU B	Time TMU C	Hand In Motion B	Wt. Allowance Wt. (lb.) Up to	Wt. Allowance Dynamic Factor	Wt. Allowance Static Constant TMU	CASE AND DESCRIPTION
3/4 or less	2.0	2.0	2.0	1.7				
1	2.5	2.9	3.4	2.3	2.5	1.00	0	
2	3.6	4.6	5.2	2.9				A Move object to other hand or against stop.
3	4.9	5.7	6.7	3.6	7.5	1.06	2.2	
4	6.1	6.9	8.0	4.3				
5	7.3	8.0	9.2	5.0	12.5	1.11	3.9	
6	8.1	8.9	10.3	5.7				
7	8.9	9.7	11.1	6.5	17.5	1.17	5.6	
8	9.7	10.6	11.8	7.2				
9	10.5	11.5	12.7	7.9	22.5	1.22	7.4	B Move object to approximate or indefinite location.
10	11.3	12.2	13.5	8.6				
12	12.9	13.4	15.2	10.0	27.5	1.28	9.1	
14	14.4	14.6	16.9	11.4				
16	16.0	15.8	18.7	12.8	32.5	1.33	10.8	
18	17.6	17.0	20.4	14.2				
20	19.2	18.2	22.1	15.6	37.5	1.39	12.5	
22	20.8	19.4	23.8	17.0				
24	22.4	20.6	25.5	18.4	42.5	1.44	14.3	C Move object to exact location.
26	24.0	21.8	27.3	19.8				
28	25.5	23.1	29.0	21.2	47.5	1.50	16.0	
30	27.1	24.3	30.7	22.7				
Additional	0.8	0.6	0.85		TMU per inch over 30 inches			

TABLE IV – GRASP – G

TYPE OF GRASP	Case	Time TMU	DESCRIPTION	
PICK-UP	1A	2.0	Any size object by itself, easily grasped	
	1B	3.5	Object very small or lying close against a flat surface	
	1C1	7.3	Diameter larger than 1/2"	Interference with Grasp
	1C2	8.7	Diameter 1/4" to 1/2"	on bottom and one side of
	1C3	10.8	Diameter less than 1/4"	nearly cylindrical object.
REGRASP	2	5.6	Change grasp without relinquishing control	
TRANSFER	3	5.6	Control transferred from one hand to the other.	
SELECT	4A	7.3	Larger than 1" x 1" x 1"	Object jumbled with other
	4B	9.1	1/4" x 1/4" x 1/8" to 1" x 1" x 1"	objects so that search
	4C	12.9	Smaller than 1/4" x 1/4" x 1/8"	and select occur.
CONTACT	5	0	Contact, Sliding, or Hook Grasp.	

TABLE III A – TURN – T

Weight	30°	45°	60°	75°	90°	105°	120°	135°	150°	165°	180°
	Time TMU for Degrees Turned										
Small – 0 to 2 Pounds	2.8	3.5	4.1	4.8	5.4	6.1	6.8	7.4	8.1	8.7	9.4
Medium – 2.1 to 10 Pounds	4.4	5.5	6.5	7.5	8.5	9.6	10.6	11.6	12.7	13.7	14.8
Large – 10.1 to 35 Pounds	8.4	10.5	12.3	14.4	16.2	18.3	20.4	22.2	24.3	26.1	28.2

TABLE III B – APPLY PRESSURE – AP

FULL CYCLE SYMBOL	TMU	DESCRIPTION	COMPONENTS SYMBOL	TMU	DESCRIPTION
APA	10.6	AF + DM + RLF	AF	3.4	Apply Force
			DM	4.2	Dwell, Minimum
APB	16.2	APA + G2	RLF	3.0	Release Force

MTMA 101
PRINTED IN U S A

Figure 8.6. Motion study by MTM analysis. (Reprinted by permission of the MTM Association for Standards and Research. No reprint permission without written consent from the MTM Association, 16-01 Broadway, Fair Lawn, NJ 07410.)

to measure various elementary micromotions such as reach, grasp, turn, etc. These times (each TMU) are stated in 0.00001 hour. The time it takes to reach, for example, is listed as a function of the distance and the "clarity" of the object being reached for (if it is moving, very small, covered, etc.).

The MTM procedure is thus to break each job down into the required elemental motions for both left and right hands. A chart similar to a *simo chart* (refer back to Figure 7.21) is then constructed and TMU's assigned to the elemental motions in order to obtain a final normal time for the job. The obvious advantage of MTM is avoiding the need for a time or work sampling study. Nevertheless, a time study may still be easier to do than the rather complex MTM.

8.3 PHYSIOLOGICAL ENVIRONMENT OF THE WORKPLACE

Considering the complete workplace environment.

In this section we focus upon the workers' *environment* as it relates to work design and productivity. We consider the workplace arrangement itself of course, such as proper seat height, as well as temperature, noise, illumination, and so forth. But we also consider neurological factors, such as the design of hand controls, and other such concerns that may affect the workers' safety or health. We will divide our discussion of workplace design among anthropometric factors (body measurements), neurological factors, muscular factors, temperature and humidity, illumination, noise, and safety and health.

Anthropometric Factors

The necessity of body measurements.

In designing the workplace, information concerning the proper desk height, handrail size, tool length, and so on must all be available. Without knowing standard body measurements, and variations in those sizes, it would be impossible to design the cab for a truck, or the faucets for a sink. Much of the data available concerning the body measurements of people was originally gathered for special purposes such as cockpit sizes for pilots in World War II. Nevertheless, such data has been put to extensive use in many other organizations and situations.

Note that simple average values will not suffice. An average value for the height of a chair is acceptable but not for the size of a door, or the weight of a fire extinguisher. For these items it is desired that some very large fraction of the population be able to use the item so knowing the variation in widths of people, and their lifting strengths, is required. Then a doorway large enough to accept 99.9 percent of all people, or an extinguisher that can be lifted by 99.98 percent of all people, can be designed. Standard figures and tables of average body dimensions and fifth and ninety-fifth percentiles for both males and females are available in References 2, 13, and 17.

Neurological Factors

Many of the tasks that workers perform relate to sensory perception, speed of reaction, and ability to perform simultaneous tasks. All these tasks are concerned with *neurological* responses and the design of the workplace can improve or hinder such responses considerably. For example, Figure 8.7 illustrates two ways to set dials, marked with a shaded "normal reading" range, in a panel. At the top, the dials are set uniformly with all the *zeros* up. When activated, the dials read as shown on the right, every pointer aimed in a different direction. At the bottom, the dials are set with the *shaded ranges* all at the top and the pointers askew. When *this* panel of dials is activated, an incorrect pointer value shows up immediately because the pointer is out of line with the rest that are all pointing up. Dials set according to the latter procedure can be read much faster than the former.

Designing knobs and dials.

There are many similar such considerations (see References 13 and 17) but, in general, workplace controls should be designed to operate in the manner a worker would expect: turning a handle clockwise to *shut off* a flow, pushing a lever to *increase* a mechanism, and so forth.

Controls should operate as expected.

Muscular Factors

Although less common than in earlier days, workers' muscular abilities are sometimes important. Similar to anthropometry tables, there are also tables of muscular strengths available (see Reference 11).

Of more probable importance than strength in workplace design is the consideration of fatigue. Unfortunately, very little progress has been made in this area although many studies have been conducted. One of the main problems is that fatigue is not totally a muscular reaction—boredom, anxiety, and stress play important roles as well. To date the most common approach has simply been the use of larger allowances for more fatiguing work.

Fatigue considered through allowances.

Temperature and Humidity

Although the normal human body temperature is 98.6°F, workers attempting to produce in an environment which is that warm are extremely ineffective. According to studies reported in McCormick [13] the limit of efficient human peformance is at

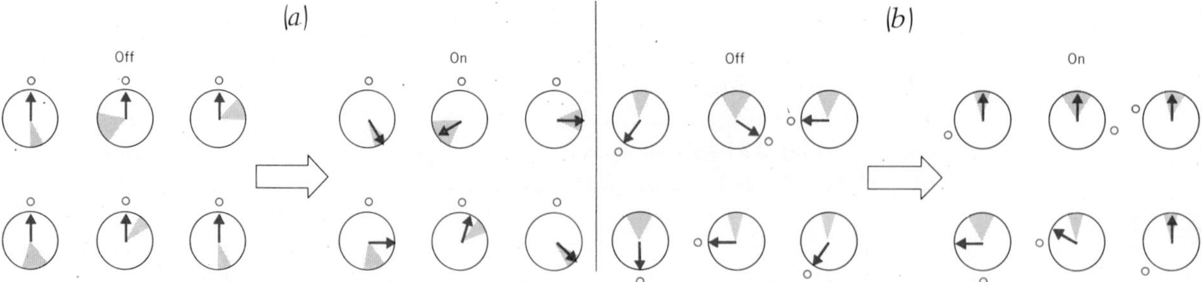

Figure 8.7. Dial alignments in a panel. Based on Reference 13. (*a*) Zero values aligned. (*b*) Shaded ("normal") ranges aligned.

Limit of efficient human performance is 92°F.

about 92°F; beyond this temperature performance degrades rapidly. The reason is that our 98.6-degree body temperature is maintained by the "burning" of fuel (food) in a normal external environment of lower temperatures.

Heating and cooling the workplace.

In the past, it has been common for organizations to heat their work areas during cold periods of the year. In recent years many organizations also air condition during the hot (or smoggy) period of the year as well. Even advanced technological equipment often requires close environmental monitoring of temperatures. For the human, however, temperature is not the only important environmental variable. Humidity is important as well, as illustrated by the **comfort zone** in Figure 8.8.

Due to the simultaneous occurrence of a natural gas shortage and several severe winters, many organizations have found it necessary to lower average temperatures in offices and factories. In fact, many factories have had gas allotments cut by 80 percent and more. The effect of working in significantly lower than "normal" temperatures is not yet known, but it is bound to have some impact on worker productivity.

Illumination

The proper lighting of the workplace, in intensity, contrast, and color, is an important element of work design. Few things are as irritating as not being able to see what you are doing. Table 8.2 lists the accepted illumination levels for various situations and tasks based on American Illumination Engineering Society standards.

Natural versus artificial lighting.

Workers generally prefer natural to artificial light, perhaps as much for claustrophobic reasons as anything else. But natural light varies considerably in intensity, from 800 footcandles on a bright summer day to 50 footcandles during rainy ones. And windows are expensive to clean, repair, and insulate.

Minimizing glare.

Glare and color are two other aspects of illumination that are important in workplace design. Glare should be minimized by moving or diffusing the source, or raising visors or shields to block it. The use of color in the workplace is often helpful, as well as psychologically beneficial. Table 8.3 lists the **OSHA** (Occupational Safety and

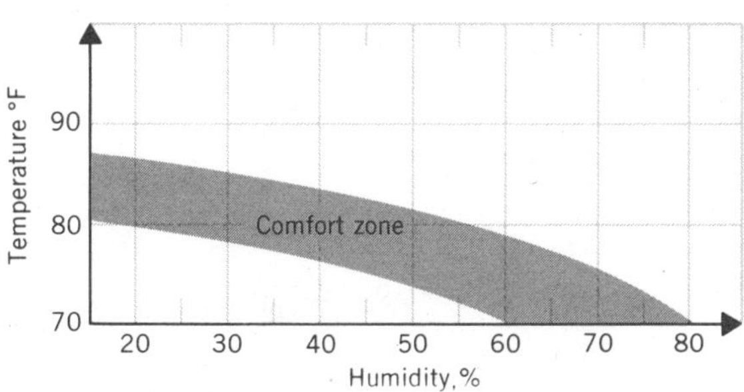

Figure 8.8. Temperature-humidity comfort zone.

TABLE 8.2 GENERAL ILLUMINATION LEVELS

Illumination, (fc)	Task
1800	Operating room surgery
1000	Welding (at work point)
500	Detailed inspection of fine work
300	Fine assembly work
200	General machining, drafting
100	Sewing
80	Polishing, typing, benchwork, art
50	Filing papers, general reading and writing, assembly
20	Rough machining, dining
10	Shipping and receiving, general lighting
5	Soft lighting, back lighting
0.5	Moonlit night
0.1	Movie theater

Health Act) color standards for marking facilities, pipes, and equipment as an example of the utility of color.

The uses of color.

The psychological use of color in hosptials, banks, and modern offices is a recent trend also. Brightly colored furniture is often used to promote a sense of sureness or progressiveness. Frequently the cool colors, blues and greens, will be used for quiet and rest areas while the warm colors, yellows, oranges, and reds are used for active areas. In addition, light colors reflect illumination well and give a sense of spaciousness to rooms.

TABLE 8.3 OSHA COLOR STANDARDS

White	Red	Orange	Yellow
Traffic lines	Fire equipment	Dangerous machinery	Caution lights
Refuse locations	Flammable liquids	Energized equipment	Guard rails
Room corners	Barricade lights	Enclosed mechanisms	Construction equipment
Food and drink dispensing	Emergency switches	Start buttons	Suspended fixtures
	Alarm boxes		Pillars, posts
			Combustible scrap containers
Green	**Black**	**Blue**	**Purple**
Safety	Traffic lines	Equipment under repair	Radiation hazards
First aid	Direction signs	Inoperative controls	Radiation storage
Go lights		Faulty valves	Radiation disposal
			Radiation equipment

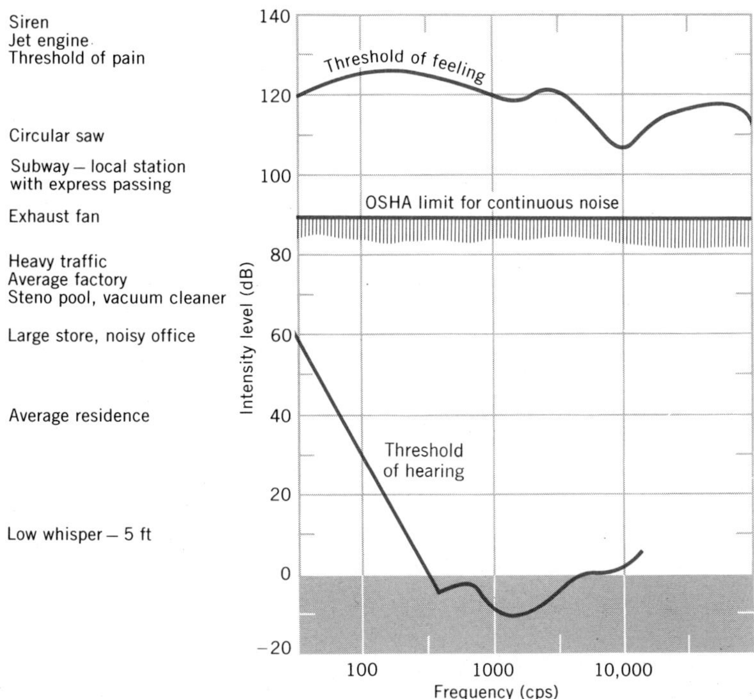

Figure 8.9. Decibel levels of some common noises. (Adapted by permission from W. E. Woodson and D. W. Conover, *Human Engineering Guide for Equipment Designers*, Second Edition, University of California Press, 1966.)

Noise

A logarithmic decibel scale.

There are two serious negative effects of noise: potential hearing loss and workplace inefficiency. Noise is typically measured in **decibels (dB)** where each increase of 10 decibels means a *tenfold* increase in intensity. Some common noise levels are given in Figure 8.9. We see that a vacuum cleaner at 70 decibels is 10 times as loud as a noisy office (60 decibels), that heavy traffic is 100 times as loud, an exhaust fan 1000 times, a circular saw 100,000 times, and a siren 100,000,000 times as loud. Included in the figure is the OSHA limit for continuous noise.

OSHA permissible noise levels.

Table 8.4 lists the permissible noise levels for shorter durations also. For example, a circular saw (110 decibels) is permissible for ½ hour, or a passing subway train for 2 hours (a very long train). But intensity of noise is not the only distraction; high pitched or irregular noises are also distracting. Some methods of dealing with noise have been

- **Controlling** the noise by reduction of vibration, and so forth.
- **Isolating** the noise.
- **Protecting** the worker through ear plugs, helmets, or even carpets and drapes.
- **Piping** in music to provide a pleasant background for working.

TABLE 8.4 OSHA PERMISSIBLE NOISE LEVELS

Duration per day (hr)	Sound Level (dB)
8	90
6	92
4	95
3	97
2	100
1½	102
1	105
½	110
¼ or less	115

Safety and Health

OSHA began in 1971.

Frequently in the discussions above we referred to the *OSHA standards* for various workplace design factors such as color, or noise. In 1971, the U.S. Occupational Safety and Health Act (OSHA) took effect. This act provides for much tighter safety and health regulations of organizations than ever before. The Department of Labor, which administers OSHA, has the authority to inspect workplaces, issue citations for violations of standards, and even obtain court orders closing down operations until unsafe practices are corrected. OSHA initially earned a negative reputation because of some poor judgments in its early regulatory activities, but most of this has now been cleared up. In addition to safety responsibilities, OSHA is also responsible for unsafe noise and chemical regulations.

The expense of accidents.

Designing for safety in the workplace is of special importance—not only accident-related safety but health as well. Management knows that health and accident expenses can be tremendous, not only to the worker but also the organization. It thus behooves the operations manager to try to anticipate and prevent both accidents and health hazards. Since we are becoming more and more aware of work environments that can produce health problems (mining of various minerals, asbestos production and use, spray painting, arc welding) it is reasonable to expect more and more regulations and precautions against materials and occupations that result in long-term health problems.

Accidents as two unsafe acts.

Most accidents seem to be combinations of multiple unsafe events: an unsafe act in the presence of unsafe conditions, or two unsafe acts occurring simultaneously. This is why accidents do not occur more often than they do. In some sense, it also explains why people are lulled into thinking accidents only happen to someone else—they have often done unsafe acts themselves and never had an accident. Since it is usually *two* unsafe events that produce accidents, there is an early opportunity to prevent accidents by watching for the *first* unsafe event. In addition to observation, another way to identify unsafe events is by a review of all previous accidents. It has generally been found that, for every major injury, there were over 300 noninjury accidents. If the location and nature of these noninjury accidents can be identified, it might be possible to prevent a major injury.

300 noninjuries per injury.

TOOLS AND APPLICATIONS

8.4 ORGANIZATIONAL AND MANAGERIAL ASPECTS OF WORK DESIGN

Work design for a robot.

Up to this point, in our discussion of work design we have considered the layout of the workplace, the uses of mechanization and automaton, the productivity of the worker and how to measure and improve it, and the environment within which the worker must operate. In a sense, this views the worker as an automaton—motivation, peer groups, and leadership pose no problem. But in most organizations just the opposite is the case.

Effect of organization and management.

In this section then, we consider the effect of organization and managerial style upon the worker. There is a tremendous amount of information in this area and we will only briefly survey the high points. The interested reader should consult some of the works in the bibliography such as References 3 and 8 for further details.

Organizational Design

There are three primary concepts in organizational design that relate directly to the design of work: division of labor, span of control, and organizational structure. We will consider each of these in turn.

Division of labor

Line derived from the chain of command.

We have, in previous chapters, spoken at length about the **division of labor** concept stemming from Adam Smith's advantages of specialization. We have also discussed the negative aspects of specialization, such as boredom. However, another aspect of the division of labor concept is the distinction between **line** and **staff**. The idea of a line originated in military and religious organizations and describes the **chain of command**, of authority and responsibility, from the lowest worker to the organizational head.

The development of staff, on the other hand, served the purpose of relieving the line managers of increasingly burdensome duties, especially when society and technology advanced to the point that specialists were required in these areas (such as legal counsel, R&D, public relations, taxation) to properly serve the organization. A continuing problem often exists between line units and staff over authority and responsibility and top management must carefully delineate the duties of each unit.

Committees, a special kind of division of labor, are formally organized to deal with a special issue. The members are often chosen, not because of their homogeneity, but almost the opposite—to represent different interests and positions. Work design for committees often proceeds according to the same standard formula: a chairperson follows an agenda, Roberts' rules of order are used, and the most aggressive or vocal member usually gets the results he or she wants. The advantage of committee work is that all factions (theoretically) have an input to the process.

Roberts' rules versus adversary process in committees.

There are other ways to run effective committees however. One way conforms to the legal "adversary" process. For each issue, advocates speak pro and con until all points of importance have been put forth. The chairperson then seeks a consensus. If no consensus can be found then a majority opinion is written *and* a minority opinion is included. The advantage of this process is twofold: 51 percent of the group is not imposing its will upon the other 49 percent. And better decisions may be made based on the two opinions—there is not simply the report of a "yes" or "no" vote on a particular, apparently black-and-white, issue.

Nominal and Delphi groups.

Another method for running an effective committee is called a **nominal group process**. (**Delphi panels** are nominal groups.) In this situation the committee members need not meet face to face and the typical drawbacks of committee meetings, such as generating irrelevant information, getting sidetracked, and being dominated by one member, are thereby avoided. Nominal groups exist in *name* only and tend to generate more relevant information, are more tolerant of minority views, and avoid domination. They typically communicate with the chairperson in writing, who may then summarize the viewpoints and relay this information, perhaps with new questions, back to the members. This process may be repeated until some form of consensus is reached or else positions on an issue do not change further.

Span of control

Ranges in spans of control.

The number of managerial levels within a hierarchy in an organization is inversely related to the **span of control**. With very few levels (a short chain of command) a manager must be responsible for many subordinates (that is, have a large span of control), and with more levels, the span of control can be reduced. Two extreme spans of control to direct eight workers are illustrated in Figure 8.10.

The "best" span of control depends on a number of factors.

1. Task complexity: if the work is simple and repetitive a span of control of 30 or more may be possible.

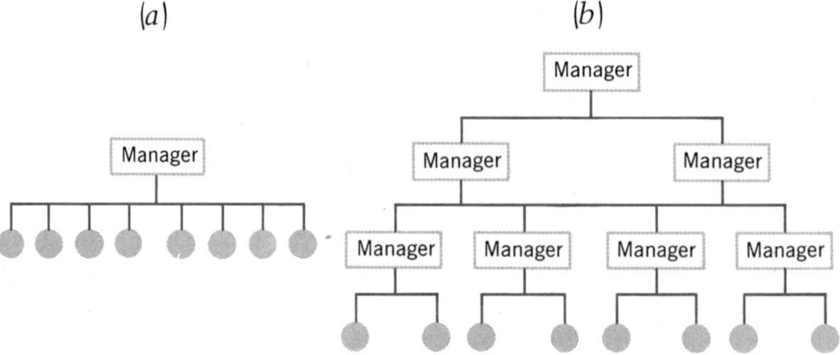

Figure 8.10. Relation between number of levels and span of control. (*a*) One level; large span of control. (*b*) Three levels; small span of control.

2. System efficiency: with an efficient set of working policies, procedures, and support systems the span of control can be enlarged.
3. Managerial ability: some managers can effectively handle more subordinates because of his or her individual energy, smooth working relationships, and experience in the work situation.

Six people a natural span of control.

It has been postulated that a "natural" span of control is approximately six people because, in almost any grouping, if more than six people are put together, the group will typically divide into two sets of conversation, work, relationships,and so forth.

Decentralization through delegation.

Long chains of command tend to be avoided since they are more expensive, involve more communications and red tape, delay the transmittal of critical information, and encourage formality, bureaucracy, and internal "politics." A more desirable approach, if large spans of control are impossible, is **decentralization**, delegating authority to lower level managers. This is widely used in geographically dispersed organizations and in those organizations with a few, very different outputs. The advantages of decentralization include using decisions that are made by people "on the firing line," having lower level support for decisions, and providing a feeling of importance and belonging to all levels in the organization. The disadvantage, of course, is the loss of central control.

A balance of centralization and decentralization.

From studies of organizations it appears that the more successful organizations are neither highly centralized nor decentralized. Apparently, a point of diminishing returns of managerial, output, and behavioral advantages is reached with decentralization and the loss of further control with more decentralization results in hurting the organization.

Effect of computers on centralization.

The use of system-wide computers as a basis for management information systems (MIS) has given top management the ability to extend their control and a trend toward *recentralization* was, at one time, taking place. Two new elements have now, however, entered the arena, which continue the trend toward decentralization. The first, the advent of minicomputers (discussed in Chapter 19I), favors decentralization of data processing functions into independent units and the second, "distributed data processing" (linking all of the organization's computers together through a computer network), promotes decentralized processing but with centralized "monitoring."

Organizational structure

Avoid reorganizing.

There are many different structures that have been adopted by organizations and a good structure for one organization may be poor for another. Furthermore, the best structure at one stage of an organization's development might be the worst at some other stage. An important managerial rule is to avoid reorganizing when faced with a problem unless the organizational structure itself can be identified as the problem. Too often reorganization is used as a solution for a problem that is not structurally related. In that case, a change in structure cannot help the problem and only further delays the correction of the real problem.

Some of the more common structures used by organizations are briefly outlined below.

Common organizational structures.

- **Functional:** Organizing according to the traditional functions such as finance, marketing, production, and so forth.
- **Output (product):** Organizing around the types of distinct products or services such as trees, plants, lawn, seeds, landscaping, mowing, and spraying, for a nursery.
- **Process:** Organizing according to the operation involved: drilling, stamping, milling, and so forth.
- **Geography:** Central, Northeast, South, West, Foreign.
- **Client:** Different types of clients (industrial versus military versus consumer; men's versus women's versus children's wear) have different needs, may require different marketing approaches, and so on.
- **Project:** This is similar to product organization except that the scale and complexity are much greater. Dams, military operations, and other such projects are considered here.
- **Mixed:** Many organizations are structured in different ways at different organizational levels. For instance, they may be divided by product initially, sales region next, and by function thereafter. Thus, there would be an accounting department for southern television sales and an accounting department for southern appliances.
- **Matrix:** A special type of mixed structure that has received considerable attention is the **matrix organization**, which is organized functionally but also by project "across" the functions. Each project has a manager who requests the temporary assignment of individuals from the functional units to his or her project until that particular phase of the project life cycle is completed whereupon they return to their functional unit. This structure, often used in defense and aerospace companies, is illustrated in Figure 8.11.

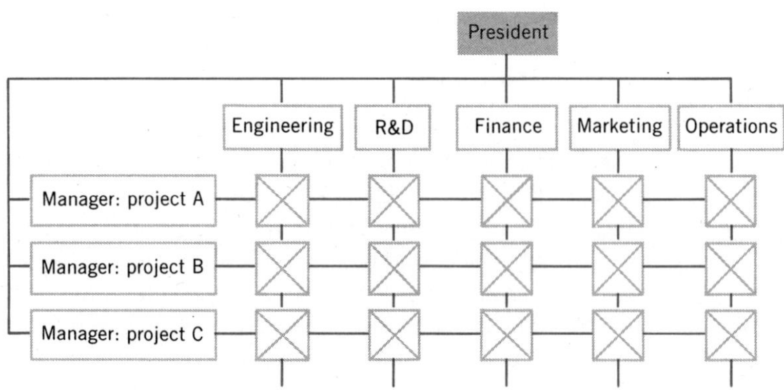

Figure 8.11. A matrix organization.

The Informal Organization

The above discussion has concerned the design of the *formal* organization that will direct and reward the worker and coordinate his or her efforts with other workers. However, it is not only the formal organization that affects the worker's activities—the **informal organization**, consisting, in large part, of the worker's peers, also influences the worker's activities through **the grapevine**, peer pressure, organizational politics, and other such invisible mechanisms. In the design of work these informal organizational mechanisms should also be recognized and allowed for.

The importance of the informal organization.

The peer group

One of the most powerful forces in the workplace is the group to which the worker belongs. It may be a formal or informal group, large or small, but it plays a large part in determining the worker's productivity. When work groups are given the chance to control their own work they frequently come up with excellent work methods. To illustrate this, any manager only has to let a work group know that when they have finished a standard amount of production for the day they may go home.

At the same time, if a work group is opposed to a change that management would like to implement, the change will probably not succeed, at least in the long run. Groups exert a strong amount of peer pressure, which keeps the members loyal to the group and protects the group as a whole.

The effects of peer pressure.

You need only consider the importance of peer pressure upon yourself and your friends. If everyone in the class "decides" to party instead of studying for next week's quiz, it's amazing how justified you can feel in deciding not to study either.

Organizational politics

Politics versus games.

One of the most dysfunctional aspects of the informal organization is **organizational politics**. Politics in the workplace plays an extremely important role, even threatening workers with the loss of their jobs, and should certainly not be ignored. Before proceeding, politics should be distinguished from *games*—the two are not really the same. With games everyone knows the rules, and the probable outcomes, and people are *assumed* to participate in them—such as overstating travel expenses, asking for more in the budget than is really needed, and so forth. Also, games are "portable" and are often carried from one organization to another.

Danger in politics.

Politics is entirely different. No one is usually aware of a worker who is playing politics—there are no rules and every situation is different. Also, the stakes are usually much higher. Lower level politics are sometimes played by relatively new, young workers trying to get ahead but the most vicious politics are typically played by long standing, established managers who are afraid their jobs have outgrown them.

Minimizing politics.

It has been found that politics is minimal in aggressive, dynamic organizations and worst in large, mature, declining organizations. The message for organizational design in minimizing the opportunity for politics to develop is to keep a lean organization with considerable responsibility placed on the individual and appropriate remuneration for extra effort. For further discussion of this interesting aspect of informal organization refer to References 6, 12, or 14.

Management

Importance of the management system.

Of all the elements of work design we have discussed so far few have as direct or important an impact on the productivity of the worker as the nature of the organization's management system. Unfortunately, this element is also one of the most difficult to plan or design. We can arrange a workplace, install air conditioning, buy labor-saving equipment, design smooth workflows, and even organize for effective work and minimal politics but we can never be sure of the managerial "style" that the workers are experiencing from day to day. Nor, for that matter, is it even clear *what* managerial "style" should be used in a given situation. Organizational behavior researchers in the area of **contingency theory** are attempting to answer exactly that question. The contingency theorists believe that there is no single managerial style, or even a set of rules of management, that is best for any situation. Rather, the best management approach depends on the situation, and the study of management should include knowing which managerial approach to use in which situation.

Taylor's motivation system; higher wages.

The goal is to provide an environment that will motivate workers to be highly productive. What properly constitutes that environment has been the subject of researchers for the last 80 years. Frederick Taylor's answer was simple: higher wages for more work, in conjunction with training and development. And for many years that was sufficient.

Human relations

Motivation through the work group.

In the 1930s another motivating force was "discovered" by Mayo and Roethlisberger [15] at the now-famous Hawthorne Plant of Western Electric. These researchers found that social and interpersonal factors also had a significant effect on worker productivity. Cohesive work groups and managerial expressions of interest and attention could improve worker performance considerably. However, it has since been found that cohesive work groups can also *restrict* output considerably and that managerial interest and attention may please the workers but, by themselves, do not necessarily increase productivity.

Maslow's needs hierarchy

Many of the contemporary theories of motivation are based on the foundation of Abraham H. Maslow's theories of human needs [11]. Maslow's theory is based on the following assumptions.

1. Man constantly attempts to satisfy his needs.
2. Only *unsatisfied* needs determine behavior.
3. There is an important **hierarchy of needs** that exists and man strives to satisfy more basic needs first.

Maslow's hierarchy of needs as illustrated in Figure 8.12 includes

1. Physiological needs.
2. Safety needs.
3. Social needs.
4. Esteem needs.
5. Self-actualization needs.

Physiological needs include food, water, shelter, clothing and other necessities for survival. Safety needs include physical protection, the general feeling of security in an emotional sense, and freedom from ill health. These two needs are material needs and in most cases can be satisifed by simply having a secure job. That is, money earned through organizational membership can be used to buy clothing, medical care, food, and a house in a "safe" neighborhood. Once these needs have been satisfied, the individual becomes concerned with psychological needs.

Basic needs satisfied by the organization.

The social need is the individual's need to be a part of a social group. People need to be accepted by others, to have companionship, affection, and friendship. Within these social groups people need to be recognized. The esteem need is concerned both with recognition of worth by others and also self-esteem, the feeling of personal worth and importance. Social and esteem needs suggest that work designed around other workers, or groups, and work in which the worker can take pride should be a major consideration in the design of tasks and the workplace.

Work design for social and esteem needs.

Maslow's highest level need, **self-actualization**, is the need to use to the fullest the talents and capabilities that one possesses. Self-actualization relates to a worker's fulfilling his or her complete potential. Clearly, such fulfillment requires high level, challenging work in the first place.

Need for fulfillment on the job.

Organizations are typically very good at providing the means for satisfaction of the lower order needs. Salaries and fringe benefits usually provide enough to satisfy

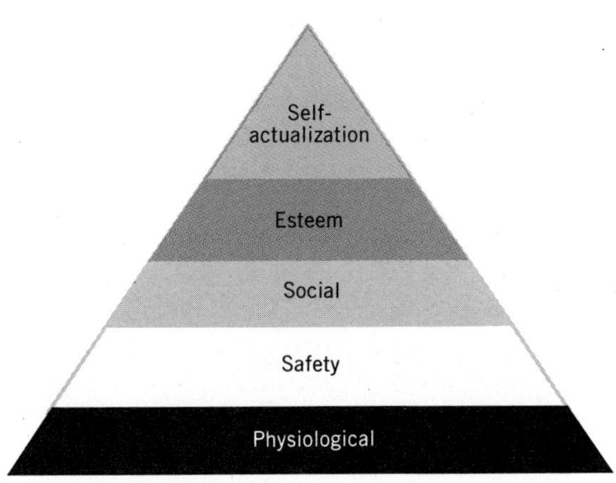

Figure 8.12. Maslow's needs hierarchy.

the physiological and safety needs of individuals, and the organization itself contributes to the social needs. The esteem and self-actualization needs are less well satisfied by typical organizations.

The order hierarchy of needs is not intended to be taken strictly but only in a general sense. Clearly, people attempt to satisfy various needs at various times, in multiples at times, and out of Maslow's order at times, depending on their current situation. Also, each of these needs differ from person to person in their relative importance. To some, material needs are dominant and others much less important. There are no magic amounts or recipes that will satisfy all of the people all of the time.

Job enrichment and enlargement

Two approaches to designing more fulfilling work, which have had some success, are "job enrichment" and "job enlargement." In job **enrichment** the worker is more fully integrated into the *vertical* elements of the task such as inspection responsibility, scheduling, and planning of the work. For example, rather than just attaching the cover on a pump, the worker may assemble the entire pump.

Job enrichment for greater responsibility.

The objective is to build into the work an opportunity for personal challenge, achievement, growth, and recognition. The process typically entails giving the worker a natural and complete "module" of work, removing restrictions from the worker while increasing autonomy and accountability, and giving the worker (rather than the manager) performance evaluation reports for feedback purposes. Ford [4] reports that considerable success has been achieved with job enrichment programs at AT&T.

Job enlargement to combat specialization.

Job **enlargement**, originated at IBM [5], is an attempt to counteract the trend toward greater and greater specialization (and the resulting boredom, monotony, and fatigue) by increasing the number of tasks a worker is responsible for. Two methods are typically used: (1) adding a greater *variety* of tasks to the worker's responsibility, perhaps even consisting of producing the entire output; and (2) *rotating* workers among a variety of tasks. The goal of job enlargement is to give up some efficiency for more pride in workmanship, more motivation, and more overall job satisfaction among workers. Not all jobs are amenable to successful enlargement however and mixed results have been reported with the approach [10].

Goal congruence

Design work for consistency between organization's and worker's goals.

Organizations can use incentives or motivators that can contribute to the accomplishment of one or more individual needs to promote **goal congruence**. That is, work should be designed to encourage consistency between organizational goals and individual's goals. The control system should be designed so that actions that are in the best interest of the organization are also perceived by the individual to be in his or her own best interest. Clearly, complete goal congruence will never be achieved, but work should not be designed to encourage behavior that is against the best interests of the organization.

Some of the research findings in the area of incentives and motivators include

1. Positive incentives (satisfying a need) are better motivators than negative incentives (depriving an individual of a need satisfaction).
2. Top management interest and involvement in control systems is important to the extent that subordinates see this interest as contributing to the esteem need.
3. Money is a motivator but diminishes in importance as the amount increases. Money is often less important than nonmonetary incentives, but *relative* pay among workers is an important incentive or disincentive (e.g., John was very pleased with his $3000 raise until he found out that Tim, an employee who, he felt, was less industrious, received a $4000 raise).
4. Incentives are of diminishing value as the time between performance and reward (or punishment) increases. (Do not give a Christmas bonus for a job well done at Easter.)
5. Goals are best that are achievable, but challenging. If goals are either easily attained or impossible, motivation is weak and frustration usually results.

Each of these findings holds meaning for the design of a motivating work environment. One conclusion is clear. No one motivation system will work under all conditions. For example, monetary rewards for performance may work well at one level of the organization and poorly at another.

Herzberg's two-factor theory

Even with a well structured motivational system integrated into the organization's control system, it is still possible, according to Frederick Herzberg [7,8], that employees will not act in the best interest of the organization. Herzberg has developed what is known as the **two-factor theory** of motivation based upon his research into the satisfaction of employees on the job.

Dissatisfying job factors.

His first conclusion is that certain conditions of a job act primarily to dissatify an employee when they are *not* present. That is, presence of these conditions is expected and only if they are not present is dissatisfaction felt. No positive value is placed on these conditions and therefore they are of no value as motivators. They only serve to dissatisfy and not to satisfy. Herzberg called these factors **maintenance** (or **hygiene**) **factors**

1. Company policy and administration.
2. Technical supervision.
3. Interpersonal relations with supervisor.
4. Interpersonal relations with peers.
5. Interpersonal relations with subordinates.
6. Salary.
7. Job security.

8. Personal life.
9. Work conditions.
10. Status.

Motivating job factors.

The second conclusion is that certain job conditions that Herzberg called **motivational** factors often create high levels of motivation by being present, but do not cause dissatisfaction simply by being absent. These factors are

1. Achievement.
2. Recognition.
3. Advancement.
4. The work itself.
5. Possibility of personal growth.
6. Responsibility.

These sets of factors are illustrated in Figure 8.13.

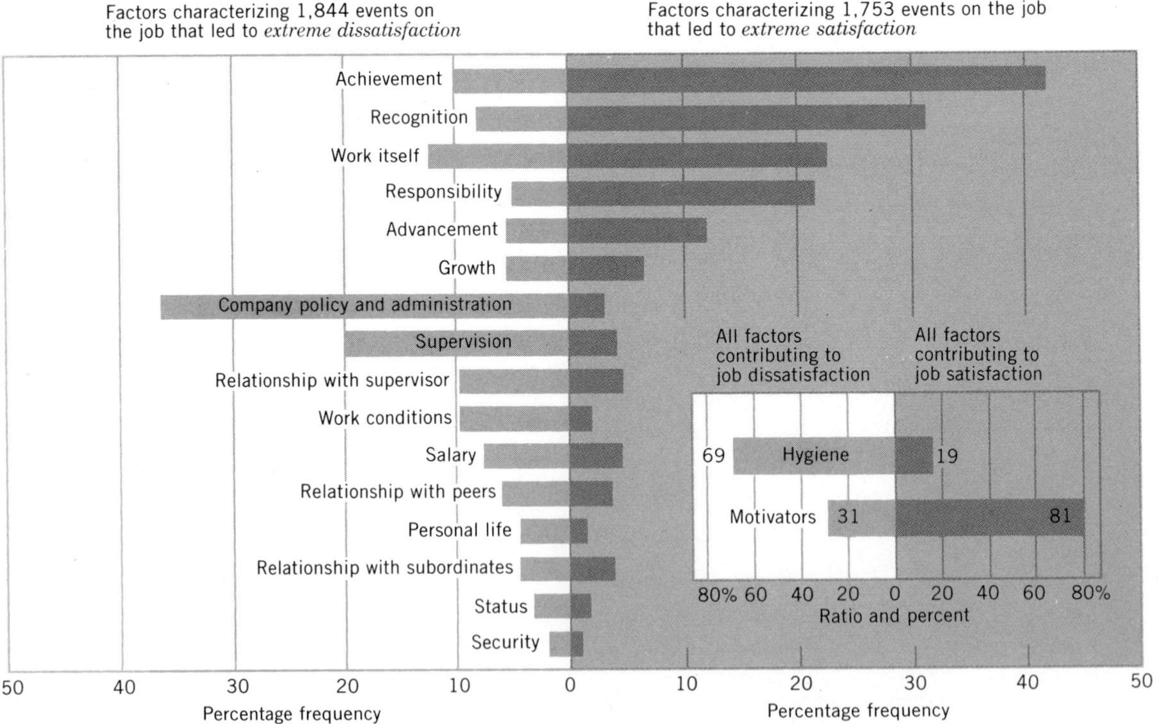

Figure 8.13. Hygiene and motivational factors. (Reprinted by permission. From Frederick Herzberg, "One More Time: How Do You Motivate Employees?" *Harvard Business Review*, vol. 46, no. 1, 1968, p. 57.)

It is worth noting that these guideline factors are not infallible. For instance, it is well known that some workers do *not* want meaningful, challenging work. They simply want to earn their wages as easily and painlessly as possible so they may leave the workplace and participate in what *is* meaningful to them in their lives. On the other hand, it may be argued that such workers are simply inappropriately employed, and given proper employment, would desire the work to be meaningful and challenging. As an extreme example of what a worker may find meaningful in life, even Al Capp's classic cartoon character Li'l Abner, found appropriate work for his major interest in life (sleeping)—testing mattresses.

While Herzberg's theory is somewhat controversial (e.g., some researchers claim that for blue-collar workers, salary and job security are motivational factors) there is little doubt that those factors that relate most to Maslow's top two needs, the motivational factors, are important considerations in the design of work. For example, a job or task that is not challenging (or for which the performance standard has been established too low) may produce less satisfaction than a more difficult task.

Expectancy theory

The previous theories of motivation are known as "content" theories because they attempt to identify those factors that motivate high performance. No attempt is made to explain or describe the process or what initiates it. In contrast Victor Vroom's **expectancy theory** [16] of motivation does.

Explaining motivation.

"They told me I'd be a plant supervisor. . . ."

(*Source: Industry Week*, August 1, 1977. Reprinted, courtesy of *Industry Week.*)

Motivation = expectancy × valence.

Vroom argues that motivation is the product of two forces. One is the *expectancy* that a particular act (such as hard work) will be followed by a particular outcome (such as more pay or satisfaction). The other is the strength, or **valence**, of a worker's preference for the outcome. The amount of motivation is the product of the two forces and if either force is zero there will be minimal motivation. The message for the manager is that to motivate the worker the reward must be desired (whether a low level or high level need) and the worker must be assured his efforts will be fairly rewarded by receiving what is desired.

8.5 SUMMARY

The benefits of high productivity in organizations can be obtained through proper work design that integrates the technical job needs with human needs. That is, work design involves the social and psychological aspects of the organization and management style as well as the physical and physiological environment of the workplace.

The tools of motion study, such as therblig analysis, have been developed to aid in improving worker's efficiency in their tasks. On the other hand, the time study tools, such as work sampling, are required to determine a standard output rate for the organization.

In the design of the workplace and its environment, anthropometric and neurological factors are considered for tool sizes, knobs, and dials, as well as fatigue, temperature and humidity, illumination and color, noise, and safety factors. Many standards for these factors have been set by OSHA.

The design of the organization in terms of the division of labor and span of control, as well as its functional sructure, also has an influence on the workers' productivity. And the informal organization, consisting primarily of peers, is especially influential. But probably of greatest importance is the management of workers. In spite of a number of theories about motivation and general guides to aid in designing motivational work environments there is very little information to aid the manager in knowing how to motivate workers in specific situations.

8.6 READINGS

OSHA: Hardest to Live With

One of the most sweeping recent efforts to regulate industry for social ends came with the establishment six years ago of the Occupational Safety & Health Administration. OSHA's job is worker protection, and its mandate covers a staggering 4 million companies.

Equally sweeping is the criticism that businessmen level against the agency. No one, of course, sounds off against the concept of worker protection. But attacking the way in which OSHA goes about its tasks is another matter altogether. Businessmen point to the agency as their quintessential example of regulatory overkill. "The principle of OSHA is sound," concedes Thomas F. Green Jr., administrative vice-president for Norton Co. But its standards, he charges, have been applied "widely and arbitrarily . . . OSHA has become a burden."

That burden has little to do with worrying what OSHA inspectors may do if they find a plant violating any of the agency's myriad rules. According to The Diebold Group Inc., a management consulting firm, OSHA levied only $12.4 million in fines over the past 12 months. Since the agency is responsible for policing so many companies, simple division demonstrates that the average fine must be laughably small.

The costs of complying with OSHA standards far outweigh the costs of violating them. To meet OSHA's 90-decibel factory noise standard—one of the agency's most disputed rules—could cost industry as a whole $13 billion, according to one study. As OSHA's departing chief, Morton Corn, notes: "In general, the concerns of the public sector are directly proportional to the costs of compliance with OSHA standards."

The furor over the noise rule reaches to the heart of industry's disaffection with OSHA. The agency has specified so-called engineering controls—machine enclosures and the like—as the only acceptable way to meet the standard. But businessmen point out that for many plants the installation of such controls is economically prohibitive. They feel that their judgment should be paramount as to when personal hearing protection for workers (ear muffs and the like) are sufficient. Continental Can Co., for one, has appealed, OSHA has counter-appealed, and the issue is now in the courts.

A LEGAL ALBATROSS

Any Monday morning quarterback looking back at the agency's inception on Dec. 31, 1970, could predict the current battle over industry discretion vs. OSHA's fiat. At that time, Congress charged the fledgling OSHA with assuring, "so far as possible, every man and woman in the nation safe and healthful working conditions." In effect, this language instructed OSHA to seek absolute safety for everyone instead of simply trying to minimize the inevitable risks of an industrial society. Furthermore, it encouraged the new agency to impose its judgment on employers instead of leaving them any choice between different approaches to safety precautions. Like old-fashioned building codes, OSHA's rules prescribe details rather than performance.

They also lean heavily on the same standards industry has claimed to follow all along. OSHA's enabling legislation gave the agency a Hobson's choice: It could either follow a brutal 22-step procedure to develop "consensus" standards of its own, or it could use the myriad of existing industrial guidelines that were sprinkled through various other laws and codes. In a rush to meet its mandate, OSHA adopted many of the existing Walsh-Healy standards—the safety and health rules for companies with government contracts—and made laws of the voluntary guidelines issued by the American National Standards Institute. "The overregulation really began," notes the safety engineer for a Southeastern textile company, "when OSHA made voluntary standards mandatory."

OSHA is still carrying those ANSI standards as an albatross around its neck. Some of them, such as rules specifying the height at which fire extinguishers should be hung on walls, have more to do with property protection than with safety. Others are simply antiquated. ANSI's test method for determining the strength of safety shoes, for example, has not been changed since it was adopted in 1944. Even B. Everett Gray, chairman of an ANSI committee that is currently revising the test, admits: "No one knows how they chose the test procedure or the parameters." Understandably, businessmen spot the anachronisms and the outright silliness of some of these tests and standards, extrapolating them to the agency as a whole.

The standards themselves are not only unrealistic at times. Their sheer volume is almost unmanageable for OSHA and industry alike. The steel industry, for one, is staggering under a load of 5,600 regulations from 27 different agencies—and OSHA alone accounts for 4,000 of those rules. "I'm not poking fun at the efforts to protect the health of our people," says Edgar B. Speer, U. S. Steel Corp.'s chairman, "but some of these requirements run from the ridiculous to the extreme."

Ironically, OSHA officials readily admit that industry has been unfairly harassed. But they point to signs of internal change at OSHA to prove that cries for the agency's dismemberment should not be heeded. Until he handed over the reigns to Eula Bingham this month, Corn did everything he could to get the agency back on the right track. He instituted better training programs for inspectors, started moving the agency to a clear emphasis on health problems, and tried to weed out foolish standards. And Corn encouraged a program, already being tested for machinery safety standards, that not only would simplify the rules but would also give employers more latitude in deciding how they should be met.

GUIDE, NOT POLICEMAN

Corn's moves helped, but they did not solve all the problems. "He made a conscientious effort," notes Ronald A. Lang, executive secretary of the Synthetic Organic Chemical Manufacturers Assn., "but he was not there long enough to make a significant change."

Businessmen worry that Bingham will not follow through on Corn's good start. She hails from the University of Cincinnati's environmental health department, and her academic training may have ill-prepared her to handle OSHA's formidable administrative problems. What is more, Bingham was proposed for her job by the AFL-CIO, and she headed the OSHA committee that set the controversial coke-oven emissions standards that have so infuriated steel executives. All told, numerous businessmen view her background as decidedly antibusiness.

For her part, Bingham remains close-mouthed about specific plans. But she has repeatedly said she will continue with the streamlining programs Corn initiated, and industry has every reason to expect OSHA to change for the better.

Probably the brightest side to the outlook for OSHA is the agency's professed desire to shed its role of policeman and become a guidance counselor for industry. Under current law, OSHA inspectors must give citations—or at least warnings—on their first visit to a plant that is in violation of rules. Not surprisingly, plant managers are reluctant to let an OSHA inspector in the door. In fact, a state court recently ruled that the agency's practice of warrantless searches is unconstitutional. The Labor Dept. has appealed, but the Supreme Court has not yet agreed to hear the case.

The whole question would be moot if Congress were to change OSHA's enabling legislation to permit the agency's inspectors to advise businesses on how to make plants truly safe. The move could dissipate some of the growing animosity between OSHA and the companies its inspectors visit. It would also give industry longer lead times between agency visits and final compliance. If these steps were taken, many of the arguments against OSHA would lose their sting.

Source. Reprinted from the April 4, 1977 issue of *Business Week* by special permission,

8.7 KEY TERMS

Concepts

productivity (p. 252)
automation (p. 253)
mechanization (p. 253)
sociotechnical (p. 256)
redundancy (p. 255)
motion study (p. 260)
therblig analysis (p. 261)
micromotion study (p. 261)
microchronometer (p. 262)
memomotion (p. 262)
chronocyclegraph (p. 262)
time study (p. 260)
snapback timing (p. 262)
elemental times (p. 264)
machining center (p. 254)
NC (p. 254)
normal time (p. 264)
standard time (p. 265)
allowance (p. 265)
performance rating (p. 264)
work sampling (p. 266)
MTM (p. 266)
TMU (p. 266)
predetermined standards (p. 266)
anthropometric (p. 269)
neurological (p. 269)
comfort zone (p. 271)
OSHA (p. 271)
decibel (dB) (p. 273)

Tools and Applications

chain of command (p. 275)
span of control (p. 276)
nominal group (p. 276)
Delphi panel (p. 276)
decentralization (p. 277)
mixed organization (p. 2 3)
matrix organization (p. 278)
functional organization (p. 278)
informal organization (p. 279)
peer group (p. 279)
organizational politics (p. 279)
grapevine (p. 279)
valence (p. 286)
division of labor (p. 275)
line (p. 275)
staff (p. 275)
human relations (p. 280)
needs hierarchy (p. 280)
self-actualization (p. 281)
job enlargement (p. 282)
job enrichment (p. 282)
goal congruence (p. 282)
two-factor theory (p. 283)
maintenance factors (p. 283)
hygiene factors (p. 283)
motivational factors (p. 284)
expectancy theory (p. 285)
contingency theory (p. 280)

8.8 REVIEW TEST

Concepts

1. Machines have replaced labor when they became more cost-effective. (p. 252)
   a. True b. False
2. The substitution of mechanical power for human physical labor is called automation. (p. 253)
   a. True b. False
3. The sociotechnical approach to work design enlarges the alternatives by adding the human element to the system. (p. 256)
   a. True b. False
4. Productivity in the U.S. hit a peak in the early 1960s and has been declining since then. (p. 257)
   a. True b. False
5. Memomotion study is the use of a high speed camera to capture the smallest motions of workers. (p. 262)
   a. True b. False
6. Time study times job elements for increased accuracy and utility. (p. 263)
   a. True b. False
7. Aberrations during a time study are included and then subtracted out of the allowance. (p. 264)
   a. True b. False
8. For workplace measurements we need average human body dimensions that are based on a good sample of the population. (p. 269)
   a. True b. False

9. We align pointers in panels of dials so that abnormal readings can be easily spotted. (p. 270)
   a. True b. False
10. A player piano is a numerically controlled machine. (p. 254)
   a. True b. False
11. Our main approach to consideration of fatigue is through allowances. (p. 270)
   a. True b. False
12. Natural light is a strong, steady source of illumination. (p. 271)
   a. True b. False
13. Purple has been designated by OSHA as a marking for radiation materials. (p. 272)
   a. True b. False
14. A 20-decibel noise is twice as loud as a 10-decibel noise. (p. 273)
   a. True b. False
15. OSHA allows very loud noises if the duration is not too long. (p. 273)
   a. True b. False
16. Accidents are not usually caused by a single unsafe act. (p. 274)
   a. True b. False

Tools and Applications

17. The chain of command indicates how many workers report to a superior. (p. 275)
   a. True b. False
18. A Delphi panel is a type of nominal group. (p. 276)
   a. True b. False
19. A matrix organizational structure has a leader at both the top and side. (p. 278)
   a. True b. False
20. Organizational politics is its worst in aggressive, hard-driving organizations. (p. 279)
   a. True b. False
21. In Maslow's hierarchy, esteem is the highest need. (p. 281)
   a. True b. False
22. In job enlargement the worker is given more responsibility to relieve boredom. (p. 282)
   a. True b. False
23. The nature of the work itself is one of Herzberg's "hygiene" factors. (p. 283)
   a. True b. False

8.9 DISCUSSION QUESTIONS

1. How can a company justify to its stockholders the installation of air conditioning in its machine shop?
2. What type of organizational structure do you think is most prevalent at this time?
3. Federal guidelines now call for wheelchair facilities in newly constructed machine plants. Do you feel this is appropriate for all industrial plants?
4. How might the productivity of other resources than labor be defined such as: a pump, $1000, a warehouse, a kilowatt-hour, a market survey?
5. How are humans superior to computers?
6. The sociotechnical approach to work design deals with the overlap of two areas. Might you add more factors to consider in this overlap?
7. Much national concern has been voiced about the recently decreasing rate of productivity in the U.S. Has productivity really been decreasing?
8. Why is the performance rating multiplied by the time instead of divided? Does this not seem backward?
9. Since work sampling seems so much easier and less irritating to the workers, why is it not always used instead?
10. How do those workplace measurements requiring *average* dimensions differ from those requiring extreme percentiles?
11. How does *adding* background noises reduce noise distraction?
12. Is six a natural span of control?
13. Why is the nominal group process not in wider use?
14. What will the computer's ultimate effect probably be on decentralization?
15. Is there a congruence between Maslow's needs and Herzberg's factors?

8.10 PROBLEMS

Concepts

1. Mr. I. R. Service is employed by the H & R Blop income tax service. I. R. prepares 1040s, all day, every day, from January 1 to April 15 each year. Work sampling was done for one week and the following results were recorded:

Number of 1040s completed	82
Available work time	2400 min
Performance rating	95%
Actual work percentage	80%

H & R Blop uses a 10 percent allowance. Based upon this information, what should the standard time be for preparation of a 1040 tax return?

2. John Q. Injunear has performed the following time study for a bending operation on a metal press. The times are recorded using the continuous reading method.

	Cycle 1	2	3
Get sheet from stack	0.10	1.19	2.90
Place against back and side guides	0.25	1.49	3.18
Depress safety activator switches with both hands	0.80	2.39	3.74
Remove and stack part in crate	1.10	2.72	4.01

The performance ratings for the four activities are 0.90, 0.85, 1.05, and 0.95, respectively. Assuming a 15 percent allowance, what should be the standard time for a complete cycle?

3. Jake Idletime has been observed 1000 times over the last 300 hours during which time he produced 27,000 parts. Jake was busy at work 600 times, but idle 400 times. Jake is rated at 80 percent of normal efficiency and normal allowance is 10 percent. What is the standard output per hour?

4. The following time study results were obtained using the snapback method.

	Cycle 1	Cycle 2	Cycle 3
Get carton	0.02	0.03	0.03
Pick up six cans	0.08	0.10	0.10
Place cans in carton	0.13	0.12	0.15
Seal carton	0.06	0.07	0.06

If the performance rates are 1.0, 0.9, 1.1, and 1.0, respectively, and a 20 percent allowance is used, what is the standard time for one cycle?

5. How large a work sample will be required to estimate within ± 2 percent the proportion of the working day a worker spends in travel to and from the tool crib if he is expected to use about 30 percent of his day in travel and a 95 percent confidence level is required?

6. Jake's sister Jane (see Problem 3) works at the same job, but Jane has a 110 percent efficiency rating. How many parts can Jane be expected to produce in an hour?

8.11 CASE BALDWIN MOTOR WORKS INC.

Baldwin Motor Works Inc. is a manufacturer of small electric motors for model trains and cars. Their first plant was opened in Cincinnati, Ohio in 1970. Demand for Baldwin's products became so great (there are several major toy manufacturers located in the Cincinnati vicinity) that production had to be carried on around the clock. The company began making a profit after its second year of operation and has been profitable every year since.

Although employee relations have been acceptable, the workers who solder the motor lead wires to their bases have consistently been complaining. Each worker is seated in front of a large revolving table which receives motors from three assembly lines. A worker must pick up the next motor in line, place it on a solder jig, solder the two leads to the base, and place the motor on a conveyer belt, which moves on to inspection. The workers argue that, while they were able to keep up with the three production lines when the plant opened, this is no longer true due to improvements in production further up the line from them. They contend that if they are to keep from becoming a "bottleneck," they must work feverishly without time to take care of personal needs.

The plant superintendent sets production rates for all three shifts. The production rate for each shift is set at an identical level so that there are no complaints about one shift carrying the load of another shift. All three shifts complain about the solder job.

Bob Dennler, the industrial engineer for Baldwin Motor Works, has convinced management to conduct a work sampling study on the soldering job. He has decided that a sample of 2000 observations would be required to establish the degree of confidence necessary for the sample. Work samples were taken for each of the three shifts over a 20 day period (four workweeks). To remove the effect of any sampling bias, the hours of the day within each shift and the workers sampled were both randomized by using a table of random numbers. There are four soldering workers operating on each shift. The table below shows the results of the work sampling at the end of each of the four weeks.

	Total No. of Observations	No. of Observations During Which Productive Work was Being Performed
End of week 1	510	460
End of week 2	480	430
End of week 3	520	440
End of week 4	490	430

QUESTIONS FOR DISCUSSION

1. Assuming that the industry's standard for idle time ranges between 8 and 10 percent, evaluate the results of this work sampling study.
2. From your limited knowledge of the situation, what suggestions might you have to resolve or alleviate part of the problem?

8.12 REFERENCES AND BIBLIOGRAPHY

1. Barnes, R. M., *Motion and Time Study: Design and Measurement of Work*, 6th ed., New York: Wiley, 1968.
2. Dreyfuss, H., *The Measure of Man: Human Factors in Design*, New York: Whitney Library of Design, 1967.
3. Duncan, W. J., *Essentials of Management*, Hinsdale, Ill: Dryden Press, 1975.
4. Ford, R. N., "Job Enrichment Lessons from AT&T," *Harvard Business Review*, 51:97–99, (Jan.–Feb. 1973).
5. Guest, R. H., "Job Enlargement—A Revolution in Job Design," *Personnel Administration*, 17:9–16 (Jan. 1957).
6. Hegarty, E. J., *How to Succeed in Company Politics*, New York: McGraw-Hill, 1964.
7. Herzberg, F. H., *Work and the Nature of Man*, New York: Harcourt Brace & World, 1966.
8. ———, "One More Time: How Do You Motivate Employees?" *Harvard Business Review*, 46:53–62 (Jan.–Feb. 1968).
9. Ivancevich, J. M., Szilagyi, A. D., Jr., and Wallace, M. J., Jr., *Organizational Behavior and Performance*, Santa Monica, California: Goodyear, 1977.
10. Kilbridge, M. D., "Do Workers Prefer Larger Jobs?" *Personnel*, 37:45–48 (Sept.–Oct. 1960).
11. Maslow, A. H., *Motivation and Personality*, 2nd ed., New York: Harper & Row, 1970.
12. Mayes, B. T., and Allen, R. W., "Toward a Definition of Organizational Politics," *Academy of Management Review*, 2:672–677 (1977).

13. McCormick, E. J., *Human Factors Engineering*, 3rd ed., New York: McGraw-Hill, 1970.

14. Ritti, R. R., and Funkhouser, G. R., *The Ropes to Skip and The Ropes To Know: Studies in Organizational Behavior*, Columbus, Ohio: Grid, Inc., 1977.

15. Roethlisberger, F. J., and Dickson, W. J., *Management and the Worker*, Cambridge, Mass.: Harvard University Press, 1939.

16. Vroom, V. H., *Work and Motivation*, New York: Wiley, 1964.

17. Woodson, W. E., and Conover, D. W., *Human Engineering Guide for Equipment Designers*, 2nd ed., Berkeley: University of California Press, 1966.

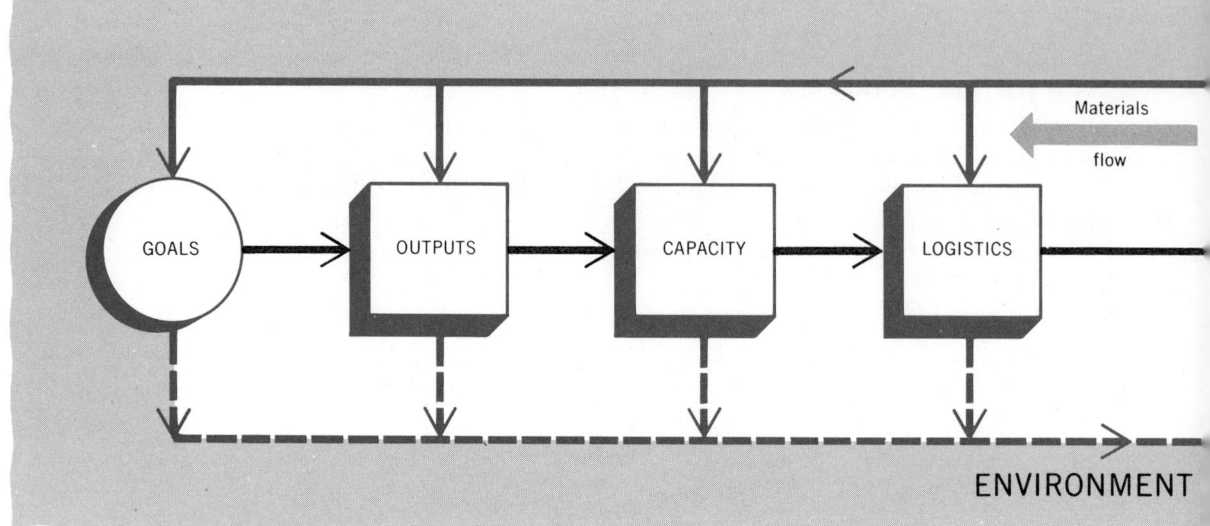

Chapter 9

Scheduling the Transformation Activities

9: Scheduling

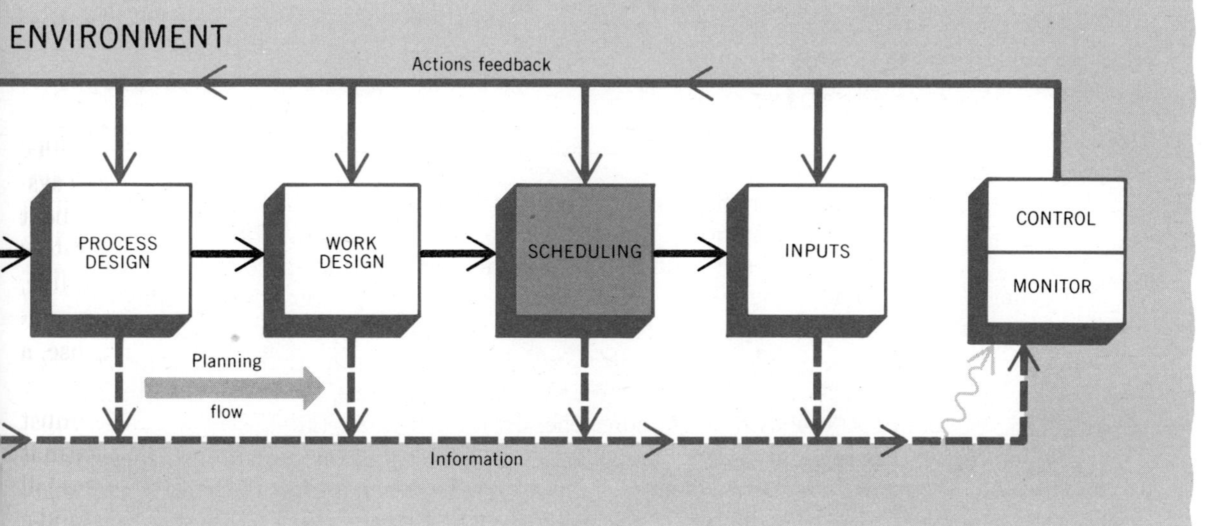

LEARNING OBJECTIVES

By the completion of the *Concepts* portion of this chapter the student should

1. Understand the sequence of activities involved in scheduling and their interrelationships.
2. Realize that scheduling adds the dynamic element of activity to the static design of operations discussed up to this point.
3. Comprehend the necessity for computers in modern scheduling systems and their advantages.
4. Realize the central importance of the master schedule in the scheduling activity.
5. Know the meaning behind the current terminology used in computerized scheduling systems.
6. Be aware of the various forms of Gantt charts.
7. Be aware of the main difference between scheduling for products and scheduling for services.
8. Understand the nature of the queuing situation and how it especially applies to services.
9. Comprehend the difference between project scheduling and scheduling of the other types of processes.

CONCEPTS

The previous four chapters have dealt with the design of the operations to produce the organization's output. But this has been a static snapshot of the operations system, with workers, machines, and materials all frozen in space and time. The next function adds the dimension of *time* to this static picture, transforming it into a running, operating set of activities that are producing products or services for live, demanding people and organizations. Ensuring that the *right* operations are conducted at the *right* time on the *right* items to produce the output is, in a sense, a matter of "orchestration," more generally known as *scheduling*.

The need for scheduling.

The scheduling function addresses the issues that the operations manager must face on a daily basis: where each input must be, when it must be there, what form it must be in, how many must be available, and other such details. These activities fall under such headings as scheduling, aggregate planning, sequencing, loading, and a number of other terms that we will soon encounter.

Scheduling—bringing together all the inputs.

Our approach in this chapter will be to first describe the scheduling function in detail from the perspective of organizations that have formally organized scheduling departments. Following this we treat scheduling where the function is not so formally addressed, such as in service organizations, and point out some significant differences in the scheduling problems that organizations face. Lastly we address scheduling in the project organization, which is again a significantly different problem.

9.1 THE SEQUENCE OF SCHEDULING ACTIVITIES

In most organizations there is a department (or individual) specifically responsible for scheduling the organization's operations. In product organizations it is frequently called **production planning and control**, or some similar name. The breadth of this department's responsibility varies considerably and may consist only of planning gross output levels, for example, or may include all of the scheduling activities illustrated in Figure 9.1.

The Production Planning and Control Department.

This figure does not describe a *standardized* scheduling system, such as might exist in an available computer package, but rather the complex of activities and terms that are often grouped under the phrase "scheduling." Many of these have only become major activities since the advent of computerized scheduling. Prior to that, the activities were simply judgmental ones (as some of the activities still are). Let us look at each of the scheduling activities on the chart and their interrelationships; in the remaining sections of the chapter we will then look more intensively at some of the major activities and describe some approaches in dealing with them.

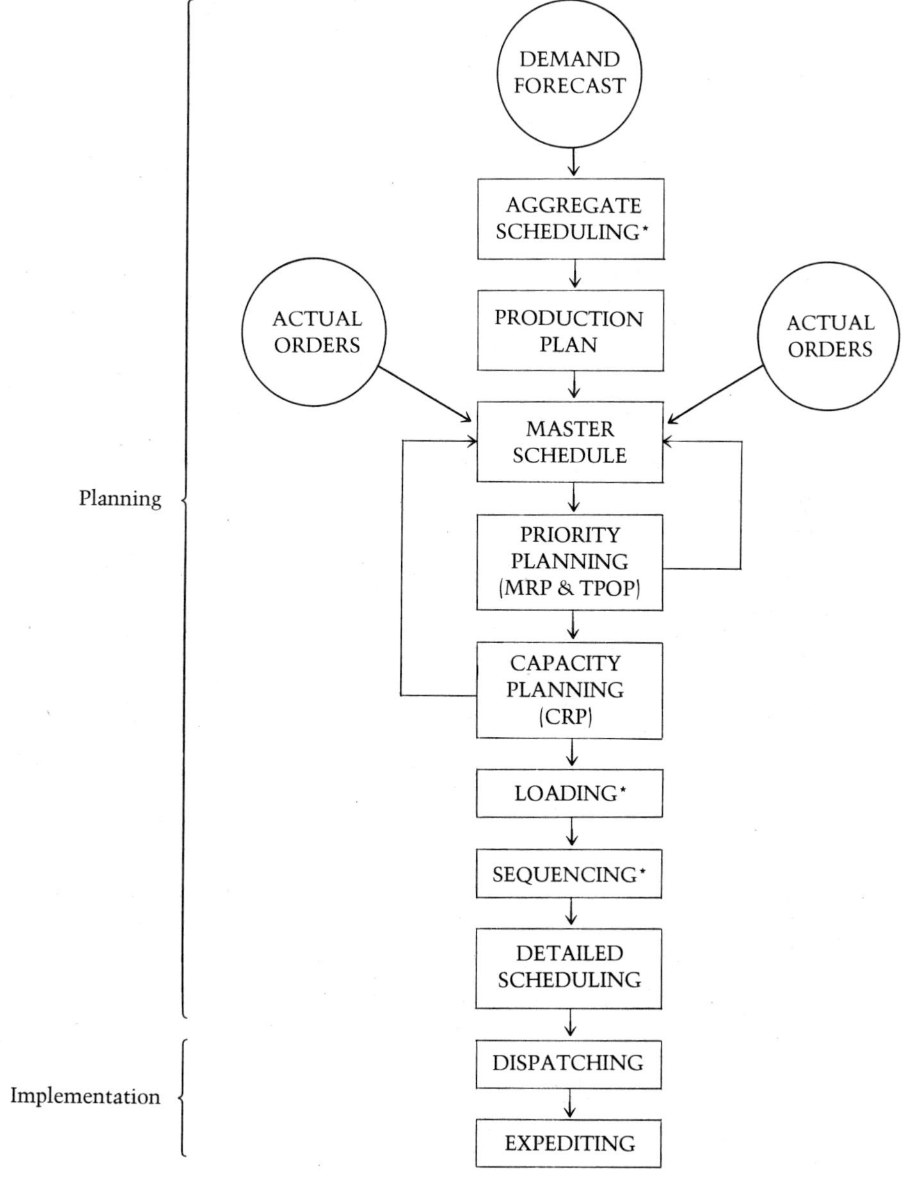

Figure 9.1.Scheduling activity relationships. (*Described in greater detail in later sections.)

Demand forecast. The foundation that supports the entire scheduling process is, in most cases, the forecast of demand for the upcoming planning horizon. In some organizations, such as the machine tool industry, customers place orders up to a year ahead of time because of the long lead times and order backlogs. Thus only minimal forecasting, if any, is conducted and organizational operations are scheduled on the basis of actual customer orders instead.

Demand forecast as the basis for scheduling.

Most organizations do not operate in such a fortunate environment, however, and their success often hinges heavily on the accuracy of their forecasts of demand. In these cases the forecasting concepts and techniques illustrated in Chapter 4 are especially relevant for the scheduling functions.

Aggregate scheduling a first rough-cut.

Aggregate scheduling. The **aggregate schedule** is a rough-cut schedule of an organization's overall operations that will satisfy the demand forecast at minimum cost. Planning horizons are often one year or more. This is because one of the purposes in aggregate scheduling is to minimize the short-sighted effects of day-to-day scheduling where material may be ordered from a supplier and workers laid off one week, only to have to reorder more material and rehire the workers the following week. By taking a longer term perspective of resource use, short-term changes in requirements can be minimized with a considerable cost savings.

The basic approach in minimizing short-term variations is to work only with "aggregate" (grouped or bunched together) units. Aggregate resources are used, such as total number of workers, hours of machine time, and tons of raw materials, as well as aggregate units of output: gallons of product, hours of service delivered, number of patients seen, and so on, totally ignoring the fact that some are blue and others are red, some soft and some hard, and so forth. That is, neither resources nor outputs are broken down into more specific categories—that occurs at a later stage.

On occasion, the units of aggregation are somewhat difficult to determine, especially if the variation in output is extreme (such as when a manufacturer produces dishwashers, clothes washers, and dryers). In such cases, **equivalent units** are usually determined based on value, cost, manhours input, or some similar basic measure. For the appliance manufacturer above, the aggregate schedule might be: January—5000 "appliances," February—4000 "appliances," and so forth.

Aggregate scheduling to minimize total costs.

The resulting aggregate scheduling problem is to minimize the long run costs of meeting forecasted demand. The relevant costs are typically those of hiring and laying off workers, storing finished goods if a product is involved, wages and overtime charges, shortage and **backordering** costs, subcontracting costs, and so on. As it turns out, the use of inventory to buffer production against variations in demand is an extremely important managerial option. In service organizations this option is usually not available since services, such as plane trips, typically cannot be inventoried. The result is increased cost to produce the service with a resulting increase in the price of the service.

The topic of aggregate scheduling will be discussed in considerably more detail in Section 9.2.

The output of aggregate scheduling is the production plan.

The production plan. The result of the aggregate scheduling task is the organization's **production plan** for the planning horizon used by the organization (e.g., one year). Sometimes this plan is broken down (i.e., **disaggregated**) one level into major output groups (still aggregated); for example, by models but not by colors. In either case, the production plan shows the resource requirements and output changes over the future: hiring requirements, capacity limitations, the relative growth and decreases in materials inventories, the output rate of goods or services.

The master schedule. The driving force behind the scheduling process is the **master schedule** There are two reasons for this.

1. It is at this point that *actual* orders are incorporated into the scheduling system.
2. This is also the stage where aggregate scheduled outputs are broken down into individual scheduled output groups (called **level zero items**) by model, size, color, and so forth, specifically checked against lead time (time to produce or ship the items) and operations capacity (if there is enough equipment, labor, etc.) for feasibility.

The actual scheduling itself is usually an iterative process, with a preliminary schedule being drawn up, checked for problems, and then revised. Initial schedules are usually obtained by either **forward scheduling**, where jobs are scheduled in the order they come in, or by **backward scheduling**, where due dates are used to determine the *latest* possible time a job can be started. Problems typically checked are

1. Does the schedule meet the aggregate plan?
2. Does the schedule meet the end item demand forecasts?
3. Are there priority or capacity conflicts in the schedule (see next two scheduling activities)?
4. Does the schedule violate any other constraints regarding equipment, lead times, supplies, facilities, and so forth?
5. Does the schedule conform to organizational policy?
6. Does the schedule violate any legal regulations or organization-union rules?
7. Does the schedule provide for flexibility and backups?

The major role of the master schedule.

It is the master schedule then that specifies *what end items* are to be produced *in what periods* to *minimize costs*, and gives some measure of assurance that such a plan *is feasible*. Clearly, such a document is of major importance to any organization—it is, in a sense, a blueprint for future operations.

Priority planning for materials.

Priority planning. This term, popularized by Oliver Wight [38], relates not to giving priorities to jobs (a topic included under "sequencing"), but rather to determining *what material* is needed *when*. For a master schedule of production to be feasible, the proper raw materials, purchased materials, and manufactured or purchased subassemblies must be available when needed, top priority going to immediate needs. The key to production planning is the "needed" date. Previous scheduling attempts concentrated on **order launching**; that is, when to *place* the order. Priority planning concentrates on when the order is actually needed and schedules *backward* from that date. For example, if an item is needed July 18 and requires a two-week lead time then the order is released July 4 and not before. Why store inventory needlessly?

TPOP system for independent demand.

The systems that have been devised for accomplishing this task are inventory control sytems based on lead times and expected demands. The classical inventory systems are most appropriate for organizations **producing to stock** (e.g., continuous flow organizations). These are called "order point" systems because new orders for materials are sent out when the inventory on hand reaches a certain low point. Although delivery lead time is *generally* known, as well as a distribution of demand, the *specific* demand for materials cannot be easily anticipated. Materials must therefore be stocked in quantity to meet this random or "independent" demand. For example, demands for spare parts is typically independent of current orders. Manual systems based on **economic order quantities** (to be discussed in Chapter 12) have followed this approach for years; recent trends have been to computerize this mass of order quantities and reorder points for the thousands of items organizations normally use. These systems are now called *time-phased order point* (**TPOP**) systems.

MRP systems for dependent demand.

For organizations that **produce to order** (e.g., many job shops), materials requirements are known with almost certainty because they are tied to specified outputs (thus known as **dependent demand**). For example, every car requires four wheel covers—the number of wheel covers *depends* only on the number of cars. For these situations the computer has unlocked an undreamed of world to the production scheduler. Computerized *materials requirements planning* (**MRP**) systems have just recently been developed to anticipate materials needs, consider lead times, release purchase orders, and schedule production in accord with the master schedule, a capability almost unimaginable a dozen years ago. MRP is also useful in producing "to stock" when demands are again dependent. That is, the critical issue in choosing between an MRP system and a TPOP system is not *how* the item got ordered but whether the demand is *dependent* or *independent*.

If insufficient lead time exists to produce or obtain the necessary materials, under either TPOP or MRP systems, or other problems arise, the master schedule must be revised or other arrangements made. These inventory systems are discussed in much greater detail in Chapters 12 and 13.

Checking the master schedule against the CRP.

Capacity planning. The inventory control system and master schedule drive the *capacity requirements planning* (**CRP**) system. This system projects the job orders and demands for materials into equipment, manpower, and facility requirements and finds the total required capacity of each over the planning horizon. That is, during a given week how many nurses will be required, how many hours of kidney machine operation, how many syringes, and so forth.

This may or may not exceed *available* capacity. If it is within capacity limits then the master schedule is finalized, **time-phased work orders** are released according to schedule, materials orders are released by the priority planning system, and **load reports** are sent to work centers listing the work facing that area based on the CRP system.

Human intervention if capacity limits are exceeded.

However, if the capacity limits are exceeded then something must be changed. Either some jobs must be delayed, a less demanding schedule devised, or extra capacity obtained elsewhere (e.g., by hiring more workers or using overtime). It is the role of Production Planning and Control to solve this problem.

Allocating jobs to work centers.

Loading. **Loading** means deciding which jobs to assign to which work centers. Although the capacity planning system determined that sufficient gross capacity existed to meet the master schedule, no *actual assignment* of jobs to work centers was made. Some equipment will generally be superior for certain jobs and some equipment will be less heavily loaded than other equipment. Thus, there is often a "best" (fastest, or least costly) assignment of jobs to work centers. We will consider the loading problem in more detail in Section 9.7.

Properly ordering the execution of the jobs through priority rules.

Sequencing. Even after jobs have been assigned to work centers, the *order* in which to perform the jobs must still be decided. Unfortunately, even this seemingly small final step can have major repercussions on the organizations's workload capacity and the timeliness of job completions. A number of **priority rules** have been researched in this regard and some interesting results are available which will be discussed in Section 9.3.

A final schedule, at last.

Detailed (Short-Term) Scheduling. Once all the foregoing has been specified, detailed schedules itemizing specific jobs, times, materials, and workers can be drawn up. This is usually only done for a few days in advance however since changes are always occurring and detailed schedules become outdated quickly. It is production planning and control's responsibility to ensure that when the job is ready to be worked on, all the items, equipment, facilities, and information (blueprints, operations sheets, etc.) are available as scheduled.

Releasing the work orders.

Dispatching. All of the previous activities constitute the schedule *planning*; no production, per se, has taken place yet. **Dispatching** is the physical **release** of a work order from production planning and control to operations. The release may be manually, from the **dead load file**, as it is called, or through the computerized master scheduling system.

Checking on delays.

Expediting. Once production planning and control has released a job to operations (or the *shop floor*, as it is sometimes called) they usually have no more responsibility for it and it is the operations manager's task to get the job done on time. As jobs fall behind schedule, managers have historically tended to use *expediters* to help push these "hot" jobs through the operations.

The overuse of expediters.

Before computerized scheduling techniques, the extensive use of expediters was common (and still is in many organizations). The problem was the impossibility of

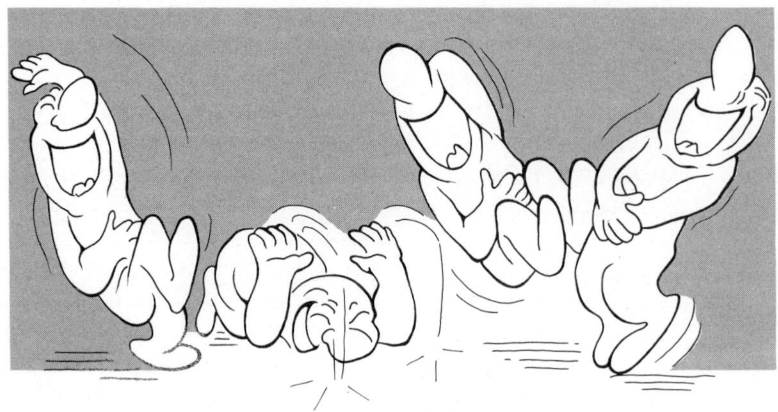

YOU WANT IT WHEN ? !

the scheduling task facing production planning and control. Not only could they not determine a good production schedule; they often could not even tell when insufficient capacity existed. Operations managers thus relied heavily on expediters to gather all the necessary materials together (often cannibalizing parts from other jobs) in order to get important jobs completed. Of course this further delayed the remaining jobs so that more and more jobs tended to become **hot**.

Instances are common of the use of yellow tags on jobs to label the "hot" ones until, pretty soon, all the jobs had yellow tags. To identify the "especially hot" jobs then red tags were used. After a while the operation's area resembled a rainbow whereupon no new orders were accepted, the backlog was worked off, and the cycle started from scratch.

The need to de-expedite.

It may be presumed that a clear indication of the failure of a scheduling system is the existence of a great many expediters. One of the problems of the informal scheduling system, of course, was the lack of a **de-expediting** (delaying jobs that have dropped in priority) system to reflect changes in required due dates and, thus, in the priorities and schedules for jobs. This process has been built into the computerized scheduling systems.

The Role of Computers in Scheduling

The critical importance of the computer.

Requirements-based scheduling systems, because of their relatively large scale and complex nature, necessitate the use of a computer system for implementation. The rule of the computer here is extremely important. The concept of requirements-based scheduling is not novel; it simply was heretofore too cumbersome to pursue in a clerically oriented system. Construction management has for years recognized the need for detailed requirements planning and scheduling. If material, labor, or equipment was at the job site in the wrong sequence or at the wrong time, not only would bottlenecks be unending but wasted time and material losses from weather damage and theft would raise the cost of construction to unreasonable levels. The computer has simply allowed all of these clerical data processing activities and file handling tasks to be accomplished more efficiently; hence, what once was conceptually feasible but technically infeasible is now both technically and conceptually possible.

The PICS scheduling system.

An example of a computerized scheduling system is the Production Information and Control System (**PICS**) designed by IBM [21]. PICS accepts a sales forecast and basic engineering data for each product and, using an MRP subsystem, develops the "time phased materials requirements." Once this information is available, the purchasing, capacity planning, and operations scheduling components of PICS take over to produce purchase order requirements, route the product through the operations, generate capacity requirements by individual operations, and load and schedule operations for production.

We might ask how the system handles the inevitable last minute changes such as breakdowns or rush orders. When these changes are input to the computer, the program works *backward* to see what new resources are needed, or what old resources are now not needed, and *time phases* (schedules) the requirements. When an order is scheduled earlier, this is called "expediting"; when an order is intentionally delayed it is referred to as "de-expediting." One of the Production Planning and Control (PP&C) Department's important tasks is to determine the need for reasons for expediting and de-expediting. That is, an equipment failure input to the system may indicate the need to delay (de-expedite) a particular job. However, PP&C should not simply let the system delay the job but should attempt to find alternative ways to maintain the original schedule, if possible.

Net change versus regenerative systems.

If changes, such as the above, are input to the MRP system on an immediate basis, then this is called a **net change** system and is always up to date (at a cost for computing time and program complexity). If such changes are stored until, for example, a weekend, and then the entire MRP program rerun, this is called **regeneration**. Clearly, this latter system will always be somewhat out of date, except on Monday morning.

The importance of data base integrity.

Generally speaking, the integrity of the **data base** is the most critical element in computerized scheduling systems. If incorrect data is fed to the system, the confidence of the workers in the validity of the schedule will be lost and they will turn once again to an expediter to identify the hot jobs. The use of the computer to handle and store the massive amounts of data concerning the hundreds of jobs and thousands of items is a revolution in the information base available to operations managers.

Now that we have looked at the overall scheduling system, let us consider some of the more technical components in greater detail. First, we will consider aggregate scheduling.

9.2 AGGREGATE SCHEDULING

The aggregate scheduling problem.

The aggregate scheduling problem arises in the following context. The manager of operations has a month to month forecast of total demand for all outputs combined for the next year or so. She or he is expected to capitalize on this demand by supplying that portion of it that will maximize long run profitability. That is, not all of the demand need be satisfied if attempting to fill it will result in lower overall profits. But a loss of market share might thereby result, which, in turn, may reduce long run profitability.

The manager has a set of productive facilities and workers with some maximum capacity to supply demand. There may also be some finished output available in inventory to help meet the demand but there may, as well, be a backorder of unsatisfied demand. The manager must decide how to employ the resources at his or her disposal to best meet the demand. If excess capacity is available the manager may lease it out, sell it, or lay off workers. If insufficient capacity is available, but only for a short time in the future, she or he may employ overtime or part time workers, subcontract work, or simply not meet the demand.

As discussed in Chapter 5, there are a number of ways of changing the capacity available to the manager to meet demand at minimum cost such as

1. Overtime.
2. Additional shifts.
3. Hiring or laying off workers (including part time).
4. Subcontracting.
5. Building up inventories during slack periods.
6. Leasing facilities and/or workers.
7. Backlogging demand.
8. Changing demand through marketing promotions or price changes.
9. Undersupplying the market.

The need for a long range view.

Each of these strategies has advantages and disadvantages associated with it and perhaps certain restrictions on its use (such as legal or union regulations). The manager must plan his or her strategy carefully because a short-sighted strategy, such as laying off workers when they will later be needed again, can be very expensive to rectify. However, an excessively long range perspective may also be incorrect, such as keeping an idle worker for a year when she or he could much more cheaply be layed off and then rehired.

Pure Strategies

Two baseline strategies.

There are two **baseline** aggregate scheduling strategies, known as *pure strategies*, which, although rarely used in practice, can give the manager a feel for some upper limits on costs. They are

I. **Chase demand.** In this strategy, production is identical to the expected demand for the period in question. This is typically obtained either through overtime or hiring and laying off. The advantage of this policy is that there is no finished goods inventory cost (except perhaps for *buffer*, or *safety, stock* as discussed in Chapter 12) or shortage cost.

II. Level production. Here finished goods inventories (or backlogged demand) are used to meet variations in demand, at the cost of inventory investment and shortage or stockout expense. The advantage is steady employment with no workforce or overtime expenses. Since service outputs cannot generally be inventoried, this strategy results in a constant, but poorly utilized, workforce of a size large enough to meet peak demand (e.g., repair crews, firefighters).

The vast majority of realistic aggregate scheduling strategies achieve much lower costs than the baseline costs of these pure strategies by trading off investment in finished goods inventories for capacity level changes or vice versa. Let us demonstrate with an example.

Aggregate Scheduling Example

Demand forecasts for each of the quarters of the year for your product are 40, 60, 30, 10, with this pattern repeating in the future as far as can be foreseen. The current workforce is three and each worker can produce 10 units per quarter. Inventory costs are \$10 per unit per quarter while shortage costs for expediting backorders are \$13 per unit per quarter. Hiring and layoff costs have been estimated as \$100 per worker but idle workers effectively cost \$150 per quarter. The cost to produce units on an overtime basis is an additional \$15 each. Find the best production plan if all demand *must* be met, either immediately or through backorders.

ANALYSIS. Figure 9.2 displays the expected demand over a two-year (eight-quarter) period, and the two extreme production strategies.

I. Production equal to demand.

II. Level production at a rate equal to the average demand of (40 + 60 + 30 + 10)/4 = 35 units per quarter. (Producing in excess of this would continue to build up unnccessary inventory, producing less than this would build up a continuing backlog.)

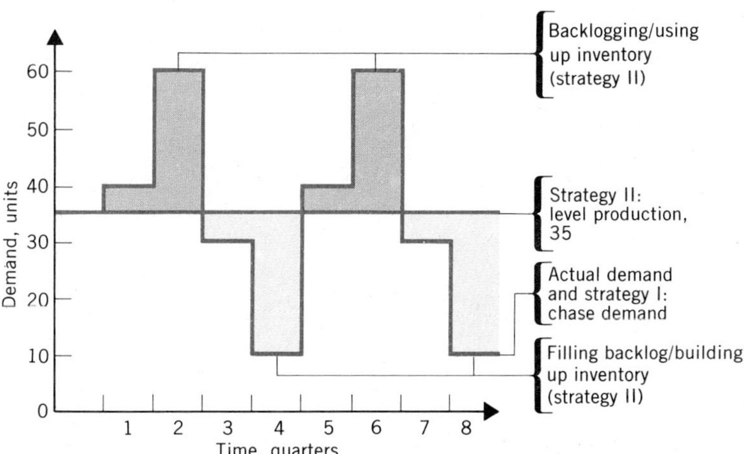

Figure 9.2 Quarter production and demand.

The shadings in the figure illustrate periods of inventory use (or backlog) and then buildup under a 35 unit level production strategy.

Figure 9.3 illustrates the resultant inventory level for the given demands under strategy II as either positive or negative (or alternately both), depending upon the quarter during which you begin to market your product. If production and sales *began* in quarter 3, for example (i.e., you entered the market in quarter 3), then inventory level under the constant 35 unit production would always be at or above zero. But if production and sales began in quarter 1, then the inventory level would be permanently at or below zero using the same production level. That is, there would always be backorders simply because sales exceed production in both of the first two quarters and production is level at 35 units thereafter.

Note that the shape of the inventory curves are identical. *When* you start production simply shifts the curve up or down in proportion to the amount of inventory initially on hand. As another example, suppose you entered the market in quarter 2. Then by the end of that quarter your inventory level would be −25 (a backlog). The message here is that strategy can be changed from, for example, one of backlog to inventory buildup by "reentering" the market at a different point. This may be done by temporarily dropping out of the market (at the risk of losing market share), working overtime to "catch up" on the market, subcontracting, or any number of other *mixed* strategies, which we will consider below.

Mixed Strategies

Using a cumulative chart for mixed strategies.

A way to combine Figures 9.2 and 9.3 in order to obtain a working graph for better analysis is the "cumulative" chart shown in Figure 9.4. Here, both demand and production are accumulated so positive inventories with level production strategies are

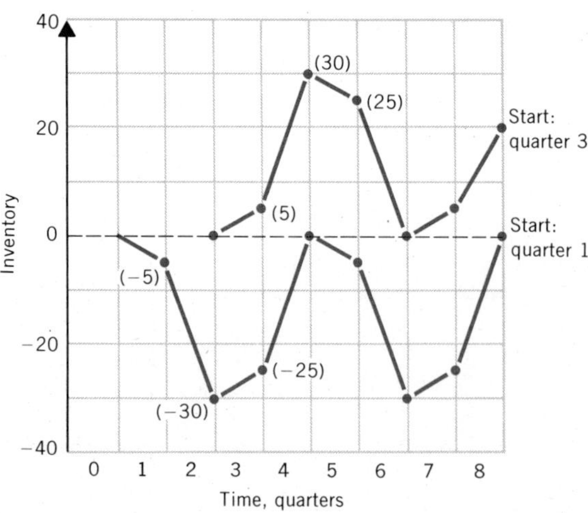

Figure 9.3. Inventory accumulation for two level-production strategies.

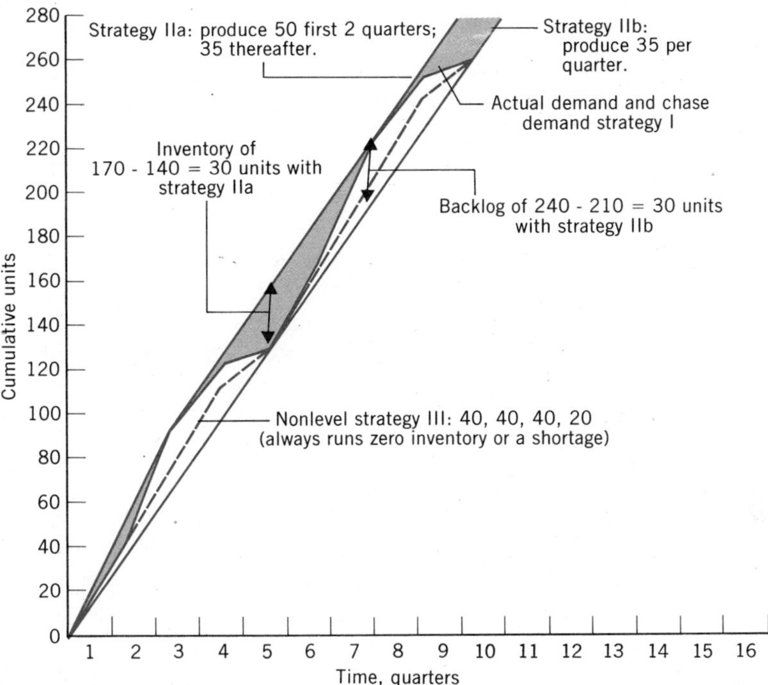

Figure 9.4. Cumulative demand and production strategies.

shown (shaded) *below* any production line and shortages (unshaded) *above* it. The two solid heavy lines are level production strategies. The top one, strategy IIa, represents a production of 50 units in the first two quarters and then levels at 35; it never has shortages. The bottom one, strategy IIb, is 35 units continuous production and never has positive inventory. The dashed line, strategy III (a better strategy), represents production of 40, 40, 40, and 20 units per quarter. Lastly is the chase demand strategy (produce an amount each quarter identical to the demand). (If buffer stock existed then the chase demand strategy would parallel demand but be above it by the amount of the buffer.)

The total costs for some of the strategies shown in Figure 9.4 are derived in Table 9.1 for varying situations.

Ia. Chase demand using overtime and idle time: $900 total cost.

Ib. Chase demand by hiring and laying off: $1,000.

IIa. Level production (three workers) and overtime (start regular cycle in quarter 3): $900.

III. Produce 40, 40, 40, 20 (four workers): $690.

IV. Produce 50, 50, 30, 10 (four workers) and overtime: $1000.

In cases III and IV the cost of *permanently* hiring the fourth worker increased the cost by $100 for one year only. This increase was *amortized over an infinite horizon* and thus effectively added nothing to the total annual costs. Hiring and laying off is only expensive when used as a *continuing* strategy to balance production and demand.

As seen in Table 9.1, the pure chase demand strategy Ia only incurs overtime and idle cost. To produce 40 units with three workers requires 10 units from overtime at $15 for a cost of $150. In quarter 4, two workers were idle (20 units of production) for an "effective" cost of 2 × $150 = $300.

Strategy Ib is also a pure chase demand strategy but accomplished in a different way (with a different cost) through hiring and laying off workers. The cost calculations are skipped in quarter 1 because the previous quarter's work-force is unknown at this point; it will be determined later from quarter 4. We therefore start calculating costs in quarter 2 when we have to hire two workers beyond the four we had in quarter 1 at a cost of $100 per worker. The total cost of achieving the chase demand strategy in this manner is seen to be $100 per year more expensive than with strategy Ia.

Strategy IIa uses extra workers (or overtime) to reach quarter 3 where regular operations (and our calculations) then begin with three workers and overtime. Five units are always produced on overtime for a constant cost of 5 × 15 = $75 every quarter. Inventory builds up 5 units in quarter 3 plus another 25 units in quarter 4 and then is drawn down in quarters 5 and 6.

Strategies III and IV employ four workers with combinations of either shortage and idle time cost or inventory with overtime and idle time costs. Strategy III is the least costly of those investigated, but there are undoubtedly even better policies. Note the difficulty of even such a simple problem: constant (from year to year) demands, clear-cut costs, limited strategies, and all for only a *single "aggregate" product*.

In the *Tools and Applications* portion of this chapter we present four approaches that have been developed for analyzing the aggregate scheduling problem.

9.3 SEQUENCING

The next scheduling topic we will consider is sequencing, which is most appropriate for intermittent and batch processes with independent demands. For dependent demands the MRP capacity planning routine predetermines the sequencing before the master production schedule is derived. Sequencing refers to ordering the jobs so as to achieve some operations goal such as maximizing job throughput, minimizing job lateness, and so forth. An introduction to the nature of the severity of the sequencing problem was given in Chapter 5 where the effect of sequencing was shown to restrict capacity quite seriously.

Approaches to efficient job ordering.

In this section we will consider first the historical use of Gantt charts to pictorially aid in the sequencing problem and then look at some priority rules that have been extensively tested to determine their value in maximizing facility utilization, getting jobs through the operations, and minimizing late deliveries. We will then conclude by examining the sequencing/lot size problem of batch production of multiple outputs on a standard set of facilities.

TABLE 9.1 RELEVANT COSTS FOR VARIOUS STRATEGIES

Case	Quarter	Demand	Production	Inventory Cost	Overtime Cost	Idle Cost	Shortage Cost	Hire-Layoff Cost	Total
Ia.	1	40	40	0	10 × $15 = 150	0	0	0	$150
	2	60	60	0	450	0	0	0	450
	3	30	30	0	0	0	0	0	0
	4	10	10	0	0	2 × $150 = 300	0	0	300
									$900
Ib.	1	40	40	0	0	0	0	(Calculate in quarter 5)	
	2	60	60	0	0	0	0	2 × $100 = 200 (hire 2)	$200
	3	30	30	0	0	0	0	300 (layoff 3)	300
	4	10	10	0	0	0	0	200 (layoff 2)	200
	5	40	40	0	0	0	0	300 (hire 3)	300
									$1000
IIa.	3	30	35	5 × 10 = 50	5 × $15 = 75	0	0	0	$125
	4	10	35	(5 + 25) × $10 = 300	75	0	0	0	375
	5	40	35	(30 − 5) × $10 = 250	75	0	0	0	325
	6	60	35	(25 − 25) × $10 = 0	75	0	0	0	75
									$900
III.	1	40	40	0	0	0	0	0	$ 0
	2	60	40	0	0	0	20 × $13 = 260	0	260
	3	30	40	0	0	0	130	0	130
	4	10	20	0	0	2 × $150 = 300	0	0	300
									$690
IV.	1	40	50	10 × $10 = 100	10 × $15 = 150	0	0	0	$250
	2	60	50	0	150	0	0	0	150
	3	30	30	0	0	1 × $150 = 150	0	0	150
	4	10	10	0	0	3 × $150 = 450	0	0	450
									$1000

Gantt Charts

The flexibility of Gantt Charts.

Probably the oldest, most useful, and yet most eaily understood method for conveying the sequence and status of operations is the **Gantt chart**, developed by Henry L. Gantt, a scientific management pioneer, around 1917. The Gantt chart usually shows planned *and* actual progress on a number of items displayed against a horizontal time scale. The items may be jobs, machines, departments, parts, staff, and so forth. A variety of symbols may be added to the chart, depending on the activity being charted. Some common symbols are given in Figure 9.5 and their use illustrated in Figure 9.6. This latter figure illustrates job loadings for three facilities. As of July 15, 5 P.M., job 481 was completed as planned, even with the shutdown of facility A-2 July 9; and job 502, although completed, took half a day longer than expected. Job 563 was delayed one day due to lack of materials and still is incomplete and job 459, besides starting late, was delayed for repairs. Lastly, job 496 is half a day ahead of schedule.

Squencing by Gantt chart.

The use of a Gantt chart for sequencing is illustrated in Figure 9.7. In this situation the jobs to be considered over the next two weeks with their facility and time requirements, in order, are as shown below the figure.

Figure 9.7 shows only one possible sequencing; a better one might have been to put job 703 on facility A-2 first at day 6½ and then job 717 on A-2 so facility A-5 would be better utilized over the two-week duration. What is "best" depends on a number of factors such as the importance and due dates of the jobs, the relative expense of the facilities, and so on. If the objective is to meet due dates, **backward scheduling** is often useful. Here, tasks are first assigned to the *final* operation so as to just meet the due dates for each job. The next to last operation is then considered, and so on. Scheduling in this fashion allows maximum flexibility in early operations while still guaranteeing that due dates will be met. This is basically the approach of *priority planning* techniques, such as *materials requirements planning* (MRP), which we discuss in detail in Chapter 20.

Backward scheduling to meet due dates.

A number of variations of the basic Gantt chart have been developed with the use of pegs, colored string, colored tape, and so forth. Nevertheless, the purpose remains the same: to clearly communicate the current status of operations, facilities, and jobs for purposes of expediting, sequencing, resource allocation between idle and bottleneck facilities, and so forth.

⌐	:	scheduled start of an operation
¬	:	scheduled completion date of an operation
⋈	:	time unavailable for scheduling (e.g., preventive maintenance)
—	:	scheduled worktime
▨	:	actual progress
V	:	date of last charted progress
M	:	delay caused by materials
R	:	delay caused by repairs
T	:	delay caused by tool trouble
A	:	operator absent

Figure 9.5. Gantt chart symbols.

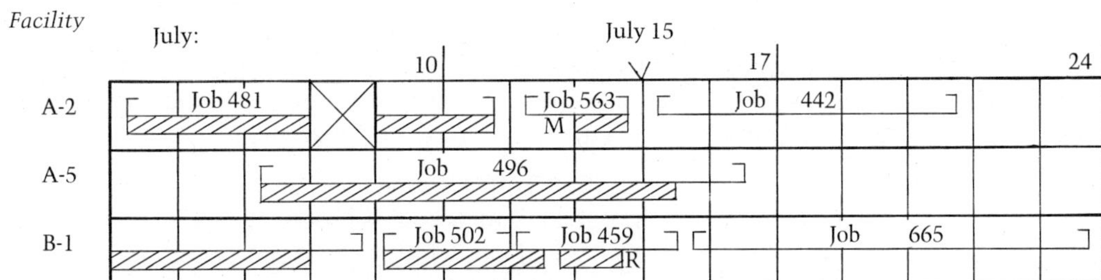

Figure 9.6. Typical Gantt status chart.

Although the Gantt chart performs the function of communicating job and facility status quite well, it is not especially useful in determining the best sequence of activities, or for rescheduling activities, in some special situations. Other approaches, described below and in the *Tools and Applications* sections have been found more useful for these situations.

Priority rules for Sequencing

Best sequence depends on goals.

An ideal sequencing rule would be one that resulted in all jobs being completed on time, with maximum facility utilization, but minimal in-process inventory. Since no rule is perfect, the task is then to identify that rule which minimizes the sum of these interrelated costs. In some organizations, the cost of lateness will far overshadow the other costs (e.g., ambulance services) while, in other organizations, equipment utilization (e.g., machine shops), or inventories (e.g., retailers), will result in the largest cost. It may also be that, at different times in an organization's life, different factors will be of first importance and so the "best" priority rule will change.

There are quite a few priority rules; for example, Conway investigated 92 of them [9]. Such rules can be categorized on a number of different bases, such as on the costs they most often minimize. Another basis is whether they are static (based on situa-

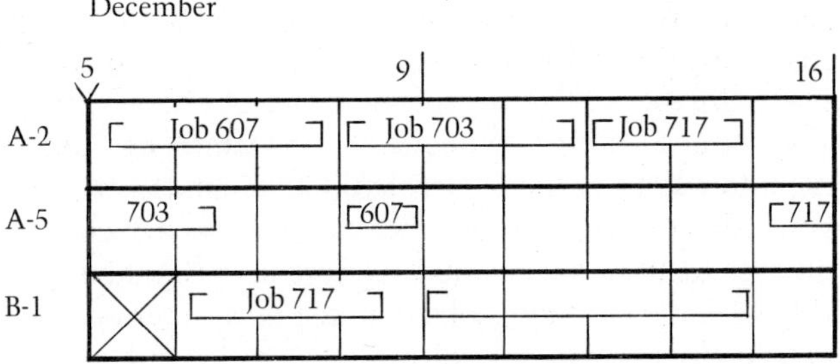

Job 607: Facility A-2 (3 days); Facility A-5 (1 day); Facility B-1 (4 days)
703: Facility A-5 (1½ days left); Facility A-2 (3 days)
717: Facility B-1 (2½ days); Facility A-2 (2 days); Facility A-5 (6 days)

Figure 9.7. Sequencing by Gantt chart.

tions existing at the time the job came in, such as order of acceptance) or dynamic (taking current events into account such as delays and rush orders).

A number of researchers [2, 6, 11, 16, 23] have investigated the characteristics of many of the more common priority sequencing rules and have come to some interesting conclusions. The rules in most common use are

- **FCFS** First come, first served. The first job to arrive at a work center (*not* into the organization) is processed first. This rule is based on "fairness" to all jobs waiting at the same work center.
- **FISFS** First in the system (organization), first served. The assumption here is that a job entering the organization first will be given an earlier due date. The rule is justified to recipients on the basis of "fairness": "His job came in first—then yours is next."
- **SOT** Shortest operation time. Do the short, easy jobs first and get them out of the way.
- **LOT** Longest operation time. The longer jobs are often the bigger, more important (and profitable) ones and should be done first.
- **SS** Static slack. Slack here equals the due date minus the time of arrival at the work center. Jobs with the smallest "slack" are done first.
- **SS/RO** Static slack per remaining operation. If two jobs have the same static slack but one has more operations remaining to be completed, it should have the higher priority because it will require more setups.
- **DS/RO** Dynamic slack per remaining operation. The dynamic slack is defined as the remaining time until the due date *less* the remaining expected processing time.
- **COVERT** Priority is given to the job with the *highest* ratio of cost of delay, c, over processing time, t (c over t). This rule attempts to operate like the SOT rule but to also consider the cost of delays, c.
- **RAND** Random order.

The general superiority of the SOT rule.

In terms of maximizing work flow through the operations, maximizing facility utilization, and minimizing lateness, the SOT rule was often found to be the best. Not considering the COVERT rule for the moment (which was not included in most of the research), the SOT rule results in more jobs being finished early, earlier average completion times, shorter, in-queue waiting times, and higher labor and equipment utilization. In addition, the SOT rule ranks second only to the DS/RO rule in minimizing the percent of jobs completed late. It is this one characteristic of the SOT rule that hampers its use—when short jobs are always taken before long jobs there will invariably be some *very* long jobs that just *never* seem to get done. Perhaps this is a legitimate justification for expediting.

Improving the SOT rule.

Researchers have attempted to devise SOT-type rules that would negate this one drawback of SOT. And that, of course, was the basis for devising the COVERT rule

[6]. However, the determination of the "cost" of delay is a difficult matter and not easily identified with a particular job once it is in processing. Also, such modifications to the SOT rule destroy one of its most important characteristics—its simplicity of use. Any worker by him or herself can usually tell which job among those available is going to be easiest, thereby eliminating the sequencing task for the operations manager and freeing him or her to handle bottlenecks, overdue jobs, and so forth.

In addition to the formal priority rules above, there are also informal priority systems as well. Examples are: most important customer first, most profitable item first, most crucial subassembly first. There is also a special priority rule called the **critical ratio** used in situations where there is a production lead time for self-manufactured items that are kept in stock for later use. This ratio is used to compare the rate at which stock is being used up to the rate at which it is being resupplied. The stock usage factor is

A critical ratio rule for lead time items.

$$A = \frac{\text{stock still available}}{\text{reorder point value}}$$

and the resupply factor is

$$B = \frac{\text{production time still required}}{\text{total normal production time for a lot}}$$

The critical ratio is then just A/B. For critical ratios above or near 1.0, we are not usually concerned because stock is being used up slower or at about the same rate as production time. But for values near 0.8 or less, the stock is being used significantly faster than production time (and thus resupplies) and there is a good chance of a shortage. Clearly, the lower the critical ratio the greater the priority, and the greater the need for management intervention.

Although responsive to lateness considerations, the critical ratio rule often delays the processing of items until the need is more critical. This may then result in increasing the in-process inventory investment significantly. For situations where this investment is a major cost, the SOT rule is again usually the best priority rule. Although well justified, these priority rules are sometimes not used at all in organizations. Instead, "chaos" rules. That is, a worker may be told to start on one job, and 15 minutes after a customer's call, told to work on his or her job instead. This **hat switching** often consumes more of a day than actual productive work.

The hat switching problem.

9.4 SCHEDULING SERVICES

In this section we consider the scheduling of services. Much of what was said above applies to the scheduling of services, as well as products, but here we consider some scheduling issues of particular relevance to services.

Up to now we have dealt primarily with situations where the jobs (or recipients) were the items to be loaded, sequenced, or scheduled. There are, however, many

Resource scheduling when the *jobs* cannot be scheduled.

operations where scheduling of the jobs themselves is either inappropriate or impossible, and it is necessary to concentrate instead on scheduling one or more of the input resources. Therefore, the staff, the materials, or the facilities are scheduled to correspond, as closely as possible, with the expected arrival of the jobs. Such situations are common in service systems such as libraries, supermarkets, hospitals, urban services, colleges, restaurants, and airlines.

The complications of scheduling staff.

In the scheduling of jobs we were primarily interested in minimizing the number of late jobs, minimizing rejects, maximizing the throughput, and maximizing the utilization of available resources. In the scheduling of resources, however, there may be considerably more criteria of interest, especially when one of the resources being scheduled is staff. Staff desires in terms of shifts, holidays, and work schedules become critically important when work schedules are variable and not all employees are on the same schedule. In these situations there are usually exist schedules that will displease everyone and schedules that will satisfy most of the staff's more important priorities—it is crucial that one of the latter be chosen rather than one of the former.

Approaches in Resource Scheduling

Match the resources to demand.

The primary approach to the scheduling of resources is to match resource availability to demand on the resources (e.g., 7 P.M.–12 A.M. is the high fire alarm period). In so doing we are thus not required to provide a continuing high level of resources that are poorly utilized the great majority of the time. However, this requires that a good forecast of demand be available for the proper scheduling of resources. If demand cannot be accurately predicted then the resulting service with variable resources might be worse than using a constant level of resources.

Methods to increase resources.

Methods used to increase resources for peak demand include using overtime and part-time help and leasing equipment and facilities. Also, if multiple areas within the organization tend to experience varying demand, use of **floating workers**, or combining departments to minimize variability, is often helpful. On occasion, the employment of new technology can aid the organization such as 24-hour computerized tellers and bill paying by telephone.

Changing demand through promotion.

And, as mentioned previously, the use of promotion and advertising to shift *demand* for resources is highly practical in many situations. Thus, we see **off-peak pricing** in the utilities and communication industries, summer snowblower sales in retailing, and cut rates for transportation and tours in both the off-peak seasons (fall, winter) and off-peak times (weekends, nights). Let us now consider how some specific service organizations approach their scheduling problems.

Hospitals

Selective admissions to control demand.

There are multiple scheduling needs in hospitals. Although patient arrivals (the jobs) are in part uncontrollable (e.g., emergencies) they are, to an extent, controllable through selective admissions for hernia operations, some maternity cases, in-hospital observation, and so on. By selective admissions the hospital administrator can smooth the demand faced by the hospital and thereby improve service and increase the utilization of the hospital's limited resources. For an overview of hospital admission systems refer to Reference 30.

Scheduling equipment.

Very specialized, expensive equipment such as a kidney machine is also carefully scheduled to allow other hospitals access to it, thus maximizing its utilization. Two-stage scheduling may thus exist in some cases: equipment availability may be scheduled for a hospital only during certain periods of various days of the week (such as 7–11 A.M. Mondays; 9 P.M.–4 A.M. Thursday–Fridays; and 2–6 P.M. Sundays), and the job (patient) scheduling for those periods of availability may be conducted by the hospitals (Mr. R. from 2–2:30 Sunday the sixth; Miss S. from 2:30–5).

By sharing such expensive equipment among a number of hospitals, more hospitals have access to modern technology for their patients at a reasonable level of investment.

Scheduling the nursing staff.

Of all the scheduling needs in hospitals the most crucial is probably the scheduling of the nursing resources. This is because: (1) it is mandatory, given the nature of hospitals, that nurses always be available, (2) nursing resources are a large expense for the hospital, and (3) there are a number of constraints on the scheduling of nurses such as the number of days per week, hours per day, weeks per year, hours during the day, and so on.

Approaches to nurse scheduling.

Abernathy et al. [1] review the difficulty of the nurse scheduling problem, point out the deficiences in present practices and conclude that an integrated scheduling system is what is required to solve the problem. Warner and Prawda [37] approach the nurse scheduling problem in terms of a programming model that determines the number of nursing personnel of each skill level to allocate among wards and shifts. In a pilot test of their model they reduced nursing costs by two-thirds (primarily in the night shift) and increased service by a factor of three.

Urban alarm services

Scheduling police, fire, and rescue services.

In those urban services that respond to alarms, such as police, fire, and rescue, the jobs (alarms) appear randomly and must be quickly serviced with sufficient resources or else extreme loss of life or property may result. In many ways this problem is similar to the hospital problem in that the staffing cost of personnel is a major expense but floating fire companies and police S.W.A.T. units may be utilized where needed and some services (such as fire inspection) can be scheduled to help *smooth* demand.

Scheduling duty tours.

However, there is sometimes a major difference that vastly complicates some of these services (particularly fire) and that is the use of **duty tours** of extended duration, as opposed to regular shifts, which run over consecutive days. These tours typically vary from 24 to 48 hours in teams of two to four personnel each. Common schedules for such services are "two on and three (days) off" and "one on and two off" with every fifth tour, or so, off as well (for a running time off, every three weeks, of perhaps 3 + 2 + 3 = 8 days). Because living and sleeping-in are considered part of the job requirements, the standard workweek is in excess of 40 hours with common values being

50 and 54 hours. Clearly, the scheduling of such duty tours is a complex problem, not only because of the unusual duration of the tours but also because of the implications concerning overtime, temptations of "moonlighting," and other such issues. For further discussion of such problems consult References 19, 25, and 28.

Educational services

The scheduling requirements of schools.

Colleges and universities have scheduling requirements for all of the various types of transformation processes: intermittent (such as counseling), continuous (English 1), batch (committee meetings), and project (regional conferences). In some of these situations the jobs (students) are scheduled, in some the staff (faculty, administrators) are scheduled, and in some the facilities (classrooms, convention centers) are scheduled.

The difficulty of scheduling classes.

The primary scheduling problem, however, involves the scheduling of classes, assignment of students, and allocation of facility and faculty resources to these classes. Three difficult elements must be coordinated in this process to obtain a manageable schedule.

1. An accurate forecast of student class demand.
2. The limitation on available classroom space.
3. The multiple needs and desires of the faculty such as

- Number of "preparations."
- Number of classes.
- Timing of classes.
- Level of classes.
- Leave requirements (sabbatical, without pay, etc.).
- Release requirements (research, projects, administration).

The need for a multicriteria approach.

Due to the number of objectives in such scheduling problems, a variety of multicriteria approaches have been employed to aid in finding acceptable schedules including simulation [24], goal programming [18], and interactive modeling [12].

In summary, the scheduling approach to services is usually to attempt to match resources to the forecasted demand for service. Since the demand cannot be controlled, inventory buildup ahead of time is impossible, and backordering is usually infeasible. Careful scheduling of staff, facilities, and materials is employed instead with (limited) flexibility achieved through floating, part time, and overtime labor and off-peak rates to encourage leveling of demand.

Scheduling techniques for services similar to scheduling jobs.

Scheduling techniques for resources are similar to those used for scheduling jobs: the use of indexes, weights, priorities, programming, simulation, heuristics, and so forth. Simulation appears to be an especially relevant approach since it can handle multiple criteria in highly varied situations [15, 24, 33]. The main advantage of simulation is that the reality of operational conditions—equipment breakdowns,

Simulation as an important aid.

emergencies, and so forth—can be easily included to determine their effect. Various schedules can be tested and their impact on resource utilization and level of service under varying distributions of demand can be found with ease. The "best" schedule is often not the one that optimizes the use of resources or minimizes lateness for the expected demand but rather the one that gives acceptable results under all likely operating conditions.

The tendency of queues to form.

An important element in the scheduling of operations to produce either products or services concerns the waiting lines, or **queues**, that tend to build up in front of the operations. With an unpaced production line, for example, buffer inventory between operations builds up at some times and disappears at other times due to the natural variability in the difficulty of the operations.

In the production of services this variability is even greater because of both the amount of highly variable human *input* and the variable service *requirements*. What is more, the "items" in queue are often people, who tend to complain and make trouble if kept waiting too long. Thus it behooves the operations manager to provide adequate service to keep long queues from forming. This, however, costs more money for service facilities and staff. But long queues cost money also, for in-process inventory, unfinished orders, lost sales, and ill will. The tradeoffs in these two costs

1. *The cost of waiting*: in-process inventory investment, ill will, lost sales, which decreases with service capacity.
2. *The cost of service facilities*: equipment, supplies, staff, which increases with service capacity.

The tradeoff between ill will and cost of service.

are conceptually illustrated in Figure 9.8 as a function of the capacity of the service facility. At some point the total of the two costs is minimized and it is at this point that managers typically wish to operate. The field of *queuing theory*, presented in the *Tools and Applications* section, has developed to address exactly these kinds of situations.

9.5 PLANNING AND SCHEDULING PROJECTS

How project scheduling differs from other processes.

The scheduling of project activities is highly complex due to (1) the number of activities required, (2) the precedence relationships among the activities, and (3) the limited-time nature of the project. Project scheduling is similar to that discussed earlier in some ways but still differs significantly. For example, the basic network approaches, **PERT*** (Program Evaluation and Review Technique) and **CPM*** (Critical Path Method), are based on variations of the Gantt Chart.

But a project is a one-time operation. Its scheduling typically differs in that the complexity does not involve handling a large number of separate jobs, all requiring different operations and materials, but rather an enormous number of different operations and materials that must be coordinated with each other in such a way that

* PERT was developed by the U.S. Navy with Booz-Allen Hamilton and Lockheed Corporation in the late 1950s to manage the Polaris missile project. CPM was develped independently in the same time period by DuPont, Inc.

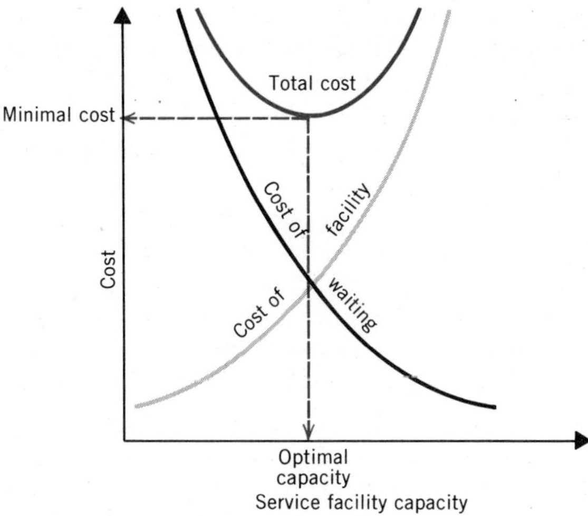

Figure 9.8 The relevant queuing costs.

following activities can take place and the entire project (job) be completed by the due date. For example, the use of a shortest operation time (SOT) priority rule would be entirely inappropriate here. Rather, the *critical* operation, which must precede all the remaining operations, should be performed next. PERT and CPM have been most extensively used in the construction, defense, and aerospace industries.

SOT vs. PERT.

The scheduling procedure for project operations must not only be able to identify and handle the variety of tasks that must be done but also dovetail their time sequencing as well. In addition, it must be able to integrate the performance and timing of all the tasks with the project as a whole so that control can be exercised, for example, by shifting resources from operations with **slack** (permissible slippage) to other operations whose delay might threaten the project's timely completion. (Project control will be discussed in Chapter 15.) The three main tasks involved in scheduling and controlling project operations are thus

1. *Planning*: the determination of *what* must be done and which tasks must *precede* others.
2. *Scheduling*: the determination of *when* the tasks must be completed; when they *can* and when they *must*, be started; which tasks are *critical* to the timely completion of the project; and which tasks have *slack* in their timing and how much.
3. *Control*: the ability to replan and reschedule the tasks when things start going wrong, and knowing how to shift resources between tasks to keep the project on schedule.

The PERT approach to planning and scheduling project activities is developed in detail later in the *Tools and Applications* portion of this chapter. First, however, we will look again at aggregate scheduling.

TOOLS AND APPLICATIONS

9.6 SOLUTION APPROACHES FOR THE AGGREGATE SCHEDULING PROBLEM

A number of interesting approaches for the aggregate scheduling problem have been developed, especially with the increased power of the computer, and we will investigate some of these in detail.

Linear Programming

The use of **linear programming** to meet aggregate production demands was first developed by Bowman [3] in 1956. The objective is assumed to be to minimize the costs of monthly production plus storage, subject to the constraints of meeting monthly sales demands, capacity limitations, and desired initial and ending inventory levels. The model is quite flexibile in that productive resources may include regular time production, overtime production, outside subcontracting, extra shifts, inventory stockpiling between periods, and backordering. Constraints on productive capacity in each period may also be included. And infeasible allocations, for any reason, may simply be dropped and not considered.

The transportation model for aggregate scheduling.

Bowman recognized that the format of this problem matched that of the **transportation model** (Chapter 6I) of **linear programming** and thus presented it in that form. An example illustrating the capabilities of such a format is depicted in Figure 9.9 for the three-month period June, July, and August. Across the top of the matrix the months are listed, with the monthly demands shown at the bottom of the matrix. Demand in the final month, September, represents the required August ending inventory. A dummy column for unused (idle) capacity picks up any slack in the productive abilities of the three sources, shown in the far right column as "available."

Along the left side of the matrix are the three productive sources of supply for each month: regular time, overtime, and subcontracting. In the upper right corner of each cell is listed the cost of using that supply source for each month's sales requirements. Note that backordering is possible (e.g., July production for June), but at a cost of $5 extra per unit per month. Subcontracting is also possible for future months but with an inventory carrying charge of $2 per unit per month, as with regular production.

Backordering and subcontracting available.

An advantage of this approach to aggregate planning is that multiple outputs may be included in the model if their demands can be transformed to aggregate units (such as hours of work). There are also some limitations to the model, however; the most important of these is that workforce hiring and firing costs are not included when production changes are significant (as demand is between June and July). If production is fairly steady then this limitation does not become a problem.

		June	July	August	(Sept)	Unused	Available
	Begin. Invent.	0	2	4	6	0	200
June	Regular Time	50	52	54	56	0	500
	Overtime	60	62	64	66	0	100
	Subcontract	65	67	69	70	0	300
July	Regular time	55	50	52	54	0	500
	Overtime	65	60	62	64	0	100
	Subcontract	70	65	67	69	0	300
August	Regular time*	60	55	50	52	0	250
	Overtime*	70	65	60	62	0	50
	Subcontract	75	70	65	67	0	300
	Demand	1000	700	500	150	250	2600

* Two week vacation in August.

Figure 9.9. The linear programming approach to aggregate planning.

Other limitations enter through the lack of shortage costs when demand is lost and the linearity of the cost functions with output level (which undoubtedly are not strictly proportional); however, the approximations may be sufficiently close for the situation at hand. Extensions of Bowman's approach include workforce hiring and firing costs and shortage costs through a general linear programming model.

The Linear Decision Rule

In the early 1950s a group of researchers at the Carnegie Institute of Technology developed a set of managerial "decision rules" to aid managers in determining two aspects of aggregate scheduling: the least cost monthly production and workforce levels for their organizations [6, 20]. These rules were simple linear equations involving

1. The size of the workforce the preceding month.
2. The ending inventory in the preceding month, less any units on backorder.
3. Demand forecasts for the next 12 months.

The rules were derived from a process that minimized the total monthly cost of

1. Regular payroll.
2. Hiring and layoffs.
3. Overtime.
4. Carrying inventory and incurring stockouts.

These costs were approximated by a series of curves, as shown in Figure 9.10. Note that some of the relationships are straight (linear) whereas others are **parabolic**

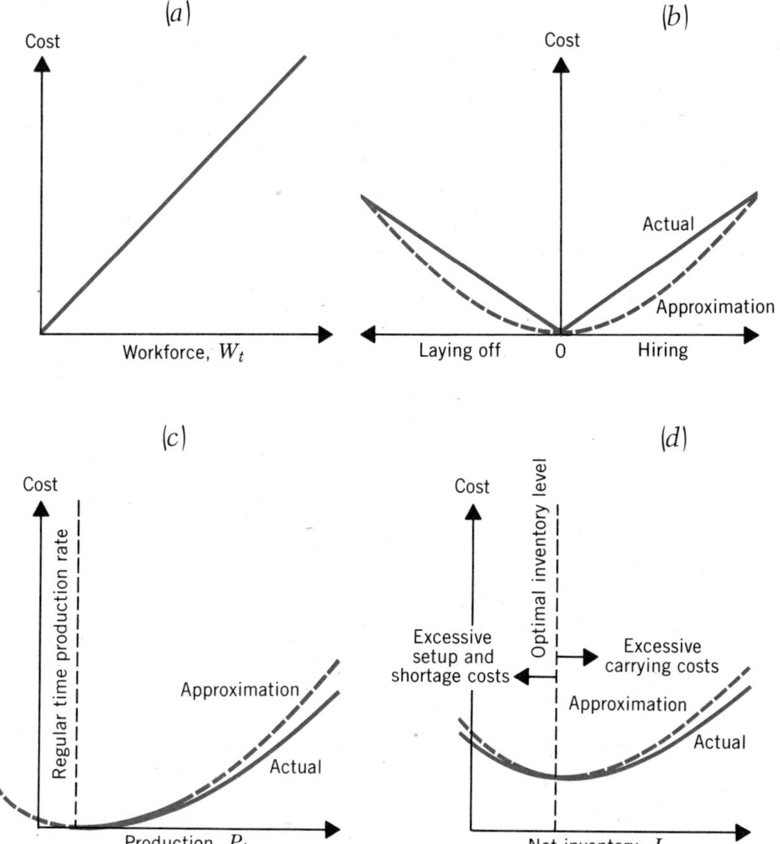

Figure 9.10. Cost approximations in the linear decision rule. (*a*) Payroll cost approximation. (*b*) Workforce cost approximation. (*c*) Overtime cost approximation. (*d*) Inventory cost approximation.

Approximating costs with quadratic equations.

(**quadratic** or of *second degree*). Due to the simple form of these four curves, there exists a minimum point on the monthly *total* cost curve (i.e., the sum of the four curves for each month), which can be located through calculus to give the least cost values of monthly production and workforce levels.

The simplicity of LDR in use.

Although perhaps difficult to generate the initial cost curves, the linear decision rule is a simply applied approach to aggregate production planning. To use the rules, the manager or production scheduler solves two simple equations at the beginning of every month. For the actual company considered by the researchers, the use of the rules would have lowered production costs significantly. The criticism of the approach, beyond the difficulty of collecting the cost data, is that it does not consider many contraints such as overtime restrictions, capital limitations, and so forth.

For the company data used by the researchers, the resulting decision rules looked like

$$P_t = (aF_t + bF_{t+1} + \cdots + lF_{t+11}) + mW_{t-1} + nI_{t-1} + p$$
$$W_t = (qF_t + \cdots + wF_{t+11}) + xW_{t-1} + yI_{t-1} + z$$

where

$a, b, \ldots, z =$ constants
$P_t =$ the production rate for the upcoming month t
$W_{t-1} =$ the workforce in the preceding month
$I_{t-1} =$ the ending inventory level of the preceding month less any outstanding backorders
$F_t =$ the forecast demand for month t

Although these equations look overwhelming, they are not really difficult. The analysts studying the operations are responsible for deriving the constants $a, b, \ldots, z$. For simplicity, suppose all the constants are 0.2. And let us also suppose production last month was 30, the workforce was 20, and the ending inventory was 20. And lastly, suppose the forecast of demand for every month in the future is 9. Then the linear decision rules say that next month's production should be

$$[.2(9) + .2(9) + \cdots + .2(9)] + .2(20) + .2(20) + .2 = 29.8$$

and the workforce should be

$$[.2(9) + .2(9) + \cdots + .2(9)] + .2(20) + .2(20) + .2 = 29.8$$

or, use 30 workers (hiring is required) to produce 30 units. In the next month the forecasts, workforce, and inventory would be updated to produce new production and workforce values.

Management Coefficients Heuristics

Use of heuristics.

A **heuristic** decision rule is usually developed on the basis of a rigorous analysis of a situation, possibly including experimentation. Although similar to rules of thumb, the latter are more likely to have been developed on the basis of trial-and error-experience instead. In the world of organizational operations it is probably true that most decisions are based on heuristics and rules of thumb.

PEANUTS® **By Charles M. Schulz**

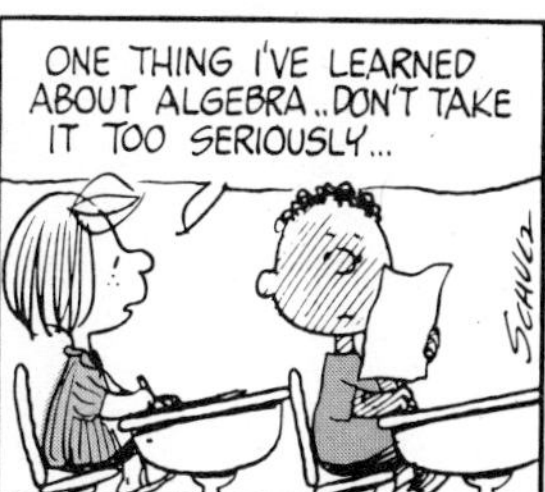

The use of rule-of-thumb heuristics. (Reprinted by permission of United Feature Syndicate.)

It might be expected that the managers faced with operational decisions would themselves know best what the critical variables were in those decisions. Thus, there would somehow be a way of synthesizing their experience to capitalize on this knowledge.

Using managers' own decision rules to improve the decisions.

A number of interesting studies have been conducted that analyzed the performance of managers with the aim of trying to uncover their heuristic decisions rules (e.g., see References 29, 34, and 39). The research process used in these studies is usually the same. The researcher talks with a number of managers involved in the decision situation and generates a list of all the possible variables that the managers feel might bear on the decision. Historical data relating to the occurrence of the decision in the past and all of the identified variables are then collected for analysis. A **multiple regression analysis** (Chapter 4), or some other analytical method, is then used to uncover the significant variables and how, on the average, they affect the decision. This model is thus an approximation to the manager's decision heuristic. The last step is to try this heuristic on historical data and new decision data to see how well it imitates the manager's actual decisions.

Multiple regression to find the heuristic rules.

When these heuristic rules were *reapplied* to the same historical data the managers had worked with, performance was usually improved *significantly*. The major reason for such a result was the erratic, though normal, behavior on the part of the manager. That is, interruptions, headaches, lack of time, and other such facts of managerial life were more typically the cause of bad decisions than lack of managerial skill. On the other hand, models employing the skills distilled from the manager are not subject to the same pressures and problems.

Bowman conducted a study of this sort relating to aggregate production planning [4]. He adopted the variables used in the linear decision rule but, instead of using the calculus derived coefficents, he derived them by multiple regression, as described above. His general results were excellent.

Search Methods

Another way to approach the aggregate production planning problem is to formulate the exact costs as accurately as possible, program them on a computer, and then attempt various production plans to see which one has the least cost. The problem, of course, is that in this trial and error method there are an unending number of plans that might be tried (c.f. Table 9.1). The basis of "search" methods is thus to develop efficient procedures for picking trial alternatives from the infinite number of possible aggregate production plans and identifying the best one.

Computer search.

There are a number of heuristic procedures for searching a set of decision variables to identify extreme (e.g., least cost) points. Some of these, known as **hill-climbing** or **gradient** methods, start at one spot and check the effect of changing one variable at a time *just a little* to see the effect on cost. The most promising variable (the one that reduces cost most quickly) is thereby identified and is changed first (sometimes combinations of favorable variables are used).

Hill-climbing and gradient heuristics.

The next question concerns *how much* to change the variable. Again, this is answered by testing. The selected variable is changed a bit more than it was the previous time. This information tells the computer routine *how fast* the selected variable is lowering the cost and thus lets it approximate how much to change the variable. For example, suppose the first change was to add one worker and the effect was to reduce the total cost by 3 percent (more than any other change). And suppose the second change, adding another worker, reduced the total cost another 2 percent. The computer would then conclude that the next best aggregate plan to examine would be to add three workers (expecting to thereby reduce the total cost 6 percent). In the chemical industry, one such method is known as "evolutionary operation." Production variables are changed on the basis of earlier successes and failures and the process "evolves" in a rational manner, improving at almost every step.

Search techniques to locate an optimum.

Evolutionary operation in the chemical industry.

Sometimes this elementary logic does not work. In those cases the search routines use varied strategies. The rule may be to backtrack to the previous best (least cost) point (adding two workers) and reinitialize the search. Or, alternatively, go half the distance instead and examine that point.

One problem with search methods is that they do not guarantee that the *best* solution has been located. There may be another point with quite different values of the variables that has a lesser cost.

Taubert used this type of search methodology, called the **Search Decision Rule**, to test its performance on the company data used for the linear decision rule [35]. The results were gratifying in that the search rule converged to essentially the same results as the linear decision rule.

Of the above methods considered for solving the aggregate scheduling problem, the search decision rule (SDR) has the greatest potential. It is not limited in its assumptions as the other rules are and the full power and cost effectiveness of the computer can be brought to bear on the problem. Lee and Khumawala [26] tested the above methods against actual company decisions in a capital goods job shop and found all of them superior to actual results, with the search decision rule improving profits the most (14 percent increase).

The superiority of the SDR.

9.7 LOADING

For continuous process systems such as assembly line operations and chemical processors, loading is a moot problem because all output goes through essentially the same processes. And the load on each facility is fairly constant. But in electrical power generation an interesting loading problem arises where an organization places a "load" on the utility at various times and in various amounts throughout the day. Linear programming-type models are currently being used in conjunction with mini- and microcomputers to optimally allocate the load so as to minimize energy cost. One IBM publication [22] indicates that a supermarket with $3000 per month electrical bills (for lighting, cooling food cases and freezers, etc.) can reduce costs up to 20 percent and more through proper scheduling of compressor use to produce an optimal load on the utility.

Allocating intermittent and batch jobs to facilities.

But for many intermittent and batch transformation systems there is considerable choice in determining which facilities should handle which jobs. Some choices are much better than others, however, because particular processes are more efficient for some jobs than for other jobs. It is desirable to process the operations as quickly as possible, both to minimize job lateness and to minimize facility use time.

The Assignment Model

Allocation by the assignment model.

When the problem consists of deciding which of a number of jobs to allocate among a number of facilities on a one-to-one basis, the **assignment model** is a useful aid. For example, suppose the costs of producing five jobs at each of five different work centers is as shown in Table 9.2. Use of the assignment method will indicate which job should be allocated to which work center in order to minimize costs.

Solution procedure

Inspection is insufficient.

Although the problem appears simple enough, the solution is not always easy to obtain. For example, in Table 9.2 it appears by inspection that job 3 should go to center S. It costs less to assign job 3 to center S than any of the other jobs, *and* assigning job 3 to center S is cheaper than assigning it to any other center. Nevertheless, this would be a poor assignment, as we will soon see. Overall, it is less expensive to assign job 4 to center S, even though it costs $20 more initially. This is because in making one assignment we eliminate the possibility of making another, later assignment at, perhaps, a much lower cost. A better procedure than simple inspection is derived from the following logic.

TABLE 9.2 COSTS OF ASSIGNING JOBS TO VARIOUS WORK CENTERS

Work Centers / Jobs	1	2	3	4	5
R	$ 30	$ 50	$40	$ 80	$20
S	90	40	30	50	70
T	110	60	80	100	90
D	60	100	40	120	50
F	30	50	60	40	90

Using *relative* costs.

Since the assignments are on a one-to-one basis, then adding (or subtracting) a *constant* to every cost in the same row, or the same column, will not alter the relative costs of the assignments. For example, adding $10 to all the costs in column 1 of Table 9.2 still leaves the cost of assigning job 1 to center S $20 cheaper than to center T. Therefore, the least cost solution (which job to which center) will be unchanged by this process even though the *values* will be different.

One way then to identify good assignments is to subtract amounts from the rows and the columns so as to generate zeros in some of the cells, being careful not to generate negative numbers in the process. Then, if a feasible assignment can be made to only zero-valued cells this will result in the lowest possible cost assignment. The assignment method uses the essence of this approach in a five-step procedure. We will illustrate it with the example.

Step 1. Subtract the lowest cost in each row from all the other costs in that row (Table 9.3).

Step 2. Next, subtract the lowest remaining cost in each column from all the other costs in that column. (Steps 1 and 2 may be reversed.) See Table 9.4.

Step 3. Since all costs at this point are non-negative, the minimum possible assignment cost using these "new" cost elements would be zero. *If* a one-to-one assignment can be made to only cells with zero costs then this would be an optimal assignment. Rather than attempting to make an optimal assignment by trial and error we follow a special procedure: cover all the zeros in the matrix with the *fewest* possible number of straight horizontal and vertical

TABLE 9.3 ROW REDUCTION

	1	2	3	4	5
R	30 − 20 = 10	50 − 20 = 30	40 − 20 = 20	80 − 20 = 60	20 − 20 = 0
S	90 − 30 = 60	40 − 30 = 10	30 − 30 = 0	50 − 30 = 20	70 − 30 = 40
T	110 − 60 = 50	60 − 60 = 0	80 − 60 = 20	100 − 60 = 40	90 − 60 = 30
D	60 − 40 = 20	100 − 40 = 60	40 − 40 = 0	120 − 40 = 80	50 − 40 = 10
F	30 − 30 = 0	50 − 30 = 20	60 − 30 = 30	40 − 30 = 10	90 − 30 = 60

TABLE 9.4 COLUMN REDUCTION

	1	2	3	4	5
R	10	30	20	60 − 10 = 50	0
S	60	10	0	20 − 10 = 10	40
T	50	0	20	40 − 10 = 30	30
D	20	60	0	80 − 10 = 70	10
F	0	20	30	10 − 10 = 0	60

TABLE 9.5 OPTIMALITY TEST

10	30	20	50	0
60	10	0	10	40
50	0	20	30	30
20	60	0	70	10
0	20	30	0	60

lines. If the number of lines is equal to the number of rows (or columns) an assignment can be made. (The *minimum* number of lines never exceeds the number of rows or columns.) If not, then it is possible to improve the solution. (In Table 9.5 all the zeros can be covered with only four lines; hence, it is possible to improve the solution.)

Step 4. If an assignment can be made, go to step 5. Otherwise, inspect the values *not* covered by lines and select the lowest one (10 in Table 9.5). *Subtract* this value from all the *uncovered* values and *add* it to the values at the *intersections* of the lines. Return to step 3. (See Tables 9.6 and 9.7. We find that, following the first improvement, it requires five lines to completely cover all the zeros in Table 9.7. An optimal assignment can therefore be made.)

Step 5. To identify the optimal assignment, make the first assignment, if possible, to a row or column with only one zero in it. Delete that row and column and then continue the procedure. If more than one optimal solution exists, this process will quickly indicate that fact. (Table 9.8 illustrates the procedure. Assignments R-5 or D-3 are identified first. In this case there is only one solution: R-5, S-4, T-2, D-3, F-1, with a minimum cost, from Table 9.2, of 20 + 50 + 60 + 40 + 30 = $200.

The most economical assignment of jobs to centers will therefore cost $200. The assignment method is quite flexible in handling special assignment conditions. Prohibited assignments, for example, can simply be marked out with an X without disrupting the solution process. The *maximization* problem can be treated simply by converting it to a minimization problem. This is accomplished by subtracting every entry in the original table from the largest entry. Once the optimal assignment is found, the original values (to be maximized) are used to determine the value (profit) of the solution.

TABLE 9.6 FIRST IMPROVEMENT

10 − 10 = 0	30 − 10 = 20	20	50 − 10 = 40	0
60 − 10 = 50	10 − 10 = 0	0	10 − 10 = 0	40
50	0	20 + 10 = 30	30	30 + 10 = 40
20 − 10 = 10	60 − 10 = 50	0	70 − 10 = 60	10
0	20	30 + 10 = 40	0	60 + 10 = 70

TABLE 9.7 SECOND OPTIMALITY TEST

0	20	20	40	0
50	0	0	0	40
50	0	30	30	40
10	50	0	60	10
0	20	40	0	70

The Index Method

Allocation through use of an efficiency index.

A simple variant of the assignment model can be used where more than one job is assigned to each work center. The approach, called the **index method**, is to calculate an "efficiency" index for each job on each work center and then to load the centers with those jobs that have the best indexes for that center. Simply put, this method assigns jobs to the centers best able to do them. Let us demonstrate with a simple example.

Stereo Re-Pairs, Inc.

Bill, owner-manager of Stereo Re-Pairs, employs three part-time electrical engineering students, John, Mary, and Bo, to service the stereos customers bring to the shop. Bill knows that the three students have different experience on the various stereo brands and also knows on which stereo each of the students works best. Bill can usually estimate their repair times fairly accurately. On this particular Monday, six stereos, brought in on Saturday, are awaiting repair. Table 9.9 shows Bill's estimate of the repair times for each unit, depending on who services it, and the weekly hours each student works for him.

Assuming the students are all paid equally, it is desirable to load the tasks on the students who are expected to be fastest on that repair. Letting the smallest repair time take an index value of 1.00 and giving other times an index equal to the ratio of repair time to the minimum repair time gives the results shown in Table 9.10.

We now attempt to load the tasks on those facilities where the index is 1.00. Notice, however, that if Bo is loaded first, the total hours will exceed the 5 hours available, so the procedure is initiated with John, who has the most hours available. John then gets the Panasonic, Juliette, and Heathkit for a total of 6 hours, leaving 20

TABLE 9.8 OPTIMAL SOLUTION

	1	2	3	4	5
R	0	20	20	40	0
S	50	0	0	0	40
T	50	0	30	30	40
D	10	50	0	60	10
F	0	20	40	0	70

TABLE 9.9 STEREO REPAIR TIMES IN HOURS

Stereo	John	Mary	Bo
Lloyds	4	3	3
Panasonic	2	3	2
Sound Design	5	(?)	3
Juliette	1	1	1
Heathkit	3	4	5
Realistic	2	3	1
Total hours available	20	15	5

− 6 = 14 hours available for the rest of the week. Many next takes the Lloyd (3 hours), leaving the Sound Design and Realistic to Bo (4 hours total).

In case a facility with the lowest index becomes overloaded, jobs are simply shifted to that facility with the next lower index which is not already overloaded. In some situations the work may have to be split between facilities. For example, if Mary only had 1 hour available to spend on the Lloyds and then was to leave the rest of the job to John, he would *not* spend (Mary's remaining) 2 hours on it. Rather, he would have two-thirds *of the job* to do which would take him ⅔ × 4 = 2.67 hours.

The model is simple enough that pay rates can also be easily included. This is done by deriving indexes based on Bill's *labor* cost (rate × hours) rather than just the hours. The hours available would still constrain the allocations, however, not the labor cost per student.

9.8 JOHNSON'S RULE FOR SEQUENCING JOBS

Sequencing two jobs on two facilities.

The general sequencing problem usually involves getting jobs through the operations as quickly as possible. The dual objectives are to (1) maximize facility utilization by smoothly processing a large number of jobs, and (2) avoid excessively delaying any one job. As a simple motivating example, consider the situation of two jobs, J_1 and J_2,

TABLE 9.10 INDEX LOADING PROCEDURE

Stereo	John		Mary		Bo	
	Hours	Index	Hours	Index	Hours	Index
Lloyds	4	(4/3 =) 1.33	3	1.00	3	1.00
Panasonic	2	1.00	3	1.50	2	1.00
Sound Design	5	1.67	(?)	—	3	1.00
Juliette	1	1.00	1	1.00	1	1.00
Heathkit	3	1.00	4	1.33	5	1.67
Realistic	2	2.00	3	3.00	1	1.00
Hours remaining:	14		12		1	

going through two facilities in the *same order*: F_1 and then F_2. Suppose one of the jobs (say, J_1) requires 4 hours on F_1 and 5 hours on F_2 and the other job (J_2) requires 7 hours on F_1 and 4 hours on F_2. In what order should the jobs be run to minimize the total facility time?

This problem is simple enough so that we may enumerate both of the possible solutions: start J_1 first or J_2 first. Figure 9.11 illustrates the Gantt charts for each solution. In the case of J_1 first, Figure 9.11*a*, we see that due to our scheduling there exists some delay on facility 2 before the second job can begin. Hopefully, scheduling job 2 first will eliminate this delay. And we see in Figure 9.11*b* that indeed it does; however, even with the delay eliminated, it takes *longer* to process both jobs: 16 hours with J_2 scheduled first compared to 15 hours with J_1 first.

Upon further examination we can see the reason why. No matter which job was scheduled first, the two jobs completed work on facility 1 in 11 hours. Therefore, if the job with the longest time on facility 2 is scheduled last, the overall duration for completion of both jobs would be greatest. The message then is clear: schedule the job with the *shortest* time on facility 2 *last*.

Scheduling the shortest jobs.

By the same token, it would be well to get jobs *started* on facility 2 as soon as possible. Hence, the *short* jobs on facility 1 should be scheduled as *early* as possible. These intuitive conclusions have been formalized by S. M. Johnson [23] in a form now referred to as **Johnson's Rule**, which deals with the task of optimally sequencing N jobs through two facilities in the same order.

Johnson's Rule.

If the shortest time for a job is on the first *facility, schedule the job as* early *as possible. If it is on the* second *facility, schedule it as* late *as possible. Delete that job and repeat the procedure.*

Let us consider an example.

Sickle Cell Screening

Five patients who had positive tests on "sickledex" are to be scheduled for definitive testing by "electrophoresis" and then consultation with a physician for genetic education. A mobile laboratory is to be used, starting at 8 A.M. Naturally, it is desirable to

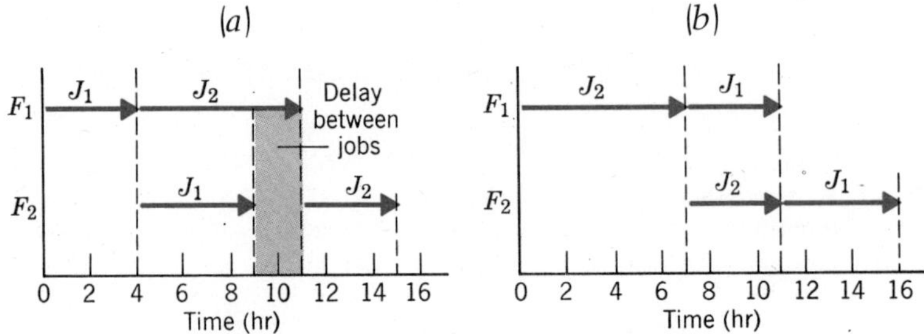

Figure 9.11. The result of two sequencing possibilities. (*a*) J_1 first. (*b*) J_2 first.

TABLE 9.11 SICKLE CELL SCREENING TIME ESTIMATES IN MINUTES

Patient:	1	2	3	4	5
Lab (electrophoresis):	120	30	20	40	60
Genetic education:	10	60	120	30	60

conclude the screening and education tasks as quickly as possible, so that the mobile lab may be used elsewhere. Based on the sickledex results, the nurse estimates that the screening and education times listed in Table 9.11 will be required. In what order should the patients be scheduled and when may the work be expected to be completed?

ANALYSIS. Applying Johnson's rule, the shortest time is 10 minutes in the second task with patient 1. Thus, this patient should be scheduled last. The problem now appears as

~~P_1~~	P_2	P_3	P_4	P_5
~~120~~	30	20	40	60
~~10~~	60	120	30	60

				P_1

The next shortest time is for P_3 on task 1 (20 minutes), so it is scheduled first. Deleting this patient, the next shortest time is 30, but this appears twice. In general, ties may be broken arbitrarily; but here there really is no problem, since for P_2 the 30 is on the first task and for P_4 it is on the second. Hence, P_2 is scheduled right after P_3 (see below) and P_4 just before P_1, leaving P_5 in the middle. The resulting schedule is illustrated in Figure 9.12; it appears that the mobile lab will be able to leave by about 1 P.M.

P_3	P_2	P_5	P_4	P_1

The multiplicity of optimal schedules.

Although Johnson's rule will find an optimal schedule, it is not necessarily the *only* optimal schedule—there may be others also, but none will finish *sooner*. It should also be noted that there are extensions to Johnson's rule concerning the case of two jobs and N facilities, and for certain N jobs—three facilities situations, but there is not a solution to the *general* sequencing problem. In fact, the general sequencing problem is not just limited to jobs undergoing the same sequence of operations.

The need for a policy.

Under certain conditions the more general sequencing problem can be formulated and solved by linear programming (see Eilon [13]), but, by and large, such decisions must be made on the spot and often by someone who is not a manager but "just works there." What is needed then is a *policy*, rather than a solution model, which will give good results most of the time under real operating conditions. This is

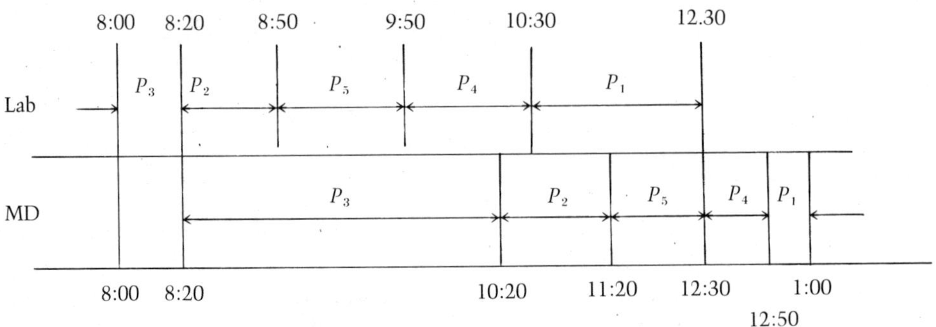

Figure 9.12. Mobile lab schedule.

the purpose of the priority rules discussed in Section 9.3. It might be noted that some of these priority rules are based on the general approach embodied in Johnson's rule.

9.9 THE QUEUING SITUATION

What descriptive queuing theory will determine.

The pioneer analyst in queuing theory was a Danish telephone engineer named A. K. Erlang who developed the theory in the 1920s to predict telephone call service. Given an arriving population and a service facility (or facilities) with a certain speed of service, the theory will determine, given certain assumptions, the expected (average): length of the queue, the number of people or items in the queue, the idle time of the facility, and other such criteria of service facility performance.

The structure of the queuing system.

The structure of the queuing system to be considered here is illustrated in Figure 9.13. It is assumed that the arrivals wait in *one* queue (or take a number for service or add their names to a list) and, as they come to the front of the line, go to the next available service facility. (This system is called first come, first served, FCFS, and is commonly adopted for reasons of fairness.) The arrivals are assumed to come at random, with the average rate λ (arrivals per unit time). Service is also assumed to be random, with the average rate μ (services per unit time).

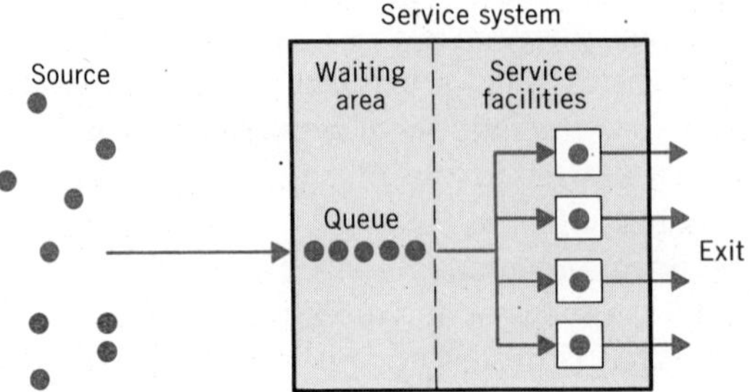

Figure 9.13. Queuing system structure.

If the service can be performed *before* the recipient arrives and then stored until his or her arrival, a queue will *not* form (unless the demand rate exceeds the service rate). For example, if punch is being served as a refreshment at a party where people arrive for refreshments, on the average, every 4 seconds and it takes 4 seconds to pour a drink there will never be a queue, over the long run (say, after at least 10 minutes). This is because even when people are not coming for a drink the server keeps on pouring drinks; then, when a batch of people all come at once, the drinks are ready.

How a queue tends to form.

However, if mixed drinks are being served so that the mix cannot be poured *until the person gives his or her order*, a queue will tend to form under exactly the same conditions. To see this, let us assume that people arrive consecutively 2 and then 6 seconds apart (thereby averaging 4). The results are tabulated in Table 9.12.

As seen in the table, following the arrival of person B there is never a time that someone is not waiting for a drink. On many occasions there is a queue of one person waiting to be served (while another is being served). Starting from the arrival of B at 8 seconds there are 11 seconds (out of 50 − 7 = 43 seconds or 11/43 = 26 percent of the time) when a person is waiting to be served. The *expected queue length* in this case is thus said to be 0.26 × 1 = 0.26 persons.

TABLE 9.12 THE FORMATION OF A QUEUE

Time (sec)	Waiting	Time (sec)	Waiting
1	—	26	G, F
2	A	27	G, F
3	A	28	G
4	A	29	G
5	A	30	G
6	—	31	G
7	—	32	H
8	B	33	H
9	B	34	I, H
10	C, B	35	I, H
11	C, B	36	I
12	C	37	I
13	C	38	I
14	C	39	I
15	C	40	J
16	D	41	J
17	D	42	K, J
18	E, D	43	K, J
19	E, D	44	K
20	E	45	K
21	E	46	K
22	E	47	K
23	E	48	L
24	F	49	L
25	F	50	M, L

Assumptions and Results of Queuing Theory

Queuing theory can determine the expected queue length, and many other such variables, for situations much more realistic than this—such as for variable service and arrival rates, and for more than one server. There are, however, some basic assumptions that must be satisfied.

- *The system is in **steady state**.* Note in the example above that we ignored the 7 second **start-up transient** in Table 9.12. This time to reach "steady state" is usually a small fraction of an ongoing service system and may be ignored. (However, some systems, such as banks, may always be in transient states such as 9:00 A.M. start-up, 10:00 A.M. coffee break, 11:30 A.M.–1:30 P.M. noon rush, 2:00 P.M. break, 2:30 P.M. closing rush. In these cases queuing theory is inappropriate and simulation must be used.)
- *First come, first served **priority discipline**.* We assume people (items) are served in the order they join the queue and only one queue exists, even if there are multiple service facilities.
- *An unlimited source exists.* We assume we never run out of recipients from the source. Chapter 18 includes an approach for queuing situations where the source *is* limited (e.g., machines that are breaking down and must be repaired).
- *Unlimited queue space is available.* We assume there is sufficient space in the (single) queue to hold any recipient who desires service.
- *Standard queue behavior which prohibits*:

  Balking—refusing to join the queue.
  Reneging—leaving the queue before being served.
  Jockeying—switching between queues as their lengths vary.
  Cycling—returning to the queue following service.
- *Random arrivals and service.* As stated earlier, the **random arrivals** occur at the average rate λ and the services at the average rate μ.

Although some limited results have been obtained for situations that relax some of the above restrictions, we will not consider them here. The interested reader is referred to References 17 and 36.

Poisson arrivals and services.

The assumption of random arrivals and services results in a *particular* distribution of arrival and service rates known as the **Poisson distribution**. With the assumptions given above, these distributions allow us to find a number of characteristics (discussed below) that describe the waiting line and the service process. Since these characteristics are usually related, only one of them need be found and then the others follow from it.

Here we choose as the major characteristic the expected (average) length of the queue, L_q, that is waiting for service (not including those being served). This characteristic is presented in Figure 9.14 as a function of two parameters of the queuing situation.

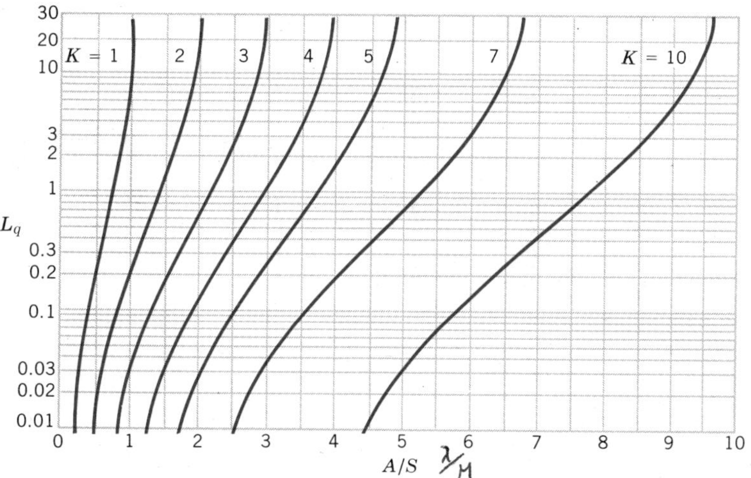

Figure 9.14. The multichannel queue. (Reprinted by permission from Efraim Turban and Jack R. Meredith, *Fundamentals of Management Science* (Dallas, Texas: Business Publications, 1977, p. 432. © 1977 by Business Publications, Inc.)

- K—the number of servers or service facilities, known as **channels** (four shown in Figure 9.13) in the service system.
- λ/μ—the **utilization** of the facility. If the arrival rate λ exceeds the service rate of a single server μ the queue will grow indefinitely unless more than one server is available.

Note in Figure 9.14 that as curves of constant K reach values of $\lambda/\mu = K$ (near the top of the chart), the length of the queue, L_q, gets larger and larger. This is because the arrivals tend to fully utilize the capacity of the system. For example, if the arrival rate is twice that of the service rate this will keep two servers busy full time.

Finding the other queue characteristics.

Once a value for L_q is found, many other interesting characteristics describing the process can be derived from it.

1. The *average number of items in the system*, both in the queue and in service combined, L. The number being served, on the average, is simply the utilization of the service facility, λ/μ. Thus,

$$L = L_q + \frac{\lambda}{\mu} \tag{9.1}$$

2. The *expected waiting time in the queue*, W_q. This is *not*, as might be expected, simply the average length of the queue times the service time. Rather another relationship is used: the average *length* of the queue will equal the average *waiting time* multiplied by the average *arrival rate*: $L_q = W_q\lambda$. Rearranging terms

$$W_q = \frac{L_q}{\lambda} \tag{9.2}$$

3. The *expected total time in the system*, W. This will be the queuing time plus the service time, $1/\mu$.

$$W = W_q + \frac{1}{\mu} \tag{9.3}$$

4. For service systems composed of a *single server* (channel) we can determine the *probability of n items occupying the system* (both queuing and in service).

$$P_n = \left(\frac{\lambda}{\mu}\right)^n\left(1 - \frac{\lambda}{\mu}\right) \quad \text{for } K = 1 \tag{9.4}$$

Note that when $n = 0$ this reduces to the *probability that the system is empty*.

$$P_0 = 1 - \frac{\lambda}{\mu} \quad \text{for } K = 1 \tag{9.5}$$

The *probability that the system is busy*, otherwise known as the *utilization* of the facility, is thus $1 - P_0$ or

$$P_{\text{busy}} = \frac{\lambda}{\mu} \quad \text{for } K = 1 \tag{9.6}$$

Unexpected results.

One of the most confounding aspects of waiting line analysis is that it defies normal expectations. For example, if a service system with one server results in an average queue length of 12 recipients then most people expect that adding a second server will cut the queue in half, to 6 recipients. But consider the following situation. A one-person service facility can serve on the average, 10 customers per hour and customers arrive, on the average, every 7.5 minutes. What will happen if a second server is added?

ANALYSIS

$$\lambda = \frac{60}{7.5} = 8/\text{hr}, \qquad \mu = 10/\text{hr}, \qquad \frac{\lambda}{\mu} = 0.8, \qquad K = 1$$

From Figure 9.14, $L_q = 3$, approximately. If a second server is added then reading from Figure 9.14 at $K = 2$ and $\lambda/\mu = 0.8$ we find $L_q = 0.14$. That is, the expected line length reduces by

$$\frac{3.0 - 0.14}{3.0} = 0.95$$

Queue reduction much greater than expected.

or 95 percent. This is much greater than just one-half (50 percent). The reason is because of the randomness of the arrivals and the fact that services cannot be produced during idle periods and stored for use in busy periods. A second server is no help when the facility is idle or only one customer is being served but when *groups of people* arrive, the second server is a *great* help.

Let us consider an example now of a more realistic managerial type of situation.

Kee Pon Trucking, Ltd.

Mr. Kee Pon is trying to estimate the best number of work crews to employ in a local excavating job at Bandini, India. The crews can each load, on the average, four trucks per hour but cost $10 per hour in total wages. (Only one crew can work on a truck at one time.) On the other hand, the idle time of trucks is charged at $16 per hour. If the trucks arrive every 20 minutes, on the average, how many crews should Mr. Pon hire? (Assume loading and arrivals rates are random.)

ANALYSIS

$$\lambda = 60/20 = 3/\text{hr}$$
$$\mu = 4/\text{hr}$$
$$\frac{\lambda}{\mu} = 0.75$$

One crew. From Figure 9.14 at the intersection of $\lambda/\mu = 0.75$ and $K = 1$, we find $L_q = 2.3$. Hence: $W_q = 2.3/3 = 0.77$ hours per truck. At three trucks per hour, the total hourly waiting cost of the trucks is

$0.77 \times 3 \times \$16$	= $37
	+ $10 (cost of one crew)
Total	$47/hr

Two crews. From Figure 9.14 T $L_q = 0.12$

$$W_q = \frac{0.12}{3} = 0.04$$

waiting cost of trucks:	$0.04 \times 3 \times \$16 = \$2$
cost of two crews:	$20
Total:	$22/hr

Three or more crews. The most that can now be saved from the cost of waiting trucks is $2 so clearly it is not worthwhile to add another $10 crew. The best answer is, therefore, *two* crews.

Scheduled Services

When jobs can be scheduled by appointment.

There are some situations where the recipients do *not* arrive randomly but are *scheduled*, as in medicine and dentistry. If possible, appointments in such a case should be scheduled such that the first recipient has the most *definite* required service time and the last recipient the most *variable* service time. For similar types of recipient needs, the variability is often proportional to the expected length of service. That is, a 10-minute appointment may run 5–15 minutes but a 4-hour appointment may run 3½ to 4½ hours. Scheduling in this manner then minimizes the potential wait for all *following* recipients, as was discussed earlier.

9.10 PERT/CPM FOR PROJECT SCHEDULING

An integrated methodology is used.

Although PERT and CPM originally had some differences in the way their activities were determined and laid out, many current approaches to project scheduling minimize these differences and present an integrated view of an approach instead, as we shall see here. It will be helpful to define some terms first.

- **Activity**—one of the project operations, or tasks, that requires resources and takes some amount of time to complete.
- **Event**—the completion of an activity, or series of activities, at a particular point in time.
- **Network**—the set of all project activities graphically interrelated through the precedence relationships. In this text we let the network lines (or **arcs**) represent the activities, the connections between the lines (called **nodes**) represent the events, and arrows on the arcs represent the precedence relations. (This is typical of the PERT approach; in CPM the nodes represent the activities.)
- **Path**—a series of connected activities between two events.
- **Critical**—activities, events, or collections of activities and events, which, if delayed, will delay the entire project. The **critical paths** of a project are those continuous paths from the start to the finish of a project that contain the critical activities and events.

We will use an example to illustrate the PERT/CPM technique.

Black Cross Plan "E"

The Black Cross is a volunteer organization recently formed in California to prepare for and respond to the long-overdue earthquake expected there in the last decade. They have developed a single, efficient, uniform response plan (termed "plan E") consisting of 10 major activities for all cities where the earthquake causes major damage. Clearly, completing the project activities as quickly as possible is crucial in saving lives and property and aiding victims in distress. The staff of Black Cross has determined not only the most likely times for each activity but the probably fastest (termed **optimistic**) and slowest (termed **pessimistic**) **times** that might be encountered by a project team out in the field. The project operations and the optimistic, most likely, and pessimistic times, in hours, are listed in Table 9.13 along with the activities that must precede them.

Three activity time estimates.

Construction of the Network: Ordering the Activities

Following precedence in constructing the network.

A project "network" illustrating the activities and their interdependence is constructed by first examining Table 9.13 for those activities that have no activities preceding them. These activities *a*, *b*, and *c*, are all drawn out of a starting node, which, for convenience in Figure 9.15, we have labeled **1**.

Next, the activity list is scanned for activities that require only that activities *a*,

TABLE 9.13 PLAN "E" ACTIVITY TIMES (HOURS)

Project Activity	Optimistic Time, t_o	Most Likely Time, t_m	Pessimistic Time, t_p	Required Preceding Activities
a	5	11	11	none
b	10	10	10	none
c	2	5	8	none
d	1	7	13	*a*
e	4	4	10	*b,c*
f	4	7	10	*b,c*
g	2	2	2	*b,c*
h	0	6	6	*c*
i	2	8	14	*g,h*
j	1	4	7	*d,e*

b or *c* be completed. Thus, activities *d* through *h* can be drawn in the network next. Activity *d* can be drawn directly out of node **2**, and activity *h* can be drawn out of node **4**. But if node **3** indicates the completion of activity *b*, how can activities *e, f,* and *g* be drawn since they also depend upon the completion of activity *c*? This is accomplished by the use of a **dummy activity** from event **4** to event **3** which indicates that event **3** depends on activity c (event **4**) being accomplished as well as activity *b*. The dummy activity, shown as a dashed line in Figure 9.15, requires no time to accomplish, but the linkage is necessary, so that activities *e, f,* and *g* cannot start before *both* activities *b* and *c* are completed.

The use of dummy activities.

What if activity *e* did *not* require that activity *c* be completed whereas *f* and *g* did? If this was the case, the diagram would be drawn as shown in Figure 9.16. Care must be taken to ensure that the *proper* precedence relations are drawn in the diagram; otherwise, the project might be unnecessarily delayed.

The remainder of the diagram is drawn in the same manner. Activity *i*, which depends upon activities *g* and *h*, comes out of node **5** that represents the completion of *g* and *h*. A similar situation occurs with activity *j*. All of the remaining activities without completion nodes, (*f, i,* and *j*) are then directed to the project completion node **7**.

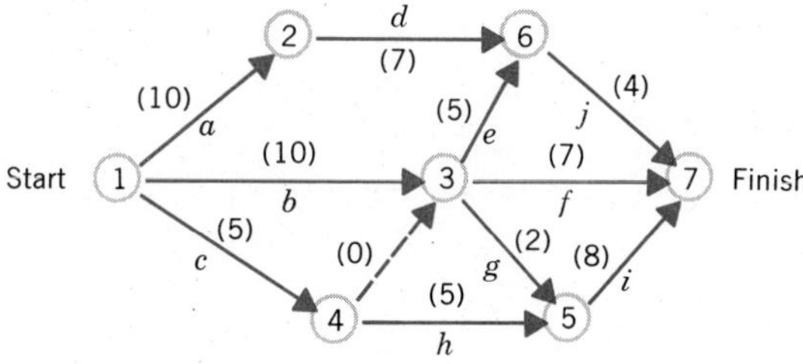

Figure 9.15. Plan "E" project operations network.

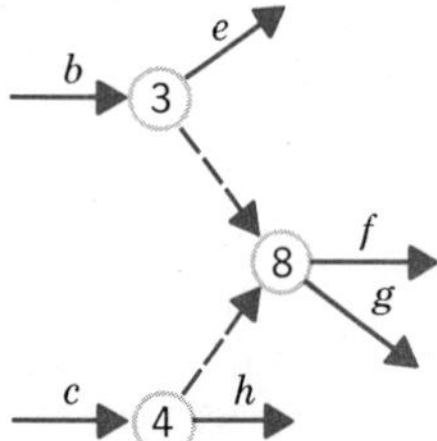

Figure 9.16. Proper use of dummy activities.

Calculating Activity Durations

We have now completed a *graphic* network representation of the precedence information shown in Table 9.13. We next need to place expected activity times on the network so we can see which activities must be scheduled first and when they must be completed for the project not to be delayed.

An *expected completion time*, t_e, for each activity is found from the three time estimates in Table 9.13 by the following formula.

$$t_e = \frac{t_o + 4t_m + t_p}{6} \tag{9.7}$$

Note in the table that, for some activities, their durations are known with certainty (e.g., activity *b*). The results of this calculation are shown in Table 9.14 and indicated, with parentheses, on the network of Figure 9.15. It is also possible to calculate

TABLE 9.14 ACTIVITY EXPECTED, VARIANCE, AND SLACK TIMES

Activity	Expected Time t_e	Variance, σ^2	Slack (* on CP)	
a	10	1	0*	
b	10	0	0 + 10 + S + 2 + 8 = 21	1
			0 + 10 + S + 7 = 21	
			0 + 10 + S + 5 = 17	
c	5	1	0 + 5 + S + 5 = 17	3
			0 + 5 + S + 5 + 8 = 21	
			0 + 5 + S + 7 = 21	
			0 + 5 + S + 2 + 8 = 21	
d	7	4	0*	
e	5	1	10 + 5 + S = 17	2
f	7	1	10 + 7 + S = 21	4
g	2	0	10 + 2 + S + 8 = 21	1
h	5	1	5 + 5 + S + 8 = 21	1
i	8	4	12 + 8 + S = 21	1
j	4	1	0*	

a measure of "uncertainty" in the activity duration, its variance, σ^2, and this is given by

$$\sigma^2 = \left(\frac{t_p - t_o}{6}\right) \tag{9.8}$$

which is also included in Table 9.14.

Project Completion and Critical Paths

Calculating early start time.

To determine the expected completion time of the entire project, **early start times** are calculated for each of the event nodes in the project, working from the *start* node on the left and progressing to the right. The early start times are the soonest that *all* activities leading into each node can be completed. These times are shown next to each of the nodes in Figure 9.17. Starting with 0 at node **1**, nodes **2** and **4** are simply the times of the activities preceding them. However, node **3** is the *latest* of activity *b* or *c* since *both* of these activities must be completed before activities following event **3** can begin.

Similarly, event **5** is the later of the two paths **3-5** or **4-5**. Thus, the time for event **5** is 12 (10 + 2 for **3-5** is greater than 5 + 5 for **4-5**). Completing the project nodes, it is found that node 7, project completion, has a time of 21 (hours); this is then the soonest that the project can be completed. The activity path that resulted in this value (and sometimes there is more than one) is identified as the *critical path* of the project and is shown with a heavy arrow in Figure 9.17. This means that any delay in the activities along this path will delay the entire project. In addition to a project critical path, each node has its own critical path. For example, the critical path to node **5** is **1-3-5** since this is the path that defines the earliest that node **5** can be realized and the activities following it begun.

Slack Time

Finding the slack in activities.

All activities on the critical path have zero slack—that is, there is no room for delay in any activity on the critical path without delaying the entire project. Activities off the critical path may delay up to a point where further delay would delay the entire project. This is called their **slack**. A number of ways exist to calculate this slack but

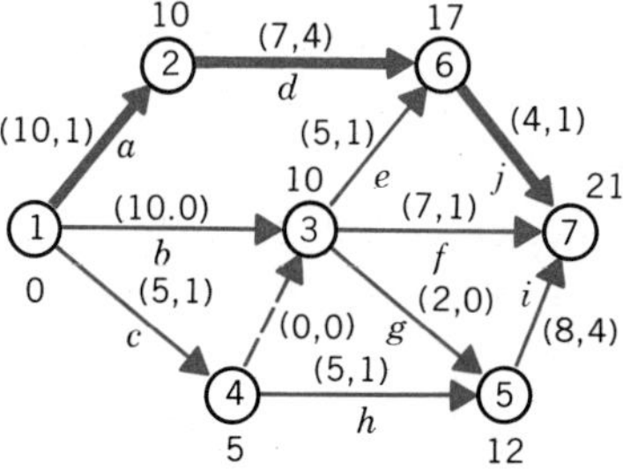

Figure 9.17. Early start times and critical path.

one of the easiest is to simply calculate the values of the slacks, S, in the activity that would delay the project by *all* of the various paths that return to the critical path. (Any activity that delays the *critical path* will necessarily delay the project completion.)

For example, in activity g, the only way that this activity can delay the project is by delaying activity i and thus delaying node 7. The maximum delay permissible is thus

$$\begin{aligned} &\text{early start at node } \mathbf{3} + \text{activity g time} + \text{slack} + \text{activity i time} = 21 \\ &10 + 2 + S + 8 = 21 \\ &\text{or} \quad S = 1 \text{ hr} \end{aligned}$$

This value of slack is listed in Table 9.14. In activity b, however, there are *three* ways to delay the project, resulting in the following equations.

$$\left.\begin{array}{lll} \mathbf{1\text{-}3\text{-}5\text{-}7} & 0 + 10 + S + 2 + 8 = 21 & \rightarrow S = 1 \\ \mathbf{1\text{-}3\text{-}7} & 0 + 10 + S + 7 = 21 & \rightarrow S = 4 \\ \mathbf{1\text{-}3\text{-}6} & 0 + 10 + S + 5 = 17 & \rightarrow S = 2 \end{array}\right\} S = 1$$

Since *each* of these calculations computes a *maximum* permissible delay, the *smallest* of the maxima gives the true slack in the activity: 1 in this case. That is, any delay in activity b beyond 1 hour will delay project completion through path **1-3-5-7**. Knowing these slacks then allows the manager to transfer resources from noncritical to critical activities in order to keep the project on schedule. But in doing so, she or he must not delay a noncritical activity in excess of its slack.

Probabilities of Completion

Finding the probability of completing the project on time.

Knowing the variance in each activity (the variance in Table 9.14) we can compute the likelihood of completing the project in a given time period, assuming the activity durations are independent of each other. The distribution of completion times will be approximately normally distributed with a mean and variance found from the critical path. The mean time along the critical path was found to be 21 hours. The variance is found by summing the variances of each of the activities on the critical path. In our example, this would be

$$\begin{aligned} V &= \sigma_a^2 + \sigma_d^2 + \sigma_j^2 \\ &= 1 + 4 + 1 \\ &= 6 \end{aligned}$$

The probability of completing the project in, say, 23 hours is then found through the table of the standard normal probability distribution in the appendix with a standard normal deviate of:

$$Z = \frac{\text{desired completion time} - \text{mean completion time}}{\sqrt{V}} \tag{9.9}$$

$$= \frac{23 - 21}{\sqrt{6}}$$
$$= 0.818$$

which results in a probability (see Figure 9.18) of 79 percent.*

Application

A number of weaknesses have been pointed out in the literature regarding the application of PERT/CPM methods (validity of the assumptions, availability of data) [8, 10]. Nevertheless, the approach has found considerable use in some areas (such as construction) for the planning and control of complex projects and remains, to date, the primary technique.

9.11 SUMMARY

Scheduling the transformation operations consists of a number of separate activities starting with the demand forecast and ending with expediting the jobs if they become delayed. The first activity is aggregate scheduling to minimize overall costs of operation and obtain first-cut approximations to resource requirements.

Two easily understood aggregate scheduling strategies are "chase demand" and "level production." However, these strategies are not typically the least costly and a number of other approaches, such as linear programming, have been developed to identify better aggregate scheduling strategies. One of the most realistic is called the "search decision rule."

The aggregate schedule is typically broken down further into individual output groups, including actual orders, in the master schedule. The master schedule is then checked against lead time for materials via priority planning and operations capacity

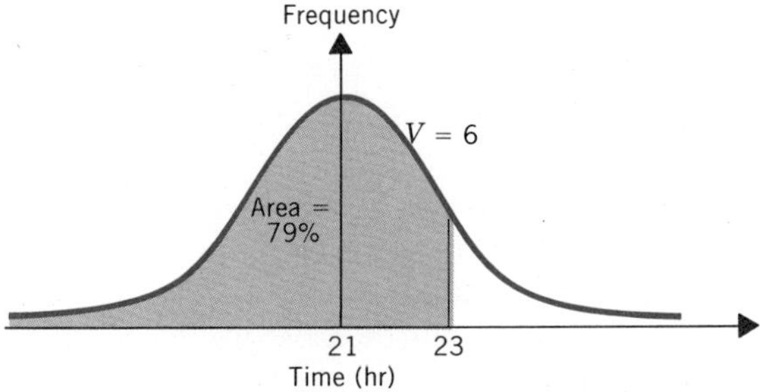

Figure 9.18. Probability distribution of project completion times.

* The variance of "almost-critical" paths should also be investigated if they might affect the probability of completion in the desired time. For further details, refer to [36].

via capacity requirements planning. Priority planning systems typically consist of time-phased order point systems for continuous processes and material requirements planning systems for intermittent processes.

Following the construction of the master schedule, the next step is loading the jobs onto the best work centers to maximize utilization of the facilities and minimize cost and delays. Here the assignment model and its variations may be helpful in minimizing costs.

Once the jobs have been assigned to work centers they must be appropriately sequenced with the same goals again in mind—maximize utilization and minimize cost and delays. Historically the Gantt chart has been of value in this task but current attention has focused on the numerous priority rules that have been proposed. Of all of them, the shortest operation time rule, an extension of Johnson's method, has frequently exhibited the best overall performance. For repetitive batch scheduling problems, the critical ratio method has proven useful.

At this point a detailed schedule can be drawn up listing the times and locations of resources and start and finish dates of jobs. In accord with the detailed schedule, jobs are then released to operations. Should delays set in, expediting of the jobs may then prove necessary to meet scheduled delivery dates.

Much of the scheduling clerical work of the past has been relieved through application of the memory and speed of the computer to store scheduling and materials information in the first place, and then speedily update the information when the inevitable last-minute changes and delays take place. Prior to this, the coordination task was virtually impossible and large reserves of resources had to be maintained in case they were suddenly needed.

The scheduling of services and projects are significantly different from other transformation processes. Since many service demands occur on a random basis and the services cannot be inventoried ahead of time or backordered, the organizational resources must be scheduled to meet this demand instead. The best utilization of these resources occurs when they are scheduled in proportion to demand, thereby necessitating an accurate forecasting system.

Attempting to schedule staff presents special problems involving equity, compensation, and so forth. In some services the use of "duty tours" for staff further complicates the scheduling process. To the extent that advertising and promotion can shift demand from peak periods and smooth resource requirements, this problem is helped.

Also due to the inability to store services, waiting lines tend to form for service. The problem facing the manager is to determine the proper size service facility to minimize the cost of ill-will due to waiting and the cost of service. Queuing theory can aid in this process by predicting the expected queue lengths and waiting time for different sized service facilities.

The main difficulty in project management is planning a tight schedule of activities to expedite completion of the project. PERT/CPM is a planning and scheduling methodology that can identify the critical activities, determine event completion times, calculate activity slacks, if any exist, and compute probabilities of project completion for any times of interest.

9.12 READINGS

Scheduling is Not the Problem

KENNETH L. CAMPBELL
Honeywell Information Systems, Inc.
Cleveland, Ohio

ABSTRACT

It has often been said that scheduling is no problem, but rescheduling can kill you. In this article, the author supports this theme and points out the causes and penalties of rescheduling. He also makes pertinent suggestions as to how to avoid the causes and reduce the penalties.

At a conference on shop scheduling, the principal speaker was extolling the virtues of a particularly complex scheduling system when one of the attendees spoke up and said, "Scheduling is no problem, it's the rescheduling that kills me".

While that remark may have sounded facetious to the speaker, it is a concise statement of fact. When one stops to analyze the situation, it becomes quite clear how well that comment expresses a truly profound observation.

WHAT IS A SCHEDULE?

When we isolate the act of scheduling from its related activities, such as loading, dispatching and rescheduling, it becomes clear that scheduling is, in fact, no problem.

First, it is an abstract. It cannot be specifically related to a real life situation. The schedule, as prepared for a manufacturing organization, is based on a given capacity, the availability of specific materials or a given job content. In most cases, due to the lapse of time between the conception and the execution of a schedule, one or more of these factors has changed.

The typical schedule in itself is not dynamic, and is, therefore, a poor instrument to associate with the usual manufacturing shop which, as we all know, is a dynamic beast, continually out of control and continually going off in an unpredictable direction.

Schedules come in a large number of varieties. They can be grouped into three major families: forward, backward and (for the lack of a better word) non-directional. In the first family, we begin with where we are and find out when we will arrive. In the second, we decide when we wish to arrive and determine when we should get started.

With the third family, the non-directional, we may start now to get there by then without any regard to the route, the terrain, or the other travelers who may be encountered along the way. (Sound silly? Check the systems where the Sales Department dates the customers orders!)

Scheduling techniques are often described as being related to finite or infinite capacity. Some aren't (or can't be) described at all in terms of capacity.

Some schedules are based on very sophisticated rules and formulas, some on very simple ones, and, of course, some are based on no rules at all.

There are, in the first category, scheduling systems that take into consideration such factors as the order quantity, resource capacity, material availability, set up and process time, in-house transportation delays and even order values.

In the second category, one would group those having only one or two factors to consider: perhaps the product complexity, the current shop loading, or the time of the year. Into the third group, we could toss the schedules based strictly on external factors: customers requested date, a sales forecast and Joe's best guess.

WHAT ARE THE PROBLEMS OF RESCHEDULING?

The majority of the problems caused by the need to reschedule can be divided into three groups: (1) cost, (2) capacity, (3) confusion.

Naturally, cost, in terms of reduced dollar profits, is the major concern of every red-blooded manufacturing man. And rescheduling can be a real drain on the profits. In most shops, a rescheduling can involve untold manhours of both direct and indirect labor. If there is any doubt about this, count the number of "expediters" found on our payrolls. "Expediters prevent rescheduling", you say? Well, perhaps that viewpoint does have some merit, but, at the same time, it supports our premise that rescheduling does cost profit dollars—otherwise we would not be willing to spend so much money on the salaries of the expediters.

Rescheduling also costs labor dollars when it involves the premature breakdown of a set-up, the paying of overtime, or the use of a less efficient resource.

When capacity utilization is adversely effected by rescheduling, it is lost forever. If a resource is in short supply, its scheduling is critical and extreme care must be taken to be sure that rescheduling will not waste any of the resource.

Confusion, for most people, is a detractor and has a detrimental effect on their morale, their production and their respect for those who are responsible for its creation or permit its prolonged existence. If it could be quantitatively expressed, confusion would undoubtedly increase exponentially with the amount of rescheduling.

Now that we have considered the problems associated with rescheduling, what should we do about them?

RESCHEDULING IS HERE TO STAY

At first thought, it would seem as though the best solution to the rescheduling dilemma would be to eliminate the practice of remaking our schedule and stick to it come what may. Unfortunately, this solution could soon put most manufacturers out of business. This is primarily due to the source of some of the causes of the failure of our scheduling systems. A list of some of the causes of schedule failures would include such things as:

1. Materials Not Available. The vendors have failed to meet deliveries or the previous operation has not been completed.
2. Tools Are Not Available. They haven't been received or they have not been repaired.
3. Machines Have Broken Down. An alternate is not available or is less efficient.
4. Customers Requirements Have Changed. Order quantities have changed or new delivery dates are required.
5. Overloaded Capacity. Unrealistic master schedules or promise dates have been prepared without regard to available capacity.
6. Loose Discipline in Job Selection. A good schedule is ignored for such reasons as make-out, personal preferences or simply unawareness of the need for first-things-first.

Obviously, some of the listed causes are external and, as such, *are not fully* under control of the organization. Others, such as overloaded capacity, are internal and can be controlled by management once they are recognized and the problem given some attention.

In either case, it is only practical to acknowledge the fact that things do happen to upset even the best, well prepared, schedule and, as a consequence, rescheduling will be necessary.

REDUCE THE PROBLEMS OF RESCHEDULING

There are a few basic things that can be done in any shop and using any system that will reduce the penalties caused by the act of rescheduling. Included among these are:

1. Release Fewer Jobs

In many shops the manufacturing information is prepared, typed, duplicated and distributed to the shop floor as rapidly as it can be done, without regard to *start dates, due dates* or *capacity*. This creates a large portion of the problem when rescheduling is necessary.

Someone must scurry about the shop locating the paperwork, collecting, correcting or replacing it with updated information. Naturally, the more jobs in the queue, the more likely changes will be required and, therefore, the more involved the task. Likewise, the more jobs in the queue, the more likely a rescheduling will be *required*. This may mean rescheduling shop orders which have been previously rescheduled.

When the situation gets too far out of control, it is natural that we throw in the towel and no longer attempt to keep the dates (start and/or finish) corrected. Instead, a Hot List is published and we hire more expediters to get the jobs on the list pushed to the front of the queue.

Where the system is computerized, it is logical to delay the preparation of all the maufacturing information until the last practical moment. The storage of the basic facts within the computer will permit it to be factored into the scheduling system (or rescheduled) as often as required, with or without changes.

Some scheduling systems distinguish between "PLANNED" orders and "RELEASED" orders. In those systems a planned order is one which has been entered into the computer but not yet "exposed" to the shop thru the preparation of shop papers. Planned orders may be altered (date or quantity) or cancelled for any reason. Released orders are those for which the shop papers have been prepared and distributed to the shop. On these orders, it takes a virtual act of congress to change them and they will be cancelled only by feeding back the information that they were "completed" with an increased quantity or "closed out short".

It pays then, to release orders only far enough in advance to permit the tools, materials and resources to be "staged" soon enough to prevent lost time between jobs. Where the processing cycle is longer than the staging time, the optimum would be to release only the next job ahead of each machine, production line or employee. When the processing time is shorter, it would be best to have several released orders ahead.

2. Demand Shop Floor Discipline

Assuming that it is not practical at this time in your shop to release only the next job, it is then necessary to enforce a system of job selection. The lack of such discipline generally makes effective scheduling difficult. Perhaps, in such cases, each job entering a particular queue should be given a sequence number and a firm rule be established that jobs be started in order of their sequence numbers.

Good scheduling systems should be directly associated with a corresponding monitoring system in which job completions are fed back in a timely manner. Systems permitting time or labor banks will suffer unless, of course, the payroll input is divorced from the scheduling feedback. Naturally, that would be a duplication of effort and is not recommended.

Overruns should be controlled since they will generally be an unnecessary drain on available resources. Overruns are often again the result of releasing too many shop orders to a given machine, particularly when the orders have identical raw materials and the material is not clearly "bundled" by order.

3. Use Realistic Dating Procedures

If your shop orders from a master schedule, the persons preparing that schedule should be aware of the time required to process the quantities on that schedule. They must also be aware of the capacities available on the various resources involved.

A two-way exchange between the master scheduling function and the shop scheduling system is desirable. Using a computer, it is quite easy to "explode" the master schedule into its requirements and to those requirements against available capacity. Where conflicts exist the master schedule can be adjusted to avoid them.

If, on the other hand, your shop load is basically the direct result of customer orders, it is prudent to withhold the promise date until a similar test has been made of the required resources.

These systems need not be complicated. They can be very effective even when available capacity and capacity requirements are only roughly known.

One company, using a small computer, has developed a loading system which permits the computer to automatically apply promise dates to customer orders up to a predetermined amount (say 85%) of capacity. Unless a "special" date is requested, the computer assigns the date of the next available time period. The sales department has the option of assigning the remainder of the available capacity (in this example 15%) to rush orders, etc.

When it comes time to schedule the orders for the next week's production, a tentative schedule for that week is produced along with a list of the orders loaded into the next time period. The total accumulated required machine time is printed. If less than 100% of capacity is scheduled for the coming period, the scheduler has the authority to select orders from the following period to make up a full schedule of 100% of capacity. If, for some reason, the tentative schedule shows more than 100% of capacity, the scheduler can make the necessary adjustments (overtime or rescheduling) to get a workable schedule.

The benefits of such systems include realistic schedules, fewer overdue shipments, less panic and more profits. The system is relatively uncomplicated and easily administered by those responsible for getting the job done.

SUMMARY

Since rescheduling is really the problem, scheduling systems *should* be so designed to recognize the need for and make it as convenient as possible to reschedule. In designing such a system, every factor should be considered. However, only those factors of major importance may need to be used in the scheduling rules. To attempt to use all factors may make the logic too complex, and therefore, impossible to administer.

Source. Production and Inventory Management, 3rd quarter, 1971. American Production and Inventory Control Society,

9.13 KEY TERMS

Concepts

aggregate scheduling (p. 298)
production planning and control (p. 296)
backordering (p. 298)
equivalent units (p. 298)
production plan (p. 299)
disaggregate (p. 299)
master schedule (p. 299)
produce to stock (p. 300)
produce to order (p. 300)
CRP (p. 300)
capacity planning (p. 300)
time-phased work orders (p. 300)
loading (p. 301)
sequencing (p. 301)
priority rules (p. 301)
detailed scheduling (p. 301)
short-term scheduling (p. 301)
dispatching (p. 301)
dead load file (p. 301)
expediting (p. 301)
hot jobs (p. 302)
de-expediting (p. 302)
data base (p. 303)
PICS (p. 303)
net change (p. 303)
regeneration (p. 303)
chase demand (p. 304)
order launching (p. 300)
load reports (p. 301)
hat switching (p. 313)
releasing (p. 301)
level zero items (p. 299)
priority planning (p. 299)
TPOP (p. 300)
MRP (p. 300)
dependent demand (p. 300)
economic order quantity (p. 300)
Gantt chart (p. 310)
baseline (p. 304)
level production (p. 305)
PERT (p. 317)
slack (p. 318)
CPM (p. 317)
floating workers (p. 314)
off-peak pricing (p. 314)
duty tours (p. 315)
queues (p. 317)
forward scheduling (p. 299)
backward scheduling (p. 310)
FCFS (p. 312)
FISFS (p. 312)
SOT (p. 312)
LOT (p. 312)
SS (p. 312)
SS/RO (p. 312)
DS/RO (p. 312)
COVERT (p. 312)
RAND (p. 312)
critical ratio (p. 313)

Tools and Applications

Johnson's rule (p. 330)
transportation model (p. 319)
assignment model (p. 325)
linear programming (p. 319)
linear decision rule (p. 320)
quadratic (p. 322)
parabolic (p. 321)
management coefficients (p. 322)
heuristic (p. 322)
multiple regression analysis (p. 323)
gradient (p. 324)
search decision rule (p. 324)
hill-climbing (p. 324)
index method (p. 328)
steady state (p. 334)
start-up transient (p. 334)
priority discipline (p. 334)
balking (p. 334)
reneging (p. 334)
jockeying (p. 334)
cycling (p. 334)
random arrivals (p. 334)
Poisson distribution (p. 334)
channels (p. 335)
utilization (p.335)
slack (p. 341)
event (p. 338)
network (p. 338)
arc (p. 338)
node (p. 338)
path (p. 338)
critical path (p. 338)
optimistic time (p. 338)
pessimistic time (p. 338)
dummy activity (p. 339)
early start time (p. 341)

9.14 REVIEW TEST

Concepts

1. By the term "scheduling" we may be referring to any one of a number of activities. (p. 296)
   a. True b. False
2. The scheduling approaches discussed for products are inappropriate for the scheduling of services. (p. 313)
   a. True b. False
3. The aggregate schedule is a first approximation. (p. 298)
   a. True b. False
4. Actual orders become incorporated into the schedule in the production plan. (p. 299)
   a. True b. False
5. Priority planning helps determine the proper ordering of work on jobs. (p. 299)
   a. True b. False
6. TPOP systems are typically for continuous flow organizations with dependent demand items. (p. 300)
   a. True b. False
7. If a master schedule exceeds capacity limits the standard computer response is to delay some items. (p. 301)
   a. True b. False
8. Dispatching is the attempt to speed up delayed jobs. (p. 301)
   a. True b. False
9. Computerized scheduling is a novel concept. (p. 302)
   a. True b. False
10. One of the aggregate scheduling alternatives available to the manager is to simply not produce enough. (p. 304)
    a. True b. False
11. The "chase demand" strategy will have one clear-cut baseline cost that other strategies can be compared against. (p. 304)
    a. True b. False
12. *When* you enter a market may dictate whether you tend to backlog demand or build up inventories. (p. 306)
    a. True b. False
13. An M on a Gantt chart means a delay caused by a manager's interruption. (p. 310)
    a. True b. False
14. A major complication in the scheduling of services is scheduling the staff. (p. 314)
    a. True b. False
15. The approach in scheduling for services is to match resource schedules to expected demand. (p. 314)
    a. True b. False
16. Sleeping during continuous duty tours is permissible. (p. 315)
    a. True b. False

Tools and Applications

17. Priority rules such as "shortest operation time" have proven helpful in loading problems. (p. 325)
    a. True b. False
18. Management coefficient heuristic methods can never do quite as well as the manager since they simply model him or her. (p. 323)
    a. True b. False
19. Johnson's rule is to schedule the shortest job on the first machine first and the longest job on the second machine last. (p. 330)
    a. True b. False
20. The theory of queues presented here includes multiple service facilities where more than one queue exists. (p. 332)
    a. True b. False
21. Queuing theory can find the expected length of the waiting line before a service facility reaches steady state. (p. 334)
    a. True b. False
22. Random arrivals imply that the arrival distribution is Poisson. (p. 334)
    a. True b. False
23. Adding a second server, contrary to expectations, does not *begin* to cut the queue length in half. (p. 336)
    a. True b. False

24. If arrivals can be scheduled, the longest one should probably be scheduled first. (p. 337)
    a. True b. False
25. A critical event is one of the project nodes lying on the critical path. (p. 338)
    a. True b. False
26. Dummy activities are only used to show precedence. (p. 339)
    a. True b. False
27. There can be only one critical path in a network. (p. 338)
    a. True b. False
28. There is a critical path to every node in a network. (p. 341)
    a. True b. False

9.15 DISCUSSION QUESTIONS

1. What scheduling techniques for products also apply to services?
2. What are some practical ways of matching staff availability to expected demand?
3. How do overtime and moonlighting become issues when duty tour scheduling is used?
4. Under what other conditions can queues form besides when the service cannot be stored ahead of time?
5. Why is balking disallowed in queuing theory?
6. Why is λ/μ called the "utilization" of the facility?
7. Why is the expected waiting time in the queue not simply L_q/μ?
8. Can you explain why adding a second server does not cut the queue length in half?
9. Why can the SOT rule not be used for projects?
10. What is the difference between PERT and CPM?
11. What might a "late start time" indicate? What could it be used for?
12. Could there ever be negative slack?
13. Some texts define a term called "free slack" along a path. What might this be?
14. Can the variance of a "near-critical" path possibly invalidate a computed probability of completion based on the critical path? How?
15. Do you think people's estimates of the optimistic or pessimistic activity times are the most accurate?
16. Might some of the scheduling techniques be extended into other realms such as investment analysis and information systems planning?
17. How could top management overcome lower level resentment of the installation of a computerized scheduling system?
18. How would the scheduling of bottleneck operations involving a single machine (printing press, computer) be accomplished?
19. Do the available priority rules differ in product and service organizations?
20. Given the immensity of the computerized scheduling task, how did it ever get accomplished previously?
21. What are the implications of the use of multiple expediters for the value of inventory and utilization reports to management?
22. Why is de-expediting important?
23. What are the advantages of "net change" versus "regeneration" scheduling systems?
24. In what sense is "chase demand" a "pure" aggregate scheduling strategy?
25. To what other areas might management coefficients heuristics be applied?
26. Why do loading and sequencing not apply as well to continuous processes?
27. What problems arise when the SOT rule is used?

9.16 PROBLEMS

Concepts

1. Find a better aggregate schedule than those shown in Table 9.1 for the example problem.
2. Data Tronics produces custom engineered testing equipment. The following four orders are currently in the design department.

Order No.	Due date	Date Order Received in Design Dept.	Operations Time (hr)	No. Operations Remaining
1	12/1/79	10/15/79	30	1
2	1/15/80	11/15/79	40	3
3	2/10/80	11/5/79	20	5
4	1/30/80	11/1/79	35	2

In what sequence should these four orders be processed through the design department if the following priority rules are used?

1 FCFS
2 SOT
3 SS
4 FISFS
5 SS/RO

3. Two fastener items have reached their reorder points, and production has started on both. Based upon the critical ratio, which should receive management attention?

	Inventory on Hand	Reorder Point	Lead Time To Produce Standard Batch	Lead Time Required To Complete Batch
Item 1	100	150	6 hr	4 hr
Item 2	200	200	4 hr	3.5 hr

4. Demand forecasts for each of the quarters of the year for your product are 120, 140, 110, 90 with this pattern repeating in the future as far as can be told. Current workforce is 11 and each worker can produce 10 units in a quarter. Inventory costs are $10 per unit per quarter while shortage costs with backordering are $13 per unit per quarter. Hire and fire costs are each $100 per worker but idle workers cost $150 a quarter. Cost to produce units on overtime is an additional $15 each. Find the best long-term production plan if all demand must be met.

Tools and Applications

5. John, Mary, and Henry have been asked to work this Saturday morning but the union contract calls for double time pay on Saturday. Since the work must get out, the production supervisor has decided to load the three jobs so as to minimize the total cost of overtime. The jobs and the time required for each person are shown below. John earns $12 per hour, Mary $16 per hour, and Henry $20 per hour on overtime.

	John	Mary	Henry
Job 1	2	1.5	1.5
Job 2	1.5	1.5	1
Job 3	1	2	1

Who should do which job if one job is assigned to each worker?

6. Solve Problem 5 using the index method. Note that none of the employees is willing to work more than 4 hours on Saturday morning.
7. Chippo Bakery Co. has five cakes which must be produced today for pickup this evening. Each cake must go through the bakery department and then the decorating department. Each department can process only one cake at a time. If the following estimates are available for production in each department, in what order should the cakes be scheduled?

	Baking (min)	Decorating (min)
Cake 1	30	30
Cake 2	20	15
Cake 3	20	45
Cake 4	15	35
Cake 5	15	15

8. Your are a manager in a large consulting firm. Fees billed to clients are based upon total hours spent on each project. For one client you have four projects going. How would you assign the four projects to four groups of consultants to minimize the time spent in total on the projects?

Project	1	2	3	4
Group 1	3	6	1	3
2	1	5	4	8
3	5	2	2	5
4	7	3	2	2

9. The emergency room of a local hospital employs three doctors. Emergency patients arrive randomly at the average rate of 3.5 per hour. Service is good and averages about ½ hour per patient so the hospital is considering reducing the number of doctors to two. What effect would this have on patient waiting time?

10. Jim sells tickets at a counter where the customers randomly arrive, on the average, every 2 minutes. He finds that he can service no more than 10 customers per hour. For management to maintain an average queue length of no more than one customer, how many more ticket sellers must they provide to help Jim?

11. Given the following project find the probability of completion by 17 weeks. By 24 weeks. By what date is management 90 percent sure completion will occur?

		Times (Weeks)	
Activity	Optimistic	Most Likely	Pessimistic
1-2	5	11	11
1-3	10	10	10
1-4	2	5	8
2-6	1	7	13
3-6	4	4	10
3-7	4	7	10
3-5	2	2	2
4-5	0	6	6
5-7	2	8	14
6-7	1	4	7

12. If the firm in Problem 11 can complete the project within 18 weeks it will receive a bonus of $10,000. But if the project delays beyond 22 weeks it must pay a penalty of $5,000. If the firm can choose whether or not to bid on this project, what should its decision be if the project is only a breakeven one normally?

9.17 CASE MICROSERVICE INC.

In January 1978, Rollie Bolton, who had been a customer engineer for both Burrows Corporation and IB2 Corporation, opened the doors to his new microcomputer service company. Rollie had spent 14 years repairing computers and peripheral hardware for Burrows and IB2 and had spent a considerable amount of time learning the microcomputer business. He was the immediate past president of the Tri-City Computer Club, which was made up principally of computer hobbyists.

Within Rollie's "service area" there were 8 microcomputer stores selling to small businessmen and hobbyists. Only three of those stores provided service for the equipment that they sold.

Rollie's business grew rapidly over the first 18 months, but at that point he began to falter. Rollie was receiving subtle hints from many of his friends in the computer club that service times were becoming longer than acceptable. Several of the computer stores were complaining that they were unable to sell hardware because of the rumored poor service.

Rollie recognized the problem and knew that lack of staff was not the answer. His staff were often idle waiting for the testing and diagnostic equipment. Rollie currently had five microcomputers or components in his shop. He estimated the amount of time required for each of the operators to complete their respective tasks. These estimates are shown in the table below. Rollie wants to minimize the amount of waiting time, and minimize the time required in total to get the five components shipped out the door. He is, however, uncertain as to the sequencing of these five components to accomplish his objective.

Equipment	Diagnostic Check (hr)	Repair/Part Replacement (hr)
TRS-80	9	8
IMSAI	12	6
Tektronics Printer	10	3
Adds Terminal	8	7
Ohio Scientific	14	2

QUESTIONS FOR DISCUSSION

1. How should Rollie sequence the computer equipment through his shop to minimize the waiting time and the total time taken?
2. Provide Rollie with a scheduling method to use in place of his trial and error scheduling.

9.18 REFERENCES AND BIBLIOGRAPHY

1. Abernathy, W. J., Baloff, N., and Hershey, J. C., "The Nurse Staffing Problem: Issues and Prospects," *Sloan Management Review*, 13:87–109 (Fall, 1971).
2. Baker, K. R., *Introduction to Sequencing and Scheduling*, New York: Wiley, 1974.
3. Bowman, E. H., "Production Planning by the Transportation Method of Linear Programming," *Journal of the Operations Research Society*, Feb. 1956.
4. ———, "Consistency and Optimality in Managerial Decision Making," *Management Science*, 9:310–321 (1963).
5. Buffa, E. S., "Aggregate Planning for Production," *Business Horizons*, 10:87–97 (Fall, 1967).
6. ——— and Miller, J., *Production-Inventory Systems: Planning and Control*, 3rd ed., Homewood, Ill: Irwin, 1979.
7. Campbell, K. L., "Scheduling is Not the Problem," *Production and Inventory Management*, 11:53–59 (No. 3, 1971).
8. Clayton, E. R., and Moore, L. J., "PERT vs. GERT" *Journal of Systems Management*, 23:11–19 (1972).
9. Conway, R. W., Maxwell, W. L., and Miller, L. W., *Theory of Scheduling*, Reading, Mass: Addison-Wesley, 1967.
10. Davis, E. W., *Project Management*, Norcross, Ga.: American Institute of Industrial Engr., PP&C Monograph #3, 1976.
11. Day, J. E., and Hottenstein, M. P., "Review of Sequencing Research," *Naval Research Logistic Quarterly*, 27:11–39 (March, 1970).
12. Dyer, J. S., "A Time-Sharing Computer Program for the Solution of the Multiple Criteria Problem," *Management Science* 19:1379–1383 (1973).
13. Eilon, S., *Elements of Production Planning and Control*, New York: Macmillan, 1962.
14. ———, "Five Approaches to Aggregate Production Planning," *AIIE Transactions*, 7:118–131 (1975).
15. Fetter, R. B., and Thompson, J. D., "The Simulation of Hospital Systems," *Operations Research*, 13:689–711 (1965).
16. Gavett, J. W., "Three Heuristic Rules for Sequencing Jobs to a Single Production Facility," *Management Science*, 11:B166–176 (1965).
17. Gross, D., and Harris, C. N., *Fundamentals of Queuing Theory*, New York: Wiley, 1974.
18. Harwood, G. B., and Lawless, R. W., "Optimizing Organizational Goals in Assigning Faculty Teaching Schedules," *Decision Sciences*, 6:513–524 (1975).
19. Heller, N. R., McEwan, J. T., and Stengel, W. W., *Computerized Scheduling of Police Manpower*, Vol.

I and II, St. Louis: N. R. Heller and Assoc., March 1973.

20. Holt, C. C., Modigliani, F., Muth, J. F., and Simon, H. A., *Planning Production, Inventories, and Work Force*, Englewood Cliffs, N.J.: Prentice-Hall, 1960.

21. IBM, *The Production Information and Control System*, GE20-0280-2.

22. ———, "Shopwell's One Million $ Promise," *Viewpoint*, 8:26–28 (July-August, 1978).

23. Johnson, S. M., "Optimal Two and Three Stage Production Schedules with Set-up Time Included," *Naval Research Logistics Quarterly*, 1:61–68 (March, 1954).

24. Judy, R. W., and Levine, J. B., *A New Tool for Educational Administrators*, Toronto: University of Toronto Press, 1965.

25. Larson, R. C., *Urban Police Patrol Analysis*, Cambridge, Mass.: MIT Press, 1972.

26. Lee, W. B., and Khumawala, B. M., "Simulation Testing of Aggregate Production Planning Models in an Implementation Methodology," *Management Science*, 20:903–911 (1974).

27. Mellichamp, J. M., and Love, R. M., "Production Switching Heuristics for the Aggregate Planning Problem," *Management Science*, 24:1242–1251 (1978).

28. Meredith, J., and Shershin, A. C., *EMS and Fire Activities in the South Florida Region*, Working paper 75-4, School of Business, Florida International University, November 1975.

29. Miller, M. H., and Orr, D., "An Application of Control-Limit Models to the Management of Cash Balances," in Robicheck, A. A., ed., *Financial Research and Management Decisions*, New York: Wiley, 1967.

30. Milsum, J. H., Turban, E., and Vertinsky, I., "Hospital Admission Systems: Their Evaluation and Management," *Management Science*, 19:646–666 (1973).

31. Nanot, Y. R., "An Experimental Investigation and Comparative Evaluation of Priority Disciplines in Job Shop-Like Queuing Networks," Unpublished Ph.D. Dissertation, UCLA, 1963.

32. O'Brien, J. J., *Scheduling Handbook*, New York: McGraw-Hill, 1969.

33. Reitman, J., *Computer Simulation Applications*, New York: Wiley, 1971.

34. Simon, H. A., and Newell, A., "Heuristic Problem Solving: The Next Advance," *Operations Research*, 6:1–10 (1968).

35. Taubert, W. H., "Search Decision Rule for the Aggregate Scheduling Problem," *Management Science*, 14:343–359 (1958).

36. Turban, E., and Meredith, J. R., *Fundamentals of Management Science*, Dallas: Business Publications, 1977.

37. Warner, D. M., and Prawda, J., "A Mathematical Programming Model for Scheduling Nurses," *Management Science* 19:411–422 (1972).

38. Wight, O. W., *Production and Inventory Management in the Computer Age*, Boston, Mass.: Cahners, 1974.

39. Willoughby, T., Paterson, W., and Drummond, G., "Computer Aided Architectural Planning," *Operational Research Quarterly*, 21:91–99 (1970).

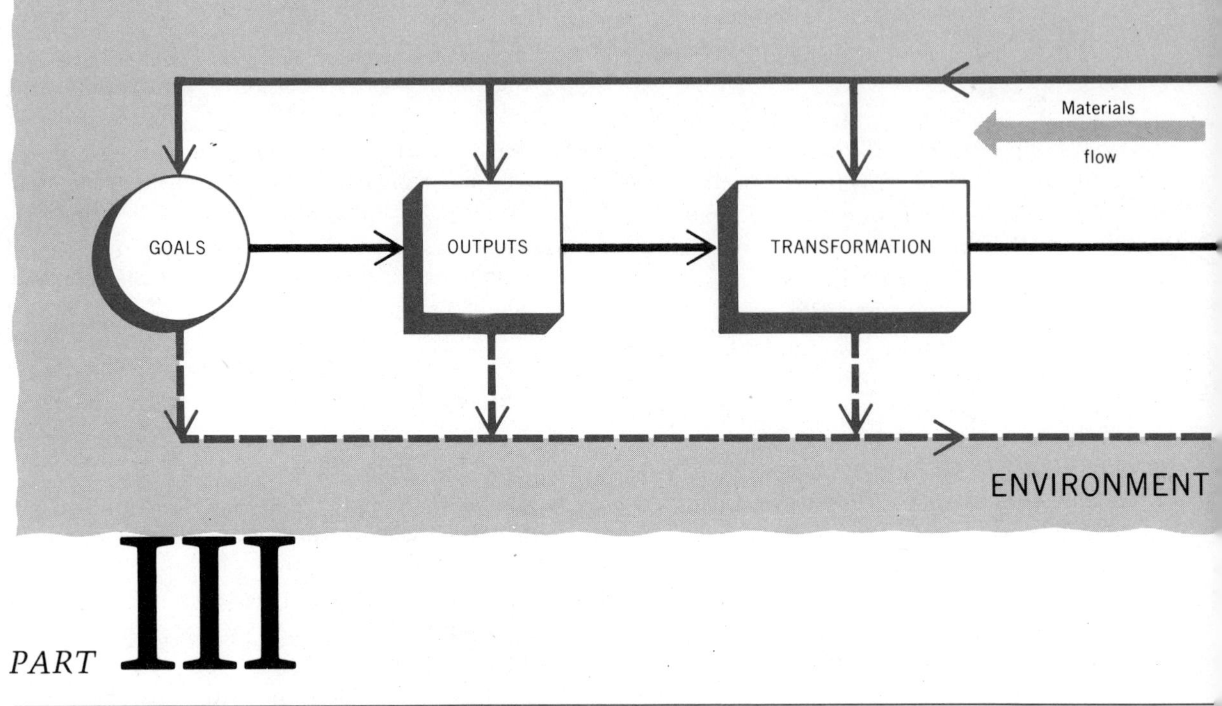

PART III

ACQUIRING THE INPUTS

At this point in the text we have discussed the design of the operations system and, in terms of operational activities, now are ready to consider the design of those sytems that will obtain the required inputs. We consider three inputs of special importance to operations: facilities (particularly capital equipment), staff (workers), and materials. Although these are clearly areas of major importance to operations management they are typically organized into separate functional areas within the organization—namely: finance, personnel, and operations/purchasing. Thus, this part of our study will briefly focus on these three interfaces, each of which is complex and important enough to justify a book-length discussion.

Our perspective in looking at the acquisition of facilities is not an engineering one but rather the financial perspective of capital budgeting. Rather than considering smokestack scrubbers to eliminate air pollution, equipment longevity under torsional vibration, and so on, we focus instead on the "bottom line," or *management*, aspects of when and how to acquire the organization's plant and equipment. Thus, we examine costs and benefits over the investment's life cycle, the effects of deprecia-

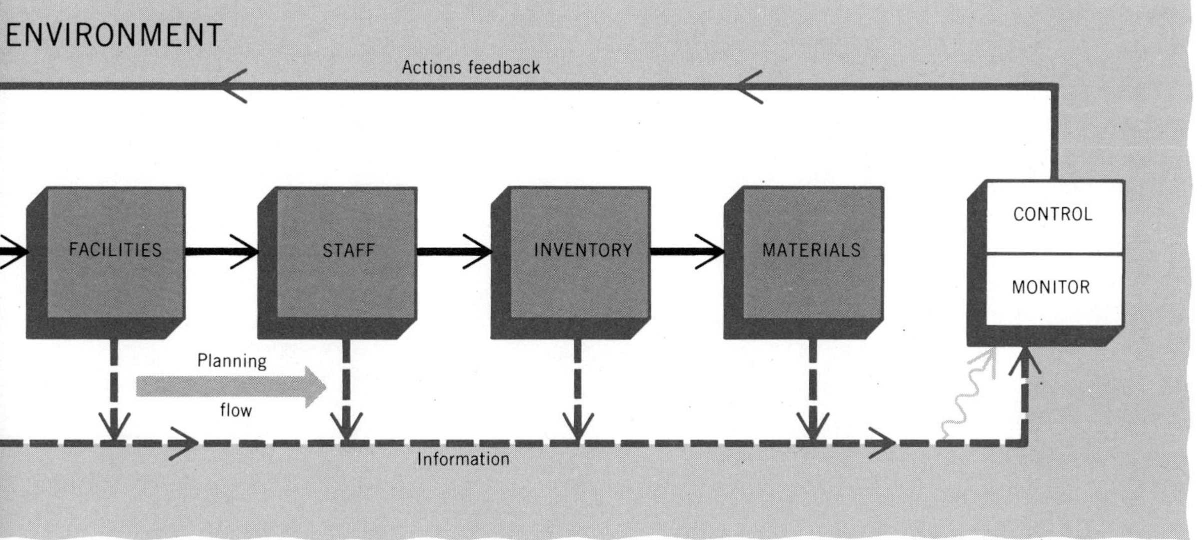

tion and taxes on the present value of investments, the advantages of leasing over purchasing, and other such matters that impact strongly on the operations facilities which are finally selected.

Our view of the acquisition of human resources is again one of operations *management*. We therefore stress topics such as "manpower" forecasts, training, and motivation rather than arbitration, bargaining, and such; that is, the emphasis is on "personnel management" rather than "labor relations." Other topics included are recruitment, development, evaluation, and termination.

For the acquisition of materials, expendable tools, and supplies we take an operations/purchasing perspective. (Purchasing is usually not involved in the acquisition of major capital facilities.) In operations we consider the multiple complexities of materials management including inventory ordering, safety stocks, lead times, reorder points, bills of materials, product structures, and dependent versus independent demand. In purchasing we consider the procurement system and its procedures, supplier selection and evaluation, and pricing of materials.

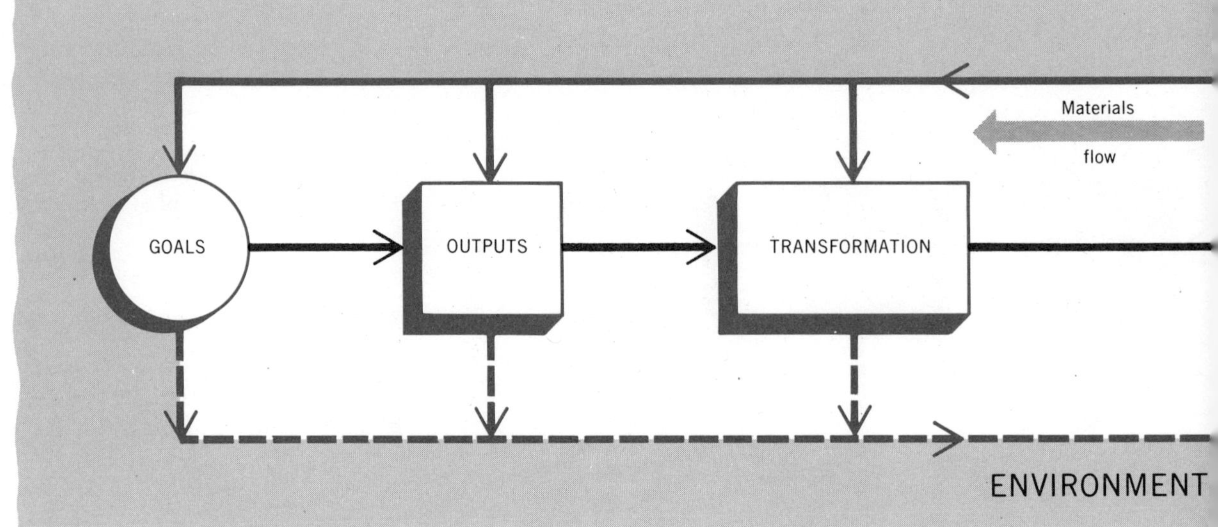

Chapter 10I

The Financial Interface: Acquiring Facilities

CONCEPTS

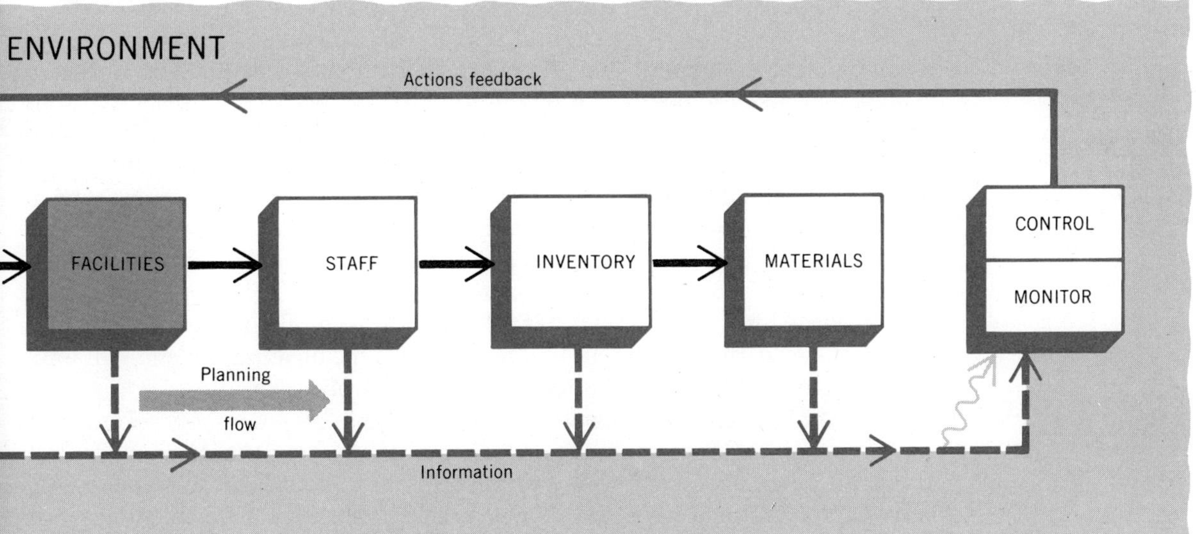

LEARNING OBJECTIVES

By the conclusion of this chapter the student should

1. Be familiar with the nature of capital budgeting for fixed assets.
2. Understand the steps in life cycle costing and why it is preferred to the "low bid" method.
3. Know how to compare investment alternatives by the "payback" and "net present value" methods and be able to use present value tables.
4. Be aware of the interacting effects of depreciation and taxation.
5. Know how to calculate depreciation by the three major methods.
6. Comprehend the implications of leasing and its advantages and disadvantages as compared to ownership.
7. Be able to use the breakeven model for capacity-investment analysis of alternative asset proposals.

Primacy of capital asset investment.

Acquiring plant, equipment, and other such capital items is particularly important for operations management and is deserving of special attention for several reasons. First, all other inputs, including materials and labor, are dependent upon the types of capital resources acquired. For example, a high speed electronic conveyer system will reduce the materials handling labor requirements and the amount of transit inventory required. Second, capital investments usually involve large amounts of money that must be committed for extended periods of time. An incorrect decision might unnecessarily tie up organizational resources and adversely affect the returns to the organization. Third, capital investment decisions are typically irreversible; once the decision is made, the investment will remain with the organization and will influence (often mandate) the future direction of the firm's operations.

Capital budgeting for fixed assets.

Capital items such as buildings and large machines are commonly referred to as **fixed assets** in that they are used up over a number of years rather than in one operating cycle of the organization. The process of generating capital investment alternatives, comparing and evaluating them, and selecting the best investment proposals is known as **capital budgeting**. Although the acquisition of equipment is only one type of capital investment alternative among many in the capital budgeting decision, it is one that the operations manager is very concerned with.

All too often, production and operations managers send new equipment requests to the controller, vice president of finance, or to the corporate capital budgeting committee. Whatever the appropriate channel through the organization, those proposals with the strongest justification are the ones most likely to be approved. The subjects discussed in this chapter constitute a minimum body of knowledge for the operations manager to prepare and present financially sound capital budgeting requests. In the next section we discuss a capital investment approach known as **life cycle costing**

10.1 LIFE CYCLE COSTING

Life cycle costing now favored over "low bid."

While it is found less often in capital procurement procedures of private organizations than it is in state and local governments and in not-for-profit organizations, the "low bid" decision rule is still widely utilized. The **low bid** rule states simply that the vendor submitting the bid with the lowest initial purchase price is awarded the order. The federal government, through the Department of Defense and other organizations (such as the Logistics Management Institute) is now, however, encouraging the use of life cycle costing (LCC) instead.

LCC considers the lifetime cost.

Kaufman [3] describes LCC as "the total cost of ownership of a system during its operational life." LCC includes the initial purchase price of a piece of equipment but also includes implementation, support, maintenance, operation, and training costs resulting from the acquisition of the equipment. It is thus particularly relevant to operations management. To determine the LCC of various alternative capital investments every conceivable cost must be identified and measured.

The notion of life cycle costing is of extreme importance to the operations manager. Very often in large corporate settings, capital budgeting decisions are relegated to financial analysts and planners who have a less-than-adequate understanding of many aspects of the operations function. A capital expenditure project that appears to be very sound on a financial basis may prove to be completely unworthy when such intangibles as ease of operations and maintenance, local parts inventory availability for repair of breakdowns, setup time, operation speed, and quality of the product are all considered.

While, in practice, some of the following steps (from Reference 3) might be condensed, there are essentially seven steps in the formulation of the LCC for a given piece of equipment.

1. Establish the operating profile.
2. Establish utilization factors.
3. Identify all cost factors.
4. Calculate all costs at current prices.
5. Escalate current labor and material costs.
6. Discount all costs to a base period.
7. Sum up all discounted and undiscounted costs.

Same operating profile used.

The *operating profile* describes, in calendar form, the planned timing of equipment operations. At any given time, the equipment can be either operating or not operating. It can be in a start-up mode, in steady state, or in overhaul. The important consideration is that each machine being evaluated should be considered with the same **operating profile** except for those elements not planned by management but dictated by the equipment itself (e.g., preventive maintenance, expected breakdown rate).

The **utilization factor** varies with operating profile. During an operating mode a machine may run 75 percent of the time and be stopped for loading and unloading 25 percent of the time. For setup, the machine may be utilized 20 percent of the time and stopped 80 percent of the time.

Lifetime costs identified and inflated or deflated.

Next, all costs are identified and estimated at current prices. Since costs are unlikely to decrease for any of the cost elements, estimates should be made of the costs over the operating life of the equipment. Various multipliers such as specific industry price inflators might be used here.

Smoky Flats Electric Company

To illustrate these first five steps, consider the case of the Smoky Flats Electric Company which is considering the installation of a new generator system. Two contractors have made proposals on the new system based upon the prescribed operating profile. The profile calls for continuous operation with twice annual 24-hour preventive maintenance sessions. The equipment has to be able to produce peak power at twice the rate of the called for average daily output. These peaks are expected to occur during the high use service months and especially during the early afternoon hours. When the equipment is "down" for maintenance it is totally nonproductive.

The cost factors involved are

1. Initial purchase.
2. Coal consumption.
3. Labor requirements.
4. Semiannual maintenance costs.

For systems A and B these costs are estimated as follows (on an annual basis):

	A	B
Initial purchase	$165,000	$200,000
Coal consumption	30,000	26,000
Labor cost	18,500	20,100
Maintenance cost	14,000	6,500

The life of each system is estimated to be 8 years and coal cost is estimated to increase at the rate of 8 percent per year. Labor cost is expected to increase at the rate of 10 percent per year and maintenance cost is estimated to grow at 5 percent per year.

Based upon this information, Table 10.1 and 10.2 present the total life cycle costs of these two systems.

The time value of money recognized.

The last two steps are based upon the concept of the time/value of money. A banker, for example, is willing to pay interest to you for money deposited in your savings account. A dollar today is worth more than a dollar next year, because (1) it can be invested today to earn a profit or return, and (2) it inflates. Therefore, dollars of cost paid out in the future are less valuable dollars than current dollars. We *discount* future dollars to present terms using the appropriate **discount rate**. This discounting process results in the **present value** of the total costs. The initial purchase price (or the initial payment) is in current dollars and is, therefore, not discounted. But all future costs are discounted to the current period using the discount rate.

TABLE 10.1 LIFE CYCLE COSTS FOR SYSTEM A

	Coal	Labor	Maintenance	Total
Initial purchase cost				$165,000
Year 1	$30,000	$18,500	$14,000	62,500
2	32,400	20,350	14,700	67,450
3	34,992	22,385	15,435	72,812
4	37,791	24,623	16,206	78,620
5	40,814	27,085	17,017	84,916
6	44,079	29,794	17,868	91,740
7	47,606	32,773	18,761	99,140
8	51,414	36,051	19,699	107,164

TABLE 10.2 LIFE CYCLE COSTS FOR SYSTEM B

	Coal	Labor	Maintenance	Total
Initial purchase cost				$200,000
Year 1	$26,000	$20,100	$ 6,500	52,600
2	28,080	22,110	6,825	57,015
3	30,326	24,321	7,166	61,813
4	32,752	26,753	7,524	67,029
5	35,372	29,428	7,900	72,700
6	38,202	32,371	8,295	78,868
7	41,258	35,608	8,710	85,576
8	44,559	39,169	9,146	92,874

What discount rate?

The discount rate is usually determined judgmentally. Factors entering into the decision of the appropriate discount rate are industry rate of return estimates, inflation rates, cost of debt and equity money to the company, and the degree of risk in the investment.

Purchase price only 20–60 percent of total.

Clearly, this procedure is more complicated than simply determining the lowest bid and awarding contracts on that basis. But as Kaufman points out, the costs beyond the initial purchase price are often much more important to the determination of LCC. In fact, for most industrial equipment, purchase price is normally between 20–60 percent of LCC [3]. In order that the equipment selected be the least costly, in a "real" sense, a method that considers the costs of an investment over its total life should thus be employed rather than the "lowest bid" method.

We will return to the subject of present value as introduced and described above later, but first we will consider a less complicated decision rule called "payback" which has historically been used in operations management for capital investment selection decisions.

10.2 THE PAYBACK METHOD

Payback: years to recover cost.

Because of its simplicity, the **payback** method of investment selection has for many years been the most popular method of analyzing alternative investment possibilities. Simply put, the method computes the number of years required to recover the cost of the investment, either through increased revenues or decreased costs (savings) or a combination of the two. A company using the payback method will usually have determined a standard minimum payback period (e.g., three years) and all investment proposals will be compared against this standard. Proposals with payback periods in excess of the standard are typically rejected, or at least are subjected to more study before adoption.

The operations manager can use this simple investment evaluation technique to "self-critique" his or her own proposals for new equipment. Payback provides a quick check on the financial reasonableness of an investment. For an operations manager to argue for the purchase of a new machine because it "reduces variable costs by 80 percent" is not sensible if the payback is 10 years and company policy is a 4 year maximum.

The Salt and Shotgun Mining Company

This company uses a payback standard of three years. Two equipment proposals, A and B, are being considered by Salt and Shotgun's management. Their net cash savings and their initial costs are shown in Table 10.3. Machine A has a payback period of 2⅓ years ($400,000 in two years + $100,000 in the first third of the third year) while machine B has a payback period of 3¼ years ($180,000 in three years + $20,000 in the first quarter of the fourth year). Based on this simple analysis, investment A is the only acceptable alternative (i.e., less than a three year payback).

Two problems with payback.

But, as a wise philosopher once said, "There are no simple solutions to complex problems, only simple-minded solutions." Payback, while simple, suffers from two very real limitations. First, the method does not recognize timing of the repayment. Second, the method does not recognize differences in the total return from a project. Consider the following two examples, depicted in Tables 10.4 and 10.5.

Ignores timing of returns.

In Table 10.4 both projects have a payback period of four years and, therefore, the method indicates that the organization should be indifferent between the two alternatives. Clearly, alternative B generates the return much more rapidly than A, and, because of the time value of money, should therefore be preferred.

Ignores returns beyond horizon.

In Table 10.5 both projects have two-year payback periods. But again, a rational investor would not be indifferent as the decision rule indicates that she or he should, because project B returns $15,000 more than project A over its total life.

Net present value is better.

Both of these flaws in the logic of the payback method are the result of little or no consideration of time. Returns *past the payback year* and the *timing of returns* are not properly considered. However, the *net present value* method overcomes these two shortcomings of the payback method.

TABLE 10.3 CASH FLOWS FOR TWO INVESTMENTS

	Equipment Proposals	
	A	B
Initial investment	$500,000	$200,000
Savings,[a] year 1:	$150,000	50,000
Savings, year 2:	250,000	60,000
Savings, year 3:	300,000	70,000
Savings, year 4:	200,000	80,000
Savings, year 5:	200,000	90,000

[a] Savings are due to decreased labor.

TABLE 10.4 SAME PAYBACK, B PREFERRED FOR RATE

	A	B
Initial investment	$100,000	$100,000
Return, year 1:	25,000	75,000
Return, year 2:	25,000	10,000
Return, year 3:	25,000	10,000
Return, year 4:	25,000	5,000

10.3 THE NET PRESENT VALUE (NPV) METHOD

As we discussed earlier in our presentation of the life cycle costing concept, costs and returns over the life of a system's operation should be discounted to their present values using an appropriate discount rate. We discount future costs and returns because future dollars are of less value to us than present dollars.

To illustrate, consider the investment of $1 today at an interest or inflation rate of 10 percent. The amount, A_1, at the end of one year is

$$A_1 = 1 + 0.1(1) = \$1.10$$

or, if we let A_0 equal the amount of the initial investment and i equal the interest rate, then

$$A_1 = A_0 + iA_0$$

or

$$A_1 = A_0(1 + i)$$

The amount at the end of the second year is A_2.

$$\begin{aligned} A_2 &= A_1 + iA_1 \\ &= (1 + i)A_1 \end{aligned}$$

TABLE 10.5 SAME PAYBACK, B PREFERRED FOR AMOUNT

	A	B
Initial investment	$ 50,000	$ 50,000
Return, year 1:	30,000	30,000
Return, year 2:	20,000	20,000
Return, year 3:	10,000	10,000
Return, year 4:	0	5,000
Return, year 5:	0	5,000
Return, year 6:	0	5,000

But $A_1 = A_0(1+i)$. Therefore

$$\begin{aligned} A_2 &= (1+i)[A_0(1+i)] \\ &= A_0(1+i)^2 \\ &= 1(1.1)^2 \\ &= \$1.21 \end{aligned}$$

In general, the *amount* A_n at the end of n periods is

$$A_n = A_0(1+i)^n \tag{10.1}$$

From this example we see that receiving $1.21 at the end of two years is only worth $1.00 now (presuming an interest or an inflation rate of 10 percent), because that $1.00 invested today would grow to equal $1.21 by the end of two years.

In order to discount each annual cost or revenue back to its present value in current dollars we simply solve Equation 10.1 above for A_0, the present value of the amount A_n.

$$\begin{aligned} A_0 &= \frac{A_n}{(1+i)^n} \\ &= A_n\left(\frac{1}{(1+i)^n}\right) \end{aligned} \tag{10.2}$$

The discount factor.

The term $1/(1+i)^n$ is called the "discount factor." To demonstrate, $1.00 received three years from now with an available interest rate of 5 percent is worth only

$$A_0 = \frac{1}{(1.05)^3} = \$0.86$$

in current dollars.

Rigid Box, Inc.

Rigid Box is considering the purchase of a new carton folding machine which would save $10,000 per year for five years in labor costs. The machine costs $35,000 to be paid as follows.

$20,000 at time of purchase.

$10,000 at end of first year.

$ 5,000 at end of second year.

If the company requires a 5 percent return on new equipment purchases, what is the net present value of this investment? Data for this problem is presented in Table 10.6.

Positive versus negative NPV.

The NPV for the Rigid Box Company problem is $9234.82, which is computed as the *sum* of the discounted net cash flows over the five-year useful life of the machine. Having a *positive* NPV means that the actual return on the investment is greater than the 5 percent return required by the company.

The present value of an annuity.

The computations become quite cumbersome for projects with longer lives. If the future cash flows are equal amounts, the flows can be considered to be an **annuity**

TABLE 10.6 FOLDING MACHINE CASH FLOWS

(1) Year	(2) Cash Outflow	(3) Cash Inflow	(4) Net Cash Flow	(5) Discount Factor	(6) Discounted Cash Flow (4 × 5)
0	$20,000	0	−$20,000	$1/(1 + 0.05)^0$	−$20,000.00
1	10,000	10,000	0	$1/(1 + 0.05)^1$	0
2	5,000	10,000	5,000	$1/(1 + 0.05)^2$	4,535.15
3	0	10,000	10,000	$1/(1 + 0.05)^3$	8,638.38
4	0	10,000	10,000	$1/(1 + 0.05)^4$	8,226.03
5	0	10,000	10,000	$1/(1 + 0.05)^5$	7,835.26
					$ 9,234.82

and the determination of the present value simplifies to calculating just the the following equation.

$$A_0 = A\left(\frac{1 - \dfrac{1}{(1+i)^n}}{i}\right) \tag{10.3}$$

where A is the equal cash flows each year. Rather than computing the discount factor for each of the n years, one discount factor (the term in parentheses in the above equation) is computed.

For example, the net present value at 10 percent of a project which saves $3000 per year for four years and costs $10,000 initially is computed as −$10,000 plus

$$\begin{aligned} A_0 &= 3000\left(\frac{1 - \dfrac{1}{(1+0.10)^4}}{0.10}\right) \\ &= 3000\left(\frac{1 - 0.683}{0.10}\right) \\ &= 3000\left(\frac{0.317}{0.10}\right) \\ &= 3000(3.17) \\ &= \$9510 \end{aligned}$$

or

$$-\$10{,}000 + 9510 = -\$490$$

This project does not earn the required 10 percent return.

10.4 PRESENT VALUE TABLES

Appendix tables for present values.

To even further simplify the computations of present values, two tables are available. Table A1 in the appendix is called the "present value of $1" table. To use it we simply read the discount factor in the body of the table corresponding to an interest rate of i and number of years n and multiply this factor times the cash flow in the nth year. For example, \$10 received in year 4 at 10 percent interest is worth $10 \times 0.683 = \$6.83$.

Table A2 in the appendix is the "present value of an annuity of \$1" table. From it we read the discount factor for an interest rate of i and annuity life of n.

For example, to compute the present value of a \$100 annuity for 10 years at an 8 percent interest rate we find the discount factor 6.71 corresponding to the 10 year row and 8 percent column of Table A2 and multiply the factor times the amount of the annuity, \$100.

$$A_0 = 6.71 \times 100 = \$671$$

Return to Smoky Flats

If the Smoky Flats Electric Company uses an 8 percent discount rate for new investment projects, which of the previously analyzed systems should be selected on a life cycle costing basis? The discount factors to be used can be found in Table A1 under the 8 percent column heading. They are

Year	Discount Factor
1	0.926
2	0.857
3	0.794
4	0.735
5	0.681
6	0.630
7	0.583
8	0.540

Applying these factors to the two project cost flows yields the following present values for systems A and B.

System A \$627,569

System B \$595,153

Since System B has the lowest life cycle cost, it should be selected by Smoky Flats. Notice that system A has the lowest initial cost and, according to the "low bid" rule, would have been selected.

10.5 DEPRECIATION AND TAXES

For the most part, the major expenditures requested by the operations manager will be for capital assets. These assets cannot be expensed in the year required, but must be **depreciated** over their useful lives. This depreciation simply reflects the "using up" of the asset and matches the cost of this use with the revenue-generating, or productive, capability of the asset. The operations manager must recognize that this depreciation, while being a bonafide expense and deductible for income taxation purposes, does not result in any out-of-pocket cash flow. Understanding the effect on cash flows of depreciation and taxes will aid significantly in the preparation of capital budgeting requests and will often produce a stronger argument for the operations manager.

Effect of taxes.

In our previous examples of net present value we ignored the very real consequences of taxes and tax deductible expenses such as depreciation. For example, if a corporation paying taxes at the rate of 50 percent of net income were to increase net income by \$100,000 per year, the cash benefit would be only \$50,000 since 50 percent of the additional earnings would be paid out in income taxes. Since only the actual net cash flows are relevant to a capital budgeting decision, the role of income taxes must be considered.

Effect of depreciation.

Also, since certain expenses do not result in an actual cash outflow, the tax savings generated are also important to the investment decision. Depreciation on capital items, including equipment and buildings, is a major noncash expense, which results in a reduction in tax payments for a business. Depreciation expense is simply the accounting allocation of the initial cost of an asset over its useful life. It does not result in actual cash outflows, yet it is a deductible expense for the purposes of computing taxable income.

Three depreciation methods.

There are three major depreciation methods: **straight-line, sum-of-year's-digits** and **double-declining balance**

Straight-Line

Under this depreciation method, cost is allocated equally to every year of the asset's life. The depreciation amount D, is computed as

$$D = \frac{A - S}{L} \tag{10.4}$$

where A is the initial asset cost and S is the salvage value at the end of its life, L years from now. For a \$20,000 asset with a 10-year life and \$5,000 salvage value, the annual depreciation is (\$20,000 − \$5,000)/10 = \$1500 per year. This type of depreciation schedule is appropriate to an asset which is used up equally over its lifetime.

Sum-of-Year's-Digits

This approach is appropriate when the asset loses more value in the early years of its lifetime. The annual depreciation charge is

$$D = \frac{Y}{T}(A - S) \tag{10.5}$$

where Y is the number of years of remaining useful life in the asset, and T is the sum of all the Y values from L to 1. For the example used above, T would be $10 + 9 + 8 + 7 + 6 + 5 + 4 + 3 + 2 + 1 = 55$ and the first year's depreciation would be

$$\frac{10}{55}(\$20{,}000 - \$5{,}000) = \$2727$$

whereas the second year's depreciation would be

$$\frac{9}{55}(\$20{,}000 - \$5{,}000) = \$2454$$

and the last year's depreciation would be

$$\frac{1}{55}(\$20{,}000 - \$5{,}000) = \$272.73$$

Double-Declining Balance

This approach also writes off more value in the early years but has a built-in salvage value factor and hence does not specifically include salvage in the annual depreciation formula.

$$D = \left(\frac{2}{L}\right) V \tag{10.6}$$

where V is the remaining value of the asset. Again using the example data above, the first year's depreciation would be

$$\left(\frac{2}{10}\right)(\$20{,}000 - 0) = \$4000$$

and the second year's depreciation expense would be

$$\left(\frac{2}{10}\right)(\$20{,}000 - \$4000) = \$3200.$$

Figure 10.1 indicates the relationship between the three depreciation methods for the example above. The figure illustrates the early write-off advantage (in year 7) of the double-declining balance method. Next we will consider a brief taxation-depreciation example.

Abacus Computer Services (ACS)

ACS is considering the purchase of a computer system which has an initial cost of \$120,000 and a useful life of five years (no salvage value). Abacus' tax rate is 50 percent and they plan to depreciate the system using the straight-line method. The asset is assumed to have no salvage value at the end of its five-year life. The machine is expected to produce a net income before depreciation and taxes of \$35,000 per year and Abacus uses a 7 percent interest rate on all investment proposals. Cash flows for each year are given in Table 10.7.

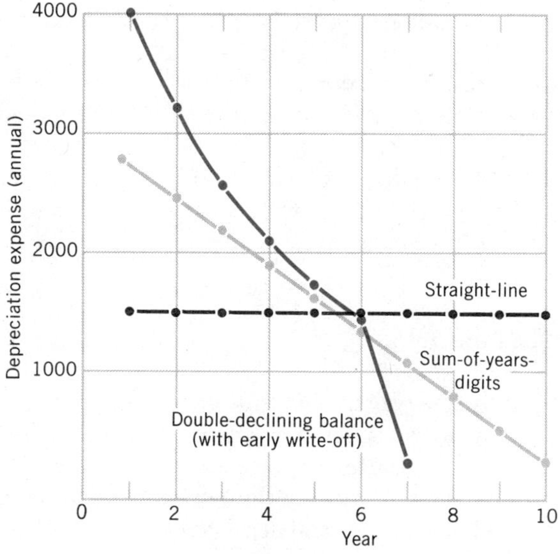

Figure 10.1 Comparison of depreciation methods—simple five-year project.

Calculations for the first year are as follows.

Net income before depreciation and taxes	$35,000
Less: depreciation expense*	24,000
Net income before taxes	11,000
Less: taxes (50 percent)	5,500
Net income after taxes	5,500
Plus: depreciation expense	24,000
Cash inflow	$29,500

* Computed as ($120,000)/5 = $24,000

TABLE 10.7 NET PRESENT VALUE OF ABACUS' COMPUTER INVESTMENT

(1) Year	(2) Cash Inflow	(3) Cash Outflow	(4) Net Cash Flow	(5) Discount Factor	(6) Discounted Cash Flow
0	0	$120,000	−$120,000	1	−$120,000
1	$29,500	0	29,500		
2	29,500	0	29,500		
3	29,500	0	29,500	4.1[a]	120,950
4	29,500	0	29,500		
5	29,500	0	29,500		
				Net present value	$ 950

[a] Since all cash inflows are equal amounts, we use the present value of an annuity discount factor (Table A2).

Depreciation is added back for cash flow.

Note that the depreciation expense is "added back" in our calculations. The reason for this is that depreciation is deductible as an expense for taxation purposes, but actually does not result in an outflow of cash. The general rule for cash flow calculations is to begin with accounting income after taxes and add back all "noncash" expenses.

Since the present value is positive ($950), the project meets (even though just barely) the company's 7 percent return policy and, therefore, should be adopted, presuming other more profitable investments are not available.

10.6 LEASE VERSUS PURCHASE

Lease, lessee, leasing, lessor.

Purchasing is only one way of obtaining capital equipment. Another alternative is leasing. Leasing involves a series of payments made by the **lessee** (the party acquiring use of the equipment) to the **lessor** (the party who owns the leased equipment) for the *use* of the equipment rather than for the *ownership* of the equipment.

There are both advantages and disadvantages to capital equipment leasing. The advantages include

1. Low initial investment by lessee allows liquidity to be maintained.
2. Reduced risk of owning obsolete equipment, or equipment with too little or too much capacity.
3. Reduced commitment to equipment/test period before purchasing.
4. Lease rentals are expenses for income tax purposes.

The disadvantages include

1. The total lease cost is likely to be higher than the total purchase cost.
2. There are usually restrictions imposed on the use of the equipment by the lessor.

The operations manager should recognize that leasing is a very reasonable alternative, particularly when company cash flows are tight or when technology advances are progressing quickly. The computer operations manager has recognized this fact for a number of years. In less than 20 years the data processing world has seen four computer generations arrive. The manager who owned his or her own equipment was committed to a long-term use of the hardware. Once a new generation was announced, preceding generations became virtually worthless.

Owning equipment that has a high risk of becoming obsolete can jeopardize the operations productivity of a firm. A competitor who leases and can take advantage of the newly available technology will have a competitive advantage over the firm that owns obsolete machinery. The operations manager must recognize the tradeoff inherent here. For the reduction in risk of obsolescence, the firm must typically pay a premium price for the use of the equipment.

Abacus Computer Services (Continued)

Consider again the Abacus Computer Services problem of the last section. Suppose that the computer manufacturer has just initiated a lease plan that will allow General to lease the same computer that it has been considering for purchase at a lease rate of $30,000 per year, payable at the end of each year. However, to obtain this rate ACS must provide its own maintenance and servicing. Table 10.8 presents the lease data for this problem; the calculations for year 1 are shown below.

Net income before lease payment and taxes	$35,000
Less: lease payment	30,000
Net income before taxes	5,000
Less: taxes (50 percent)	2,500
Net income after taxes (net cash flow)	$ 2,500

Clearly, in this example, leasing is the better alternative. The NPV of the lease is $10,250 compared to only $950 for the outright purchase of the machine.

10.7 INVESTMENT FOR CAPACITY

Problems of too little, and too much, capacity

Breakeven for equipment comparison.

Operations managers must always consider capacity requirements when contemplating the acquisition of new equipment. Both too much and too little capacity present problems for operations. Purchasing more capacity than is necessary results in idle time, poor utilization of equipment, and, possibly, operational inefficiencies, all of which are real costs to the organization. Too little capacity can mean lost revenues, lost customer goodwill, increases in overtime, and production scheduling problems. Again, the costs to the organization are tangible and must be considered prior to any capital investment decision. The breakeven model for comparing cost alternatives (presented in Chapter 5) can be used to compare the costs of various pieces of equipment with different capacities, as illustrated below.

TABLE 10.8 NET PRESENT VALUE OF ABACUS' LEASE ALTERNATIVE

Year	Net Cash Flow	Discount Factor	Discounted Cash Flow
0			
1	$2,500		
2	2,500		
3	2,500	4.1	$10,250
4	2,500		
5	2,500		
		Net present value	$10,250

Cutter Machining Co.

Cutter Machining Company is looking for equipment to do precision machining on a new part. Machine A is a large capacity, high speed horizontal milling machine, which will produce the required parts at a variable cost of $3.00 per unit. The annual fixed cost for machine A is $30,000. Machine B is a smaller capacity machine, which can produce the required parts at a cost of $5 each and has annual fixed costs of only $14,000. Plotting production volume on the horizontal axis and cost on the vertical axis results in the cost-volume chart shown in Figure 10.2.

As can be seen, the total cost of operation for machine A is greater than that for machine B for annual production volumes less than 8000 units. Beyond 8000 units machine A is the least costly alternative. Based upon the annual demand forecast, management can now select the most appropriate machine; that is, the one with the lowest total cost for the estimated annual volume. Even though machine A can produce the required parts for 40 percent less than machine B, production must be quite high before machine A becomes the optimal alternative. Fixed costs add significantly to the total cost of operations, yet too often operations managers are attracted to investments solely on the basis of low *variable* costs. And often, it is after production has begun that they realize that their volume is not sufficient to reap these low variable cost rewards.

10.8 SUMMARY

The topic of facility acquisition is of major importance to operations management because it commits the organization to a specific transformation process over the

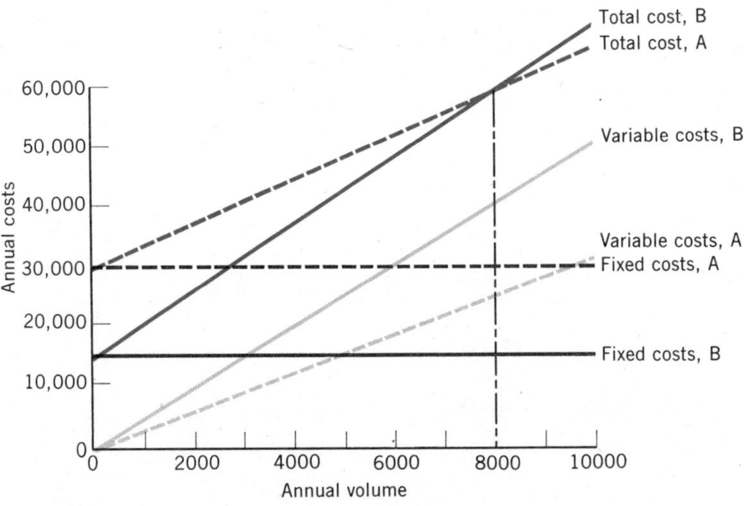

Figure 10.2. Cost-volume graph for machines A and B.

long term. The acquisition of productive facilities, plant and equipment, is a major part of the capital budgeting process. Life cycle costing, which relies heavily on present value concepts of lifetime costs, is an important new approach for capital budgeting.

Other financial concerns of importance to operations managers are the effects of depreciation and taxation on the acquisition of capital assets, and on the value of leasing compared to ownership of the assets.

The cost-comparison-of-alternatives form of the breakeven model is useful in facility acquisition for comparing capacity-investment tradeoffs to identify the most appropriate investment for organizations.

10.9 READINGS

Cautious Companies

Firms Like Monsanto Give Capital Projects Tough Second Looks

Executives Sharpen Methods Of Picking Outlay Plans, Hold Up Many Proposals

Putting Stress on the Future

BY DAVID P. GARINO
Staff Reporter of The Wall Street Journal

ST. LOUIS—Two years ago, Monsanto Co. confidently laid plans for a major increase in capital spending.

The plans called for spending to jump nearly 70% from 1974 to a record $525 million in 1975, to $600 million in 1976 and to more than $650 million in 1977. Projections for 1975 and 1976 proved accurate. But 1977 is a different story; the big chemical company recently shelved several major projects, and 1977 spending plans have been slashed to a range of $500 million to $525 million.

. . .

For the time being, at least, a hard second look is being taken at spending relating to textiles, a new plastic bottle and foreign investments. Monsanto also has decided to concentrate only on markets in which it can be a meaningful factor; accordingly, in recent years it has eliminated several marginally profitable operations with small market shares.

In short, what's happening at Monsanto, and at many other companies, is that management apparently is becoming more sophisticated about allocating capital resources and more concerned than ever about return on investment.

Laying capital-spending plans is inherently difficult work. It takes two or three years for a plant, once approved, to come on stream. "You're betting your money on a market that mightn't be there two or three years from now," a Monsanto executive explains.

LONG-TERM PLANS

So rather than merely reacting to immediate problems in specific markets, Monsanto recently has been emphasizing forecasts of the long-term potential of a product line. Thus, even if a market is currently soft, the company may expand its capacity to manufacture a product with a bright future. "We try to make our decisions without being affected unduly by present economic conditions," says H. James Lawler, director of corporate planning.

This, too, is difficult. "It's obvious that you're more inclined to spend when things are good, and vice versa," Mr. Lawler says. In fact, Monsanto executives think the recession taught businessmen in many industries a lesson. "In 1973 and 1974, there were shortages all around and some companies were coining profits," Mr. Kerley says. "Managers aged 40 and under had never seen anything but up, up and away." But that "euphoria has worn off," he adds. On the other hand, when the economy is weak, Mr. Lawler says, "we don't want to tell someone with a good project to go away."

Monsanto also is putting much emphasis on avoiding the "sawtooth effect" evident in its capital spending several years ago. The chemical industry had expanded rapidly in the late 1960s with little concern about demand two or three years out; when, of course, the plants began production. The results were oversupply, price-cutting and slumping profits. After Monsanto's earnings plunged in 1970, its capital expenditures fell to $205 million in 1971, $168 million in 1972 and $205 million in 1973 and didn't even reach the level of depreciation.

Then, when demand surged in 1973 and 1974, Monsanto and other chemical companies lacked adequate production capacity. The results were shortages and lost profits. To a large extent, Monsanto's 1974-76 expenditures reflected a catch-up on capacity that should have been built earlier.

NEW SYSTEM

To avoid a repetition of this ragged performance, Monsanto now periodically reviews capital-spending proposals to ensure, among other things, that markets haven't deteriorated or that some other problem hasn't arisen.

Moreover, projects are initiated with greater care than in the past.

. . .

PRESSING AHEAD

Still, Monsanto is going ahead with projects when current economic conditions aren't favorable. For instance, money is being spent on large, acrylonitrile expansions at Texas City, Texas, and in Britain, even though demand has softened. Besides using acrylonitrile in several of its products, Monsanto peddles it on the open market. Says one official, "This expansion will make us the world's largest maker of acrylonitrile. Whether we can sell it will tell us if we made the right choice."

Moreover, the company is looking actively for ways to spend money, most notably for crop-protection chemicals. "We have a good technical base and demand for food and protein will be a sharply growing market world-wide," Mr. Kerley says. Monsanto actually is building excess capacity to avoid shortages such as those in the early 1970s. Monsanto's eagerness in this area isn't hard to understand. Last year Monsanto Agricultural Products Co. accounted for only 15% of corporate sales but contributed nearly 50% of operating earnings.

James H. Senger, general manager, technical devision, of the agricultural products unit, observes, "Implicit in our planning is that no operating unit has a fixed capital budget. We don't say. You have X millions of dollars to spend and don't come back for more. Each project must stand on its own."

Also stressing that "each new dollar spent must bring in a satisfactory rate of return," Mr. Kerley adds that the company's earlier projection of $3 billion in capital spending for 1976-80 "is still reasonable, but I won't say that the make-up won't change."

Source. Reprinted by permission of *The Wall Street Journal*,

10.10 KEY TERMS

capital budgeting (p. 360)
fixed asset (p. 360)
capital assets (p. 360)
life cycle costing (p. 360)
low bid (p. 360)
operating profile (p.361)
utilization factor (p. 361)
discount rate (p. 362)
present value (p. 362)
payback (p. 363)
annuity (p. 366)
depreciation (p. 368)
straight-line (p. 369)
sum-of-year's digits (p. 369)
double-declining balance (p. 369)
lessee (p. 372)
lessor (p. 372)

10.11 REVIEW TEST

1. Fixed assets are those that are seen as fixed, long-term costs. (p. 360)
   a. True b. False
2. Life cycle costing is preferable to low bid because it considers the costs over the asset's lifetime. (p. 360)
   a. True b. False
3. One discount factor that can be used is an organization's current cost of capital. (p. 363)
   a. True b. False
4. In spite of its faults the payback method has been popular because of its simplicity. (p. 363)
   a. True b. False
5. An annuity is appropriate only when payments are made annually. (p. 366)
   a. True b. False
6. Straight-line depreciation is higher in the later years than sum-of-year's-digits. (p. 370)
   a. True b. False
7. An advantage of leasing is the lower risk of investing in the wrong assets. (p. 372)
   a. True b. False
8. Managers are often lured into an asset investment by low variable costs and neglect the high fixed costs. (p. 374)
   a. True b. False

10.12 DISCUSSION QUESTIONS

1. What are other types of capital investments besides capital assets?
2. Enumerate the reasons LCC is preferred to "low bid."
3. What is the difference between the discount factor and the interest rate?
4. What other methods besides payback and NPV exist for comparing investments?
5. Why does depreciation reduce taxes even though it is a noncash expense?
6. How does double-declining balance automatically handle salvage value and how is it eventually terminated?
7. What are other advantages and disadvantages of leasing?
8. Why would otherwise rational managers tend to err on the side of low variable cost equipment?
9. How does the energy crisis affect facilities investment when an organization is highly mechanized?
10. Should other bidding companies be allowed to file suit against low bidders on government contracts to prove they can perform within bid and not cause a loss to taxpayers?

10.13 PROBLEMS

1. Standard Tool and Die, Inc. is considering the purchase of a minicomputer to maintain its accounts receivable records and to send out monthly statements. Standard is currently using a local computer service bureau for this service. The service bureau charges a flat monthly fee of $80 plus $0.10 per transaction posted to the accounts receivable file. The monthly cost of the minicomputer and the programs necessary to operate it will be $200, but the cost per posted transaction will be only $0.03 since Standard can hire a part-time key punch operator at this rate. If standard anticipates a monthly volume of transactions of 1500, should they continue with the computer service or purchase the mini? What minimum volume of transactions is required to warrant the minicomputer purchase?

2. Doyle Mining Co. is about to replace several coal trucks. They have received two proposals from truck distributors. The first proposal is for the purchase of a truck with an annual hauling value of 300,000 ton miles. The truck has a price of $100,000 and a salvage value at the end of its three-year life of $10,000. Annual operating costs are expected to be $0.10 per ton mile and revenues are forecast to be $0.80 per ton mile. The second proposal is for an identical truck, but for a three-year lease instead of a purchase. The lease payments are $30,000 at the beginning of each of the three years and a final payment of $35,000 at the end of year 3. With this final payment, deed to the truck is passed to Doyle. Doyle can borrow from the local bank at a 10 percent interest rate.

a. Ignoring taxes, which proposal should be accepted?

b. Presuming that the $30,000 lease payments are tax deductible and that $25,000 of the final payment is deductible for tax purposes, which proposal is the best? Doyle is in the 50 percent bracket, uses straight line depreciation, and has other income to offset any losses.

3. Hiway Motel is deliberating about enclosing their outdoor swimming pool so that it can be used year around. Hiway's manager believes that with this change annual revenues would increase by $18,000 while pool operating expenses would rise by only $3500. The enclosure is expected to cost $30,000 and has a 10-year life. If another of Hiway's investment opportunities promises to return 12 percent, should the pool cover be constructed? What is the payback period for this investment?

4. Crittenden County operates eight swimming pools, each of which is due to have the filtration system replaced. There are two filter systems which will work on these pools. Their characteristics are listed below.

		Filter Systems	
		1	2
Characteristics	Initial purchase price	$3000	$1800
	Chemicals used ($)	$ 350	$ 500
	Annual cleanings required	2	3
	Cost per cleaning	$ 120	$ 90
	Useful life	5 yr	3 yr

Two county councilmen are debating over the merits of the two filtration systems. Jones argues that cost per cleaning is higher for 1 than for 2 and also that its purchase price is higher. Smith contends that 2's life is shorter and that the chemicals used are greater, as is the "total" cleaning cost. The mayor states that he will settle this argument by invoking an age old rule—the minimum bid gets the business. How would you advise the county council regarding this problem? What role does life cycle costing play in this analysis?

5. Rat Trap Homes, Inc., has just purchased a new bulldozer for use in excavating basements for new homes. The purchase price of the dozer was $37,000. Delivery and initial setup and adjustment by a factory service man costs an additional $2200. The expected life of the dozer is eight years, and it is anticipated that its salvage value will be $5000 at that time. Compute the depreciation using

a. Straight-line.

b. Sum-of-year's-digits.

c. Double-declining balance.

What is the difference in tax advantage between the straight-line and the double-declining balance depreciation for the first year if Rat Trap is in the 48 percent tax bracket?

6. Two molding sanders are available to The Wooden Tree, a custom molding and trim manufacturer. Model 101 has fixed operating costs of $4500 per year and variable costs of production of $0.005 per linear foot of sanding. Model 201 has $6200 fixed costs each year but $0.0037 per linear foot of sanding. Doug Bush, the owner, has come up with the following estimates for annual sanding volume over the next 10 years.

Volume	Probability
200,000 linear ft	.2
400,000	.5
600,000	.3

Which machine is expected to produce the lowest annual cost?

10.14 CASE SAVEWAY FOODSTORES

John Grashoff, President of Saveway Foodstores, has recently returned from a supermarket industry convention during which he attended a presentation on computerized energy management. John knew that energy costs for motors, compressors, conveyers, lights, heating, air conditioning, and so forth, were quite high for his six stores, but he always looked upon this expense as simply being a cost of doing business. John returned from the seminar convinced that a computerized energy management system would be beneficial for his stores.

Upon his return, John invited a computer salesman to visit several of his locations and together they figured that the cost of installing an energy management system in each store would be $21,000 per store. They also estimated that energy consumption and peak loading charges could be reduced from 12 to 18 percent per month. The table below presents the average per store energy consumption costs for the last 12 months.

John estimates that energy costs will increase at an annual rate of 7½ percent over the next seven years. His required rate of return is 2 percentage points over the prime interest rate which is 12.5 percent. John will depreciate the assets over a seven year life using a straight-line depreciation method, and will also use seven years as the project life. His effective tax rate is 22 percent.

Month	Average Cost per Store
Mar	$4800
Apr	4100
May	3900
June	4100
July	4800
Aug	5300
Sept	4700
Oct	4100
Nov	4200
Dec	5100
Jan	5600
Feb	5400

QUESTIONS FOR DISCUSSION

1. How would you advise John regarding the installation of an energy management system in his stores?
2. What other factors would you consider, or what cautions would you give to John, before placing an order for six systems?

10.15 REFERENCES AND BIBLIOGRAPHY

1. Hamel, Henry C., *Leasing in Industry*, New York: National Industrial Conference Board, 1968.
2. Horngren, C. J., *Cost Accounting: A Managerial Emphasis*, 4th ed., Englewood Cliffs, N.J.: Prentice-Hall, 1977.
3. Kaufman, R. J., "Life Cycle Costing: Decision Making Tool for Capital Equipment Acquisitions," *Journal of Purchasing*, 5:16–31 (August 1969).
4. National Association of Purchasing Agents, Inc., *Leases versus Buying*, New York, 1963.
5. Weston, J. Fred, and Brigham, Eugene F., *Managerial Finance*, New York: Holt, 1972.

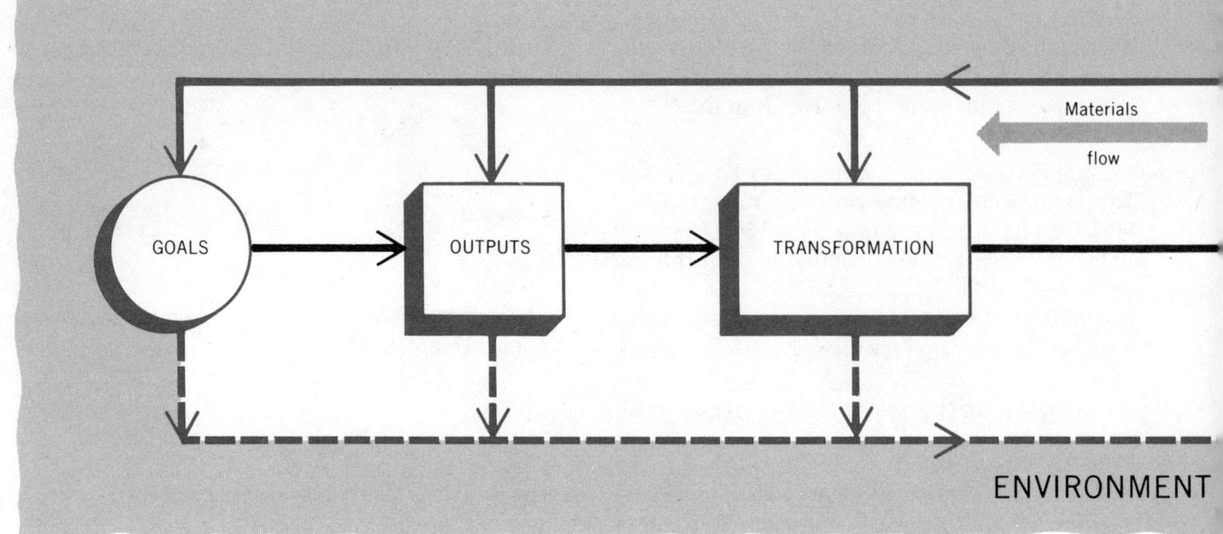

Chapter 11I

The Personnel Interface: Acquiring Staff

CONCEPTS

11.1 Manpower Planning
- Plans
- Current Resources
- Losses
- Forecast
- Actions

11.2 Job Evaluation

11.3 Recruitment, Selection, and Placement
- Recruitment
- Selection
- Placement

11.4 Compensation

11.5 Training and Development
- Training
- Development

11.6 Employee Evaluation, Termination
- Evaluation
- Termination

11.7 Summary

11.8 Key Terms

11I: Personnel

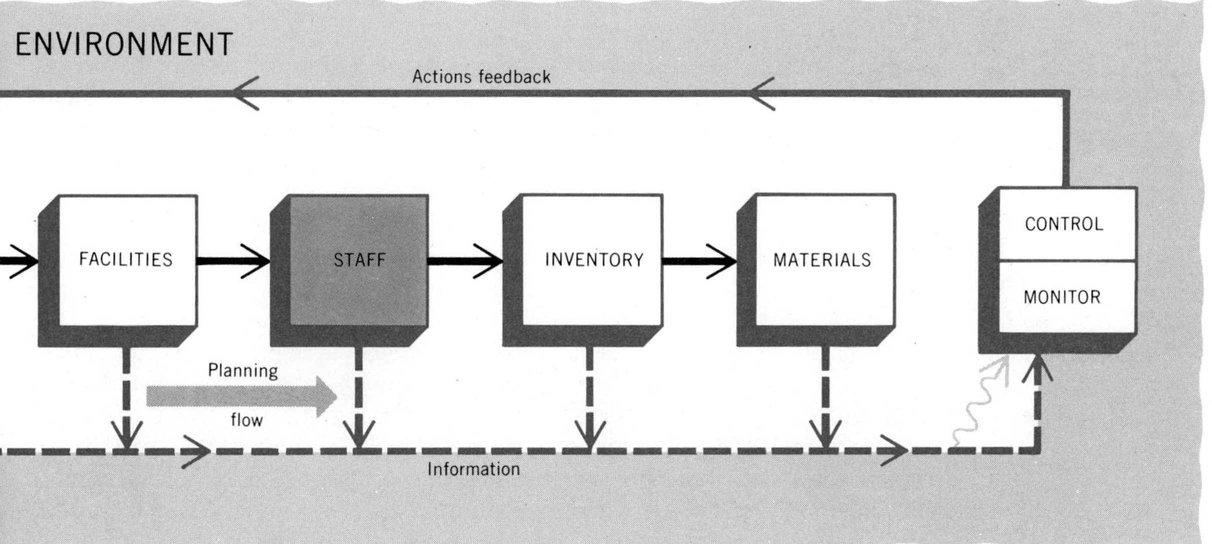

LEARNING OBJECTIVES

By the conclusion of this chapter the student should

1. Be aware of the importance of the various personnel functions to the proper management of the operations area.
2. Know how to develop a manpower plan and put it into action.
3. Be familiar with the standard methods of job evaluation and be able to develop wage rates for various job classifications.
4. Understand the techniques for recruiting, selecting, and placing applicants into jobs and know the organizational attractions for workers.
5. Comprehend the wide range of compensation and incentive plans in use in today's organizations.
6. Appreciate the importance of informal, as well as formal, training and development programs.
7. Understand the methods of evaluation and termination interviews and their value to the organization, as well as to the employee.

People are the key.

One of the major determinants of the success of the operations function in an organization is the quality of its human resources. These are the people who will plan, produce, and sell the organization's output and will determine its quality, cost, and rate of production. Without their cooperation and effort, no production, inventory, or quality system will operate the way it was intended. For example, General Electric and Westinghouse corporations were once the same size and had equal access to financing, similar product lines, and nearly identical physical assets. Now General Electric is more than twice the size of Westinghouse and at least one GE insider claims that human motivation was the major factor in GE's growth.

Personnel functions.

The primary function of the personnel department is to provide the appropriate personnel to staff the organization so that organizational goals can be met efficiently and effectively. While the personnel function in many organizations is often burdened with small matters of company operations such as administering the company cafeteria and vending machines or running the company picnic, there are several major functions included in personnel administration in general. The functions of particular importance to operations include: manpower planning, job evaluation, recruitment, selection, placement, compensation, training, development, employee evaluation, and, on occasion, termination.

11.1 MANPOWER PLANNING

Manpower planning objectives.

Simply put, the objective of **manpower planning** is to ensure that the organization has the correct *number* of people, with the appropriate *skills*, at the right *time* and in the proper *location*. Five steps are required in good manpower planning.

1. Analyze short and long range organizational plans.
2. Determine current manpower resources.
3. Determine probable losses.
4. Develop a short and long range manpower forecast.
5. Develop action plans to meet the forecast.

Plans

Manpower plans tied to organizational goals.

All plans are based upon organizational goals and specific organizational objectives. The short and long range production plans are based upon these underlying directions and, therefore, the manpower plan is "tied to" organizational goals through these plans. Manpower requirements are determined by the actions the organization expects to take in the future (e.g., new output mix, higher volume, better quality), and, if not achieved, can severely limit the organization's ability to act on higher level plans.

Importance of timing in training.

Meeting skill and timing requirements are critical and often elusive objectives of manpower planning. For example, a large regional fast-food chain is growing rapidly. Financing for expansion and profits are both good. A plan to open 50 new stores each year for the next three years must be severely altered because of poor manpower planning. Cooks and counter help are available, but store managers, who require six months training, and district and regional managers, requiring one to two years training, will not be available. The necessary backscheduling of manpower was not done and opening without adequate managerial skill is a sure route to failure. As seen, the production plan and the manpower plan are interdependent. The production plan must recognize the current manpower status for short range actions and the manpower planning system must react to new production plans or changes in them.

Current Resources

Human resource audit.

To paraphrase the Cheshire Cat, as mentioned earlier, "If you don't know where you are going, any path will get you there." Equally important in "getting there" is knowing where you are. Before beginning any manpower plan, a complete manpower inventory should be available. This inventory should include at least the following information about all present personnel.

Name
Age
Sex
Department or organizational unit
Education
Job category
Experience on current job
Other experience
Performance rating
Promotability to other positions

Predicting changes.

This basic information about current employees enables manpower planners to anticipate possible promotions, and to plan training and additional experience to upgrade existing employees into expected future positions. It also provides the base line data from which needed personnel additions can be determined. Manpower inventory information also pinpoints job categories which will experience declines and for which layoffs or job transfers will be required.

Losses

Manpower losses usually result from deaths, disabilities, retirements, employee terminations (voluntary or otherwise), and intracompany transfers. Deaths, disabilities, and retirements can be predicted with reasonable accuracy based upon past organizational history and current trends. Quit rates are generally higher for employees in the first two or three years of employment, and for younger employees. The expected rate of termination due to unacceptable performance is dependent upon availability of good employees in the community and upon the system of employee selection used. A poor selection system will result in a higher rate of termination. Transfer losses are not net losses to the organization, but are clearly redistributions of manpower needs. This problem is particularly burdensome in governmental organizations for which the Civil Service system allows high employee mobility between government departments and agencies. While a transfer from HUD to the DOD is not a loss for the federal government, the HUD planning unit has lost an employee.

Forecast

Anticipates requirements.

The manpower forecast is based upon the production plans and the current manpower inventory, adjusted for expected losses. The manpower forecast begins with the estimate of operational activity requiring labor. For example, a fast-food restaurant may operate two shifts of four employees and a store manager for each shift. One district manager has a span of control of eight stores and each regional manager, six district managers. Therefore, to open 50 new stores next year will require

$50 \times 4 \times 2 = 400$ cooks and counter helpers
$50 \times 2 = 100$ store managers (50 day, 50 night)
$50 \div 8 = 7$* district managers
$8 \div 6 = 2$* regional managers

As for timing, the regional and district managers need to be employed and involved in most of the planning for the new stores. The store managers will be hired six months prior to the opening of a new store so that they can be adequately trained, and cooks and clerks will begin two weeks to one month prior to opening.

Actions

Personnel activities to meet plans.

Finally, once the manpower forecast exists, the personnel manager must develop plans to meet the forecasted needs. Parts of this plan might include such activities as college campus recruiting, newspaper advertising, and employee training and development programs. An obvious necessity in developing these plans is a consideration of equal employment opportunity laws and affirmative action programs to upgrade the skills and employment levels of women and minorities.

As you can well imagine, this manpower planning process requires a significant amount of information and also necessitates the integration of numerous objectives, assumptions, and quantitative factors into an overall planning system. Once the manpower requirements for an organization have been estimated, it still remains to implement a plan of action to meet these requirements. An early element in this plan of action is job evaluation to determine the rates of pay of the various jobs.

* Assumes a new manager is required after each preceding manager reaches specified span of control. Thus, $50 \div 8 = 6.25$, or 7 district managers.

11.2 JOB EVALUATION

Job evaluation versus employee evaluation.

Job evaluation is an analysis of a particular job to determine the appropriate rate of pay. Worker or **employee evaluation**, on the other hand, is concerned with determining how well a given worker is performing a job. Here we will discuss job evaluation and defer worker evaluation until a later section.

Know the job requirements.

For a proper job evaluation a description of the job duties, working conditions, and prevailing wage levels must be known. The evaluation takes into consideration educational requirements, skill levels, working conditions, responsibilities to be assumed, and necessary experience required for the job. Such evaluations are frequently conducted by a committee which includes the worker or union representatives. Four general systems are in use.

Base on key jobs in composite.

Artificial job levels.

Factor rating relative to key jobs.

- **Job ranking:** In this simple method a number of *key* jobs are analyzed in detail and ranked in order of their importance and worth to the organization. Maximum and minimum competitive rates are then set for these jobs and all other jobs are then rated relative to these key jobs. Jobs are considered in composite and not on the basis of relative factors. The main drawback of this system is that it is relatively subjective.
- **Job classification:** This is also a composite system. It involves the artificial construction of a set of levels or "classes" of jobs that act as benchmarks by which all jobs may be evaluated and then classified. This system has the widest use in federal and military organizations and is typified by the 18 General Schedule (GS) rating classifications (GS-1 to GS-18) used for most federal employees.
- **Factor comparison:** This method is generally more accurate than the previous two methods. It consists of ranking a set of **key jobs** on a set of factors, typically five: responsibility, mental requirements, skill, physical effort, and working conditions. Each key job is ranked (see Figure 11.1) on a partial wage scale for

Partial Wage	Responsibility	Mental	Skill	Physical	Conditions
$1.00	S	S	S		
0.80	T	T	T	T	C
0.60	R	C		C	T
0.40	C		R	S	S
0.20		R	C	R	R
S:	Secretary (1.00 + 1.00 + 1.00 + 0.40 + 0.40) =			$3.80	
T:	Typist/dictation			$3.80	
R:	Receptionist			$1.60	
C:	Clerk			$2.60	

Figure 11.1. Factor comparison scales.

each factor such that the sum of the partial wage amounts equals the total wage for each key job. Other jobs are then located on each factor relative to the key jobs and a resulting total wage may then be found.

Factor and point relations between key jobs.

- **Point method:** This method is the most widely used of the four. It is similar to the factor comparison method but uses more factors to enlarge the organizational applicability of the approach (such as creativity, hazards, equipment, skills, shorthand) and points rather than wages. A brief example is shown in Figure 11.2. Different requisite levels of each factor are associated with different points. The point total for key jobs with known prevailing wages then identifies the appropriate wage for any job in question through the use of a point-to-wage graph as in Figure 11.3.

For example, suppose one of the key jobs in a particular company is that of a foreman. For this position the minimum educational level is high school and two years on the job. For the particular job the working conditions are basically good. From Figure 11.2 the points associated with this job are

high school education:	30
skill of 24 months experience:	60
good working conditions:	10
total job points:	100

For the position of foreman in this company the wage range varies as shown in Figure 11.3. The job points for the "job in question," in this case a foreman, are 100 as calculated above. By analyzing a number of such jobs, the curve and set of rectangles shown in Figure 11.3 may be determined.

11.3 RECRUITMENT, SELECTION, AND PLACEMENT

Recruitment

Attracting candidates.

This is the process of attracting a broad range of applicants for the position in question, and selection is the process of "filtering" them to identify the appropriate choices. **Recruitment** is typically based on organizational policies regarding sources and types of applicants such as college interviews, minority hiring, internal promotion, and so on. There are a large number of recruitment methods. Advertising in

Factor	Scale	Level/Points				
Education	Attainment	Eighth/15	High school/30	B.S./45	M.S./60	Ph.D./75
Skill	Months	3/20	9/40	24/60	60/80	120/100
Conditions	Hazards	Ideal/5	Good/10	Poor/15	Bad/20	Dangerous/25

Figure 11.2. Factor point assignment.

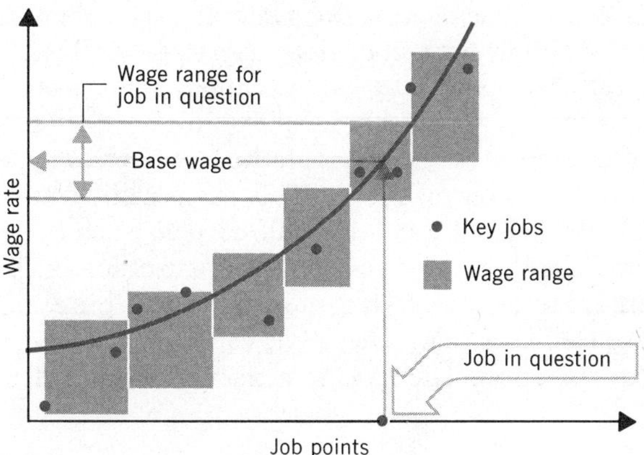

Figure 11.3. Point-wage relation.

local newspapers, trade magazines, and business publications often brings in numerous responses and at a relatively low cost per applicant. Employment agencies can often be helpful in locating candidates for higher level or hard-to-fill positions. Employees themselves are often good sources of other potential employees. Walk-ins and write-ins provide candidates for positions, although their timing is seldom in agreement with organizational needs. But, if an organization enjoys a good reputation, the number of unsolicited candidates can be quite large.

Encouraging and discouraging applicants.

The best recruitment procedure will be one that entices *the most appropriate* candidate to apply and discourages all others. It is extremely expensive to recruit, select, train, and place the wrong worker in a job, only to have him or her quit for more appropriate employment soon thereafter. Not only has there been a large, unnecessary personnel cost incurred by the organization, but a number of other costs as well.

- The entire process must be repeated, and done better this time, to get the *right* worker.
- A significant, perhaps irreparable, loss of time has occurred in permanently filling the position.
- The reputation of the organization for selecting appropriate workers, and keeping them, has suffered.

The above points are especially true for organizations that are trying to keep minorities and women on their staff. Such candidates are commanding extremely high salaries and no organization wants to incur these salary costs, plus training costs, for a year or so only to have these valuable employees quit and go to a competitor as soon as they are ready to produce.

Organization attractors.

The need for appropriate recruitment is therefore extremely high. Table 11.1 lists a number of *general*, as well as *specific*, **attractors** that organizations frequently use to attract candidates. In spite of the fact that organizations find they have to offer

Fast track employees.

extremely favorable general attractions in order to get the types of workers they desire, this often is simply not sufficient to *keep* those workers. The *best* workers want challenging, fulfilling, promising jobs *regardless* of the general work attractions. If a highly desirable worker finds that in spite of his or her high salary and prestigeous working conditions, he or she is not on the **fast track** to upper management in the organization, that worker may leave. This is especially true in organizations with a long, carefully worked out executive training plan (such as two years in the plant, a year in the branch office, three years in the home office, etc.). Herzberg [4] has conducted extensive research which demonstrates that the *general* attractors in Table 11.1 are those elements that, if negative, can lead to worker *dissatisfaction* with a job but *not* satisfaction. The *specific* attractors are the elements that lead to job satisfaction.

Selection

Identifying applicants to extend offers.

Selection is the process of evaluating, screening, and choosing the candidate for a specific position. For example, a campus recruiter is likely to interview from 10 to 100 students during a campus visit, and will do likewise on numerous college campuses. From this list of candidates several may be asked to make site visits to the organization offices or plant and from these some will be given offers, others not. Finally, some offers will be accepted and others rejected by the candidates. Screening and selection criteria differ with the type of position being filled. Clearly, for college recruiting, grades and extracurricular activities play an important part in initial screening as does the candidate's manner and communication skills during the brief campus interview.

Recruitment and selection are closely interdependent to the extent that if a very fine selection screen is used, perhaps all of the applicants will be screened out of the position and hence further recruitment will be necessary. Similarly, in an oversupplied market the recruitment process may result in many more applicants than can even be properly screened.

Overqualified workers.

Perhaps one of the most important aspects of recruitment and selection is correctly deciding just what type of worker is required for a particular job. There has been a long-established tendency to select overqualified workers for jobs, only to have

TABLE 11.1 ORGANIZATIONAL ATTRACTORS FOR WORKERS

General	Specific
Salary	Nature of the work
Benefits (insurance, vacation, etc.)	Advancement possibilities
Geography and climate	Challenge, responsibility
Organizational image	Fulfillment
Working environment	Opportunity to aid others
Growth and education	Personal recognition, prestige, power

them leave soon thereafter and then have to repeat the search. Time spent initially in determining the *minimum* qualifications for the job and the characteristics of a *successful* worker should pay good dividends later.

The organization typically fills a position according to standard selection policies. These may include specific or general tests, sequential interviews, reference checks, educational or work history analysis, even "pirating" from other organizations known to have quality recruitment, selection, and training programs but slow advancement "tracks." Mention should be made of the fact that testing is coming under heavy federal scrutiny these days after years of use, and sometimes abuse, by organizations, and, therefore, any testing program used by an organization should be justified in terms of specific job requirements.

Legality of testing.

Placement

Promoting internally.

Placement is the selection process used when positions are filled internally. Many organizations have adopted policies of **promoting from within** rather than going outside the company for upper level positions. This process is an important one and one that can be highly sensitive. The personnel manager must assure that fairness prevails in announcing vacancies and in selecting the candidate to fill the vacant position. A common problem that must be handled carefully is the employee who was not selected to fill the vacancy. While she or he may have been perfectly happy up to that point, being passed over for a better job can lead to resentment, reduced performance, and possibly even resignation.

"My ultimate goal? Retirement."

11.4 COMPENSATION

Compensation plans are invariably of two types, either time-based or output-based (sometimes the latter is called "incentive wages"). When members of organizations are paid for their services, they are often considered to be either salaried or hourly. All salaried and most hourly workers are compensated on a **time-based system**, typically weekly, biweekly, or monthly. The advantages of a time-based system are that compensation is easy to calculate, precise output standards do not have to be calculated, recordkeeping is minimal, workers are generally considered to be self-motivated by standards of professionalism or fairness, labor relations are smoother (since output-based "incentive" wages do not exist), and quality need not suffer in attempts to increase quantity.

Time-based systems.

Output-based systems.

The primary disadvantage of time-based systems is that no direct incentive exists for working harder than "average." Only far-removed merit increases and possible promotion provide "direct" incentives for working harder, but they also provide incentives for "playing politics," "favoritism," and a host of other dysfunctional organizational behaviors. Of course, in many types of work, the nature of the work itself, the working conditions, and other such factors provide natural motivation to the workers.

Although the main advantage of **output-based compensation systems** is that a direct incentive is applied to increase output, there are also many disadvantages.

- The determination of "standard" output is difficult.
- The system itself requires a considerable amount of time and cost to develop and implement.
- Loopholes frequently exist in such systems and are quickly exploited by workers.
- Quality and service may decrease in an attempt to increase the output rate.
- Workers resent the manipulative aspect of such plans.
- Record keeping becomes a monstrous task.
- The calculation of compensation becomes extremely complicated.
- The plan is often the subject of grievances, and union contract negotiations.
- Not all jobs can be put on incentive systems and charges of unfairness often result.
- Social problems and peer pressure may be encouraged.
- An incentive is created for the worker to devise improved work methods and equipment but keep both secret from management so the standard will not be raised.

In addition to these disadvantages, management must be careful that the increased output can be profitably used. For example, if automobile production is 60 per hour there is little value in putting transmission workers on an incentive system that increases transmission output to 100 per hour.

Individual incentive plans.

The simplest **incentive plan** is the straight **piece-rate system** where the worker, such as a harvester, is paid for the amount of output produced (bushels picked). Modifications to this basic system also exist. A **base-rate system** (also called **100 percent premium plans**) guarantees the worker a minimum wage based on standard output with a *piece-rate* bonus beyond the standard. In some cases, instead of a piece-rate bonus beyond the standard; a **sharing plan** (e.g., Halsey plan, Rowan plan) is used where the organization shares the increased value of the output at some rate, such as 50:50, with the worker.

Group incentive plans.

In addition to individual incentive plans, there are also **group plans** wherein a particular group can earn a bonus, as in the **Scanlon plan**, where all the organization's workers gain, as in profit sharing. To illustrate, the basis of the Scanlon plan is the formation of committees who seek out ways in which the organization can cut labor costs. The group is then rewarded on the basis of the value of their suggestions. Some controversy has arisen with this plan when worker committees make suggestions regarding unproductive *managerial* policies and inefficiencies. Nevertheless, top management has usually encouraged such constructive criticism.

Some useful guidelines to aid in setting up incentive plans are

1. The bonus should follow the action as soon as possible.
2. The plan should be simple and the bonus easy to calculate.
3. The plan should be fully communicated to all the workers.
4. Precise standards should be stated and guaranteed to remain unchanged for some period of time.
5. The manner and time points of reevaluating standards should be specified.
6. Clear policies should be given regarding bonuses under conditions beyond the control of the worker, such as when a machine breaks down.
7. No upper limit should exist on bonuses.
8. Standards should be monitored for fairness in case of changes in products, production methods, quality requirements, or equipment.

11.5 TRAINING AND DEVELOPMENT

Training involves preparing the worker for a particular position. This might include the acquisition of certain skills, experience, or education. **Development** means the continuing improvement of the worker, sometimes in order to transfer or promote him or her.

Training

Formal and informal orientation.

Training programs can vary from none at all, typically for very low (or very high) skilled jobs to multiyear rotational programs as mentioned previously. Most organizations include some form of **orientation** for new members so that they may quickly learn what is happening within the organization, who does what, formal organizational rules and regulations, and similar such useful, generalized information. This information may be conveyed through films, tours, pamphlets, talks by some of the organization's key staff, and so on. The purpose is to ease the member's entry into the work situation and eliminate potential stumbling blocks before they present a problem. If the new member is fortunate, he or she will get another, informal "orientation" from a protective secretary or experienced "old timer" that is often more useful than the formal orientation. This orientation, of a rather secretive nature, will inform the new member for whom to watch out, who *really* runs things, how to get around the rules, and so forth.

Training program problems.

Skill-oriented training programs are of all types: on-the-job, laboratory-classroom, subcontracted (with local technical schools or universities), apprenticeships, and so on. Too often, training programs bore and "turn off" the very workers for whom they are designed. Instead of getting on with the job for which they were hired, they must instead wait for some inadequate training program to end. If training programs are to be used by organizations, they should be kept as short as possible, use only enthusiastic, well-qualified instructors, provide the proper facilities and equipment, and be constantly reevaluated in light of their success—including member evaluation.

Development

Improving skills.

Development is the process of improving the worker's skills so he or she becomes more productive. Some common development techniques are local educational seminars, relevant regional or national conferences, special courses offered by universities, or even leaves of absence to obtain new skills or advanced degrees.

11.6 EMPLOYEE EVALUATION, TERMINATION

Evaluation

Importance of evaluation.

Members of an organization are typically evaluated regarding their performance on a regular basis, usually annually. The purpose of these evaluations is to give the worker some formal feedback on his or her performance and also provide an opportunity for the worker to identify, for management, any problems that are impairing the employee's ability to perform. These sessions are usually held in connection with changes in pay and or promotion. Union guidelines concerning the conduct and frequency of these sessions are often spelled out since promotions, raises, tenure, terminations, and other such personnel actions may be **bargaining issues**.

In some organizations the evaluation interviews are held with a superior *two* grades higher so that the worker can air any complaints regarding an immediate superior, and correspondingly, any criticism of the worker's performance will have more authority and seem less like personal criticism. Both good and bad performance are normally identified and the best method for growth on the part of the worker is spelled out—skill requirements, further education, and so forth.

EMPLOYEE PERFORMANCE EVALUATION SHEET

Performance	Exceeds Job Requirements	Meets Job Requirements	Needs Some Improvement	Does Not Meet Minimum Requirements
Quality	Leaps tall building with a single bound	Requires running start to leap tall buildings	Can leap short buildings only	Can only leap candlesticks
Timeliness	Is faster than greased lightning	Is faster than a greased pig	Is faster than a pig in molasses	Is slower than molasses
Drive	Works in overdrive	Works in high gear	Works in low gear	Works in reverse gear
Adaptability	Walks on water consistently	Walks on water in emergencies	Swims in water	Requires flotation device
Communication	Talks with God	Talks with the angels	Talks to animals	Talks to self

Termination

Value of termination interviews.

One of the most opportune times for management to learn of organizational problems is at the time an employee decides to leave. This **exit interview** may be the only chance the organization will get to identify weaknesses in its managerial structure by which it may be losing valuable and well-trained workers. Although perhaps disgruntled, terminating workers can often shed light on managerial practices and policies that may be generally aggravating to other workers as well. The terminating worker has very little reason to withhold information or criticisms and can often be a vital source of information regarding employee morale, management deficiencies, wage inequities, and other such unsuspected problems.

11.7 SUMMARY

In many ways, the personnel department holds the key to the efficient and effective functioning of the organization's operations. Obtaining the proper workers at the right time with the appropriate skills is a very complex task and is even futher complicated by equal opportunity and affirmative action laws and regulations.

Manpower planning is a sequential process that ties manpower needs to organizational goals, audits existing organizational human resources, predicts changes and losses, forecasts net needs, and then takes action to supply those needs. These actions include job evaluation, recruitment, selection, placement, compensation, training, development, evaluation, and, sometimes, termination.

Four general job evaluation systems to determine rates of pay are in use. The most common one is a point method related to key job factors. Different levels of each factor receive different points. The point total for key jobs with known prevailing wages then identifies the appropriate wage for other jobs.

Recruitment concerns attracting the most appropriate candidates and selection is choosing the candidates to whom job offers will be made. Placement is the procedure of promoting from within.

Compensation plans are usually either time-based or output-based. The former is easier to administer but lacks output incentive. The latter types of plans may be piece-rate, base-rate, sharing, or even group incentive plans.

Training may be highly formalized or entirely informal. Even with a formal training program, however, the informal orientation received from fellow workers may be more valuable. Development is the process of improvement of worker's skills through education, conferences, and so forth.

Evaluation and termination interviews are especially valuable to the organization, as well as the employee, for their information regarding potential improvements in efficiency, effectiveness, motivation, and so forth.

11.8 KEY TERMS

manpower planning (p. 382)
human resource audit (p. 383)
termination (p. 393)
job ranking (p. 385)
job classification (p. 385)
factor comparison (p. 385)
point method (p. 386)
key jobs (p. 385)
recruitment (p. 386)
selection (p. 388)
piece-rate (p. 391)
placement (p. 389)
attractors (p. 387)
promoting from within (p. 389)
time-based compensation plans (p. 390)
output-base compensation plans (p. 390)
incentive plans (p. 391)
Scanlon plan (p. 391)
base-rate system (p. 391)
sharing plan (p. 391)
group plan (p. 391)
training (p. 391)
development (p. 391)
orientation (p. 391)
evaluation (p. 385)
bargaining issue (p. 392)
exit interview (p. 393)
fast track (p. 388)
100 percent premium plan (p. 391)

11.9 REVIEW TEST

1. In some organizations it is personnel's duty to run the vending machines. (p. 382)
   a. True b. False
2. A personnel audit identifies current manpower resources. (p. 383)
   a. True b. False
3. Job evaluation is analyzing the job skills necessary so the best candidates can be identified. (p. 385)
   a. True b. False
4. General attractors can often lead workers to overall satisfaction with their job. (p. 388)
   a. True b. False
5. Psychological testing by organizations is now often illegal. (p. 389)
   a. True b. False
6. Placement is the final assigning of a worker to a specific job. (p. 389)
   a. True b. False

7. Incentive wage systems are always output-based compensation plans. (p. 391)
   a. True b. False
8. Informal orientations are less important for the job than the formal programs. (p. 392)
   a. True b. False
9. Termination interviews are usually emotional affairs and of little value to an organization. (p. 393)
   a. True b. False

11.10 DISCUSSION QUESTIONS

1. Why is manpower procurement so much more difficult than materials procurement?
2. How long should company orientation programs be?
3. Should companies require new employees to contract to work a specified number of years after the training program?
4. If an organization has developed good work systems why are the personnel so important? And if the personnel are that important why bother to develop good work systems?
5. The accounting profession has recently been conducting human resource audits in addition to their other audits. Comment on the value of these audits.
6. What other job evaluation schemes might you envision?
7. What checks can be used to ensure you are getting the proper balance between recruitment and selection?
8. How can inappropriate candidates be discouraged from applying?
9. What might the drawbacks be in group incentive plans such as Scanlon's?
10. How can organizations identify legitimate gripes in termination interviews?

11.11 PROBLEMS

1. Peoplepower, Inc., a new temporary employment service, is expanding toward the West Coast. Peoplepower operates each local office with one full-time recruiter, a secretary, a sales person, and a manager. A district manager is used to manage four local offices and each regional manager has a span of control of six district managers. To open local offices in 25 cities next year, how many district managers have to be trained? What manpower forecast would you provide?
2. Factory job pay rates at the Fair Wage Company are based upon the factor comparison method. Each job is rated on skill required, strength required, fatigue factor, working conditions, and responsibility. Each rating is on a five-point scale and each point is worth $0.40 of partial wage (e.g., a rank of 4 gives a $1.60 partial wage). Consider the following jobs and ranks.

	Skill	Strength	Fatigue	Conditions	Responsibility
Laborer	1	4	3	4	1
Light machine operator	5	3	3	3	3
Lead man	4	2	2	2	5

What will each worker be paid?

3. Using the factor point assignment table (Figure 11.2) in the text, and the point-wage graph below, what base wage will each of the following people earn?

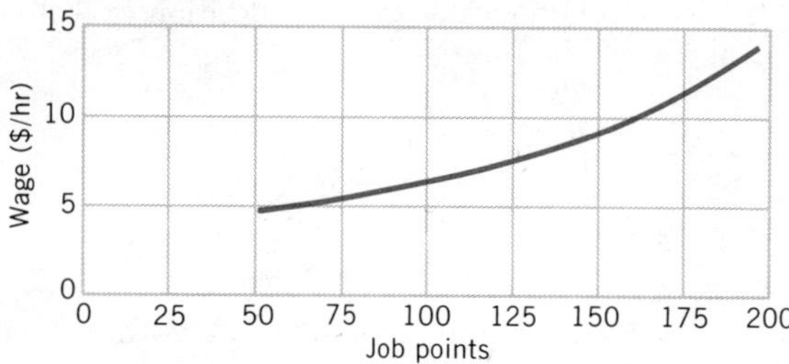

Chuck Lasher, a maintenance man, high school education, 10 years experience, good working conditions.
Dr. Barbara Judy, the plant psychologist, Ph.D. from Passemout U., six month's experience, ideal working conditions.
Robert Lee, plant superintendent, M.S. in electrical engineering, 2 years experience, ideal working conditions.

Comment on the ability of the three factors to explain or determine appropriate wages for company employees.

11.12 CASE TICK AND TYE, CPA'S

Tick & Tye, CPA's is a regional public accounting firm with four offices located in four major cities in North Carolina. The central office is located in Greensboro, North Carolina and the other three offices are located in Winston-Salem, Raleigh-Durham, and Danville, North Carolina. The firm has been growing rapidly over the last eight years since Harold J. Tick and Michael Z. Tye merged their respective practices. Their billing volume in 1979 was $3,200,000. This represented an increase of 22 percent over the previous year.

Tick & Tye has recently begun a major recruiting emphasis with the University of North Carolina and with the University of Virginia. The effort is directed toward developing strong enough relationships with the accounting faculty in both institutions so as to be able to attract the highest quality students needed in a growing accounting practice. The four firm offices are not equally attractive to prospective incoming employees, nor are they equally attractive to the existing members of the firm. Each of the offices is managed by a partner-in-charge of the office, with that partner having primary responsibility for the growth and development of the practice within that office. The firm's overall direction is established by an executive committee made up of senior members of the partnership. There are 14 partners in the firm and the firm employs a total of 127 people.

At a recent executive committee meeting the financial statements for the preceding year were being discussed. Of particular note was the poor performance of the Danville office. While volume had increased over the previous year by approximately 8 percent, the Danville office showed a net loss of $43,000. One senior partner, who practiced out of the Greensboro office, contended that the Danville office staff was too large. The partner-in-charge of the personnel committee argued that the Danville office was absolutely swamped during tax season but that there was not sufficient audit work to be conducted during the remainder of the year. As a result there was substantial down time during eight months of the year. The executive committee decided to hold a general partners meeting for the following month to discuss the situation of the Danville office and other staff scheduling and assignment problems.

During the general partners meeting there was much discussion about recruiting, staffing, scheduling, and assignment. The partner-in-charge of the Greensboro office gloated over his very favorable profit statistics and claimed that the profit was a direct result of keeping a "very lean" staff. The partner-in-charge of the Raleigh-Durham office argued that "people are our most important resource." His philosophy was to hire the best talent that could be hired out of the University of North Carolina and to make every effort to keep them busy. But, he contended that "we can't use profit as our only measure of performance. Some of this down time should be charged to professional development and training since that is the way it is used." Someone chimed in that "maybe we could use up some of the slack time in other offices."

QUESTIONS FOR DISCUSSION

1. What personnel policies do you see presented in this case?
2. How might manpower planning assist in solving Tick & Tye's problems?
3. How can staff scheduling and work assignment be used to resolve part of this problem? What problems do you see in using these methods to alleviate manpower peaks and valleys?

11.13 REFERENCES AND BIBLIOGRAPHY

1. Cassell, Frank H., "Corporate Manpower Plans," *Bulletin*, Stanford, California: Stanford Graduate School of Business, Summer, 1965.
2. French, Wendell, *The Personnel Management Process*, 2nd ed., Boston: Houghton Mifflin, 1970.
3. Geisler, Edwin B., "Manpower Planning: An Energy Staff Function," New York: American Management Association, *AMA Management Bulletin*, 1967.
4. Herzberg, F., "One More Time: How Do You Motivate Employees," *Harvard Business Review*, 46:53–62 (Jan.-Feb., 1968).
5. Kellogg, M.S., *What to Do About Performance Appraisal*, New York: American Management Association, 1965.
6. Wortman, Max S., and George Willeried, *Labor Relations and Collective Bargaining*, Boston: Allyn & Bacon, 1969.
7. Yoder, Dale, *Personnel Management and Industrial Relations*, 6th ed. Englewood Cliffs, N.J.: Prentice-Hall, 1970.

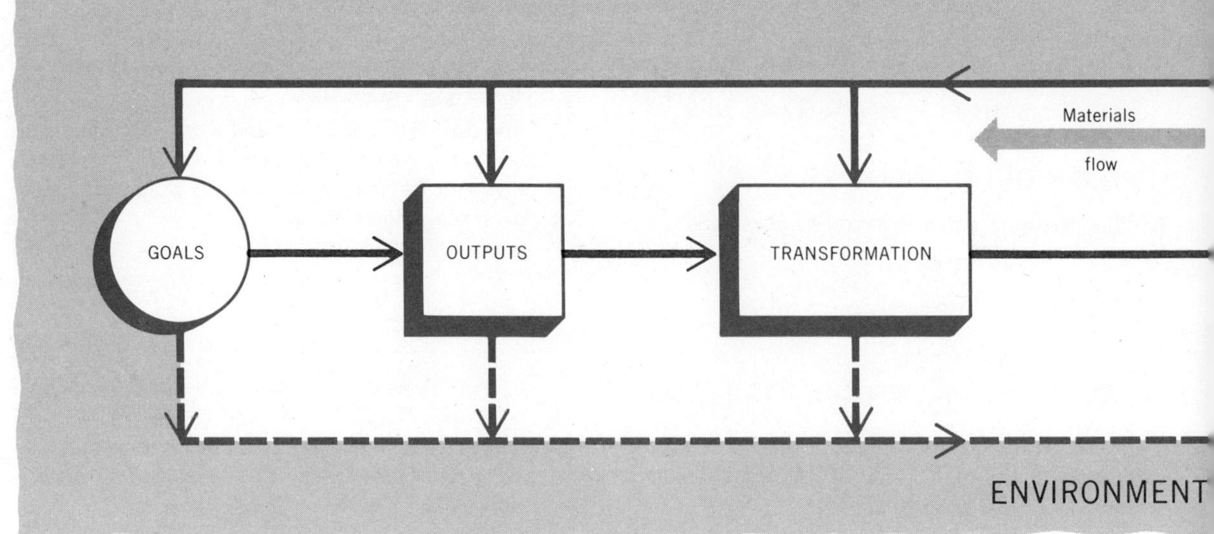

Chapter 12

Inventory Management: Concepts and Models

CONCEPTS

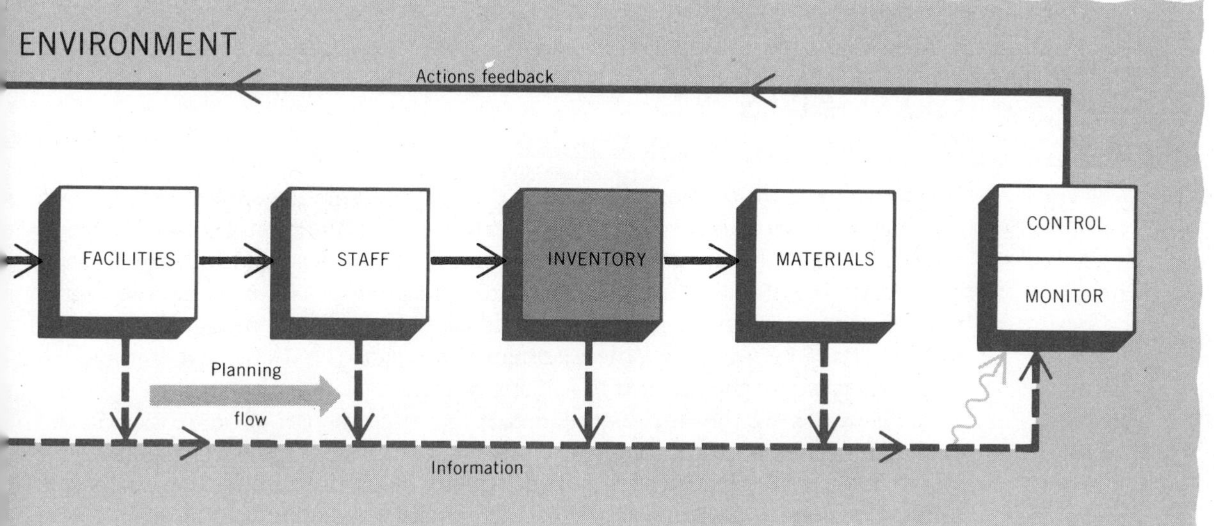

TOOLS AND APPLICATIONS

12.6 The Economic Order Quantity
    Finding an Optimal Policy
    Cautions Regarding EOQ Computations
    Using the EOQ in Reorder Point and Periodic Review Inventory Systems
12.7 The Economic Production Lot Size
12.8 Lot Sizing for Multiple, Recurring Batches
12.9 EOQ with Quantity Discounts
12.10 Uncertainty in Both Demand and Lead Time: The Service Level Concept
    Analytical Approach
    Simulation Approach
12.11 Uncertainty and Normally Distributed DOLT
12.12 Summary
12.13 Readings
12.14 Key Terms
12.15 Review Test
12.16 Discussion Questions
12.17 Problems
12.18 Case
12.19 References and Bibliography

LEARNING OBJECTIVES

By the completion of the *Concepts* portion of this chapter the student should

1. Understand the purposes for holding inventory.
2. Recognize the value of inventory in a manufacturing situation.
3. Know the costs involved in inventory decisions.
4. Recognize the relationships between order costs and holding costs.
5. Understand the differences between reorder point and periodic review inventory systems.
6. Know how flexibility is added to an operations system through the use of various types of inventory.
7. Recognize the impact of demand uncertainty on the order quantity of a perishable item.
8. Understand the meaning and use of safety stock.
9. Understand the notion of service level in an inventory system.

CONCEPTS

Up to now in our discussion of acquiring the inputs we have addressed the interface functions of finance and personnel for acquiring capital (and capital goods) and labor, respectively. Before we consider the purchasing interface for acquiring the final major input, materials, it will be useful to first consider the design of the inventory systems that will dictate when the materials should be purchased and how much should be ordered at a time. Inventory management is a major operations function and we devote this chapter and the next to its consideration.

Inventories as stocks of goods.

Inventories are the stocks of materials that become part of or are used in the production of the organization's output. A retail store stocks dresses and slacks for sale to final consumers. An auto parts distributor stocks inventories of parts for sale to retail outlets. A furniture manufacturer stocks wood, glue, and fabrics, among other items, to be used in the production of lounge chairs. And, a government office stocks supplies of forms to be used in providing its particular services.

Different attitudes toward inventories.

While inventory is inanimate, the topic of inventory and inventory control can arouse completely different sentiments in the minds of people in various departments within an organization. The sales people generally prefer large quantities of inventory to be on hand. In this way they can meet customer requests without having to wait. **Customer service** is their primary concern. The accounting and financial personnel see inventory in a different light. High inventories do not translate into high customer service in the accountant's language; rather, they translate into large amounts of tied-up capital which could otherwise be used to reduce debt or for other more economically advantageous purposes. From the viewpoint of the operations manager, inventories are seen as a tool that can be used to promote efficient operation of the production facilities. Neither high inventories nor low inventories, per se, are desirable—they are simply allowed to fluctuate so that production can be adjusted to its most efficient level. And top management's viewpoint is with "the bottom line"—what advantages the inventories are providing versus their costs.

In this chapter we will discuss some of the more important types of inventories and describe the essential characteristics of a good inventory management system. In addition, several inventory management concepts will be presented and demonstrated by examples.

12.1 GENERAL INVENTORY CONSIDERATIONS

Types of Inventories

There are often many purposes for holding inventory but, in general, there are only five types of inventories that an organization can use to accomplish these purposes. The student should be aware that these various types of inventories will not be identified and segregated within the organization and that not all types will be represented in all organizations. The five types are

1. Transit (pipeline) inventories.
2. Buffer inventories.
3. Anticipation inventories.
4. Decoupling inventories.
5. Cycle inventories.

Transit inventories

Inventories to fill the pipeline.

Transit inventories exist because materials must be moved from one location to another. (These are also known as **pipeline** inventories.) Five hundred tons of coal moving slowly on a coal train from the mines of southeastern Kentucky to an industrial northeastern city cannot provide customer service by powering furnaces or generators. This inventory results because of the transportation time required. If no time were necessary for transport (e.g., inventory could be "beamed" from factory to warehouse a la Star Trek) then transit inventories would be unnecessary.

Transit inventories also exist between facilities of the same organization. For example, transmissions assembled in the Cincinnati Ford transmission plant are shipped to numerous assembly plants via truck and train. While they are in transit (and with continuous production and shipping, some are *always* in transit), they cannot be used by assembly plants in the production of new autos and therefore provide no value or service as do other types of inventory.

Buffer inventories

Inventory as a cushion.

Variation in demand for items.

Another one of the purposes of inventories is to protect against the uncertainties of supply and demand. **Buffer** inventories or, as they are sometimes called, **safety stocks** serve to cushion the effect of unpredictable events. The amount of inventory over and above the *average* demand requirement is considered to be buffer stock held to meet any demand in excess of the average. A grocery store manager may know that average daily demand for rye bread is 58 loaves. Does that mean that she or he can stock 58 loaves of bread each morning and be assured of having enough for that day's customers? Obviously not. Even though *average* demand and *average* delivery time are known, actual demands and deliveries vary from these averages and therefore can never be predicted perfectly. These fluctuations in demand and lead time are normally protected against by carrying more inventory than is necessary just to meet "average" demand.

Inventory provides safety against stockouts.

Stockouts and backorders.

The higher the level of inventory, the better the customer service; that is, the fewer the **stockouts** and **backorders**. A stockout exists when a customer's order for an item cannot be filled because the inventory of that item has run out. Some systems allow backorders in such a case: an order for the demanded item that will be filled as soon as the next shipment of the item is received. In many cases, backordering is practical (such as in a clothing store or a furniture store) and results in a minimum loss of customer goodwill.

Backordering not always practical.

But, there are many cases in which backorders are not practical, either because of the clerical expense involved in keeping track of what is on backorder or because of the customer's basic unwillingness or inability to wait. For example, gas stations cannot backorder gasoline because the customer can find many substitutes and would be unwilling and generally unable to wait. Better yet, what would you think of a McDonald's manager who has just run out of Big Mac's but wants to backorder one that you can pick up tomorrow?

Buffer inventories are unavoidable because we can never perfectly predict the level of demand or supply for a given period. In Section 12.5 we will consider methods for determining the optimum amount of buffer inventory to be maintained.

Anticipation inventories

Inventory buildup for surges in demand.

An anticipated future demand is the reason for holding anticipation inventories. Rather than operating with excessive overtime in one period and then allowing the productive system to be idle or shut down because of insufficient demand in another period, inventories can be allowed to build up before an event and consumed during or after the event. Examples of the use of **anticipation inventories** are numerous. Manufacturers, wholesalers, and retailers build anticipation inventories prior to occasions such as Christmas and Easter when demand for specialized products will be high. Anticipation inventories are built up when strikes are expected in a supplier's plant, when a supply price increase appears imminent, or when a large sales promotion is expected to significantly increase demand.

Inventories increase resource utilization.

In addition, without anticipation inventory a manufacturing plant would have to produce goods to meet immediate demand, and only immediate demand. For services this is most generally true since the services themselves cannot be inventoried. A painting contractor cannot produce and store "painted walls" and then wait for a customer to demand them. A hospital surgical team cannot produce and store open heart surgeries in their spare time and then use them later when a patient requires one. But, a bathing suit manufacturer could produce bathing suits all year long or it could produce them only during the three-month bathing suit buying season. If corporate policy stated that no inventories of bathing suits were to be stocked then the company would have to produce only to meet demand.

What this means to the utilization of equipment and manpower can be seen from Figure 12.1. In order to keep inventory level at zero all year long, as depicted in Figure 12.1*b*, the company must only produce during the buying months and must produce only the amount that will be demanded. Thus, the production level remains at zero for 9 of the 12 months of the year and increases to the level of demand for the three buying months. This would pose obvious problems. However, if inventory is allowed to fluctuate over the year as in Figure 12.1*a* then production (and workforce levels) can be maintained at a year-round constant level. The *annual* amount of production will equal the amount of demand over the *three-months* buying period. Figure 12.1*a*

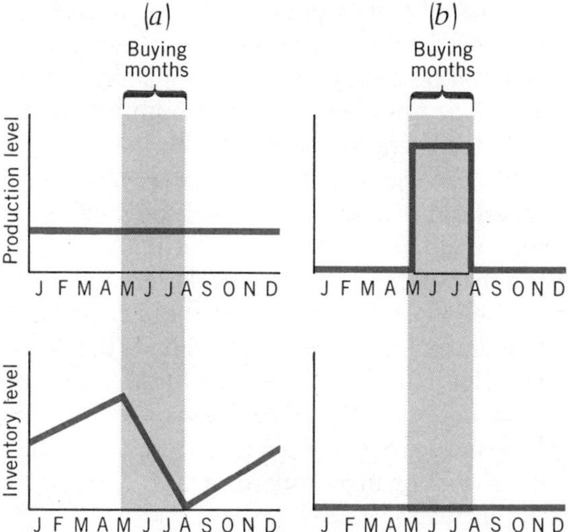

Figure 12.1. Producing for seasonal demand. (*a*) Year-round production. (*b*) Production to meet demand.

also illustrates the effect on the inventory level. Inventory is depleted, due to sales, at the end of July and begins to increase at a constant rate from August through April. Then, beginning in May, demand outstrips production so that inventory falls and continues to decline until the end of July, at which time the cycle begins again. Production is going on at all times whether or not demand exists.

What efficiencies are produced in this example by allowing a capital investment of inventory to accumulate? First, the productive capacity of the operations system can be one-fourth the size of the system required if no inventories are allowed. Second, the costs of hiring, training, and firing employees are avoided (as well as union trouble) with year-round production. Third, production capacity is used continuously rather than being allowed to sit idle for nine months out of the year. There are indeed some costs associated with keeping inventory, but, as we shall see in this chapter, they must be balanced against other costs, such as the three just mentioned.

Decoupling inventories

Smoothing production through in-process inventories.

It would be a rare production process in which all equipment and personnel operated at exactly the same rate. Yet, if you were to take an inspection tour through a production facility you would notice that almost all of the equipment and people were producing. Products move smoothly even though one machine can process parts five times as fast as the one before or after it. Inventories of parts between machines, known as **decoupling inventory**, act to disengage the production process. That is, inventories act as shock absorbers, or cushions, increasing and decreasing in size as parts are added to and used up from the stock. Even if a preceding machine were to break down, the following machines could still produce (at least for a while) since an "in-process inventory" of parts would be waiting for production. Magee [4] has argued that the more inventories that management "carries between stages in the manufacturing-distribution process, the less coordination is needed to keep the process running smoothly." Clearly, there is an optimum balance between inventory level and coordination in the operations system.

Paced lines without inventory.

But without decoupling inventories, each operation in the plant would have to produce at an identical rate (a **paced line**) to keep the production flowing smoothly and when one operation broke down, the entire plant would come to a standstill. Figure 12.2 illustrates two machines that produce at different rates and the inventory between them which is used to disengage these two machines. If machine A, for example, could produce twice as fast as machine B, then A could possibly be used to produce other parts for a third machine after running an appropriately large batch of inventory for B to work on. If A produced at a *slower* rate than B, then more type A machines would be needed or else B would sit idle. Thus, there is no place or capacity for maintaining decoupling inventory in a paced line; the system must always run smoothly, or not run at all.

Cycle inventories

Inventory lots to minimize total costs.

Cycle inventories or, as they are sometimes referred to, lot-size inventories exist for a different reason than the others just discussed. Each of the above types of inventories typically serve one of the major purposes for holding inventory. Cycle inventories, on the other hand, result from management's attempt to minimize the total cost of carrying and ordering inventory. If the annual demand for a particular part is 12,000 units, management could decide to place one order for 12,000 units and maintain a rather large inventory throughout the year or place 12 orders of 1000 each and maintain a lower level of inventory. But the costs associated with ordering and receiving would increase. Cycle inventories are the inventories that result from ordering in batches or "lots" rather than from an "as needed" basis.

As you can see from the above discussion, the inventory system and the operations system within an organization are strongly interrelated. Inventories affect customer service, facility and equipment utilization, capacity, and labor efficiency. Therefore the plans concerning the acquisition and storage of materials, or "inventories," are vital to the production process. This chapter initiates the discussion of these plans. A recurring point of focus in the discussion is: How *much* to order and *when*. All of the analyses and plans eventually boil down to addressing these two issues, as we shall see.

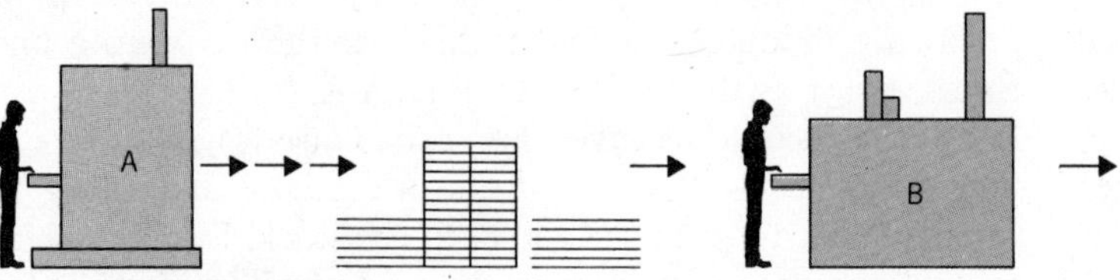

Figure 12.2. Inventory used to disengage and smooth production.

Inventory Classes

Inventories are also usually classified into four groups, some of which correspond directly with the previous inventory types but some of which do not.

1. Raw materials.
2. Spares, supplies.
3. Work-in-process.
4. Finished goods.

Raw Materials

These are the objects, commodities, elements, and items that are received (usually purchased) from outside the organization to be used directly in the production of the final product. Typically, when we think of raw materials we think of such things as sheet metal, flour, paint, structural steel, chemicals, and other basic materials. But nuts and bolts, hydraulic cylinders, engines, frames, integrated circuits, and other assemblies purchased from outside the organization would also be considered part of the **raw materials inventory** of an organization.

Spares, supplies

Spares are sometimes produced by the organization itself rather than being purchased. These are usually machine parts or supplies, crucial to production. The term "supplies" is often used synonymously with inventories. The general convention, and the one that we will adopt in this book, is that supplies are stocks of items used in the production of goods or services but not directly as a part of the finished product. Examples are carbon paper, staples, pencils, and packing material.

Work-in-process

Work-in-process inventory consists of all of the materials, parts, and assemblies that are being worked on or are waiting to be processed within the operations system. Decoupling inventories are an example of work-in-process. That is, they are all of the items which have left the raw materials inventory but which have not yet been converted or assembled into a final product.

Finished goods

The finished goods inventory is the stock of completed products. Goods, once completed, are transferred out of work-in-process inventory and into the finished goods inventory. From here they can be sent to distribution centers, sold to wholesalers, or sold directly to retailers or final customers.

Another class of inventory that should also be considered is *components*. Components are subassemblies of a finished product, that is, some assembly of parts that enter as a unit into the final assembly of the product. Components can be found in each of the preceding classes of inventories. Some components are purchased directly from outside the organization and stocked in raw materials inventory. Other components are produced from raw materials by the organization and are stocked until needed in final production. Still other components are stocked as replacement parts in finished goods inventory. General Motors, for example, must produce engines, transmissions, doors, fenders, and other components of each style of automobile produced, to be sold as replacement and maintenance parts. These components are classified as finished goods, even though they are not automobiles, but parts of automobiles.

12.2 DESIGN OF OPTIMAL INVENTORY SYSTEMS

The inventory system balances the costs of inventory with its advantages.

The ultimate objective of any inventory system is to produce decisions regarding the level of inventory that will result in an optimum balance between the purposes for holding inventories and the costs associated with them. Typically, we hear inventory management practitioners and researchers speaking of "total cost minimization" as the objective of an inventory system. If we were able to place dollar costs on interruptions in the smooth flow of goods through the operations system, on not meeting customer demands, or on failures to provide the other purposes for which inventories exist, then "total cost minimization" would be a reasonable objective. But, since we are unable to assign costs to many of these subjective factors, we must be satisfied with obtaining a good "balance" between inventory costs and inventory functions.

Costs Involved in Inventory Decisions

Five inventory costs.

There are essentially five broad categories of cost associated with inventory system decisions. These are

1. Ordering or setup costs.
2. Carrying or holding costs.
3. Stock-out costs.
4. Capacity-associated costs.
5. The cost of the goods themselves.

Ordering or setup costs

Ordering costs are the costs associated with the outside procurement of material, and **setup costs** are the costs associated with the internal procurement (i.e., the internal manufacture) of parts of material. Ordering costs include the cost of writing the order, processing the order through the purchasing system, postage, invoice processing, accounts payable processing, and receiving department costs such as handling, testing and inspection, and transporting. Setup costs also include order writing and processing for the internal production control system, the cost of the setup labor, the machine downtime due to a new setup (i.e., cost of an idle, nonproducing machine), the cost of parts damaged during setup (e.g., actual parts are often used for tests during setup), and costs associated with the employee learning curve (i.e., the cost of early production spoilage and low productivity immediately after a new production run is started). Learning curve costs are often referred to as "hat switching" costs.

Inventory carrying or holding costs

Three components of carrying costs.

Inventory carrying or **holding costs** consist of the following major components.

1. Capital costs.
2. Storage costs.
3. Risk costs.

Capital costs include interest on money invested in inventory and in land, buildings, and equipment necessary to hold and maintain the inventory. If these investments were not required, the organization could invest the capital in an alternative which would earn some return on investment.

Storage costs include rent, taxes, and insurance on buildings, depreciation of buildings, maintenance and repairs expense, heat, power, light, salaries of security personnel, taxes on the inventory, labor costs in handling inventory, clerical costs of inventory recordkeeping, taxes and insurance on equipment, equipment depreciation, equipment fuel and energy costs, the costs of repairs and maintenance, and so forth.

Inventory risk costs include the costs of obsolete inventory, insurance on inventory, physical deterioration of the inventory, and losses from pilferage.

Carrying costs are frequently 20 percent of the value of the inventory.

While some of these costs are relatively small, the total costs of carrying items in inventory can be quite large. Studies have demonstrated that the cost for a typical manufacturing firm are frequently as large as 20 percent of the cost of the inventoried items. A large portion of this cost is typically the cost of the invested capital.

Stockout costs

The cost of not having inventory when it is needed.

If inventory is unavailable when customers request it, or if inventory is unavailable when it is needed for production, a stockout occurs. There are several costs associated with each type of stockout. A stockout of an item demanded by a customer or client can result in lost sales or demand, lost client goodwill, and costs associated with backorder processing (such as extra paperwork, expediting, special handling, and higher shipping costs). A stockout of an item needed for production results in production rescheduling costs, costs of down time and delay caused by the shortage, the cost of "rush" shipping of needed parts, and possibly the cost of substituting a more expensive part or materials.

Capacity-associated costs

Capacity-associated costs are those costs incurred because a change in productive capacity is necessary or because a temporary shortage or excess in capacity exists.

Why would capacity be too great or too small? If, for example, a company tried to meet seasonal demand (or any fluctuations in demand) by changing production level rather than by allowing inventory level to increase or decrease, capacity would have to be increased during high demand periods and reduced during low demand periods.

Inventory-capacity tradeoffs.

Capacity-associated costs include the overtime required to increase capacity, the costs of hiring, training, and terminating employees, the cost of using less skilled workers during peak periods, and the cost of idle time if capacity is *not* reduced during periods when demand decreases. The tradeoffs in these costs were considered earlier in Chapter 9 in terms of aggregate scheduling.

Cost of goods

Lastly, the goods themselves must be paid for. Although they must be acquired sooner or later anyway, *when* they are acquired can influence their cost considerably, such as through quantity discounts.

Decisions in Inventory Management

As we have stated, the objective of an inventory management system is to make decisions regarding the appropriate (optimal) level of inventory and changes in the level of inventory. To maintain the appropriate level of inventory, essentially two questions must be answered.

Two questions an inventory control system must answer.

1. When should an order be placed to replenish the inventory?
2. How many items should be ordered when inventory is reordered?

Various types of inventory management systems use different methods for making the "**when**" and "**how much**" decisions. Some are time dependent and others are dependent upon the level of inventory, but the essential decisions are the same. Even when complexities, such as uncertainty in demand and delivery times, are introduced into the inventory management problem, the "how many" and "when to order" decisions still remain the basis of sound inventory management.

Types of Inventory Management Systems

Three types of inventory control systems.

All inventory systems can be classified as one of three varieties, based upon the approach taken to the "when to order" decision.

1. Reorder point systems.
2. Periodic review systems.
3. Material requirements planning (MRP) systems.

Before we describe these three systems, let us consider a simplified inventory management situation to provide a background for our subsequent discussion.

Consider the Hard Charger Corporation, a wholesaler that sells 1000 generators per month to auto parts retailers in the Southeast. Demand for generators is constant throughout the year. Suppose that Hard Charger has a policy of ordering 2000 generators per order and that they have just received a shipment of 2000, bringing their inventory level to 2000.

Hard Charger sells 1000 generators per month, and therefore the beginning inventory of 2000 units will be depleted by the end of the second month. In order to keep from "stocking out" an order must be placed and shipment received prior to the end of the second month. To keep the costs of carrying inventory as low as possible, it is desirable to schedule receipt of the order at the time that the previous inventory supply is exhausted. Assuming this perfect scheduling and "instantaneous replenishment" (the immediate resupply of the order quantity when the inventory level reaches zero), a graph of the inventory level as it changes over time would appear as in Figure 12.3.

Inventory is used at the rate of 1000 per month and orders are received so that the inventory level is replenished before a stockout can occur. No stockouts occur and the inventory level never exceeds the order quantity of 2000. As we progress through this chapter we will eliminate the unrealistic assumptions of constant demand and instantaneous replenishment and introduce other more "realistic" assumptions into our discussion. For now, let us turn to a discussion of the three types of inventory control systems.

Reorder point systems

Reorder points and lead times.

In reorder point systems an inventory *level* is specified at which a replenishment order for a fixed quantity of the inventory item is to be placed. Whenever the inventory on hand is placed for a predetermined inventory level (or **reorder point**) an order is placed for a prespecified amount as illustrated in Figure 12.4. The reorder point is established so that the inventory on hand at the time an order is placed is sufficient to meet demand during the **lead time** (i.e., the time between placing an order and receipt of the shipment). The quantity of inventory to be ordered is typically based upon the **economic order quantity** (EOQ) concept (one answer to the "how much to order" question), an approach illustrated in the *Tools and Applications* portion of this chapter. But, other "how much" decision rules such as ordering "six-weeks supply" are also used in reorder point systems.

The "two-bin" system.

A simplified and much used variation of the reorder point system is the **two-bin** system. In this system, parts are stored in two bins, one large and one small. The

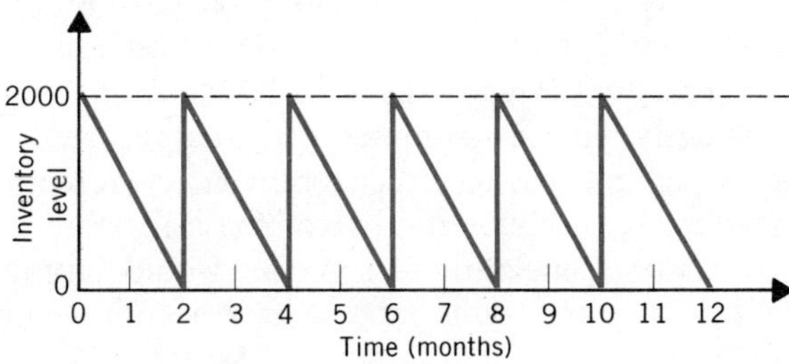

Figure 12.3. Inventory fluctuation.

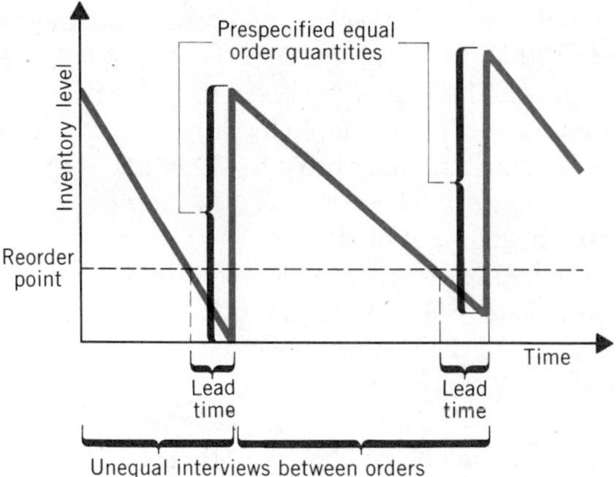

Figure 12.4. A reorder point system illustrated.

small bin usually holds sufficient parts to satisfy demand during the replenishment lead time. Parts are used from only the large bin until it is empty. At that time, a replenishment order is placed and parts are used from the small bin until the replenishment order is received.

Who should reorder?

Two-bin systems have been developed in many variations. In some systems it is simply the responsibility of the employee who removes the last item from the large bin to place a materials requisition with the purchasing department or with his or her supervisor. In others, a completed requisition is placed at the bottom of the larger bin and only needs to be picked up and submitted when the last item is removed. In others, an 80-column computer card is affixed to a wrapped quantity of items in the small bin. When these items are opened, the card is removed and sent to data processing to generate an order. The advantage of the two-bin system is that no detailed records of inventory use (a **perpetual** inventory system) must be kept and inventory level need not be continuously recounted to determine whether or not a reorder should be placed.

The perpetual inventory system. Constantly checking the inventory level.

This latter point is important. A perpetual inventory system requires either a manual card system or a computerized system to keep track of daily usage and daily stock levels. Also, each day the cards or computer file must be "searched" to find all items whose balances have fallen below the reorder point. Note that these are clercial functions that remove the burden of assessing proper inventory levels from the people who use the inventory. Typically, perpetual systems run into problems because those who use the inventory fail to report the use. Management controls over the inventory system must be fairly rigid to assure that perpetual records remain accurate and, in turn, result in proper orders being placed for inventory. A reorder point system could not perform adequately without either a two-bin type system or a perpetual inventory control system. Without one of these, someone would have to record the inventory balances for all items each day in order to have accurate counts and, therefore, to know when to order.

Periodic review systems

The periodic review system.

On-hand plus on-order.

In **periodic review** systems the inventory level is reviewed at equal time intervals and at each review a reorder is placed to bring the inventory level up to a desired quantity. The amount of the reorder is based upon a "maximum" level established for each inventory item. The quantity that should be reordered is the amount necessary to bring the **on-hand** inventory plus the **on-order** quantity to the maximum level. That is

$$\text{reorder quantity} = \text{maximum level} - \text{"on-hand" inventory} - \text{"on-order" quantity} \qquad (12.1)$$

Is an order due in?

The on-hand inventory is the amount actually in stock. If the system allows back orders, then on-hand could be negative, at least in concept. If back orders are not used, then a stockout condition simply results in a zero on-hand quantity. The on-order amount is the quantity for which purchase orders have been issued, but delivery has not yet been made. We deduct the on-order quantity to assure that an order is not placed for the same goods. Figure 12.5 illustrates such an occurrence. At review point A an order is placed for Q_A, the amount necessary to bring the inventory up to the maximum level. At review point B, the first order has not arrived so an order for Q_B is placed to bring the inventory to the maximum. No attention was paid to the on-order quantity. Now, some time later, Q_A is received, and then Q_B. At review point C, inventory exceeds the desired maximum.

Fixed review period or fixed reorder amount?

In periodic review systems the *review period* (and therefore reorder period) *is fixed* and the *order quantity varies* (see Figure 12.6) according to the above rule. This system is most appropriate when it is difficult to keep track of inventory levels and the cost of stockouts or safety stock is not excessive. In reorder point systems the *order quantity is fixed* and the *reorder period varies* (see Figure 12.4). This system is best where a continuing watch of inventory levels is feasible and stockouts or safety stock would be expensive. If demand increases during the period the reorder point

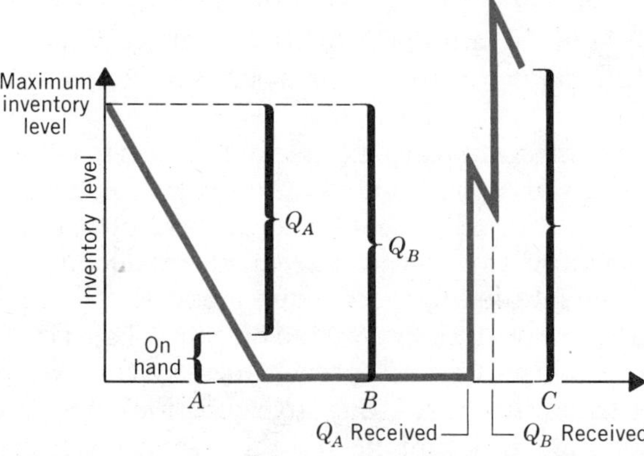

Figure 12.5. Periodic review systems without considering on-order quantity.

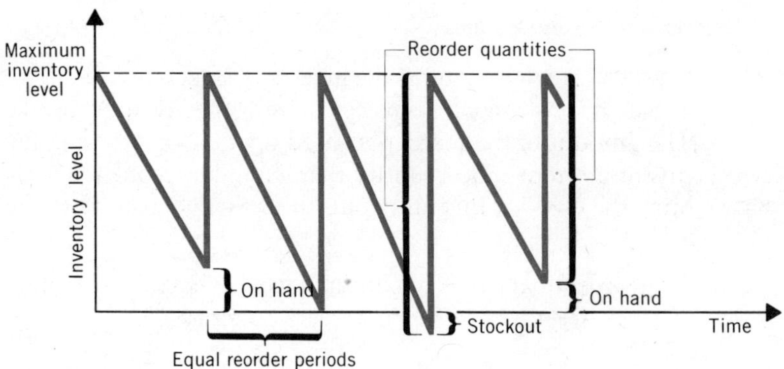

Figure 12.6. Periodic review system illustrated (assumes none on order at time of reorder).

system would simply place an order sooner than normal. The periodic review system would review and place an order at the regularly scheduled time but for a larger than normal quantity. However, in both systems there is a risk that a stockout will occur because the demand during the lead time may be greater than the amount "on hand" at the time the order is placed. As we shall see later in the chapter, there are ways to compensate for this risk.

Material requirements planning (MRP) systems

MRP for independent demand.

The two previously discussed systems operate best for inventory items with fairly constant, and independent, demand. **Independent demand** simply means that demand for an item is not based upon demand for some other item. Examples include clothing, furniture, automobiles or retail items, and supply type items (paper, pencils) in a manufacturing or office environment. The most likely applications for the two previous systems are for finished goods inventories and for some continuously used raw materials. But, for a wide range of raw materials, component parts, and subassembles, the **MRP** system, a materials application of the requirements planning concept presented in Chapter 9, produces better results. MRP was primarily designed by Joe Orlicky of IBM in the early 1960s to take advantage of the capabilities of computers for storing and monitoring the millions upon millions of parts requirements of modern production.

Order dependent demand items when they are needed.

For most component parts and assemblies used in production, demand tends to be intermittent rather than continuous because demand for those components is *dependent* upon demand in another stage of the operations system. For example, many manufactured products are entered into production in batches, the size of the batches and the scheduling of entry into production being dependent upon anticipated orders for the product. Entering an order for a batch of 100 Model X-72 room air conditioners would result in a (dependent) demand for 100 "wood grained" front covers. There is little sense in stocking large quantities of these covers if they will only be demanded a few times throughout the year. A better inventory strategy would obviously be to order the 100 covers so that they will be received just prior to the time they are needed in production, that is, the last stage of assembly prior to packaging. We will discuss the MRP approach in detail in Chapter 13.

12.3 PRIORITIES FOR INVENTORY MANAGEMENT: THE ABC CONCEPT

Varying importance of inventories.

In practice, all inventories cannot be controlled with equal attention. Some inventories are simply too small or too unimportant to warrant intensive monitoring and control activity. Additionally, in implementing new inventory management systems a priority ranking must be developed to allow management to decide the order in which to include the inventoried items in the control system. One simple procedure of common use is the ABC classification system.

The **ABC** classification system is based upon the annual dollar purchases of an inventoried item. As can be seen from Table 12.1, a relatively small proportion of the total items in an inventory account for a relatively large proportion of the total annual dollar volume, and a large proportion of the items account for a small proportion of the dollars. This phenomenon is often found in systems in which large numbers of different items are maintained, and is also in evidence in marketing where a small number of customers represent the bulk of the sales, in complaint departments where a large volume of complaints come from a relatively small group, and so forth.

Three value classes.

The three classifications used in the ABC system are

A. High value items—the 15–20 percent of the items that account for 75–80 percent of the total annual inventory value.

B. Medium value items—the 30–40 percent of the items that account for approximately 15 percent of the total annual inventory value.

C. Low value items—the 40–50 percent of the items that account for 10–15 percent of the annual inventory value.

This classification is presented in the ABC chart of Figure 12.7, which presents the cumulative distribution of the dollar value of inventory items.

TABLE 12.1 INVENTORY VALUE BY ITEM

Number of Items	Percentage of Total Items	Annual Dollar Purchases	Percentage of Total Purchases
521	4.8	$15,400,000	50.7
574	5.3	6,200,000	20.4
1,023	9.4	3,600,000	11.8
1,145	10.5	2,300,000	7.6
3,754	34.0	1,800,000	5.9
3,906	36.0	1,100,000	3.6
10,923	100.0	$30,400,000	100.0

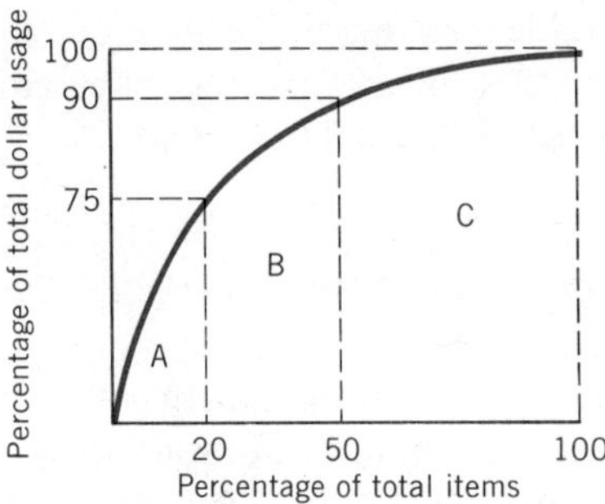

Figure 12.7. ABC inventory categories.

Annual usage important also.

A common misconception is that the ABC classification is based upon the dollar value of the individual items. Relatively costly items can still be classified as C items if the annual usage is low enough. Table 12.2 presents a simple table of cost/volume combinations and the inventory class likely to result.

ABC levels of control.

The ABC classification is management's guide to the necessary control priority of inventory items. A items should be subject to the tightest control with detailed inventory records being maintained and accurate, updated values of order quantities and reorder points being employed. B items are subject to normal control with order quantities being set by EOQ (as shown in the next section) but with less frequent updating of records and review of order quantities and reorder points. C items are subject to little control; orders are commonly placed for six month's to one year's supply so that relatively little control must be exercised and inventory records can be kept simple. Essentially, the control time and effort saved by *not* controlling C items is used to tighten control of A items.

Practical Aspects of Inventory Management

Inventory managers often pride themselves in the fact that they have been ordering quantities very near to the EOQ, even before an EOQ system was implemented. This

TABLE 12.2 CLASSIFICATION OF INVENTORY ITEMS

Dollar Value/Unit	Volume/Year	Category
High	High	A
High	Medium	A
Medium	High	A
High	Low	B
Medium	Medium	B
Low	High	B
Medium	Low	C
Low	Medium	C
Low	Low	C

should not come as a surprise since the natural forces within an organization tend to produce reasonable, if not optimal, inventory policies. That is, the sales people desire large quantities of inventory, accounting and financial personnel desire low quantities of inventory, and the operations manager desires fluctuating inventories so that production can operate most efficiently. The combination of these forces tends to produce an inventory policy that is a compromise of all of the individual departmental (and, thus, organizational) objectives. But, if one of the department managers is significantly more influential than the others (and this is often the case) an imbalance, and possibly a poor inventory policy, will come about.

Setting inventory levels by compromise.

12.4 MANAGING INVENTORIES IN AN UNCERTAIN ENVIRONMENT: THE SINGLE-PERIOD, "NEWSBOY" PROBLEM

Introducing uncertainty into the inventory situation.

In the previous sections we discussed the fundamental concepts and terminology of inventory management. The systems we described presumed an absoute knowledge of the parameters that determined optimal order quantities. We also discussed the notion of an order point based upon a known demand and a known lead time. Now it is appropriate to relax these assumptions so as to consider more realistic inventory situations. That is, we will introduce uncertainty into the inventory environment.

Demand uncertainty for a perishable commodity.

First, we will consider a problem that has been traditionally referred to as the "newsboy" problem, but which is applicable in numerous situations in which a *perishable* commodity is purchased in some order size (before demand is known) and is then either sold or scrapped, depending on the demand level. The following example will clarify the problem.

Clark Kent has, for three years, sold newspapers each morning at the corner of Upper and Downer Streets. Clark purchases the morning edition of the *Daily Planet* at 6:00 A.M. and stands on the corner from 6:30 to 8:30 each morning before walking two blocks to school. Clark buys the newspapers for $0.10 each and sells them for $0.15. Even though Clark is making a good profit on each newspaper sold and has developed quite a sizable bank account for a lad his age, he knows that he can do better.

Overstocking versus understocking.

It seems that he is always running out of papers before 8:30 A.M. and therefore missing potential sales, *or* having several papers left over that cannot be sold or returned to the newspaper company. He reasons that there must be some "best" order quantity to stock each day which will produce the largest average profit over the long run. Clark knows that he cannot perfectly predict daily demand and that he is bound to run out on some days and to overstock on others. But, he is sure that a consistent policy will maximize his expected profit over the long run. How many newspapers should Clark stock each day?

To answer this question we must first consider the demand for newspapers on Clark's corner. Suppose that Clark has kept a record of the number of papers demanded each day for 100 days. That is, even when he ran out of papers, Clark remained on the corner until 8:30 A.M. to count the number of people who asked for a

TABLE 12.3 CLARK'S NEWSPAPER DEMAND

Demand (newspapers)	Frequency (days)	Relative Frequency
28	10	.10
29	20	.20
30	35	.35
31	25	.25
32	10	.10
	100	1.00

paper, even though he had to tell them he had none left. His summary of the 100 days' demand is presented in Table 12.3.

Clark's lowest demand was for 28 newspapers and his highest demand was for 32. Therefore, he at least knows that he should never order more than 32, nor less than 28.* But, Clark could order any of the five quantities in between on any given day. Which number will maximize profits? Table 12.4, which is called a **payoff table** presents the daily profit for each "order/demand" combination.

The rows of Table 12.4 are labeled with the five potential order quantities and the columns are labeled with the five potential demands. Each combination of order quantity and demand will result in a different payoff, as seen in the body of the table.

Each entry in the payoff table is computed as follows. If Clark orders enough to equal or exceed demand, then

$$\text{profit} = \text{no. demanded} \times \$15 - \text{no. order} \times \$0.10 \qquad (12.2)$$

For example, if he orders 30 and 28 were demanded

$$\begin{aligned}\text{profit} &= 28 \times \$0.15 - 30 \times \$0.10 \\ &= 4.20 - 3.00 \\ &= \$1.20\end{aligned}$$

TABLE 12.4 PAYOFF TABLE FOR THE NEWSBOY PROBLEM

	Demand				
	28	29	30	31	32
Order quantity					
28	$1.40	$1.40	$1.40	$1.40	$1.40
29	1.30	1.45	1.45	1.45	1.45
30	1.20	1.35	1.50	1.50	1.50
31	1.10	1.25	1.40	1.55	1.55
32	1.00	1.15	1.30	1.45	1.60

* We are making the assumption here that 100 days history is enough to predict the future. Obviously, demand can change; Clark must simply be aware of the possibility and monitor for it.

If Clark orders less than is demanded on a given day, then he can only sell what he has in stock and therefore

$$\text{profit} = \$0.05 \times \text{no. ordered} \tag{12.3}$$

If 32 were demanded and he had ordered only 30

$$\begin{aligned}\text{profit} &= 0.05 \times 30\\ &= \$1.50\end{aligned}$$

With the information provided in the payoff table, Clark now knows the profit that will be earned for each of the potential order quantities and each of the possible daily demands. He can now determine the best order quantity by determining the expected profit to be earned using each order quantity.

Clark knows the relative frequency of occurrence of each level of demand. On the average, 28 newspapers are demanded 10 percent of the time, 29 newspapers are demanded 20 percent of the time, 30 newspapers are demanded 35 percent of the time, and so on. If Clark plays it safe and orders 28 newspapers each day, then the expected daily profit will be

$$\begin{aligned}E(P_{28}) &= 0.1(1.40) + 0.2(1.40) + 0.35(1.40) + 0.25(1.40) + 0.1(1.40)\\ &= \$1.40\end{aligned}$$

That is, his expected daily profit is *$1.40* if he orders 28 newspapers each day and the relative frequency of the demand levels remains as it was for the 100 day data collection period. This result is obvious since he is sure of selling at least 28 papers at a nickel profit each.

If Clark orders 30 newspapers each day his expected daily profit is

$$\begin{aligned}E(P_{30}) &= 0.1(1.20) + 0.2(1.35) + 0.35(1.50) + 0.25(1.50) + 0.1(1.50)\\ &= \$1.44\end{aligned}$$

Therefore, even though he will not sell all of the 30 newspapers each day (in fact, he will not sell all of them 30 percent of the time) his expected long run daily profit is greater than the more conservative approach.

Table 12.5 contains the expected profits for each of the five possible order quantity decisions. Since the expected profit for the "order *30*" decision is the greatest, the optimal policy is to order 30 newspapers each day.

TABLE 12.5 CLARK'S EXPECTED PROFITS

Order Quantity	Expected Daily Profit
28	$1.400
29	$1.435
30	$1.440 (best)
31	$1.392
32	$1.307

Does this mean that Clark will never run out of newspapers, or that Clark will never have bought more than he can sell? The obvious answer is NO! In fact, Clark can expect to *run out* 35 percent of the time; that is, the times that demand is 31 or 32, and to stock *more* than he needs 30 percent of the time, the times that demand is 28 or 29. This policy, though, is one that produces the greatest long run profit.

The newsboy problem in other situations.

This problem is a common one. Retailers purchase seasonal clothing, perishable foods, and other items such as Christmas trees, Valentine candy and cards, and fruit and vegetables in anticipation of demand. If too little demand is realized then the remaining goods are scrapped if not salable or "reduced-for-clearance," either at a loss or a reduced profit.

12.5 SAFETY STOCK FOR UNCERTAINTY IN DEMAND: STERLING'S JEWELERS

In the newsboy problem, the concern was with ordering quantities of a perishable commodity for a *single* period. The reorder point model, on the other hand, is concerned with *multiple* periods. Clark was forced to order each day because of the nature of his product but, on the other hand, he had no holding costs. Here we will introduce *demand* uncertainty into the problem. The case of *lead time* uncertainty is treated in the *Tools and Applications* portion of the chapter.

Sterling's Jewelers sells a relatively inexpensive man's watch, which it orders directly from a New York distributor. Tom O'Malley, the store's owner, recently attended a conference on inventory control, learned about EOQ's, and immediately decided to put this concept to work in his store. Tom collected the demand data shown in Table 12.6 for 20 weeks and computed an average weekly demand of 13 watches. Order cost was determined to be $30 and holding cost was calculated to be $2 per watch per year. The EOQ (for a 50-week year) was calculated to be (refer to Section 12.6) 140 watches. Lead time was known to be one week so Tom instituted the EOQ system with a reorder point of 13.

Soon after implementing this new policy Tom started receiving complaints from his clerks and customers that this particular watch was often out of stock. Steinberg's has constantly advertised a policy of always meeting customer demand so this problem especially concerned Tom. After two months he realized that he was losing numerous sales and that something must be wrong with his new inventory policy.

Uncertain demand over lead time.

Figure 12.8 presents a graph of the actual inventory level of the watches which Tom has recently placed on the 13 watch reorder point policy. As you can see, the inventory level is not constantly decreasing, as in the inventory graphs of the previous sections, but decreases randomly. Tom's inventory policy was based upon a constant demand (and therefore a constant rate of decrease in inventory level) since this is one of the EOQ assumptions. The numerous stockouts were the result of insufficient inventory available to meet the demand *between* the time the order was placed and the time the shipment was received. This demand is known as the "demand over the lead time" and is abbreviated as **DOLT**. As you can see from Table 12.6, weekly demand ranges from 10 to 16 watches. If an order is placed at the reorder point of 13 watches and either 14, 15, or 16 watches are demanded, there will be a stockout.

TABLE 12.6 WATCH DEMAND FOR STERLING'S JEWELERS

Week	Weekly Demand
1	10
2	13
3	12
4	16
5	11
6	13
7	16
8	13
9	14
10	12
11	15
12	10
13	16
14	14
15	15
16	13
17	11
18	12
19	13
20	11
	260

Average weekly demand = 13 units

Safety stock to protect against demand uncertainty.

In order to avoid stockouts, Sterling's must maintain a *safety stock* of watches. That is, a certain number of watches must be kept on hand solely to act as a buffer against the uncertainty in demand. For example, since Sterling's demand ranges up to 16 watches per week, a three (3) watch safety stock [calculated as: maximum demand over lead time (16) – reorder point (13) = 3] would result in zero stockouts. The appropriate level of safety stock depends upon the number of stockouts management is willing to allow each year. No stockouts is the ideal but, because of the increased holding cost resulting from the safety stock, can also be an expensive policy.

How many stockouts a year is acceptable?

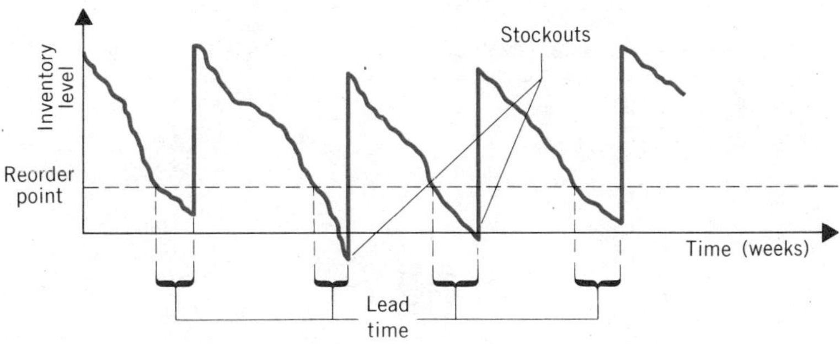

Figure 12.8 Graph of inventory level for Sterling's Jewelers.

Sterling's lead time from the New York distributor is one week. Since demand has been reordered on a weekly basis we can use the data in Table 12.6 to construct a frequency distribution for *demand over lead time*. You will recall that demand over lead time is the name we have given for the number of units demanded per lead time period (in our example, one week). Table 12.7 presents the frequency distribution for demand over lead time (DOLT).

The demand over lead time, DOLT.

Sterling's recently implemented inventory policy of ordering 140 watches results in 4.64 orders being placed per year

$$\frac{13 \text{ watches/week} \times 50 \text{ weeks}}{140} = 4.64$$

Stockout exposure.

or a recorder every 365/4.64 = 79 days. At the time an order is placed, presuming that a perpetual inventory system is maintained, the number of units on hand will equal the reorder point of 13 watches. But, within the one week period until the next shipment arrives, Sterling's is **exposed** to a stockout. If they do not maintain safety stock the risk of a stockout is greater than if an adequate safety stock level is being held.

Suppose Mr. O'Malley has decided that one stockout every year is the maximum that he will allow. That is, he is willing to take one chance in 4.64 exposures or a 1/4.64 = 21.55 percent chance of a stockout at each exposure. Using Table 12.7, constructed from Table 12.6, we can determine the probabilities of a stockout for any given reorder point. The probability of a stockout is calculated as 1.00 minus the probability shown in the right-hand column of the table that demand will be less than a given demand over lead time.

These probabilities of a stockout for each reorder point are shown in Table 12.8. From this table we can see that in order to have less than a 21.55 percent chance of a stockout (that is, more than 78.45 percent chance of demand over the lead time being *less* than the reorder point, the units on hand when an order is placed) the reorder

TABLE 12.7 STERLING'S FREQUENCY DISTRIBUTION FOR DEMAND

Demand over Lead Time, DOLT	Frequency	Relative Frequency	Cumulative Frequency (i.e., Probability that Demand Will Be Less Than or Equal to DOLT)
10	2	.10	.10
11	3	.15	.25
12	3	.15	.40
13	4	.20	.60
14	3	.15	.75
15	2	.10	.85
16	3	.15	1.00
	20	1.00	

The service level concept.

point will have to be set at 15 watches and therefore the safety stock is 15 − 13 = 2 units. With this reorder point, the probability of no stockout is 85 percent. This "probability of no stockout" is referred to as the **service level** for this inventory policy, and is the same as the cumulative probability column of Table 12.7.

TABLE 12.8 PROBABILITY OF A STOCKOUT FOR EACH REORDER POINT

Reorder point	Safety Stock	Probability of Stockout	Service Level (%)
10	−3	.90	10
11	−2	.75	25
12	−1	.60	40
13	0	.40	60
14	1	.25	75
15	2	.15	85
16	3	0	100

If Mr. O'Malley were to decide that a 25 percent chance of a stockout is the maximum acceptable (that is, he wants at least a 75 percent service level) then the reorder point would be set at 14 and the safety stock would be reduced to one (14 − 13) watch.

We have now covered the basic concepts of inventory management. In the next part of the chapter we will derive and apply some more sophisticated inventory management models, beginning with the basic EOQ model.

TOOLS AND APPLICATIONS

12.6 THE ECONOMIC ORDER QUANTITY

EOQ to balance ordering and carrying costs.

The *economic order quantity* (**EOQ**) concept applies to inventory items that are replenished in *batches* or *orders* and are not produced and delivered continuously. While we have identified a number of cost categories associated with inventory decisions, only two, the carrying cost and the ordering cost, are considered in the elementary EOQ model. The shortage and capacity-associated costs are not relevant because shortages and changes in capacity should not occur if demand is constant, as we assume in this elementary case. And the cost of the goods is considered to be fixed (for the moment) and, hence, does not alter the correct decisions as to *when* inventory should be reordered or *how much* should be ordered.

The Hard Charger Corporation

Let us again consider the Hard Charger Corporation, which sells 1000 generators per month (30 days) and purchases in quantities of 2000 per order. Lead time for the receipt of an order is six days. The cost accounting department has analyzed the inventory costs and has determined that the cost to place an order is $60 and that the annual cost of holding one generator in inventory is $10. Under its present policy of ordering 2000 per order, what is Hard Charger's total annual inventory costs?

Hard Charger's inventory pattern is represented by the "sawtooth" curve of Figure 12.9. For simplicity of presentation, let us define the following notation.

Q = order quantity
U = annual usage
C_O = order cost per order
C_H = annual holding cost per unit

In order to determine the total annual incremental cost of Hard Charger's current inventory policy we must determine two separate annual costs, the total annual holding cost and the total annual ordering cost.

The *ordering cost* is determined by C_O, the cost to place one order ($60) and the number of orders placed per year. Since Hard Charger sells 12,000 generators per year and orders 2000 per order, they must place six (12,000/2000) orders per year for a total ordering cost of $360 (6 orders per year × $60 per order). Using our notation, the annual ordering cost is written as

$$\text{annual ordering cost} = \frac{U}{Q} \times C_O \qquad (12.4)$$

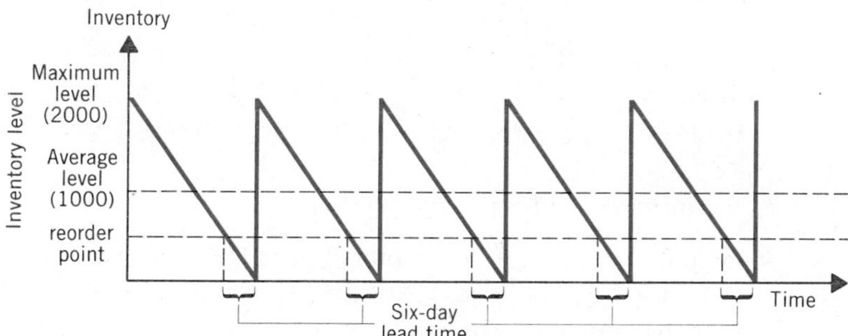

Figure 12.9. Hard Charger Corporation's inventory pattern.

The annual holding cost is determined by C_H, the cost of holding one generator for one year ($10) and the number of generators held. Notice that the inventory level is constantly changing and that no single generator ever remains in inventory for an entire year. On the average, though, there are 1000 generators in the inventory. Consider one cycle of Hard Charger's inventory graph as shown in Figure 12.10.

The inventory level begins at 2000 units and falls to 0 units before the next cycle begins. Since the rate of decline in inventory is constant (i.e., 1000 per month), the average level is 1000 units or simply the arithmetic average of the two levels: (2000 + 0)/2 = 1000.

If, on the average, there are 1000 generators in inventory over the entire year, then the annual inventory holding cost is $10,000 ($10 per unit × 1000 units). Or, in our general notation, the annual holding cost is

$$\text{annual holding cost} = \frac{Q}{2} \times C_H \tag{12.5}$$

Adding the annual ordering cost and the annual holding cost gives the following equation for total annual cost (TAC)

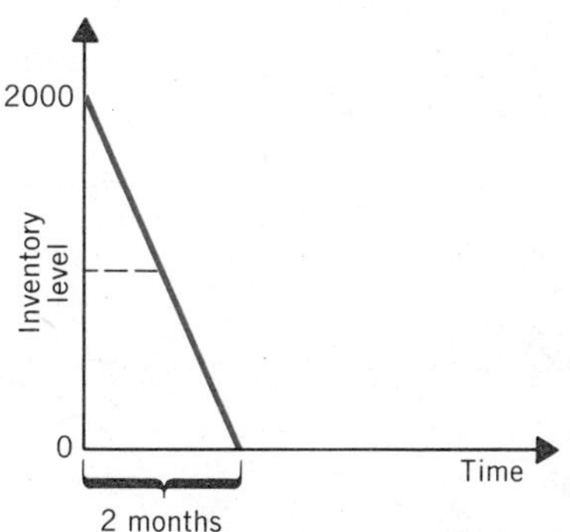

Figure 12.10. Hard Charger's inventory graph.

$$\text{TAC} = \left(\frac{Q}{2}\right) C_H + \left(\frac{U}{Q}\right) C_O \qquad (12.6)$$

For Hard Charger, the TAC is \$360 + \$10,000 = \$10,360.

Improving Hard Charger's Inventory Policy

Hard Charger's current inventory policy of ordering quantities of 2000 generators is costing \$10,360 per year. Is this the best policy or can it be improved? Using a simple trial and error approach we can answer this question.

First, let us see what happens if we increase the order quantity to 5000 units.

$$\begin{aligned} \text{TAC} &= \left(\frac{5000}{2}\right) 10 + \left(\frac{12{,}000}{5000}\right) 60 \\ &= 2500 \times 10 + 2.4 \times 60 \\ &= 25{,}000 + 144 \\ &= \$25{,}144 \end{aligned}$$

The annual holding cost increases and the ordering cost decreases, but the overall result is a significant increase in the total annual inventory cost. This is clearly an uneconomical choice. Let us try some other values. The resulting costs are given in Table 12.9.

We see from the table that 100 units is too small and the costs are beginning to increase again. But, we have bounded the range of solutions. The best order quantity is somewhere between 100 and 1000 items.

Finding an Optimal Policy

As you can imagine, the trial and error approach used above could go on for quite some time before an optimal policy is determined. A more straightforward approach to finding an optimal policy is to use the graphical approach or an algebraic solution.

We can graph the annual holding cost and annual ordering cost as a function of the order quantity as shown in Figure 12.11. Since the annual holding cost is $(Q/2)C_H$, which can be written $(C_H/2)Q$, we see that holding cost is linear and increasing with respect to Q. Annual order cost is $(U/Q)C_O$, which can be rewritten as $(UC_O)/Q$. We can see that ordering cost is nonlinear with respect to Q and decreases as Q increases.

TABLE 12.9 COSTS OF VARIOUS ORDER QUANTITIES

Order Quantity	Annual Holding Cost	Annual Ordering Cost	Total Annual Cost
2000	\$10,000	\$ 360	\$10,360
5000	25,000	144	25,144
1000	5,000	720	5,720
500	2,500	1440	3,940
100	500	7200	7,700

Now, if we add together the two graphed quantities for all values of Q we have the TAC curve as shown in Figure 12.11. Note that the TAC first decreases as ordering cost decreases but then starts to increase quickly. The point at which the TAC is a minimum is the optimal order quantity; that is, it gives the quantity Q which provides the least total annual inventory cost. This point is called the *economic order quantity*, or the EOQ, and, for this inventory problem, happens to occur where the order cost curve intersects the holding cost curve. From Figure 12.11 we can see that the EOQ is approximately 400 generators per order.

Finding the EOQ where the curves intersect.

We can compute an accurate value algebraically, by noting that the value of Q at the point of intersection of the two cost lines is the EOQ. We can find an equation for the EOQ by setting the two costs equal to one another and solving for the value of Q that satisfies the equality. That is,

$$\left(\frac{Q}{2}\right) C_H = \left(\frac{U}{Q}\right) C_O$$

Multiplying both sides by Q gives

$$\left(\frac{Q^2}{2}\right) C_H = UC_O$$

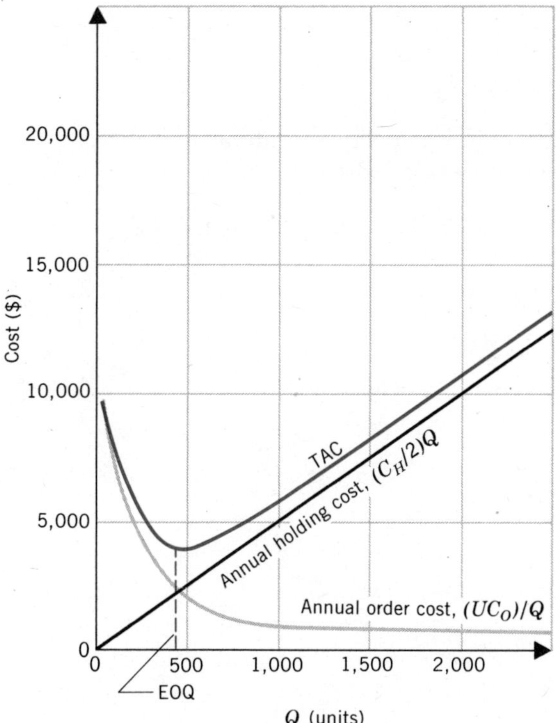

Figure 12.11. Annual inventory costs graph.

and dividing both sides by $C_H/2$ gives

$$Q^2 = \frac{2UC_O}{C_H}$$

Finally, taking the square root of both sides gives

$$Q = \sqrt{\frac{2UC_O}{C_H}}$$

The Q is the economic order quantity* and is most often written as

$$\text{EOQ} = \sqrt{\frac{2UC_O}{C_H}} \qquad (12.7)$$

For the Hard Charger Corporation we can compute the EOQ as

$$\text{EOQ} = \sqrt{\frac{2(12{,}000)60}{10}} = \sqrt{144{,}000} = 379.5$$

Obviously, since we cannot order half a generator, the order quantity would be rounded to 380 units.

The total annual cost of this policy would be

$$\begin{aligned}\text{TAC} &= \left(\frac{380}{2}\right)10 + \left(\frac{12{,}000}{380}\right)60 \\ &= 1900 + 1894.74 \\ &= \$3794.74\end{aligned}$$

Note that this is an improvement in total annual cost of $6565.26 over the present policy of ordering 2000. But also note that the optimal policy of ordering 380 per order

* For those students with an understanding of calculus, we could find the minimum of the TAC equation by taking the first derivative and setting it equal to zero as follows.

$$\text{TAC} = \left(\frac{Q}{2}\right)C_H + \left(\frac{U}{Q}\right)C_O$$

$$\frac{\partial \text{TAC}}{\partial Q} = \frac{C_H}{2} - \left(\frac{U}{Q^2}\right)C_O$$

Setting this equal to zero we have,

$$O = \frac{C_H}{2} - \left(\frac{U}{Q^2}\right)C_O.$$

or:

$$\left(\frac{U}{Q^2}\right)C_O = \frac{C_H}{2}$$

$$UC_O = \frac{Q^2C_H}{2}$$

$$\frac{2UC_O}{C_H} = Q^2$$

$$\sqrt{\frac{2UC_O}{C_H}} = Q$$

provides only a $145.26 savings over the "order 500" policy which we considered in our trial and error procedure. Actual inventory situations often exhibit this relative "insensitivity" to quantity changes in the vicinity of the EOQ. To the operations manager what this means is added flexibility in order quantity decisions. If, for example, shipping and handling was more convenient or economical in quantities of 500 (perhaps the items are wrapped in quantities of 250), the additional 120 units per order would only cost the organization an extra $145.26 per year.

Cost insensitivity in the EOQ region.

Cautions Regarding EOQ Computations

The GIGO rule.

The EOQ is a computed minimum cost order quantity. As with any model or formula, the GIGO rule (garbage in-garbage out) applies. If the variables used in computing the EOQ are inaccurate, then the EOQ will be inaccurate. EOQ determination relies heavily on two variables that are subject to considerable misinterpretation. These are the two cost elements, holding cost (C_H) and order cost (C_O). In the derivation of the EOQ we assumed that by ordering fewer units per order that the cost of holding inventory would be reduced. Likewise, it was assumed that by reducing the number of orders placed each year that the cost of ordering could be proportionately reduced. Both of these assumptions must be thoroughly questioned in looking at each cost element that is included in both C_H and C_O.

For example, if a single purchasing agent is employed by the firm, and orders are reduced from 3000 per year to 2000 per year, does it stand to reason the purchasing expense will be reduced by one third? Unless the person is paid on a "piece-work" basis the answer is clearly NO. Likewise, suppose that we rent a warehouse that will hold 100,000 items and we currently keep it full. If the order sizes are reduced so that the warehouse is only 65 percent occupied can we convince the owners to charge us only 65 percent of the rental price? Again, the answer is NO. Clearly then, when costs are determined for computations, only real, out-of-pocket costs should be used. Those costs that are committed or "sunk," no matter what the inventory levels or number of orders are, should be excluded because they violate the assumptions of the EOQ model.

Use only out-of-pocket costs in the EOQ.

Using the EOQ in Reorder Point and Periodic Review Inventory Systems

As we mentioned in the previous section, both reorder point systems and periodic review systems rely upon the EOQ concept for reorder level and review interval. Consider first the inventory level graph for the optimal "order 380" policy shown in Figure 12.12.

Hard Charger's maximum inventory level will be 380 units. Selling at the rate of 1000 per month, or 33.34 per day, the beginning supply of 380 will be sold in 11.4 days. An order must be placed six days (the **lead time**, LT) prior to the time the original supply will be exhausted so that an order will be received in time to avoid stockouts. In order to avoid stockouts, therefore, Hard Charger must reorder when the inventory level falls to 200 units (6 days × 33.34 per day). We can also see this result from Figure 12.12. If the inventory is used uniformly (this is one of the assumptions we have

The reorder point is based on LT.

made), then six days prior to the time the inventory level will fall to zero, the inventory level must be 200 units in order that 33.34 units can be sold (on the average) in each of those remaining days before an order is received.

For the periodic review system our concern is not with the optimal order quantity, but with the *time interval* for review and reordering. Using information provided by the EOQ model we can derive an effective period review policy. If Hard Charger orders 380 generators per order then, on the average, they will place 31.6 orders per year. That is, since the number of orders is given by U/Q, Hard charger will place 12,000/380 = 31.6 orders. The review period in a periodic review inventory system is constant; only the order quantity changes. Therefore, to equally space 31.6 orders throughout the year Hard Charger should order every 7.91 working days (practically, this would be rounded to 8 for convenience). That is, 250 working days per year/31.6 orders per year = 7.91.

12.7 THE ECONOMIC PRODUCTION LOT SIZE (ELS)

ELS for continuous production and use.

If an internally used part or assembly is also manufactured internally, rather than being procured from an outside vendor, it is often possible to use individual items *as they are produced* rather than waiting for an *entire lot*, such as a caseload, to be produced. The economic lot size model is used to determine the optimal inventory policy under these conditions. The following example will clarify the **ELS** problem.

Brush and Ladder Paint

Consider the Brush and Ladder Paint Manufacturing Company, which manufactures and sells latex interior wall paint. B&L is a small local company selling through three retail outlets in the same city as the manufacturing plant. Because B&L's largest selling paint (80 percent of all sales) is eggshell white, management wishes to establish an inventory policy for this one product. Demand for eggshell white has averaged 300 gallons per day. The setup cost for production of a new paint color is $250 including downtime of the machines, cleanup, and setup labor. The annual holding cost of a gallon of paint is $1.50. B&L's production management wants to know how many

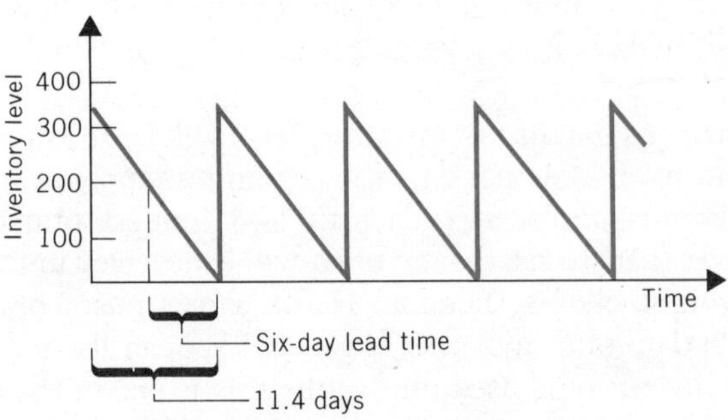

Figure 12.12. Optimal inventory pattern for Hard Charger Corporation.

gallons of eggshell white should be produced in each lot in order to minimize the combined total annual cost of holding inventory and setting up for production.

Let us use the following notation.

Q = production lot size
U = annual demand rate
P = annual production rate
C_O = setup cost per lot
C_H = annual holding cost

When a new order for paint production is given to the factory the previous lot of paint is terminated, all machines are disassembled for complete cleaning, all adjustments are made and the machines set up for the new production run. Once the setup is complete, production will begin and filled cans will exit the filling line at the rate of 800 one-gallon cans per day. These cans are moved by conveyer belt to the finished goods storeroom, from which sales and shipments to the three retail outlets are made. The system is graphically represented in Figure 12.13. Note that cans are available for use as they leave the filling line. The storeroom does not have to wait for a completed batch before using the paint.

Inventory level in the finished goods storeroom will simultaneously increase at the rate of 800 gallons per day and decrease at the rate of 300 gallons per day (the average daily sales), for a net increase of 500 gallons per day while the eggshell white is being produced. At the end of the production run, the inventory level will continue to decrease at the rate of 300 gallons per day until production of eggshell white resumes. In our notation, inventory will increase at the rate of $P - U$ while the lot is being produced and will decrease at the rate of U when eggshell white is not being produced.

One final question remains to be answered before we can draw the inventory level graph for B&L's eggshell white paint. We must know the duration of a production run in order to compute the maximum inventory level. If the production lot size is Q gallons and the facility can process and fill P gallons per year, then it will take the fraction Q/P years to complete the production run. The inventory level will grow to a maximum, computed as

$$\text{maximum inventory level} = (P - U) \times \frac{Q}{P} \quad (12.8)$$

which can be rewritten as

$$\left(1 - \frac{U}{P}\right) Q$$

Figure 12.13. B&L production system.

That is, the maximum inventory level is achieved at the point where eggshell white production terminates, the fraction Q/P years after it starts. Since the rate of increase in finished goods inventory is $(P - U)$, the maximum level is given by the rate of increase times the duration or $(P - U)$ times Q/P. We can now present the inventory level graph, Figure 12.14, for eggshell white paint.

For this inventory pattern the holding cost and setup (ordering) costs are computed similarly to the computation of these costs in the outside procurement (EOQ) model. Annual holding cost is computed as the average inventory level times the annual holding cost per unit in inventory. Using our notation

$$\text{average inventory level} = \frac{1}{2}\left(1 - \frac{U}{P}\right)Q$$

$$\text{annual holding cost} = \frac{1}{2}\left(1 - \frac{U}{P}\right)QC_H$$

Annual setup cost is computed as the number of annual setups times the individual setup cost.

$$\text{number of setups} = \frac{U}{Q}$$

$$\text{annual setup cost} = \left(\frac{U}{Q}\right)C_O$$

The total annual cost (TAC) is therefore given by

$$\text{TAC} = \frac{1}{2}\left(1 - \frac{U}{P}\right)QC_H + \left(\frac{U}{Q}\right)C_O \tag{12.9}$$

The optimal lot size is determined, in a fashion similar to that used for the EOQ model, to be*

$$\text{ELS} = Q = \sqrt{\frac{2UC_O}{\left(1 - \frac{U}{P}\right)C_H}} \tag{12.10}$$

For B&L, the economic production lot size for eggshell white paint is (assuming 250 working days per year)

$$\text{ELS} = \sqrt{\frac{(2(75{,}000)250}{\left(1 - \frac{300}{800}\right)1.50}}$$

* The first derivative of the TAC equation is

$$\frac{\partial \text{TAC}}{\partial Q} = \frac{1}{2}\left(1 - \frac{U}{P}\right)C_H - \left(\frac{U}{Q^2}\right)C_O$$

Setting this expression equal to zero and solving for Q gives

$$Q = \sqrt{\frac{2UC_O}{(1 - U/P)C_H}}$$

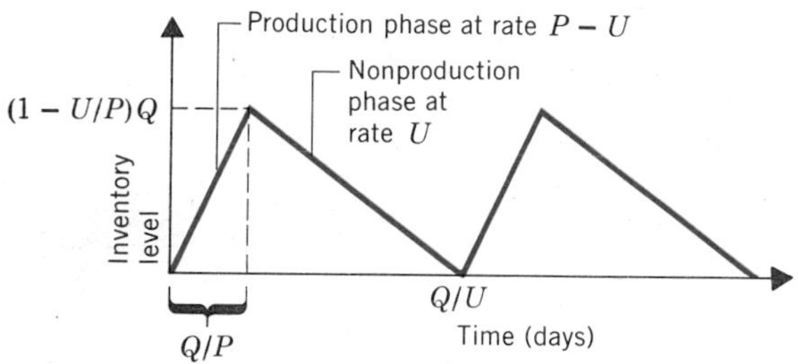

Figure 12.14. Inventory level graph for B&L.

$$= \sqrt{\frac{37{,}500{,}000}{0.9375}}$$

$$= \sqrt{40{,}000{,}000} = 6325 \text{ gallons}$$

Using this lot size the maximum inventory level will be

$$\left(1 - \frac{300}{800}\right) 6325 = 3953 \text{ gallons.}$$

The length of a production run will be

$$\frac{6325}{800} = 7.91 \text{ days}$$

and the total annual inventory cost will be

$$\begin{aligned} \text{TAC} &= \frac{1}{2}\left(1 - \frac{300}{800}\right) 6325 \times 1.50 + \left(\frac{75{,}000}{6325}\right) 250 \\ &= 2964.84 + 2964.43 \\ &= \$5929.27 \end{aligned}$$

12.8 LOT SIZING FOR MULTIPLE, RECURRING BATCHES

The problems of scheduling batches.

The two basic problems of multiple batch production are (1) what size batches should be produced? and (2) how should the batches be sequenced and scheduled? These two problems are highly interrelated however—specifying the batch size to a large extent fixes the schedule, and vice-versa.

Lot sizes for multiple batches.

For multiple batches, more than one output is competing for the *same* facilities. Inventories of the various outputs are used up (demanded) at different rates, can be produced at other rates, and undoubtedly have different "economic lot sizes." Given that the production capacity is limited, what are the "best" batch sizes for each of the products?

Consider the following very simple situation. A manufacturer has limited equipment available to produce two products, A and B, which have the demand rates, production rates, and economic lot sizes shown in Table 12.10. Note that the manufacturer can produce all the monthly demand for A in half a month (demand rate/production rate = 100/200 = 0.5) and all the demand for B in 2/5 (or 0.4) months. In total, production of both A and B only requires 0.9 months and, therefore, productive capacity seems quite adequate. The economic lot size for A is only 20 units which takes 20/200 = 0.1 months to produce and will last for 0.2 months. The economic lot size for B is 180 units so this requires 180/500 = 0.36 months to produce. Presuming A is scheduled on the equipment first, A finishes at 0.1 months and product B finishes at 0.46 months (0.1 for A + 0.36). In the meantime, however, product A will suffer a stockout (at 0.3 months). This situation is illustrated in Figure 12.15 for greater clarity.

Inferiority of ELS for multiple batches.

The conclusion is that "economic lot sizes" computed for products on a single item basis are not at all "economic" when other products compete for the same production equipment. One way to avoid this problem is by producing in lots other than the economic lot size—for example, in lots for each product that last an equal length of time.

In the two product case above, this would mean producing A for some fraction of a month and then B for the remainder of the month so that the units of A and B produced would each last X months. The amount to be produced within the month would thus be

$$100X \text{ units of product A} + 200X \text{ units of product B}$$

The amount of time to produce the A product would be $100X/200$ months and for the B product would be $200X/500$ months. Considering a one month production plan

$$\frac{100X}{200} + \frac{200X}{500} = 1$$

or

$$0.5X + 0.4X = 1$$

and therefore

$$X = \frac{1}{0.9} = 1.11 \text{ months}$$

$100X$ = 111 units of A taking 111/200 = 0.555 months to produce and

$200X$ = 222 units of B taking 222/500 = 0.444 months to produce

TABLE 12.10 DEMAND AND PRODUCTION RATES FOR TWO PRODUCTS

Product:	A	B
Monthly demand, units	100	200
Production rate, units/month	200	500
Economic lot size, units	20	180

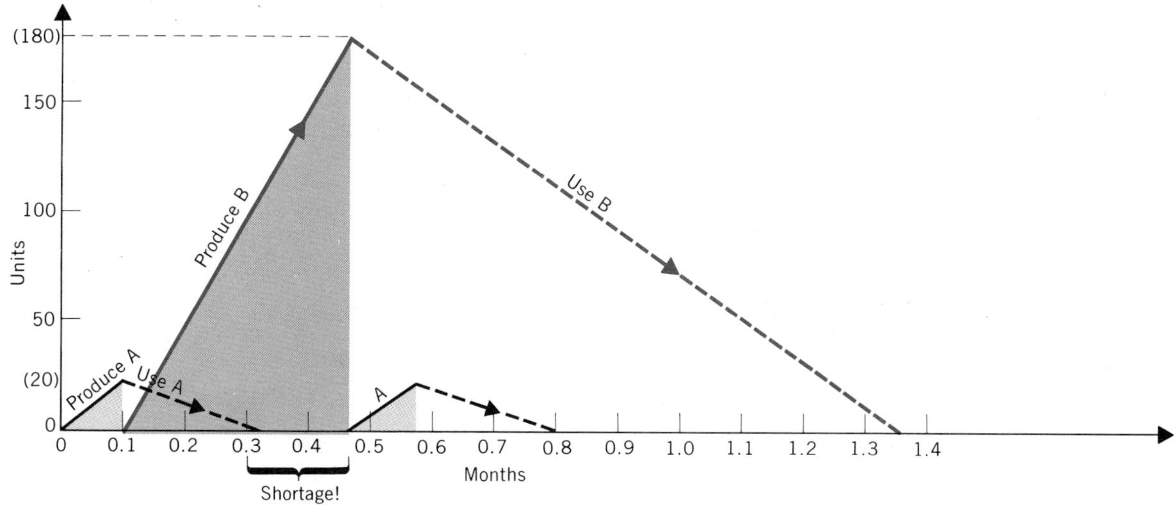

Figure 12.15. Two-product scheduling by economic lot size.

This schedule is shown in Figure 12.16. As seen, due to the extra capacity of the equipment it can be shut down (for maintenance, etc.) during 0.11 months every cycle. Although shown in Figure 12.14 as following the production of B this shutdown could be divided between the two runs or allocated in any other manner. And although Figure 12.16 represents a *feasible* schedule it is not very efficient (although the ease of scheduling may outweigh any loss in cost efficiency). More complex tech-

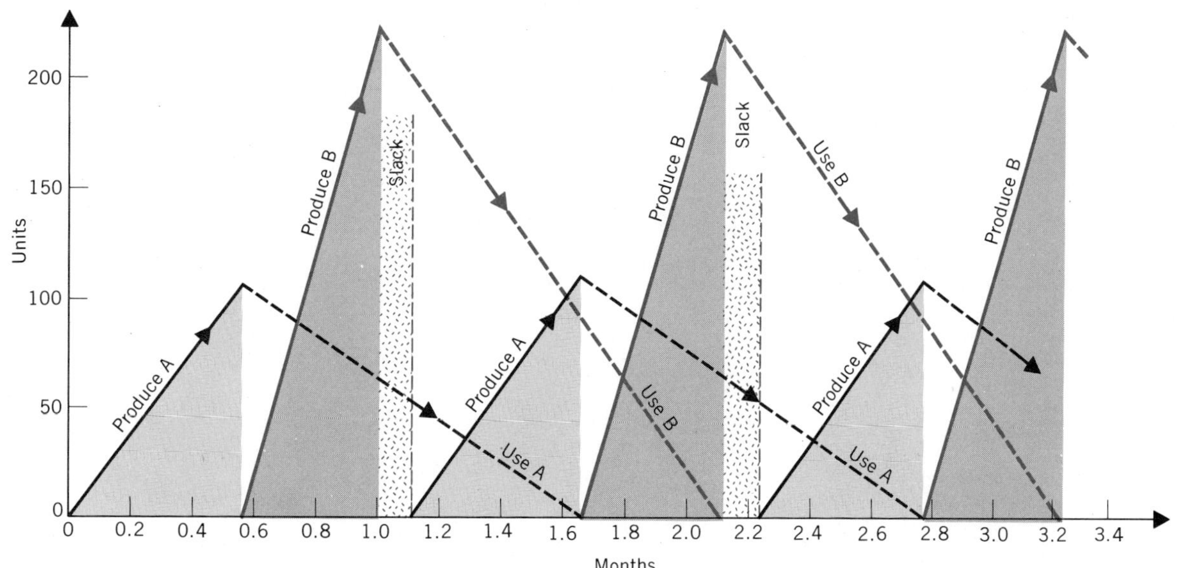

Figure 12.16. Two-product scheduling for equal usage periods.

niques do exist for determining economic lot sizes for multiple-product batches operations however (see Reference 1).

12.9 EOQ WITH QUANTITY DISCOUNTS

As briefly noted earlier, our total annual cost equations for the EOQ model have not included a term for the cost of the item itself. The reason for this omission is that we have assumed a constant unit cost for all of the items ordered or produced and therefore this unit cost does not change with changes in the order quantity.

Quantity discounts affect optimal order sizes.

In practice, though, this assumption is often not true. **Quantity discounts** are common practice in many businesses and are used by selling companies as incentives for purchasing companies to buy in larger quantities. With quantity discounts the total annual cost of the items purchased *does* change with changes in the order quantity and therefore unit cost must be considered in the EOQ model.

The Pinchpenny Co.

Consider the Pinchpenny Company which uses a small alloy casting in the production of one of its machines. Currently, annual usage of this item is 500 parts. The cost accountant has estimated that the cost to place an order is $49 and the inventory carrying cost is $1 per casting per year. Pinchpenny's supplier of castings, Buymorfromus, Inc., has just released the following discount schedule (Table 12.11) to the purchasing agent of Pinchpenny. The current policy employed by Pinchpenny is to order in EOQ's. Pinchpenny's purchasing agent must answer two questions regarding his purchasing policy now that discounts have been offered. Should they change this policy on the basis of the new discounts offered? If so, what should the new order quantity be?

The total annual cost equation for Pinchpenny, including the cost of the casting, is

$$\text{TAC} = \left(\frac{Q}{2}\right) C_H + \left(\frac{U}{Q}\right) C_O + UC \tag{12.11}$$

where C is the unit cost of the castings and the other notation is as defined earlier.

A rather simple two-step procedure is used to determine the answers to the above two questions. First, we compute Pinchpenny's current EOQ. If the EOQ is large

TABLE 12.11 DISCOUNT SCHEDULE FROM BUYMORFROMUS

Order Quantity	Unit Cost of Casting, C
0– 999	$5.00
1000–2499	$4.85
2500–over	$4.75

enough to receive the greatest discount, there is no problem to solve; the current EOQ will be maintained *and* the best discount will also be received. But, if the EOQ is less than the minimum order size to qualify for the largest discount (in our example, 2500) then the second step is entered. The current EOQ for the alloy casting is

$$\text{EOQ} = \sqrt{\frac{2(5000)49}{1}} = 700$$

which falls in the lowest class and, therefore, qualifies for no discount.

In the second step, we establish trial order quantities equal to the minimum order quantities qualifying for each discount level. For Pinchpenny's casting the two trial order quantities are $Q_1 = 1000$ and $Q_2 = 2500$ corresponding to the minimum order quantities that qualify for the \$4.85 and 4.75 prices from Buymorfromus. Then, we evaluate the total annual cost of the current EOQ and these two trial order quantities.

If we order the EOQ, the annual cost is

$$\begin{aligned} \text{TAC} &= \left(\frac{700}{2}\right)1 + \left(\frac{5000}{700}\right)49 + 5000(\$5) \\ &= 350 \quad + 350 \quad + 25{,}000 \\ &= \$25{,}700 \end{aligned}$$

If we order 1000, the total annual cost is

$$\begin{aligned} \text{TAC} &= \left(\frac{1000}{2}\right)1 + \left(\frac{5000}{1000}\right)49 + 5000(4.85) \\ &= 500 \quad + 245 \quad + 24{,}250 \\ &= \$24{,}995 \end{aligned}$$

If we order 2500, the total annual cost is

$$\begin{aligned} \text{TAC} &= \left(\frac{2500}{2}\right)1 + \left(\frac{5000}{2500}\right)49 + 5000(4.75) \\ &= 1250 \quad + 98 \quad + 23{,}750 \\ &= \$25{,}098 \end{aligned}$$

The costs for each of the three policies are summarized in Table 12.12.

Table 12.12 shows the results of changing the order quantity from 700 to 1000 and 2500, respectively. In both cases the ordering cost decreases and the holding cost

TABLE 12.12 TAC FOR THREE ORDERING POLICIES

Order Quantity	Annual Holding Cost	Annual Ordering Cost	Annual Purchase Cost	TAC
700	350	350	25,000	25,700
1000	500	245	24,250	24,995
2500	1250	98	23,750	25,098

increases. The decrease in holding cost is more than offset by the increase in ordering cost, for both trial order costs, resulting in net increases in cost. But, the annual cost of purchasing the castings decreases enough for the order 1000 policy to more than offset the net increase in the other inventory costs. Such is *not* the case in moving from 1000 to 2500 per order. The order quantity of 1000 has the minimum total annual cost of the three and therefore the Pinchpenny policy should be changed to "order 1000."

But, how do we know that some other quantity, such as 1500, or 3000, would not result in an even lower cost? In this case the EOQ for all three prices breaks was, we assumed, at the same quantity: 700. Therefore, for quantities greater than 7000, at the same unit cost, the TAC would be increasing. Figure 12.17 illustrates this point.

Sketching the TAC curves is a useful device for determining the best order quantity in more complex situations. More than two price breaks are common, which adds to the computation involved. Also, it is often true that the inventory carrying charge is related to the cost of the items being carried. If this is so, then the EOQ must be recomputed for each price rather than simply for the base price.

To illustrate, consider this simplified price break situation.

Quantity	Unit Cost
1–99	\$2.00
100 and over	1.00

where inventory carrying cost is computed as 20 percent of the value of the item, 250 items are used per year, and order cost is \$5. Computing the two EOQ's we have

$$\text{EOQ}_{\$2.00} = \sqrt{\frac{2(250)\,5}{0.2(2)}} = 79$$

$$\text{EOQ}_{\$1.00} = \sqrt{\frac{2(250)5}{0.2(1)}} = 112$$

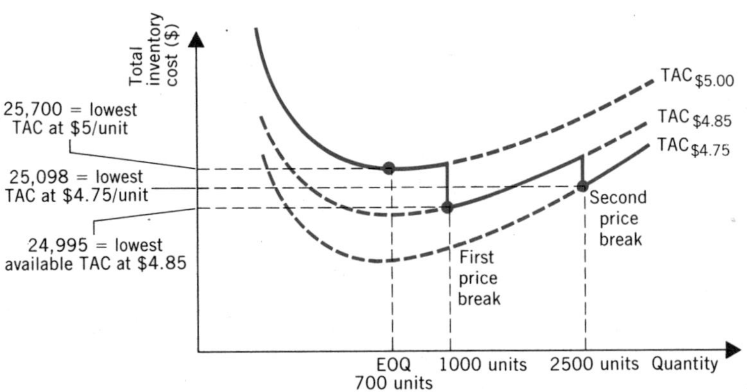

Figure 12.17. Illustration of Pinchpenny quantity discount problem.

Note that the optimal order quantity for the $1.00 price is 112 units and not 100, the minimum quantity that qualifies for the lower price. Figure 12.18 illustrates the TAC graph for this situation in which the EOQ changes as the unit cost changes (i.e., where the holding or carrying charge is computed as a percent of the unit cost).

12.10 UNCERTAINTY IN BOTH DEMAND AND LEAD TIME: THE SERVICE LEVEL CONCEPT

In the *Concepts* section of the chapter, the Sterling's Jewelers example was used to illustrate the impact of unknown demand over the lead time period. But, for Steinberg's, the lead time was assumed to be known. If lead time is also uncertain the problem of determining the proper amount of safety stock takes on an added dimension. We can approach this problem from two directions; attempting either to determine a solution *analytically* (as we have done in all of the previous inventory control situations discussed so far) or through **simulation**. We will use the following example to demonstrate both approaches.

Analytic and simulation approaches.

Great Gusher Oil and Gas Exploration Co.

The Great Gusher Oil and Gas Exploration Co. has been drilling oil and gas wells, working at one site at a time, for the past three years. Weekly use of diamond tipped drill bits over the past year has been between zero and three units per week as shown in Table 12.13. The supplier is located several hundred miles from Great Gusher's primary drill site and the drilling foreman has tabulated lead times for bit delivery to the site. Based on this data he has developed the probability distribution shown in Table 12.14.

Over the past three years Great Gusher has never stocked out of the required drill bit, primarily because an excessively high inventory of the units has always been maintained. The foreman wants to reduce the investment in the inventory by reducing the safety stock currently being held. He reasons that some number of stockouts

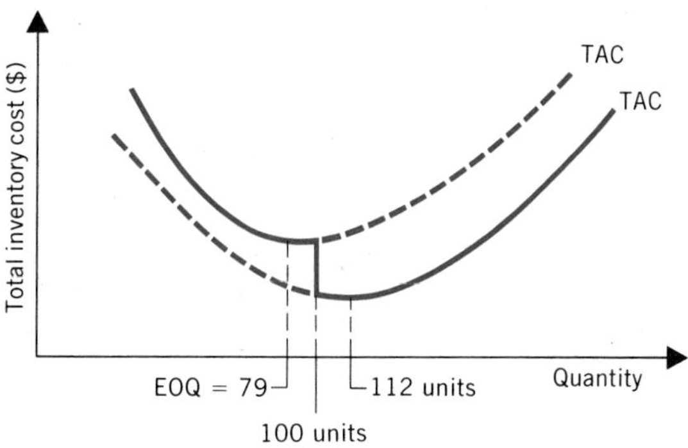

Figure 12.18. Quantity discounts and EOQs when holding cost is computed as a percentage of the unit cost.

TABLE 12.13 PROBABILITY DISTRIBUTION FOR WEEKLY DRILL BIT USE

Number Required	Probability
0	.10
1	.40
2	.30
3	.20
	1.00

is acceptable since, in an emergency, he could "borrow" a bit from any of six other drilling companies working in adjacent areas. Because of the number of personnel and the investment in equipment, shutdowns of the drilling rig must be avoided.

Analytical Approach

Using the joint probability distribution.

The foreman initially needs to know the probability distribution for demand over lead time (DOLT). Just as with Sterling's Jewelers, the distribution of DOLT is essential in determining the risk of a stockout associated with each of the various levels of safety stock which could be maintained. Because both weekly usage and lead time are uncertain, the distribution of demand (usage) over lead time is a function of the probability distributions of *both* lead time and demand. This DOLT distribution is known as a **joint probability distribution** which, for relatively simple problems like the Great Gusher example, can be computed using a simple tree diagram.

Figure 12.19 presents the tree diagram used to compute Great Gusher's drill bit DOLT distribution. To illustrate the computations involved in the tree, consider the branch "$LT = 2$ weeks." The probability that lead time will be two weeks is .3. If lead time is two weeks then there will be two weeks during which demand can be either 0, 1, 2, or 3 units each week. Hence, there are two levels or branches after the "LT = 2 weeks" branch in the figure. That is, demand can be 0, 1, 2 or 3 units in week 1 and 0, 1, 2 or 3 units in week 2, each weekly demand being determined by the probability distribution shown in Table 12.13. For example, if lead time is two weeks, the probability that demand will be 3 units the first week and 1 unit the second week is .2 ×

TABLE 12.14 PROBABILITY DISTRIBUTION FOR DRILL BIT LEAD TIME

Number of Weeks from Order to Delivery	Probability
0	.20
1	.50
2	.30
	1.00

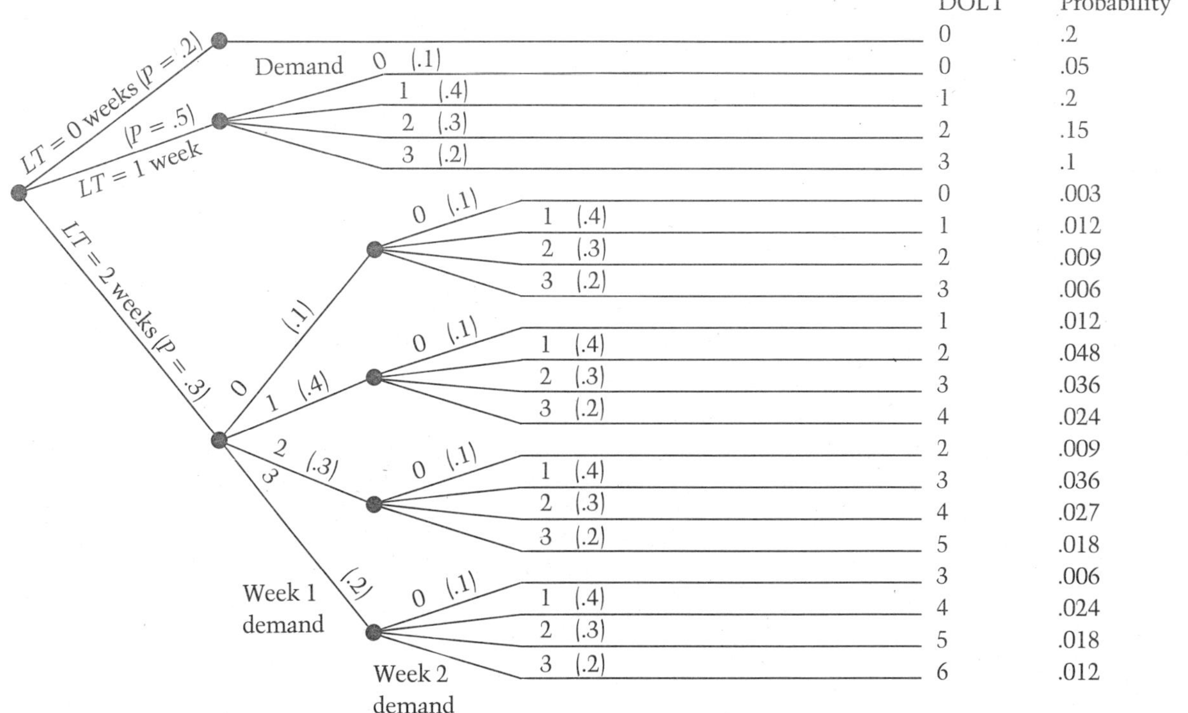

Figure 12.19. Tree diagram for drill bit demand over lead time distribution.

.4 = .08. The probability of the *joint* occurrence of $LT = 2$ weeks *and* 3 units demanded in the first week *and* 1 unit demanded in the second is .3 × .2 × .4 = .024. The probabilities for each of the other branches of the trees are computed in an identical manner.

The last two columns of data labeled "DOLT" and "Probability" provide the data necessary for the construction of the DOLT probability distribution. You will notice that there are several ways in which to get a total demand over lead time equal to a specific number of units. For example, to get a DOLT of 4 drill bits, lead time must be two weeks and demand for weeks 1 and 2 could be either 1 and 3, 2 and 2, or 3 and 1, respectively. Since the end result of each of these demand patterns is the same (i.e., DOLT = 4 drill bits) we simply add the probabilities for all like DOLT's to find that the probability of DOLT equaling 4 is .075 (i.e., .024 + .027 + .024). The final result of these calculations is shown in the DOLT probability distribution, Table 12.15.

We can now use this DOLT probability distribution just as we did in the earlier example with Sterling's Jewelers. First we construct the cumulative probability distribution for demand over lead time as shown in Table 12.16. We can now use this distribution to determine safety stocks and reorder points given the foreman's desired maximum risk of stockout; that is, his service level.

Safety stock based on desired service level.

TABLE 12.15 DEMAND OVER LEAD TIME DISTRIBUTION FOR DIAMOND DRILL BITS—GREAT GUSHER OIL AND GAS EXPLORATION CO.

Demand over Lead Time	Probability
0	.253
1	.224
2	.216
3	.184
4	.075
5	.036
6	.012
	1.000

For example, if the foreman wished no more than a 10 percent chance of stockout (that is, at least a 90 percent service level), the reorder point should be set at 4 units (see Table 12.16). Since *average* demand (computed from Table 12.13 as $0 \times .40 + 1 \times .40 + 2 \times .30 + 3 \times .20 = 1.6$) is 1.6 drill bits per week, the safety stock is thus 2.4 units ($4 - 1.6$). To have a 99 percent service level requires a reorder point of 6 units and if an 87.7 percent service level is acceptable (stockouts are expected to occur on 12.3 percent of exposures) the reorder point can drop to 3 units.

Simulation Approach

The second approach to inventory problems with uncertainty in both demand and lead time is simulation. Clearly, the tree diagram approach would become quite cumbersome if lead time exceeded three or four weeks (e.g., adding a lead time of three weeks to Great Gusher's problem would add 64 branches to the tree). Also, if the distributions of demand and lead time were continuous probability distributions rather than discrete distributions, as we have used here, the tree approach would be impossible and the mathematics required to form the joint distribution for DOLT quite complex.

TABLE 12.16 CUMULATIVE PROBABILITY DISTRIBUTION FOR DOLT

Demand, D	Service Level or P (DOLT $\leq D$)
0	.253
1	.477
2	.693
3	.877
4	.952
5	.988
6	1.000

TABLE 12.17 SIMULATION FOR WEEKLY DEMAND

If Random Number Is Between	Demand Equals
00–09	0
10–49	1
50–79	2
80–99	3

Testing inventory policies by simulation.

Simulation is a simple, descriptive technique that can handle extreme problem complexity. It requires the development of a model of a real situation or process and then the experimentation on that model using different policies (refer to Chapter 7) to determine the best policy. To give an example, we will manually simulate the Great Gusher problem for several periods.

Suppose that the economic order quantity of diamond drill bits is 15 and that the foreman wishes to try a policy of reordering when the inventory level falls to 2 units. Using a table of two-digit random numbers (see Appendix) the foreman can simulate lead times and weekly demand using Tables 12.17 and 12.18 (even one-digit random numbers could have been used here).

Now let us manually simulate the Great Gusher system starting with a beginning inventory of 15 drill bits and none on order. We begin by generating the first week's demand. We will use the random numbers in column 4 of Table 12.19 as demand random numbers and the numbers in column 9 as the lead time random numbers. The first random number is 39, therefore demand for week 1 is 1 unit (Table 12.17). Ending inventory for the week is therefore 14 units (15 − 1), and since it is not less than or equal to the reorder point of 2, no order is placed. Demand for week 2 is 2 units, found by using the second random number. Ending inventory is 12 which is still not below the reorder point. Table 12.19 presents the results of the simulation for 20 weeks. At the end of the eighth week the ending inventory has fallen to 1 unit and therefore, an order for 15 drill bits is placed between weeks 8 and 9. The lead time random number (column 9) of 76 generates (Table 12.18) a lead time of two weeks and therefore receipt of the order is scheduled between week 10 and 11. The simulation continues until the end of week 20 at which point it is discontinued. Typically, in a computer simulation we would continue for a long period of time, perhaps 50 to 100 weeks before terminating. From Table 12.19 we can see that the average inventory under the "order 15 when ending inventory reaches 2 units" policy is 8.55 drill

TABLE 12.18 SIMULATION FOR LEAD TIME

If Random Number Is Between	Lead Time Equals
00–19	0
20–69	1
70–99	2

TABLE 12.19 GREAT GUSHER SIMULATION

(1) Week No.	(2) Receipts	(3) Beginning Inventory	(4) Random No.	(5) Demand	(6) Ending Inventory	(7) Stockouts	(8) Order Placed	(9) RN	(10) Weeks To Arrive
0					15				
1	0	15	39	1	14				
2	0	14	73	2	12				
3	0	12	72	2	10				
4	0	10	75	2	8				
5	0	8	37	1	7				
6	0	7	02	0	7				
7	0	7	87	3	4				
8	0	4	98	3	1		15	76	2
9	0	1	10	1	0				
10	0	0	47	1	0	1			
11	15	15	93	3	12				
12	0	12	21	1	11				
13	0	11	95	3	8				
14	0	8	97	3	5				
15	0	5	69	2	3				
16	0	3	41	1	2		15	23	1
17	0	2	91	3	0	1			
18	15	15	80	3	12				
19	0	12	67	2	10				
20	0	10	59	2	8				
Total		171				2			
Av		8.55							

bits and that two stockouts occurred in two exposures. Using this simulation model the foreman could test any policy that he chooses and in this way select the policy which appears to be most reasonable to him.

Testing other policies.

For example, using the above policy of "order 15 when ending inventory reaches 2 units," the simulation model showed that the service level would be relatively poor. That is, a stockout occurred during both exposures. An alternative policy of "ordering 15 when the inventory level reaches 3 units" could be simulated to determine the impact on both average inventory level, the number of orders required in a given time period, and the service level provided. By varying the two decision variables (i.e., reorder point and order quantity) the foreman can determine the best policy without ever actually altering his current inventory control methods.

12.11 UNCERTAINTY AND NORMALLY DISTRIBUTED DOLT

If DOLT is normally distributed.

An assumption that is often made in determining safety stock is that demand over lead time is normally distributed. This assumption, which should always be tested before it is employed, significantly reduces the complexity of safety stock determination.

Dry Gulch Metropolitan Police Department

The Dry Gulch Metropolitan Police Department orders accident report forms from a printing company in a nearby town. Lead time has remained constant at one week and the demand per week has averaged 500 forms with a standard deviation of 250 forms. Figure 12.20 illustrates the distribution of demand over lead time for the accident report forms. The police chief has been ordering in quantities of 2600 units (two cartons). After much deliberation, the chief has decided that a policy of no more than one stockout in four years is appropriate. What reorder point (and safety stock) will satisfy the chief's policy?

ANALYSIS. First, the annual demand is 500/week × 52 weeks = 26,000 forms/year. Ordering 2600 forms per order leads to 10 exposures per year and the chief will allow one stockout in four years, or one stockout in 40 exposures. This translates into an allowable stockout probability of 2.5 percent or alternatively as a 97.5 percent (100 percent − 2.5 percent) *service level.*

The required safety stock can be determined by multiplying the **standard normal deviate**, Z, for a 97.5 percent service level times the standard deviation of demand over lead time.* Figure 12.21 presents the normal distribution of DOLT with the 2.5 percent probability area shaded. This shaded area represents the probability that DOLT will exceed the order point, which is the unknown in the problem. The order point is determined by finding the amount of safety stock which will have to be maintained. The value of Z for a 97.5 percent service level is 1.96; therefore the safety stock is

$$\begin{aligned} \text{safety stock} &= \mathbf{Z\ factor} \times \text{standard deviation of DOLT} \\ \text{safety stock} &= 1.96 \times 250 \qquad (12.12) \\ &= 490 \end{aligned}$$

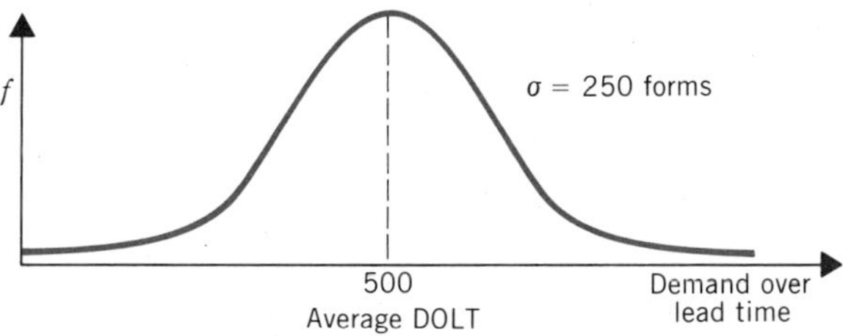

Figure 12.20. DOLT for Dry Gulch Police Dept.

* See Appendix B on probability and statistics if this procedure confuses you.

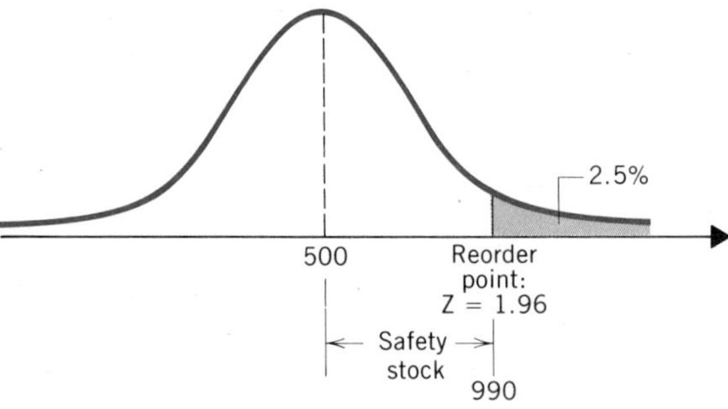

Figure 12.21. Normal distribution of DOLT.

and the reorder point is therefore

$$\begin{aligned} \text{reorder point} &= \text{average DOLT} + \text{safety stock} \\ \text{reorder point} &= 500 + 490 \\ &= 990 \end{aligned} \tag{12.13}$$

If an order is placed when 990 units are on hand, the chance of running out before receiving the order is 2.5 percent.

12.12 SUMMARY

In this chapter we have introduced the concepts and terminology of modern inventory control. The purpose of carrying inventory includes providing good customer service, smoothing production flow, protecting against uncertainty in supply and demand, and effectively utilizing equipment and personnel.

The various types of inventory include transit, buffer, anticipation, decoupling, and cycle inventories. In terms of inventory system design, the cost categories of holding costs and ordering costs are often the major quantifiable costs. In addition to these, other inventory costs are stockout costs, capacity-associated costs, and the cost of the goods themselves. Reorder point, periodic review, and material requirements planning are the main types of inventory systems.

We also introduced the more realistic condition of uncertainty in demand. We considered two situations under which demand uncertainty can be a problem. In the "newsboy" problem, we considered the single period problem of ordering a perishable commodity where demand for that commodity was uncertain. We also considered the situation of uncertainty in demand for a durable commodity that was ordered for multiple periods. Each situation, when combined with uncertain demand, results in reorder point uncertainty. Thus, we introduced the ideas of safety stock and service level to determine the appropriate reorder point under uncertain conditions.

The economic order quantity (EOQ) and the economic production lot size (ELS) models were derived to address the "how much" question of inventory control. The EOQ model was also used under the situation of quantity discounts.

Uncertainty in both demand and lead time simultaneously was addressed with both analytical and simulation models. The power of simulation as a general method of modeling inventory systems with uncertain parameters was also demonstrated.

12.13 READINGS

How getting sacked could be your bag

BY SI CORNELL
Post staff reporter

If you're left holding the bag these days, you'd better hang on to it.

The grocery bag and the carry-out sack, mainstays of American consumer life, may become a scarce item.

Retailers are being warned by suppliers to be prepared for a real paper bag shortage in the next few months.

"There is a definite shortage of paper of all kinds," according to S. David Shor, board chairman of Duro Paper Bag Manufacturing Co., this area's only paper bag producer.

"If the strikes on the West Coast continue another month things will be a lot worse," he said.

Workers in big West Coast paper and pulp mills have been striking up to three months. Even some union lumberjacks are out. Other paper mills scattered around the country, many of which are owned by the West Coast giants, have been sending portions of their production West to fill the gap, tightening supplies in the Midwest and East.

National reports on the present shortage blame not only current strikes but a decline in paper bag production. Gulf States Paper Corp., which once produced nearly 10 percent of all paper bags, closed its plant at Tuscaloosa, Ala., and quit the business entirely on grounds it required too much capital investment for the profit involved.

Crown Zellerbach Corp., based in San Francisco, closed its bag plant in Bogalusa, La., and pulled out of the eastern and midwestern markets.

Duro supplies Kroger's and Shor said "we're taking care of our customers."

Any shortage likely will hit smaller stores harder than big chain operators. A Kroger official said the firm buys months ahead and isn't worried about bags for the holiday rush. Kroger's uses 500 million bags a year.

Frisch's Restaurants uses 7.6 million carry-out bags a year and an official said a good stockpile is on hand. But prices are going up. Frisch's says it had been informed of a 15 percent price increase on the next order.

Bernard Strunk, vice president of Saalfeld Paper Co., which supplies Frisch's sacks, said it now is taking eight weeks or more to get paper bag orders filled at the mills. Deliveries in the past have been as quick as one week.

Jack B. Schneider, executive vice president of Diem & Wing Paper Co., said he expected paper towels and toilet tissue to remain unaffected in any shortage. But he says shopping bags, millinery bags, quality paper for lithography and fine printing, paper tape and even supplies for corrugated boxes might become scarce.

"Lithographers and industrial plants with printing operations have doubled and tripled their supplies," he said. "It's a very complex situation."

Local department stores report adequate shopping bag supplies on hand. If they suffer any scarcity at all it likely would be in small, colorfully printed specialty sacks.

Fred Michell, sales promotion director for Champion Paper, said paper bags have increased 30 per cent in price since last Jan 1.

"The problem begins with the finest paper," he said. "Magazines and business catalogs have increased the number of their pages tremendously."

What with more demand, strikes, plant closings, there isn't much cheap paper around at the moment to make the lowly paper sack which becomes important only when you try to go home from the store.

Source. "Focus" September 19, 1978. Reprinted courtesy of *The Cincinnati Post*.

SORRY, NO BAGS
FRIES
KETCHUP
B. SCHILMEISTER

12.14 KEY TERMS

Concepts

customer service (p. 400)
smoothing production flow (p. 403)
work-in-process (p. 405)
raw material (p. 405)
transit (p. 401)
buffer (p. 401)
anticipation (p. 402)
decoupling (p. 403)
cycle (p. 404)
setup (p. 406)
holding (p. 407)
stockout (p. 407)
capacity-associated cost (p. 407)
reorder point (p. 409)
periodic review (p. 411)
paced line (p. 404)
service level (p. 421)
DOLT (p. 418)
order cost (p. 406)
on-hand (p. 411)
on-order (p. 411)
back order (p. 401)
when? (p. 408)
economic order quantity (p. 409)
how much? (p. 408)
two-bin (p. 409)
perpetual (p. 410)
lead time (p. 409)
independent demand (p. 412)
MRP (p. 412)
ABC (p. 413)
safety stock (p. 401)
exposure (p. 420)
payoff table (p. 416)
pipeline (p. 401)

Tools and Applications

EOQ (p. 422)
ELS (p. 428)
quantity discount (p. 434)
simulation (p. 437)
Z factor (p. 443)
standard normal deviate (p. 443)
joint probability distribution (p. 438)
lead time (p. 427)

12.15 REVIEW TEST

Concepts

1. The more inventory in a system the less the flexibility. (p. 403)
   a. True b. False
2. Transit inventories are the inventories that exist between two machines on a production floor. (p. 401)
   a. True b. False
3. Stockout costs are equal to the cost of the merchandise not sold. (p. 407)
   a. True b. False
4. The ABC analysis system is concerned only with inventory values. (p. 413)
   a. True b. False
5. Safety stock is the average amount of inventory left when an order is finally received. (p. 418)
   a. True b. False
6. A periodic review inventory system gives the same results as a reorder point system (p. 411)
   a. True b. False
7. A two-bin system is a version of the reorder point system. (p. 409)
   a. True b. False
8. The "newsboy" problem is concerned with order quantities for perishable items. (p. 415)
   a. True b. False
9. Service level is equal to the probability that an item will be in stock when demanded. (p. 421)
   a. True b. False
10. Safety stock computations are based only on rates of demand. (p. 421)
    a. True b. False
11. An exposure to a stockout occurs every time the inventory level approaches the reorder point. (p. 420)
    a. True b. False
12. The two major inventory questions are when to order and how much to order. (p. 408)
    a. True b. False

13. The safety stock is the difference between the reorder point and the average demand over lead time. (p. 421)
    a. True b. False
14. Inventory systems in organizations tend to be nonoptimum and, hence, large savings can be expected through implementing an EOQ system. (p. 409)
    a. True b. False
15. An MRP system is designed to handle dependent demand situations. (p. 412)
    a. True b. False

Tools and Applications

16. The EOQ minimizes total order cost. (p. 422)
    a. True b. False
17. The cost of the goods themselves is never considered in inventory models. (p. 434)
    a. True b. False
18. DOLT is always normally distributed. (p. 422)
    a. True b. False
19. Simulation is conceptually less complicated than analytical solutions to uncertainty problems, but does not guarantee optimal solutions. (p. 442)
    a. True b. False
20. In a quantity discount situation, the EOQ will never be the best order quantity. (p. 436)
    a. True b. False

12.16 DISCUSSION QUESTIONS

1. Grocery stores have traditionally operated on a periodic review basis for inventory control. What type of system can (will) be maintained with the new automatic sensing equipment being installed at checkout counters?
2. Discuss the limitations of the EOQ model.
3. Is certainty in demand and lead time a reasonable assumption?
4. What effect(s) on the types of inventories would "beaming" a la Star Trek produce?
5. Discuss the use of EOQ type models in such places as hospitals (blood banking, gauze, pacemakers, etc.) and pharmacies. What type of service level is appropriate?
6. If you were implementing a new inventory system on a computer and top management wanted to get the most "value" from the new system in the first week of installation, what priority would you give the order of entry of the inventory items on the master file?
7. Discuss why the reorder period will vary in a reorder point system.
8. What inflexibilities are forced on service organizations as a result of their inability to inventory their output? Is it possible to inventory any of these outputs? Give examples.
9. Why is the decision tree not practical for solving inventory problems with a large number of uncertain demand and lead time possibilities?
10. With the two probability distributions of demand and lead time, how can the distribution of DOLT be found? Under what conditions can (should) each be used?
11. Why would a marketing program that would "stabilize" demands benefit inventory levels?
12. Describe what service level means from the perspectives of the marketing manager and the inventory control manager.
13. List two organizations which have high service levels and two which should probably have low service levels. Why would you expect these service levels in each case?
14. What happens to total annual inventory cost as lead time uncertainty increases? As demand uncertainty increases?
15. What other inventory situations are similar to the "newsboy" inventory situation discussed in the chapter?

12.17 PROBLEMS

Concepts

1. Mario's Pizza, across from the campus main gate, serves pizza by the slice and does a substantial lunch business. The following table provides demand information based upon an analysis of the last six month's activity. Mario's direct cost in a pizza is $2.00. He sells each pizza for a total revenue of $5.00. If Mario want to maximize profits, how many pizzas should he make each day?

Demand	Probability
45	.15
46	.15
47	.25
48	.20
49	.15
50	.10

2. Lead time for delivery of frozen hamburgers to a fast-food restaurant is known to be three days. Daily demand has been charted as follows.

Daily demand	Probability
1200	.30
1300	.20
1400	.50

If a service level of at least 85 percent is desired, what safety stock should be held? What is the reorder point?

3. Demand for strawberries at McDonald's Berry Patch, Inc., has been recorded as follows.

Demand (quarts)	Probability
13,000	.1
15,000	.5
18,000	.2
20,000	.1

McDonald's orders berries on Monday morning from a large wholesaler and pays $0.40 per quart. Any berries not sold at the retail price of $0.95 per quart are sold for $0.30 per quart to a local family which makes strawberry jelly for sale at the flea market. How many quarts of berries should McDonald's purchase to maximize profits?

4. John operates a boring mill and Frank a hone. John's parts, when finished, are placed in crates and moved to Frank's location where they are honed to remove internal burs. Both men are on an incentive system that requires the company to pay for at least two hours of work for each person when a machine fails. That is, if John's boring mill were to stop, Frank would continue working until parts ran out, but would get paid for at least two hours even if parts did not last that long. Frank can hone one part in two minutes and set up the next in a half-minute. If the company policy is to have enough parts so that Frank must work the full two hours for which he will be paid, how much inventory must be maintained between the two workers?

5. In the following list of inventory items, which would you consider to be C items?

Cost	Sales/Year
$10	3,000
$12	80,000
$ 6	15,000
$ 3	1,200
$10	18,000
$ 4	4,000
$18	10,000
$27	8,500

Tools and Applications

6. For the following distributions, determine the DOLT distribution.

Lead Time (Weeks)	Probability	Demand/ Week	Probability
1	.7	3	.6
2	.3	4	.4

7. What service level would be expected if a reorder point of 7 were used with the data in Problem 6?

8. Weekly demand for gasoline at a local service station is normally distributed with a mean of 6000 gallons and a standard deviation of 800 gallons. If order cost is $50 and holding cost is $0.02 per gallon per year, what order quantity and reorder point should be used to provide an 85 percent service level? Assume lead time is one week.

9. The Frame Up, a self-service picture framing shop, orders 3000 feet of a certain molding every month. The order cost is $40 and the holding cost is $0.05 per foot per year. What is the current annual cost? What is the maximum inventory level? What is the EOQ?

10. The Discount Drum Co. buys used 55 gallon drums from several chemical companies and cleans and resells them. One supplier has offered the following quantity discount schedule.

0–49	$3.00
50–99	2.75
100 and over	2.50

The order cost is $100 and holding cost is $0.50 per drum per year. If Discount can sell 8000 drums per year, what order quantity should they use?

11. Happy Days Jacket Company manufacturers 1950s vintage leather jackets. They can produce jackets at the rate of 5000 per year. Sales average 3000 per year. What production lot size should be used if setup costs are $200 and holding costs are $3 per jacket per year?

12. The Quick In-Quick Out Corner Convenient Store receives orders from its distributor in three days from the time an order is placed. Lighter Than Air beer sells at the rate of 860 cans per day (they can sell 250 days of the year). A six pack of Lighter Than Air costs QIQOCCS $1.20. Holding cost is 10 percent of the cost of the beer. Order cost is $25.00. What is QIQOCCS's EOQ and what is the reorder point?

13. The Efficiently Operating Quarry Company places orders for blasting caps once each month. The order quantity is 500 per month. The purchasing agent has just learned of the EOQ model and wants to try it out. He determines that order costs are $150 and that holding cost is $8 per cap per year. What is the EOQ? Should they change their order quantity to the EOQ? Base your answer on economic and practical grounds.

14. Wing Computer Corp. uses 15,000 keyboards each year in the production of computer terminals. Order cost for the keyboards is $50.00 and holding cost for one keyboard is $1.50 per unit per year. What is the EOQ? If Wing ordered 1250 per month, what will the total annual cost be? What is the average inventory level?

12.18 CASE VETTER CORPORATION

Vetter Corporation manufactures tables and work stations for the ever-growing computer industry. Vetter began operations three years ago with a single product, a cathode ray tube (CRT) stand which sold for $98. That product was designed by Vetter, completely subcontracted for manufacture of parts and assembled at the Vetter plant.

Since that beginning, Vetter has continually developed new products and has made efforts to vertically integrate their production and assembly operations. Currently, Vetter manufactures all of their own tops, does all laminating work and all sheet metal work with the exception of chromed tubular steel table legs. These legs are manufactured by a large company located approximately 120 miles away. Vetter's demand has been growing at such a rate that supplies of table legs have been constantly short. Vetter's expeditors have been pressed to keep a supply of legs in stock. Vetter uses 300 sets of table legs per day in the manufacture of two different CRT stands. Because of the delays and delivery uncertainties, Vetter has been considering manufacturing these legs themselves. Vetter has been using an economic order quantity of 6000 sets. The annual holding cost per set is $1.20. Vetter's industrial engineer estimates that with the proper equipment they can produce 800 leg sets per day. Setup costs for the equipment will be $750.

Jim Lochary, the production supervisor, is in favor of self-production by purchasing the new equipment. He argues that "being able to produce the legs ourselves will result in virtually no inventory being on hand. Our inventory holding costs will drop substantially." Peter Thomsen, the purchasing agent, argues that "if we are the only source of supply, downtime will surely kill us." Bobby Smith, the warehouse supervisor, contends that "we simply don't have space to increase inventory any more. If making them ourselves will help to solve the space problem, I'm all for it."

QUESTIONS FOR DISCUSSION

1. What production lot size is justified if Vetter decides to purchase the leg manufacturing equipment?
2. How would you approach the problem of resolving these inventory level comments?

12.19 REFERENCES AND BIBLIOGRAPHY

1. Buffa, E. S., and Miller, J., *Production-Inventory Systems: Planning and Control*, 3rd ed., Homewood, Ill.: Irwin, 1979.
2. England, W. B., and Leenders, M. R., *Purchasing and Materials Management*, 6th ed., Homewood, Ill.: Irwin, 1975.
3. Hadley, G., and Whitin, T. M., *Analysis of Inventory Systems*, Englewood Cliffs, N.J.: Prentice-Hall, 1963.
4. Magee, J. F., *Production Planning and Inventory Control*, New York: McGraw-Hill, 1958.
5. Plossl, G. W., and Wight, O. W., *Production and Inventory Control*, Englewood Cliffs, N.J.: Prentice-Hall, 1967.
6. Wagner, H. M., *Statistical Management of Inventory Systems*, New York: Wiley, 1962.
7. Wight, O. W., *Production and Inventory Management in the Computer Age*, Boston: Cahners, 1974.

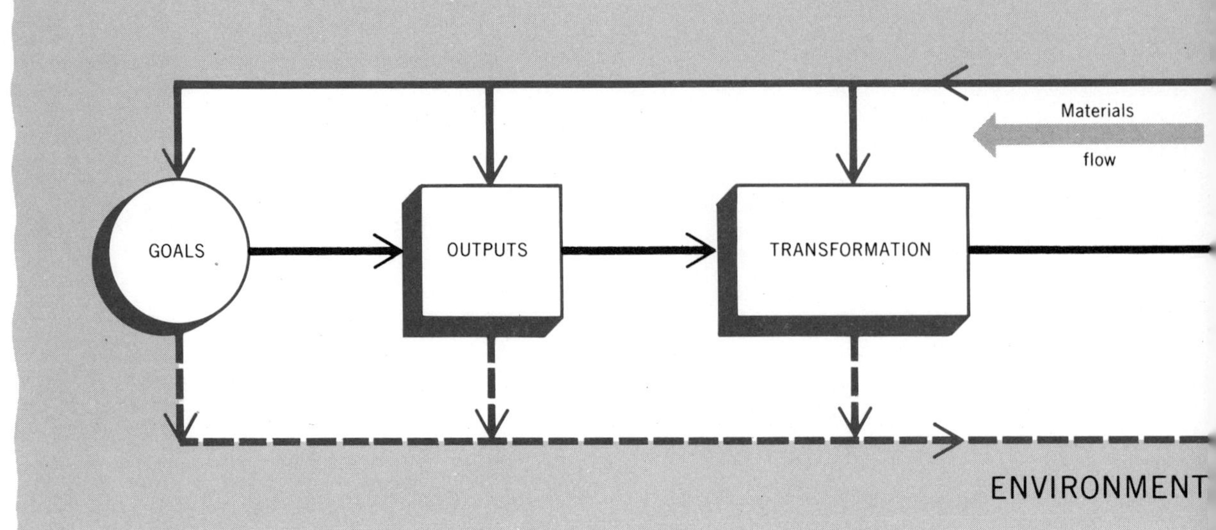

Chapter 13

Inventory Management for Dependent Demand

CONCEPTS

13: MRP

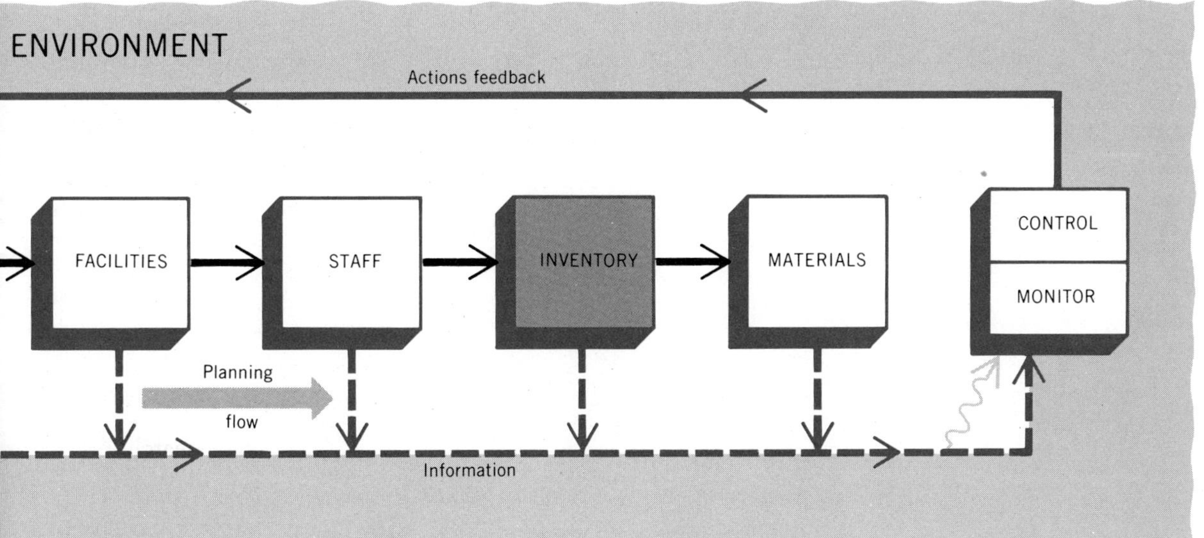

TOOLS AND APPLICATIONS

LEARNING OBJECTIVES

By the completion of the *Concepts* portion of this chapter the student should

1. Understand the difference between dependent and independent demand.
2. Realize that dependent demand situations typically require a different method of inventory management.
3. Be aware of the significant role of the computer in dependent demand inventory management.
4. Know the MRP approach to inventory management and be able to conduct an MRP analysis.
5. Be able to solve a lot sizing problem using the part period balancing method.
6. Understand the role of computerized files in the MRP process, what the various files are, and how they must be maintained.

CONCEPTS

This chapter introduces a relatively new concept in inventory control, that of **dependent demand**. In the previous chapter we discussed the use of reorder point and periodic review inventory management systems. We concentrated our attention on the problem created and the solutions for systems with unknown periodic demand and uncertain lead times. But, as we have previously indicated, these *statistical* or *probabilistic* inventory management systems perform best for demands of finished goods inventories and for some raw materials inventories. That is, inventories such as men's slacks and shirts in a retail store, cases of cereal from a wholesale grocery, and demand for airline flights from a given city are independent of other demands. Also, some raw materials, such as nails in a modular home assembly plant or latches in a storm window manufacturing facility, can also be considered as independent because they would be used in equal quantities no matter what product is being produced. Statistical reorder systems, though, have typically proved themselves inadequate for many types of raw materials and for assemblies and subassemblies used in producing a "higher level" product.

Independent demand materials.

The key to this lack of performance has been pointed out and researched by Dr. Joseph Orlicky [5,6] and has been further developed and promoted by such other noted inventory management specialists as George Plossl and Oliver Wight [6,7]. As these and other researchers and practitioners have noted, statistical methods perform well for "smooth" or "constant" demand; that is, demand with rather normal fluctuations around an average value or a trend value. But they perform poorly if demand is "lumpy"; that is, if demand remains fairly constant for a period, then surges for a short duration, and then returns to its previous constant level. Examples of constant and **lumpy demands** are shown in Figure 13.1. For the constant demand case, demand varies around the average (shown by the dashed line). A standard deviation can be calculated and a reorder point determined which will provide a specific level of assurance against a stockout. But, for the "lumpy" demand case, using the same statistical

Smooth versus lumpy demand.

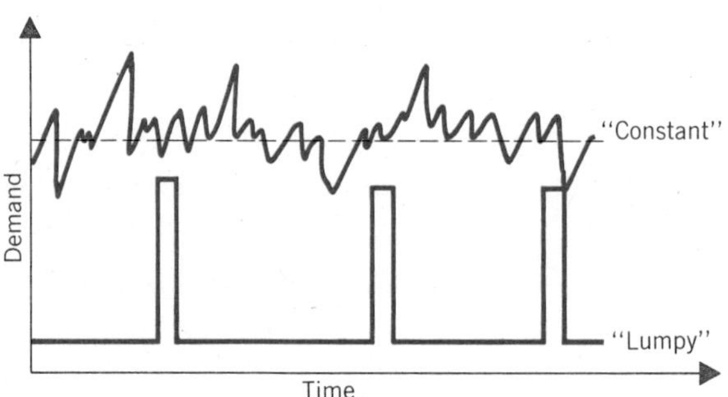

Figure 13.1. Constant and lumpy demand.

approach results in average inventory levels that are much too high. The example in the next section will illustrate this point. The entire focus of this chapter is material requirements planning (**MRP**), which is a system designed specifically for the "lumpy" demand situation when the "lumps" are known about beforehand, typically because the demands are "dependent."

13.1 INDEPENDENT VERSUS DEPENDENT DEMAND

Independent finished goods but dependent subassemblies and raw materials.

Many items, particularly *finished products* that are demanded in many small quantities by customers (e.g., General Motors auto sales to dealers, sales of ice cream at a local grocery, etc.), are said to experience "independent" demand. That is, the demand cannot easily be related to or traced to a known or predictable requirement. Demand appears to be random, or caused by chance events. But most *raw materials, components*, and *subassemblies* are "dependent" upon demands for finished goods and other (sub)assemblies. This is because production is usually done in lots or batches, and when a lot is ordered for production in the factory, all materials and components needed for production are ordered at the same time, hence a "lump" in demand. For example, in a wooden door production facility, reorders of (finished) doors may be based upon a reorder point system. When the number of finished doors on hand reaches the reorder point, R, then an order of quantity Q is placed into production on the shop floor. Figure 13.2*a* illustrates this inventory time pattern.

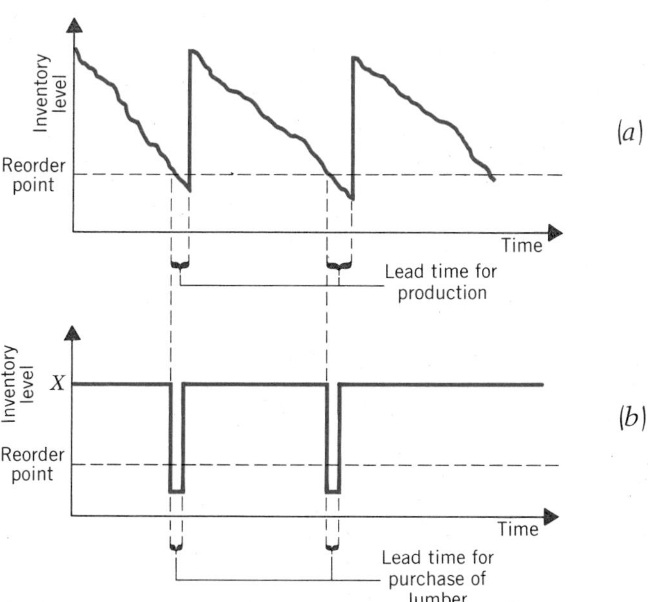

Figure 13.2. Relationship between finished item inventory and raw material/subassembly item inventory—reorder point approach. (*a*) Finished doors. (*b*) Lumber.

Lumpy demand for lumber.

If a reorder point system similar to the one used in managing the finished door inventory were used in managing the inventory of lumber used in the production of the finished doors, the inventory patten shown in Figure 13.2*b* would result. Notice that in Figure 13.2*b* the "normal" inventory level is *X* units. When the finished door inventory in Figure 13.2*a* reaches its reorder point and a production order is released to the shop, a requisition for the required quantity of lumber is made against that inventory. The inventory level will drop by the quantity used in producing the lot, thus causing the raw materials inventory to fall below its reorder point. This triggers a reorder for a quantity of lumber resulting in replenishment of the inventory after its purchase lead time.

Order for when needed.

As you can see, the average inventory level for the lumber is quite high, and most of this inventory is being held for long periods of time without being used. A logical approach to the reduction of the inventory level is to anticipate the timing and quantities of demands on the lumber inventory and then to schedule purchases to meet this requirement. Figure 13.3 illustrates the results on the lumber inventory level of this anticipation-of-demand approach. Figure 13.3*a* illustrates the same finished product "inventory" pattern as Figure 13.2*a*. Figure 13.3*b* depicts the scheduling of receipt of lumber just prior to the time when it is needed. The impact on average inventory level is obvious.

All reorder point systems presume (even though implicitly) that demand for each item in inventory is independent of the demand for a finished item or any other items in the inventory. Reorder point approaches work well when this presumption holds,

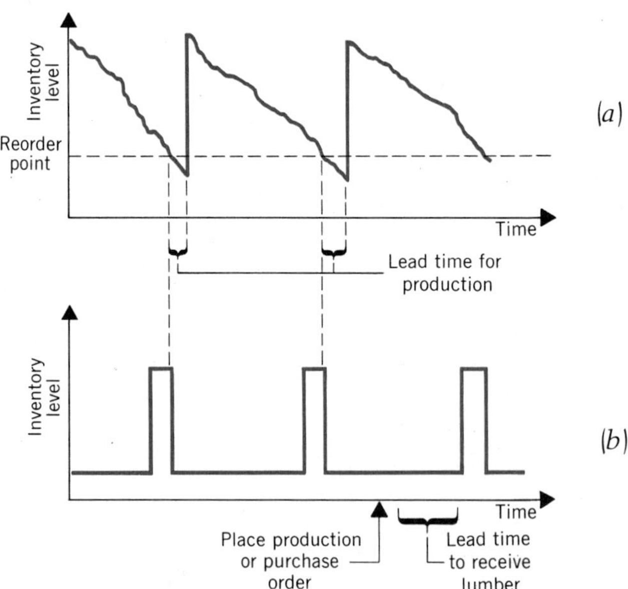

Figure 13.3. Relationship between finished item and subassembly/raw material item inventories—a requirement planning approach. (*a*) Finished doors. (*b*) Lumber.

but work rather poorly for items whose demands are dependent upon higher level items. Material requirements planning is the fundamental method used in inventory management systems for dependent inventory items.

The student should note that dependent demand is not the only cause of "lumpy" demand. Demand can appear in lumps if only a small number of customers exist for the item and their purchasing habits are discontinuous. MRP is not a solution to the general lumpy demand case since no basis exists for development of the materials plan unless the demand is dependent upon something that a planner can either measure or forecast.

13.2 PRECOMPUTER VERSUS POSTCOMPUTER INVENTORY MANAGEMENT

The availability and practicality of MRP systems is related directly to the advent of relatively inexpensive computer power. Without the electronic computer, operations managers would simply be unable to perform all of the calculations and maintain all the schedules necessary to perform requirements planning. A simple example will illustrate this point.

The need for a computer.

The Breakneck Company

The Breakneck Company produces skateboards known as the Sidewalk Suicide Special. The Special is made up of one fiberglass board and two wheel assemblies. The lead time to assemble a special from its two major components is one week. The first component, the board, is purchased and has a three-week delivery lead time. The second major component, the wheel assembly, is assembled by Breakneck. Each wheel assembly is made up (with a one-week lead time) of one wheel mounting stand (manufactured by Breakneck with a four-week lead time), two wheels (purchased with a one-week lead time), one spindle (manufacured by Breakneck with a two-week lead time), and one chrome plated locknut (purchased with a one-week lead time). The product structure (or **product tree**) is shown in Figure 13.4.

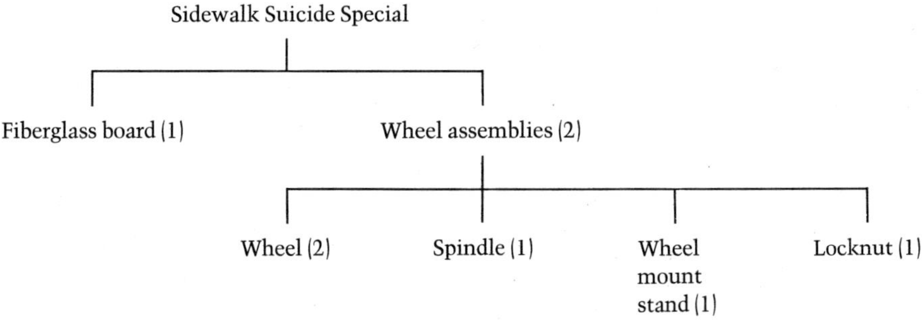

Figure 13.4. Skateboard product tree.

To produce an order for 50 Special skateboards, the materials requirements are computed as follows.

$$
\begin{aligned}
\text{Fiberglass boards: } 1 \times \text{no. of specials} &= 1 \times 50 = 50 \\
\text{Wheel assmblies: } 2 \times \text{no. of specials} &= 2 \times 50 = 100 \\
\text{Wheels: } 2 \times \text{no. of wheel assemblies} &= 2 \times 100 = 200 \\
\text{Spindles: } 1 \times \text{no. of wheel assemblies} &= 1 \times 100 = 100 \\
\text{Wheel mount stand: } 1 \times \text{no. of wheel assemblies} &= 1 \times 100 = 100 \\
\text{Locknut: } 1 \times \text{no. of wheel assemblies} &= 1 \times 100 = 100
\end{aligned}
$$

Furthermore, presume that the master schedule indicates that an order for 50 Specials is due to be delivered in 10 weeks. The calendar in Table 13.1 illustrates the timing of due dates and the necessary order dates (presuming the lead times stated earlier) that must be met in order to deliver in the tenth week.

Lower level items.

Note that MRP is a highly *logical* system. Knowing that 50 Specials must be shipped at the end of week 10 means that 50 boards must be placed on order for outside procurement at the end of week 6, that an order for 100 mounting stands must be placed in the shop at the end of week 4, and so forth. Ordering later than these dates would result in late shipment (or working overtime and otherwise expe-

TABLE 13.1 SUICIDE SPECIALS DEMAND

		Week									
		1	2	3	4	5	6	7	8	9	10
Suicide Specials											50
	Date needed									50	
Boards	Order date						50				
Wheel	Date needed									100	
Assembly	Order date								100		
	Date needed								200		
Wheels	Order date							200			
	Date needed								100		
Spindles	Order date						100				
Mounting	Date needed								100		
Stands	Order date				100						
	Date needed								100		
Locknuts	Order date							100			

diting the order) and ordering earlier would result in inventory being available (and occupying space, requiring paperwork and other holding costs) before it is needed. MRP looks at each end product and the dates when each is needed. From these due dates, needed dates for all lower level items are computed, and from these due dates starting or order dates are determined.

While the overall idea is simple, consider the extreme complexity of operating an MRP system on a manual basis. In this simple example with only one end product the calculations and record keeping requirements are straightforward. But, for a large firm that manufactures hundreds of end items with thousands of intermediate components, only a computer can keep up with the processing volume. This is an important point, for it is not that MRP is a revolutionary idea. The basic idea has been around for quite some time. It is and has been practiced for construction projects (from a single house to a mammoth skyscraper) that are scheduled according to a "right materials to the right place at the right time" philosophy. MRP has come of age in manufacturing and assembly operations with large numbers of end and intermediate items because large scale and relatively inexpensive computer power is available.

MRP not a new idea.

Precomputer Inventory Management

Precomputer inventory management was characterized by the following.

1. Concentration on order quantities.
2. Concern for "when to order."
3. Expediting "late" orders.
4. Production control and inventory management viewed as separate functions.

Concentration on order quantities

The concern for order quantities stemmed primarily from the emphasis on ordering economic order quantities (EOQ's). Numerous articles in trade and industrial magazines touted the praises of ordering in economic quantities. Claims of substantial savings in inventory cost were common. But, upon further scrutiny it has been found that in situations where the demand for the inventory item is dependent, the EOQ methodology was less helpful. Good order quantities for "constant" demand items are not necessarily good for "lumpy" demand items. As Oliver Wight points out, "Getting the right quantity at the wrong time does not accomplish anything." Timing is particularly important in situations where subassemblies must be available to assemble the finished product.

Concern for "when to order"

The concern for "when to order" was typically answered by reorder point calculations. The reorder point was calculated, as we saw in the last chapter as

Reorder point = demand over lead time + safety stock

But, this "when to order" concern was typically translated into **order launching**; that is, orders were sent out into production or to a vendor or supplier simply on the basis of a reorder point. Consideration was not given to when the items were needed.

As a result, items not needed again until six months from now may have been ordered today if the order point was reached. Likewise, an item needed in two weeks, but with a production lead time of eight weeks may not have been ordered until today—again, when the reorder point was reached. While logical managerial "override" should have prevailed to assure that such ridiculous results did not occur, these possibilities were (and are) real failures of the statistical reorder point approach. And since for very large inventories, the attention necessary to assure that such blunders did not take place was prohibitively expensive, these types of errors in fact occurred.

Expediting of "late" orders

Expediting of late orders also became the rule. The job of the expediter in a production system was to push jobs along in the shop which were either needed for another stage of production or to satisfy a customer's demand. All "launched" orders were presumed to be of equal priority unless they were being expedited. A common occurrence on factory floors was the RUSH ticket. Orders tagged with a RUSH ticket were to receive special treatment (e.g., moving ahead of other orders waiting to get on a particular machine, special handling from work station to work station, etc.). But, an equally common occurrence was the use of RUSH tickets on 50 to 80 percent of the jobs in the shop and also the introduction of the RUSH-RUSH and the RUSH-RUSH-RUSH ticket. Obviously, everything cannot have first priority and thus, such methods often result in confusion for the operations manager and almost no improvement in getting jobs out the door.

Rush-rush tickets.

Production control separate from inventory management

Production control and inventory management were viewed as independent functions. Those concerned with inventory management were concerned with calculating "correct" or "scientific" order quantities and order points. But the production control personnel were concerned with moving items through the operations to produce the outputs in the right quantities and at the right time. Clearly, these two functions have an impact on one another. Without the raw materials, purchased components, work-in-process inventory, subassemblies, and so forth, the production control personnel would have nothing to schedule and control through the facility. Likewise, the inventory management personnel had no purpose except to assume that inventory was available to meet demand.

Postcomputer Inventory Management

Postcomputer inventory management, and particularly MRP, is characterized by

1. Concern for "when needed."
2. Concern for order "priorities."

3. Deexpediting as well as expediting.
4. Production control and inventory management viewed as integral functions.

Concern for "when needed"

Once the computer was available to handle the myriad calculations and multiple data files, it was not long until the production control and inventory management functions were considered to be integral. The integration of thinking between these two functions resulted in a shift in concern to **when needed** rather than a direct concern for "when to order." If the operations manager has good information regarding the due date for an order, the ordering and scheduling of parts and components to make up that order becomes a matter of "back scheduling," as we have shown in the Breakneck Company example, from the due date for each part and operation.

Concern for order "priorities"

There has also been the realization that all orders on the shop floor do not have the same **priority**. Certain products are more important than others and certain customers take precedence over others. Knowing the priority of individual orders relative to the others allows scheduling to fulfill these priorities.

Deexpediting orders

Recognition of different priorities also results in the concept of **deexpediting**; that is, holding up production or order release for items that were scheduled earlier, but are now found to be due at a later date. Expediting and deexpediting work hand in hand to maximize the throughput of operations. If an order for skateboard wheels had been assigned a high priority because they were needed in the production of a particular order of skateboards, then it should be deexpedited if the original order has been cancelled or rescheduled for later delivery. Failing to reduce the priority or to deexpedite the order provides misinformation to the production department, and will perhaps cause incorrect schedules to be developed.

13.3 THE MECHANICS OF MRP

MRP inputs.

Material requirements planning is a production/inventory management system. As such, it requires both production and inventory information in order to produce its primary output—a schedule or plan for orders, both released and pending, which specifies actions to be taken now and in the future. Figure 13.5 illustrates the flows of information within an MRP system.

Figure 13.5 indicates three primary inputs to the MRP computer system.

1. The Master Production Schedule.
2. The Bill of Materials File.
3. The Inventory Master File.

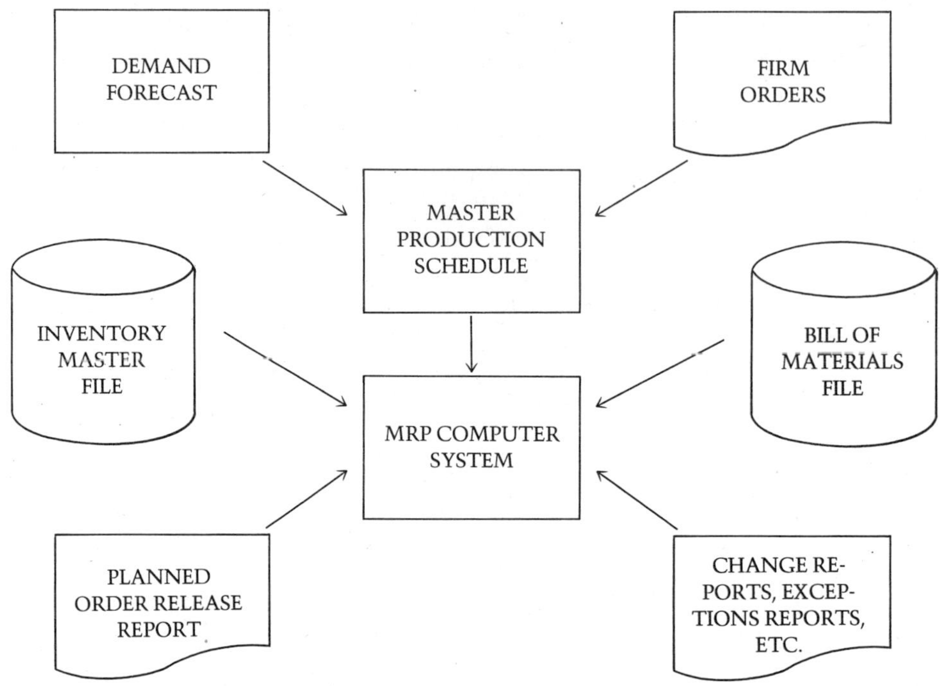

Figure 13.5. Schematic of MRP system.

MRP outputs.

A major output from the MRP computer system is the planned order release report although there are other change reports, exceptions reports, and reports used for deexpediting orders already released.

The MRP system, in summary, operates as follows.

1. The **Master Production Schedule** is prepared based upon "actual" customer orders and predicted demand. This schedule indicates exactly when each ordered item will be produced to meet the firm and predicted demand; that is, it is a time-phased production plan.
2. For each item in the Master Production Schedule, a bill of materials exists. The **Bill of Materials File** indicates all of the raw materials, components, subassemblies, and assemblies required to produce an item. The MRP computer system accesses the bill of materials files to determine exactly what items, in what quantities, are required to complete an order for a given item.
3. The **Inventory Master File** contains detailed information regarding the number/quantity of each item on hand, on order, and committed to use in various time periods. The MRP computer system accesses the inventory master file to determine the quantity available for use in a given time period, and, if enough are available to meet the order needs, commits these for use during the time period by updating the inventory record. If sufficient items are not available, the

system includes this item, with the necessary quantity for an EOQ or ELS, on the planned order release report.

The MRP Inputs

As indicated earlier, the MRP inputs are the Master Production Schedules, the Bill of Materials File, and the Inventory Master File. Because these items are crucial to the operation of an MRP system, we will discuss each in more detail below.

The master production schedule

The Master Production Schedule is a summary of planned end product needs for specific future time periods. The schedule is based upon **firm customer orders** which are typically submitted by salesmen or received directly from the customer. These orders include the quantity that the customer desires and, typically, a promised delivery date. The schedule is also based upon forecasts of future demand for which orders have not yet been received. These formal projected orders are summed by time period and these time-phased requirements then make up the Master Production Schedule.

It should be noted that this schedule is only a trial schedule. There is no guarantee that production capacity will be available to produce according to the schedule. Therefore, this trial schedule is used as input to the MRP computer system to produce the Planned Order Release Report. Based upon the orders to be released in specific time periods and the total capacity available during these periods the schedule is modified. If capacity is insufficient, the schedule is modified and tried again. When a reasonable schedule is achieved, the Planned Order Release Report will outline a detailed production schedule that is feasible for the resources and capacity available.

The bill of materials file

Once a master schedule is available, MRP uses a *Bill of Materials File* to determine all of the individual items that will be required to complete production on the product represented in the Master Production Schedule. A bill of materials is a structured parts list. The Bill of Materials File is the set of all structured parts lists for all items that an organization produces. Rather than simply listing all of the parts necessary to produce one finished product, the bill of materials shows the way a finished product is put together from individual items, components, and subassemblies. For example, a product with the product structure illustrated in Figure 13.6 would generate the bill of materials illustrated in Figure 13.7.

Parent, or zero level, items.

This bill of materials shows the finished product (sometimes called the **parent item**) at the highest, or zero, level. Subassemblies and parts that go directly into the assembly of the finished product are called level 1 components, while parts and subassemblies that go into level 1 components are shown as level 2 and so on. Thus, when a Master Production Schedule shows a requirement for a given quantity of finished products for a certain due date, production planners can **explode** the bill of materials for that finished product to determine the number, due dates, and necessary order dates of subcomponents that are required to meet the time and quantity require-

Exploding the BOM.

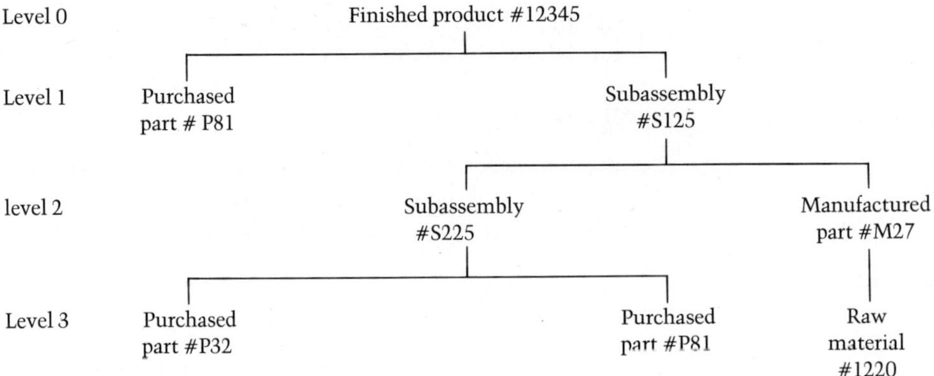

Figure 13.6. Product structure tree.

ments. Exploding a BOM (bill of materials) simply means stepping down through all the levels of the bill of materials and determining the quantity and lead time for each item required to make up the item at that level. The result of exploding a bill of materials for a given item is a time-phased requirement for specific quantities of each item necessary to produce the finished product. We exploded an order for skateboards earlier in this chapter, although we had not formally introduced the notion of a bill of materials.

Note in Figures 13.6 and 13.7 that purchased part number P81 is used both as a level 1 and a level 3 component and is specifically identified in both locations in the product tree and bill of materials. Purchased part number P81 could perhaps be a stainless steel nut and bolt assembly which is used to produce subassembly number S225 as well as to complete the assembly of the finished product 12345 by assembling with subassembly number S125. We do not aggregate the number of P81's used to produce a single finished product (that is we do not show part number P81 as requiring 3 to produce finished product number 12345) because aggregating would not allow us to identify the specific number of P81's necessary to produce a lot of S225

Level 1 Parts	Level 2 Parts	Level 3 Parts	Description	Quantity	Source
#P81				1	Purchased
#S125				1	Manufactured
	#S225			1	Manufactured
		#P32		1	Purchased
		#P81		2	Purchased
	#M27			1	Manufactured
		#1220		3 lb	Purchased

Figure 13.7. Bill of materials for a three-level product.

subassemblies. It would also preclude knowing how many P81's would be necessary to complete final assembly of S125 subassemblies into finished products.

The inventory master file

The Inventory Master File is made up of all of the individual inventory records, one for each finished product and item in the bill of materials. While these records can be quite lengthy and contain a significant volume of data, the primary requirements for MRP are the master data and item status segments of the record. The master data is the typically unchanging portion of the record (e.g., identification, make, description, cost, EOQ or ELS, setup time, etc.). The status segment contains information used in time phased planning. Specifically, this segment contains the gross (actual quantity needed during the period) and net (the gross less the quantity available) requirements for each period, the planned receipts of inventory scheduled by time period, the number currently on hand, and the planned orders to be released by time period.

The Inventory Master File is kept up to date through periodic updates which post the receipts of purchased and manufactured items into inventory, the release of items onto the production floor for production, the losses due to scrap, the orders that have been cancelled or expedited/deexpedited, and so forth.

MRP System Outputs

Three specific MRP system outputs constitute the plan of action for released and pending orders. These are

1. The Order Action Report.
2. The Open Orders Report.
3. The Planned Order Release Report.

The Order Action Report indicates which orders are to be released during the current time period and which orders are to be cancelled. The Open Orders Report shows which orders are to be expedited or deexpedited. This report is typically an exception report listing only those open orders for which action is necessary. The **Planned Order Release** Report is the time-phased plan for orders to be released in future time periods. It is this report that determines whether a master production schedule is feasible or not.

MRP Computations

An order for 100 of a finished product due 12 weeks from today may or may not be cause for action in the production/inventory system. If 1000 are currently on hand and planned order deliveries for 350 are scheduled between now and 12 weeks from now, 650 will be available from which the order for 100 can be shipped. But if 400 are now available and 350 will be shipped between now and the due date for the order of 100, action is necessary.

Gross versus net requirements.

MRP computations are based, in large part, on **gross** and **net requirements**. The order for 100 to be shipped in 12 weeks is a gross requirement. Actions, though, should be based on net requirements. In the first instance, the net requirement is −550 (i.e., 100 − 650); thus, there is no production requirement. But in the second case, the net requirement in the twelfth week is 50 (100 − 50). Since there is a net requirement for 50 units, at least that quantity will have to be produced to meet the shipping requirement for 50. These quantities are based upon the following two formulas:

Net requirements for planning period = gross requirements for the planning period − planned on hand at planning period (13.1)

and

Planned **on-hand** at planning period = current on-hand + scheduled receipts prior to planning period − scheduled requirements prior to planning period (13.2)

Backtracking through lead times.

Using the lead times that are available in the inventory file, order release dates are calculated by backscheduling or time phasing from the planning period (the due date) by the amount of the lead time. Orders are scheduled to be received when needed to meet the due date(s). If the net requirements for the planning period are positive, then an order must be scheduled to be received in time for use in the planning period. MRP answers the question of "when to order" by first determining when items are needed, and then scheduling an order release so that the items will be received just prior to the needed date. On the other hand, if the net requirements are negative or zero, no order is necessary.

Each successively lower level item that goes into production of the 100 parent items is scheduled in an analogous fashion. A planned order release at one level generates requirements at the next lower level. The differences in on-hand inventory at each level, the order quantities used at successively lower levels, and the number of different finished products that use a particular lower level component result in different order cycles for items at the various levels.

For example, suppose that in the order for 100 items in week 12, the planned on-hand quantity is 50 and the lead time for production (assembly) of level 1 items is three weeks. Then, an order for at least 50 (and possibly more, depending upon the company's policy to order in economic lot sizes) would be placed in week 9. The material requirements plan at level 0 of the product is shown in Table 13.2.

At level 1, a purchased hose may be required and therefore a requirement plan must be developed for this item as well. But, the same hose may be used on another product. Therefore, the requirements plan for the hose must incorporate the requirements generated from all higher level items in which it is used. The material requirements plan for the purchased hose is shown in Table 13.3. Lead Time is four weeks.

But notice the demand in week 10 for 200 of the hoses. Presume that these are required to produce subassemblies used in an entirely different end product. The requirements for both uses are aggregated and an order planned in week 10 − 4 = 6 for 250. The order, again, could have been for an EOQ.

TABLE 13.2 0 LEVEL MRP

Week	1	2	3	4	5	6	7	8	9	10	11	12
Gross requirements		50			150			50	100			100
On hand 400	400	350	350	350	200	200	200	150	50	50	50	50
Net requirements	—	—	—	—	—	—	—	—	—	—	—	50
Planned order receipts												50
Planned order releases									50			
Lead time = 3 weeks												

At each level this same procedure is followed. All requirements from higher levels generate needs at lower levels. These needs are aggregated at each level for each item and a requirements plan established using the formulas and tables outlined above.

Daily changes affect the MRP plan.

The MRP system is not complete when a requirements plan is finally prepared. Whenever the master schedule changes or priorities on scheduled orders change, rescheduling of order releases takes place. Since the order release generates all requirements for items at lower levels, changing an order release requires the regeneration of new requirements plans. Also, released orders may be expedited or deexpedited based upon schedule changes, changes in priorities, and cancellation of orders.

Lot Sizing

How many to order?

In conjunction with scheduling orders to be released (i.e., the "when to order" decision), the second major inventory management question "How many to order?" must

TABLE 13.3 LEVEL 1 MRP

Week	1	2	3	4	5	6	7	8	9	10	11	12
Gross requirements									50	200		
On hand 100	100	100	100	100	100	100	100	100	100	50	100	
Net requirements	—	—	—	—	—	—	—	—	—	150		
Planned order receipt										250		
Planned order releases						250						
Lead time = 4 weeks												

also be answered. Determining the appropriate **lot size** for the production of intermittently demanded products is more complex than using the simple EOQ or ELS models presented in Chapter 12. But, the general objective of balancing ordering or setup costs with inventory holding costs is the same.

The difficulty stems again from the lumpy nature of demand in a dependent inventory situation. Both the EOQ and ELS models assumed a constant demand. Therefore, the rate of decline of the inventory level over time could be predicted with relative certainty. Since the costs of holding and ordering inventory are related to inventory levels over time and to the rate at which inventory is consumed, logical calculations could be made on the basis of this constant rate (you might want to refer back to Chapter 12, particularly to the discussion of the number of orders placed each year and to the average inventory level). But, with lumpy demand neither the rate of use nor the average level of inventory can be easily predicted. Instead of a formal equation for determining the appropriate order quantity or lot size, several heuristics have been used.

Trial and error.

One approach is to determine, through trial and error, the best order quantity by trying every possible order quantity which meets the master schedule requirements. This is obviously a large and tedious problem since there are so many feasible possibilities. Another method, known as the *Wagner-Whitin algorithm* [3], systematically determines optimal lot sizes by evaluating all possible ways of ordering to meet the master schedule. Note that this procedure is an optimizing technique. The major drawback to the method is the rapid increase in computational time as the number of ordering alternatives increases.

Optimization via Wagner-Whitin.

Accumulation.

Another approach simply tries the lot sizes determined by accumulating the time-phased requirements. That is, suppose requirements of 100, 40, and 75 units were scheduled for weeks 13, 18, and 21, respectively. This approach would simply evaluate the three order quantities 100, 140 (100 + 40), and 215 (100 + 40 + 75).

The evaluation would compare the costs of ordering three times (quantities of 100, 40, 75), two times (quantities of 140, 75) and one time (quantity of 215) with the costs of holding the extra inventory above the first 100 units after weeks 13 and 18. While this appears to be a logical approach, and is certainly better than performing no evaluation at all, it does not consider all alternatives (e.g., 100 + 75), (40 + 75) and therefore does not guarantee an optimal solution.

Part period balancing.

The *part period balancing method* provides a more systematic solution procedure which uses the same general approach. **Part period balancing** attempts to equate the cost of placing a single order with the cost of holding the inventory produced by that order. You will recall from our discussion of EOQ and ELS that the optimal order quantity was that quantity for which order cost equaled holding cost. The part period balancing method recognizes this relationship and attempts to use it to find an order quantity, from those available, for which the order and the holding cost associated with that order are approximately the same.

While this method is not guaranteed to produce optimal order quantities, it does produce satisfactory approximations and with much less computational difficulty than required of the methods that produce optimal solutions. For example, in one study [3], Berry compared the Wagner-Whitin algorithm (which does produce optimal results) with the part period balancing method and found that the cost of the optimal solution was only 7 percent lower than the solution developed with the part period balancing heuristic. We will demonstrate the approach with an example.

Limp Spring Co.

Limp Spring Company manufactures a variety of compression springs for use in automobile rocker arm assemblies. Current orders for the x-250 model used in several V6 engines are as follows.

Week 28	10,000
Week 31	18,000
Week 40	12,000

Setup of the spring winding equipment for a production run costs approximately \$700. The cost of holding an x-250 spring in inventory for a week is considered to be \$0.0025.

Under the part period balancing method, the three lot size alternatives available before week 28 are

Alternative:	1	2	3
Produce in week 28:	10,000	28,000	40,000

Part period balancing selects the alternative for which holding cost is closest to the order cost of \$700. The three holding costs are

$$C_H(10{,}000) = 0$$
$$C_H(28{,}000) = 3 \text{ weeks} \times 18{,}000 \text{ excess units} \times \$0.0025\text{/unit/week} = \$135$$
$$C_H(40{,}000) = 3 \times 18{,}000 \times 0.0025 + 12 \times 12{,}000 \times 0.0025 = \$495$$

Because producing all 40,000 springs in one lot results in most closely matching order cost with holding cost, the third alternative should be chosen.

To summarize, the MRP system follows these steps.

1. Determine requirements of finished products, the Master Production Schedule, from firm orders and sales forecasts.
2. Using the bill of materials, calculate the gross requirements for each item, beginning with the item at level zero.
3. Determine, using the Bill of Materials File and the Inventory Master File, the order release dates and the order quantities for each item necessary to meet the Master Production Schedule.
4. Regenerate the MRP on the basis of changes in the Master Production Schedule or in order priorities.

The complete MRP procedure is illustrated with an example in the *Tools and Applications* portion of this chapter.

TOOLS AND APPLICATIONS

13.4 LEE KEY VALVE CO.

To illustrate the MRP procedure, consider the Lee Key Valve Company, which manufactures industrial valves and fittings. Lee Key has decided to implement a material requirements planning system throughout its production facilities and is planning to first test the operation of the system using one finished product, the #3303 check valve. Table 13.4 presents the master production schedule for the #3303 check valve. It is based upon existing orders and promised shipping dates as well as anticipated sales of the valve. This schedule indicates the number of valves required to be shipped by the end of each of the indicated weeks. The master production schedule is prepared every week for the current week and next 10 weeks. The "past due" column indicates the number of valves that are currently back ordered (in this example, none). Suppose that the current inventory of #3303 check valves is 800 units. Table 13.5 shows a partially completed MRP for the #3303 check valve. The MRP will be completed once the lot sizes are determined.

Determining Lot Size

Because this is a relatively simple situation in which only one item is being considered, all three possible order quantities can be evaluated to determine the best production lot sizes. Suppose that Lee Key's cost accounting department has determined setup cost to be $90 and holding cost per unit per week to be $0.08. If Lee Key produced one batch for each required shipment there would be no excess inventory, but the total setup cost over the next 10 weeks would be $270 (3 × $90). Producing 3200 for week 21 plus the 3000 required for week 24 in one batch would result in a savings of one setup ($90) but would increase holding cost by $720 (3 weeks × 3000 units ×

TABLE 13.4 #3303 CHECK VALVE: MASTER PRODUCTION SCHEDULE

Item no.: #3303
Description: check valve.
Current inventory level: 800.

Week no.	Past due	18	19	20	21	22	23	24	25	26	27	28	29
Gross requirements	0	0	0	0	4000	0	0	3000	0	0	0	6000	0

TABLE 13.5 PARTIALLY COMPLETED MRP FOR #3303 CHECK VALVE

Week no.	Past duc	18	19	20	21	22	23	24	25	26	27	28	29
Gross requirements	0	0	0	0	4000	0	0	3000	0	0	0	6000	0
On hand: 800		800	800	800	800								
Net requirement					3200								
Planned order receipts													
Planned order releases													
Lead time = 3 weeks													

\$0.08 per unit per week). Combining all three shipping requirements results in a savings of \$180 (\$2 × \$90) in setup costs, but additional holding costs of \$4080 (3 weeks × 3000 × 0.08 + 7 × 6000 × 0.08) are incurred. Clearly, for this situation a policy of ordering in lot sizes equal to the requirements each period is the best policy since this results in the lowest total cost.

The part period balancing method, which attempts to equate the cost of placing a single order and the cost of holding the inventory produced in that order, requires the computation of the holding cost of the three lot size possibilities.

3200
6200
12200

The part period balancing decision rule requires that Lee Key select the lot size for which holding cost is closest to the order cost, \$90. The part period balancing computations are

$$C_H\ (3200) = 0$$
$$C_H\ (6200) = 3 \text{ weeks} \times 3000 \text{ excess units} \times \$0.08/\text{unit/week} = \$720$$
$$C_H(12200) = 3 \times 3000 \times 0.08 + 7 \times 6000 \times 0.08 = \$4080$$

Clearly, the holding cost of zero is closest to \$90 and thereore the order size of 3200 (as recommended previously) would also be selected by the part period balancing method.

Presuming a lead time for assembly of the #3303 check valve of 3 weeks, orders should be released in weeks 18, 21, and 25 for order quantities of 3200, 3000, and 6000, respectively. Table 13.6 illustrates the completed MRP for the # 3303 check valve.

TABLE 13.6 MRP FOR #3303 CHECK VALVE

Week no.	Past due	13	14	15	16	17	18	19	20	21	22	23	24	25	26	27	28	29
Gross requirements										4000			3000				6000	
On hand: 800							800	800	800	800	0	0	0	0	0	0	0	
Net requirement										3200			3000				6000	
Planned order receipts										3200			3000				6000	
Planned order releases							3200			3000				6000				

Lead time = 3 weeks

Parts Explosion for Scheduling

Lee Key, having determined the order quantities and release dates of finished #3303 valves, must now determine the quantities and timing of orders for the component parts and subassemblies that make up the #3303 check valve. This determination begins with a *bill of materials*, which is the structured list of all required parts needed to produce one #3303 valve. Table 13.7 illustrates the multilevel bill of materials (in this case there are two levels of items). Figure 13.8 shows the same bill of materials as a product tree. Note in Table 13.7 the column labeled "Quantity." The number that appears in this column indicates the number of that item required to produce one of the next higher level of items. For example, two locknuts are required to produce one poppet assembly and two poppet assemblies are necessary for one #3303 check valve. Therefore, four locknuts are required for one #3303 valve. The parts in the second level are used to produce a subassembly (e.g., one valve body and one valve seat are assembled to produce one valve body assembly) and the subassemblies in turn are coupled with other first level parts to produce the finished product.

TABLE 13.7 BILL OF MATERIALS: #3303 CHECK VALVE

First Level Part No.	Second Level Part No.	Description	Quantity	Source
79221		Valve body assembly	1	Manufacturing
	82392	Valve body	1	Manufacturing
	64103	Valve seat	2	Manufacturing
30468		Spring	2	Purchasing
84987		Poppet assembly	2	Manufacturing
	29208	Stem	1	Manufacturing
	91182	Facing	1	Purchasing
	73919	Locknut	2	Purchasing

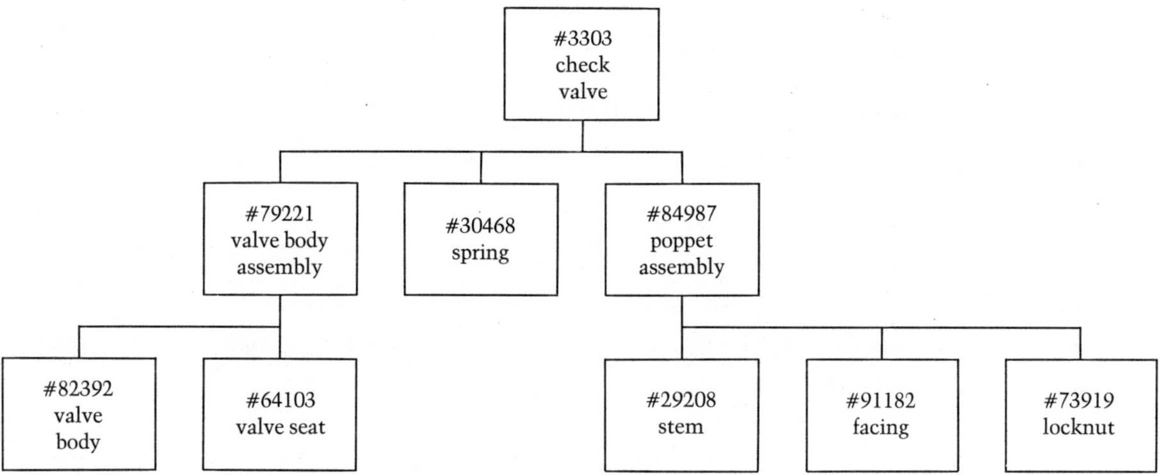

Figure 13.8. Product tree for #3303 check valve.

In addition to the bill of materials information, two pieces of information are required from the Inventory Master File for each item used in the production of the #3303 check valve. This information, the quantity on hand and the lead time (for assembly, manufacture, or purchase, as appropriate), is presented in summary form in Table 13.8.

Now that the three information soruces are available (i.e., master production schedule, bill of materials, inventory master information) the MRP system can produce a requirements plan. Presume, for this example, that all order quantities will be exactly the quantity necessary to meet net requirements. Table 13.9 shows the MRP for a complete #3303 check valve including all items at all levels. The entire MRP is developed by

1. Referencing the bill of materials to determine the number of each level of item necessary to produce 3200, 3000, and 6000 check valves, respectively.

TABLE 13.8 INVENTORY MASTER FILE INFORMATION FOR MRP

Final Product: #3303 — Quantity on Hand: 800
Description: Check Valve — Lead Time for Assembly: 3 Weeks

Item No.	Quantity on Hand	Lead Time (Weeks)
79221	1000	1
82392	2200	2
64103	500	1
30468	800	2
84987	1000	3
29208	500	1
91182	1200	2
73919	2000	2

TABLE 13.9 CHECK VALVE REQUIREMENTS PLAN

a. #3303 Check Valve

Week number	Past due	13	14	15	16	17	18	19	20	21	22	23	24	25	26	27	28	29
Gross requirement										4000			3000				6000	
On hand 800							800	800	800	800								
Net requirement										3200			3000				6000	
Planned order receipts										3200			3000				6000	
Planned order releases							3200			3000				6000				
Lead time = 3 weeks																		

b. #79221 Valve Body Assembly

Week number	Past due	13	14	15	16	17	18	19	20	21	22	23	24	25	26	27	28	29
Gross requirement							3200			3000				6000				
On hand 1000						1000	1000											
Net requirement							2200			3000				6000				
Planned order receipts							2200			3000				6000				
Planned order releases						2200			3000				6000					
Lead time = 1 week																		

c. #30468 Spring

Week number	Past due	13	14	15	16	17	18	19	20	21	22	23	24	25	26	27	28	29
Gross requirement							6400			6000				12000				
On hand 800					800	800	800											
Net requirement							5600			6000				12000				
Planned order receipts							5600			6000				12000				
Planned order releases					5600			6000				12000						
Lead time = 2 weeks																		

d. #84787 Poppet Assembly

Week number	Past due	13	14	15	16	17	18	19	20	21	22	23	24	25	26	27	28	29
Gross requirement							6400			6000				12000				
On hand 1000				1000	1000	1000	1000											
Net requirement							5400			6000				12000				
Planned order receipts							5400			6000				12000				
Planned order releases				5400			6000				12000							

Lead time = 3 weeks

e. #82392 Valve Body

Week number	Past due	13	14	15	16	17	18	19	20	21	22	23	24	25	26	27	28	29
Gross requirement						2200			3000				6000					
On hand 2200				2200	2200	2200												
Net requirement									3000				6000					
Planned order receipts									3000				6000					
Planned order releases							3000				6000							

Lead time = 2 weeks

f. #64103 Valve Seat

Week number	Past due	13	14	15	16	17	18	19	20	21	22	23	24	25	26	27	28	29
Gross requirement						4400			6000				12000					
On hand 500					500	500												
Net requirement						3900			6000				12000					
Planned order receipts						3900			6000				12000					
Planned order releases					3900			6000				12000						

Lead time = 1 week

g. # 29208 Stem

Week number	Past due	13	14	15	16	17	18	19	20	21	22	23	24	25	26	27	28	29
Gross requirement				5400			6000				12000							
On hand 500			500	500														
Net requirement				4900			6000				12000							
Planned order receipts				4900			6000				12000							
Planned order releases			4900			6000				12000								
Lead time = 1 week																		

h. #91182 Facing

Week number	Past due	13	14	15	16	17	18	19	20	21	22	23	24	25	26	27	28	29
Gross requirement				5400			6000				12000							
On hand 1200		1200	1200	1200														
Net requirement				4200			6000				12000							
Planned order receipts				4200			6000				12000							
Planned order releases		4200			6000				12000									
Lead time = 2 weeks																		

i. #73919 Locknut

Week number	Past due	13	14	15	16	17	18	19	20	21	22	23	24	25	26	27	28	29
Gross requirement				10800			12000				24000							
On hand 2000		2000	2000	2000														
Net requirement				8800			12000				24000							
Planned order receipts				8800			12000				24000							
Planned order releases		8800			12000				24000									
Lead time = 2 weeks																		

2. For each item, the inventory record is accessed and both the current inventory level and the lead time are determined.
3. Using the current inventory level, the gross and net requirements are calculated.
4. Using the lead time, the order release date is determined by "backscheduling" the amount of the lead time from the needed date.

The MRP for the finished #3303 check valve is shown in Table 13.9a. The MRP for all items is developed from this requirement plan by first generating requirement plans for level 1 items and then, from each of these, the level 2 items are generated. Tables 13.9b through i are the requirements plans generated from this finished item plan. The arrows at the left of the figures indicate the order and relationship of one plan to the other.

To clarify the development of these plans, let us consider the plan for valve seats. To meet the shipping requirements for 4000 check valves (Table 13.9a) in week 21, component parts to assemble 3200 must enter production in week 18 (a three-week lead time). In order to release an order for 3200 in week 18, 2200 *additional* valve body assemblies (Table 13.9b) must be produced by that time. To do this, an order for 2200 must be placed in week 17 (a one-week lead time). Finally, to produce 2200 additional valve body assemblies, 4400 valve seats (2 × 2200) must be available. Since 500 are currently on hand (Table 13.9f), 3900 must be produced by week 17. With a one-week lead time, this means that an order for 3900 must be released in week 16. Required order releases for each level 1 and 2 component is planned in exactly the same manner.

We began this example by assuming that Lee Key was experimenting with the use of MRP on the #3303 check valve. When the company decides to include all products in the system, the situation is further complicated. The major difference is that some subassemblies and components will be used in more than one end product. Therefore, for example, the MRP for an item such as the 73919 locknut would include in the "Net requirement" row all of the requirements from all final products. Orders would be scheduled simultaneously to meet all of the requirements rather than being scheduled on a product-by-product basis. The necessity of using a computer becomes obvious when one considers a situation in which there are over 1000 finished products with perhaps as many as 30000 purchased and manufactured components. The need for rapid computation and summarization of requirements as well as handling of massive bills of materials and inventory master files is obvious.

13.5 SUMMARY

Inventory management systems for items with independent demand can successfully utilize reorder point/order quantity procedures. But, for items with dependent demand, which are in the vast majority in production and assembly environments, material requirements planning is a preferred approach. MRP concentrates its attention on "when needed" rather than "when to order." Orders are scheduled for release on the basis of the orders' priority, the lead time for production, and the due date for use in the next production level.

To utilize MRP, an operations manager must develop bills of material for all finished products and must also know current inventory levels and production and purchasing lead times for parts and subassemblies. A computer is essential for realistic MRP applications since the volume of data and calculations would simply overwhelm most production and inventory control staffs.

MRP is no panacea. Many companies have tried materials requirements planning and have failed. The reasons have been numerous, but more often than not the failures are human failures. MRP requires a very disciplined approach to production and production scheduling. Bad record keeping, inadequate manpower to update billing materials files and production and purchase lead times, lack of attention to detail, or poor follow-up on expediting and deexpediting can effectively cripple an MRP system. MRP is a logical and worthwhile approach to inventory management in many companies, but it is also a complex and expensive system to implement. Without full management support and adequate resources for this implementation, MRP is likely to be nothing more than another futile effort to resolve chronic production and inventory control problems.

13.6 READINGS

Production Control: MRP Ends Guessing at Southwire

CHARLES H. BOYER, Assistant Editor, *Industrial Engineering*

When Stan Morgan, Manager of Corporate Production Control at the Southwire Company, discovered that a work-in-process inventory item had been sitting around for two long years, he knew their decision to install a computerized material requirements planning (MRP) system was the right one. A major manufacturer of utility cable and building wire, Southwire, like most larger corporations, has long utilized a computer data base to control finished goods inventory, sales order entries, and certain raw materials and parts storage. Now, they have turned their attention to controlling the critical mid-point between raw materials and final products: the manufacturing inventory (or, as they refer to it at Southwire, work-in-process inventory).

Proponents of MRP systems claim sizable potential savings in reduced inventory levels, better control, and less reliance on inherently expensive and inefficient reorder point schemes. Also, with the advent of the powerful, relatively inexpensive small computers, MRP systems now feature, as their primary function, methods for updating and revising production schedule priorities.

At Southwire, finished goods inventory and shipping allocation information was being maintained on-line with a Burroughs 3500 computer and remote terminals. And some finished goods were warehoused in a computer-controlled automated storage and retrieval system. "We had both ends of our system under control." says Morgan. "We wanted to do the same with our work-in-process inventory, and at the same time improve our production control procedures.

"Our production planners were running the show by the seat of their pants. Reordering for the manufacturing plants was being done by a mishmash of safety stock levels and gut feelings. And some of the production data, such as manufacturing specifications, had to be transferred onto production orders from hard copy. The system was slow and cumbersome."

DECISIONS, DECISIONS

The decision to go with an MRP system was not made by a strict financial comparison of alternatives. In 1973, Group VP of Operations, Gordon Johnson, appointed a special committee to study production control problems. Should the company use a computerized system, a manual system, or a combination computer/manual system? Corporate Information Systems Analyst Roger Brown cochaired the committee with Morgan. Brown had designed the company's on-line order entry and shipping allocation system. Corporate IE, Inventory Control, and Research and Development were represented on the committee.

The committee members decided on a computerized MRP system using Burroughs advanced PCS II (Production Control System) software as a starting point. Eventually, many of the final programs were done in-house. "It was not a pure financial choice," Morgan explains. "First, the MRP system is not an isolated, integral function. It was built upon systems that had been in use for some time, both batch and on-line. To analyze the total cost, we would have to go back and compute the cost of those systems. It would be very difficult to isolate them, both as a function and in relation to time. That is, at what point in time would you evaluate the system's economics? Six months or two years after start-up? Secondly, and most importantly, we had to consider the company and its place in the market. Starting from scratch, literally, Southwire has grown at an annualized rate of 25%, from one small plant in 1950, to nine major production facilities today, manufacturing and distributing its products all over the world. We currently supply final products to 48 distribution centers. And we are not yet a mature company. We intend to continue growing. The decision to put in a computerized MRP system was born out of business necessity—survival. Manual methods could not cope with our expanding volume and complex product mix." The target for the initial system was the company's Building Wire Plant in Carrollton, GA. John Norman, a 14-year veteran with Southwire, is Materials Manager for the plant.

INSTALLING MRP

Three things must be known before implementing an MRP system:

1. Demand
2. Inventory
3. Bill of materials: Processing times, Routing, and Manufacturing Specifications.

"At the time we first examined MRP," says Norman, "our WIP inventory accuracy was around 69%; that's not nearly good enough for MRP use."

Accuracy is vital to the success of an MRP system. Essentially, MRP compares the planned production schedule with the bill of materials needed to make the products, then examines the manufacturing inventory to see which parts and raw materials are on hand and which have to be ordered. It then time phases the necessary orders for manufacturing inventory so it is available when needed at the work center. Ideally, all manufacturing inventory would arrive no sooner than when it is needed, thus reducing the amount of work-in-process inventory. The system reexamines the production schedule, either continuously or periodically, to keep it current, thus reducing or eliminating the need to stockpile large quantities of inventory in the production area. Without accurate control of the manufacturing inventory, the system will not work.

Accuracy at Southwire's Building Wire Plant means tight control over 4,900 unique stock numbers. That's 700 different final products with approximately seven components on each product's bill of materials. A tagging system was implemented to carefully track the manufacturing inventory after it entered the plant. Production, purchasing, and design specification information on 3,000 of the 4,900 stock items was transferred from microfiche to disk file, the necessary software modules were written, or modified, and the MRP system was "cranked up."

Stan Morgan tells what happened then: "Our first output from the system was garbage. We soon found out why. It's the computer analyst's axiom: garbage in—garbage out. The information we were feeding the system was not *accurate*. One major problem was our work-in-process tagging system. The tags were not taken seriously by the employees. Consequently, the number and type of tags turned in from the shop floor did not match the inventory consumed. We implemented an improvement program, with management emphasis, to educate everyone as to the importance of the tag system. Tags released on the shop floor are now accounted for at release, at turn in, and once during every shift. David Abercrombie, Systems Manager for the MRP system, reports: "Our accuracy on the WIP inventory went from 69% to 96% after we improved the tag control. We consider 96% the minimum acceptable level." A special block house was constructed on the shop floor to house an on-line terminal for recording tag information.

GETTING EDUCATED

There are many small problems encountered in the practical implementation of any idea. MRP is no exception. One problem confronted early in the year and a half required to start-up and debug Southwire's system was employee education. Several teaching aids, including videotape presentations and plant manager seminars, were used to demonstrate the advantages of MRP and gain wholehearted employee support. But it wasn't easy. After all, a conscientious foreman wants to be sure he has enough materials on hand to meet his production orders. There is a natural tendency to stockpile and hoard inventory. "It's a tough problem," says Morgan. "You don't really convince people at the front end, you convince them after you demonstrate that the system works. And you get the system working with management's help."

Roger Brown points out another problem encountered during the start-up: "When the system first goes on-line, it immediately calls up inventory needed to meet the production schedule. In the first few months, this actually increases your total work-in-process inventory, because now necessary inventory is being added to the unnecessary inventory previously stockpiled. It takes a few months before the total inventory volume in the manufacturing area begins to decline. But for a while, it appears the system is not working. This is another reason it is not easy to inspire employee confidence in the early stages."

THE OUTPUT

Southwire is using a "schedule regeneration" MRP system. Their key production planning document, the Planned Order Report, is updated whenever necessary, usually two or three times a week, to accommodate changes in the production schedule. The other major type of MRP system is the "net change." This type of system updates automatically with the slightest change in the production schedule. Net change was considered too sensitive for the Building Wire Plant, which is a combination continuous manufacture and job shop operation. "We thought "net change" would be too nervous for our type of production," says Morgan. "We prefer to regenerate our key production document—the Planned Order Report—whenever *we* deem it's necessary." Old planned order reports are discarded after updated ones are generated. Production orders that have been released to the shop floor are not subject to MRP updates.

Recently, Southwire changed their on-line final products inventory and order entry systems from Burroughs 3500 computers, using disk forte storage, to Burroughs 6700 computers using integrated DMS (data management system) file structure. The heart of the MRP system, the PCS II and Southwire software, operates on a 24-hour batch system. Sometime in the next three years, as MRP is expanded to corporate-wide use, this system will be placed on line also. Since MRP system startup began, the number of unique stock items in WIP inventory has been reduced 50%, and the better than 96% accuracy level of inventory control has eliminated the need for taking manual inventory counts in the future. Total work-in-process inventory volume is expected to be reduced by 30%.

Source. Reprinted from *Industrial Engineering,* March 1977.

13.7 KEY TERMS

Concepts

dependent demand (p. 454)
lumpy demand (p. 454)
MRP (p. 455)
deexpediting (p. 461)
when needed (p. 461)
priority (p. 461)
master production schedule (p. 462)
bill of materials (p. 462)
inventory master file (p. 462)
planned order release (p. 465)
firm order (p. 463)
net requirement (p. 466)
gross requirement (p. 466)
explode (p. 463)
parent item (p. 463)
on-hand (p. 466)
lot sizing (p. 467)
part period balancing (p. 468)
product tree (p. 457)
order launching (p. 460)

13.8 REVIEW TEST

Concepts

1. MRP is only suitable for purchased items. (p. 455)
a. True b. False

2. Net requirements equals the gross requirements less on-hand less planned order receipts. (p. 466)
a. True b. False

3. The master production schedule indicates the quantity and timing of forecast orders. (p. 463)
a. True b. False

4. Deexpediting means stalling the customer. (p. 461)
a. True b. False

5. The inventory master file contains product structure information. (p. 464)
a. True b. False

6. Part period balancing guarantees optimal order quantities. (p. 468)
a. True b. False

7. MRP is a statistical order point method. (p. 455)
a. True b. False

8. Lead times for all items at all levels are subtracted from the due date for the parent item in arriving at planned order release dates. (p. 466)
a. True b. False

9. Once an order is released in MRP, only a priority change should change its schedule. (p. 461)
   a. True b. False
10. Dependent demand is typically lumpy demand. (p. 454)
   a. True b. False
11. Key figures in the development of MRP are Joe Orlicky, Oliver Wight, and George Plossl. (p. 454)
   a. True b. False
12. MRP can only be used without a computer if the number of parent items is under 1000. (p. 459)
   a. True b. False
13. A product tree is another way of illustrating a bill of materials. (p. 457)
   a. True b. False

13.9 DISCUSSION QUESTIONS

1. Why would record accuracy, particularly in bills of material and inventory records, be important in MRP?
2. What types of "demand" are considered formally in MRP?
3. In your own terms, distinguish between dependent and independent demand.
4. What is the meaning of the term "planned order release"?
5. Why has MRP taken so long to develop since it is such a logical and straightforward idea?
6. Contrast the ideas of "order launching" and "when needed."
7. Once an order is "launched" in MRP, how is it controlled?
8. Explain why the part period balancing method will not guarantee optimal order quantities.
9. Is MRP or EOQ best for smooth, dependent demand? For lumpy, independent demand?

13.10 PROBLEMS

Concepts

1. Product 101 consists of three 202 subassemblies and a 204 subassembly. The 202 subassembly consists of one 617, a 324 subassembly, and a 401. A 204 subassembly consists of a 500 and a 401. The 324 subassembly consists of a 617 and a 515.
   a. Prepare a product tree.
   b. Prepare an indented bill of materials.
   c. Determine the number of each subassembly/component required to produce fifty 101's.
2. Item #6606.

Week number	5	6	7	8	9	10	11	12	13	14	15	16	17	18
Gross requirement				100			50	30			80			
On hand 100														
Net requirement														
Planned order receipts														
Planned order releases														
Lead time =3 weeks														

Complete the MRP for item #6606.

3. Suppose that in Problem 2 the company wishes to maintain a safety stock of 50 #6606's. Complete the MRP.

4. Conduct a part-period lot sizing for part 1098 given the following demand schedule and the facts that holding a 1098 part in inventory for a week costs $1 and the ordering and shipment costs (0 lead time) total $100 for any size order.

Week:	16	17	18	19	20	21	22
1098 Demand:	85	40	25	40	105	75	80

Tools and Applications

5. Develop the MRP for Lee Key Valve Company presuming that lead time for the assembly of valve body assemblies increases to four weeks.

6. Fractured Frame Co. sells two 8 × 10 inch picture frames complete with backs and glass. The standard model uses a thin black frame and the deluxe model uses a gold trim frame. The backs and glass are the same for both. Assembly lead time for the complete process from frame material, glass and back is two weeks for either model. Frame material is ordered (2.5 feet for each frame) from a local supplier and has a one-week lead time. Glass is purchased, cut to size, and has a three-week lead time. Backs are purchased finished from a hardboard manufacturer with a two-week lead time. The master production schedule for the two models is shown below.

Week	8	9	10	11	12	13	14
Standard frame				100	150		300
Deluxe frame			200		200		150

The on-hand inventory is

Deluxe frame material	300 ft
Standard frame material	150 ft
Glass plates	150
Backs	50
Standard frames (complete)	75
Deluxe frames (complete)	100

Prepare the MRP to exactly meet the demand schedule.

7. Given the following, how many #1342 items should be purchased and when?

Item	Lead times	On Hand	Demand in Week No. 11	12	13	14	15
19	1 week	100	100	0	100	200	0
1342	2 weeks	200	0	500	0	0	0
102	1 week	0	50	0	0	0	0
312	2 weeks	0	5	0	0	10	0

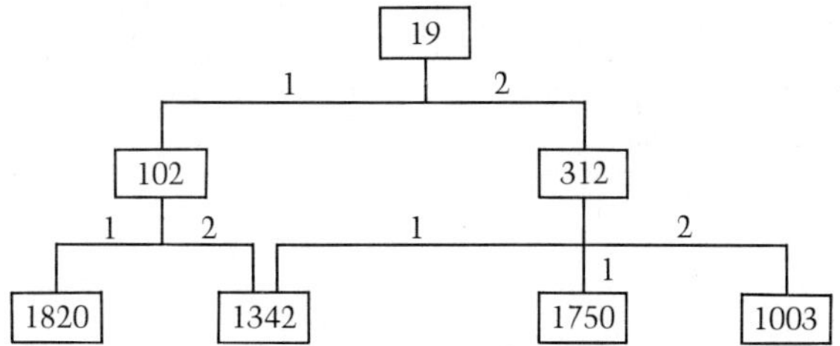

13.11 CASE ANDREW JACOBS & COMPANY

Andrew Jacobs & Company employs approximately 280 people in the manufacture of a number of "add-on appliances for residential heating and air conditioning units." The company began 15 years ago producing a home humidifier and has since expanded into the dehumidifier and air purifier lines. They currently produce 30 different models but, because of heavy competition, engineering changes are constantly taking place and the product line is often changing. Each model is made up of between 40 and several hundred different parts which range from purchased nuts and bolts and prefabricated subassemblies to internally manufactured components.

Andrew Jacobs purchases over 2,500 parts and manfactures over 1,000 parts and assemblies of its own. Many of the parts are used on several different models and some parts such as nuts and bolts are used on over 75% of the finished products.

The finished goods inventory is kept relatively

small. Sales are forecast on a month-to-month basis and production is scheduled according to actual sales orders and the sales forecast. For this reason, production lots placed in the final assembly line are usually for relatively small quantities.

Rather than producing manufactured parts and subcomponents and purchasing other parts according to the sales forecast, parts, sub-assemblies, and purchased items are ordered on a reorder point/economic order quantity basis. Since it is imperative to maintain accurate control of these raw materials and sub-assembly items, all parts and materials stored in the main supply area are controlled with the use of perpetual inventory cards which are maintained by the scheduling department. Each card contains the reorder point, the economic order quantity, and the lead time for outside procurement or internal manufacture. Both receipt of new inventory into the main supply room and use of items from the supply room are recorded on the inventory card.

The scheduling department is reponsible for checking the availability of inventory on the inventory cards. Approximately 3 weeks before a final assembly order is to be placed on the floor, the scheduler checks all the cards for parts needed in that assembly to determine whether issuing the number required to complete the assembly will reduce the inventory of the sub-assembly or part below the reorder point. If the scheduler determines that the projected final assembly order will result in hitting the reorder point, a production order or a purchase order is issued.

Physical inventories are taken every quarter and there are usually a substantial number of small adjustments which must be made. The quarterly physical inventory was suggested after a series of major inventory shortages occurred several years ago. The company's current policy allows any worker to enter the main supply area to remove needed parts. The workers are to fill out materials requisitions and to sign for all parts removed, but they are frequently in a rush and fail to complete the inventory requisitions accurately. There have been several cases where parts staged for final assembly of one product were removed and used on the assembly of another item.

To adjust for many of these problems, the production schedulers often add a safety factor to the reorder point when placing orders and have typically increased the order quantity from 10 to 25 percent over the economic order quantity. Their justification for this is that "it is less expensive to carry a little extra inventory than to shut down the production facility waiting for a rush order."

QUESTIONS FOR DISCUSSION

1. Evaluate and critique the existing system used by Andrew Jacobs & Company.
2. How might MRP work in a situation like this?
3. Suppose that a computer is unavailable and that MRP cannot be sensibly implemented without one. What improvements can you suggest to the existing system to help alleviate Andrew Jacobs' problems?

13.12 REFERENCES AND BIBLIOGRAPHY

1. APICS Special Report, *Material Requirements Planning by Computer*, APICS, Washington, D.C., 1971.
2. ———, *Material Requirements Planning Report*, APICS, Washington, D. C., 1973.
3. Berry, William L., "Lot Sizing Procedures for Requirements Planning Systems: A Framework for Analysis," *Production and Inventory Management*, 2nd Quarter 1972, pp. 19–34.
4. Davis, Edward W., *Case Studies in Materials Requirements Planning*, APICS, Washington, D.C., 1978.
5. Orlicky, Joseph, *Material Requirements Planning*, New York: McGraw-Hill, 1975.
6. Orlicky, Joseph A., Plossl, George W., and Wight, Oliver W., *Material Requirements Planning*, IBM Publication No. 6320-1170, 1971.

7. Plossl, George W., and Wight, Oliver W., *Material Requirements Planning by Computer*, APICS, Washington, D.C., 1971.

8. Wacker, J. and Hills, F. S., "The Key to Success or Failure of MRP: Overcoming Human Resistance," *Production and Inventory Management,* 17:7–15 (No. 4, 1977).

9. Wight, Oliver W., *Production and Inventory Management in the Computer Age*, Boston: Cahners, 1974.

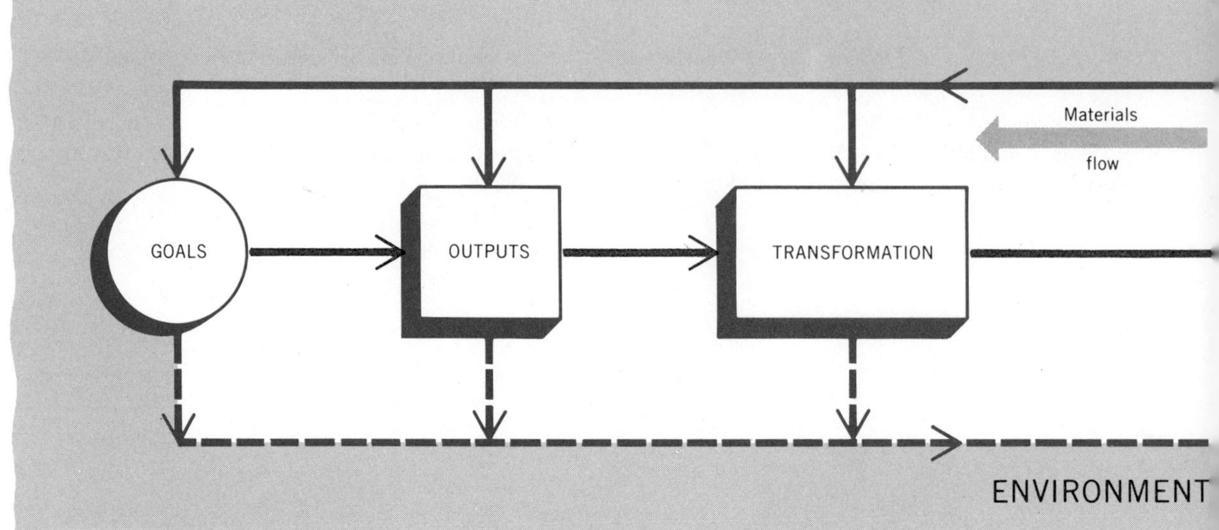

Chapter 14I

The Purchasing Interface: Acquiring Materials

CONCEPTS

14I: Purchasing

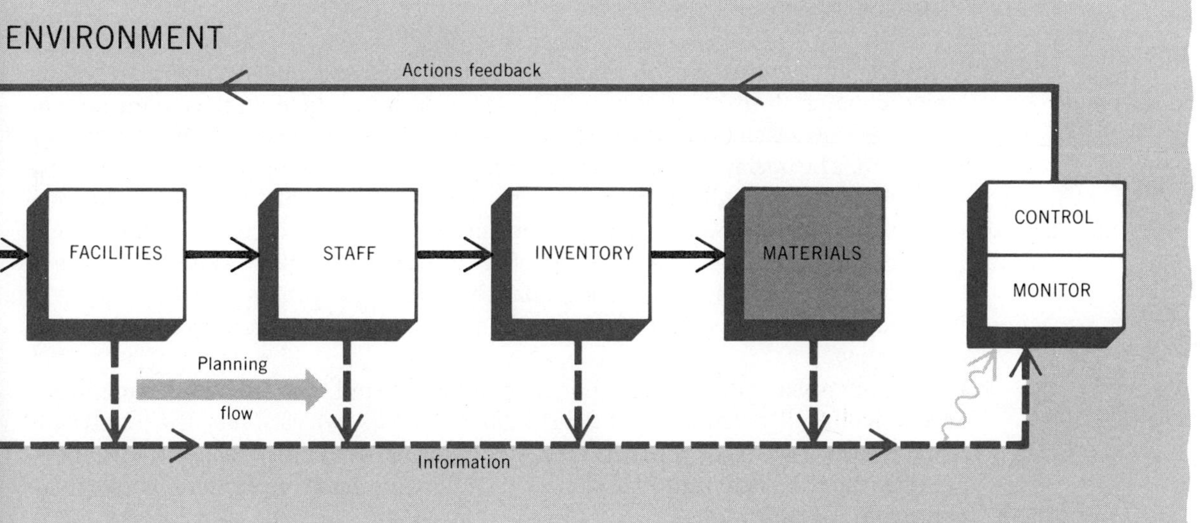

LEARNING OBJECTIVES

By the completion of this chapter the student should

1. Be aware of the potential of purchasing in contributing both to the objectives of operations management and to cost reduction in the organization.
2. Understand the many differences between organizational purchasing and individual purchasing.
3. Be familiar with the requisition and order forms used in purchasing.
4. Know the evaluation criteria and the basis for some of the models used by purchasing in selecting vendors.
5. Know the types of discounts available to organizations.
6. Understand how fair prices are determined through engineering cost analysis and the learning curve.

This chapter covers the final design task in the resource acquisition process: obtaining the materials. In the last two chapters we designed the materials *management* system—now, again following the design approach, we address the issue of *purchasing* them. The operations function depends heavily on the purchasing area to dependably obtain materials by the time they are needed in the production process. Purchasing must make some important tradeoffs in this process. Particularly in the current age of shortages of raw materials and other resources, the purchasing operations of matching varying prices, qualities, quantities, and lead time to meet the needs of production, inventory control, quality control, and other operations functions is a crucial one.

Importance of purchasing.

Many organizations, particularly wholesale, retail, and manufacturing firms, spend half their revenues for outside materials and services. Thus, the purchasing system also has a major potential for cost/profit improvement, perhaps the most powerful within the organization. Consider the following data concerning a simple manufacturing organization.

Profit potential.

$$
\begin{aligned}
\text{total sales} &= \$10{,}000{,}000 \\
\text{purchased materials} &= 7{,}000{,}000 \\
\text{labor and salaries} &= 2{,}000{,}000 \\
\text{overhead} &= 500{,}000 \\
\text{profit} &= 500{,}000
\end{aligned}
$$

To double profits to $1,000,000, one or a combination of the following five actions could be taken.

1. Increase sales by 100 percent.
2. Increase selling price by 5 percent (same volume).
3. Decrease labor and salaries by 25 percent.
4. Decrease overhead by 100 percent.
5. Decrease purchase costs by 7.1 percent.

Although 2 above looks best, it may well be impossible since raising prices almost always reduces the sales volume. In fact, raising prices often *decreases* the total profit (through lower volume). Alternative 5 above is thus particularly appealing.

Decreasing the cost of purchased material provides significant profit leverage. For every 1 percent decrease in the cost of purchases, a 14 percent increase in profits results. This potential is often neglected in both business and public organizations.

Procurement defined.

Another common term for the purchasing function is **procurement**. Whereas "purchasing" implies a *monetary* transaction, "procurement" is simply the responsibility for acquiring the goods and services the organization needs and thus may include, for example, scrap, as well as purchased materials.

Individual versus organizational purchasing.

Organizational procurement is quite different from the consumer purchasing of an individual; for example

1. The volume and dollar amounts are much larger.

2. The buyer may be larger than the supplier, whereas in consumer purchases the buyer is typically smaller than the supplier.
3. Very few suppliers exist for certain organizational goods whereas many typically exist for consumer goods.
4. Certain discounts are available for organizations (discussed later).

14.1 PURCHASING FORMS AND PROCEDURES

Purchase requisitions for departments.

Purchasing forms and procedures in most organizations have become relatively standardized. **Purchase requisitions** are the forms sent to the purchasing department from another department within the organization authorizing it to obtain needed materials, supplies, or equipment. The standard purchase requisition usually includes the items indicated in Figure 14.1. On occasion, a **traveling requisition** is used when a standard item must constantly be resupplied. This form is simply a heavy duty card with the standard information listed on it which can just be pulled and sent to purchasing when new items are needed.

Purchase orders for vendors.

In some computerized production systems, such as MRP systems, vendor lead time, dependability, price, and so forth, are stored internally and when an item is determined to be in need a computerized *purchase order* is automatically generated. In manual systems purchasing will draw up the purchase orders authorizing a vendor to ship items, directly from the requisitions (see Figure 14.2). The required information is similar to that for the purchase requisition and is also shown in Figure 14.1. For items that are in constant need, there is a **blanket purchase order** (corresponding to the traveling requisition) through which the originator in an organization can order without having to go through purchasing. This order system is usually negotiated by purchasing with individual suppliers for a year's duration at a time. Blanket purchase orders are also used for small-valued purchases where the cost of purchasing might even exceed the cost of the item.

Standard Purchase Requisition		Standard Purchase Order
*Identification number		*P.O. no.
*Date of request		*Date of issuance
*Originator		*Vendor name, address
*Billing account and authorization		*Item description and amount
*Item description and amount		*Delivery date
*Date needed		*Carrier
*Vendor information:	Name	*Price, terms, conditions
	P.O. no.	
	Carrier	
	Promised delivery	

Figure 14.1. Standard purchase forms information.

25275 - INSTRUCTIONS TO DEPARTMENT: COMPLETE FORM IN FULL. USE TYPEWRITER ONLY. THIS FORM CAN BE USED ONLY WHEN THE TOTAL AMOUNT OF GOODS OR SERVICES BEING REQUESTED IS $25.00 OR LESS, MULTIPLE ORDERS MUST NEVER BE USED AS A MEANS OF CIRCUMVENTING THE $25.00 LIMITATION. THIS FORM MUST

BE AUTHORIZED (SIGNED) BY THE DEPARTMENT HEAD BEFORE SEPARATING AND DISTRIBUTING ALL COPIES. MAIL ORIGINAL COPY TO VENDOR, SEND THIRD COPY TO PURCHASING DEPARTMENT, AND RETAIN SECOND AND FOURTH COPIES. IMMEDIATELY UPON RECEIPT OF INVOICE, DEPARTMENT MUST COMPLETE SECOND COPY (RECEIVING REPORT AND RECOMMENDATION FOR PAYMENT) AND FORWARD THIS COPY ALONG WITH THE INVOICE TO OFFICE OF CONTROLLER FOR PAYMENT. FOURTH COPY SHOULD BE RETAINED FOR DEPARTMENTAL FILES.

A-116 20M 7-75

UNIVERSITY OF CINCINNATI

DEPARTMENTAL PURCHASE ORDER

Cincinnati, Ohio 45221

No. D 38374

DATE ____________

TO: ____________ VENDOR NAME

____

____________ ADDRESS

____________ CITY STATE ZIP CODE

DELIVER & INVOICE TO: ____________ NAME OF ORIGINATING DEPARTMENT

____

____________ ADDRESS

____________ DEPARTMENTAL TELEPHONE NUMBER

QUANTITY	DESCRIPTION	PRICE	AMOUNT

1. **Invoice in duplicate to Department issuing order.** Do not invoice for partial shipments; send one invoice only upon completion of order.
2. The articles specified herein are to be used exclusively by the University of Cincinnati and are not subject to Ohio State Sales Tax or Federal Excise Tax.
3. This order is valid only if the total amount of purchase is twenty five dollars ($25.00) or less.
4. PLEASE READ DIRECTIONS on reverse side.

VENDOR CAUTION!

Do not accept this order 1) unless it has been signed, 2) unless you know its bearer, 3) unless you have been paid for all previous shipments made to the department shown above. Contact the originating department concerning any overdue payments or the validity of this order.

DO NOT WRITE IN THIS SPACE

Authorized By:

____

Department Head Signature
(Order Valid Only When Signed)

Figure 14.2 A typical purchase order.

For high cost and high volume items, an intensive analysis is usually conducted before a decision is made as to which vendor will receive the purchase order. Bids are usually solicited from vendors and an analysis of all bidding suppliers conducted to aid in the supplier selection decision. The considerations in such an analysis will be discussed in the next section.

Bidding.

14.2 THE SUPPLIER SELECTION DECISION

Supplier qualifications.

Dickson [3] has listed a number of evaluation criteria which are used in the supplier (**vendor**) **selection** process. His list contains many of the qualifications of a good supplier. Some of these general characteristics are

1. Deliveries on time, of the quality, and in the quantity specified. This maintains the consistent flow of processing operations for the purchasing organization.
2. A fair price.
3. Able to react to unforeseen changes such as an increase or decrease in demand, quality, specifications, or delivery schedules, all frequent occurrences in operations.
4. Continually improving products and services.

Suppliers with all of these characteristics are difficult to find. The purchasing function must recognize these selection criteria and not be swayed by cost/price considerations alone.

The vendor evaluation and selection process can be divided into two segments: evaluating existing suppliers and evaluating potential new suppliers.

Evaluating Existing Suppliers

Evaluation factors for existing suppliers.

Current suppliers can be evaluated monthly or quarterly on the basis of three elements of objective data and one subjective assessment. The objective variables are

- Price.
- Percentage of material rejected.
- Percentage of delivery dates met.

The subjective data can be gathered through periodic questionnaires to company engineers, purchasing agents, and others within the organization. This subjective information relates to the level and quality of technical and service help provided by the vendor. Vendors who fall below the acceptable standards should be notified and, if improvement is not forthcoming, dropped as a supplier.

Evaluating Potential Suppliers

Evaluation factors for potential suppliers.

Evaluating *potential* sources of supply is less objective but, according to the *Guide of Purchasing* of the National Association of Purchasing Management, Inc. [7], it can be divided into four major areas.

1. Technical and engineering capability.
2. Manufacturing strengths.
3. Financial strengths.
4. Management capability.

Each of these four areas can be evaluated through generally available information and through meetings with the potential vendor. The vendor's technical and manufacturing capability can often be evaluated through meetings with engineering and manufacturing personnel, through bid evaluation, plant tours, and through the use of a trial order.

Capability.

Financial strength.

Financial strength is an important consideration, for even though a company is technically competent, it may not be financially sound enough to meet deliveries. Recent examples of this problem include Rolls Royce's difficulty in delivering jet engines and Lockheed's difficulty delivering jet planes to buyers. An analysis of financial statements, including financial ratio analysis of ability to repay short- and long-term debt, profitability, and the general trend of the capitalization structure of the firm, should also be undertaken.

Management strength.

Management strength is paramount in long-term and high dollar contracts. For example, management of construction contractors for buildings, bridges, and highways, or airframe manufacturers for aircraft, must be evaluated to detemine their ability to successfully complete the project. The technical capability may well exist, but managerial talent and organization may not be available to guide the project. Even for short-term arrangements, the ability of the vendor's management to control its own operations will lead to better prices, delivery performance, and quality.

14.3 VENDOR SELECTION MODELS

One method of combining the various decision factors for several vendors is to use a simple expected value model. Suppose the vendor selection decision is to be determined on the basis of three decision criteria.

1. Ability to meet price.
2. Ability to meet shipping date.
3. Ability to meet quality specifications.

A simple selection model.

Importance scores can be assigned to each of the three criteria and *probabilities* of meeting each criterion can be estimated for each vendor. The vendor with the greatest expected importance score should be selected.

Smith versus Jones

A simple example will illustrate the procedure. Two suppliers, Smith and Jones, are being evaluated. Their chances of meeting the three criteria are shown in Table 14.1.

TABLE 14.1 SUPPLIER SELECTION

		Smith	Jones
Criterion Number	1	.8	.7
	2	.6	.85
	3	.9	.75

The importance scores for the three criteria are

1. Ability to meet price, 5.
2. Ability to meet shipping date, 10.
3. Ability to meet quality specifications, 8.

A score of 0 is given for failure on any of the three criteria. The expected score for Smith is computed as

$$.8(5) + .6(10) + .9(8) = 17.2$$

and for Jones

$$.7(5) + .85(10) + .75(8) = 18$$

On the basis of this simple analysis, the best supplier is Jones, with an expected importance score of 18.

This kind of decision model is important in selection decisions such as the vendor selection problem and for other purchasing problems such as specification selection. Because there are multiple criteria and most of them are subject to uncertainty, a decision analysis, or expected value, approach is often useful.

Other evaluation models.

Other models are the aviation industry's CASE program [6], General Motor's SPEAR program [4], and Ford Motor Company's Q-101 program [6]. These and other methods, such as those used by the Department of Defense, offer a significant addition to the precision of at least one component of the purchasing function.

Other Considerations

Using local vendors.

Other factors often considered by purchasing managers are the location of vendors and the use of multiple vendors for the same item. Local vendors are often preferred to nonlocals for two primary reasons. First, expediting orders is often less complicated if the purchasing agent can easily travel to the supplier's plant. Communications are less difficult, and a better rapport can be established between the representatives of the two organizations. Second, for less tangible reasons, a local vendor is often desirable. The economic condition of the community affects the company and its employees. **Buying local** means that the local economy is stimulated, causing tax receipts to increase and thus improving the lot of employees through better schools, parks, and other public services. It also improves the general social conditions of the community, making it a more desirable place to locate and thus improving the organization's ability to attract good employees.

Using multiple vendors.

Multiple vendors are often desirable, assuming that more than one feasible source exists. The reasons for using more than one vendor include

1. Reduced risk compared with **sole source** buying.
2. Competition among vendors.

Risk of stockout.

Buying from one vendor increases the risk of missed deliveries due to a strike, natural catastrophe, or equipment failure. Diversification of purchasing reduces this risk since it is unlikely that all vendors would be affected at the same time. Also, knowledge on the part of the vendor that other suppliers are getting some of the business increases the vendor's sense of competition and keeps all of the suppliers aware of the need for good performance.

Competition.

The "80-20 rule."

Lastly, a word might be said about keeping good relations with suppliers. The **80-20 rule*** works in purchasing just like everywhere else: 80 percent of the materials will come from 20 percent of the suppliers. Thus, it behooves purchasing management to stay on good terms with their major suppliers.

14.4 COST/PRICE ANALYSIS

Role of price.

Price is an important element in any purchase. Whether the item being purchased is a new dress or a ton of coal, the purchaser is expected to search for the best value possible for himself/herself or the organization. As we have already discussed, price is not the only consideration. A great price cut is meaningless if the material purchased is of insufficient quality to be used or is not delivered on time to meet operations schedules.

Discounts

Discounts.

There are typically four standard types of discounts that purchasing managers should take advantage of.

1. **Trade discounts.** These are discounts to the retailer from the distributor, or to the wholesaler from the manufacturer. Only the final customer ever buys at the "manufacturer's suggested price."
2. **Quantity discounts.** These discounts are available for buying in large quantity and thus should be especially important to purchasing. They were analyzed in detail for inventory purposes in Chapter 12.
3. **Seasonal discounts.** These discounts are available to purchasers for buying in the "off" season and help the vendor or manufacturer level out their production. If storage is available, excellent discounts can be obtained in this fashion.

* Also known as Pareto's rule and is the basis of the ABC concept (see Chapter 12): 20 percent of inventory represents 80 percent of the value; 20 percent of the customers make 80 percent of the complaints.

4. **Cash discounts.** These are for cash and "near cash" purchases (prompt payment). The most common is "2/10, net 30" which means a 2 percent discount if the bill is paid within 10 days; otherwise the entire amount is due in 30 days. Such discounts represent a 36 percent annual cost savings to organizations and should rarely be passed up.

The right price.

A purchasing manager is also concerned with determining the price that will ensure a reliable source of supply in the right quantities, quality, and timing. She or he must be able to enter negotiations with suppliers with a reasonable estimate of the price the organization is willing to pay and must be aware both of prices which are excessive or prices which cannot possibly earn the supplier a profit.

Federal pricing regulations.

While discussing materials pricing, mention should be made of the Robinson-Patman and other such federal acts affecting pricing in interstate commerce. While originally intended to curb discriminatory practices of large retailers, the Robinson-Patman Act has also become applicable to manufacturers. The effect of the act has been to make it illegal, in most circumstances, for sellers to offer different customers different prices for the identical material in the same quantities. In addition to the Robinson-Patman Act, there are many others (Miller-Tydings, Clayton, Sherman) of importance the operations manager should be acquainted with. For further information, consult References 1, 2, and 5.

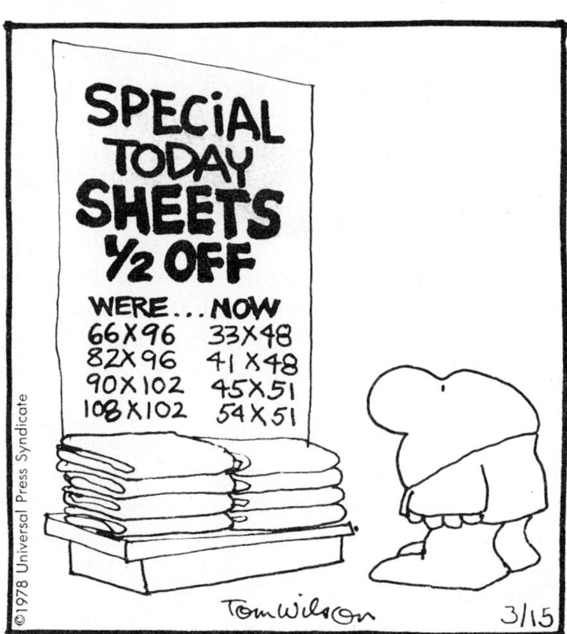

(Copyright © 1978 Universal Press Syndicate. Reprinted by permission.)

Economically, every supplier must receive a price for its product which will cover all costs and which will provide some margin of profit. If this return is not forthcoming to the vendor, it will inevitably be forced out of business. A purchasing manager must be able to estimate the total cost of an item and be aware of industry profit margins if she or he is to be successful in price negotiations. Two methods of cost determination which are frequently employed are: engineering cost analysis and learning curve analysis.

Engineering Cost Analysis

Engineering cost analysis attempts to break down the price of an item into its component parts.

Direct material.

Direct labor.

Overhead.

General and administrative expense.

Profit.

Direct material cost.

Direct material cost is easily estimated from the list of component parts and raw materials (commonly called a **bill of materials**) used to produce the item to be purchased. The price/cost analyst can compute materials cost by multiplying quantity used of each material by the unit price. While the unit price may vary somewhat due to the supplier's own quantity buying policies, a reasonably accurate materials cost estimate can usually be determined.

Direct labor cost.

Direct labor costs are not as easily estimated as direct material. Depending upon the level of mechanization and automation that the supplier employs, more or less labor will be used. While labor rates (the wages paid to various categories of labor) are more easily determined, and time estimates can be made for the operations needed to complete a unit of the product, there are several factors that complicate direct labor cost estimates. The size of the production runs, the number of different products run through the same machine or department, the experience of the operator(s) (which is adversely affected by high employee turnover) all tend to increase direct labor costs. These factors are difficult to estimate even if the analyst has direct knowledge of the details of the supplier's operation. Also, geographical differences result in differences in wage rates, although many of these differences, particularly between U.S. and foreign labor, are diminishing rapidly.

Overhead costs.

Overhead costs are allocated costs because they are not directly assignable to a given product. Overhead items include depreciation on equipment, heat, light, power, taxes, research and development costs, maintenance costs, and many others. Depending upon the basis for allocation, a given product may receive a disproportionate share of the company overhead. Again, the cost/price analyst will find it difficult to estimate the exact amount of overhead without an intimate knowledge of the supplier's operations and their cost allocation methods.

G&A costs.

General and administrative (G&A) expenses include salaries for non-operations executives and service functions within the organization (such as the accounting department, the personnel department), selling, advertising, legal expenses, and so on. Like overhead costs, general and administrative expenses are usually not attributable to a specific product, and, therefore, must be allocated to all products.

Profit rate.

Profit is the difference between price and the sum of the four cost factors. A reasonable profit, as we have discussed, is desirable, but profit margins which appear to be out of line with industry averages should be questioned by the purchasing manager.

Learning Curve Analysis

Including learning effects in price per unit.

We saw in Chapter 5 how **learning curves** could be used by a manager to estimate the time required to complete future operations. For new products, or new vendors of an existing product, the learning curve is likely to result in a decreasing cost of the units produced as experience is gained. This knowledge should be used in determining the price of units to be purchased.

Mr. Mushy Ice Cream

The Mr. Mushy Ice Cream Co. wishes to upgrade all of the soft ice cream made in its 150 national locations over the next three years by the use of an ingeniously designed new machine. Figure 14.3 shows the 90 percent learning curve Mr. Mushy's purchasing manager has estimated that the machine's manufacturer should experience in the production of the 150 units. Clearly, Mr. Mushy should not be willing to pay at the rate of the first units produced nor should the manufacturer be willing to sell at the rate of the one-hundred fiftieth unit.

Either a price should be negotiated which covers the long run average cost to produce all 150 units or a price per 100 units could be used with prices declining over the three year period to reflect the learning rate.

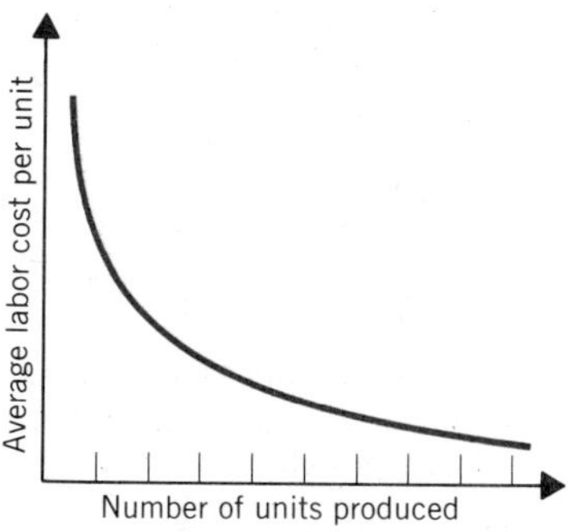

Figure 14.3. Learning curve for Mr. Mushy ice cream machines.

14.5 SUMMARY

The purchasing function, or procurement as it is sometimes called, is of special importance to operations management because of the effect of materials availability and quality on the transformation process. In addition, purchasing can be a major contributor to reducing organizational costs.

Organizational purchasing is considerably different from individual consumer purchasing in a number of ways. Organizations employ purchase requisition forms to communicate departmental needs and purchase orders, which go to vendors.

Supplier selection is a major task of purchasing and is usually a function of price, on time delivery, flexibility, and quality. Some weighted-score types of selection/evaluation models are available to aid in this process. However, purchasing usually favors local vendors and using multiple vendors rather then "sole-sourcing."

Pricing is probably the major consideration in many purchases. Many types of discounts are available to organizations, which should be taken advantage of. In determining a fair price, engineering cost analysis is frequently employed and, where learning is expected to occur, the learning curve.

14.6 KEY TERMS

procurement (p. 488)
purchase requisition (p. 489)
traveling requisition (p. 489)
blanket purchase orders (p. 489)
vendor selection (p. 490)
importance scores (p. 492)
buying local (p. 493)
sole source (p. 494)
80-20 rule (p. 494)
trade discount (p. 494)
quantity discount (p. 494)
seasonal discount (p. 494)
cash discount (p. 495)
engineering cost analysis (p. 496)
learning curve (p. 497)
bill of materials (p. 496)
overhead (p. 496)

14.7 REVIEW TEST

1. The profit improvement potential of purchasing is also important in not-for-profit organizations. (p. 488)
   a. True b. False
2. Procurement and purchasing are identical. (p. 488)
   a. True b. False
3. Organizational purchasing is identical to individual purchasing but on a larger scale. (p. 488)
   a. True b. False
4. A purchase requisition is sent to a vendor to obtain materials. (p. 489)
   a. True b. False
5. A traveling requisition is a single form that is periodically circulated through departments to request out-of-stock materials for purchasing. (p. 489)
   a. True b. False
6. A blanket purchase order allows a department to bypass the purchasing department. (p. 489)
   a. True b. False
7. An important qualification of a good supplier is that she or he is continually improving products and services. (p. 490)
   a. True b. False

8. Evaluating existing suppliers is more objective than evaluating potential suppliers. (p. 490)
a. True b. False

9. Vendor selection models are typically based on simple expected values. (p. 492)
a. True b. False

10. Multiple vendors are desirable because they increase the competition for serving an organization. (p. 494)
a. True b. False

11. A cash discount is only obtainable when payment is made in cash. (p. 495)
a. True b. False

12. Organizations should shy away from vendors whose prices are extremely low. (p. 495)
a. True b. False

13. Direct labor costs are, like direct material costs, fairly easy to estimate. (p. 496)
a. True b. False

14. The learning curve is primarily useful in costing *new* products and services. (p. 497)
a. True b. False

14.8 DISCUSSION QUESTIONS

1. How might a weak purchasing department hinder operations managers?
2. In what other ways might organizational purchasing differ from individual purchasing?
3. What other types of purchasing forms are there? What are they used for?
4. Can you add some additional qualities desirable in a supplier?
5. On what basis would you evaluate a potential supply source?
6. What are the disadvantages in using local vendors? Multiple vendors?
7. When might an organization *not* wish to take advantage of each of the four types of discounts?
8. What elements of an engineering cost analysis are subject to high risk? Why?
9. Should a company prohibit its purchasing agent from socializing with vendors?

14.9 PROBLEMS

1. Musik Manufacturing Co. is evaluating two potential suppliers of plastic fasteners. Musik uses an expected importance score model to select suppliers based upon three criteria.
a. Price.
b. Impact strength.
c. Shipping date.

The three criteria have importance weights of 3, 5, and 2 respectively. If the probabilities of meeting the three criteria are as follows, which vender should be selected?

	Vendor A	Vendor B
Probability of meeting price quote	.8	.5
Probability of meeting impact strength quote	.3	.9
Probability of meeting shipping date quote	.5	.7

2. Suppose that Buildo Construction is interested in having five construction office trailers manufactured to their specifications. Buildo's purchasing agent is negotiating with Movable Modulars, Inc., a custom trailer manufacturer. Movable Modulars estimates that an 80 percent learning curve is appropriate for a project of this size. If they compute the price of the first trailer to be $8000, what should the fifth one cost if the savings are passed on to Buildo? What average price per unit should Movable Modular charge? (Assume the cost of materials is negligible here.)

3. The purchasing department of the City of New Old is negotiating with two contractors for the construction of five sewage treatment plants. Sledge, Inc., estimates that their learning rate will be 65 percent and that the cost of the first plant will be $128,000. Dis-Poz, Inc., estimates a first plant cost of $106,000 and a learning rate of 80 percent. Based upon the total cost of all five units, which contractor should receive the bid?

14.10 CASE CLASSIC AUTO PARTS COMPANY

Classic Auto Parts Company began eight years ago when Don Murphy, frustrated at his inability to find needed parts for his 1961 356B Porsche, purchased two rusted Porsches for parts. Don had always been a sports car enthusiast and the 356B was the third of his auto restoration attempts. Parts for the old Porsches were extremely scarce and prices for available components were at a premium.

Don was able to complete his restoration with the parts obtained from the two parts cars. He was also able to sell, with no advertising, all the usable parts of the two cars which he did not need. He wound up with a 2000 percent profit on the purchase of the two cars. He also received numerous phone calls about parts long after the two cars were both "parted out" and their remains shipped off to the junk yard.

Don began to search for old Porsches that were not in restorable condition and purchased as many as he could find. He called his company Classic Auto Parts and placed an ad in the yellow pages of several telephone books in the surrounding communities. After two years in business, Don quit his full time job and devoted his entire attention to Classic Auto Parts.

Calls were coming in constantly for body components (fenders, rocker panels, lower pans, hoods, trunk lids, doors, etc.) which were typically rusted on the cars which Don had. Don approached a local sheet metal fabrication company with the idea of manufacturing stamped floor pans identical to those of the original Porsches. The dies for the press were manufactured at a cost of $8200 and Don had 100 floor pan sets produced. His cost in the floor pans (including the cost of the die) was $140 each. He sold all the sets within the first six months at a selling price of $175 each. With this initial experience, Don decided to become actively involved in the NOS (new-old stock) business. Since that time, Don has taken on several additional suppliers for sheet metal parts and has produced floor pans for all model Porsches including the newer 911's and 912's, and is producing fender panels, inner fender wells, trunk lids and deck lids, rocker panel assemblies, and a variety of chrome and rubber body parts. The business has grown from an initial part time activity to a $13 million per year business.

Dick Sandmeyer, Don's vice president in charge of purchasing, has recently secured quotes on NOS battery hold-down brackets. Four suppliers have bid on the order for one thousand brackets and have quoted the following prices.

Supplier	Price	Terms	FOB	Tooling Cost
A	$8.62	2/10 net 30	Shipping Point	$ 750
B	7.50	1/10 net 30	Classic Auto Parts	550
C	9.01	net 30	Classic Auto Parts	1000
D	7.40	net 30	Shipping point	500

Dick has only specified that the battery hold-down bracket be equivalent in construction and workmanship with the original Porsche hold-down bracket. The vendors have not been given prints or other engineering specifications from which to develop their bid. Classic has purchased previously from vendors A and C, and has not purchased from Vendors B and D. Dick feels that a fair price for the part would be in the $8.50 to $9.00 range. He has some doubts about vendor D's ability to produce the part although they are doing NOS work for several companies specializing in NOS Chevrolet parts. The two vendors that Classic has used before have both called to talk with Dick and have indicated that their prices have gone up due to inflation in both labor and materials costs.

Vendor A is located 800 miles from Classic's plant. Vendor C is located in the same city as Classic. Vendor B is located 300 miles away and vendor D is located 75 miles away. The part weighs approximately 3 pounds.

QUESTIONS FOR DISCUSSION

1. Which supplier should Classic choose? Make whatever assumptions and analysis that are necessary.
2. What special studies might be useful here?
3. What cautions would you give to Dick in making his decision to select one of the new vendors?

14.12 REFERENCES AND BIBLIOGRAPHY

1. Aljian, G. W., ed., *Purchasing Handbook*, 3rd ed., New York: McGraw-Hill, 1973.
2. Ammer, D. S., *Materials Management*, Homewood, Ill.: Irwin, 1974.
3. Dickson, G. W., "An Analysis of Vendor Selection Systems and Decision," *Journal of Purchasing*, 2:5–17 (February, 1966).
4. Edwards, M. G., "Supplier Management Evaluation," *Journal of Purchasing*, 3:28–41 (February, 1967).
5. England, W. B., and Leenders, M. R., *Purchasing and Materials Management*, Homewood, Ill.: Irwin, 1975.
6. Lamberson, L. R., Dredenck, D., and Wuori, J., "Quantitative Vendor Evaluation," *Journal of Purchasing and Materials Management*, 12:19–28 (Spring, 1976).
7. National Association of Purchasing Agents, Inc., "Vendor Supplier Evaluation," *Guide to Purchasing*, New York, 1967.

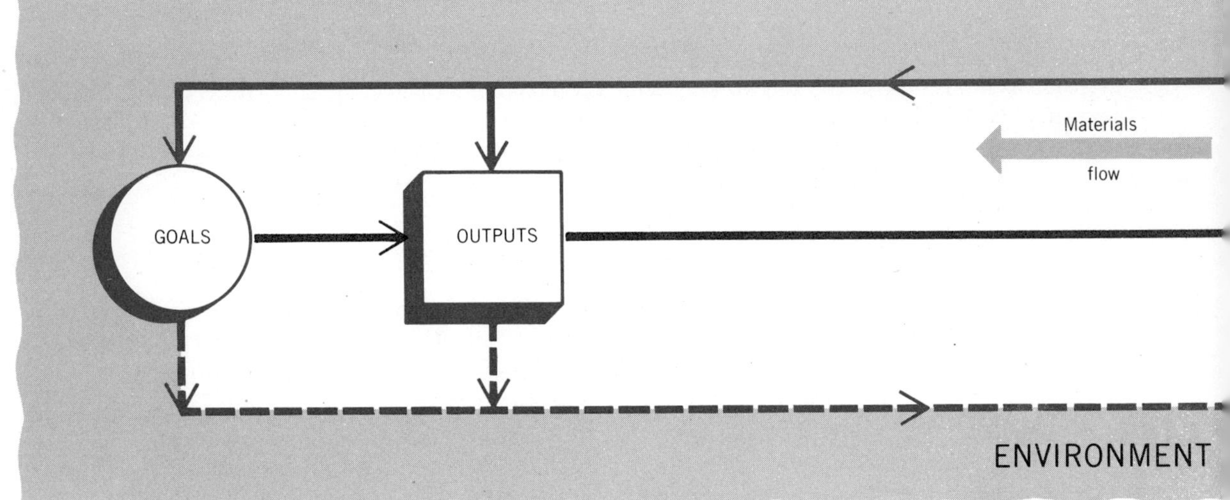

PART IV

CONTROLLING THE SYSTEM

At this point in the text, the discussion of the design of the operations activities is largely complete. However, no system operates for long in the way that it was designed. Thus, it is necessary to also consider the design of *control* systems that will keep operations on course as reality deviates from expectations to assure their efficient and effective achievement of the organization's goals. In essence, these systems monitor internal operations and the external environment through the information system, feed back this information for comparison against a master plan, note serious deviations, and apply *control* to correct for these deviations.

In Chapter 15 we discuss two general control processes—preventive control and feedback control. This chapter also presents techniques to determine whether or not a system is actually out of control. The chapter con-

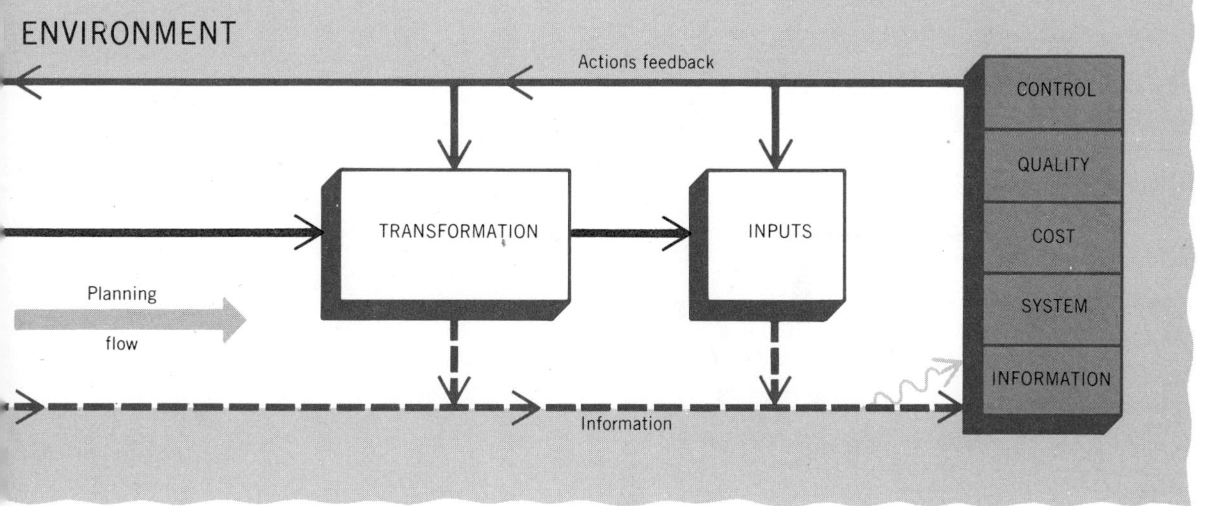

cludes with a discussion of some specialized forms of control systems.

The next four chapters investigate the control of three crucial organizational elements. Chapter 16 considers the many facets of quality control. In Chapter 17I the topic of cost control and the interface with the accounting function are discussed. Then the control of the overall system in terms of maintaining its reliability is examined in Chapter 18.

The information system to monitor organizational activities is held until last so that a discussion of all the organization's activities can be completed first. The use of computers in this and certain other functions is also included here. This then represents the systems interface—the computer and information system tie-in to all the organization's activities.

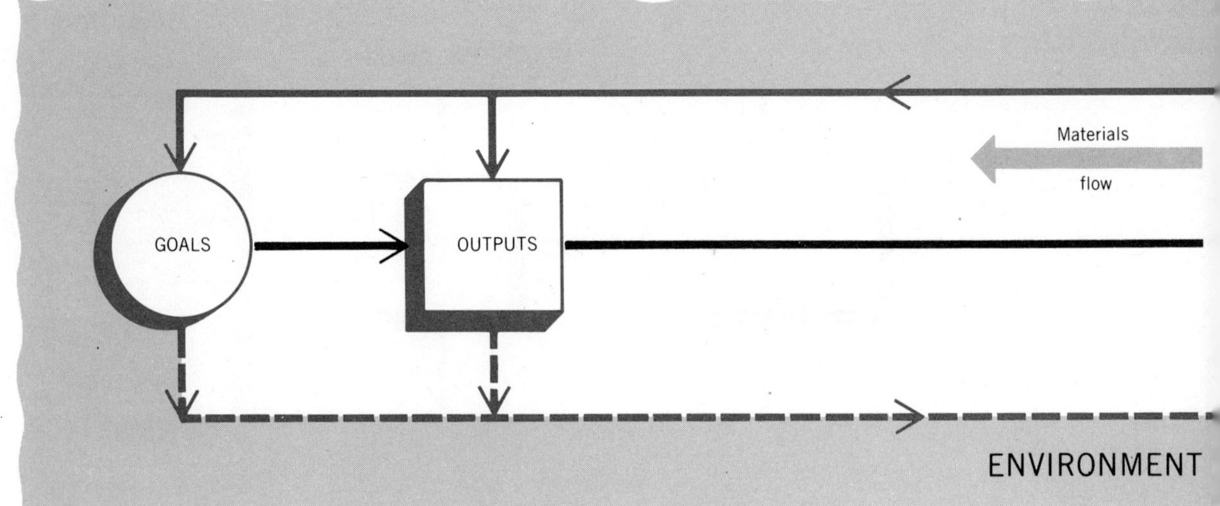

Chapter 15

Organizational Control Systems

CONCEPTS

15.1 The Control Process
Preventive Control
Feedback Control in Organizations
Information Lag
15.2 Control Charts for Feedback Control
15.3 Order Control for Intermittent Operations
15.4 Flow Control for Continuous Operations
15.5 Block Control for Batch Operations
15.6 Load Control for Bottleneck Operations
15.7 PERT/CPM for Project Operations

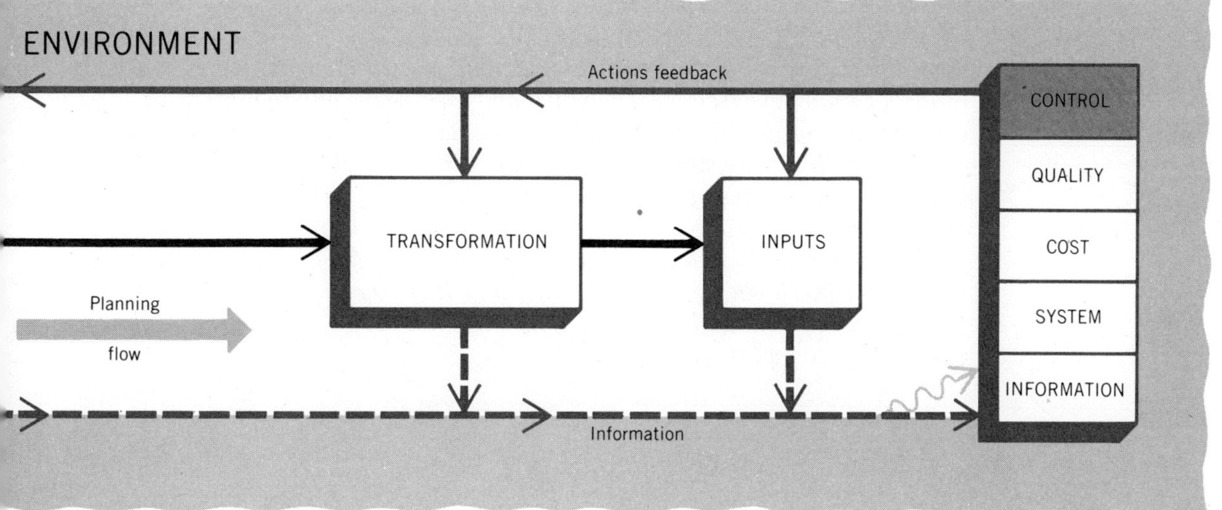

TOOLS AND APPLICATIONS

LEARNING OBJECTIVES

By the completion of the *Concepts* portion of this chapter the student should

1. Understand the difference between preventive control systems and feedback control systems and what each is typically used for.
2. Realize the importance of information lag in feedback control systems.
3. Be familiar with the activities that organizations attempt to control, both internally and externally.
4. Know how to use control charts for feedback control systems.
5. Comprehend the differences between order, flow, block, and load control and the organizational situations for which they are appropriate.

Basically the job of general manager in a small industrial organization . . . is like running a multiringed circus. Daily demands and decisions emanate from all parts of the organization. One must at one and the same time be involved in production activities, selling, personnel issues and day to day financial management. Most information gathering and decision making occurs on an interpersonal basis characterized by brevity and verbal communications. The time and information available for detailed and indepth analysis is nonexistent. One must have some basic priorities and/or strategy clearly in mind to be able to handle the constant flow of interruptions and decisions. Otherwise it is very simple for the total operation to go rapidly out of control.

— J. R. M. Gordon, in "Perspectives," (Academy of Management), 5:19 (Fall, 1977).

CONCEPTS

Definition of control.

In order for an organization to accomplish its goals, the efforts of the individuals and systems comprising it must be coordinated. That process of coordination of effort, which we call "management," requires *control:* assuring that actual performance conforms to plan. Anthony and Reese [1] state it in even simpler terms: "Control is assuring that desired results are attained."

Planned versus desired results.

Control worthwhile?

Planned and actual results are very often not the same. Plans are based upon imperfect information and upon estimates about the future. Once activity begins to take place and plans are implemented, the organization may learn that original expectations were too ambitious or not ambitious enough. On occasion, of course, it is not necessary to control because the activity is not significant enough to affect organizational performance. On other occasions, the *cost* of control may not warrant the benefits to be obtained. Management may be faced with changes in the environment or other circumstances which were not indicated when plans were originally adopted. In these cases, it may be more desirable to modify the original plan than to continue using it.

Internal control.

Control may either be directed internally or externally. Internal control usually is focused on the following.

- *Inputs:* The quantity and quality of materials, staff, equipment, facilities, and information acquired by the organization.
- *Activities:* The scheduling and performance of the transformation operations and distribution activities occurring within the organization.
- *Outputs:* The characteristics of the intended outputs, and unintended outputs (pollution, scrap, waste), of the organization.

Controlled activities.

Although the breakdown above clearly illustrates the *requirements* for internal control, it does not indicate the relative organizational emphasis accorded the various activities. In terms of managerial responsibility, internal control is more commonly divided according to the following breakdown.

- *Quality:* The control of the *quality* of incoming materials, internal processing operations, and the output. (This material is covered in Chapter 16.)
- *Cost:* the control of *costs* and the organization's *financial resources*. (This is discussed in Chapters 10 and 17.)
- *Materials:* Controlling the acquisition of materials through purchasing (Chapter 14I).
- *Staff:* Controlling the acquisition of staff through personnel (Chapter 11I) and their *performance* (Chapter 8).
- *Inventories:* Controlling raw, in-process, and finished materials (Chapters 12 and 13).
- *Rates and schedules:* The coordination function (Chapter 9).
- *System reliability:* Guaranteeing the proper functioning of the overall system (Chapter 18).
- *Information:* The need, quantity, and quality of information for reporting and decision making (Chapter 19I).

External control.

External control is usually directed to environmental demand for the output and competition (a marketing function), sources of input supplies (a purchasing and personnel function), capital availability (a financial function), new technology (an engineering and R&D function), new laws and regulations (a legal function), and other, similar considerations. In some cases, control can be attempted, as through pricing or lobbying, but in other cases the organizational environment can only be monitored, the results being reported back to management.

15.1 THE CONTROL PROCESS

Feedback versus preventive control.

Control systems in organizations are of two major types: **preventive control** systems and **feedback control** systems. Preventive control systems operate to prevent the occurrence of deviations from plan. That is, preventive controls attempt to keep deviations from happening through good system design. Feedback is simply information about a process which is returned to a decision maker (or controller) as input to a "control" decision. In a feedback control system a plan or standard is adopted, the actual performance of the system is monitored and measured, and the system status is fed back to a decision maker. Significant deviations from plan indicate the need for adjusting action (control) to put the system back on course. Feedback control systems are known as **dynamic** systems. Since no feedback occurs in preventive control systems they are considered **static** systems.

Clearly, both types of control systems will typically be used in the control of organizational activities. Although either type, by itself, *could* exercise sufficient control for most situations, if well designed, the experience of the system designer is usually too limited to design a system that is acceptable under all conditions. Preset traffic lights are a good example of preventive control systems that are typically well designed. Nevertheless, in many cities it has been found to be necessary to augment these systems with pedestrian and in-roadway switches. These switches provide *feedback* to a nearby electrical controller, which overrides the preset light sequence if traffic becomes too heavy.

Preventive Control

Preventive control procedures.

The preventive control systems of an organization consist, in large part, of the policies, procedures, rules, budgets, and regulations of the organization. Many of these systems are described in training and procedure manuals given out to new employees but many more are communicated simply by word of mouth, or even nonverbally (a frown), through the informal organization. ("Committee meetings are *never* set for Friday," "Where's your safety helmet, Bob?")

In addition to formal procedures, numerous other means of communicating preventive controls are also employed, the most formal of which is, of course, one's immediate superior. But even the yellow lines painted on the warehouse floor, the goggles hanging near the machine's switch, the one-way theater turnstile, and the supermarket railings that are just slightly narrower than the shopping carts are preventive control systems.

Design for preventive control.

A considerable amount of thought goes into the design of such systems to make them as foolproof as possible, thus requiring minimal supervision. This, for example, is the basis for the numerous franchises in the fast-food business, the chain drugstores, and other such standardized multilocation organizations. An efficient system is developed that closely controls the activities of the employees, and, on occasion, the recipients as well, thus guaranteeing a certain quality of output. The scoop is designed to hold just enough french fries to fill a bag, the camera requires the librarian to simultaneously actuate a switch with *each* hand before it will take a picture of the borrower's library card (so that idle fingers do not cover the lens by accident).

Use of both types necessary.

As mentioned, preventive control systems are rarely sufficient in all cases, however. They must usually be supplemented by feedback control systems to handle exceptional circumstances. It should be noted that even dynamic feedback systems may not be adequate to control some activities—in these cases we may need to resort to higher levels of control (lawsuits, firing, police, army).

Feedback Control in Organizations

Figure 15.1 illustrates the major components of an organizational feedback control process for internal control. The process begins with *goals* and *plans*, without which control is meaningless. Control implies maintenance of a direction toward a specific target. Without an identified target there is nothing for the organization to be guided

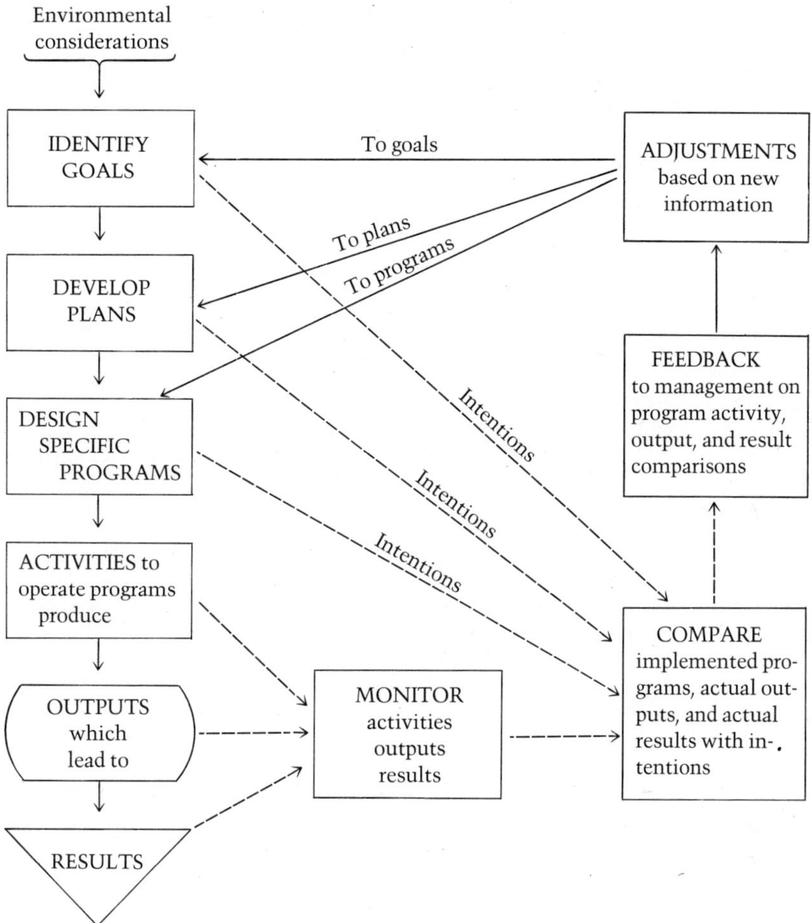

Figure 15.1. The feedback process.

toward. Hence, planning and control, although they are different activities, are closely related and interdependent.

Feedback control process.

Within organizations, major activities are identified as *programs*. These programs are the specific methods by which the organization intends to carry out its strategic plans. For example, to increase consumer awareness of a new product, an organization might implement an advertising program. To prevent the outbreak of certain childhood diseases, a local health department might organize an immunization program. And, to develop new methods of providing necessary energy, an organization may develop an energy research program. Each program is designed to undertake certain *activities* and to produce specific *outputs*. These activities and outputs are intended, in conjunction with other programs and environmental conditions, to produce some desired outcome or *result*.

The feedback control process is made up of four major activities.

1. Monitoring.
2. Comparing.
3. Feedback.
4. Adjusting.

Monitor.

The **monitoring** activity in a feedback control process serves as a data collection activity. Data regarding the activity of a program, the outputs produced by the program, and the results accomplished by the production of these outputs are routinely measured and processed to provide specific reports. This monitoring activity is provided, in part, by the organization's accounting system which captures and processes economic data about activities and outputs. Other subsystems of the organization's information system* measure and record various nonfinancial data.

Monitoring results for most organizations is less routinized than for activities and outputs. Even in business organizations (wherein one of the many results is "level of profit"), the results of specific activities and outputs are very seldom systematically collected. For example, neither the pollution damage resulting from one of an organization's activities nor the societal good achieved by an equal employment opportunity program or a life-saving product are systematically measured.

Monitoring outputs instead of inputs.

For not-for-profit organizations the monitoring problem is even more acute. Taxpayers would like to know the *results* of a legal system or a mental health system, not how many assets were used or how many mental patients have been hospitalized. These measures are clearly difficult to develop, but without them the organization is less able to intelligently control operations.

Comparator.

Simply knowing that activities, outputs, and results have been accomplished is still not enough for control. The organization must *compare* these accomplishments with what is intended. Typical questions which need to be asked and answered are

1. Are we working as many hours as we had planned?
2. Are we producing as many services with the available resources as had been intended?
3. Are our outputs being translated into the kinds of results we want?

Effector.

These comparisons provide the basis for *feedback* and **adjustment** through managerial action. Both negative and positive answers to these questions are important. It could be the case that management's original plans were too conservative and that opportunities are being missed to produce more with the available resources. Also, comparison can also show that, while activity levels are up to expectation, the outputs of that activity are not. Perhaps some inefficiencies have crept into the system, or the environmental conditions that existed when the program was envisioned have since changed and goals need to be adjusted.

* We will further discuss information systems in Chapter 19I.

Feedback control systems, being dynamic, are easy to identify in organizations: alarms on "FIRE EXIT ONLY" doors, roving managers, end of aisle mirrors, employee performance evaluations, report cards, votes of confidence, time clocks, theater tickets, sales receipts, complaint departments, Gallup polls, shareholder's reports, applause, and so on. **Budgets** are also control mechanisms and are typically used in both a preventive and feedback context. Another financial control system historically used to monitor and compare organizations' finanaical health is **ratio analysis**: liquidity ratios, turnover ratios, profit ratios, and so forth. The use of ratios for control is not limited to financial aspects but is also used in operations control for line balancing, facility utilization, and scheduling as discussed in earlier chapters.

Financial control.

As might be expected, the majority of feedback systems involve human intervention, usually in the adjusting activity, but also frequently in the monitoring, comparing, and feedback activities. The result is that feedback control systems are typically much more expensive than prevention systems. This is also because prevention, if effective, is usually simpler than correction (e.g., fires, diseases, accidents).

Human intervention in feedback control.

"An ounce of prevention is worth a pound of control."

Information lag

Effects of information lag.

A critical aspect of the monitoring-feedback process is the **information lag** that is built (usually unintentionally) into a system. The effect of lag on management control can be similar to the effect of switching electric blanket controls on the occupants of a double bed. As the left occupant gets too warm and turns down the thermostat (right side's), the right occupant gets too cold and turns *up* the (left side's) thermostat. This makes the left occupant warmer still, resulting in a further lowering of the right side thermostat, and so on.

Industrial dynamics.

To investigate the result of information lag in systems, Jay Forrester of MIT used a computer simulation technique called "industrial dynamics" [4]. He investigated the effect of a permanent 10 percent increase in retail sales on the response of a retailer-distributor-manufacturer, distribution-production system. The inventory-reordering lags between levels of the system were about 15 days each and response lags were about 5 days each. The total information lag in the distribution system from the retailer's view was thus almost two months.

The result of the 10 percent January sales increase is shown in Figure 15.2 by the curves ① through ⑤ with curve ① representing the 10 percent sales increase. The retailer's response in terms of ordering is shown by curve ② and reaches an anticipation-of-further-sales-increases peak of 18 percent in March. The distributor, seeing an increase in orders from his or her retail customers, also overanticipates (curve ③) and reaches a 34 percent peak in early April. The manufacturer also overresponds (curve ④) and peaks at 51 percent in late April. By the time the factory can respond to the continuing increase, each level has started to realize their mistake and cut back their orders, resulting in a factory production peak (curve ⑤), in June of only 45 percent, less than the 51 percent originally ordered in April.

As the retailer cuts back from his or her 18 percent peak toward the actual 10 percent increase (curve ②, June) the distributor, and manufacturer as well, cut back

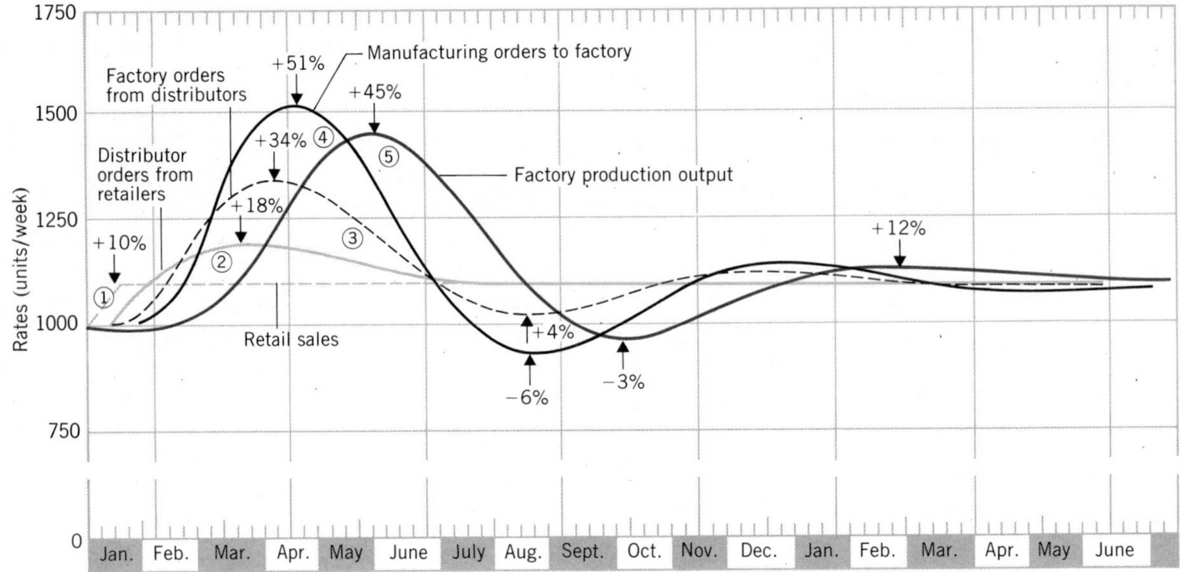

Figure 15.2. The effect of lags in the feedback control system. *Source:* Reprinted from *Industrial Dynamics* by Jay Forrester by permission of The MIT Press, Cambridge, Massachusetts. Copyright © 1961 by the Massachusetts Institute of Technology.

also, again amplifying the lower level effect. The result is a 6 percent drop below the new 10 percent level (curve ③, August) for the distributor (4 percent above original level), a 16 percent drop below the new 10 percent level (curve ④, August) for the manufacturer (6 percent below original level), and a final 13 percent actual drop in production in October (curve ⑤, 3 percent below original).

Stable versus unstable (explosive) systems.

By now, however, the distributor realizes she or he has cut back *too* far and starts to increase again, repeating the entire cycling process but at a much *lower* level. The oscillating cycles finally stabilize at the 10 percent level in the following June, a year and a half after the initial effect. In this particular case, the following oscillations were at lower levels than the original peaks and valleys thus leading to what is termed **damped** oscillations or a **stable** system. In some cases however, as with the electric blanket example, the oscillations tend to get *higher* each time and the unstable system becomes **explosive**

Positive versus negative feedback.

Explosive systems usually result from **positive feedback** systems where the feedback action or adjustment, increases, rather than decreases the external effect (as with the electric blanket). But information lag in a **negative feedback** system can also, on occasion, result in an explosive system if the lag, and resulting adjustments, are sufficient. By reducing either the strength of the adjustment, or the length of the lag (e.g., by improving the information system) an explosive negative feedback system can usually be dampened.

15.2 CONTROL CHARTS FOR FEEDBACK CONTROL

In or out of control?

Library control.

One of the feedback control system elements that is the most difficult to design is the feedback block of Figure 15.1 where the manager must decide whether or not an activity is "out of control" and needs adjustment. Consider the task of managing the operations of a large city library. To manage such an organization will require monitoring and controlling the flow and inventories of library materials (books, periodicals, records, cassettes, etc.), the condition of facilities and equipment (building, chairs, shelves, tables, phonographs, utilities, duplicating machines, perhaps even a computer system for book-borrower records), the hours and performance of employees (payroll, personnel records, interview forms), user information (book requests, reference calls, monthly borrowings, returns), and so on.

What information should be monitored?

The majority of this information need not be closely controlled since it either varies slowly (condition of the building), has little to do with direct performance (personnel records), or will be brought to the attention of the staff if it becomes serious (condition of phonographs). Of more importance, however, are ongoing measures of activity that will affect budgets, personnel, scheduling, and user service. Examples of such measures are daily book checkouts, percentage of overdue books, and the number of daily requests for reference information.

Control charts to identify systems out of control.

To monitor the performance of measures similar to these at Bell Telephone Laboratories in the 1920s, Walter A. Shewhart developed the concept of statistical **control charts** to aid in distinguishing between **chance variation** in a system and variation caused by the system being "out of control," called **assignable variation**. Should a process go out of control it must first be detected, then the assignable cause located, and, finally, the appropriate control action or adjustment made. The control chart is used to detect when a process has gone out of control.

Normal distribution of variations.

A repetitive process or operation will seldom produce *exactly* the same quality, size, or other measure to be controlled; rather, with each repetition the process will generate variation around some average. Because this variation is usually due to a large number of small, uncontrollable sources, the pattern of variability is often well described by the **normal distribution**, shown plotted against the vertical scale in Figure 15.3.

Checking the mean for control.

The succession of measures that result from the continued repetition of the process can thus be thought of as a **population** of numbers that is normally distributed with some mean and standard deviation. As long as the distribution remains the same, the process is considered to be "in control" and simply exhibiting chance variation. One way to help determine if the distribution is staying the same is to keep checking the mean of the distribution—if it changes to some other value then the process may be considered to be "out of control."

Sampling to reduce cost.

The sample must be representative.

The problem, however, is that it is too expensive for oganizations to keep constantly checking operations. Therefore, *samples* of the operation's output are checked instead. When sampling output for inspection, it is imperative that the *sample* fully *represent* the population being checked; therefore, a *random sample* should be used. A **random sample** is one taken in such a way that every item in the population has an

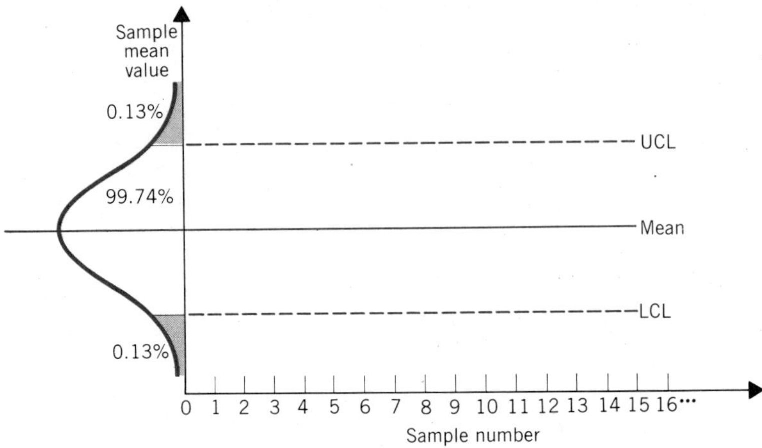

Figure 15.3. Control chart with the limits set at three standard deviations.

equal chance of being included in the sample. An important caution here regards a common sampling technique known as **systematic sampling**; for example, every tenth name in a phone book is drawn at random. Although this sampling method may result in a random sample of phone listings, it may not result in a random sample of *households*, because unlisted numbers are not included in the sample, nor are households that do not have telephones.

Biased samples.

For example, if such an approach is used to inspect items coming off an assembly line, it may result in a *very* biased sample. It may be that in some particular plant, final assembly is conducted by five workers who sequentially place their finished work on the conveyor belt. Therefore, every fifth, tenth, fifteenth, and so on, item has been assembled by the *same worker*, and if every tenth item is inspected, then only one person's work is being checked.

Risk introduced.

But when checks are only made of sample averages, rather than 100 percent of the output, there is always a chance of having selected a particular sample with an unusually high, or low, mean. The problem facing the operations manager is thus to decide what is *too high*, or *too low*, and should be considered as a process out of control. Also, the manager must consider the fact that the more samples eventually taken, the more likely that a sample will accidentally be selected that has too high (or low) a mean *when the process is actually still in control.*

Setting the values of the UCL and LCL.

The values of the mean selected by the manager as too high or low are called the upper **control limit** **UCL**) and the lower control limit (**LCL**), respectively. These limits generally allow a **management by exception** approach to control since theoretically, no action need be taken by the manager unless a **sample mean** exceeds the control limits. The control limits most commonly used in organizations are plus and minus three **standard deviations** (or occasion, two or even one standard deviation). We know from statistics (see Appendix A) that the chance of a simple mean exceeding three standard deviations, in either direction, due simply to chance variation, is only 0.3 percent (i.e., three times per 1000 samples). The equivalent values for two and one standard deviation are 4.55 percent and 31.73 percent, respectively. Figure 15.3 illustrates the use of control limits set at three standard deviations. Of course, using the higher limit values (three or more) increases the risk of not detecting a process that is only slightly out of control.

There are other rules, besides simply finding a data point outside the control limits, which should warn a manager of a potential "out of control" condition. These are listed in Figure 15.4, generally known as the **2-5-7 rules.** Note in the first two figures that even *improvement* in a chart should be investigated, not just loss of control. Perhaps a new method or tool has been discovered by a worker that could be applied to other, similar processes. (Or maybe the worker is throwing away defective items.) In the third figure it appears that there has been a definite, and permanent, change in the process which should clearly be investigated.

General utility of control charts.

It should be noted that the control chart approach, although originally developed for quality control in manufacturing, is applicable to all sorts of repetitive processes in any kind of organization. Thus, it can be used for services as well as products, people or machines, cost or quality, and so on, as illustrated in the *Tools and Applications* portion of this chapter.

15.3 ORDER CONTROL FOR INTERMITTENT OPERATIONS

As discussed in Chapter 7, there are basically four primary ways of organizing operations: intermittent, continuous, batch, and project. Specific means of controlling each of these forms, as well as operations characterized by special problems (such as "bottlenecking"), have been developed and will be discussed in the following sections.

Order control derives its name from the fact that in intermittent operations most output is "made to order." For example, in a sheet metal fabricating company each manufactured part is produced because a customer order exists for that part. Even in organizations that produce items in anticipation of demand (i.e., before an order actually is received), the product is usually produced as a result of a "shop order" for a certain amount of the item. In either instance, order control is called for.

Organization of orders.

Organizations based upon order control use copies of the orders to run the organization. The accounting is based on orders, scheduling of staff and equipment is derived from the orders sitting in the "load files," financing needs are based on the orders (especially large ones), purchasing issues purchase orders based on the customer orders, and so forth. In other words, to find out almost anything in the organization requires knowledge of the appropriate order.

Preventive and feedback controls.

Order control is made up of a rather large number of specific preventive and feedback controls which attempt to assure that the operations are coordinated to produce the desired quantity of the product, delivered to the appropriate location by

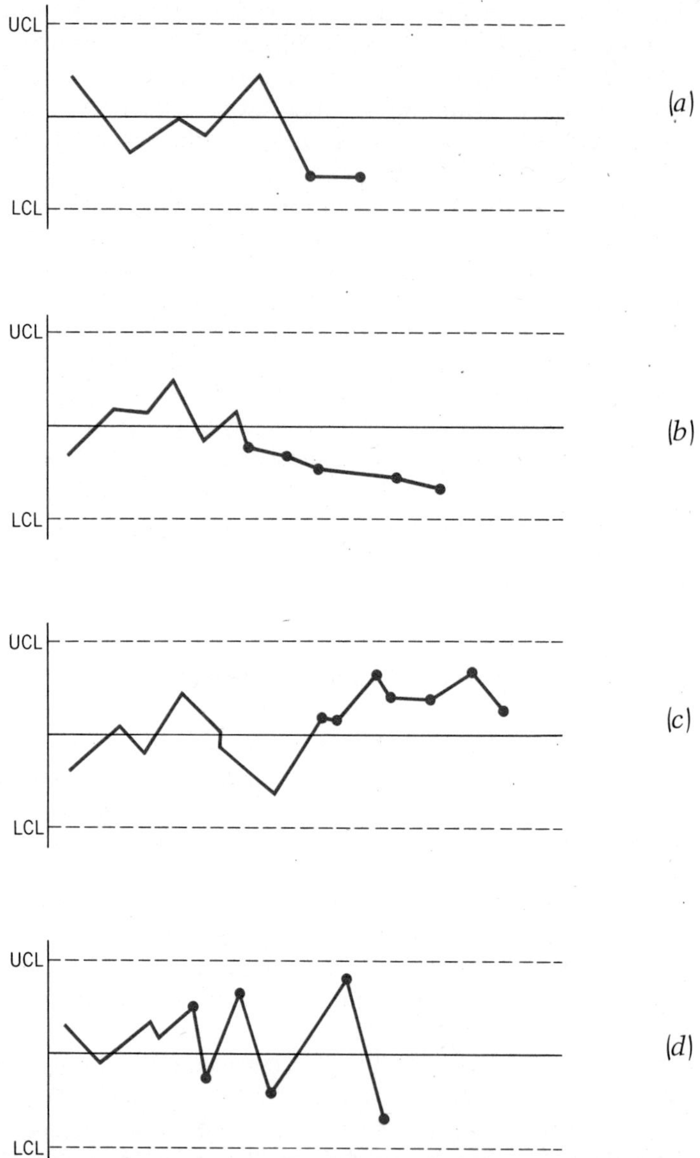

Figure 15.4. Special conditions warranting investigation. (*a*) Two consecutive points near a control limit. (*b*) Five consecutively decreasing (or increasing) points. (*c*) Seven consecutive points on one side of central line. (*d*) Worsening erratic behavior.

the desired due date at the agreed-upon price. An example of a preventive control in an order control situation is a scheduling policy which calls for establishing order dates for raw materials by backscheduling from the due date some amount of time based upon delivery time for the raw material and production time for the item. A feedback control in an order control environment is provided by monitoring and reporting systems that "track" the order's progress through the system, comparing actual progress with planned progress, such as when using critical ratio or slack time rules.

Order control is applicable to service delivery as well as manufacturing. For example, control of a patient's stay in the hospital (the patient being the "order") requires the same general type of control as the production of a manufacturing order. Likewise, controlling the operations of any computer center, restaurant, or university registration system requires some form of order control.

Order control systems are simple conceptually, but difficult to implement. Each order is unique and therefore requires special action to assure its progress through the organization. For example, an order for 100 mattresses in a mattress factory will require different buying (purchasing) decisions, different production methods, different quality assurance plans, different cost control, and so on, than an order for 100,000 of the same mattresses.

11.4 FLOW CONTROL FOR CONTINUOUS OPERATIONS

Major concerns in flow control.

Flow control, on the other hand, is used in continuous and semicontinuous operations. In semicontinuous operations the volume of production seldom changes drastically, and output is of a similar type day after day. The major control method in flow control is feedback. Actual output costs, quality, and so forth, are constantly compared with planned levels of performance and deviations reported so that corrective actions can be implemented. Much of the control in continuous operations centers around scheduling of operations so the delays in the process are avoided.

The basic principal behind flow control is that jobs started into a system will progress most efficiently if work in process is kept low. To do this, the organization must know its capacity limitations and release jobs to the operations area on a due date priority basis. From a practical side, clear reporting of finished jobs and jobs waiting to be started, along with reports on delayed or late jobs, are necessary to keep the system moving.

Flow control by feedback and scheduling.

Many specific types of feedback controls have been devised for continuous operations, depending on the activity concerned. Inventory control is one of the major activities of this nature and was discussed at length in Chapters 12 and 13. Similarly, quality control is another such activity and will be considered in Chapter 16. The control of materials, equipment, and staff through careful scheduling to maximize their utilization was discussed in Chapter 9.

15.5 BLOCK CONTROL FOR BATCH OPERATIONS

Output in batches.

Although batch operations frequently use both flow and order control, on occasion *block control* is more appropriate. **Block control** is a modification of flow control used in operations which produce the same output and require the same steps or processes, but which process the output in batches or "blocks." That is, for operations in which variations in the output do not cause significant variations in the transformation process, block control is used. An example of a setting in which block control is appropriate is in shoe and garment manufacturing. The processes required to produce a pair of slacks are essentially the same, no matter what the colors, sizes, or styles. Yet, any one of these variables might be used to "batch" or "block" an order and thus require that all production on the block be completed in a given department before equipment can be reset for the next block.

The sizes of departments usually are manipulated so the production throughput can be continuous. That is, each department is given equal capacity so that a block requiring 3 hours in department A will require 3 hours in each of the other departments. This approach keeps production moving smoothly through the shop without major bottlenecks between departments.

15.6 LOAD CONTROL FOR BOTTLENECK OPERATIONS

Bottlenecks in all types of organizations.

Load control may be necessary in intermittent, continuous, batch, or even project type operations. It is used in any operation that requires the use of one piece of equipment or one department that essentially limits the throughput of the entire operation. This constraining factor is typically an expensive resource which cannot economically be duplicated, but which is necessary for all production. A good example of such a resource is the computer. The objective of load control is to maximize the throughput of the system by making the most effective use of the constraining resource. Essentially what this means is scheduling all other operations and equipment so that the limited resource never waits because of lack of work or because of a **bottleneck** in some earlier stage of the operation. If an organization changes product or service mixes, the bottleneck resource may also change, thereby necessitating a dynamic load control policy.

Load control is frequently observed with printing presses, physicians, judges, presidents, surgery rooms, sauna baths, and some high capacity construction equipment. Often, the scarce resource may be shared between many organizations so as to maximize the utility of the resource, even frequently at the expense of efficiency.

15.7 PERT/CPM FOR PROJECT OPERATIONS

Difficulty of project control.

In both continuous and intermittent operations, the specific tasks, functions, procedures, and processes are routine and in many cases very repetitive. Control in these situations is less difficult than in the project environment. A project is a large and complex assembly of tasks designed to produce some large scale result. Building of the World Trade Center or the Hoover Dam are two examples of large scale projects. NASA's space program which led to the landing of a man on the moon and D-Day in World War II were large scale and complex projects.

Control to meet deadlines.

Project control is used to assure that the combination of tasks necessary for "project completion" by a given due date are accomplished. (Penalties for late completion are often large.) Resources at the disposal of the project manager—machinery, money, and employees—are allocated to the sequence of tasks (and reallocated throughout the duration of the project) to ensure that the due date is met. Project controls are essentially of the feedback variety, comparing actual accomplishments with planned deadlines. **PERT**, which has been discussed in Chapter 9 as a planning and scheduling method, will be reintroduced here in a project control context.

Control through the critical path.

The PERT technique provides information both for feedback control and for preventive control. In general, the project objective underlying the PERT technique is finishing the project on time. The control phase of PERT begins with the determination of the *critical path*, the longest path through the network. Along this path lie the *critical* jobs or tasks which must be accomplished on schedule if the project is to be completed on time. There is no slack in the schedule for each job along the critical path, so in order to *prevent* a delay in the project completion, the manager knows that resources must be scheduled first to these jobs and then to others not on the critical path. This PERT information, the jobs or tasks on the critical path and their necessary start and finish dates, is information useful for preventive control before the project ever begins.

Feedback control is employed after the project is started. Comparisons of planned completion of activities from the PERT chart and actual performance allows managers to adjust schedules through resource reallocations so as to keep the project on course when delays have been experienced. Analyzing the cause of the difference and correcting or adapting to it is basic to the feedback control function of PERT. The speeding up of critical activities is known as **crashing** and is derived from the original concepts employed in the critical path method, **CPM.** The technique is described as follows.

Crashing activities.

Cost of crashing.

Activities can be **expedited** (or **crashed**) up to a limit, at some increase in cost. The assumption is usually made that the activity duration-cost relationship is linear between the "normal" schedule and the "crash" schedule. For example, a normal 3 week activity may cost \$2000 and a crash 2 week schedule may cost \$3000. Then a 2.8 week duration is assumed to cost \$2200. Each activity usually has its own minimum duration and expediting cost, some activities being more efficient than others.

As the more efficient *critical* activities are expedited (there is no point in crashing noncritical activities—they will not speed up the delayed project), more and more activities and paths become critical and must be simultaneously expedited to further reduce the project duration. Thus, the cost for expediting the project increases faster and faster until the point is reached where the project can be expedited no further: all activities on one (or more) critical path are at their crash point. An application of this concept is included in the *Tools and Applications* portion of this chapter.

TOOLS AND APPLICATIONS

15.8 CONTROL CHART EXAMPLE: ROLLINS DATA PROCESSING

Rollins data Processing, a large computer service bureau, employs 450 keypunch operators. The average daily output over the past six months, based on daily samples of size 20, has averaged $\bar{\bar{X}} = 115{,}200$ keystrokes per data entry operator (Table 15.1). Rollins' data entry manager has been concerned with controlling production output since Rollins is now operating at full staffing levels and any further expansion will necessitate finding new office facilities.

To detect any changes in output per employee the data entry manager has decided to maintain a keystroke output control chart. At the end of each day, the average number of keystrokes for the random sample of 20 operators will be computed from the formula

$$\bar{X} = \frac{\sum X_i}{n} \tag{15.1}$$

TABLE 15.1 SIX RANDOM WEEKS OF SAMPLED KEYSTROKE OUTPUT

Day	Week	$\bar{X}_j$(1000)	$(\bar{X}_j - \bar{\bar{X}})$	$(\bar{X}_j - \bar{\bar{X}})^2$(1000)	Week	X_j(1000)	$(\bar{X}_j - \bar{\bar{X}})$	$(\bar{X}_j - \bar{\bar{X}})^2$(1000)
M	1	116.0	800	640	17	114.9	− 300	90
T	1	115.5	300	90	17	115.0	− 200	40
W	1	115.8	600	360	17	114.8	− 400	160
H*	1	115.3	100	10	17	114.4	−800	640
F	1	114.8	− 400	160	17	115.2	0	
M	7	116.2	1000	1000	23	115.1	− 100	10
T	7	115.2	0		23	114.6	− 600	360
W	7	114.2	− 1000	1000	23	115.6	400	160
H	7	115.4	200	40	23	115.1	− 100	10
F	7	115.2	0		23	115.8	600	360
M	13	115.3	100	10	24	115.2	0	
T	13	115.4	200	40	24	115.0	− 200	40
W	13	114.6	− 600	360	24	114.7	− 500	250
H	13	115.2	0		24	115.2	0	
F	13	115.6	400	160	24	115.7	500	250
Total		1729.7		3870		1726.3		2370

Average, $\bar{\bar{X}} = \sum \bar{X}_j/m = (1{,}729{,}700 + 1{,}726{,}300)/30 = 115{,}200$

Sample standard deviation, $S_X = \sqrt{\sum(\bar{X}_j - \bar{\bar{X}})^2/(m-1)} = \sqrt{(3{,}870{,}000 + 2{,}370{,}000)/29} = 464$

* H means Thursday

where

$\overline{X}$ = the sample mean for that day
X_i = the daily output of each operator i
n = the 20 operators

and plotted on the chart. The control chart will be constructed as follows:

First, the average number of keystrokes per day (115,200) is plotted as a horizontal center line on the control chart as in Figure 15.3. Then, upper and lower control limits will be plotted for three standard deviations. The standard deviation of the distribution of sample means is given by

$$S_{\overline{X}} = \sqrt{\frac{\sum(\overline{X}_j - \overline{\overline{X}})^2}{m - 1}} \tag{15.2}$$

where

$S_{\overline{X}}$ = the sample standard deviation among all the daily sample means
$\overline{X}_j$ = the sample mean for day j
$\overline{\overline{X}}$ = the average of all samples
m = the number of days in the sample

and is calculated in Table 15.1 as $S_{\overline{X}} = 464$ keystrokes.

Therefore, control limits set at plus or minus one standard deviation would be

$$\overline{\overline{X}} \pm S_{\overline{X}} = 115{,}200 \pm 464 = 115{,}664 \text{ and } 114{,}736$$

and at three standard deviations would be

$$\overline{\overline{X}} \pm 3S_{\overline{X}} = 115{,}200 \pm 3(464) = 116{,}592 \text{ and } 113{,}808.$$

These two sets of limits are shown in Figure 15.5, along with the last two weeks of data. As can be seen, none of the data exceeds the $\pm 3S_X$ limits (none were expected to) and 4 points exceeded the $\pm 1S_{\overline{X}}$ limits ($0.3173 \times 10 = 3.173$ were expected to). Thus, the process currently appears to be in control.

Rollins can now use this control chart to determine when output volume appears to actually be out of control. This can be done in a "management by exception"

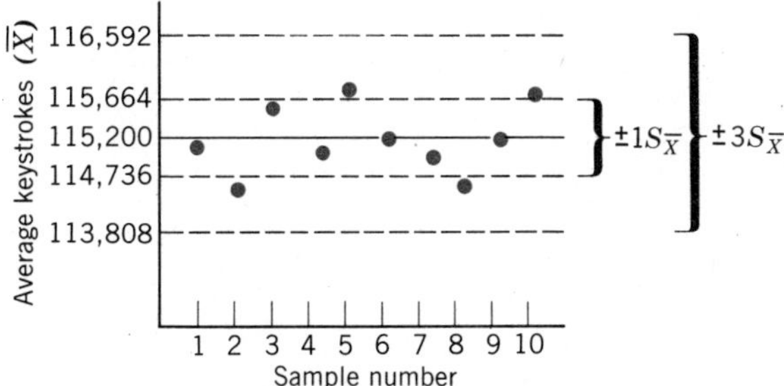

Figure 15.5. Rollins' keystroke control chart for the last two weeks.

context by only reporting to the data entry manager those times that the sample mean is outside the control limits. Thus, only when there is an apparent problem, with an assignable cause, will the data entry manager have to be concerned with keystroke volume.

15.9 SETTING OPTIMAL CONTROL LIMITS

Optimal control limits.

As mentioned, control limits are usually set at $\pm 2S_X$ or $\pm 3S_X$, with $\pm 3S_X$ being used very frequently in quality control settings. These control limits are essentially rule-of-thumb measures. Ideally, control limits should be set in accordance with the costs and benefits to be derived from alternative settings. Let us consider a formal analysis of the problem of determining optimal control limits.

Cost of control.

Suppose that Rollins' data entry manager has developed the following information regarding control conditions and investigations.

1. Cost of investigation, whether the process is in or out of control is \$100. (It is assumed that investigation will always determine the cause if the process is out of control.)
2. Cost of correcting the system, if it is out of control is \$300.
3. Cost of not correcting (in "present value" terms) if the system is out of control is \$1500.

This problem can be formulated as a problem of decision making under uncertainty. First, define the two possible states of the system as follows.

θ_1 = system is "in control"
θ_2 = system is "out of control"

and define the two possible actions that can be taken after each sample is observed as

a_1 = investigate
a_2 = do not investigate

Based upon the information listed above, a "payoff" *matrix* (Table 15.2) can be developed. Note that when the system is out of control and a decision is made to investigate, the total cost is \$400 (\$100 for investigation and \$300 for correction).

TABLE 15.2 PAYOFF MATRIX OF COSTS

Actions \ States	θ_1 in control	θ_2 out of control
a_1 investigate	\$100	\$100 + \$300
a_2 do not investigate	0	\$1500

If we let

$P(\theta_1)$ = the probability that the system is in control

and

$P(\theta_2)$ = the *critical probability* that the system is out of control

then

$$P(\theta_1) = 1 - P(\theta_2)$$

Also, let $E(a_1)$ equal the expected value of investigation after observing a sample $\overline{X}$. Now, we can determine the critical probability for this situation and use this probability in establishing our control limits.

Essentially, what we are asking is "at what value of the *critical probability*, $P(\theta_2)$ will the manager be indifferent between his two available actions, investigate and do not investigate?" We can find this probability by setting the expected values of these two actions equal to one another.

The expected value of the action *investigate* is

$$E(a_1) = 100 \times P(\theta_1) + 400 \times P(\theta_2)$$

or, in terms of $P(\theta_2)$

$$E(a_1) = 100 \times [1 - P(\theta_2)] + 400 \times P(\theta_2)$$

The expected value of the action, *do not investigate* is

$$E(a_2) = 1500 \times P(\theta_2)$$

Now, setting these two expected values equal to one another we can solve for $P(\theta_2)$, the critical probability, as follows

$$100 \times [1 - P(\theta_2)] + 400P(\theta_2) = 1500P(\theta_2)$$

or

$$P(\theta_2) = .083$$

That is, control limits should be set so that an investigation is made if the probability of being out of control is 8.3 percent or greater, which conversely means that the probability of being in control is 91.7 percent or less. If the control limits are set at a probability exceeding 8.3 percent the manager will be investigating, at a cost of $100 each time, more often than is worthwhile. Similarly, if the limits are set at a probability less than 8.3 percent the manager will be risking a $1500 out-of-control situation too often.

If we consider Figure 15.3, which we used to show the relationship between $\pm 3S_{\overline{X}}$ limits and a normal distribution, what we want are control limits that cut off 8.3 percent of the area under the normal curve in the two tails combined. Conversely, 91.7 percent of the area will be between the control limits.

Referring to the table of the normal distribution in Appendix A we can find the value of Z beyond which 4.15 percent of the area under the curve lies (one-half of 8.3

percent). That is, 1 − .0415 = .9585 gives the appropriate Z value, 1.73. For the costs involved in Rollins' investigation decision, control limits of $\pm 1.73 S_{\bar{X}}$ should be used. These limits are

$$\begin{aligned} \text{UCL} &= 115{,}200 + 1.73(464) \\ &= 116{,}003 \\ \text{LCL} &= 115{,}200 - 1.73(464) \\ &= 114{,}397 \end{aligned}$$

15.10 PROJECT CONTROL: THE BONFIRE BOYS

Local fathers and their sons in Brood 22 of the Bonfire Boys are planning a special Biannual Bonfire Blast beginning in three days. However, there are a number of expensive and time-consuming project activities remaining before the Blast can get underway, as shown in Table 15.3. Every day the Blast is delayed will be discouraging to the boys. But every extra \$10 spent unnecessarily will be discouraging to the fathers. What is the minimum cost of expediting the remaining activities for various project durations?

The network and critical path are shown in Figure 15.6; note the **dummy activity**. In the figure, activity c is shown for its actual two-day duration to the arrowhead and then the line thinly continued to node 5 to show project completion.

Inspecting the critical activities a, d, and e in Table 15.3 for the most efficient activity to crash in order to gain one day in completion time, activity e is best. The six-day schedule from expediting activity e by one day is shown in Figure 15.7. Note that there are now *two* critical paths—a-d-e and a-b-dummy.

To expedite completion by another day will require expediting *both* critical paths. This can be done in this case by expediting activities *common* to both paths (such as activity a, for \$20) or separate activities on the two paths (b and d, for \$10 + \$30 = \$40, or b and e, for \$10 + \$10 = \$20). Either way, a reduction of one day (five days total) will cost at least \$20 and then \$20 again for another day (four days total). The final result of both \$20 reductions is shown in Figure 15.8.

TABLE 15.3 NETWORK TIME-COST TRADEOFFS

		Normal		Crash		
Activity	Precedence	Duration (Days)	Cost (\$)	Duration (Days)	Cost (\$)	Cost/Time "Slope" (\$/Days)
a	—	2	20	1	40	\$20
b	a	4	30	1	60	10
c	a	2	10	2	10	—
d	a	2	10	1	40	30
e	d	3	10	1	30	10
			Total = \$80		Total = \$180	

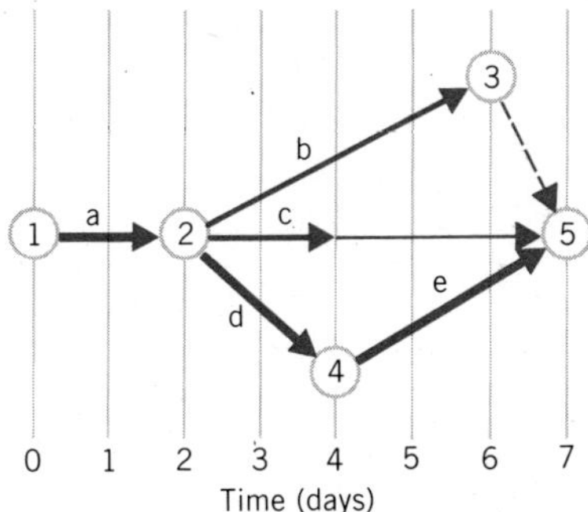

Figure 15.6. All normal, seven-day schedule.

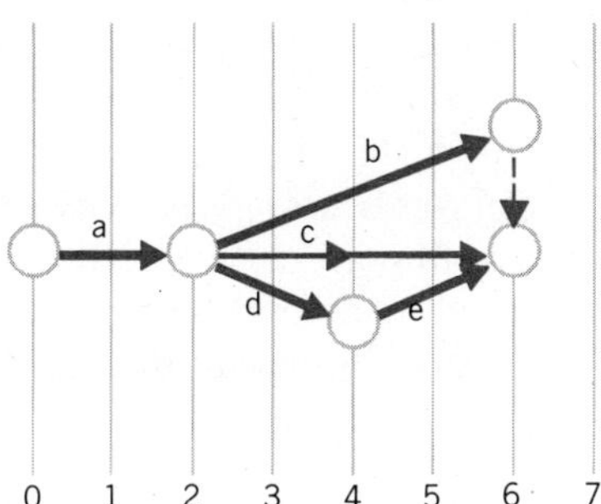

Figure 15.7. Two-critical path, six-day schedule.

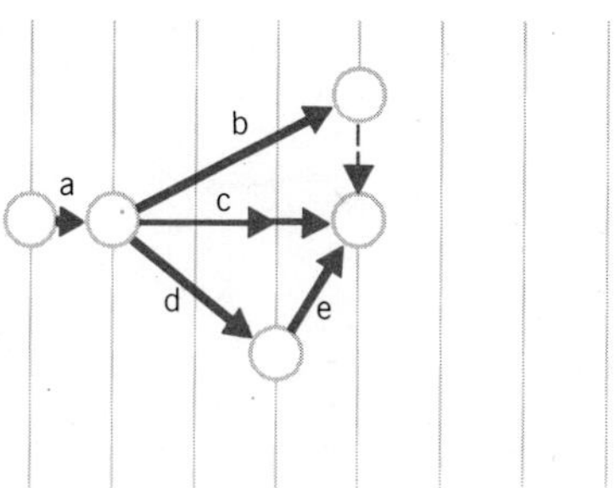

Figure 15.8. Second and third reduction, four-day schedule.

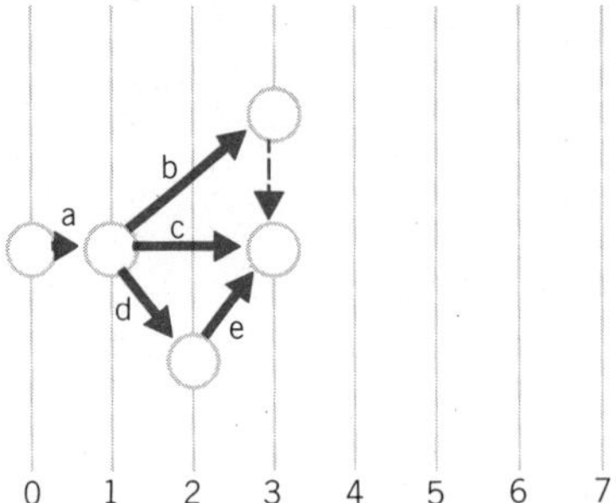

Figure 15.9. Final reduction, three-day schedule.

One more day's reduction can only come about by expediting activities b and d; activities a and e are already fully crashed. The cost of this reduction, to three days project duration, is \$10 + \$30 = \$40. The result, shown in Figure 15.9, is the maximum reduction possible because all activities along critical path a-d-e have been crashed. In addition, path a-c is now also critical and cannot be further reduced. Figure 15.10 shows the cost increases as a function of the shortened project duration.

It should be noted that for use as a feedback control technique the crashing of activity a would probably not be applicable since it is the *first* activity that might be delayed. That is, by the time control was necessary, activity a would probably already be completed. Of more use for control purposes would be the reduction possible in activities b and e and the initial slack in activities b and c. Thus, for example, one day's delay in activity d could be negated by expediting activity e.

15.11 SUMMARY

In this chapter we introduced the concept of control of activities to ensure that results occur as planned. Two major types of control used by organizations are preventive

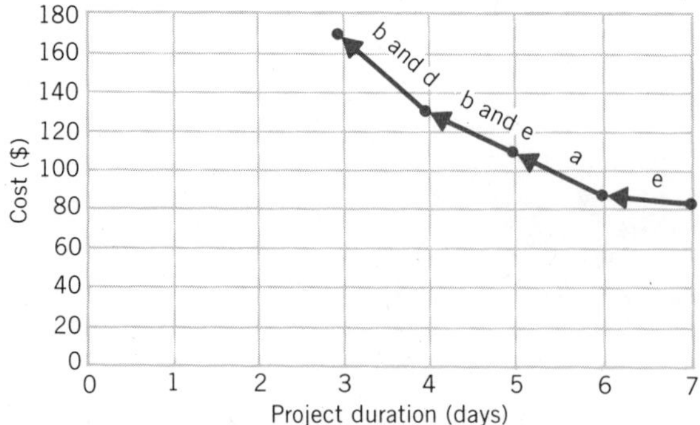

Figure 15.10. Project cost duration.

control and feedback control. The role of information lag in feedback control systems is particularly critical in assuring a stable control system.

To aid the manager in deciding when an activity is out of control and needs adjustment, the concept of the statistical control chart has been found to be useful. An element of risk is inherent in all such control decisions since, on the basis of chance variation in the data, the manager may decide to attempt to correct an activity that is actually "in control" or, similarly, may not realize an activity is "out of control" until serious damage has been done.

Particular types of control systems have been developed for operations organized along specialized forms. For intermittent operations the actual orders themselves serve as the point of control. In continuous operations, flow control is practiced through feedback systems and care in scheduling. Block control is used when the output is processed in batches and load control is applied when maximizing the utilization of scarce, single item resources that otherwise would tend to be a bottleneck in processing.

For the area of project control the PERT/CPM network representation provides an excellent control vehicle. By transferring resources from noncritical activities, and crashing those that are critical, due dates are maintained and late completion penalties are avoided.

15.12 READINGS

TEACHING TACTICS

Some School Systems Use Business Methods To Make Pupils Learn

---

They Set Proficiency Goals, Put Onus on Instructors; Indian Hill's Rigid Plan

---

'Quality Control' on the Line

BY WILLIAM M. BULKELEY
Staff Reporter of THE WALL STREET JOURNAL

Indian Hill, Ohio—If the students in Shirley Seifirth's fourth-grade class at Shawnee elementary school here don't learn to add fractions with common denominators by the time the school year ends next Tuesday, they'll have to repeat the subject in September. And Mrs. Seifirth, not the students, might be called to the principal's office.

The school system in this affluent suburb of Cincinnati has pledged to parents that it will teach students certain skills at certain times. Teachers have to quiz their students after each new area has been covered—such as adding those fractions—using standardized tests. The results are then turned over to the school administration.

EDUCATION AS A BUSINESS

Indian Hill's approach to education has made it a leader in a national movement to run school systems somewhat like a business: by setting learning goals, meeting quotas of students who have mastered skills and making schools accountable for the children who pass through their classes.

Despite strong opposition from teacher organizations, teachers in school systems across the country are being evaluated partly on the basis of what their students learn. In Indian Hill, evaluations have led to several teachers being advised to leave.

This tough approach to education is the result of the national alarm over declining aptitude-test scores and over high-school graduates who can't read newspapers or fill out job applications. "Educators couldn't care less about teaching. They get paid no matter what," says E. Dennis Barnes, a realtor in Upper Sandusky, Ohio, who is the leader of a group seeking to force the state to hand over control of education to school districts.

WILL IT RUN LIKE A CAR?

Thus, say advocates of making schools accountable, it simply makes sense to examine schools on the basis of what their product should be: educated students. Leon Lessinger, dean of the College of Education at the University of South Carolina, who helped formulate this idea about 10 years ago, says that accountability means "establishing quality control; we're seeing how many units at the end of the line look like a car but won't run like a car."

Five years ago, a committee of residents decided that the school system was inefficient. There wasn't, for example, a precise, sequential curriculum: Teachers taught whatever they felt appropriate, and there was no systematic evaluation of their performance.

The school board reacted by forcing out the superintendent and hiring a corporate recruiter to find a superintendent with a more businesslike approach to education. School board president Philip Casper points out that Procter & Gamble is based nearby in Cincinnati, and indeed several of its executives live in Indian Hill. The company "tests everything it puts out, and the same attitude permeates parents in this district," he says.

The school board found the man they wanted in Robert Boston, an expert in relating expenditures to academic achievement and a former researcher for the U.S. Office of Education. Mr. Boston is the sort of executive who uses phrases like "management by objective" and who takes a tough stance on how schools should work. "We know if we're failing," he says. "We can change the program, change the books or change the teachers."

DEFINING GOALS

Mr. Boston's first task was to define general goals that could be turned into curricula. To do this he set up a committee of 50 parents, school administrators, teachers and students. For nearly a year the committee talked to parents and even polled them on what they thought their children should be learning. Teachers then turned these goals into a sequential school program for students at the elementary level.

Reading, writing and arithmetic were the first subjects to be planned in this fashion, with each subject broken down into specific objectives. For example, a second-grade teacher knows that her students must learn to recognize the main idea in a simple, four-sentence story. Fourth-grade students must be able to "interpret the basic emotions of the characters in a story." At each point along the way, teachers give students quick, four-question, multiple-choice tests.

The elementary schools soon will be teaching natural science and social studies in this fashion. Goal-setting for physical education (learning to trap a kicked ball in the second grade, for instance) already has been introduced, and programs for art and music are planned. The school system plans to use the program in the high schools so that eventually there will be goal-setting curricula from kindergarten through 12th grade.

The goal system clearly puts a good deal of pressure on the teachers. Teachers whose pupils consistently fail the skills tests are given help by the principal or even by other teachers. But those teachers who can't keep up with the new standards are asked to leave. In just the last three years, 15 Indian Hill teachers have, in Mr. Boston's words, been "counseled out."

Mr. Boston feels that the implicit threat of being fired keeps teachers on their toes. Although Indian Hill teachers are not supposed to be evaluated on the basis of test results, some teachers worry that in time the tests will become the yardstick for measuring performance. "It would be dangerous if the tests were used as a threat to the staff," says one high-school teacher. And Debra Hunter, president of the Indian Hill Classroom Teachers Association, says that "with the present changes occurring in the district, teachers are somewhat apprehensive."

But generally, the teachers and parents seem happy with the program. "One thing that's been lacking in education is defining what you're trying to do. In the past it's been kind of hit or miss. This is an effort to alleviate that problem," says David Terrel, a junior-high math teacher.

"Rather than just saying we've covered it, we're saying the kid has mastered it," says Michael Grawe, a second-grade teacher. "I feel I'm teaching more efficiently, with more direction. I have objectives just like any other job."

Source. The Wall Street Journal, May 23, 1978. Reprinted by permission of *The Wall Street Journal*,

15.13 KEY TERMS

CONCEPTS

feedback control (p. 507)
dynamic (p. 507)
static (p. 507)
preventive control (p. 507)
monitoring (p. 510)
adjustment (p. 510)
budgets (p. 511)
ratio analysis (p. 511)
information lag (p. 511)
damped (p. 512)
stable (p. 512)
explosive (p. 512)
random sample (p. 513)
positive feedback (p. 512)
negative feedback (p. 512)
control chart (p. 513)
chance variation (p. 513)
assignable variation (p. 513)
normal distribution (p. 513)
population (p. 513)
UCL, LCL (p. 514)
systematic sample (p. 514)
control limit (p. 514)
standard deviation (p. 514)
crashing (p. 519)
sample mean (p. 514)
order control (p. 515)
flow control (p. 517)
block control (p. 518)
management by exception (p. 514)
load control (p. 518)
project control (p. 519)
bottleneck operations (p. 518)
PERT (p. 519)
CPM (p. 519)
2-5-7 rules (p. 515)
expedited (p. 519)

15.14 REVIEW TEST

Concepts

1. Control is always required of an activity. (p. 506)
   a. True b. False
2. Internal control is typically achieved by feedback whereas external control is usually preventive. (p. 507)
   a. True b. False
3. Preventive control is a static form of control (p. 508)
   a. True b. False
4. The feedback control process includes monitoring. (p. 510)
   a. True b. False

5. Feedback control is usually more expensive than preventive control. (p. 511)
   a. True b. False
6. Budgets can be either preventive controls or feedback controls. (p. 511)
   a. True b. False
7. Information lag in a negative feedback control system can make it respond like a positive feedback system. (p. 511)
   a. True b. False
8. Unstable systems tend to be damped. (p. 512)
   a. True b. False
9. The purpose of a control chart is to aid the manager in distinguishing between chance and assignable variation in a process. (p. 513)
   a. True b. False
10. Control limits in control charts are usually set at one standard deviation. (p. 514)
   a. True b. False
11. Block control is a type of order control. (p. 518)
   a. True b. False
12. Load control is the control form used in batch operations. (p. 518)
   a. True b. False
13. Activity expediting is a control technique used in project organizations. (p. 519)
   a. True b. False

15.15 DISCUSSION QUESTIONS

1. How would a control chart be constructed to help control stolen books in a library?
2. How does a university control the students? The faculty? The administrators?
3. What type of control system is most vulnerable to sabotage?
4. How can information lags be minimized?
5. What are some positive feedback systems?
6. What is the risk in using a computer for control?
7. What control limits should be used when x-raying for cancer?
8. What other types of control exist in projects besides expediting?
9. Name some external prevention and feedback control systems.
10. How may information lag simulate a positive feedback process?
11. Contrast block and flow control of work in process inventories.
12. Where might load and order control be used simultaneously? Load and flow control?

15.16 PROBLEMS

Concepts

1. A particular air quality hazard occurs on about 12 percent of the batches of paint prepared by the Mixit Chemical Company. The plant manager is considering two controls, one perventive, the other feedback. The preventive control is 90 percent effective, i.e., if the problem is about to occur, it will remedy it 90 percent of the time. The feedback control will remedy the situation 98 percent of the time, after it occurs for 2 minutes. If a batch runs for 60 minutes, which of the two controls provides the least total time exposure to the air quality hazard?

Tools and Applications

2. Top Management of the Security National Bank monitors the volume of activity at their 38 branch banks with control charts. If a branch deposit volume (or any of perhaps a dozen other volume indi-

cators) falls below the LCL, there is apparently some problem with the branch's market share. If, on the other hand, the volume exceeds the UCL, this is an indication that the branch should be considered for expansion or that a new branch might be opened in an adjacent neighborhood.

Based upon the 10 day samples for each of the six months below, prepare an $\overline{X}$ chart for monthly deposit volume (in terms of hundreds of thousands of dollars) for the Transylvania branch. Use $\pm\, 2\sigma$ control limits.

	Average of 10 day deposits ($\overline{X}$) (in hundreds of thousands of dollars)
June	0.93
July	1.05
August	1.21
September	0.91
October	0.89
November	1.13

3. The following PERT chart was prepared at the beginning of a small construction project.

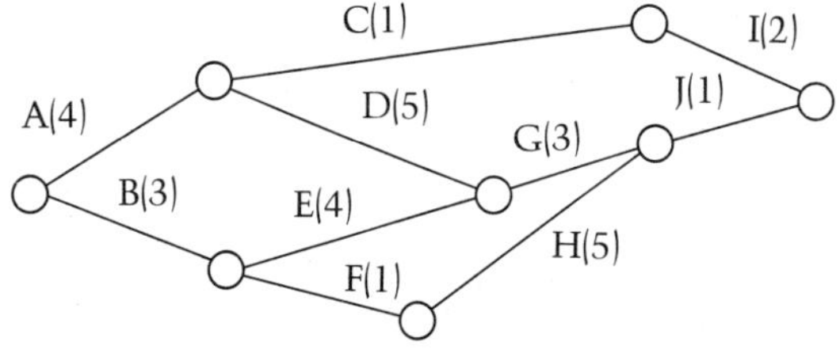

Activity	Duration (Days)
A	4
B	3
C	1
D	5
E	4
F	1
G	3
H	5
I	2
J	1

What is the critical path? Which activities should be monitored most closely?

At the end of the first week of construction, it was noted that activity A was completed in 2.5 days, but activity B required 4.5 days. What impact does this have on the project? Are the same activities critical?

4. The average cost of processing a particular computer run at a local service bureau is \$38 with an upper control limit of \$46 and a lower control limit of \$30. Consider the following four sets of observations. Are they all in control? On what rule would you base your decision?
   a. \$35, \$42, \$45, \$38, \$46.
   b. \$39, \$38, \$41, \$45, \$31.
   c. \$31, \$33, \$41, \$45, \$46.
   d. \$42, \$41, \$40, \$46, \$45.

5. Based upon the following weekly demand data for Heavyaslead beer (It's twice as fattening as our normal beer!), determine the upper and lower control limits that can be used in recognizing a change in demand patterns. Use $\pm\, 2\sigma$ control limits.

Week Number	Demand (6 packs)
1	3500
2	4100
3	3750
4	4300
5	4000
6	3650

6. Given the following control payoff matrix, what minimum probability of being out of control should be used in setting control limits?

Action \ States	In control	Out of control
Investigate	\$10	\$150
Do not investigate	0	\$300

7. Consider Problem 3, again. Suppose the duration of activities A and D can both be reduced to one day, at a cost \$15 per day of reduction. Also, activities E, G, and H can be reduced in duration by one day at a cost of \$25 per day of reduction. What is the least cost approach to crash the project two days? What is the shortest "crashed" duration, the new critical path, and the cost of crashing?

15.17 CASE PAINT TINT, INC.

In November of 1979, Jim Runnels, a salesman for the Paint Tint Corporation, was called to the plant of Townhouse Paint Company, one of his largest accounts. The purchasing agent for Townhouse Paint was complaining that the tubes of paint tint that had just been received were short weight by approximately 5 percent.

The light-weight tubes were not detected by Townhouse's receiving clerks and had not been weighed or otherwise checked by their quality control staff. The problem arose when Townhouse began to use the tubes of tinting agent and found that paint colors were not matching the specifications. The mixing charts used by sales people in Townhouse's retail stores were based upon 5-ounce tubes of tinting agent. Overfilled or underfilled tubes would result in improper paint mixes and therefore colors that did not meet customer's expectations.

In consequence, Townhouse had to issue special instructions to all their retail people which would allow them to compensate for the short-weight tubes. The Townhouse purchasing agent made it clear that a new supplier would be sought if this problem recurred. Paint Tint's quality control department was immediately summoned to assist in determing the cause of the problem. They speculated the problem may be the result of adding a second and thrid shift to the first shift operations. The first shift ran from 6 A.M. until 2 P.M. The second shift from 2 P.M. to 10 P.M. and the third shift from 10 P.M. til 6 A.M. Many of the night shift employees were new and turnover in both of the later shifts was higher than for the first shift. To help in determining the problem the quality control staff sampled 50 tubes each hour and calculated the average weight in ounces of the sample tubes. The results of that sampling are presented below.

Time	Weight (oz)	Time	Weight (oz)
6:00 A.M.	4.92	12:00 midnight	4.72
7:00	4.90	1:00 A.M.	4.64
8:00	4.84	2:00	4.64
9:00	4.76	3:00	4.72
10:00	4.74	4:00	5.00
11:00	4.82	5:00	4.72
12:00 noon	4.80	6:00	4.70
1:00 P.M.	4.84	7:00	4.84
2:00	4.84	8:00	4.88
3:00	4.97	9:00	4.96
4:00	5.01	10:00	5.00
5:00	5.00	11:00	4.98
6:00	5.00	12:00 noon	4.98
7:00	5.02	1:00 P.M.	4.89
8:00	5.03	2:00	5.00
9:00	4.98	3:00	5.04
10:00	5.00	4:00	5.10
11:00	4.86	5:00	5.00

QUESTIONS FOR DISCUSSION

1. Analyze the data and determine the tube weight problem.
2. What control techniques might you employ to resolve this problem?

15.18 REFERENCES AND BIBLIOGRAPHY

1. Anthony, R. H., and J. S. Reese, *Management Accounting*, Homewood, Ill.: Irwin, 1975.
2. Davis, E. W., *Project Management*, Norcross, Ga.: American Institute of Industrial Engineers, PP&C Monograph #3, 1976.
3. Duncan, A. J., *Quality Control and Industrial Statistics*, 4th ed., Homewood, Ill.: Irwin, 1974.
4. Forrester, J., *Industrial Dynamics*, Cambridge, Mass.: MIT Press, 1961.
5. Greene, J. H., *Production and Inventory Control*, rev. ed., Homewood, Ill.: Irwin, 1974.
6. Levin, R. I., and L. A. Kirkpatrick, *Planning and Control with PERT/CPM*, New York: McGraw-Hill, 1966.

7. Miles, R. F., *Systems Concepts*, New York: Wiley, 1973.

8. Mize, J. H. et al., *Operations Planning and Control*, Englewood Cliffs, N.J.: Prentice-Hall, 1971.

9. Plossl, G. W., "Tactics for Manufacturing Control," *Production and Inventory Management*, 15:21–30 (No. 3, 1974).

10. ———, "The Best Investment—Control, Not Machinery," *Production and Inventory Management* 18:1–7 (No. 2, 1977).

11. Plossl, G. W., and O. W. Wight, *Production and Inventory Control*, Englewood Cliffs, N.J.: Prentice-Hall, 1967.

12. Wiest, J. D., and F. K. Levy, *A Management Guide to PERT/CPM*, Englewood Cliffs, N.J.: Prentice-Hall, 1969.

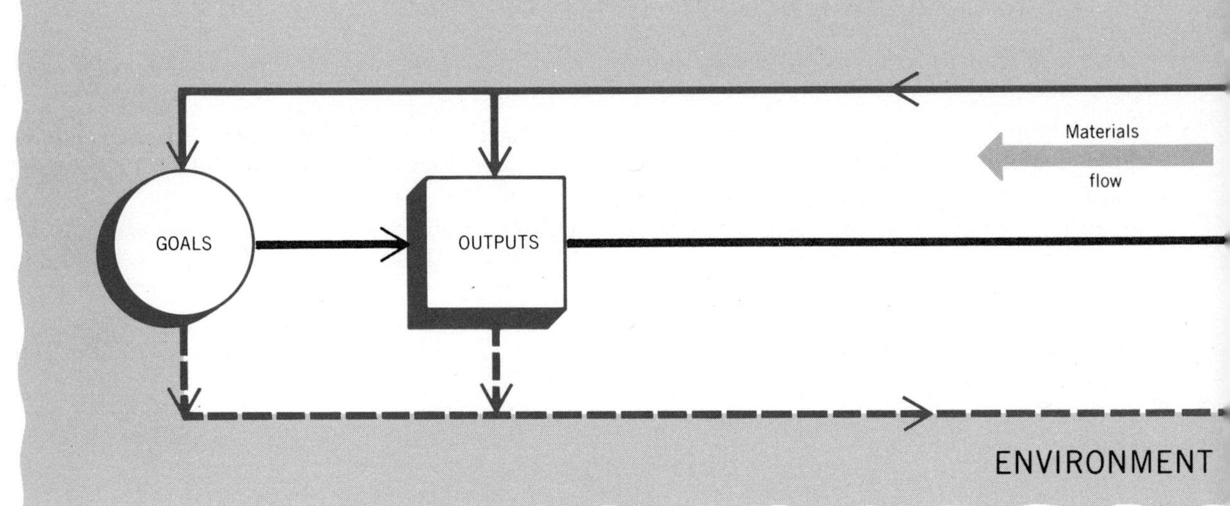

Chapter 16

Quality Control

CONCEPTS

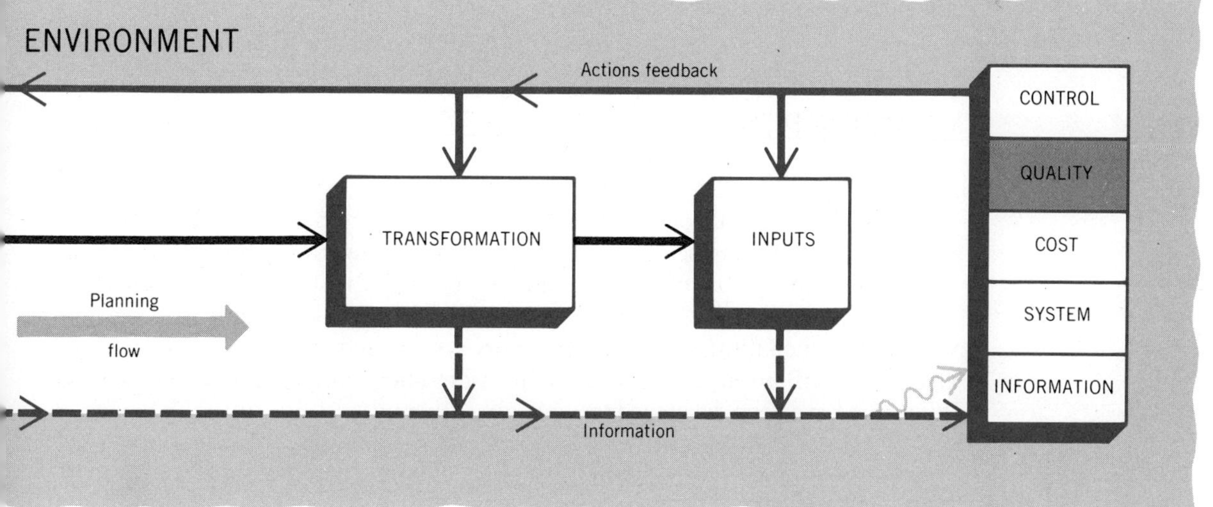

TOOLS AND APPLICATIONS

LEARNING OBJECTIVES

By the completion of the *Concepts* portion of this chapter the student should

1. Be aware of the often intangible nature of quality.
2. Appreciate the role, and difficulty, of inspection in quality control.
3. Realize how processing industries, in particular, can combine low quality outputs to improve their overall quality.
4. Be familiar with the many reasons for sampling output to determine quality rather than 100 percent inspection.
5. Understand the concepts of producer's and consumer's risk, chance and assignable variation, and variables and attributes inspection.
6. Know how to construct and use process control charts for monitoring means and ranges.
7. Know the basis for, and how to construct, a sampling plan for acceptance sampling.
8. Appreciate the value of operating characteristic curves and multiple sampling schemes.

CONCEPTS

The first topic we will consider in the controlling function is the control of the output's *quality*. This characteristic of the output is affected throughout the operations process from the quality of the raw materials, through the skill and capabilities of the workers and equipment, to the performance of the operations supporting systems such as the scheduling system, the inventory system, and the logistics system. In this chapter we will investigate how these functions affect output quality and the procedures that have been developed for controlling them.

16.1 THE NATURE OF QUALITY

In the days of the craftsmen and guilds, the quality of an individual's output was his or her *advertising*, declaration of *skill level*, and source of *personal pride* of workmanship. With the coming of the Industrial Revolution and its infinite degree of specialization and interchangeability of parts (and workers), pride of workmanship became of secondary importance to effective functioning of the individual as simply one cog in an enormous organizational "system." Quite naturally, quality deteriorated and therefore had to be specificially identified and controlled as a functional aspect of the output.

From pride of workmanship to one cog in a system.

This recognition of the need to specifically consider the quality of an output was given impetus by the adoption of statistical sampling procedures by the military in World War II through Military Standard 105. The result was a significant increase in interest in quality control in firms supplying arms and materials to the armed forces, which then spread even further into firms in the general economy.

Recognition of the need to control quality.

Quality, however, is a relative term, meaning different things to different people at different times. Depending upon the situation, an output's "quality" may refer to its *reliability* of performance, its *durability*, its *timeliness*, its *appearance*, its *integrity*, its *purity*, its *individuality*, or more likely, some combination of factors such as these. The problem of maintaining a product's or service's quality then is dependent, in part, upon knowing the end-use of the output and the conditions under which it will be judged.

Relativeness of quality.

It is usually assumed that recipients desire only "top" quality products and services. To an extent this is true, but only if the price and other characteristics can be kept at appropriate levels. If not, people will usually accept a lower quality output, trading quality for improvement in another criterion. Not only may top quality be too expensive for recipient needs—it may also be too far away, too slow, too pretentious, too much trouble, or have other negative aspects associated with it. We therefore do not all buy Cadillacs, live in Beverly Hills, or shop at Nieman-Marcus.

Top quality not always desired.

Furthermore, with our highly advanced technology, we often can not even *tell* what is high quality and what is not. Plastic flowers *look*, and sometimes *feel*, real;

Real versus imitation.

imitation walnut furniture frequently looks *better* than the real thing; and, to some consumers, "nondairy coffee creamers" are "better" than real cream. Even the old adage "You get what you pay for," may not be true these days—many people feel they are still paying, but not getting it any more.

Where is the problem?

No one really seems to be quite sure where the trouble lies. Is the quality of what we pay for indeed lower than it used to be? Or are we getting something different now for our money than we used to get—such as better service? Or perhaps, are we simply more sophisticated buyers now, demanding excellence (as the advertising promotions insist we should) from our organizations and their products and services. For that matter, perhaps the sheer variety of services available are the reason for our disenchantment with quality these days, (see the Reading Section 16.9) especially since it is so difficult to measure the quality of services. Should the quality of a police department be measured by the decrease in arrests? Or the increase? Should a student be graded in a class by what she or he knows, by how much was learned, or how hard the student tried? For that matter, is the quality of an eduction measured by the knowledge gained, the average starting salary of the graduates, or how satisfied the student was with the experience?

How is quality measured?

Traditional methods for controlling quality, especially in service organizations, have been through the establishment of goals, or standards, to guide workers in their activities. These goals are then periodically reemphasized through organizational programs, contests, posters, and the annual budget. Typical of such programs is "Zero Defects," a 1962 aerospace quality control development. This program attempts to eliminate the *cause* of errors rather than remedying them after they have been made. Better training and motivation on the part of both the worker and the manager are primary ingredients of such a program. Committees are formed, the union is involved, training review sessions are sponsored, posters are hung, contests are run, banners are pinned up, achievement dinners are given, and so forth.

Zero defects.

This type of program, however, is much more appropriate to a field such as aerospace, where one loose solder connection can abort a $100 million moon shot, than to many other areas, such as the manufacture of nails. For such other areas it is clearly not cost effective to have workers pay such extreme attention to identifying potential error sources—the price of the resulting output would simply be "out of this world," so to speak.

Appropriate quality level.

Figure 16.1 illustrates the managerial problem of quality control for the above two areas: aerospace and nail manufacturing. Note that the extremely high cost of errors due to low quality in aerospace far outweighs the cost of a quality program whereas just about the opposite holds for nails manufacturing.

Quality impacting factors.

A number of factors impact the overall quality of the organization's output. Generally these factors may be classified as stemming from either (1) the operational facility (physical conditions, building, utilities), (2) tools and equipment, (3) input materials, or, (4) the organization's staff (workers and managers). More specifically, however, quality is frequently determined by the following kinds of factors.

- *The market:* Competition is often the final factor in determining the appropriate, and necessary, level of quality of an organization's output.

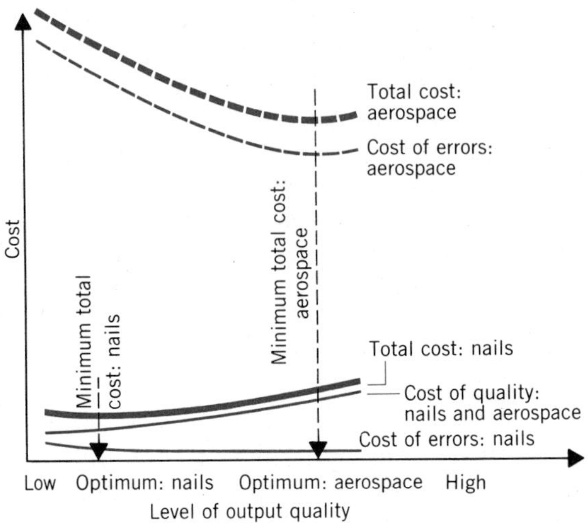

Figure 16.1. Optimal quality levels for two types of products.

- *Organizational objectives:* Is the output to be a high volume, low priced item or an exclusive, expensive one?
- *Product testing:* Insufficient testing of the output may fail to reveal important flaws.
- *Output design:* The manner in which the output is designed may itself doom the product's or service's quality from the start.
- *Production process:* The procedure for producing the output may also adversely affect the quality.
- *Quality of Inputs:* If poor materials, insufficiently trained workers, or inappropriate equipment must be used, quality will suffer.
- *Maintenance:* If equipment is not properly maintained, parts are not available in inventories, or communications kept open within the organization, quality of the resulting output will be less than it should be.
- *Quality standards:* If concern for quality throughout the organization is not apparent, no economically feasible amount of final testing or inspection will result in a high quality output.
- *Customer feedback:* If the organization is insensitive to recipient complaints and requests for repairs or service, quality will not significantly improve.

Reasons for assigning responsibility for quality.

Organizations, in an attempt to deal with the above factors, often address the quality issue by specifically assigning responsibility for quality to someone, or a number of people, within the organization. A number of reasons lie behind the creation of a specific quality control function:

1. To reduce mistakes and corrections.

2. To increase the average quality level of the output.
3. To ensure better interchangeability of parts.
4. To reduce customer complaints and returns.
5. To enable the *grading* of output (A, AA, AAA; prime, choice, good; etc.).
6. To abide by new laws or regulations.
7. To decrease the amount of defective incoming materials.

SHOE

(Chicago Tribune-New York News Syndicate, 1978. Reprinted by permission of the Chicago Tribune-New York News Syndicate, Inc.)

One of the primary methods by which organizations attempt to ensure the quality of their inputs and outputs is by testing and inspection.

16.2 THE ROLE OF INSPECTION

Inspection is an important part, although only *one* part, of a quality control program. Inspection involves the determination, sometimes by testing, of whether or not an input or output conforms to organizational standards of quality. It is not, however, inspection's role to *correct* the system deficiencies that produced the defective items, nor, for that matter, even to decide *what* to inspect or *when*.

Commonness of inspection.

Inspection is a very commonplace activity. Not only is it prominent in manufacturing organizations but clearly in processing, distributing, and service organizations as well. The wine and coffee tasters inspect their outputs for many different quality criteria. Order pickers in warehouses inspect the packaging and age of the goods they send out. And bank examiners, federal Occupational Safety and Health (OSHA) inspectors, and Food and Drug Administration agents may interrupt the activities of organizations at any time to test conformance to regulations and standards. We often even hear about licensing boards who have closed local businesses such as restaurants because their facilities could not pass inspection. And even at home, we regularly inspect the food we eat, the cars we drive, and the clothes we wear.

Because of the extent and difficulty of inspection, it can occupy a considerable amount of time. For simple, repetitive, automated production it may only require a small fraction of a direct worker's time. But in complex, technical and/or manual work, such as in computer software services, it may occupy upwards of half the direct labor hours.

Ease of missing defects.

In spite of such dedication of time to the function, it is still not uncommon for inspectors to miss half of all the defects passing by them. Most commonly, about two-thirds of the defects are caught but, depending upon the situation, this rate may vary from one in five to four in five. As an example, spend a minute with Figure 16.2.

Bear in mind that most inspectors are probably tired, not quite as enthusiastic about their work as they once were, nor as young as they used to be. To produce approximately the equivalent conditions, the exercise in Figure 16.2 should be completed during the last quarter or semester of your schooling, on a Friday night, and at about one o'clock in the morning. The correct number of "e"s in the story is 11. The typical number reported by a class of undergraduates is from 7 to 11 with an average of 10. From this it should be clear that inserting inspectors into the end of a production process is not going to miraculously improve the quality of an organization's output.

Proper screening and training required.

Better quality will be obtained through inspection if the inspectors know what to look for, have been properly trained (including human relations), and have the physical and psychological makeup required for the job. Regardless, many organizations make use of inspectors who are not properly qualified simply because they never checked to see if they *were* qualified. Instances exist, for example, where in-

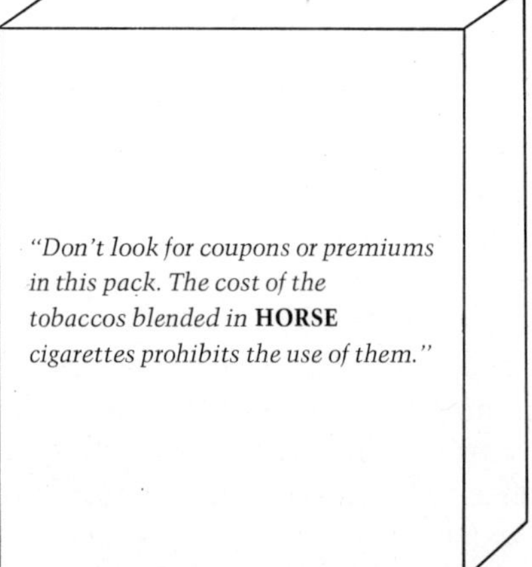

"Don't look for coupons or premiums
in this pack. The cost of the
tobaccos blended in **HORSE**
cigarettes prohibits the use of them."

Figure 16.2. Counting-the-defects exercise. During World War II, soldiers used to bet a new recruit $50 that he could not count all the "e" 's on the back of a pack of a certain brand of cigarettes in one reading. Here is an approximate rendition of what that 1940's package back stated; try it yourself for about 15 seconds.

spection jobs demanding high visual acuity were given to workers who were partially blind.

There are a number of particularly important points in the transformation process where inspection is more valuable than at other times. Some of these are:

1. Upon receipt of resources: checking the quality of raw materials and purchased parts and supplies, testing equipment for ability to meet specifications, verifying the skills of staff.
2. Before transformation processes by the worker: if the process at hand is expensive, irreversible (such as mixing food ingredients), or of a concealing nature (such as assemblies, coatings, platings).
3. When the first few items come out of an automatic process.
4. After transformation processes (inspection by the worker).
5. After transformation processes (inspection by an inspector).
6. In final inspection.
7. When customers complain, return goods, or require service.

Organizations typically cannot afford to inspect at *all* of the above points but inspection at *some* of these points should be conducted. In addition to deciding *what* is to be inspected, the organization must also decide *when* to inspect (or, equivalently, how often), *where* to inspect (on the "floor" or in one specialized area), *who* should inspect, and *how* to inspect. (The topic of when to inspect will be covered later under statistical quality control.)

Where to inspect.

The location of inspection is usually either at the workplace itself (called **floor inspection**) or in a centralized inspection area. Floor inspection usually consists of approving equipment setups before runs are made, checking "first-off" items (shaving balloons at a barber school), and checking and recording semiautomatic equipment output. Frequently, floor inspectors have the authority to halt operations that are producing excessive defectives.

Floor inspection has some clear advantages to an organization. It saves the time and cost of transporting material to a central inspection area and the resultant queuing delay once there. However, if a floor inspector is unavailable then both the worker *and* the equipment must sit idle until the inspector comes. Central inspection is typically used for tests requiring special equipment and total performance tests, such as when seniors must pass a state competency exam before graduating.

Who inspects?

The topic of *who* should inspect is important primarily in regard to who is responsible for quality control. If that person is the production manager then an obvious conflict of interest will arise. Yet is is worthwhile to give the person who is responsible for producing the output the commensurate responsibility for the quality of that output. A common resolution to this dilemma is to have the floor inspectors report to the production manager but final inspection report at a higher level in the organization. In this manner the floor inspectors will be viewed by production as aids in getting work through the *final inspection* area.

How to inspect.

How to inspect involves the tools and equipment used by both floor and central inspection. Clearly, the more expensive, sensitive, and immobile equipment will remain at central inspection while small, lightweight, or rugged gauges and instruments will often be carried by the floor inspectors.

Although inspection devices vary considerably from organization to organization, depending on the output, most of them are familiar: thermometers, questions, magnifying glasses, feel, and so forth. Some of the more esoteric tools and equipment are described in the *Tools and Applications* portion of this chapter.

Handling of defectives.

After inspection has revealed a defective item or material, what should be done with it? Typically, it is not discarded. If it is worthwhile it may be reworked and repaired, or refashioned into another output. If not, it may be sold as a "second" as is done with clothing and "second pressings" of wine. If even sale as a second is not feasible it may be recycled (e.g., shredded, remelted), if possible, and used as new raw material. Lastly, it may be sold as scrap.

Two bads equal a good.

In some instances it is possible to take a number of defective outputs and combine them to form an acceptable output. This "magic" is common in some "processing-type" industries. Grain in silos and mined coal are both tested for a number of characteristics, any one of which may be either exceeded or insufficient. For example, the moisture content of corn in one silo may be too high to qualify as top grade corn, while the sugar content of corn in another silo may be too low. By *mixing* the contents of these two silos however, a combined product is achieved which is now within *both* moisture and sugar requirements for classification as top grade corn, an interesting example of **synergism** where the whole is equal to more than the sum of the parts.

16.3 STATISTICAL QUALITY CONTROL

Reasons for sampling.

To maintain the quality of their output, organizations must inspect and test throughout their operations. However, as explained in Chapter 15, it is not usually necessary to inspect *all* the items or material during an inspection but only a **sample**. This is fortunate since there are a number of reasons for not conducting 100 percent inspection:

1. *Infinite population.* To inspect all the paper clips coming out of a factory, or all the oil from a refinery, would be virtually impossible. In the first case, the inspection would fall far behind the production rate and go on forever, and in the second, the output is not in *discrete* form but infinitely divisible.
2. *Lack of time.* The time to adequately test each item may preclude inspecting *all* the items, as with the paper clips above. Answers are needed very quickly for management decisions and late answers are worthless.
3. *Excessive cost.* Even if time were no problem, the cost of 100 percent inspection and testing is typically prohibitive.

4. **Destructive testing.** In some cases the appropriate test is by testing the output until it fails, as is sometimes done with fuses, structural beams, and light bulbs. If this testing were applied to all of the organization's output, there would be nothing left to distribute.
5. *Inaccuracy.* It was pointed out earlier that inspection does not catch all the defects. As the inspector becomes fatigued and/or bored, more defects slip by. With 100 percent inspection this would occur rather quickly. Therefore, better accuracy is usually obtained by inspecting and testing only a representative sample rather than the entire output.

When full inspection needed.

There are some instances however, when 100 percent inspection may still be called for. These infrequent cases usually fall among the following situations:

1. *Extreme cost of defects.* If, by a failure of an output, an extreme cost is incurred, such as a loss of human life in a space shot, complete inspection is called for.
2. *High variability.* In cases where the variability of the output may be extreme (typically with human inputs such as in education) but consistency is desired (thus excluding art works, musical compositions, novels, etc.) 100 percent inspection may be desirable, if not too expensive or time consuming.
3. *Operating unit assemblies.* When an assembled item is dispensed to recipients a unit at a time and is always expected to initially operate, such as a television set, automobile, or dryer, it is desirable to 100 percent check the gross performance of the output if it can be quickly and cheaply done. For example, whether a dryer heats up and spins when turned on can be checked in seconds. But checking all the various cycles of a clothes dryer could entail a major, time-consuming test.
4. *Rejected lots.* If a *lot* (binfull, gross, filled railroad car) has been sampled and rejected it may be desirable to check the entire lot, not to determine the **defect rate** of the lot, but to locate and *remove* the defective items so that those remaining can be used or sold.

Quality control like the trial process in law.

The inspection decision is identical in concept to our society's trial procedure in law. We assume that a defendant is innocent until proven guilty. Likewise, we assume that output is of acceptable quality until proven otherwise. The sampling information then determines the evidence on which a "verdict" is reached. As in the legal process, two types of errors can be made (Figure 16.3) A **type I error** is committed when an innocent defendant (a good quality lot) is found guilty (declared "defective"). A **type II error** is made when a guilty defendant ("defective" lot) is found innocent (declared of good quality). The seriousness of these two types of errors is dependent upon the organization and the type of output. Our society considers a type I error in the legal process extremely serious and goes to great lengths to prevent such a tragedy. Goods and service producing organizations, on the other hand, do not need to worry about the "rights" of their outputs and hence have more concern with the

Lot (defendent) is actually:	Inspection decision (verdict)	
	Quality (innocent)	Defective (guilty)
Quality (innocent)	Correct	Type I error
Defective (guilty)	Type II error	Correct

Figure 16.3. The inspection error possibilities.

harm that may be done by passing a lot off as good when it actually is defective. This concern is thus oriented to type II errors.

Importance of type II errors.

In the medical field, where a disease has no "rights," and the patient suffers the consequences of an inspection error, type II errors are of even more concern. The result has therefore been to utilize more and more sophisticated (and expensive) testing equipment to reduce the possibility of a patient's *having* a particular disease but being diagnosed from a test as being *disease-free*, a type II error.

Risk for both producer and consumer.

In quality control terminology, the probability of making a type I error is known as the **producer's risk** since it is the chance that the producer's product or service is incorrectly declared defective or unacceptable. The probability of a type II error is known as the **consumer's risk**. Likewise, the consumer will sometimes, because of the sampling plan, accept a lot as being of acceptable quality when it is actually defective. As we will see in a later section, one objective of a sampling plan is to balance these two risks.

Every productive process generates variability in its output. One of the goals of quality control is to assure that this variability is small enough so that the output as a whole may be deemed of acceptable quality. As mentioned in Chapter 15, this natural variability is seen as emanating primarily from two sources: **chance (random) variation** and **assignable (nonrandom) variation**.

Chance or assignable variation?

Built-in variation.

Chance variation is the variability that is built into (actually, allowed to remain in) the system. There is "play" between the gears and mechanical parts of machines. There is variation in the inputs. Processing conditions are variable. And human performance is particularly variable. When the productive operations are designed, the allowable chance variability (*tolerance* in engineering) is accounted for and the most economical system that can produce within those limits is constructed. If it later turns out that this chance variation is too great then the entire system may have to be reworked.

Identifying the cause of variation.

Assignable variation occurs because some system element or operating condition is out of control. A machine may be excessively worn, a part broken, a worker mistrained, faulty inspection gauges or instruments used, and so forth. It is this variation that quality control must identify so as to correct the faulty system element (or to refuse shipment of the goods).

If we consider the simplest possible model of an organization's operations—the input-process-output model (Figure 1.6 of Chapter 1)—we see that there are two elements, "inputs" and the "transformation process," which must both be controlled in order to control the quality variation of the output. Two separate types of control have been developed for these two elements. Taken in "design" order, process control is for the transformation process and **acceptance sampling** for the inputs.

1. *Process control:* the control of the productive operations of the organization. Upon regular examination of an output, quality control can determine if a system element is malfunctioning. A blood test, for example, can detect many anomalies in human body performance.
2. *Acceptance sampling:* the determination of acceptable and unacceptable products and services. This function is important to the organization in its acquisition of appropriate resources, especially materials, for producing its output. Although every organization must certify the acceptability of its resources, the *quality control* area typically performs this function for physical materials (parts, raw materials), *personnel* for human resources, *engineering* for plant and equipment, and so on. Since most of the nonmaterials purchases are single unit acquisitions, sampling is not usually done but each item is inspected by itself.

Variables versus attributes.

When quality control is performing an inspection it will either *measure* something, or simply determine the existence of a characteristic. The former, called inspection for *variables*, usually relates to weight, length, degree, intensity, or some other variable that can be **scaled**. The latter, called inspection of **attributes**, can also examine scaled variables but usually considers **dichotomous** variables such as right-wrong, acceptable-defective, black-white, timely-late, and other such characteristics that either can not be measured or do not *need* to be measured with any more precision than yes-no. With scaled variables the dichotomy might be light-heavy, short-long, hot-cold, weak-strong, and so forth. Both types of inspection, either for variables or attributes, can be used for either process control or acceptance sampling. The next two sections will discuss the common techniques used for process control and acceptance sampling.

16.4 PROCESS CONTROL

Control charts.

The general concept of process control by the use of control charts was covered in Chapter 15. Here we will discuss the use of this concept specifically to control quality variables and attributes of the organizaion's output.

Control of Variables

Two control charts for variables.

For the control of variables, two control charts are commonly employed.

1. A chart of the process sample **means** ($\overline{X}$) as described in Chapter 15.
2. A chart of the item **range** (R) in values indicated by the items in each sample (largest value of X – smallest).

It is important to use two control charts for variables because of the way in whicl control of process quality can be lost.

Figure 16.4 shows two patterns of change in the distribution of process values These changes might be due to boredom, tool wear, the weather, fatigue, or any othe such influence. In the top figure the variability in the process remains the same bu the mean changes; this effect would be seen in the means ($\overline{X}$) chart but not in th range (R) chart. In the lower figure the mean remains the same but the variabilit tends to increase; this would be seen in the range (R) chart but not the means ($\overline{X}$ chart.

Two ways of going out of control

In terms of quality of the output, either type of change could result in lowe quality, depending upon the situation. Regarding **control limits**, the lower contro limit (LCL) for the means chart *may* be negative (profit, temperature, etc.) but ca *never* be for the range chart (see definition of R). If calculations indicate a negativ LCL for the range chart, it should simply be set to zero.

Minimum value of LCL.

Sweetn' Cold, Inc.

Sweetn' Cold is a chain of 10 fountain ice cream stores in southern Texas. Manage ment is keenly concerned over the age of the ice cream being dispensed in their store since their ads stress "jes' like home made" as compared to that of their competitor To maintain a continuing check on this quality they have, for the last three week been selecting four stores at random from their chain each day and noting the age c the ice cream being served. Management believes that, due to the trouble of samplin a sample of 4 of the 10 stores each day will give them the best control for the troubl involved (c.f., Figure 16.1).

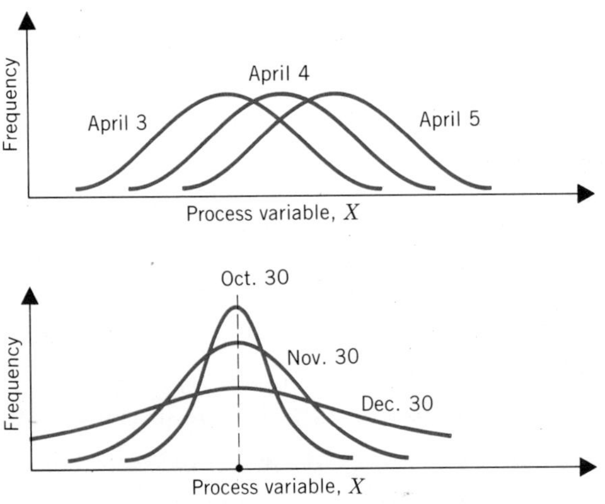

Figure 16.4 Patterns of change in process distributions.

The mean age and range in ages for each sample are presented in Table 16.1. the grand mean ($\overline{\overline{X}}$), the sample standard deviation of the means, $S_{\overline{X}}$), the average range ($\overline{R}$), and sample **standard deviation** of the ranges (S_R), are also calculated and shown in Table 16.1. As an example, the calculations for June 1 were

Main St. store:	7 days
Southside store:	2 days
Bayfront store:	20 days
West Mall store:	11 days
Total	40 days

$$\text{mean}, \overline{X} = \frac{40}{4} = 10 \text{ days}$$

$$\text{range}, R = 20 - 2 = 18 \text{ days}$$

The data in Table 16.1 can now be used to construct control charts that will indicate to management any sudden change, either for better or worse, in the quality (age) of their ice cream. Both a chart of means, to check the age of the ice cream being served, and a chart of ranges to check consistency among stores, will be used.

The grand mean and average range will give the center line on these charts and the sample standard deviations will give the control limits. Out of interest, both one

TABLE 16.1 MEAN AND RANGE OF AGES OF ICE CREAM

Date	$\overline{X}$	R	$\overline{X} - \overline{\overline{X}}$	$(\overline{X} - \overline{\overline{X}})^2$	$(R - \overline{R})$	$(R - \overline{R})^2$
June 1	10	18	−1	1	4	16
2	13	13	2	4	−1	1
3	11	15	0	0	1	1
4	14	14	3	9	0	0
5	9	14	−2	4	0	0
6	11	10	0	0	−4	16
7	8	15	−3	9	1	1
8	12	17	1	1	3	9
9	13	9	2	4	−5	25
10	10	16	−1	1	2	4
11	13	12	2	4	−2	4
12	12	14	1	1	0	0
13	8	13	−3	9	−1	1
14	11	15	0	0	1	1
15	11	11	0	0	−3	9
16	9	14	−2	4	0	0
17	10	13	−1	1	−1	1
18	9	19	−2	4	5	25
19	12	14	1	1	0	0
20	14	14	3	9	0	0
Total:	220	280		63		114

Mean, $\overline{\overline{X}} = 220/20 = 11$ days Sample standard deviation, $S_{\overline{X}} = \sqrt{63/(20-1)} = 1.82$ days

Range, $R = 280/20 = 14$ days Sample standard deviation, $S_R = \sqrt{114/(20-1)} = 2.45$ days and two standard deviation limits will initially be shown. As more data is gathered only two standard deviation limits will be used.

These charts are shown in Figure 16.5 and 16.6. In addition, the data in Table 16.1 are graphed on the charts. As seen in Figure 16.5, 10 of the $\overline{X}$ points exceed the $1S_{\overline{X}}$ limits, whereas only 7 would be expected to. However, none of the points exceed the $2S_{\overline{X}}$ limits and one is expected to. This should indicate to management that there is considerable variability in the process but of limited deviation. That is, there is considerable variation within an age limit of about 6 days (from 8 to 14 days old) but not beyond that. Whether or not this is acceptable to management is a separate question.

Interpreting the control charts.

The range chart, Figure 16.6, shows six points exceeding the $1S_R$ limits and one point exceeds the $2S_R$ limits, about what should be expected. This indicates that variability between stores does not seem to be either increasing or decreasing. Again, whether or not this normal range of variability (of 10 days) is acceptable to management is another question.

Each day, as a new sample is taken, $\overline{X}$ and R are calculated and plotted on the two charts. If either $\overline{X}$ or R are outside the given LCL or UCL, management must then decide whether to wait for another day's sample or to undertake to find the assignable cause for the variation. This decision, again, depends upon the output and the cost associated with continuing to produce for one more day a product of too low quality and the cost of the investigation.

Control charts are also used for the control of dichotomous *attributes*, as mentioned earlier. Two examples of such applications are given in the *Tools and Applications* portion of this chapter.

Although originally confined to the manufacturing setting, it should be clear that process control charts represent a significant tool for the control of *services* as well. Furthermore, because of their simplicity of use, workers can employ them to monitor their own performance, as in the example above. Thus, a positive behavioral effect can also be achieved.

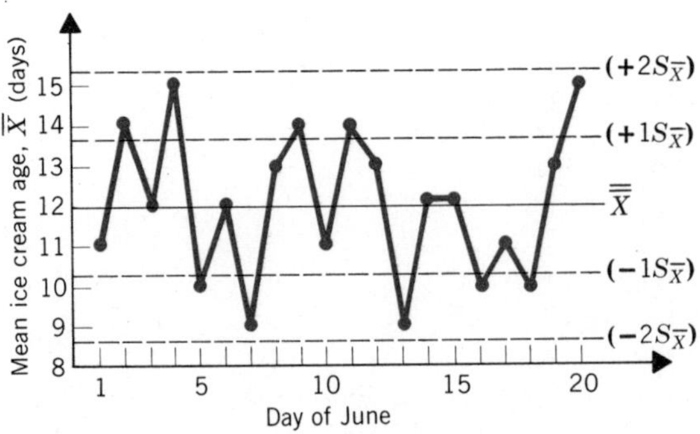

Figure 16.5. Mean ice cream age, days.

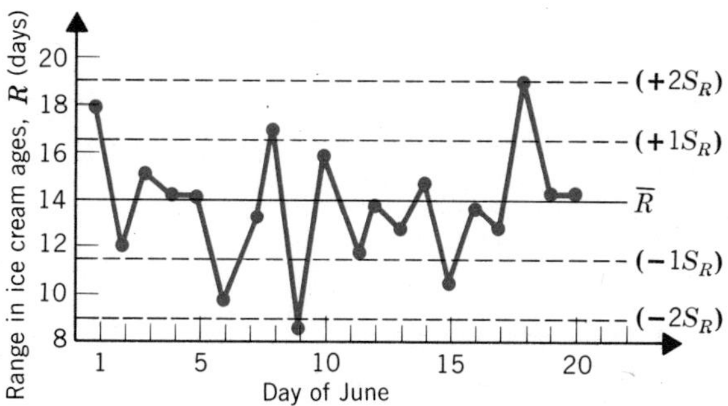

Figure 16.6. Range in ice cream ages, days.

16.5 ACCEPTANCE SAMPLING

Static control of acceptance sampling.

Whereas process quality control is a *dynamic* quality control technique, acceptance sampling, another manufacturing development, is a *static* technique for computing incoming and outgoing quality of lots. Originally developed to provide a means whereby manufacturers could efficiently decide whether to accept or reject a shipment of incoming material, the approach has utility for services as well in checking the characteristics of large groups of services in order to classify them into, for example, grades of quality. *Sampling by variables* would allow such a classification because each item is measured along a scale that can be partitioned into grades. More commonly, however, only a single bit of information is desired: whether a minimum level of quality exists or not. If not, the entire group may be returned to the supplier or else subjected to 100 percent inspection. For such a simple purpose only *sampling by attributes* is required.

Again, either variables or attributes.

Attributes most common.

Tables are available.

As opposed to control charts, it is not necessary for the organization to construct its own acceptance charts or tables. Two men, again from Bell Telephone Laboratories, H. F. Dodge and H. G. Romig, applied the theory of statistics to acceptance sampling and derived the necessary data in a form now known as the **Dodge-Romig** *Sampling Inspection Tables* [4].

Sampling plans from OC curves.

Given certain information, to be discussed later, these tables will provide an inspector with a **sampling plan** consisting of the size of the sample, n, and the maximum acceptable number of defectives, c (not to be confused with the c used in control charts). The ability of this plan to discriminate between "good" lots and "bad" lots is described by the curve of the chance of accepting the lot versus the percentage of defects in the lot, known as the plan's **operating characteristic** (OC) curve. Clearly, the greater the percentage of defects in the lot, the smaller the chance it will be accepted.

The ideal OC curve.

Ideally, such a plan would have the curve shown in Figure 16.7. In this case, the "stated" quality of the lot is 4 percentage of or less defectives. The ideal sampling plan would accept the lot if the actual percent defectives was 4 or less but reject it if more than 4. Such a result, however, could only come about by very careful inspec-

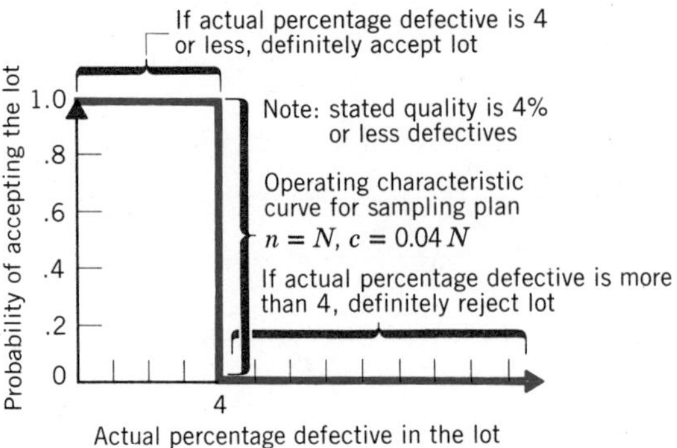

Figure 16.7. Ideal sampling plan.

tion of the *entire lot*! Only then could its *true* percentage of defectives be known (and possibly not even then) and the lot accepted or rejected according to the 4 percent figure. However, such a process would undoubtedly prove extremely expensive and very inefficient to the organization. A much better plan to minimize the total cost of both accepting defective items (cost of errors, Figure 16.1) and paying for inspection (cost of quality) would probably be to *sample* the lot and made a decision on the basis of the sample.

. . . But too expensive.

The result of implementing such a strategy is to increase the chance of making type I and type II errors, as discussed earlier, especially very near the 4 percent point in the above situation. This increased chance of error is illustrated by the shading in Figure 16.8. This figure shows a different sampling plan, which also rejects lots having samples with more than 4 percent defectives in them. In this case, the sampling plan

Trading off type I and type II errors.

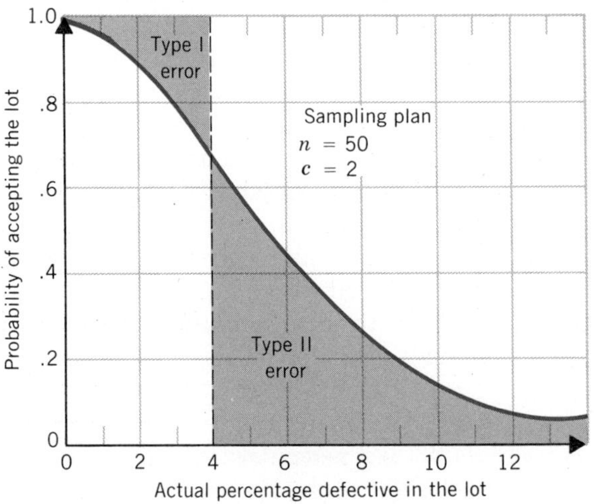

Figure 16.8. A typical operating characteristic curve.

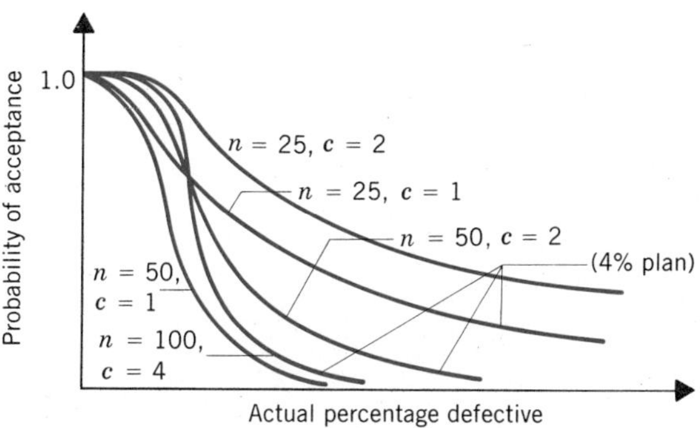

Figure 16.9. Other sampling plan's OC curves.

is to sample 50 items ($n = 50$) and reject the lot if more than two defects ($2/50 = 4$ percent) are found ($c = 2$). The figure also illustrates what the chances of accepting the lot are, depending upon the actual lot percentage of defectives. As can be seen, if the actual defect rate is 4 percent, there is about a 68 percent chance of accepting the lot. If 2 percent are actually defective the probability of acceptance is 91 percent (or a 9 percent chance of rejecting the lot even though only 2 percent are defective, a type I error called "the producer's risk") and if 6 percent are actually defective, the probability of acceptance of the lot decreases to about 45 percent (a type II error called "the consumer's risk"). Note that, with this plan, if there are just *slightly* more than 4 percent defectives the chance of making a type II error is about 2 out of 3. Even so, this may be acceptable to management, considering the cost of inspection!

Effect on n and c on type I and II errors.

Figure 16.9 illustrates the effect of changing various parameters in the plan. Note that those plans based on 4 percent are either more or less discriminating than the plan in Figure 16.8, depending on whether n is greater, or less, than 50.

Sampling plan from AQL and LTPD.

For a given lot size N, the specification (by management) of the two probabilities of making a type I and type II error determines, through the use of the Dodge-Romig tables, a sampling plan. The parameters of interest are sketched in Figure 16.10. The two parameters that must be specified by management are

AQL The **acceptable quality level.** The actual percent defective in the lot that the organization is willing to mistakenly reject (by chance) 5 percent of the time (called the "producer's risk," α) when the lot is *actually* "good" (of this quality or better). For example, in a lot of 4 percent stated quality, management might be willing to risk mistakenly returning 3 percent goods 5 percent of the time.

LTPD The **lot tolerance percentage defective**. The actual lot percentage defective the organization is willing to mistakenly accept (by chance) 10 percent of the time (called the "consumer's risk," β) when the lot is *actually* "bad." Here management might only be willing to mistakenly accept 4.5 percent goods 10 percent of the time.

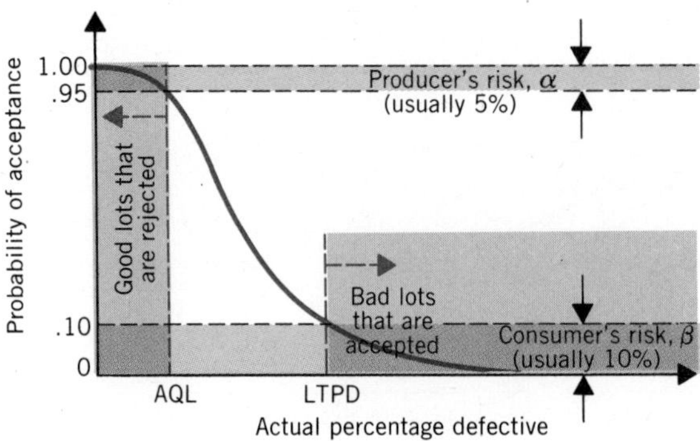

Figure 16.10. Sampling plan input parameters.

If the use of these numbers in the Dodge-Romig tables results in an "excessive" value of n (amount of sampling) to the organization then they must either be willing to risk accepting worse quality lots (increase LTPD), risk rejecting better quality lots (decrease AQL), or both. Those are the only tradeoffs possible (at this point in the discussion).

General Receivers and Shippers Co. (GRSC)

The receiving department of GRSC is under orders from the vice president of receiving to carefully inspect every order received from a new supplier, to check their honesty. For truckload sized orders of 3 percent stated quality, top management has indicated that they would be willing to risk only a 10 percent chance (consumer's risk) of accepting an order containing up to 10 percent (LTPD = 10%) defectives. On the other side, they would be willing to risk a 5 percent chance (producer's risk) of rejecting an order whose quality was as good as 1.5 percent (AQL = 1.5%).

Using this information, the acceptance sampling table A5 in Appendix A indicates that the proper sample size, n, is 50 and the limiting acceptance value, c, is 2. This sampling plan's operating characteristic curve is that sketched in Figure 16.8. If this sample size is too expensive for top management and a smaller size, say 40, is desired then they must be willing to accept an LTPD of about 11 percent (at the same AQL level) or an AQL of about 1.1 percent (at the same LTPD level). That is, either the defect rate at a 10 percent risk of acceptance must increase from 10 to 11 percent, or the defect rate at a 5 percent risk of incorrect rejection must decrease from 1.5 to 1.1 percent.

Multiple Sampling

All of the preceding discussion concerning acceptance sampling assumed, as is typically the case, that only *one* sample was to be selected and inspected. However, one method of reducing the expected sampling necessary but still maintaining the same

Reducing sample size by multiple sampling.

confidence in the sampling process is to use a **multiple sampling** plan. The idea behind this process is that, at some increase in sampling time and complexity, a small, partial sample taken first may indicate which lots are extremely good or bad (by having very few, or many, defects in the small sample) and these lots would then not need to be sampled further. For instance, if taking a half-sized sample eliminated one-third of all the lots from further sampling, the amount of sampling saved would be $\frac{1}{2} \times \frac{1}{3} = \frac{1}{6}$, or 17 percent, a considerable saving.

Double sampling.

The details of the **double sampling** procedure described above would be as follows.

Step 1 Take a sample n_1.

Step 2 If the number of defectives is greater than c_2 then reject the entire lot. However, if it is not more than c_1 (where c_1 is less then c_2), then accept the entire lot. Otherwise, take another sample of size n_2.

Step 3 Find the number of defectives in n_2. If the number of defectives in *both* $n_1 + n_2$ (that is, in both samples combined) is now greater than c_2 reject the lot; otherwise accept it.

Sequential sampling.

Sequential sampling extends this notion even further, to the point where up to only half as many samples, on the average, as with single sampling need be used (at the cost, again, of increased complexity and time). The procedure is illustrated in Table 16.2 and Figure 16.11 for a five-stage sequential sampling plan centered about 7 percent defectives. The hope, of course, is that somewhere before the fifth sample, a decision can be made, thus making it unnecessary to take all five samples. Note how, in Table 16.2, the range in percent defectives over which a "delay decision" response is appropriate shrinks toward 7 percent with the increasing number of samples. That is, the **"delay" range** begins at 20 percent ((20% − 0%) for a sample size of 40 and decreases to 6.7 percent at 120 items sampled and finally to 0.5 percent at 200 items sampled.

TABLE 16.2 FIVE-STAGE SEQUENTIAL SAMPLING PLAN

Sample No.	Sample Size	Cumulative Size	Accept if Total No. Defectives ≤:	(%)	Reject if Total No. Defectives ≥:	(%)	Delay Region (%)
1	40	40	0	0	8	20.0	7^{+13}_{-7}
2	40	80	2	2.5	10	12.0	$7^{+5}_{-4.5}$
3	40	120	4	3.3	12	10.0	$7^{+3}_{-3.7}$
4	40	160	6	3.75	14	9.0	$7^{+2}_{-3.25}$
5	40	200	14	7.0	15	7.5	$7^{+0.5}_{-0}$

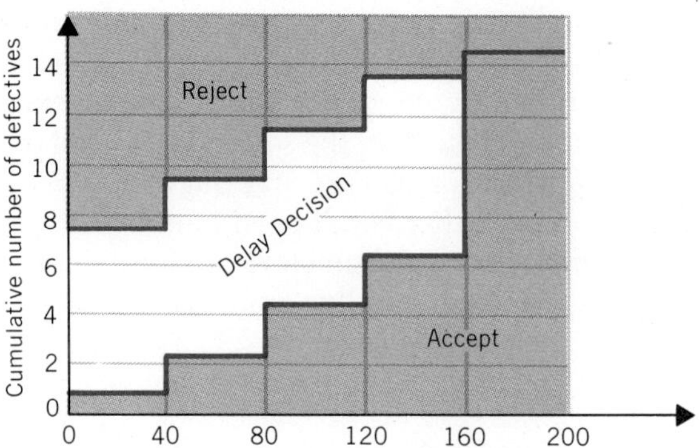

Figure 16.11. Portrayal of five-stage sequential sampling plan.

Details regarding the construction of such plans can be found in Duncan [5]. Another approach, in lieu of using the Dodge-Romig or above tables, is experimenting with different sampling plans through simulation. In addition to providing time and cost data and allowing different combinations of plans, other values of producer's and consumer's risk (α and β) than 5 and 10 percent may be tested if desired.

TOOLS AND APPLICATIONS

16.6 INSPECTION MACHINES AND EQUIPMENT

Some descriptions of relatively specialized inspection equipment are given below.

- *X-ray machines:* These machines have the ability to detect internal flaws by passing high energy waves through the medium and detecting the result on photographic film on the other side. Uses are in medicine, dentistry, and industry (for coatings and thin sheets of materials). When the density of the material becomes substantial (as in welds and castings), more powerful *gamma* rays are used instead.
- **Oscilloscopes:** These electronic machines generate a cycling electrical frequency and then input this charge into the medium and monitor what comes out the other side. (They can also monitor an internally generated electrical pulse.) In this fashion, flaws in the medium can be quite easily detected by someone who can read the "scope." However, reading a scope is not a skill based on a theory of what *should* happen but rather on experience. Therefore, a technician who can use a scope to determine if a cyclinder head in an aircraft engine is cracked would be useless in analyzing a patient's brainwaves to determine if his skull was cracked.
- **Stroboscopes:** A "strobe" emits a flashing light of high frequency to measure, typically, the motion of a moving body. Strobes are often used to measure the rpm (revolutions per minute) of rotating equipment by placing a mark on an edge of the equipment and adjusting the strobe until the mark appears to remain motionless. Reading the flash frequency of the strobe will then tell the inspector the rpm of the equipment—almost. The problem is that the equipment may also be rotating two, three, or any number of times faster as well and also appear stationary. Hence some further testing at twice the frequency, and so forth, must often be conducted by the inspector.
- *Closed circuit television:* Television cameras are used to inspect facilities and materials where it is not cost-effective to use workers or is impossible due to environmental conditions. Thus, they are used to monitor banks and prisons, inspect sunken ships thousands of feet below sea level, and relay images from inside furnaces, from outer space, and within high-radiation chambers.
- *Gauges:* Many types of gauges exist for all kinds of purposes. Some are simply meters to measure voltage, vacuum pressure, revolutions, temperature, and so forth, such as odometers, gas meters, thermometers, tire pressure gauges, clocks, speedometers, and so on. Others are mechanical instruments to

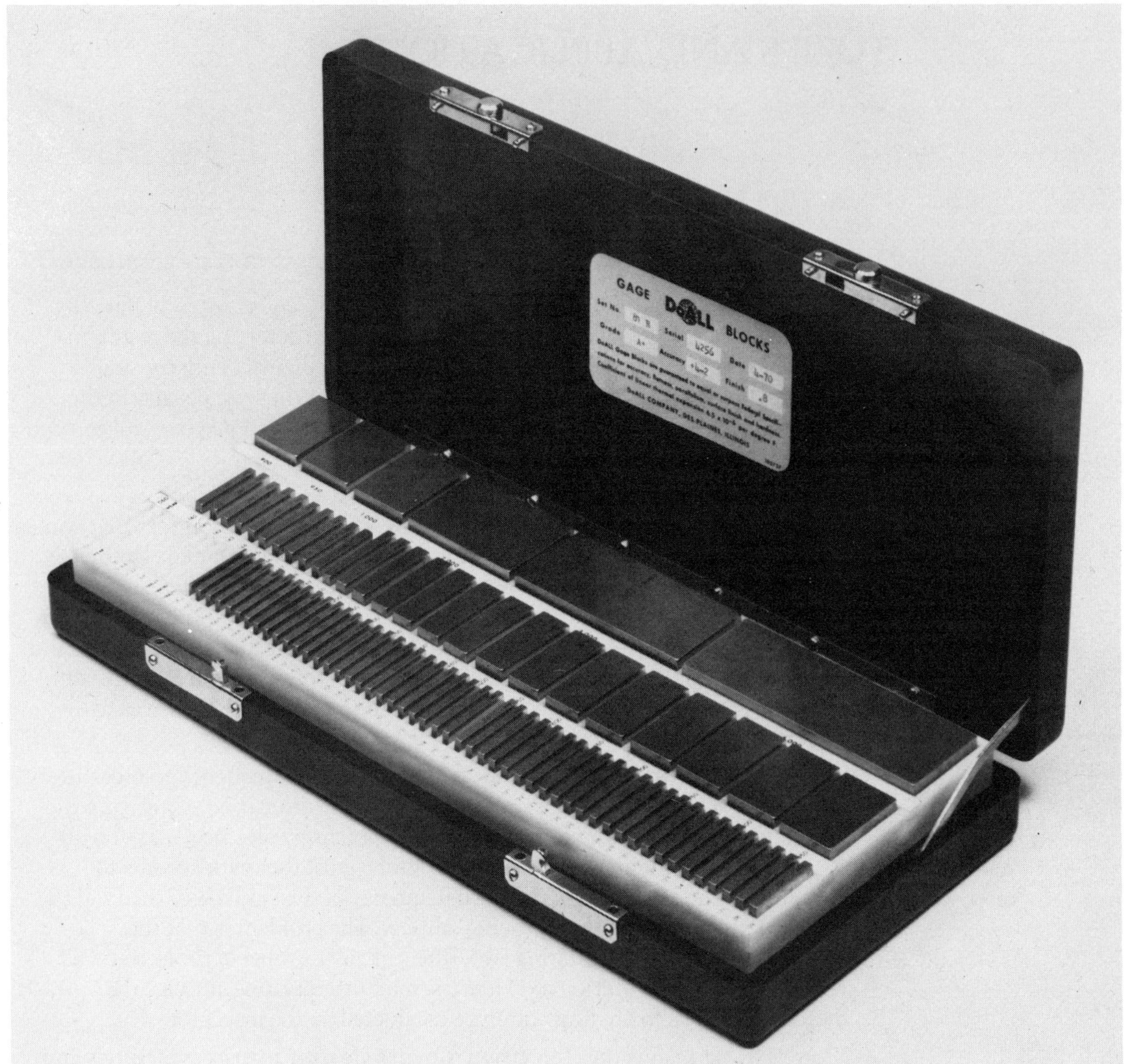

Example of a gauge block set. *Source:* courtesy of The DoAll Company, Des Plaines.

measure weight, length, hardness, and such. Here we find rulers, balances, calipers, micrometers, templates, go, no-go gauges, and gauge blocks. Some of these, such as **gauge blocks**, must be used in a laboratory where environmental conditions are controlled in order to accurately measure very precise work.

Gauge blocks, for instance, are small steel blocks calibrated to a certain size (Figure 16.12). To measure an object the blocks are stacked together to give a certain size reading. The *method* of stacking of the blocks is the crucial

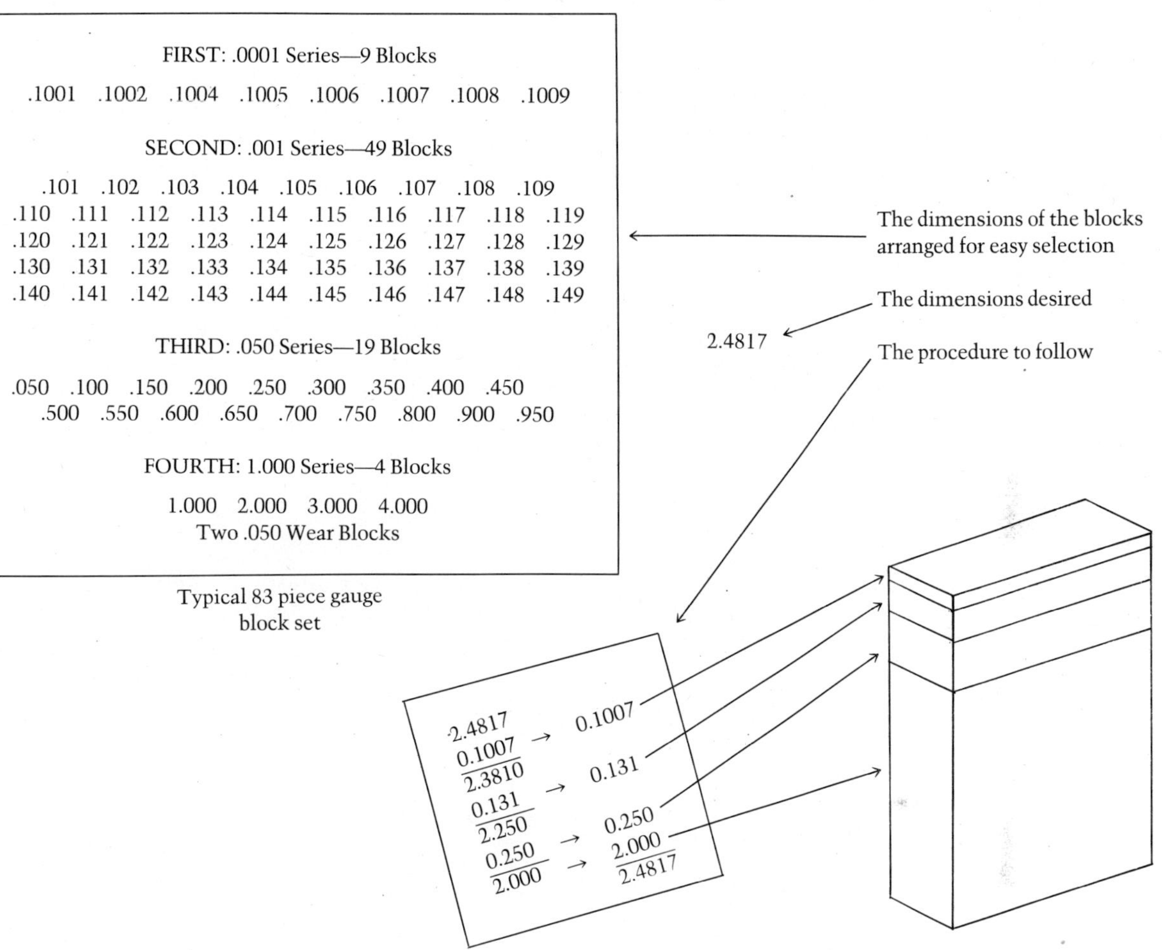

Figure 16.12. Combining gauge blocks. *Source:* T. Bush, *Fundamentals of Dimensional Metrology*, Delman Publishers, Albany, N.Y., 1964, p. 163.

element. If they are *laid* one upon the other, an incorrect (too short) measure will result. Rather, they must be "scraped" together with the proper amount of force. Too much force and the measure will be too long, however. (Also, it will be almost impossible to separate the blocks later, being held tightly together by surrounding air pressure.)

11.7 CONTROL CHARTS FOR ATTRIBUTES

Two types of attributes.

The control chart process is also valuable for controlling attributes of the output. The most common of these charts are the "fraction defective" ($\bar{p}$) chart and the "number of defects" (c) chart. these names were given to the charts from their emergence in a manufacturing context but they apply to a number of other situations as well.

Fraction Defective (p) Charts

The fraction defective chart can be used for any two-state (*dichotomous*) process such as heavy-light, big-little, and such. The control chart for p is constructed in much the same way as the control chart for $\overline{X}$. First, a large sample of historical data is gathered and the fraction having the characteristic in question (e.g., too light, defective, too old), $\overline{p}$, is computed on the entire set of data as a whole.

Large samples needed.

Large samples are usually taken because the fraction of interest is typically small and the number of items in the samples should be large enough to include *some* of the defectives. For example, when talking about defectives, a fraction defective may be 1 percent or less. Therefore, a sample size of 100 would have to be taken to expect to include even one defective item.

Since the fraction defective follows a **binomial** distribution ("bi" means two: either an item is or it is not) rather than a normal distribution, the standard deviation may be calculated directly from $\overline{p}$ as

$$\sigma_p = \sqrt{\frac{\overline{p}\,(1 - \overline{p})}{n}} \qquad (16.1)$$

where n is the uniform sample size to be used for controlling quality. Although the fraction defective follows the binomial distribution, if $\overline{p}$ is near 0.5, or n is large, the normal distribution is a good approximation and the 1, 2, or $3\sigma_p$ control limits will again represent 68, 95, and 99.7 percent of the sample observations. Again, the LCL cannot be negative. An example is given below.

Downtown Library

Downtown Library has decided to monitor the number of lost books, as a fraction of those requested, by checking daily samples of 50 books requested by their patrons. Library staff have, through the procedures described above, developed the control

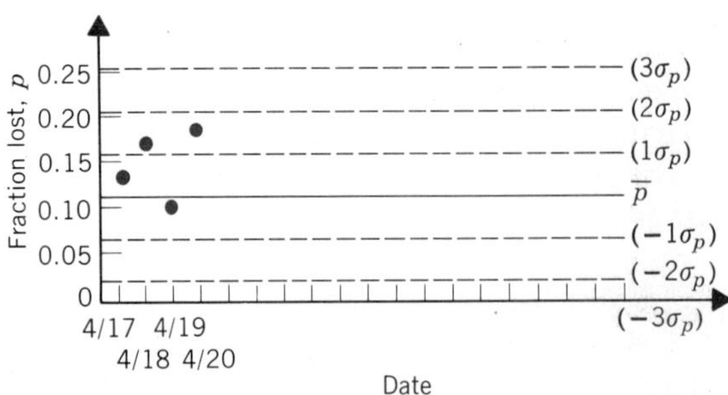

Figure 16.13. Control chart for percent of lost books.

TABLE 16.3 LOST BOOK DATA FOR p CHART

Date	Books Requested	Books That Could Not Be Located (Lost)
Feb. 7	122	15
8	91	12
9	137	13
	Total: 350	40

$$\bar{p} = \frac{40}{350} = 0.114$$

$$\sigma_p = \sqrt{0.114\,(0.886)/50}$$
$$= 0.045$$

chart illustrated in Figure 16.13 based on three typical days of requests (Table 16.3). If the library wishes to use $\pm 2\sigma_p$ limits, then no assignable variations in lost books appear to have occurred in the four days of April plotted so far in Figure 16.13.

Sample size must stay constant.

Note in this example that the data used to *derive* the control chart did not use the sample size of the samples used to determine $\bar{p}$. *Any* set of data could have been used to determine $\bar{p}$. In this case three samples were used from two months previously, one of size 122, one of 91, and the last of 137. Regardless, all the data was *combined* and then $\bar{p}$ found. However, to set control limits, the actual value of the size of the sample to be monitored (n) was used in the calculation of σ_p. If, on a particular day, less than 50 books are requested, say 40, then a new value of σ_p, and new control limits, based on the value $n = 40$, should be determined.

Number of Defects (c) Charts

The c chart is used for a single situation where any number of incidents may occur, each with a small probability. Typical of such incidents are scratches in tables, fire alarms in a city, and typesetting errors in a newspaper. Again, an average number of incidents, $\bar{c}$, is determined from combined past data. The distribution of such incidents is known to follow the **Poisson** distribution with a standard deviation of

$$\sigma_c = \sqrt{\bar{c}} \qquad (16.2)$$

Again, the normal distribution is used as an approximation to derive control limits with a minimum LCL of zero.

Stufie Bank, Ltd.

In an effort to better monitor the quality of their 24-hour teller services, Stufie Bank has instituted a charting procedure for the number of customer complaints. A quick review of the previous week's complaints gave the following.

	Number of Complaints
Monday	5
Tuesday	0
Wednesday	3
Thursday	(data missing)
Friday	8
Total:	16

$$\bar{c} = \frac{16}{4} = 4/\text{day}$$

$$\sigma_c = \sqrt{4} = 2$$

The control chart based on this one week sample of daily complaints is given in Figure 16.14. The two data points (Tuesday, Friday) out of four, on the $2\sigma_c$ limits, tend to imply the bank's quality of services is not in control. An investigation should be conducted and additional data collected.

16.8 SUMMARY

Quality is a relative term which means different things to different people. High quality is not always a desirable characteristic in an output and every organization must determine the most appropriate tradeoff between the cost of lesser quality and the cost of improving the quality of its outputs. On occasion, it is possible to combine a number of lower quality outputs together to form a higher quality output.

Inspection is an important part of controlling quality but can be a difficult and expensive task. There are a number of standard procedures and some common equipment and tools used in the inspection process.

Organizations, for a number of reasons, typically sample their outputs rather than using 100 percent inspection in quality control programs. On some occasions, however, 100 percent inspection may be called for. Because of the sampling process

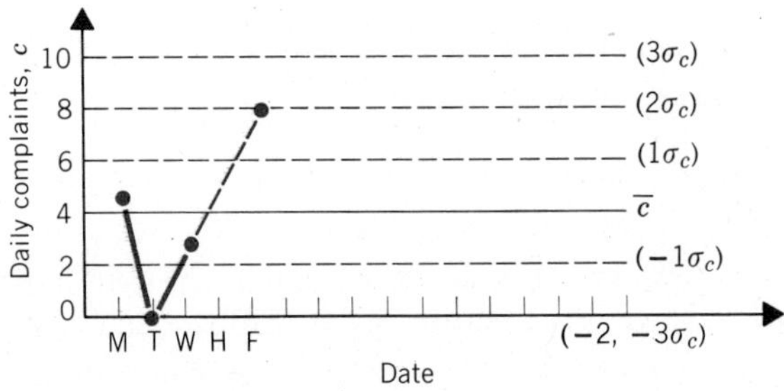

Figure 16.14. Control chart for complaints.

there is some risk of accepting groups of bad quality outputs, called the consumer's risk, and of rejecting good quality outputs, called the producer's risk. In certain instances one of these risks may be much more important than the other.

For controlling the quality of operational processes, control charts are used to determine if they are generating chance variation in the outputs or assignable variations because something is out of control. Control charts can be used to control scaled variables or dichotomous attributes. To control variables, both mean and range charts are commonly used together since these will usually detect the two primary ways processes go out of control. For the control of attributes either percentage defective (p) or number of defects (c) charts are commonly used.

Acceptance sampling of groups, or lots, of outputs is conducted by reference to Dodge-Romig sampling tables, which translate a managerially-specified operating characteristic curve into a sampling plan that can be used by inspectors. The operating characteristic curve is typically specified by giving the worst percentage defective the organization would be willing to accidentally accept 10 percent of the time and the best percentage defective the organization would be willing to accidentally reject 5 percent of the time.

At the cost of increased time and trouble, a reduced amount of sampling may result by the development of multiple sampling plans rather than single sampling. On occasion, such plans can cut the amount of sampling in half and still maintain the same confidence in results.

16.9 READINGS

Why Things Don't Work Any More

BY JOHN DIEBOLD

The need for action on today's crises of unemployment, urban decay, energy dependence, environmental pollution and . . . you name it . . . is urgent. But we had better recognize that crisis management is self-defeating when it excludes attention to what I think of as our *real* problems. These problems are part of the very machinery with which our society manages itself and the processes by which we cope with the you-name-it crises as they come along.

Energy, unemployment and welfare are real and pressing enough problems to demand our best efforts. But we need too to make the institutions of our society capable of dealing with life in the advanced industrial world in which we live, or we are going to expend increasing resources in coping with a stream of ever more demanding crises. The risk in this situation is not so much that we won't be able to make things work but that we will turn to increasingly more authoritarian governments to do so.

Things don't work any more because we rely upon brute-force solutions for crisis instead of heading off the crises by changing the *processes* with which we cope with public issues. The *processes* we use to handle problems and to make public decisions are not adequate in today's complex and demanding world.

DECLINE IN QUALITY

Some examples of what I think of as our *real* problems:

- *No matter how we organize things to produce*

management efficiency, nothing is going to keep increasingly unproductive, labor-intensive public services in important areas of life from declining. It is a paradox of our society that many public services were originally taken over by the government precisely because they were so important we wanted them available to as many citizens as possible at uniform quality. Yet today, the modern, broadly available and dependable items are consumer goods—portable color TV's, computer-driven sewing machines or cheap pocket calculators with the capability of yesterday's giant computers. Most of our *really* important activities—education, public transport, medical-service distribution, the running of cities—don't rely on advanced technology and therefore decline in quality and their costs spiral up.

The *real* problem here is not to try to force technology and modern management through the system—which is like trying to push a string—but to see if we can't find ways to create the kind of demand that stimulates innovation and high productivity in the private sector.

The problem is to learn how to define the results we want and then create incentives to achieve them. The natural ingenuity of our people, one of America's greatest strengths, will do the rest, just as it has in the things we are best at.

There are isolated examples—in various U.S. cities and towns—of privately run "public" services that reflect lower-cost, better service in response to competition and the incentive of profit. For example, a private, for-profit fire department in Scottsdale, Ariz., costs citizens substantially less than the nationwide average for similar communities. If such trendlets mean the creation in the public sector of the kind of demand-pull for science and technology that has produced such success in industrial and consumer products, we may have found the key to a wholly new approach to higher-quality public services.

• *We do not have "distant early warning systems" to anticipate future consequences of current and past decisions, to foresee the problems they may pose, and to identify the trade-offs in priority that we may have to make among alternatives right now*. Many problems don't lend themselves to forecasting—no mid 1950s projection would have included an overnight quadrupling of oil prices, the social divisiveness of Vietnam, or Watergate. But there is a great deal we could know that we don't really consider. We avoid that very act of consideration, otherwise known as "planning."

PRIORITIES FOR RESOURCES

While strong emotions and proper skepticism surround the term "national planning," we do need some imaginative political inventing to allow us to compare the alternative demands on our limited resources, to assign priorities to those ends and to create incentives and disincentives so that the play of forces in the marketplace occurs within a framework of politically agreed-upon direction. The recent creation of the Congressional Budget Office was a good step, but we need many more.

• *Attitudes toward work and personal value systems have changed radically, but few large organizations have altered their systems for managing, promoting and paying people*. Coupled with the alienation from authority and regimentation that characterizes current changing values, the productivity of our economy is declining. We need large organizations; we also need our creative younger people. Yet, the way we handle people in business and government agencies has not kept up with the changes in their values. Imaginative innovation in adapting job hours and pay to today's realities could go a long way toward unleashing the energies and creativity of many members of our society who are "turned off" by yesterday's organization concepts and practices.

Innovative approaches to manpower used abroad have proved highly successful. The key in these cases seems to be the effective identification of the employees' interests with that of industry. In Japan, employees see themselves as part of a vital working community. In Germany, they have and feel as great an economic stake in productivity and profitability as does "management." We should be able to combine the possibility of self-fulfillment with the fact of working in large organizations, building on our own traditions of individual initiative and the recognition of talent.

Diebold, chairman of the Diebold Group, Inc., an international management consulting firm, is a business leader and innovator.

16.10 KEY TERMS

Concepts

final inspection (p. 541)
floor inspection (p. 541)
synergism (p. 542)
sample (p. 542)
destructive testing (p. 543)
defect rate (p. 543)
producer's risk (p. 544)
consumer's risk (p. 544)
type I, II errors (p. 543)
chance variation (p. 544)
assignable variation (p. 544)
process control (p. 545)
acceptance sampling (p. 545)
scaled variables (p. 545)
attributes (p. 545)
dichotomous (p. 545)
means chart (p. 545)
range chart (p. 545)
control limit (p. 546)
standard deviation (p. 547)
Dodge-Romig (p. 549)
sampling plan (p. 549)
operating characteristic (p. 549)
acceptable quality level (p. 551)
lot tolerance percentage defective (p. 551)
double sampling (p. 553)
multiple sampling (p. 553)
sequential sampling (p. 553)
delay range (p. 553)

Tools and Applications

oscilloscope (p. 555)
stroboscope (p. 555)
gauge blocks (p. 556)
binomial (p. 558)
Poisson (p. 559)

16.11 REVIEW TEST

Concepts

1. The military instituted the concept of specifically considering the quality of outputs. (p. 536)
   a. True b. False
2. People can generally agree on the quality of a particular output. (p. 536)
   a. True b. False
3. Organizations should strive to improve the quality of their outputs. (p. 536)
   a. True b. False
4. Inspection is the only sure way to catch *all* the defectives in a lot. (p. 540)
   a. True b. False
5. Floor inspection and final inspection check the same things in the output. (p. 541)
   a. True b. False
6. Adding poor quality lots together gives an output with very poor quality. (p. 542)
   a. True b. False

7. We often sample rather than using 100 percent inspection because it is more accurate. (p. 543)
   a. True b. False
8. Declaring a bad output as good is a type II error. (p. 543)
   a. True b. False
9. Type I error is also known as producer's risk. (p. 544)
   a. True b. False
10. As in process control, acceptance sampling can be of either variables or attributes. (p. 549)
   a. True b. False
12. The range control chart will often miss assignable variation detected on the means chart. (p. 546)
   a. True b. False
12. The "better" OC curve is the more vertical one. (p. 549)
   a. True b. False
13. The AQL is the level the producer states for his output. (p. 551)
   a. True b. False
14. Multiple sampling is a way of decreasing the amount of sampling but still keeping the same confidence in results. (p. 553)
   a. True b. False

Tools and Applications

15. Oscilloscopes are often used to determine the speed of rotating parts. (p. 555)
   a. True b. False
16. The c chart can be transformed to a p chart by dividing the number of defects by the sample size. (p. 559)
   a. True b. False

16.12 DISCUSSION QUESTIONS

1. How could a college control the quality of their graduates?
2. What are the quality measures of a theatrical performance?
3. What quality control program would be appropriate for the post office? Include attributes and variables.
4. We often hear about the decreasing "quality of life." What does this mean?
5. What are the benefits of teaching workers to control their own quality through tools such as control charts and acceptance sampling?
6. What type of outputs do not require high quality?
7. How could a quality control program be used in American politics?
8. Why was the military the first to be concerned about quality?
9. If a plastic imitation can not be told from the real thing, what difference does it make?
10. Why are services of such poor quality these days?
11. Can adding poor quality lots together to form a higher resulting output be used outside the processing industry?
12. What are some situations where type I error is most important? Type II error?
13. Why is variables acceptance sampling not common?
14. Why is multiple sampling not increased even beyond five stages since it would continue to decrease the amount of sampling required?

16.13 PROBLEMS

Concepts

1. Connecting rods for large steam generators are x-ray tested for stress cracks. If a crack exists and is not detected, the rod will break within the first 100 hours of use and require a complete "teardown" of the generator. The x-ray test is accurate 95 percent of the time in rejecting a cracked connecting rod and

accurate 85 percent of the time in correctly "accepting" rods with no cracks. Historical data indicates that 15 percent of the rods have stress cracks. If the x-ray test result indicates that the rod should be rejectd, what is the probability that it is actually cracked?

2. In Problem 1, a complete "teardown" of a generator costs $75,000. One connecting rod costs $1500 up to the time that it is tested. Suppose that a new testing procedure is available which can improve the accuracy of accepting rods without cracks to 90 percent. How much, on a per test basis, is this procedure worth in comparison with the x-ray testing?

3. Norris Rubber Company manufactures rubber hose washers. These washers are manufactured on automatic equipment which is adjusted to produce outside diameters of 0.75 inches. Historically, the standard deviation of this diameter has been 0.01 inches. Each hour, a sample of 30 washers is selected and $\bar{X}$ is calculated and plotted on an $\bar{X}$ chart.

a. Based upon the above information, draw an $\bar{X}$ control chart for 95 percent confidence control limits.

b. For the first 5 hours the following average diameters were found: 0.7510, 0.7503, 0.7491, 0.7521, 0.7499. Was the process ever out of control?

4. Management of the Midtown Garment Outlet has decided that too many truckload lots of dresses have been accepted with too low an average quality. Midtown is a discount dress shop that sells "seconds" of famous brand merchandise. Midtown recognizes that "thirds" (not suitable for sale) often are mixed with the "seconds" merchandise, but lately too many items have been thirds. A sampling plan has been adopted with an AQL of 5 percent, with a 5 percent producer's risk and a LTPD of 15 percent with a 10 percent consumer's risk. What sample size and acceptance number of defectives should be used?

5. A local beverage bottler uses equipment to fill 12-ounce soft drink bottles. State regulations require that all bottles be filled to within ± 0.3 ounces of the 12-ounce nominal volume. The machine is adjusted to fill 12 ounces with a standard deviation of 0.3 ounces. If state inspectors check the filling machine daily using a sample size of five and shut down the machines if the average fill volume of the five bottles tested is less than 11.7 ounces or greater than 12.3 ounces, on what proportion of the days will the machine be stopped due simply to random fluctuation?

6. A fishing weight manufacturer produces ocean weights with a mean weight of 5.0 ounces and a standard deviation of 0.3 ounces. If a customer accepts the weights that weigh between 4.8 and 5.2 ounces as "5 ounce" weights, how many will the customer consider "defective" in a shipment of 1000? What limits would the manufacturer use for samples of size 10 and 2σ control limits?

7. The Tick & Tye Company, CPAs, is willing to accept a 10 percent chance of accepting a file of invoices as being properly paid when up to 5 percent were not. But they do not want to reject the file (and therefore have to audit the whole file) if the actual nonpayment rate is 1 percent or less. They are willing to accept a 5 percent chance of doing this. What sample size and acceptance value should be used?

Tools and Applications

8. Based upon the following data, prepare a $\bar{p}$ chart for the control of picking accuracy in a wholesale food warehouse.

Day	Number of Cases Picked	Number of Incorrect Picks
1	4700	38
2	5100	49
3	3800	27
4	4100	31
5	4500	42
6	5200	48

Plot 1, 2, and $3\sigma_p$ limits assuming that the sample size will be 100 cases.

9. Twenty samples of 100 were taken with the following number of defectives: 8,5,3,9,4,5,8,5,3,6,4, 3,5,6,2,5,0,3,4,2. Construct a 2σ p chart and determine if the process is in control.

10. Construct a p chart using 2σ limits based on the following results of 20 samples of size 400.

Sample Number	Number of Defects
1	2
2	0
3	8
4	5
5	8
6	4
7	4
8	2
9	9
10	2
11	3
12	0
13	5
14	6
15	7
16	1
17	5
18	8
19	2
20	1

16.14 CASE THE WESTERN HILLS DISPATCH

In April 1979 the Western Hills Dispatch was born. The objective of the newspaper was to provide an outlet for news, advertising, and community information for a rapidly growing section of a large midwestern city. The population of this western section had been growing at the rate of about 8 percent per year for the last five years. Current population is approximately 85,000. The dispatch brought together a good staff and immediately attracted a substantial readership. The current circulation now exceeds 22,000 homes. Mick Pates, editor of the Dispatch, bases the success of his newspaper on the accuracy and timeliness of his news coverage, his strong proactive editorial policy and the focus on local news with analysis of regional and national items as they impact the locality. Many others attribute the newspaper's success to Mr. Pate's own personal dedication, his ability to sell to advertisers, and his professional staff. He is widely recognized in the business as one of the best developers of newspaper talent in the business.

One of Pates' recent brainstorms has been his "Scientific Quality Control Program." He controls the quality of the type-setting output by actively monitoring the performance of three other weekly newspapers, which are distributed in adjoining communities, and basing his upper and lower error control limits on the results of his samples of these newspapers' quality.

Each Friday morning, as a paper is coming off the press, Mr. Pates randomly selects a hundred letters and counts the number of type-setting errors in the newsprint. The table below shows the results of the samples over the previous quarter.

Sample	Type-Setting Errors
1	9
2	11
3	0
4	13
5	1
6	2
7	4
8	4
9	10
10	1
11	4
12	3

QUESTIONS FOR DISCUSSION

1. What assumptions are necessary using the upper and lower control limits established by reviewing other weekly newspapers?
2. Suppose that the control limits established by reviewing other news weeklies are 0.08 and .035, respectively. Plot last quarter's data on this control chart.
3. Compare the upper and lower control limits above with the upper control limit and lower control limit calculated from the 12 samples presented in the Table.

16.15 REFERENCES AND BIBLIOGRAPHY

1. American Management Association, *Zero Defects: Doing It Right the First Time*, New York: AMA, 1965.
2. American Society for Quality Control, *Quality Motivation Workbook*, Milwaukee, Wis.: ASQC, 1967.
3. Armstrong, W. H., *Mechanical Inspection*, New York: McGraw-Hill, 1953.
4. Dodge, H. F. and H. G. Romig, *Sampling Inspection Tables*, New York: Wiley, 1959.
5. Duncan, A. J., *Quality Control and Industrial Statistics*, 4th ed., Homewood, Ill.: Irwin, 1974.
6. Grant, E. L. and R. S. Learenworth, *Statistical Quality Control*, 4th ed., New York: McGraw-Hill, 1974.
7. Hayes, G. E. and H. G. Romig, *Modern Quality Control*, Encino, Calif: Bruce, 1977.

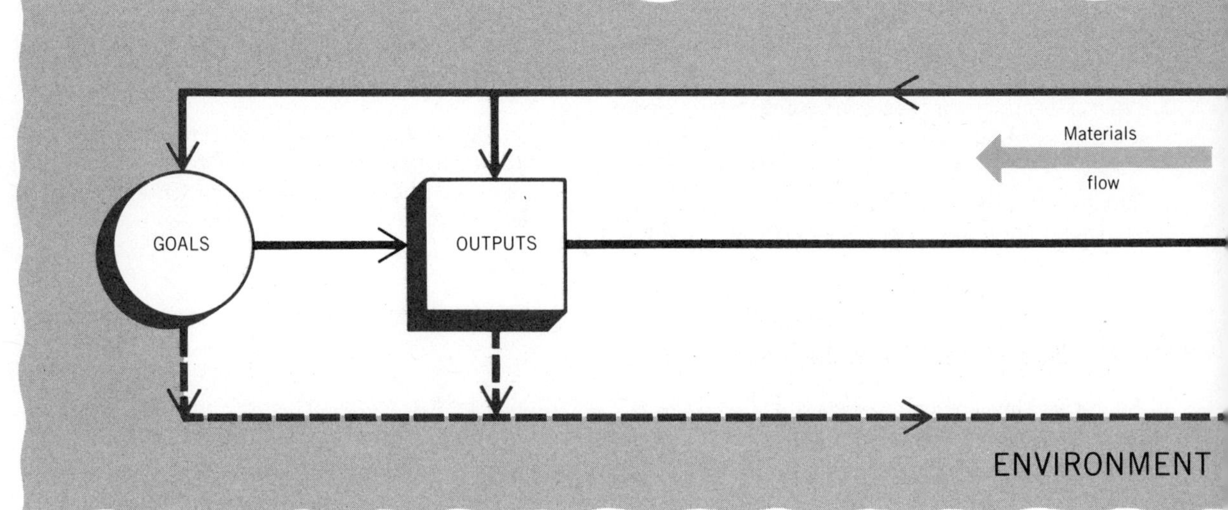

Chapter 17I

The Accounting Interface: Cost Control

CONCEPTS

17.1 Budgets and Budgeting
- Governmental Budgeting
- Types of Budgets
  - *The Operating Budget*
  - *The Cash Budget*
  - *The Capital Budget*
- Behavioral Implications of Budgets

17.2 Responsibility Accounting
- Responsibility Centers
  - *Cost Centers*
  - *Revenue Centers*
  - *Profit Centers*
  - *Investment Centers*
- Cost Classification for Responsibility Centers
  - *Controllable and Uncontrollable Costs*
  - *Direct and Indirect Costs*
- Reporting Responsibility Costs

17.3 Analyzing Performance and Reporting Results
- Materials Variances
  - *Orville's Bakery*
- Labor Variances

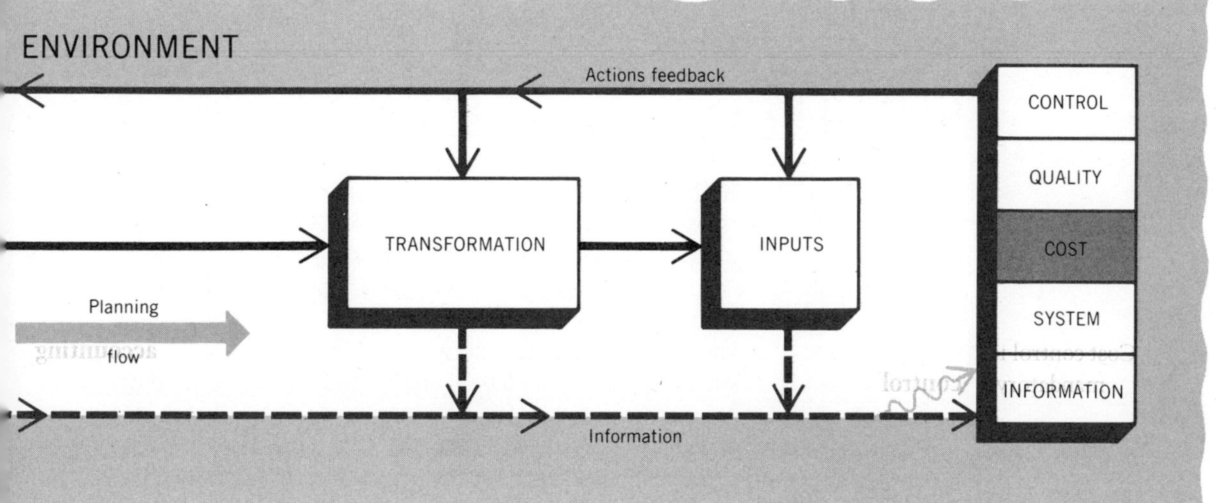

TOOL AND APPLICATIONS

LEARNING OBJECTIVES

By the completion of the *Concepts* portion of this chapter the student should

1. Understand the use of budgets, not only for control, but also for planning, communicating, and motivating.
2. Be familiar with the different types of budgets and know how they are constructed.
3. Appreciate the behavioral implications of budgets and the problems they can cause.
4. Know the different ways organizations can design responsibility centers and what their functions are.
5. Understand how costs are reported and what kinds of costs are considered controllable and what kinds uncontrollable.
6. Comprehend the variety of variances that can occur, how they are reported, and the need for being able to assign them somewhere.

CONCEPTS

Up to this point in our discussion of control we have focused attention on controlling the productive process itself in terms of flow rates, quality, feedback mechanisms, and so forth. Another aspect of operations that is just as important to control is the *cost* of producing the output. All organizations require good systems of cost control. While systems for inventory control, quality control, and so forth, are important to the operations of most organizations, cost control, and, more generally, **accounting control** (of costs, finances, profits, purchases, etc.) is mandatory. As we discussed earlier, no organization is free to spend (over the long term) more than it receives in return from its environment. To assure that it does not, and to assure that the returns received are adequate for the costs incurred, organizations make use of formal accounting control systems. The cost control system may well be the most important of the organizational control systems. Schedules can be optimized, inventory can be properly managed, quality can be appropriate, but if costs exceed revenues, or even approach revenues for an extended period, the organization's life is in jeopardy.

Cost control is mandatory.

In this chapter we consider the means by which operations costs are typically *controlled* rather than techniques for *reducing* costs (such as *value analysis* or *simplification* as discussed in Chapter 3I). The primary means by which organizations control their costs of operation are through budgets and responsibility centers. Hence, this chapter is directed toward these two topics, presented in terms of the overall accounting control system. In general, accounting control begins with organizational plans, both short- and long-term. These plans are translated into *budgets* which are quantitative statements (usually in dollars and other operational measures such as units of output, man-hours, tons of input, etc.) of the activity that the organization will undertake in the upcoming period of operations, the results it expects to achieve, and the resources it expects to consume in the process. Once operations, based upon the aforementioned budgets, begin to take place, the accounting system *collects* data regarding performance of the various divisions and segments of the organization, *analyzes* and *interprets* this data into meaningful information for management control, and *reports* this information to the appropriate levels of management so that proper control can be exercised.

Budgets for cost control.

The accounting control system is just one example of a control model such as the ones we discussed in Chapter 15. The budget is the standard against which actual results will be compared. A measurement system is necessary, and, in this instance, the accounting system is that measurement system. The accounting system often, although in less sophisticated systems not always, acts as the **comparator** as well. Actual results of operations are compared with the standard for performance, the budget, and, if significant differences exist, analysis of the causes are undertaken in an effort to locate and correct problems for operations in future periods.

Implementation via the accounting system.

Other functions of the accounting system.

Organizational accounting systems serve purposes beyond that of control. For example, various components of the system are concerned with measuring, recording, and reporting information for taxation purposes. Still others are primarily concerned with financing of the organization (i.e., its capital structure, amount of debts, common and preferred stock, etc.). In this chapter, we are concentrating on the portion of the accounting system that is devoted to planning and controlling the costs of operations.

17.1 BUDGETS AND BUDGETING

Four purposes of budgets.

Budgets are clearly a standard for performance within the organization, but they also serve other purposes.

1. In planning.
2. To communicate.
3. To motivate.
4. As a standard of performance.

Budgets for planning.

In planning an organization's activities for an upcoming period, the budgeting process, which results in the preparation of a formal set of budgets, provides a focal point for the planning effort. Budgets present a quantitative picture of the resources to be allocated to the various divisions of an organization. Because of this resource allocation dimension of the budget, most managers seek an active role in planning their activities and acquiring resources for the upcoming period. If the allocation of resources were completely separated from the process of planning, perhaps fewer managers would be so eager to become involved.

Budgets for communication.

An organization's plans, no matter how well formulated and supported by members of the organization, will not be carried out if they are not clearly understood. And, since plans are often complex, requiring the joint efforts of a large number of different departments and divisions in various geographic locations, communication and coordination are especially crucial. The budget communicates, in specific quantitative terms, the activities to be carried out, the resources available, and the timing of expenditures and expected returns. The budget specifies the amounts to be spent on materials, labor, consultant's fees, advertising, and so on, and also anticipates the receipt of various returns to the organization.

Budgets for motivation.

If the budgeting and control process is carried out in the proper atmosphere, the budget can be a powerful motivator of managers within the organization. The proper atmosphere is generally created when at least the following three factors exist.

- First, individual managers must recognize the overall goals of the organization and understand how their department's activities contribute to the accomplishment of those goals.
- Second, the manager must participate in the formulation of his or her own budget (rather than having the budget handed down from "on high") and agree (and believe) that resources are adequate to fulfill the tasks set out for the upcoming period.
- Third, the manager must be rewarded (or not rewarded) according to his or her success in achieving the agreed upon targets.

Budgets guarantee the uniformity of plans.

Consider the position of a machine shop superintendent in a large manufacturing facility. The budgeting process forces him or her to clearly delineate the expected production for the machine shop during the budget period. To prepare the budget he or she must plan the performance of the department. The specification of production levels, however, is based upon an overall organizational plan, and therefore the superintendent is reasonably assured that the personnel manager will have received and planned for the same activity level, and likewise the purchasing agent who must assure that raw material is available for machining. The same is true for all other production departments in the factory as well as other organizational units such as the marketing and accounting departments.

Governmental Budgeting

Tying the budget to goals via PPBS and ZBB.

Until recently, most governmental units and other not-for-profit organizations utilized what is known as "line-item" budgets. These are simply budgets developed by expenditure class (e.g., vehicle maintenance, office salaries, stationery, etc.) rather than by function or purpose of the expenditure. Both the planning programming budgeting system (**PPBS**) and zero based budgets (**ZBB**) are attempts to accomplish two objectives in not-for-profit budgeting.

First, these methods tie the budgeted expenditures to an objective or purpose so that budget approval and modification can be based upon the results desired rather than simply a type of expenditure. (It's always easier to delay construction of a structure than to lay off an employee!) Second, the budgets are not based upon historical budgets, but upon new justification for the function or purpose. Rather than granting blanket "across the board" budget increases, PPBS and ZBB require that each program be justified on its own continuing merits, rather than on previous merits or amounts expended.

Types of Budgets

The master budget.

The overall budget for an organization, which is most often referred to as the **master budget**, is made up of three distinct types of budgets (see Figure 17.1).

1. The operating budget.
2. The cash budget.
3. The capital budget.

Each of these three budgets and their preparation will be discussed in this section.

The operating budget.

A rolling budget for quarterly updating.

The **operating budget** provides a detailed picture of the revenues and expenses that are anticipated in the upcoming period of operations. Most companies prepare budgets once each year for the coming year. Planned revenues and expenses are usually estimated for each month of the coming period or for each quarter. Some companies, on the other hand, prepare what is known as a **rolling budget**. In a rolling budget the revenues and expenses are estimated every quarter for the upcoming four quarters.

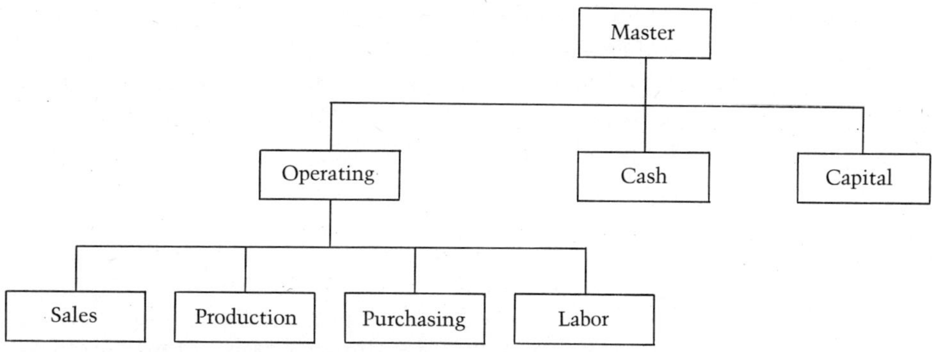

Figure 17.1. The various types of budgets.

Operating budget composed of subsidiary budgets.

Once the level of service provision and/or sales has been estimated for the period, the expense components of the operating budget can be prepared. Labor, materials, selling, and administrative expense budgets are prepared based upon the level of activity or resources required to meet the budgeted sales or service. Typically, the operating budget is further subdivided into several subsidiary (or detail) budgets which outline planned area activities in detail, such as

1. Sales budget.
2. Production budget.
3. Purchasing budget.
4. Labor budget.

Each of the last three subsidiary budgets is based upon the **sales budget**, which establishes the overall planned activity level for the period.

Review and negotiation before finalization.

A process of review and negotiation is usually undertaken after the "first round" of the operating budget development. Each manager prepares an operating budget and submits it to the next higher level of management for review and integration with other departmental and divisional budgets. Once this review has taken place, the manager and his or her superior meet to negotiate and finalize the operating budget.

Not too tight, nor too loose.

Negotiation is important if a budget is to serve as a motivating device and as a proper standard for performance. If the budget is too "tight" and not attainable, the manager preparing the budget will only feel frustrated by efforts to achieve the standard and eventually will give up trying. On the other hand, if the budget is too "loose" it will most often be met, but no real effort will have been expended. A budget that is tight but attainable provides a fair standard for performance measurement and also a motivator for improved performance.

After this negotiation process has been completed throughout the organization and a complete operating budget is prepared for the entire organization, it is submitted to top management for approval. Approval constitutes the granting of authority to act on the basis of the plans reflected in the budget and to make expenditures specified in the budget. The approved budget is communicated throughout the organization as the major guide to action in the upcoming period.

MRP as a basis for budget preparation.

You will note that the MRP system discussed in Chapter 13 provides a solid basis for the preparation of an operations budget. Because materials, equipment, and labor are scheduled in a MRP system, and since expenditures for these items can be directly tied to this scheduled use, the MRP and a sales forecast can combine to produce a very detailed operating budget.

The cash budget

The operating budget includes both revenues and expenses but does not consider the impact of these items on the flows of cash. Because organizations do not receive all revenues as cash inflows and do not expend cash for all expenses, a **cash budget** is necessary to coordinate the timing of cash inflows and outflows and to recognize and time the organization's needs for short-term borrowing. The cash budget is used to assure that the organization will have enough, but not too much, cash on hand to support operations throughout the year.

Again MRP serves as a basis for the cash budget. Timing of the use of material and labor can be directly tied to the timing of cash outflows needed to pay for these resources. In fact, it would even be possible to adopt the MRP philosophy in cash budgeting to produce a **CRP** (cash requirement plan).

The capital budget

In Chapter 10I we discussed the acquisition of major capital items and described the process of justifying the purchase of these productive assets as **capital budgeting**. The result of this process is the **capital budget**, which is simply a list of the acquisitions and projects that management intends to invest in during the operating period. Included in the list are the estimated costs of each investment and the timing of the investment.

Integrating the capital and operating budgets.

While the capital budget is prepared separately from the operating budget, the two must clearly be integrated. Plans for capital improvements such as additions to buildings and installations of new equipment, are usually disruptive to normal operations and, therefore, operations plans must reflect these interruptions. Additional overtime or subcontracting may be necessary in order to meet production schedules. Operating budgets prepared without consideration of the capital budget run the risk of underestimating costs or overestimating productive ability.

To illustrate the application of these three types of budgets, a worked out example is included in the *Tools and Applications* portion of this chapter.

Behavioral Implications of Budgets

The importance of commitment.

If all parties to the budgeting process, including superiors and subordinates, are not committed to the accomplishment of the plans it represents, the budget is likely to produce as many negative results as it does positive ones. The attitude with which the parties enter into the budgeting process, and the way in which the budget is viewed as a control tool contribute largely to success or failure in achieving the desired results from operations.

Need for flexibility.

The budget is a plan, but deviations from plans are commonplace, so changes during the operating period must be viewed in their proper perspective and not disallowed simply because "the budget does not call for that."

Similarly, if a budget is found to be unrealistic during the operating cycle, changes should be made to reflect the new information. A manager who will not allow budget modifications when real changes in environmental and/or operating conditions have come about is not only unlikely to meet the original plan, but will also promote ill will in his or her subordinates. For example, if a purchasing manager has purchased an inferior raw material than planned for in the budget, the production manager must recognize that deviations from the standard usage should be expected. The problem is not in production but in procurement, and to hold fast the previously determined use rates will only compound the problem by promoting unfair expectations to shop employees.

Participation for realism.

Also, a manager who feels that a budget unduly restricts his or her ability to react to new demands is likely to falsify budget reports and to "fatten up" his or her budget at any opportunity. This is often the response of middle managers in organizations that employ a **top down budgeting** approach in which middle and lower managers do not participate in the budget preparation process. Since they have no commitment to the budget, energy is wasted in complaining and explaining why the budget *cannot* be met.

17.2 RESPONSIBILITY ACCOUNTING

Responsibility accounting to minimize "passing the buck."

Control in organizations implies an ability to correct deficiencies once they are recognized. In an organization, each manager has one or more specific tasks to be accomplished and the budget for each manager's department identifies the resources at his or her disposal. **Responsibility accounting systems** simplify the process of recognizing significant deviations from budgeted operations and locating the root cause of the deviations.

Responsibility only for controllable costs.

A responsibility accounting system holds the manager responsible for only those costs under his or her control. For example, in a large organization, the cost of a wage increase for hourly employees is not charged to an operations manager's budget since that increase could not be controlled by him or her. Likewise, a product cost decrease that results from a wise purchasing decision for raw materials would not be credited to the operations manager responsible for manufacture of the product.

Responsibility Centers

Control through responsibility centers.

For control purposes, individual *responsibility centers* are established throughout the organization, often exactly following the organization chart. For example, the foreman in charge of welding and assembly would be responsible for controlling these budgets and would be accountable to the plant superintendent. A responsibility budget is prepared for each responsibility center and the manager of the responsibility center is given authority and responsibility for some portion of the organization's operations. An organization employing responsibility centers is usually known as a *decentralized* organization meaning that decision making in the organization is decentralized.

Four types of responsibility centers.

Responsibility centers are typically classified as being either cost centers, revenue centers, profit centers, or investment centers. The general philosophy of each of these categories of responsibility centers is the same; that is, individual managers are given authority to act and are held responsible for a certain defined section of the organization, and reporting to higher levels of management focuses upon performance of the responsibility center.

Cost centers

If an organizational unit is held responsible for the costs it incurs but not for the outputs it produces, this unit is called a **cost center**. A responsibility accounting system for such a center would collect and report cost data but would not attempt to measure and report on the outputs of the unit. Every cost center has some kind of output, but it is often difficult to measure, in monetary terms, the "value" of the output. For example, the personnel department clearly produces outputs, as discussed in Chapter 16I, but the monetary value of those outputs would be difficult to accurately measure. Therefore, personnel departments and many of the staff functions in these organizations are established as cost centers. Production operations, as well, are usually organized as cost centers since there is no formal revenue recognition by most production operations.

Revenue centers

If an organizational unit is held responsible for the revenue it generates, but not the costs incurred, the unit can be described as a **revenue center**. Revenue centers are somewhat rare; most units held responsible for revenue are also held responsible for costs. But, local sales offices for a large organization which have no control over the size of the staff, promotion, or advertising expenses would be considered revenue centers.

Profit centers

An organizational unit that is responsible for both revenues and costs is called a **profit center**. Profit centers facilitate the decentralized operations of a business organization. Each profit center is viewed as a small business entity; its reports (such as a profit center income statement) provide information that allows top management to compare divisional performance, control large operations more efficiently, and promote a degree of intracompany competition that often leads to improved performance.

Investment centers

In an **investment center** the manager is not only held responsible for the profits produced, but for the use of the assets at his or her disposal. This is essentially the furthest development of the responsibility center idea. The manager in charge of an investment center is almost in business for him or herself. She or he is held responsible for the return on the assets invested (ROI) in the investment center.

Investment center reporting provides management with information needed for resource allocation decisions, including expansion, reduction, and curtailment decisions. Not only are profits reported, but they are related to the resources required to generate those profits.

Cost Classification for Responsibility Centers

Controllable and uncontrollable costs

A cost is considered **controllable** by a responsibility center if

1. The cost is the responsibility of the manager.
2. The cost is significantly influenced by the actions of the manager.

Controllable, in our context, implies that it is both controllable by a responsibility center manager and controllable within an operating period. Costs such as overhead for administration are allocated to responsibility centers, but are not under their control and are therefore considered uncontrollable costs. Labor and materials costs, on the other hand, are considered controllable (even though the labor rate and the materials prices are relatively fixed) because a manager can exert a "significant influence" on the amounts used.

"Why can I sell it so cheap? I got no overhead!"

Direct and indirect costs

Direct costs of a department or responsibility center are those costs that are incurred by the center and are traceable to it. For example, the department foreman's salary is a direct cost of the department since it is both incurred by the department and is traceable to it. All controllable costs are direct costs, but all direct costs are not necessarily controllable. For example, the depreciation cost of a piece of equipment used solely by one responsibility center is a direct cost of that center, but it is not controllable by the operations manager if she or he does not have authority to acquire and dispose of equipment.

Reporting Responsibility Costs: Krypton Products Co.

Consider the Krypton Products Company which produces two high strength products, metal lawn chairs and ornamental railings. The company is organized into three producing cost centers and two service cost centers as follows:

Producing

1. Metal forming.
2. Welding.
3. Painting.

Service

1. Engineering and estimating.
2. Administration.

Each month the full costs of each product are reported to S. Mann, the company president, in a form similar to that shown in Table 17.1. Along with this **Full Cost Report** is a Responsibility Cost Report, illustrated in Table 17.2, which classifies the same costs reported in the Full Cost Report, but by cost center rather than by product. This information can be compared with the budget information for each cost center and for each product in order to determine the controls needed each month.

Neither of the reports by itself, is sufficient for proper management control.

TABLE 17.1 FULL COST REPORT

		Lawn Chairs	Ornamental Railings	Total
Costs	Volume (Units)	360	1820 ft	
Direct material		$15,200	$21,300	$36,500
Direct labor		7,650	8,930	16,580
Factory overhead		3,100	2,800	5,900
Service costs		6,200	3,800	10,000
Total costs		$32,150	$36,830	$68,980
Cost per unit produced		$89.30	$20.23	

TABLE 17.2 RESPONSIBILITY CENTER COST REPORT

Costs	Metal Forming	Welding	Painting	Engineering and Estimating	Administration
Direct material	$28,500	$2,200	$5,800	$ 0	$ 0
Direct labor	4,200	9,100	3,280	0	0
Indirect labor	300	500	800	1,800	2,600
Supplies	100	900	300	900	1,200
Supervision	1,200	800	600	400	1,700
Other costs	150	150	100	600	800
Total costs	$34,450	$13,650	$10,880	$3,700	$6,300

Without the Full Cost Report, management would not be able to control product costs and without the Responsibility Cost Report could not identify and correct deviations from cost center budgets.

As you can see, the total cost of producing both lawn chairs and ornamental railings ($68,980) reported in the Full Cost Report is accounted for in the Responsibility Cost Report. The Engineering and Estimating Department incurred $3700 of the service cost of $10,000 while the administration responsibility center incurred $6300 of the cost. The $5900 of factory overhead shown in the Full Cost Report was incurred by the three production departments for indirect labor, supplies, supervision, and other costs. Direct labor and material costs were only incurred by the producing departments.

If the organization used only the Full Cost Report in its manufacturing control efforts, the location of the control problem could seldom be easily recognized. For example, an increase in lawn chair unit cost from $89.30 to $93.50 could be caused by increases in cost of material, labor, supplies, supervision, or other costs for any of the three production departments or two service departments. The Responsibility Center Cost Report pinpoints causes of cost increase so that management can take any necessary corrective action needed within a segment of the operations system.

The operations manager uses this information, primarily the Responsibility Cost Report, to determine the areas most in need of improvement within his or her operations. Once each cost area is delineated within the report, deviations from budgets can easily be detected.

The concept of flexible budgeting is also useful in reporting operations performance. Reports based upon the budget, which would have been developed had the exact output been known in advance, are known as flexible budget reports. For example, suppose the operations manager expects to paint 400 lawn chairs this month. In fact, only 280 chairs are painted, but all the budgeted labor is used. A flexible budget would indicate that more labor was consumed than should have been for the output produced, while a standard responsibility center report would show that exactly the amount of labor budgeted was used.

17.3 ANALYZING PERFORMANCE AND REPORTING RESULTS

Variance reporting for control.

One of the most widely used feedback control systems in organizations is the **standard cost variance reporting system**. A standard is a performance expectation, that is, an anticipated per unit cost for items to be produced or for activity to be performed in an upcoming budget period. Standard cost variance analysis fits the traditional feedback control model as shown in Figure 17.2. Standards are determined through engineering estimates or through analysis of past performance and are established as the cost targets to be aimed for in the upcoming operating cycle. These standards are communicated to the operating system, which, as it operates, produces an "actual" cost per unit. This actual cost is monitored by some formal data collection process (part of the organization's cost accounting system) and compared with the cost standard. Feedback information is provided to a manager who can exert any necessary control if the difference between standard and actual (called a *variance*) is considered to be significant.

Cost standards for comparison.

Quantity and price variances.

Variances from a standard are divided into **quantity** or **usage variances** and **price** or **rate variances** (see Figure 17.3). The quantity or usage standard expresses the expected amount of input required for a given amount of output. The price or rate standard expresses the expected cost of the input, typically for a given amount (such as one unit). Quantity and price variances are computed for materials and labor, and, when these variances are significant, management must identify (or at least attempt to identify) an **assignable cause** for the variance. That is, the manager responsible for the control of the cost element that is at variance with the standard must study the operational process to determine why the variance occurred. This is so the proper remedy can be used to keep the variance from occurring in the next period. A correc-

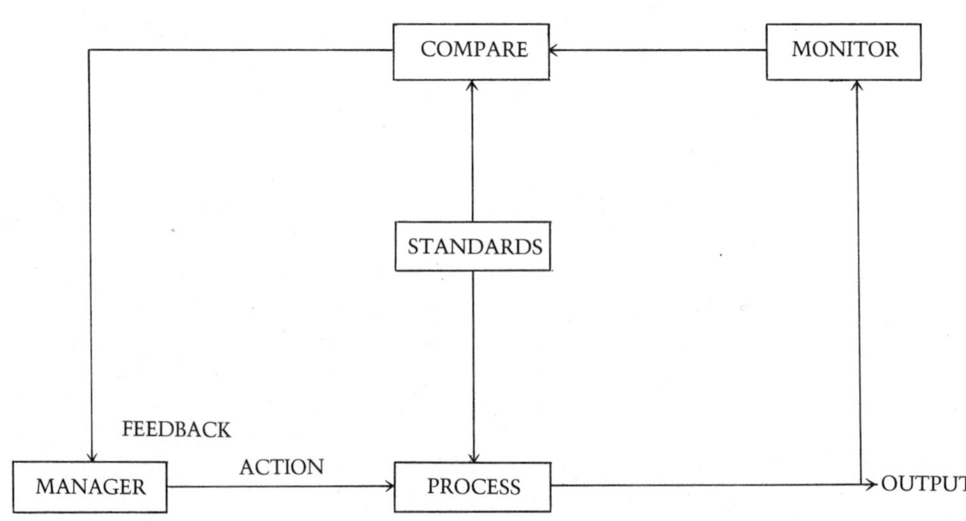

Figure 17.2. Standard cost control system.

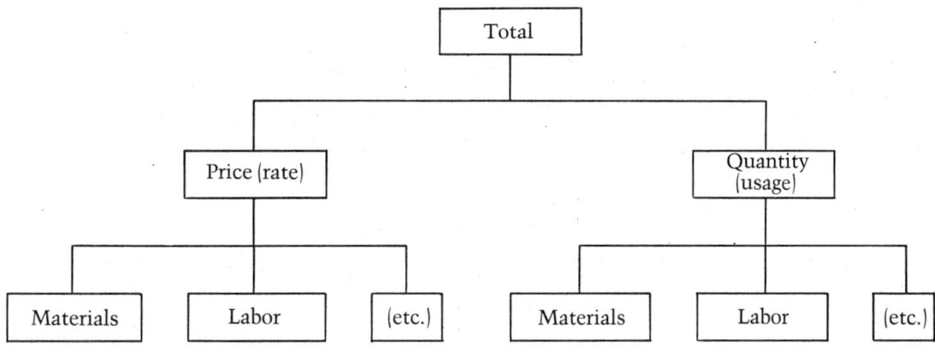

Figure 17.3. The types of variances.

tive action is called for if some inefficiency or change in the prescribed process caused the variance.

Favorable and unfavorable variances.

Variances can be both favorable and unfavorable. A significant **favorable variance** (for example, that which might have resulted from getting a large quantity discount on material) will usually not require a corrective action. But, a change in the standard itself may be necessary if an underlying condition has changed which obsoletes the current standard and will therefore continuously result in a large favorable variance.

The same is true for an unfavorable variance. An electric utility that has used a $10 per ton coal price as standard must change the standard in light of a $30 to 35 per ton price. There is no sense in planning a continued unfavorable variance.

Materials Variances

Whenever the actual price paid and the standard price of an item differ, or the actual usage and the standard usage of that item differ, a variance occurs. **Materials variances** used for control in operations are

1. The *materials price variance,* which measures the total difference between the cost of items purchased and the standard cost for the amount acquired.
2. The *materials quantity variance,* which measures the total difference between the quantity of materials used for a given output and the quantity which *should* have been used for that output.

The materials price variance is computed as follows:

Materials price variance = actual quantity of material *purchased* (units) × (actual price/unit − standard price/unit)

The materials quantity variance is computed as follows:

Materials quantity variance = standard price/unit × (actual quantity of material used − standard quantity of material used)

Materials quantity variance, the responsibility of operations.

The materials price variance is the responsibility of the purchasing agent and is therefore computed on the basis of the number of units *purchased* during the period rather than the number of units *used.* Using purchases as the basis for the computation, any variance is identified in a timely fashion so that corrective action, if necessary, can be taken. The materials quantity variance is the responsibility of the operations manager and, therefore, is computed on the basis of the number of units actually used in production of the organization's output for the period. Consider the following example.

Orville's Bakery

Orville's Bakery produces whole wheat bread. Whole wheat flour is the major ingredient in the bread, the standard cost of which is \$0.15 per pound. The standard quantity for a loaf of whole wheat bread is 0.8 pounds. During March of 1980, Orville purchased 45,000 pounds of flour at a total cost of \$7020 and used 40,000 pounds of the flour in the production of 51,000 loaves of bread. The materials variances are computed as follows.

$$\begin{aligned}\text{Materials price variance} &= 45{,}000 \text{ lb} \times (\$0.156 - \$0.15)\\ &= 45{,}000 \times \$0.006\\ &= \$270\end{aligned}$$

The \$0.156 actual cost per unit is calculated as \$7020 total cost of flour purchased divided by 45,000 pounds.

$$\begin{aligned}\text{Materials quantity variance} &= \$0.15/\text{unit} \times (40{,}000 \text{ lb} - 40{,}800 \text{ lb})\\ &= \$0.15 \times (-800)\\ &= -\$120\end{aligned}$$

(The 40,800 pounds is computed as 51,000 loaves × 0.8 pounds per loaf.)

The materials price variance is said to be an *unfavorable* variance since the purchase price of the 45,000 pounds of whole wheat flour was \$270 *greater* than the standard cost for 45,000 pounds. The materials quantity variance is said to be *favorable* since the standard cost of the flour used is *less* than the amount that would be allowed for the production of 51,000 loaves of bread. The overall variance for the month of March is \$150, unfavorable; that is, \$270, unfavorable plus \$120, favorable.

Tradeoffs between variances.

Materials variances can be caused by external factors such as changes in price for an item or increases or decreases in quantity of the material. Thus, a thorough investigation of the variance should be undertaken before responsibility for the variance is assigned. Often, materials variances are "traded." That is, a purchasing agent may be able to buy a material which, even though it costs more than the standard (resulting in an unfavorable price variance), works better in production and therefore results in a signficant reduction in use (a favorable quantity variance). As long as the overall variance result is favorable, this decision to trade variances is optimum for the organization as a whole. But, the tradeoff must be explicit or the purchasing agent will be burdened with an unfavorable variance to explain while the production superintendent receives a favorable variance through no efforts of his or her own.

Labor Variances

Unlike material, labor cannot be stored in inventory from period to period. Therefore, both **labor variances** are computed on the basis of hours used since hours used and hours purchased will always be the same. The two labor variances used to control the use of labor in operations are

1. The *labor rate variance* which measures the total difference between the wages paid and the standard wage for a given number of hours.
2. The *labor use variance* which measures the total difference between the hours used and the hours which should have been used for the output produced.

The labor rate variance is computed as follows:

Labor rate variance = actual hours of labor used × (actual wage rate/hr − standard wage rate/hr)

The labor use variance is computed as

Labor use variance = standard wage rate/hr × (actual hours of labor used − standard hours of labor used)

Labor variance the responsibility of personnel and operations.

The labor rate variance may be the responsibility of a personnel manager, whose responsibility it is to hire the proper skill levels at wage rates competitive with prevailing rates in the community. It can also be the responsibility of the operations manager (who is also responsible for the use variance) since it is his or her responsibility to assign workers to jobs requiring their requisite skills (and not higher or lower rate skills) and to train and supervise the workers to maximize the efficiency of operations.

Health care insurance

A local office of a major health insurance carrier has been experimenting with the development of labor standards for certain common office surgical procedures (generally referred to as ambulatory surgery). For one procedure the following standards have been established.

Standard hours of input/procedure = 1.3
Standard cost/hr of input = $19.60

This standard is an overall standard for the procedure. Medical personnel of several different wage rates are involved with the operation (included are physicians, physicians' assistants, registered nurses, and nurse anesthetists), but the actual amounts of contact time of each individual varies depending upon the contact time of the others. Thus, an overall standard based on total hours and an expected overall wage rate has been developed.

During the past month, 42 such procedures have been performed requiring, in total,

18 hr of physician time at $41/hr

20 hr of registered nurse time at $8/hr

13 hr of nurse anesthetists time at $11/hr

5 hr of physicians' assistant time at $6.50/hr

Total hours worked equalled 56 and total cost for these hours was $1073.50.

The labor variance is computed as follows:

$$\begin{aligned}\text{Labor rate variance} &= 56 \text{ hr} \times [\$19.17 \text{ (actual average)} - \$19.60] \\ &= 56 \times (-.43) \\ &= -\$24.08\end{aligned}$$

The $19.17 actual average rate per hour is calculated as $1073.50 divided by 56 hours.

$$\begin{aligned}\text{Labor use variance} &= \$19.60/\text{hr} \text{ (56 hr} - 54.6 \text{ hr)} \\ &= \$19.60 \times 1.4 \\ &= \$27.44\end{aligned}$$

The standard hours used is calculated as 42 procedures times 1.3 hours per procedure.

The overall labor variance for the month is $3.36, an unfavorable variance. It is made up of a favorable rate variance of $24.08 and an unfavorable use variance of $27.44.

The last step is now the reporting of these variances for the proper follow-up. In some cases, specific action will be necessary to ensure that excessive variances of the same sort do not recur. In other cases, the variances are within reason and follow-up is unnecessary. One method of determining whether or not a variance is excessive is to use the control chart discussed in Chapter 15. Upper and lower control limits can be established and only variances lying outside these limits are followed up.

Control charts for identifying significant deviations:

Whether or not follow-up is required for a particular variance, the operations manager is well advised to monitor variance reports to recognize trends and recurring variances. While immediate scheduling, inventory control, or other problems appear to be more important at the time than a "history" of last period's operations, it is this historical view that senior managers with the organization are seeing and upon which many of their decisions will be based.

Searching for an assignable cause is sometimes like looking for a needle in a haystack. But often the causes are straightforward. New employees are being trained and are not yet far enough along the learning curve. Material quality has reduced and parts now require much rework. A machine is breaking down more often than usual. Output has increased requiring the use of more overtime. All of these and many more are the first "suspects" looked to by operations managers when variances arise.

This completes our discussion of operations-related accounting concepts. Next we consider an extended example of the budgeting process we discussed earlier.

TOOLS AND APPLICATIONS

17.4 THE BUDGETING PROCESS: PEEK-A-VIEW WINDOW CO.

To illustrate the various types of budgets discussed earlier, consider the Peek-A-View Window Company (PAV). PAV manufactures three standard-size aluminum storm windows and markets these insulating windows through retail outlets in the Northeast and Midwest states. PAV's storm window sales in the first three months of 1978 and expected sales in 1979 for the three different storm window sizes are shown in Table 17.3. These estimates are based primarily upon management judgment as the market has expanded rapidly after several severe winters and with increases in energy prices.

Sales Budget

The sales budget in units is converted to a sales budget in dollars by multiplying the expected sales price for each segment times the number expected to be sold. The sales budget in dollars for the first three months of 1978 is shown in Table 17.4. Fifty percent of all sales are made on credit and 50 percent for cash. The credit sales are collected in the following month. The balance of accounts receivable on December 31, 1978 (which will be collected in January of 1979) is $22,500.

All three of the storm window models use the same materials, but in different amounts. The materials requirements for each of the three windows are shown in Table 17.5. The cost of the three materials is

Aluminum frame = $0.80/ft
Gasket material = $0.12/ft
Plate glass = $1.10/sq ft

All of PAV's purchases are on a cash basis.

TABLE 17.3 SALES (1978) AND SALES BUDGET (1979) (IN UNITS)

Month \ Size	Large 1978	Large 1979	Medium 1978	Medium 1979	Small 1978	Small 1979
Jan	4,200	5,700	9,200	9,800	12,500	13,600
Feb	4,600	5,800	9,300	10,100	12,800	14,100
Mar	5,000	6,300	9,500	10,300	13,100	14,500

TABLE 17.4 SALES BUDGET ($) FOR FIRST QUARTER OF 1979

Month \ Size	Large at $29.50	Medium at $26.00	Small at $22.50	Total
Jan	$150,450	$254,800	$306,000	$560,800
Feb	171,100	262,600	317,250	750,950
Mar	185,850	267,800	326,250	779,990

Labor cost requirements for the three windows are the same. Each window requires about 0.2 hours of assembly time and the current labor rate is $7.50 per hour. PAV wants to maintain an inventory equal to 10 percent of the current month's expected sales just in case demand exceeds the expected sales. The ending inventory of the three size windows in December 1978 is large 460, medium 920, and small 1200.

Production Budget

The production budget is derived from the sales budget and from management's desires for inventory levels. Each period the number of units to be produced can be computed as follows:

Units to be produced = planned sales + desired ending inventory level − beginning inventory level

Table 17.6 illustrates the computation of the production budget (units) for the first three months of 1979.

Information derived from this budget is important to the operations manager. For example, production must increase by 14 percent [i.e., (5870 − 5150)/5150] between January and February for large windows alone. Likewise, there are increases in medium and small window production between each of the months. The operations manager must determine the best method for meeting these requirements. Should production be subcontracted to an outside vendor? Is capacity available to increase production by 14 percent in one month? Are skilled laborers available? Would it be better to change the desired ending inventory policy and allow inventory to fluctuate while production is leveled? Discussion in previous chapters should aid the manager in solving these problems, but the production budget is the organizational device that brings these questions to the operations manager's attention.

TABLE 17.5 MATERIALS REQUIREMENTS FOR PAV'S STORM WINDOWS

Material \ Size	Large	Medium	Small
Aluminum frame	14 ft	11 ft	9 ft
Gasket	14 ft	11 ft	9 ft
Plate glass	10 sq ft	7.5 sq ft	5 sq ft

TABLE 17.6 UNIT PRODUCTION BUDGET

	January			February			March		
	Large	Medium	Small	Large	Medium	Small	Large	Medium	Small
Planned sales	5,100	9,800	13,600	5,800	10,100	14,100	6,300	10,300	14,500
+ Desired ending inventory	510	980	1,360	580	1,010	1,410	630	1,030	1,450
− Beginning inventory	460	920	1,200	510	980	1,360	580	1,010	1,410
To be produced	5,150	9,860	13,760	5,870	10,130	14,150	6,350	10,320	14,540

Purchases Budget

The purchases budget is derived from the production budget and from management's desires regarding the ending inventory levels of raw materials. PAV maintains a small raw material inventory and desires to keep the balances constant throughout the year. Monthly purchases are computed as

$$\text{Purchases} = \text{planned production} \times \text{raw material requirements/unit} + \text{desired ending inventory} - \text{beginning inventory}$$

Since PAV is going to keep the beginning and ending inventory levels constant, the last two terms of the above expression cancel out. Therefore

$$\text{Purchases} = \text{planned production} \times \text{raw material requirements/unit}$$

For example, to compute the required number of linear feet of gasket material needed for February, PAV must calculate the necessary gasket material for each of the three window sizes as follows.

$$5{,}870 \times 14 = 82{,}180$$
$$10{,}130 \times 11 = 111{,}430$$
$$14{,}150 \times 9 = 127{,}350$$

Sum these three figures to get 320,960 linear feet. Table 17.7 presents the purchases budget in units and dollars for the three months.

Again, the purchases budget provides information to the purchasing agent regarding both required amounts of materials and the timing of need of these materials. On this basis the purchasing agent can schedule delivery of materials and negotiate for quantity discounts for placing a blanket order. The purchasing budget provides coordination between the use of materials in production and the ordering and receipt of materials as controlled by the purchasing function.

Labor Budget

The labor budget, shown in Table 17.8, is developed from the production budget. Since labor cannot be inventoried, the labor consumed in each month is based exactly

TABLE 17.7 PURCHASES BUDGET (UNITS/$)

	January	February	March
Aluminum Frame			
Large	72,100/$57,680	82,180/$65,744	88,900/$71,120
Medium	108,460/$86,768	111,430/$89,144	113,520/$90,816
Small	123,840/$99,072	127,350/$101,880	130,860/$104,688
Totals	304,400/$243,520	320,960/$256,768	333,280/$266,642
Gasket			
Large	72,100/$8,652	82,180/$9,861.60	88,900/$10,668
Medium	108,460/$13,015.20	111,430/$13,371.60	113,520/$13,622.40
Small	123,840/$14,860.80	127,350/$15,282	130,860/$15,703.20
Totals	304,400/$36,528	320,960/$38,515.20	333,280/$39,993.60
Plate Glass			
Large	51,500/$56,650	58,700/$64,570	63,500/$69,850
Medium	73,950/$81,345	75,975/$83,572.50	77,400/$85,140
Small	68,800/$75,680	70,750/$77,825	72,700/$79,970
Totals	194,250/$213,675	205,425/$225,967.50	213,600/$234,960
Total purchases ($)	$493,723	$521,250.70	$541,577.60

on the units produced in that period. Each window, irrespective of size, requires 0.2 hours of assembly time at $7.50 per hour.

January's labor cost will thus be

$$(5150 + 9860 + 13760) \text{ windows} \times 0.2 \text{ hr/window} \times \$7.50/\text{hr}$$
$$= 28770 \times 0.2 \times 7.50$$
$$= \$43,155$$

Based upon the labor budget, the operation's manager can see that 276 extra hours of assembly labor will be needed between January and February. This is approximately one and three-quarters employees. The personnel department needs this information to recruit skilled assembly workers and the operation manager must schedule appropriate training and build expected "learning curve" time into his or her production schedule. Perhaps the labor budget should be modified to allow for overtime to cover for the lower production rates that newer employees are likely to have.

Considering the learning curve.

TABLE 17.8 LABOR BUDGET

	January	February	March
Total windows	$28,770	$30,150	$31,210
Assembly hours	5,754	6,030	6,242
Assembly cost	$43,155	$45,225	$46,815

An MRP system could be used by PAV as a basis for the other budgets. In order to assure that monthly output of each of the storm windows can be attained on time, the MRP can explode labor, equipment, and materials requirements into the preceding months. The cash budget will then flow directly from these other budgets.

Cash Budget

Each of the schedules from the operating budget contribute data to the cash budget. Cash sales for each month and the previous month's credit sales increase cash while each month's labor costs and materials purchases decrease cash. Table 17.9 shows the cash budget for the first three months of the year.

Investing idle cash.

From the information in PAV's cash budget it is clear that some investment decisions will have to be made regarding the use of idle cash. The cash balance should be adequate to cover operations and idle cash should be invested to earn a return. Likewise, the cash budget also serves as a borrowing plan in situations where cash disbursements for the month exceed the beginning cash balance plus receipts for the month. While these decisions are typically outside the reach of the operations manager, it is clear that operations requirements and decisions will affect the cash budget. For example, should a decision be made to level production or to order material in one large lot, the cash position will be substantially modified.

17.5 SUMMARY

In this chapter we have discussed the concepts and methods of accounting and cost control. Budgets are divided into three major types, the operating budget, the cash budget, and the capital budget. From operating and sales budgets come the production

TABLE 17.9 CASH FLOW SCHEDULE

	January		February		March	
Beginning cash balance		$22,500		$31,522		$120,921.30
Cash receipts						
Cash sales	$280,400		$375,475		$389,950	
Previous month's credit sales	265,500		280,400		375,475	
Total receipts	$545,900		$655,875		$765,425	
Cash disbursements						
Labor costs	43,155		45,225		46,815	
Purchases	493,723		521,250.70		541,577.60	
Total cash disbursements	$536,878		$566,475.70		$588,392.60	
Net cash flow		9,022		89,399.30		177,032.40
Ending cash balance		$31,522		$120,921.30		$297,953.70

budget, the purchases budget, and the labor budget. These can all be related to the information available in a materials requirements plan.

While budgets appear to be rather mundane topics, they do present several behavioral implications. People are directly affected by budgets and the standards used in developing them. Budgets that are too tight or too loose will typically prove to be of more harm than value.

Responsibility center accounting places cost control directly upon the manager responsible for incurring costs. Whether organized as cost centers or profit centers, the basic notion is the same: provide incentive for accomplishment and measure performance against predetermined budgets or standards.

Costs can be classified in various ways, among them direct versus indirect and controllable versus uncontrollable. Cost standards are performance expectations and performance against these expectations can be controlled using a variance reporting system. In this chapter we have discussed rate and usage variances for both materials and labor.

17.6 KEY TERMS

Concepts

accounting control (p. 570)
comparator (p. 570)
master budget (p. 572)
operating budget (p. 572)
cash budget (p. 574)
capital budget (p. 574)
rolling budget (p. 572)
PPBS (p. 572)
ZBB (p. 572)
sales budget (p. 573)
production budget (p. 573)
purchasing budget (p. 573)
labor budget (p. 573)
CRP (p. 574)
capital budgeting (p. 574)
"top down" budgeting (p. 575)
responsibility accounting (p. 575)
cost center (p. 576)
revenue center (p. 576)
profit center (p. 576)
investment center (p. 577)
controllable costs (p. 577)
direct costs (p. 578)
full cost report (p. 578)
standard cost variance report (p. 580)
quantity variances (p. 580)
usage variances (p. 580)
price variance (p. 580)
rate variance (p. 580)
assignable cause (p. 580)
materials variance (p. 581)
favorable variance (p. 581)
labor variance (p. 583)

17.8 DISCUSSION QUESTIONS

Concepts

1. The function of the accounting system is to control costs. (p. 570)
   a. True b. False
2. One of the purposes of a budget is to communicate the company plans to the staff. (p. 571)
   a. True b. False
3. The rolling budget is also known as the master budget. (p. 572)
   a. True b. False
4. The purpose of ZBB is to tie resource allocations to objectives. (p. 572)
   a. True b. False

5. The sales budget is part of the operating budget. (p. 573)
   a. True b. False
6. Most detail budgets are based on the sales budget. (p. 573)
   a. True b. False
7. The purpose of budget negotiations is to determine a reasonable, attainable budget. (p. 573)
   a. True b. False
8. MRP could serve as a good budgeting model. (p. 574)
   a. True b. False
9. Deviations from budgets should be investigated and corrected. (p. 575)
   a. True b. False
10. Top down budgeting encourages falsifying budget reports. (p. 575)
   a. True b. False
11. The aim of responsibility centers is to control costs. (p. 575)
   a. True b. False
12. To be considered "controllable" a cost must be a manager's responsibility. (p. 577)
   a. True b. False
13. All controllable costs are direct costs. (p. 578)
   a. True b. False
14. Either a full cost report or a responsibility center cost report is needed to control costs. (p. 578)
   a. True b. False
15. Quantity variances are concerned with materials usage. (p. 580)
   a. True b. False
16. A materials price variance is purchasing's problem (p. 582)
   a. True b. False

17.7 REVIEW TEST

1. The production manager is asked to produce a labor and materials budget each quarter of the year. He uses last quarter's sales volume to estimate his needs in the next quarter. What problems may arise from this procedure?
2. How is the cash budget used in relationships with banks and other lending institutions?
3. Responsibility cost reporting systems provide for better organizational control. Explain how.
4. How is an investment center more decentralized than a profit center?
5. Many new businesses fail within the first year of their existence due to cash budget problems. Why do you think this happens so frequently?
6. How does responsibility accounting affect a company's promotion policies?
7. What type of cost report should a company prepare for its annual report to stockholders?
8. When does the materials price and materials quantity variance for a given period sum to the total variance for the period?
9. What type, if any, of labor cost variances are due to incentive-based pay systems?
10. What type of responsibility center would be used to describe dealers for state lottery tickets?
11. How can a multinational firm prepare budgets for its foreign plants when the exchange rate on currencies and inflation rates in foreign countries are volatile?

17.9 PROBLEMS

Concepts

1. The Sugg Rug Company purchases wool each month to meet production needs in the next month. If this month's purchases are planned to be $30,000 and if beginning inventory is $8000 and desired ending inventory is $5000, how many units are planned for production if each rug requires $40 worth of wool?

2. Grippo's management has always believed in extremely tight budgets. Typically, after managers plan next period's operations and prepare their budgets, the controller's budget analysts "trim" 15 percent from each budget. What behavioral problems do you believe will result from such a policy?
3. Gina's Pizza used 25 pounds of pepperoni this month in the production of 300 frozen pizzas. The pepperoni standard calls for 0.06 pounds at $2.10 per pound. Gina paid $50 for the 25 pounds of pepperoni used. Compute the materials price and usage variances and label them as favorable or unfavorable.
4. Blue Grass Woodcrafts, Inc. produces wooden bases for awards and trophies. The controller and the president are debating about some recent labor variances. During the past month 3000 bases were produced at a labor cost of $1600 and a materials cost of $3600. The standards for the bases are

   Labor = 0.2 hr at $5/hr
   Materials = 1 board ft at $0.70/board ft

   The controller argues that the variances should be analyzed for an "assignable" cause, but the president counters that the overall variance is only $100 and therefore not worth fussing over. With whom do you agree? Why?

Tools and Applications

5. Bross Gear Works has prepared the following monthly sales budget for its major product, a plastic speedometer gear used in a major motorcycle line. Bross receives payment for gears as follows:
   a. One-third in month following sale.
   b. One-half in second month after sale.
   c. One-sixth in third month after sale.

   Variable costs are 60 percent of sales and are paid one-half in month of sale and one-half in month following sale. Fixed costs are $24,000 per year.

	April	May	June
Sales	$130,000	$180,000	$260,000

   Bross has a $100,000 line of credit at the bank, but must borrow in $10,000 increments and can repay as cash is available, in $5000 increments. Prepare the cash budget for Bross noting any required borrowing or lending. (Assume that Bross began the quarter with a $20,000 cash balance and *no* receivables.)
6. Hide, Inc. is a producer of ladies leather jackets. Because of a beef cattle farm strike, the maker of available hides is limited to 300 per month over the next three months. Hide, Inc. uses 1.4 hides per jacket at an average cost of $20 per hide, and requires 12 direct labor hours at $4.20 per hour. Suppose the demand forecast for each of the next three months is 150 jackets, 200 jackets, and 250 jackets, respectively. Prepare material and direct labor budgets as well as a "pro forma" (predicted) income statement presuming selling price is $100 per jacket.
7. Chadwick Manufacturing Co. currently has 3000 gallons of red enamel in finished goods inventory. Predicted sales for June and July are 10,000 and 12,000 gallons, respectively. Chadwick wants to have 5000 gallons on hand at the end of June and 4000 gallons on hand at the end of July. One gallon of paint requires 0.2 ounces of pigment at a cost of $0.80 per ounce. Prepare a pigment materials budget in dollars and ounces for June and July.

17.10 CASE HARRY "HATCHET" FELD

Harry Feld was hired in 1975 as the plant manager for the Indianapolis plant of a large plastics manufacturing firm. The firm specializes in the production of parts for automotive interiors. Mr. Feld had just arrived from a similar position with an automobile manufacturing firm. In that position he had developed a reputation as a cost cutter.

Feld went to work on a vigorous cost cutting program for the Indianapolis plant. His 1976 budget called for a 12 percent reduction in overhead costs, while production would be comparable with 1975. In fact, after adjusting for the slight production increase, Feld's results from 1976 indicated an approximate 24 percent reduction in overhead.

Division management for the firm was elated over

Feld's performance. Feld was given a substantial increase in salary and was personally commended by the president of the firm. During 1977, a 10 percent budget decrease was proposed, the third shift maintenance crew was cut altogether and several other indirect labor and overhead items were curtailed significantly. Feld came very close to meeting his 10 percent reduction during the second year. His actual performance showed an 8½ percent decrease in overhead. One noticeable problem was the overtime allocated to emergency repair on equipment.

While the 1978 budget was being prepared, Feld ran into a major snag in his budgeting philosophy. An automotive manufacturer, which was the major customer for Feld's plant, was finally "down-sizing" its automotive line. The result of this "down-sizing" effort was a complete change in the plastic products to be produced by Feld's plant. This called for a complete overhaul of all the assembly and production facilities. The equipment had been so poorly maintained over the last two years that it was difficult to keep one line producing all of the time. During the changeover, when one line was dedicated to producing "emergency orders" for the customer, there was significant downtime and overtime resulting in more machine failure. Since alternate lines were being changed over, Feld had no choice but to authorize the overtime.

To make matters even worse, the industrial engineering staff had been reduced to such a level that staff had to be borrowed from the Chicago and Atlanta plants to assist in redesigning the facility and laying out the new production lines. The working relationships between this "makeup" team of industrial and manufacturing engineers was not particularly good. Morale was a constant problem during the changeover and there were many failures, missed deadlines, and numerous excuses.

When the changeovers were finally complete production of the new parts was already six weeks behind schedule. Feld authorized Saturday and Sunday work, pushing his overtime costs even higher, and eventually resulting in the breakdown of three major pieces of equipment. Production schedules for three dashboard components and two different armrest brackets became backed up by more than 12 weeks. The customer was forced to find an alternative source. By mid-1978, when the production problems were finally beginning to straighten out, Feld had lost 30 percent of the production volume which had originally been produced from his plant.

Feld was replaced in August by a manager from a smaller plant.

QUESTIONS FOR DISCUSSION

1. Explain what happened to Feld. How can a budgeting system mistakenly help in promoting the kinds of mistakes that Feld made?
2. What can be done to a budgeting system to keep from promoting such behavior?

17.11 REFERENCES AND BIBLIOGRAPHY

1. Anthony, R. N., and R. Herzlinger, *Management Control in Nonprofit Organizations,* Homewood, Ill.: Irwin, 1975.
2. DeCoster, D., and E. Schafer, *Management Accounting: A Decision Emphasis,* Santa Barbara, Calif.: Wiley/Hamilton, 1976.
3. Horngren, C. T., *Cost Accounting: A Managerial Emphasis,* 4th ed., Englewood Cliffs, N.J.: Prentice-Hall, 1977.
4. A. Schick, "The Road to PPB: The Stages of Budget Reform," *Public Administration Review,* 20:243–258 (1966).
5. Welsch, G. A., *Budgeting: Profit Planning and Control,* 2nd ed., New York: Prentice-Hall, 1963.
6. Wildavsky, A., *The Politics of the Budgetary Process,* Boston: Little, Brown, 1964.

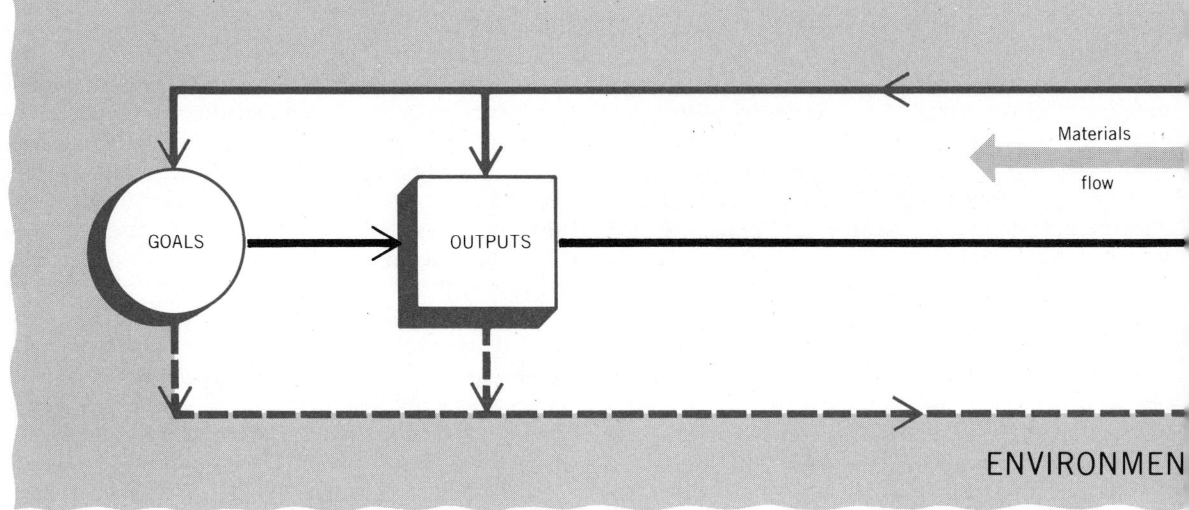

Chapter 18

System Control: Reliability and Maintenance

CONCEPTS

18.1 The Reliability Concept
Approaches to Enhancing Reliability
Independent (Series) versus Redundant (Parallel) Elements
The Use of Standbys
Beauty and Beast Hair Salon

18.2 The Maintenance Problem
Preventive versus Corrective Maintenance

18.3 The Replacement Problem
Optimal Life
Quadro Stereo
Value of a Challenger
Old Mac's Tomato Farm
Group versus Individual Replacement
Nimble Fingers Typing Service

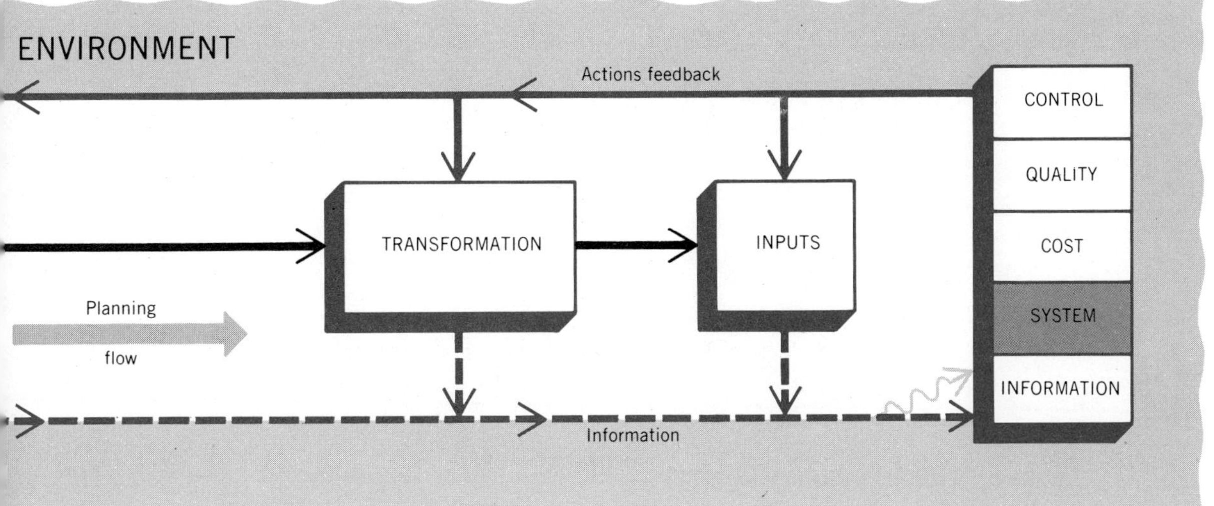

TOOLS AND APPLICATIONS

LEARNING OBJECTIVES

By the conclusion of the *Concepts* portion of this chapter the student should

1. Understand the importance of the overall reliability of a system and know the different ways in which systems can fail.
2. Comprehend the difference between systems connected in series and parallel and know how to calculate the reliability of each.
3. Be familiar with methods, such as the use of standbys and redundancy, of increasing the reliability of systems.
4. Understand the role maintenance plays in system reliability.
5. Be aware of the concepts of corrective and preventive maintenance.
6. Be able to calculate the optimum life of a deteriorating asset and the value of a challenging new asset.
7. Comprehend the group replacement situation and be able to evaluate simple replacement policies.

CONCEPTS

At this point in our discussion of the nature of operations management we have detailed a number of concepts and mechanisms for the *separate* control of the organization's various operations, its materials, and the quality and cost of its output. Now we will consider the reliability of the system as a *whole*: staff, capital, materials, equipment, facilities, and information. The basic concepts of reliability that are of use to management concerning risk, modes of failure, maintenance, and replacement are addressed in this chapter.

Controlling the total system.

18.1 THE RELIABILITY CONCEPT

Reliability defined.

Modes of failure.

The **reliability** of a system is the probability that it will perform "properly" under certain, predefined conditions. The definition of "properly" then gives rise to the consideration of the many and varied ways by which a system can fail, otherwise known as its "modes of failure."

Mode 1: **Outright failure.** In this mode a key part breaks, the firm files for bankruptcy, and the tennis ball goes into the net.

Mode 2: **Apparent failure.** The output enters final inspection bearing no resemblance whatever to the planned output, there is a large oil slick emerging from beneath your car, and the score is 15 to 0 in the bottom of the ninth, two out, no one on, two strikes, no balls.

Mode 3: **Insufficient performance.** "Chicago Slough" comes in fourth by a nose, highest bid is just under what the product cost, Jimmy misses winning the $1,000,000 state lottery by one digit.

Mode 4: **Improper conditions.** The robbers hit the bank just *after* the armored car has taken the deposits, the dentist pulls the wrong tooth, the field goal is nullified by a flag on the play.

These modes illustrate the fact that there is usually one right way for a system to perform but many, many wrong ways. Hence, it should come as no surprise that systems consisting of many parts, each of which can fail in one or more ways, will probably be unreliable unless special precautions are taken. And, of course, this is especially true of systems composed of elements with a wide range of variability in their functioning, such as people. Since the majority of services are labor intensive, it would be expected that the reliability of services, at least in terms of a standard output, would not be as high as for machine produced products. Although this is often the case, there are also many services where the human element of the system can modify its performance so as to increase the reliability of the system as well. (This, for example, is the function of the staff in a final inspection operation.)

Reliability of services.

Approaches to Enhancing Reliability

Through experience, a number of ways have been developed to enhance the reliability of a system. Below are several alternatives available to management in dealing with the reliability problem.

- *Build redundant elements into the system.* This approach results in a dramatic improvement in system reliability but often significantly increases the cost of the system as well. In situations where the same element is used many times, one backup may suffice (e.g., *one* spare tire). Or, as in the human body, the system may be designed such that the backup is used in part of the normal functioning of the system as well.
- *Increase element reliabilities.* Through special design features the reliability of the system may be enhanced. For example, special high quality materials may be used, such as self-lubricating bearings, or elements may be "overdesigned" to handle higher-than-expected loads [e.g., using thick-skinned customer relations (complaints) personnel]. Two considerations exist here: increasing the reliability of the *weakest* (most likely to fail) "link" in the system, and increasing the reliability of the *most critical* (highest expected cost) link in the system. These may well not be the same elements and proper consideration should be given to each. In a vacuum cleaner, for example, the belt is the weakest link whereas the motor is the most critical. In some models, the vacuum cleaner will continue to draw air and dirt when the belt is broken but the brushes won't turn. With a motor failure, however, *nothing* works.
- *Improve working conditions.* On occasion, it is possible to increase the reliability of a system by improving the conditions under which it must perform. Reducing the load on a system, giving more frequent breaks, improving the quality of the environment (new oil for an engine, carpeting for an office, air conditioning a plant), and other, similar attention may considerably extend the working life of the system's elements.
- *Speed the repair process.* The seriousness of a system failure may be minimized by providing sufficient facilities to repair it in case of a breakdown (extra buttons for clothes, extra needles for sewing machines). This approach is especially useful when the inherent reliability of the system is hard to increase. The repair speed can sometimes be increased by providing a larger, or higher quality, repair crew or facilities. It may also be possible to design the system for speed of repair by using, for example, modules that can be replaced quickly (television "works in a drawer") all at one time instead of having to identify the individual element that failed.
- *Provide a standby system.* As an extreme of either the module concept or the redundant concept, another alternative is to make a complete replacement system available as a backup for a failed system ("pair and a spare" stockings). Many two-car families operate on this basis, using one dependable (or even new) car and a second, unreliable jalopy for transportation to and from work. If the

jalopy fails, the good car is used until the old one can be fixed. To minimize the effective cost of such an expensive backup, it is typically used for other miscellaneous duties as well, such as around-town shopping, child chauffeuring, and so forth. The appropriateness of such backup systems will be analyzed in more detail later.

- *Isolate system elements.* At times it is possible to isolate critical or high risk system elements from the rest of the system, at least for some period of time. In a production system, for example, it may be possible to provide storage between operations for the items being processed so that the failure of one operation in the system does not stop the functioning of all the operations downstream of it. Although it is expensive to provide such in-process storage, it may well be worthwhile from a reliability standpoint.
- *Conduct preventive maintenance.* It may be worthwhile to plan, ahead of time, on shutting down the system at off-peak hours to conduct maintenance on elements that are at high risk (especially bottleneck machines such as computers). Such maintenance could consist of inspection, repair, or replacement. The costs of such programs vary considerably and their utility depends, in part, upon the seriousness of a system breakdown. This topic will be investigated in more detail in Section 18.2.
- *Accept the risk.* The final alternative we consider here is for the manager to simply accept the risk of failure. It may well be that all other alternatives appear too expensive in light of the effects of system failure. A particularly relevant topic in this regard concerns consumer product safety. The manager *must* decide at what point sufficient safety precautions have been taken in view of legal safety regulations and possible damage claims a consumer may bring against the organization.

Interdependent (Series) versus Redundant (Parallel) Elements

If a system consists of two elements, one that works 60 percent of the time (has a "reliability" of 60 percent), and the other, 40 percent of the time, then the reliability of the system is .60 × .40 = .24 or 24 percent if both elements must perform properly. Thus a system consisting of **interdependent** (or "series") elements has a combined reliability worse than any of its individual elements. Furthermore, if there are many elements, even of high reliability, the system reliability may still be poor.* Certainly, then, any common household item such as a sewing machine or radio consisting of at least 50 interdependent parts must have an extremely high part reliability, say 99.99 percent, in order for the device to operate most of the time. To an extent, the same holds true for organizations, and department operations, but the situation is more complex. For instance, in an operations department, such as final assembly, or check processing, there are a number of elements involved (people, machines, etc.), each with different reliabilities, and a number of ways (modes) the system can fail.

Reliability of complex operations.

* For example, a seven-element system with element reliabilities of 0.9 will have a system reliability of $(0.9)^7 = 0.48$.

How then can an automobile, with many thousands of parts, function so reliably? There are three answers to that. For one thing, it may not indeed be so reliable. If you have ever owned an old car you have probably experienced the irritation of needing to fix something every time you drove it. Secondly, the car will "run" even if the radio does not work, or the lights, or even third gear. That is, not all the elements are in "series," per se. So the failure of one does not necessarily lead to a failure of the whole system—just a portion of the system (perhaps critical, perhaps not).

Redundancy to increase reliability.

Lastly, intelligent designers often build **redundancy** ("parallel" elements) into a system to *increase* the reliability of the system. For example, our bodies contain numerous redundancies: redundant kidneys, eyes, hands, and so on. For example, with two eyes, seeing is easier, the field of vision is enlarged, and depth perception is possible. The loss of one eye reduces these advantages but does not render the system blind. The cardiovascular system of the body contains even more complex redundancy since it has the ability to rebuild substitutes for some injured and destroyed sections of the body.

Redundancy in automobiles.

Redundancy in an automobile is illustrated by multiple cylinders, dual headlights and taillights, spare tires, and dual brake systems (hydraulic and mechanical). Furthermore, in emergency situations there are usually even more backup systems available, at a cost. For example, if the brakes fail on your car while coming down a long, steep hill, the mechanical (parking) brakes can be used. If these also fail, the transmission can be shifted into "low" to slow the car down. If this is insufficient, the ignition can be turned off (on some cars) to further slow the car. And if the emergency is serious enough, the car can be shifted into "reverse" or "park" to lock (and probably destroy) the transmission so the wheels will not turn. Dual circuitry in computers is another common example of redundancy.

The calculation of system reliabilities for systems composed of series or parallel elements is further discussed in the *Tools and Applications* portion of this chapter. For discussion beyond the scope of this text the student should consult References 5, 6, or 13.

The Use of Standbys

If the investment cost is not excessive and **standby** equipment can be quickly moved in to take over for regular equipment breakdowns, then using standbys may be the most economical route for increasing system reliability. Let us demonstrate with an example.

Beauty and Beast's Hair Salon

Bill Beauty and Bob Beast own and manage a beauty salon near the upper-middle class suburb of a large city. The salon has a dozen relatively new hair "Kurl-n-Dri"ers, which provide the majority of the salon's income. Bob has kept track of the number of these curler-dryers out of order every day since the salon opened. Forty percent of the time none were out of order; 30 percent, one was out; 20 percent, two; and 10 percent, three. Considering this history, Bob has wondered if it might be worthwhile to keep one or even two or three spare curler-dryers on hand to recoup the inevitable

$20 daily loss of income when a regular machine is out of order. The curler-dryers cost $5 a day, on the average, over their short lifetimes.

ANALYSIS

By use of the following expected value formula we may analyze each of Bob's possible operations alternatives.

$$E(L) = \sum_{n=0}^{3} p_n(n - s)c \qquad (18.1)$$

where

$E(L)$ = the expected loss
p_n = the probability n curler-dryers are out of order
s = the number of spares available *and used* as replacements
c = the loss per unavailable curler-dryer

Current situation (0 spares). The current expected loss per day is

.4(0) + .3(1)($20) + .2(2)$20 + .1(3)$20 = $20

One spare: The expected revenue loss is

.4(0) + .3(1 − 1)$20 + .2(2 − 1)$20 + .1(3 − 1)$20	= $8
the cost of the spare	= $5
total daily cost:	$13

Two spares: The expected revenue loss is

.4(0) + .3(1 − 1)$20 + .2(2 − 2)$20 + .1(3 − 2)$20	= $2	
cost of spares	=$10	
total daily cost:	$12	(best)

Three spares: The expected revenue loss is

.4(0) + .3(1 − 1)$20 + .2(2 − 2)$20 + .1(3 − 3)$20	= 0
cost of spares	=$15
total daily cost:	$15

It is clear that four or more spares would be unnecessary. Thus, the best policy is to keep two spares handy and reduce current losses from $20 a day to $12 for an $8 per day savings.

Importance of a spare.

This type of conclusion is typical of operations problems. Often just one spare will significantly improve the production system; the spare may be raw material, equipment, finished goods, or staff and the output either a product, a service, or even a combination.

18.2 THE MAINTENANCE FUNCTION

Although the design and installation of an organization's operating system, consisting of facilities, equipment, materials, supplies, and staff, is a large and expensive

"Go ahead, hate me. It's included in the bill."
(Copyright © 1978, The Kiplinger Washington Editors, Inc.)

Maintenance for reliability.

undertaking, the trouble and expense does not end there. To keep these resources productive and reliable, constant maintenance must be performed by way of repair, rest, lubrication, replacement, inspection, and so forth. Belts wear down, grease wears thin, valves tighten up, corrosion sets in, parts crack and break, people get bored and tired, paint peels, pipes leak, and on and on. All of these items must be repaired or replaced if allowed to reach a point of failure, or failure must be prevented or retarded through certain activities if the system is to remain reliable. This is the general role of maintenance.

In the factory there is usually a maintenance engineer or manager whose job it is to keep the buildings and equipment in proper working order. In other organizations the maintenance function may be performed at random (as things break down) or by contract to an external party, or in a number of other ways.

Corrective versus preventive maintenance.

Regardless of whether the maintenance task is performed formally or informally, the function is essential. The proper role of maintenance is not only to *repair* disabled resources when they fail, termed **corrective maintenance** (CM), but to prevent their breakdown or poor performance as well. This idea of prevention, similar to our notion of preventive control, is termed **preventive maintenance** (PM) and is accomplished through inspection, service, and/or replacement of parts before they fail (all topics to be discussed in more detail later). When equipment is designed and built so that it tends to remain trouble-free and so that it is easily repaired when necessary, the system is said to have good **maintainability** [3].

Maintainability.

18.2 THE MAINTENANCE PROBLEM

Maintenance cost.

The problem facing the operations manager concerned about maintenance is, as always, how to minimize the total costs to the organization. Idled production due to an unanticipated breakdown can be very expensive; but so can a large maintenance crew* who frequently sit idle, as well as downtime due to extensive preventive maintenance. The general cost curves facing the manager are illustrated in Figure 18.1. The "quality of maintenance" axis refers to a combination of elements such as the size and ability of the repair crew, the frequency of inspection, and the frequency of replacing critical system elements through PM. As this quality goes up, the cost typically goes up even faster, while the cost of breakdowns, both in terms of number of failures and duration of idled equipment due to failure, decreases. At some point, as illustrated in the dashed "total cost" curve, a minimum is reached. This is the point the manager is trying to locate.

In many cases only a subjective estimate of this point is ever attempted, and even that is typically based on having experienced, or not experienced, a recent breakdown. By necessity, some elements of the cost of a breakdown are subjective (such as the cost of ill will) but still, many other aspects of the costs can be obtained and analyzed fairly accurately.

Preventive versus Corrective Maintenance

The expense of PM.

As noted earlier, repairing systems *before* they fail is called *preventive maintenance* (PM) and after they fail, *corrective maintenance* (CM). Performing preventive maintenance is an expensive undertaking. The commitment to regularly incurring the

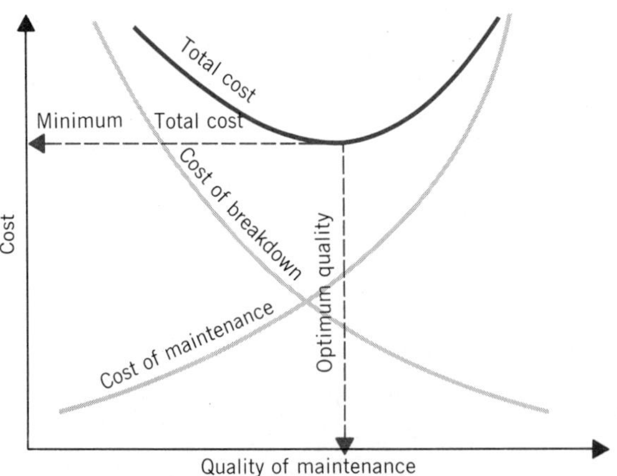

Figure 18.1 The cost factors in maintenance.

* The queuing situation, to be handled later in this section, is clear here. A service crew (facility) waits for machines (or some sort of "customer") to break down and require servicing.

high costs of skilled labor, shutting down a productive system on purpose, and replacing parts that still have some life in them is not a light one to make. Besides, there will *still* be breakdowns that happen when the system is needed—in some cases possibly even due to something that was done during PM! Let us consider the advantages.

The advantage of PM.

PM repairs are typically much cheaper than breakdown repairs. When a system fails, many other elements of the system besides the failed element, if there is one, are usually damaged in the process. For example, if a $50 motor freezes up it may destroy a $1000 pump that it powers. Even if a part does not completely fail, as one element in a system begins to deteriorate it puts more of a load on other elements in the system—a load that they typically were not designed to accommodate. If alcoholism begins to affect the comptroller of a business, purchasing will start having more trouble getting materials, finance will have problems with its credit, and so forth.

Murphy's law.

In addition to the repair costs, there are often the much more expensive costs of idled production. In some cases this loss must be made up by overtime—perhaps at time and a half or possibly even double time. As **Murphy's Law** states: "What *can* go wrong *will* go wrong." And it will go wrong in exactly the worst possible way, at the worst possible time, and in the worst possible place.

Inapplicability of PM.

PM is not, of course, always desirable. If breakdown repairs are hardly more costly, overall, than PM repairs then there is probably not a sufficient reason for PM. Or, if other alternatives are easily available when a breakdown occurs, such as standby equipment, then PM is unnecessary from a continuity-of-production viewpoint.

18.3 THE REPLACEMENT PROBLEM*

When only an economic problem.

When a system's critical element is easily reached and a breakdown is no great inconvenience then the replacement problem is simply one of economics and usually arises in either of the following forms (both of which are discussed in more detail further below):

1. *Optimum life.* The situation here is anticipating the most economic future time to replace a current asset (typically, a machine) with another identical, but new, one.
2. *Value of a "challenger."* In this situation a new asset has become available which can more efficiently perform a task that a current asset is performing. Should the old asset be replaced?

When inconvenience and trouble are involved.

However, when it is difficult or expensive to reach the critical system element then the replacement decision is more complex. "Since we got the tires off, lady, mebbe we should reline those worn brakes too. Save ya a lot of trouble and expense

* Much of this section is based on Terborgh [9].

later on." "While I'm here, Sam, why don'cha replace the filter, too." As can be seen from the above examples, early replacements derive from a situation where either the labor involved in *getting to* the critical element is significant, thereby justifying premature replacement, or else the inconvenience or cost of a later breakdown justifies the early replacement.

Group replacement.

A common example of this situation is when a large number of typically, low-priced items are more and more likely to fail with age. This is called the **group replacement decision** and relies heavily upon knowledge of the item's lifetime distribution. We will investigate somewhat later a number of the various possible replacement policies (such as item versus group replacement) but first let us consider the simpler economic policies.

Optimal Life

Minimize the average annual cost.

The analysis to determine the optimum life of an asset is one of trying to find that replacement cycle which minimizes the average annual cost of the asset. Typically, the asset deteriorates over its life, resulting in higher operating costs and loss of resale value. The behavior of these costs with asset age is illustrated in Figure 18.2. As the age of the asset increases, the operating cost increases due to reduced efficiency, wear, and maintenance. And, for much the same reasons, the salvage value of the asset decreases, but by a steadily lessening amount, year by year. In some particular year the total annual cost of the asset will be a minimum—if possible, we would like to use the asset only for *that* particular time period, but we generally cannot. Following that year the costs start rising and after a few years we have gotten "the best years" (in terms of the average annual cost) out of the asset and it is uneconomical to hold the asset beyond that point.

Identify the best years.

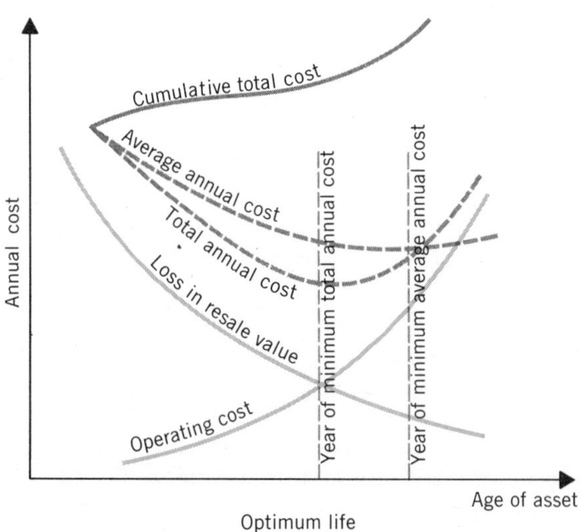

Figure 18.2 Determination of single asset optimum life.

TABLE 18.1 ESTABLISHING THE OPTIMUM LIFE OF A STEREO

Year	0	1	2	3	4	5	6
1. Resale value	600	450	370	320	290	270	260
2. Loss in resale value	—	150	80	50	30	20	10
3. Repair cost	—	70	80	100	130	170	220
4. Total annual cost	—	220	160	150	160	190	230
5. Cumulative total cost	—	220	380	530	690	880	1110
6. Average annual cost	—	220	190	176	172	176	185

The simplest way to find the optimum life is to *accumulate* the total annual costs and find that year for which the average cost (cumulative total annual cost divided by number of years) is the lowest. This calculation procedure is illustrated in the example below.

Quadro Stereo

The costs for a particular quadraphonic stereo used for background music in retail stores are listed in Table 18.1. We see that the lowest total annual cost for the stereo, $150, occurs in year 3. However, the *average* annual cost through year 3 (years 1, 2, and 3 combined) is $176, higher than the average annual cost through year 4, $172. But by year 5 the average annual cost has again risen to $176 and since this is an increase, the stereo is not worth holding through this year.

If desired, interest and present value corrections (as discussed in Chapter 10I) can also be incorporated into the figures. The point also might be noted that expected future occurrences should be factored into consideration. For example, if a retailer planned to terminate business after three years and sell his or her stereos, then the $172 average cost would not be the appropriate figure for selecting the *most economical* stereo to purchase. Rather, a three year horizon should be used, resulting in $176. In general, costs should be minimized only over the horizon of expected need for the asset. Similarly, if a much more efficient asset is expected to enter the market in the following year, perhaps the best strategy would be to delay the purchase one year and lease an acceptable asset in the interim.

The optimum life problem exists for all operations investments where the asset, unlike an antique, loses value with age and wear. On occasion, such assets may be replaced prematurely if a newer type of asset becomes available as discussed in the next subsection.

Value of a Challenger

New challengers and sunk costs.

This situation deals with the arrival of a new type of asset (called a **challenger**) which could replace the existing asset (called the **defender**) with a (typically) lower operating cost. The problem is that the challenger is expensive. Also, a considerable amount may have been paid for the defender and its book value may still be high. Managers are reluctant to part with a like-new asset unless they can obtain a good resale price for it on the used asset market; to the extent that they *cannot* the difference is called a **sunk cost**. It is important to realize that sunk costs should not enter the replacement decision; only expected future costs are relevant.

For example, suppose you bought a labor-saving machine and paid a considerable amount for it, but felt it was well worth it. Then a month later, a new type of machine becomes available that can do the same job at almost no operating cost at all and overnight makes your machine worthless. If the cost to do the job with the new machine, considering all acquisition, resale, and operating costs, is less than the operating cost alone of the old machine, then the new machine should be bought. What about the money you poured into the purchase of the original machine? That is a sunk cost and should be ignored. There is no point in using the original machine if another one will have less overall costs for the duration of need. Consider the following example.

Old Mac's Tomato Farm

Old Mac, owner and operations manager of Old Mac's Tomato Farm, is eagerly looking forward to retiring after three more years. Five years ago he purchased a mechanical tomato picker for $70,000 when they were new on the market. The machine's operating cost was $5000 last year and has steadily been increasing at the rate of $1000 each year. For a new type of harvesting machine its performance is not bad. It probably only destroys about $10,000 worth of tomatoes per year. Mac figures the machine would probably bring about $20,000 today on the used market and will bring about $4000 less each year until it is worn out (in 20/4 = 5 years).

A "second-generation" tomato picker has recently appeared on the market for $50,000. It is said to be so gentle in picking tomatoes that none at all are harmed and operating costs are only $3000 per year for at least the first five years. Mac has been considering buying one of these machines and then selling it for, he estimates, perhaps $35,000, when he retires. Money is worth 10 percent to Mac.

ANALYSIS

In this, as in probably the great majority of replacement situations, the crucial factor in the decision is the **horizon of need**. For an indefinite, continuing horizon, one decision may be best whereas for a sharply abbreviated horizon an entirely different decision may be appropriate. In this case, if Old Mac changes his retirement plans by even a year this may alter the optimal decision. For example, suppose he decides not to retire in three years after all (when he will be 62), but wait until he is 65. The crucial question in that case would be how to replace the worn out current machine in that last, sixth year.

For the existing situation we can simply compare the present value of all costs and benefits for the three-year horizon. The analysis is given in Table 18.2. The present value calculations are conducted in the same manner as explained in Chapter 10I, using the present value table in Appendix A. The conclusion is that Old Mac should definitely buy the challenger (new tomato picking machine) for a present value savings of about $25,000 (i.e., 36 − 11 = 25).

TABLE 18.2 PRESENT VALUE OF COSTS COMPARISON FOR OLD MAC

	Item ($1000's)		Present Value Factor	Present Value ($1000's)
Alternative 1:	Keep the Defender			
Year 1	Operating cost:	−6	0.9091	−5.4546
	Tomato damage:	−10	0.9091	−9.0910
Year 2	Operating cost:	−7	0.8264	−5.7848
	Tomato damage:	−10	0.8264	−8.2640
Year 3	Operating cost:	−8	0.7513	−6.0104
	Tomato damage:	−10	0.7513	−7.5130
	Resale:	+8	0.7513	+ 6.0104
	Total:			−36.1074
Alternative 2:	Purchase Challenger, Sell Defender			
Year 0	Purchase:	−50	1.0000	−50.0000
	Sell:	+20	1.0000	+20.0000
Year 1	Operating cost:	−3	0.9091	− 2.7273
Year 2	Operating cost:	−3	0.8264	− 2.4792
Year 3	Operating cost:	−3	0.7513	− 2.2539
	Resale:	+35	0.7513	+26.2955
	Total:			−11.1649

The MAPI system.

Another approach to the investment problem is provided by the Machinery and Allied Products Institute (**MAPI**). The MAPI system is composed of a number of worksheets, graphs, and a formula for easy application by managers. The result is an adjusted, one-year, after-tax rate of return relative to making the investment as compared to deferring the investment for one year. For further details consult Reference 10.

Group versus Individual Replacement

A number of policies.

The group replacement problem, one form of *preventive maintenance,* arises in situations where the cost or trouble associated with a replacement upon failure is very high. A number of policies may be considered: replace only defective items, replace defectives plus all those exceeding *x* hours of service, replace all the items.

Failure rates and infant mortality.

The most important set of data needed to address the problem is the **failure rate distribution** of the item in question. A common distribution is shown in Figure 18.3. Here there is an initially high failure rate, called **infant mortality**, followed by a drop in frequency until a fairly common wear-out period is reached where the failure frequency increases again and then finally tails off. The exact nature of this curve de-

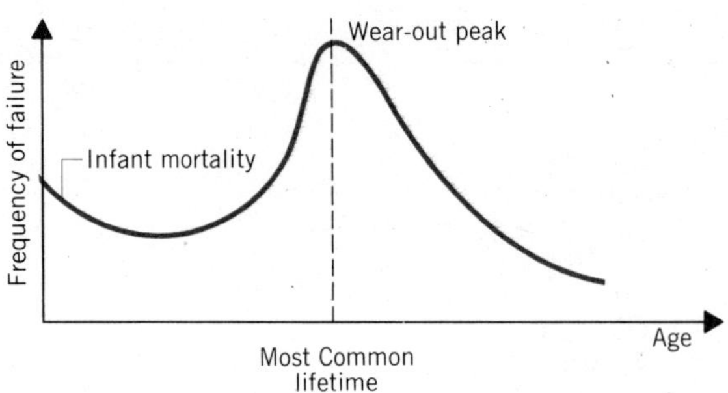

Figure 18.3 A typical failure rate distribution.

pends upon the item in question. In some cases the infant mortality peak is almost nonexistent whereas in other cases the wear-out peak is missing.

Sensitive, hard to balance.

The infant mortality peak is typified by situations where the item is highly sensitive or very difficult to adjust or balance properly and most of the failures occur from an inaccurate previous repair. If, as time goes on, fewer and fewer items are still operating, then no wear-out peak will appear.

The wear-out peak is characterized by a few items failing before this period and a few afterward, but most of the items failing right around this period. The curve of Figure 18.3 may even be considered a human mortality graph in a society with a rather high infant mortality rate.

Nimble Fingers Typing Service

Jane Nimble operates a typing service that employs 50 typists, each using an identical typewriter. The typewriters are older models, which use loose ribbons rather than snap-in cartridges and so the ribbon changing procedure is fairly time consuming. Many of the typists cannot change the ribbon and so Jane, as operations manager, personally changes all of them when they run out. Jane's typists vary in typing speeds and accuracy; hence, ribbons are used up in varying rates as shown in Table 18.3.

Jane estimates that the cost of interruption of her work and the idle time of the typist while a ribbon is being removed and replaced is $10. The ribbon cost is $2. One of Jane's typists has suggested that, rather than using corrective maintenance and replacing the ribbons only when they run out, perhaps, using preventive maintenance, they should all be replaced every evening, or every other evening. Someone

TABLE 18.3 FAILURE RATE DISTRIBUTION OF TYPEWRITER RIBBONS

Ribbon life, days	1[a]	2	3	4	5	6	7
Probability of "failure" during the day	.15	.05	.10	.15	.20	.30	.05

[a] Early failure due to defective ribbons.

could be trained to do the job at a cost of $1 per change since the machines would be idle anyway. Does the replace-each-night or every-other-night policy make sense?

ANALYSIS

The *cost of the current policy* can be computed by first calculating the expected life of a ribbon. This is

$$\begin{aligned} E(\text{life}) &= .15(1) + .05(2) + .10(3) + .15(4) + .20(5) + .3(6) + .05(7) \\ &= .15 + .1 + .3 + .6 + 1.0 + 1.8 + .35 \\ &= 4.3 \text{ days} \end{aligned}$$

The current policy therefore calls for, on the average, replacement of all ribbons at $12 each ($10 + $2 ribbon cost) every 4.3 days for a cost of

$$\$12 \times 50 = \$600$$

or, on a per day basis

$$\frac{\$600}{4.3} = \underline{\underline{\$139.53}} \text{ per day}$$

Replacing at the end of each day would result in costs of

$$\begin{aligned} \text{failures during day} &= .15 \times 50 \times \$12 = \$90 \\ \text{plus end of day replacement of all} &= 50 \times \$3 = \underline{\$150} \\ &\text{Total} \quad \$240 \end{aligned}$$

or,

$$\text{daily cost} = \underline{\underline{\$240}}$$

Replacing at the end of every other day would result in costs of

$$\begin{aligned} \text{failures during day 1} &= .15 \times 50 \times \$12 &&= \$90.00 \\ \text{failures during day 2} &= .05 \times 50 \times \$12 &&= 30.00 \\ \text{day 1 replacements failing in day 2} &= .15 \times (.15 \times 50) \times \$12 &&= 13.50 \\ \text{end of day 2 replacement of all} &= 50 \times \$3 &&= \underline{150.00} \\ \text{Total} &= &&\$283.50 \end{aligned}$$

or,

$$\text{daily cost} = \frac{\$283.50}{2} = \underline{\underline{141.75}} \text{ per day}$$

Therefore, for this problem, replacement every evening, or every other evening, are not better policies. (As an exercise, what would the average daily cost be of ribbon replacement every *third* night?)

The policies considered in the Nimble Fingers example were only three of several policies. Jane could also have used a policy of replacing those each night which appeared more than half used, or any other plan. Because the calculations become unmanageable very quickly, this problem is very amenable to a simulation solution. Through simulation, exact times until "failure" may be employed rather than "nearest day" times. Once a model has been developed for a replacement problem any number of potential policies can then be tested.

The replacement problem occurs in a number of operations settings but always where the cost of group replacement is much less than individual replacement. This is usually because the items are hard to get to, require special tools or equipment, or idle other productive resources. Examples that are seen frequently are the replacement of light bulbs; supplies such as paper, ink, toner in machines; products in vending machines; fast-wearing parts in certain equipment; and so forth.

TOOLS AND APPLICATIONS

18.4 RELIABILITY FOR ELEMENTS IN SERIES

Effect of two elements in series.

We can illustrate the effect on system reliability of multiple, interacting elements with the systems diagrammed in Figure 18.4. At the top of Figure 18.4*a* are two separate elements in **series**, A and B. In order for the system to work, both elements must operate properly (e.g., the car must start and the transmission must function). If the reliability (the probability of proper operation) of A and B are written as $R(A)$ and $R(B)$ then

$$\text{reliability of the system, } R = R(A \text{ and } B) = R(A) + 1\ R(B) \tag{18.2}$$

if the operation of the two elements, A and B, are **independent** of each other. In the special case where $R(A) = R(B) = r$ the reliability of the system will be r^2.

Reliabilty of interdependent elements.

In the bottom of Figure 18.4 are shown seven identical elements in, we shall assume, a semiseries configuration. That is, *all* the elements must function properly in order for the system to function properly. In this case the reliability of the system will be r^7.

If r, for example, is 90 percent, then the reliability, R, of the two-element system as a whole (Figure 18.4*a*) would be $(.9)(.9) = .81$ and the reliability of the seven-element system (Figure 18.4*b*) would be $(.9)^7 = .48$, both considerably less than .9. Figure 18.5 illustrates this degradation in reliability, R, as the number of interdependent (series type) elements, n, increases for a number of typical values of r. At the top of the figure is the curve for a one-element system whose reliability R is equal to the reliability of the element itself, r. Thus, at the far right where $r = 100$ percent, then R

Series reliability curve.

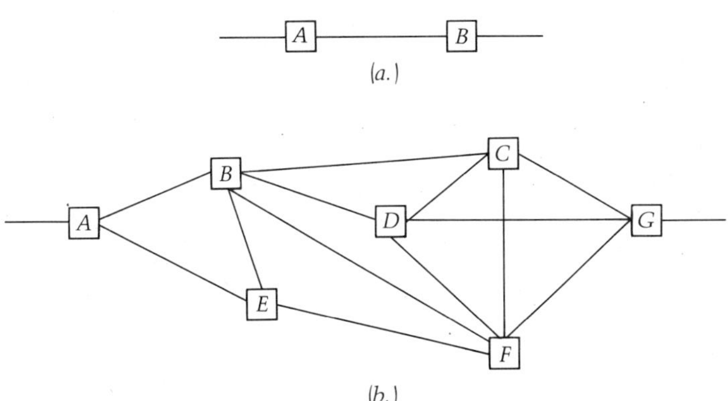

Figure 18.4 Multiple element series systems. (*a*) Two elements. (*b*) Multiple, interdependent elements.

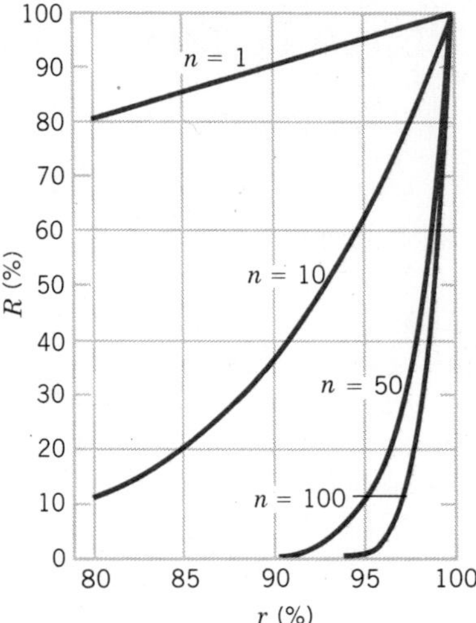

Figure 18.5 Series system reliability.

= 100 percent and at the far left where $r = 80$ percent, then R also is 80 percent. The next curve down represents a 10-element (series or semiseries) system. Again at the right, if every element has a reliability r of 100 percent the reliability of the system R will also be 100 percent. But if the reliability of each element r is only 90 percent then R is $(.9)^{10} = 35$ percent. And for element reliabilities of 80 percent R is only 11 percent.

18.5 RELIABILITY FOR ELEMENTS IN PARALLEL

The effect of **parallel** elements (redundancy) on a system's reliability is illustrated in Figure 18.6. Here, if A fails to work, B can take over and vice versa. For the system as a whole to fail, both A *and* B must fail, which is unlikely. The reliability of the system, R, in this case of, again independent, elements is

$$R = R(A \text{ or } B) = R(A) + R(B) - R(A \text{ and } B) \tag{18.3}$$

Since, in calculating $R(A)$, we have included those times when B is also working $[R(A$ and $B)]$ and in the calculation of $R(B)$ we have included those times when A is also

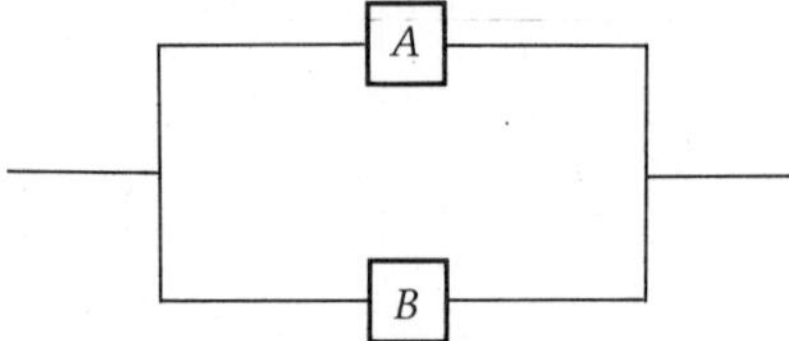

Figure 18.6 A parallel redundant system.

working [$R(A$ and $B)$], we have therefore included those times when both are properly functioning twice. To avoid this double count, we must subtract one $R(A$ and $B)$ out. This is shown in the **Venn diagram** of Figure 18.7.

Venn diagram.

The reliability of element A is given by the left circle, $R(A)$, and for element B by the right circle $R(B)$. If, as in the last subsection, *both* A and B must operate properly for the system to work (series) then this reliability is given by the cross-hatched area of overlap, $R(A$ and $B)$ or, for independent elements with identical reliabilities r, simply r^2 (as explained ealier).

But if the system will work when *either* A or B are operating properly, then $R(A$ or $B)$ is given by the total area enclosed by circles A and B. This area would normally be $R(A) + R(B)$ but, because A and B are not **mutually exclusive** (i.e., A's working does not keep B from working and vice versa) there is some overlap in their areas and this area is counted twice in the term $R(A) + R(B)$ and thus must be subtracted out once. The overall resulting reliability of the redundant, parallel system is then

Mutually exclusive elements.

$$R(A) + R(B) - R(A \text{ and } B) = r + r - r^2 = 2r - r^2 \qquad (18.4)$$

A simpler logic.

Another, easier, way to obtain this result uses the following logic: The reliability of the system is

$$1 - \text{prob } (A \text{ and } B \textit{ both fail})$$

where prob means probability. The probability that A will fail is $1 - R(A)$ or $1 - r$ and the probability for B is $1 - R(B)$ or $1 - r$ again. The resulting reliability of the system is therefore

$$1 - (1 - r)^2 = 1 - 1 + 2r - r^2 = 2r - r^2$$

This simple approach can easily be extended to any number of elements. For example, with n elements in parallel, all with the same reliability r, we have

$$R = 1 - (1 - r)^n \qquad (18.5)$$

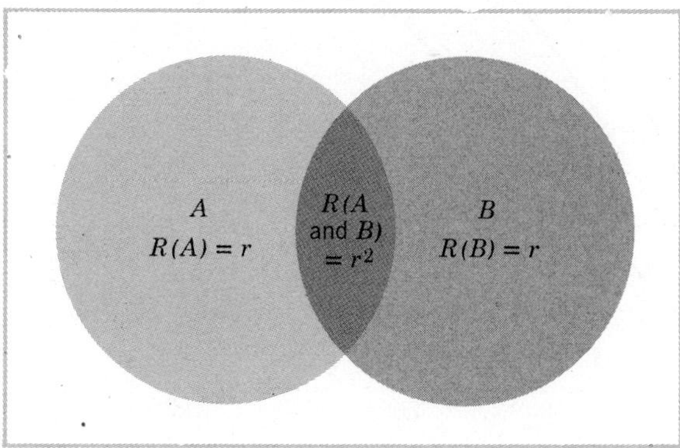

Figure 18.7 The reliability of a two-element system.

The resulting reliability figures for various values of n and r are plotted, in a fashion similar to Figure 18.5 and Figure 18.8. Note now that for three elements in parallel with reliabilities of only .9 each, the system reliability is enhanced to

$$R = 1 - (1 - .9)^3 = 1 - .1^3 = 1 - .001 = .999$$

or only one expected failure in a thousand trials.

18.6 DECISION TREES TO EVALUATE LEVELS OF RISK

Comparing reliability alternatives.

Earlier, in Chapter 5, we looked at the use of **decision trees** to aid in capacity decisions with risk involved. Decision trees are also useful in many other areas and especially for reliability considerations. The following example illustrates some of the risk-cost tradeoffs available to the manager in handling system reliability problems.

The Phlashy Phuneral Home

I. M. Macabre, operations manager for Phlashy Phuneral, has total responsibility for the operation of Phlashy Phuneral's latest model Cadillac hearse, which is used in funeral processions. Being the fanciest funeral home in a small (but wealthy) town, Phlashy has need of only one hearse but it must be absolutely the latest model available or else Phlashy Phuneral's reputation is dead (so to speak). I. M. Macabre has three choices in guaranteeing the operation of the latest model hearse for a funeral.

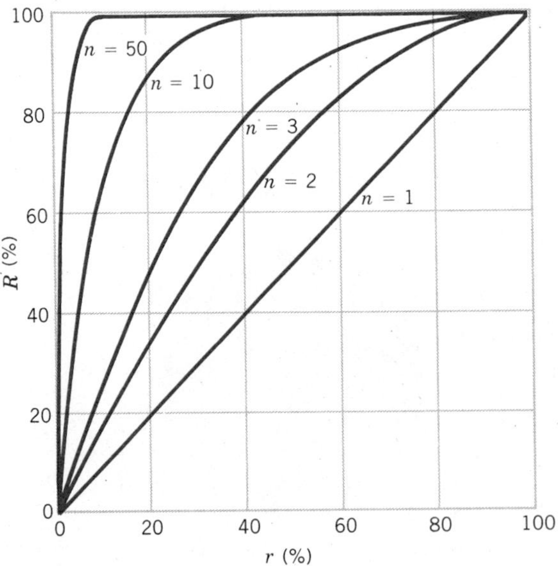

Figure 18.8 Parallel system reliability.

1. He can keep the company hearse in top condition and risk about one chance in a hundred that it will be unavailable due to a breakdown just when it is needed. In such a case he feels the future lost sales to the company and other costs due to humiliation and such would amount to one million dollars.
2. He can put a local garage mechanic on a personal retainer for $2000 a year and have only one chance in ten that the mechanic could not fix the hearse in time for the funeral.
3. He could buy a second, identical hearse as a standby which could find sufficient additional use to reduce the extra cost to $8000.

ANALYSIS

I. M. Macabre's alternatives are sketched in Figure 18.9. As can be seen, with a backup system (alternatives 2 and 3) the expected cost of the potential million dollar loss is reduced to a very small amount; so small that the cost of the backup becomes the major consideration in the decision. Since the mechanic is only $2000 compared to the $8000 for the second hearse, the mechanic is the best alternative.

It is instructive to also consider other values of the probability of hearse failure. The costs under the three alternatives for various probabilities of failure are given in Table 18.4. The best alternative depends on the probability of failure, alternatives 1 and 2 being equivalent at a probability of .00222. . . . . In this example alternative 3 cannot be "best" irrespective of the probabilities although it could be for lower values of hearse cost.

Since the decision tree concept was specifically developed for the consideration of risk, it is particularly useful for decisions regarding the reliability of operations. It can help in the analysis of providing standby machines, carrying spare parts, using "floating" personnel (e.g., floor nurses), employing larger repair crews, and so forth.

Other uses of decision trees.

TABLE 18.4 MACABRE'S EXPECTED COSTS UNDER VARIOUS PROBABILITIES OF FAILURE

	P(Fail)		
Alternative	.001	.01	.10
1	1,000	10,000	100,000
2	2,100	3,000	12,000
3	8,001	8,100	18,000

18.7 USING A REPAIR CREW

If a corrective maintenance (CM) system is adopted, one of the major issues is that of the size of the maintenance staff. When a machine or system fails, operations are generally either stopped or severely hampered. Keeping a large maintenance stafff ready for repairs will reduce this idle or "downtime" but only at a rather high fixed

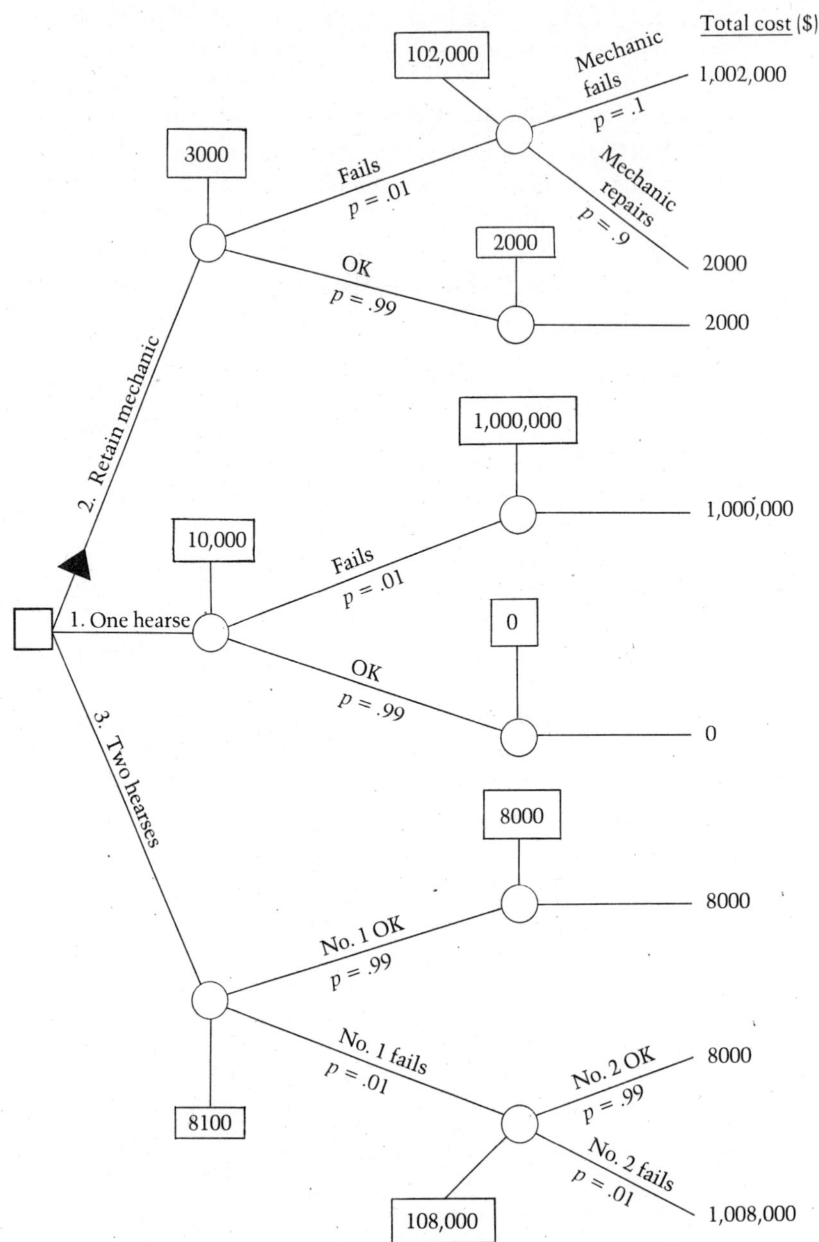

Figure 18.9 Macabre's decision alternatives.

cost of supporting that staff. **Queuing theory** represents one approach to this maintenance problem. System breakdowns can be perceived as "customers" arriving for service and the repair crew represents the servicing facility(ies). The form of this problem differs from that presented in Chapter 9 in that the breakdowns occur in a *limited number* of items, such as machines or workers, and, hence, the queue of items waiting for service cannot grow beyond some maximum value (e.g., if you have only six typewriters it is impossible to have any more than six breakdowns at one time).

Queuing theory to size repair crews.

First, we let M denote the finite number of identical "machines," λ *each* machine's "arrival" (breakdown) rate, and μ the service rate (as in Chapter 9). The same situation and assumptions discussed in Chapter 9 apply here (no jockeying; first come, first served; random arrivals and service; etc.). The only difference in this situation is that the population of customers is not infinite but limited to M. Then the expected length of the queue of machines waiting for service is given in Figures 18.10,

Queuing situation and assumptions.

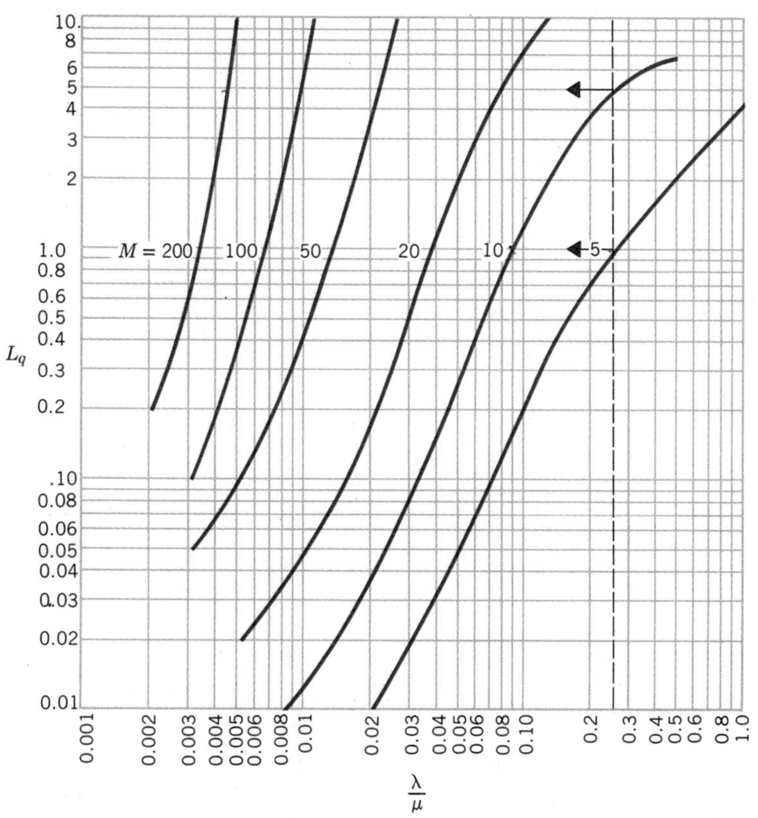

Figure 18.10. The single-server limited-source queue, $K = 1$. (*Source.* Adapted by permission from Efraim Turban and Jack R. Meredith, *Fundamentals of Management Science* (Dallas, Texas: Business Publications, 1977) p. 436.)

18.11, and 18.12 for the situation of having $K = 1$ repairman (or crew), $K = 5$ repairmen (each of whom would work on a separate machine), and $K = 10$ repairmen, respectively.

Hayseed Harvesting

One of the scenes more common around family sized farms in the last few years is the arrival, somewhat before harvesting season, of an agent representing the owner of *very* large harvesting equipment—equipment whose price is in the neighborhood of $200,000 or more! This equipment can, in the course of hours, completely harvest a farmer's entire crop at the optimum harvesting time, thus sparing the farmer the risk of weather turning bad before his family can finish harvesting the crop. Such large equipment is too expensive for a single farmer but entrepreneurs invest in such ma-

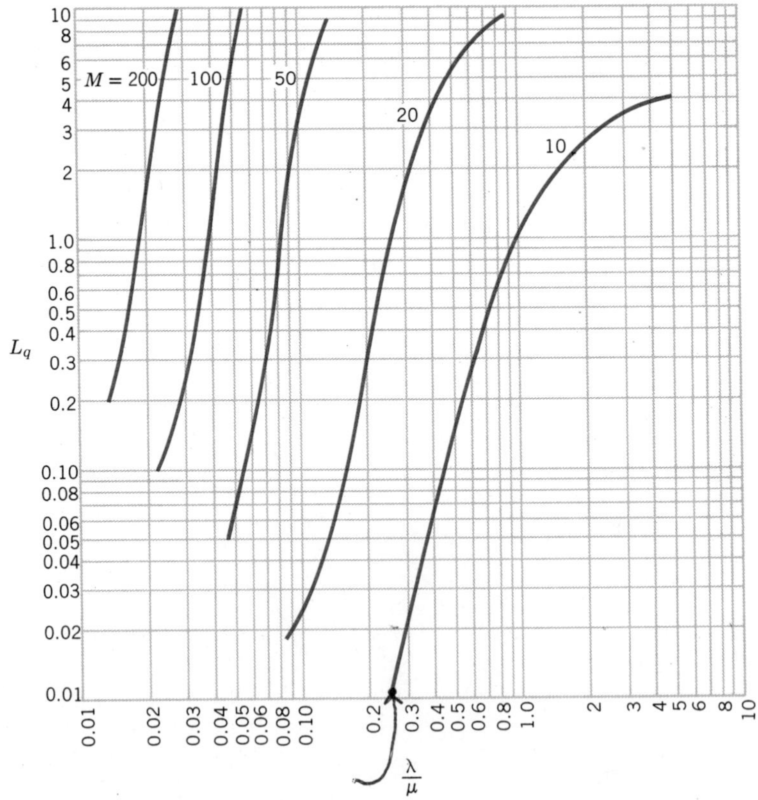

Figure 18.11. The limited-source queue, $K = 5$. (*Source*. Adapted by permission from Efraim Turban and Jack R. Meredith, *Fundamentals of Management Science* (Dallas, Texas: Business Publications, 1977) p. 437.)

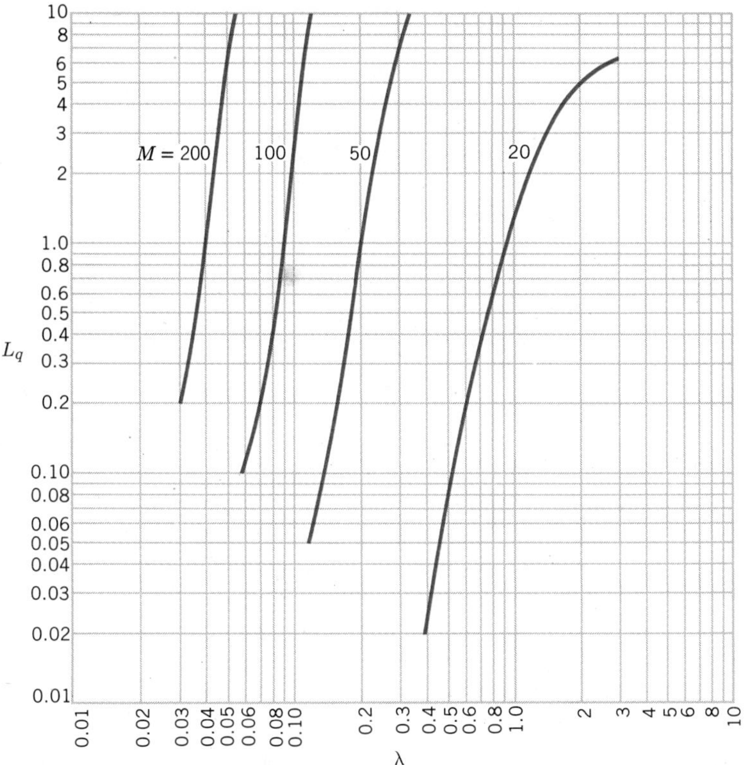

Figure 18.12. The limited-source queue, $K = 10$.

chines and then contract with *many* farmers to harvest their fields, thus increasing the utilization of the equipment so as to exceed the breakeven point. Clearly, it is mandatory that equipment be available for harvesting during those periods for which contracts have been signed. This requires a repairman to accompany the machines during their work since standby equipment is too expensive.

Suppose a very sensitive, specialized type of machine owned by Hayseed Harvesting is known to break down randomly but at the average rate of every 4 hours. Servicing by the repairman also varies randomly but requires an hour, on the average. For an upcoming one-day contract with Farmer Jones, the operations manager of Hayseed has decided that five of these specialized machines will be continuously required to harvest the crop. But if he sends only five, and a repairman, the machines will spend much of their time waiting for repairs and the harvest won't be finished by the end of the day. How many should the manager therefore send?

Figure 18.10 for one repairman can help here. The variables are

$$\lambda = 1 \text{ breakdown/4 hr} = .25/\text{hr}$$
$$\mu = 1 \text{ repair/1 hr} = 1/\text{hr}$$

Therefore $\lambda/\mu = .25$. At $\lambda/\mu = .25$ on the graph a dashed vertical line has been drawn. As can be seen, it intersects the curve $M = 5$ machines at a queue length of 1.0. This means that by sending five machines, one will always be in queue for service, on the average, with another *or less* being repaired, leaving three for harvesting. If two extra are also sent to make up for this slack, they too will probably break down and require repair. Thus, many more than simply *two* extra will be required. From the graph it is seen that the vertical line intersects the curve $M = 10$ machines at $L_q = 5$. This then says that even with 10 machines, on the average, 5 will be waiting in queue, and 1 in service, leaving 4 available for harvesting.

Another alternative, clearly, is to employ more repairmen. We can see, from Figure 18.11 that if $K = 5$ repairmen were to accompany the $M = 10$ machines the queue length would reduce to 0.012, but this solution is too expensive. Suppose instead an inexpensive "helper" is hired to aid the repairman, thereby reducing the average repair time to 48 minutes or 0.8 hours. Then $\mu = 1/0.8$ or 1.25/hr and $\lambda/\mu = .2$. From Figure 18.10 we find that $L_q = 4$ at $M = 10$ machines. The result is therefore that five or more machines, on the average, will be harvesting. For other values of M and K the tables of Peck and Hazlewood are recommended [8]. A simulation of the situation could also be conducted to gain insight into the problem.

The above situation is a very common one in operations management and occurs in service, as well as product, organizations such as police and fire departments, ambulance and hospital services, and so forth.

18.8 SUMMARY

The reliability of a system is the probability that it will perform properly under specified conditions. There are a number of ways in which a system will not perform properly, known as its "modes of failure." Systems with many interconnected elements, all of which must work for the system to function properly, will generally have very low reliabilities unless certain precautions are taken. Two of the many ways to increase reliability are through the use of standbys and adding redundant, parallel elements to the system. Decision trees can aid the operations manager in evaluating the various ways of increasing a system's reliability.

Maintenance is an especially important way to maintain a system's reliability. Corrective maintenance is the repair of an item when it fails; preventive maintenance is the attempt, beforehand, to prevent the failure of an item. Corrective maintenance procedures may at times be usefully analyzed through the aid of queuing graphs to determine expected queue lengths.

Of the various types of preventive maintenance, replacement is one of the most important. Every asset that deteriorates with use will have an optimum lifetime unless a new type of asset, called a "challenger" becomes available which can economically replace it. But the replacement approach of preventive maintenance can also be used for groups of items with well-defined lifetime distributions. Because it is difficult or expensive to replace these items individually when they fail it may well be worthwhile to replace many of them at one time, even if some of them have not yet failed.

KEY TERMS

Concepts

reliability (p. 596)
corrective maintenance (p. 601)
preventive maintenance (p. 601)
apparent failure (p. 596)
insufficient performance (p. 596)
improper conditions (p. 596)
interdependent (p. 598)
Murphy's Law (p. 603)
redundancy (p. 599)
standby (p. 599)
challenger (p. 605)
defender (p. 605)
group replacement (p. 604)
sunk cost (p. 606)
failure rate distribution (p. 607)
infant mortality (p. 607)
horizon of need (p. 606)
maintainability (p. 601)
MAPI (p. 607)

Tools and Applications

series (p. 611)
parallel (p. 612)
decision tree (p. 614)
queuing theory (p. 617)
independent (p. 611)
Venn diagram (p. 613)
mutually exclusive (p. 613)

18.10 REVIEW TEST

Concepts

1. "The surgery was successful but the patient died" is failure by insufficient performance. (p. 596)
   a. True b. False
2. The more elements in series the lower the reliability. (p. 598)
   a. True b. False
3. Redundant elements are the same as parallel elements. (p. 599)
   a. True b. False
4. One reliability alternative is to simply accept the probability of failure. (p. 598)
   a. True b. False
5. Standbys are most effective when equipment costs are high and breakdown costs are low. (p. 599)
   a. True b. False
6. The goal of preventive maintenance is to prevent the need for maintaining the system. (p. 601)
   a. True b. False
7. There are many situations where preventive maintenance would be a bad policy. (p. 603)
   a. True b. False
8. To find the optimum life of an asset the manager must consider sunk costs as well as operating and repair costs. (p. 606)
   a. True b. False
9. The infant mortality curve also applies to infants. (p. 608)
   a. True b. False
10. Group replacement is a consideration when it is a lot of trouble to replace something. (p. 607)
    a. True b. False
11. The optimum life of any asset typically exceeds its minimum-annual-cost year. (p. 604)
    a. True b. False

Tools and Applications

12. The reliability of parallel elements A and B is $R(A) + R(B)$. (p. 612)
    a. True b. False
13. The repair crew queuing problem embodies the standard assumptions of queuing theory. (p. 617)
    a. True b. False

18.11 DISCUSSION QUESTIONS

1. How do you think reliability is enhanced in NASA space equipment? In elevators?
2. Why do managers find it so hard to ignore sunk costs on expensive equipment?
3. How might group replacement analysis be used in personnel acquisition and promotion?
4. Do the replacement techniques of this chapter apply to public benefits? Other services?
5. Classify a number of failures you are familiar with according to the four basic failure modes.
6. Why are services so unreliable compared to products?
7. Draw a Venn diagram to help calculate the reliability of three parallel elements and compare it to Equation 18.5.
8. How do the reliability formulas change if the element reliabilities are not all identical?
9. Is it better to increase the reliability of the weakest link in a system or the most critical link?
10. Preventive maintenance is often viewed as a long-term approach to reliability. Why?
11. When should PM not be used?
12. For what kinds of situations is early replacement appropriate?
13. Why should an asset not be replaced at the end of its minimum annual cost year?
14. How does the horizon of need affect the replacement decision?

18.12 PROBLEMS

Concepts

1. Ray Gordon, owner-operator of a single "18 wheeler" tractor trailer has had trouble with flat tires over the past year. Ray is considering the possibility of using additional spare tires. His rig currently carries one spare. On any given trip, the probability of zero or more flat tires is given as follows.

Flats	Prob.
0	.3
1	.5
2	.1
3	.1

If Ray has more than one flat tire, a new tire must be purchased on the road, and a special "road service" fee paid to the tire company. The cost to Ray is $600. The cost per trip of each extra spare is based upon the expected tire life (even if it is not used, it is subject to dry rot so its life is not indefinite) and is anticipated to be $20 per trip. How many spares would you recommend that Ray carry?

2. The Blue Grass Computer Center provides data processing services for area businesses. Blue Grass currently contracts with a computer vendor for maintenance of the equipment. The cost is $120 per day. The probability of equipment failure on any given day is .13. The computer vendor must send a repairman from a city nearly 100 miles away; consequently, the machine is typically down for 24 hours until it is repaired. The cost of the down time is estimated to be $1000. A local computer repair company has just opened and Blue Grass has been solicited as a potential client. The local firm claims 8-hour service from machine failure to repair, but their rates are somewhat higher than the computer vendor, $160 per day. Advise Blue Grass as to the expected cost of each maintenance option.
3. The Last National Bank of Pleasantville uses a magnetic ink character reader (MICR) to process checks. The machine loses 20 percent each year in resale value (its original purchase price was $80,000) and has the following maintenance cost schedule over its 10-year useful life.

Year	1	2	3	4	5	6	7	8	9	10
Cost	8000	9000	10200	12000	15000	16500	17000	17400	17750	18000

When should the machine be replaced?

4. Solve the Nimble Fingers group replacement problem of Section 18.3 for replacements every *third* night.

Tools and Applications

5. For a new clock-radio, which you have purchased, the clock, the alarm switch, and the radio must all work in order for you to be awakened in the morning. If the reliabilities of the three independent components are .95, .90, and .92, respectively, what is the probability that the alarm clock will perform as expected in the morning?
6. If, in Problem 5, there is a backup switch (with the same reliability as the first) that will function if the primary switch fails, what is the chance of your being awakened in time?
7. A factory repair crew of 5 maintain 20 high volume pumps which break down at an average rate of 15 per week. The pumps are repaired by a single serviceperson in half a week, on the average. What is the expected number of pumps waiting for service?

18.13 CASE MID-WEST WHOLESALE

The salesman for Hardware Reliability, Inc. had just left Jim Dewberry's office. He had presented an hour long sales pitch for preventive maintenance on Jim's year old minicomputer system. The sales pitch had been quite convincing.

Jim Dewberry is the president and general manager of the Mid-West Wholesale Company. Mid-West Wholesale distributes over 300 different varieties of canned goods to 165 different independent grocery stores throughout a three-state territory. Mid-West installed a minicomputer last year to accept customer orders over touch-tone telephone systems. This system has been performing about as well as expected, but there have been five equipment failures since the hardware was installed. Maintenance services are provided by the hardware vendor, who has an office located approximately 20 miles from Mid-West's warehouse. The average downtime for the five hardware failures was 9.5 hours.

Mid-West has come to depend upon the computer system. Once orders are received from customers, the computer prints picking tickets which are used to pick orders in the warehouse and also produces the customers' invoices, a summary statement at the end of the month, and various management reports. When the machine is down, the orders are taken over the telephone for distant customers whereas nearby customers hand deliver their orders. With the computer system, each order is sorted into warehouse sequence location before the picking tickets are printed. This resequencing of the order produces quite a dramatic production increase for the order pickers since they only cover each aisle once in their filling of a single order. In all, Dewberry feels that each machine failure is costing him $5000 in lost production.

Hardware Reliability, Inc. (HRI) is offering a hardware maintenance package which includes a preventive maintenance plan for Mid-West's minicomputer system. HRI will perform a series of diagnostic checks on the hardware each month and will provide corrective maintenance service for any machine failures. The salesman has analyzed each of the five hardware failures which occurred during the first year period. He claims that the HRI diagnostic package could have detected two of those failures before they occurred and had a better than 50 percent chance of catching a third failure before it occurred. The diagnostic testing requires 1 hour of machine time each month. HRI will schedule the tests to take place at 8 o'clock in the morning, which is 1 hour prior to the time when Mid-West begins accepting customer orders. If the tests indicate the need to replace or make adjustments to any component HRI will perform the required maintenance at that time. The salesman indicated that the resulting downtime is typically cut in half.

Jim has asked the salesman to call him again next week after he has had time to think about the proposal.

QUESTIONS FOR DISCUSSION

1. What factors should Jim consider in evaluating this proposal?
2. What potential problems exist from switching the maintenance contract from the vendor to HRI (you might call several local computer hardware vendors to gain insight into this question)?
3. Can you determine a maximum amount that you would be willing to pay for HRI's services?

18.14 REFERENCES AND BIBLIOGRAPHY

1. Adam, E. E., Jr., and M. F. Pohlen, "A Scoring Methodology for Equipment Replacement Model Evaluation," *AIIE Transactions,* 6:308–314 (1974).
2. Barlow, R., and L. Hunter, "Optimum Preventive Maintenance Policies," *Operations Research,* 8:90–100 (1960).
3. Goldman, A. S., and T. B. Slattery, *Maintainability: A Major Element of System Effectiveness,* New York: Wiley, 1964.
4. Hardy, S. T., and L. J. Krajewski, "A Simulation of Interactive Maintenance Decisions," *Decision Sciences,* 6:92–105 (1975).
5. Jardine, A. K. S., *Maintenance, Replacement, and Reliability,* New York: Wiley, 1973.
6. Landers, R. R., *Reliability and Product Assurance,* Englewood Cliffs, N.J.: Prentice-Hall, 1963.
7. Morrow, L. C., *Maintenance Engineering Handbook,* 2nd ed., New York: McGraw-Hill, 1966.
8. Peck, L. G., and R. N. Hazelwood, *Finite Queuing Tables,* New York: Wiley, 1958.
9. Terborgh, G., *Business Investment Management,* Washington, D.C.: Machinery and Allied Products Institute, 1967.
10. ———, *A Practical Method of Investment Analysis: The MAPI System,* Washington, D.C.: Machinery and Allied Products Institute and Council for Technological Advancement, 1971.
11. Turban, E., "The Use of Mathematical Models in Plant Maintenance," *Management Science,* 13:342–358 (1967).
12. ———, "The Complete Computerized Maintenance System," *Industrial Engineering,* p. 20–27 (March, 1969).
13. Vonalven, W. H., ed., *Reliability Engineering,* Englewood Cliffs, N.J.: Prentice-Hall, 1964.
14. Wilkinson, J. J., "How to Manage Maintenance," *Harvard Business Review,* 46:100–111 (March–April, 1968).

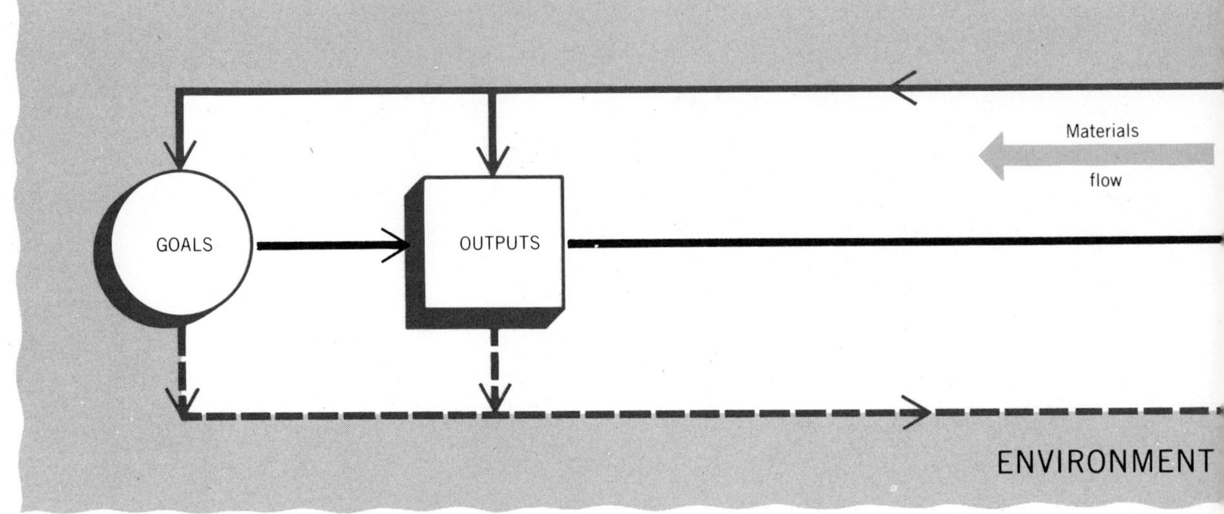

Chapter 19I

The Systems Interface: Information and Computers

CONCEPTS

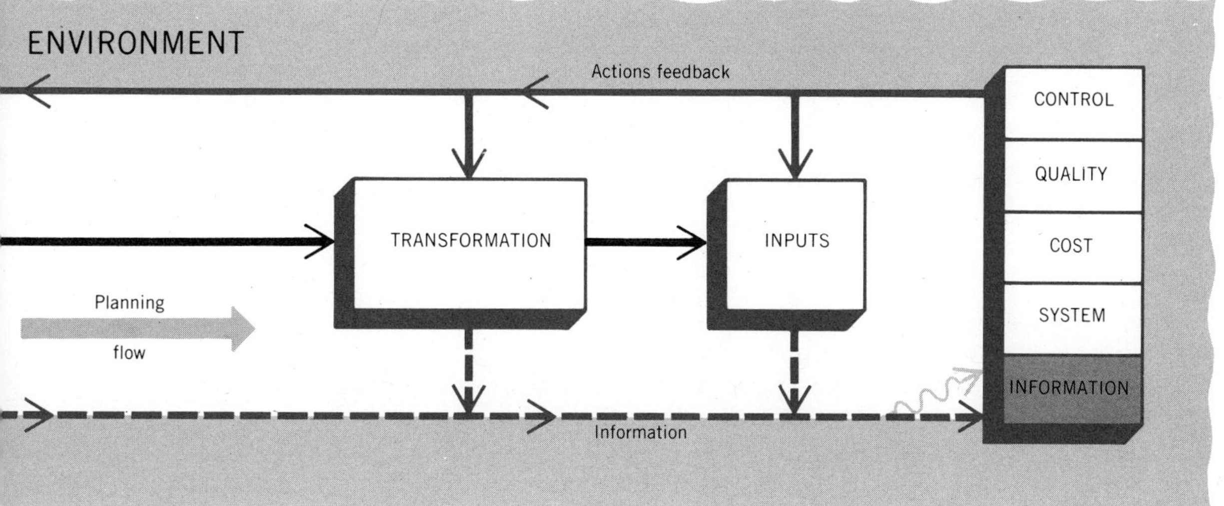

TOOLS AND APPLICATIONS

LEARNING OBJECTIVES

By the completion of the *Concepts* portion of this chapter the student should

1. Be aware of the importance and functions of information for the management of operations.
2. Understand the nature of information systems and the different types that exist.
3. Be able to derive the value of perfect information in a probabilistic situation and the other values of information.
4. Know the major categories of organizational information systems and the role of information systems in organizational operations.

CONCEPTS

We have now completed our discussion of the operations functions, as well as some others, for which special controls must be designed. Now that we know what operating systems to control we must also design an information system that will monitor the system elements and provide us with the proper information by which to exert control. That is the subject of this chapter. First we consider the general nature of information and its value, and then we relate it to organizational information systems and give some examples of such systems. In the *Tools and Applications* part of the chapter we discuss data processing systems, and the role of computers in those systems, in greater detail.

As we have discussed in many of the preceding chapters, sound management is required for an organization to succeed in accomplishing its objectives. In the planning, execution, and control of operations an information system is an absolute essential. Indeed, without information, management of the organization's operations would be impossible. The organization would be lost and totally dependent upon others for its maintenance. To an organization, management information is like a human's senses. A person who does not possess the senses of sight, hearing, taste, touch, and smell is dependent upon others for direction and maintenance. Such an individual, even though the basic intelligence exists, cannot know what his or her likes and dislikes are because they cannot be sensed. Therefore, the individual cannot rationally decide on objectives or courses of action to accomplish them. Nor can he or she sense that anything is wrong and therefore take corrective action. Without information an organization would be in a similar predicament; that is, unable to set objectives, plan courses of action, schedule, coordinate, and control operations.

The importance of information.

19.1 THE NATURE OF INFORMATION

Information is one of the basic inputs to organizations, along with materials, capital, staff, and so on. Information may be classified in any of a number of ways, one of which is external versus internal.

External and Internal Information

Sources of external information.

External information comes to the organization in many forms: through reports, manuals, newspapers, magazines; by way of salespeople, clients, consultants, stockholders, suppliers; and many such others. But probably the most important source of external information is brought to the organization through its staff in their own personal external activities such as shopping, taking classes, and the thousands of normal day-to-day activities that constitute living in a modern society.

Sources of internal information.

Of equal or even greater significance to the organization is **internal information** concerning the organization and its operation. This information consists of performance reports, directives, marketing studies, research reports, phone updates, the "grapevine" (gossip), committee conferences, and all the thousands of other ways by which the organization's staff come to obtain the information necessary to perform their duties.

The function of the operations information system.

One of the numerous internal information systems is the operations information system. This system receives and processes data relevant to the various operations activities and decisions; for example, aggregate production planning, machine loading, manpower planning, purchasing requirements, and so forth. Once information is received and processed, the operations information system can produce reports for operations planning, execution, and control. Before becoming too involved with the specifics regarding operations information, let us first discuss the nature of information in general.

"We've got all the 'Know-How.' We just don't know where it is."

(Reprinted by courtesy of Esselte Pendaflex Corporation.)

The Functions of Information

Simon [7] comments that information is used at various levels within an organization to answer three broad types of questions:

1. Scorekeeping questions.
2. Attention-directing questions.
3. Problem-solving questions.

Scorekeeping

Scorekeeping information for reporting.

Scorekeeping information allows managers to answer questions such as "How well am I doing in meeting my budget?," "What is the currently available spare parts inventory balance?," "Which department produced this defective item?" and so on. A considerable amount of organizational information is recorded and stored simply for internal and external reporting purposes and for possible later use. In some organizations the bulk of this scorekeeping information is gathered and reported by an "integrated" information system. In other organizations, special information systems (accounting, operations, personnel) produce scorekeeping information relevant to particular purposes only.

Attention-directing

Attention directing information for "management by exception."

Attention-directing information helps managers to answer the general question "Are there any problems or impending problems which I should be concerned about and/or working on?" Attention-directing information is generally less widely available within organizations than is scorekeeping information and is typically derived from special formatting, or analysis, of scorekeeping information or directly from a control system. The variance reports discussed in Chapter 17I and the control charts discussed in Chapter 15 are examples of attention-directing information used by the operations manager.

Problem-solving

Problem-solving information from data analysis.

Problem-solving information aids managers in solving specific problems, such as which machine to purchase, how many items to order in one production lot, whether to make or buy a needed subcomponent and so on. Because of the complexity of this information, usually requiring special analyses of data, it is the least likely to be systematically collected by most organizations. Numerous examples of problem-solving information have been presented in this book. In the chapters on inventory management, data on costs and volumes of use were combined to provide answers to questions of "how much" and "when" to order. In Chapters 10I, 11I, and 14I, on acquiring inputs, several information models were presented to aid management's selection of new equipment, vendors for purchased items, and even employees.

Information Systems and MIS

The IS.

It is the function of the organization's information system (IS) to provide the information necessary to answer each of the above three types of questions. In actuality, this information system consists of a number of smaller information systems, each serving a specialized purpose. The accounting information system gathers and records data for financial accountability and reporting purposes. In a similar fashion, operations and marketing each have their own information systems, which may be either formalized or quite informal. Of all the information systems perhaps the one receiving the most attention has been the *management information system* (**MIS**). The intent of this formalized system is to provide the various levels of management with the information needed to perform the following types of functions:

Management information system to provide timely information to management.

- Set goals
- Develop new products and/or services.
- Establish staffing levels for the coming year.
- Develop the aggregate production plan.
- Set inventory levels.
- Gauge individual and group performance.
- Assess market demands.
- Control operations.
- Implement decisions.
- Detect problems.

The formal MIS refers to the set of policies, procedures, people, forms, equipment, and reports required to produce information for management's needs, especially their decision-making needs. However, every manager knows that such a formal system will never provide *all* the information she or he needs and, thus, other sources and contacts, an **informal information system**, must still be maintained. For example, rumors reaching the manager faintly implying that Joe is playing politics, or that XYZ Corp. may soon be coming out with a new soap called "SWET," are extremely valuable bits of information that will probably never be found in a formalized information system, yet may provide 80 percent of the basis for a particular management decision. Gordon [5] gives an example of this from his own experience.

Formal versus informal information systems.

A critical aspect of the (management) task is determining the nature of the invisible information system which exists in any organization. In a small organization which has been staffed for many years by the same people this information system is not necessarily formalized but may be critical in sensing developments in its health. An ability to deal on a one to one basis with employees, customers, suppliers, and other contacts appears to be daily and without advance warning. Finally, the necessity of constant interaction with employees at their work stations on a personal basis is an essential form of motivating performance and at the same time gathering information.

The Value of Information

The economic value of information.

Information is usually considered in terms of its **economic value.** How much more efficiently can I produce knowing this information? How much better service can I provide with this information system? How much more well informed will my decisions be with this data? But Mock [6] has stated that: "The economic value of information concept, while being derived from a sound logical construct, has not proven to be of frequent value in the design of more effective information systems, particularly those oriented towards feedback, learning, attention-directing, and score-keeping." There are at least two other information concepts presented by Mock which may be even more valuable in information system design—the information system's **model value** and its **action-effectiveness value.**

Other values of information.

Model value of information to improve the manager's view of the world.

An information system can improve the operations manager's view of the world. That is, managers have perceptions or "models" of the way things operate, the relationships between various components of the organization, the connection between organizational and/or competitor actions and outcomes, and so on. An information system can improve a manager's subjective model of the situation within which she or he is operating. For example, an operations manager may believe that his or her department is as "productive" as ever, but a formal report might show that output per worker hour has been dropping by 2 percent per month. To the extent that this improvement in knowledge (learning) resulting from an information system increases the manager's expected environmental returns, the information system has "model value."

Action-effectiveness value of information to increase environmental returns.

Not only does the operations manager often not know the relationship between actions, states-of-the-world, and outcomes, but just as often she or he does not know the relationship between actions taken and the environmental returns received. The "action-effectiveness value" of information is defined as the expected increase in returns resulting from an information system or report which leads the manager to better understand and predict the results (in terms of environmental returns) of particular decisions or actions. As an example, an operations manager may decide to work 10-hour days each time there is a production backlog. But, with a new formal reporting system, the manager can see that working overtime does not help to diminish the backlog.

Information for goal accomplishment.

Neither of these two values of information are easily measured. We present them primarily to make the student aware of the fact that information can be useful not only for specific decisions but for learning about the organization and the environment within which decisions are made. The eventual value of all information is measured in terms of increased accomplishment of organizational goals (i.e., increasing environmental returns).

Several important conclusions regarding information systems can thus be deduced:

1. Information systems will decline in model and action effectiveness value for a given manager over time. The system may have to constantly change to keep up with the learning needs of individual managers.

2. Information systems should be designed for specific purposes (or, at least, the purposes of each report should be identified) and should be evaluated according to their success in achieving these purposes. A system designed primarily to produce action-effectiveness information should not be evaluated on the basis of economic value.
3. Information systems training for managers should stress the three roles of information, particularly the model and action-effectiveness values, as they are often initially more important than the information's economic value.

Managers have also found that voluminous amounts of data, such as in thick computer reports, effectively hide whatever value lies within. For example, it is easier to find a needle in a box of straw than it is in a box of pins. Some computerized management information systems have been corrected of their earlier "overreporting" tendencies and now print **exception reports** for managers in order to facilitate the "management by exception" concept. A production manager in a large job shop does not need a daily status report on all 300 jobs in the shop but rather a report on those jobs falling behind schedule.

Overreporting and management by exception.

Although the tendency is to think of organizational information systems as computerized, because the majority of the publicity about information systems has concerned the computer and its abilities in this capacity, most information systems are manual. In fact, computer systems analysts will caution against computerizing *any* system where an acceptable manual system has never been designed. The point is to refrain from "building in" the errors and inadequacies of previous manual systems. Rather, a computerized system should be an expansion of a successful manual (or electromechanical, as discussed in the next section) system to simply handle larger volumes of data and/or to provide more rapid compilation of needed information. There are, however, exceptions to this caution. Some systems, such as the MRP systems discussed in Chapter 13, were not feasible before the development of the economical computer. The sheer effort required to "explode" product profiles and to prepare capacity plans in a timely manner was beyond the capability of human "processors." Such systems as these are exceptions to the general rule that a good manual system should exist first.

Computerizing successful systems.

In the next section we will extend our preceding discussion and more explicitly consider the need for information about specific organizational operations. Then we will look at the design of an MIS in both a product and a service organization.

19.2 ORGANIZATIONAL INFORMATION SYSTEMS

Organizational information can be classified into five broad categories:

1. Financial information.
2. Logistical information.
3. Personnel information.

4. Marketing information.
5. Environmental information.

Information Categories

Financial information

Financial information reports on flows and stocks of financial resources within the organization. For example, a fixed assets accounting system provides information about the initial cost, book value, location, age, and, oftentimes, the maintenance, operating costs, and replacement value of the equipment owned by the organization. Other financial information systems include the payroll system, the accounts payable and accounts receivable systems, the cash management system, and the general ledger system. These systems account for the economic returns received by the organization and for other economic exchanges between the organization and the environment.

Logistical information

Logistical information reports on the flows, stocks, and schedules of physical resources within the organization. For example, in a manufacturing organization, flows and stocks of raw materials, work-in-process, and finished goods inventories are monitored, as through an MRP system, as are the locations and availabilities of productive assets such as materials handling and machining equipment. Logistics information also includes information regarding production scheduling and inventory and other resource requirements planning.

Systems typically classified as logistical systems include machine loading systems, machine utilization reporting, inventory and status systems, MRP systems, and so forth.

Personnel information

Personnel information reports on the flows and stocks of people within the organization. Included in the personnel information category is information concerning all currently employed personnel such as education, position, title, department, age, sex, and, in some systems, evaluation information and promotability. The personnel system also contains information concerning manpower budgets to guide in recruiting and training activities.

Marketing information

Marketing information reports on demand for and satisfaction with the organization's products or services. Marketing information includes information on demand for products and services, on new markets for existing organizational outputs, and on new outputs. The marketing system includes such systems as sales analysis by product line and territory, demand forecasting systems, order entry systems, and customer complaint reporting systems.

The student should keep in mind that marketing, a concept most often related only to business organizations, applies equally well to not-for-profit and governmental organizations. The objective in each of these organizations is one of meeting a societal need; only the returns are measured differently.

Environmental information

Environmental information is a broad category including such information as governmental regulatory changes, changes in consumer desires and tastes, competitor and industry actions, industry structure changes (e.g., major new entrants), supplier and raw material information, and general economic conditions.

Obviously, each of these information elements is potentially of major importance to the organization and thus must be monitored so that the organization can anticipate and react to any shifts. While the majority of information items used by an organization can be classified into one of the above five categories, it is clear that the categories are not mutually exclusive. For example, how would an organization classify the fact that "John Fritz sold $3750 worth of brand *Z* pencils to be delivered by January 1, 198X?" This information has financial, personnel, logistical, and marketing implications and could therefore be classified into each of these categories.

Information is typically not of one category.

In fact, depending upon the level of **integration** of the information system, this item of data could well be entered once into the system and impact each of the four individual systems categories. The concept of data base management around which many large scale computer systems have been developed lends itself to the single entry idea. One data element can be accessed and used with a number of systems to produce the most meaningful information to the managers using that portion of the system.

Single entry data base management.

The operations manager is not particularly concerned that John sold the pencils or what the final sale price is, but, she or he is concerned that some number of brand *Z* pencils will have to be available for shipping on January 1. The operations manager will also have to assess the logistics system to determine the current inventory level of brand *Z* pencils and may have to consider the department's capacity to produce the pencils necessary to fill the order.

Information use for operations.

Information that is typically referred to as operations information is derived from the logistical information system. While all of the other systems provide input to this system (such as customer order information from the marketing system or labor availability information from the personnel system), the logistical system produces the specific inputs used by operations managers in the performance of their roles.

The importance of logistical information to operations.

For example, customer order information, inventory status information, and sales forecasts are used in the logistical system to produce aggregate demand projections. These aggregate requests are combined with machine loading or other capacity planning information and with specific manufacturing information (i.e., equipment and labor required to produce each item) to derive master scheduling reports. This information is further utilized with inventory status, the current machine loading reports, and the capacity plan to produce the short-term schedule.

Information flow in a job shop.

Figure 19.1 illustrates the major flows of information and physical goods through a typical "make-to-order" job shop. Information flows are necessary to control the physical flows of raw materials, work-in-process, and finished goods within the system and between outside suppliers and customers. The organization is a system, and as such, we know that it is therefore made up of various parts which are interdependent. The coordination of these interdependent parts is carried out through the use of information flows between the parts.

The customer's order starts the cycle.

In order to understand the relationship between the physical flows and the information flows, let us consider Figure 19.1 for a typical make-to-order job shop. The flow of information commonly begins with the submission of an order to a sales "rep" or the marketing department by the customer. The customer's purchase order is received by the marketing department, is verified for accuracy (and oftentimes a credit check is run), and the customer's purchase order is transcribed onto an internal document, called a sales order. The sales order specifies the item identification, the quantity of each item ordered, any specifications such as size, shape, color, and so forth. Also the requested shipping date, the customer's purchase order number, and an internal sales order number are entered onto the sales order. The sales order is typically a multiple-part form with copies going to several different departments. In our example, copy 1 is sent to the production department where a production order is produced for each item on the sales order. Copy 2 is sent to the accounting department where it is filed for later billing purposes. Copy 3 is sent to the shipping department as an information copy for the shipping foreman. She or he will use this information to prepare any necessary pallets or shipping cartons which will be required. The Copy 4 is used as a file copy for the marketing department, which allows them to respond to any customer requests and (since it is numbered as the others are numbered) allows the salesman to keep track of the order in the shop.

Issuing the production order.

The production supervisor will order all items necessary for the production of each production order. Materials requisitions to central stores may be written as well as special purchase requisitions for items that are typically not stocked within the shop. Materials requisitions sent to central stores will result in one of two actions by the stores manager. She or he will either send raw materials when needed to the production department or will place orders for raw materials that are not available in stock. Purchase requisitions sent to the purchasing department will result in the production of a purchase order. As shown in Figure 19.1, the purchase order is a four-part form. The first part of the purchase order is sent to the vendor, the second part is sent to the receiving department to be matched up with the vendor's bill of lading, the third part is sent to the accounting department to be used as a control copy and the fourth part is filed in the purchasing department to be used to follow up on late and/or lost purchasing.

The vendor will eventually send the ordered items to the shop. They will be received through the receiving department which will issue a receiving report, one copy of which is sent along to the central stores with the incoming raw materials and

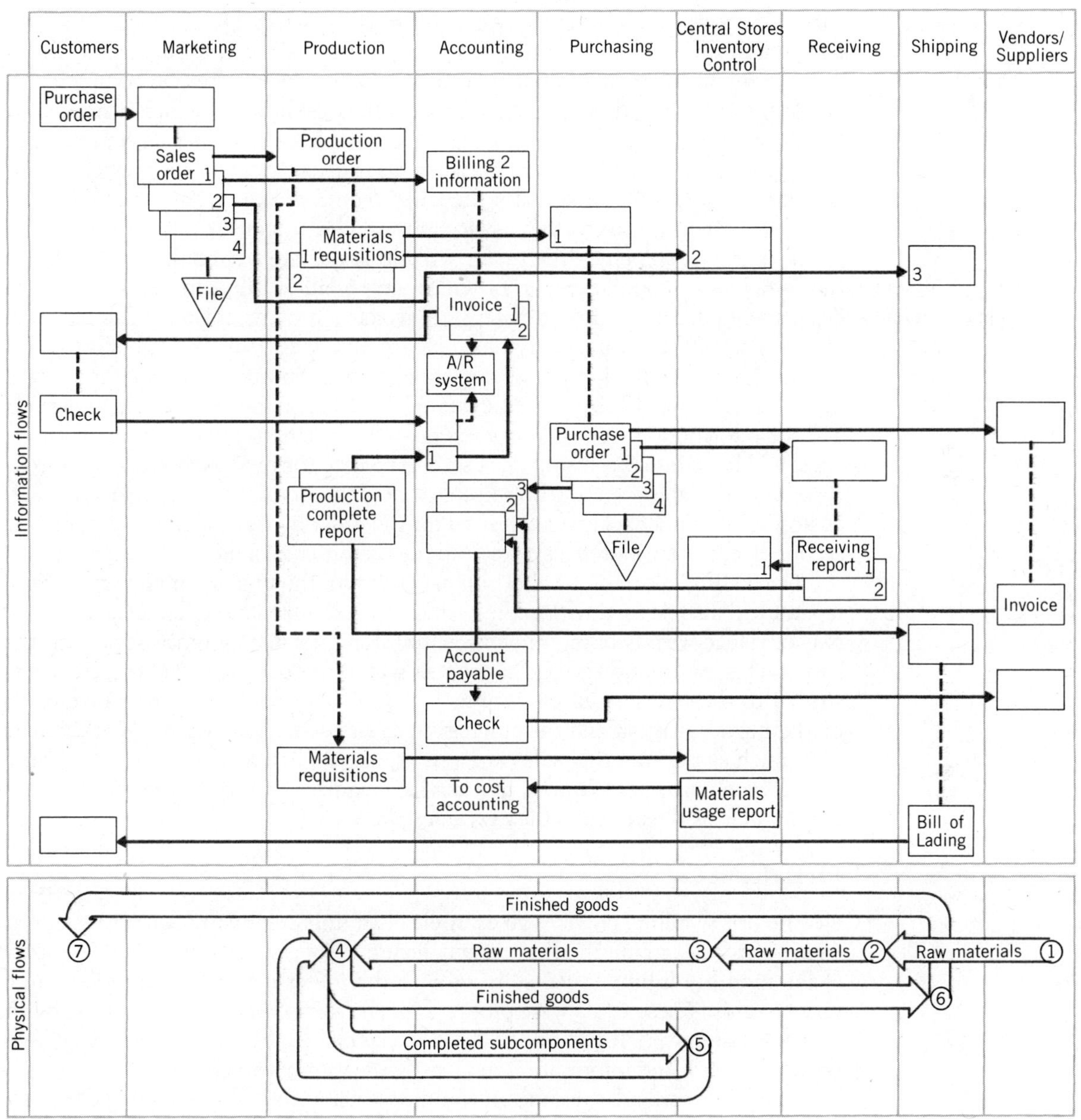

Figure 19.1 Information and goods flows in a job shop.

a second copy, which is sent to the accounting department as a control copy for payment of the vendor's incoming invoice. The central store, in turn, sends the ordered items to the production department for their use. Production completes the necessary transformation tasks resulting in a finished product, which is ready to be sent to shipping. The production department completes a production completed report, one copy of which is sent to the accounting department for the preparation of a customer invoice and possibly for the shipping bill of lading. Also the production completed report is used by the cost accounting department to evaluate performance on this job. The shipping department will either prepare a bill of lading based upon the completed production report or will receive a bill of lading from the accounting department (oftentimes in computerized invoicing systems, the bill of lading is simply one part of the invoice with the dollar amounts omitted). The bill of lading will be sent along with the shipped goods to the customer. Shortly thereafter, the accounting department will have prepared an invoice based upon the original sales order copy and the information received from the production department. One part of the invoice will be sent to the customer. A second invoice copy will be used as input to the accounts receivable system which keeps track of the amount owed and payed by each customer. When a check is submitted for the order by the customer, it enters the accounts receivable system as a credit to the customer's balance.

Shipping and invoicing complete the cycle.

Depending upon the level of sophistication of the organization, various other reports will also be used within the system. For example, the materials usage report may be issued weekly or monthly by central stores, for all jobs processed during that period. This information is used by the cost accounting department to prepare reports similar to those discussed in Chapter 17I. Similar reports can be prepared for the marketing department and the purchasing department. Also, various marketing reports such as the monthly sales analysis report can be prepared from information available on customer invoices. In a service organization the information flows are very similar, as illustrated in the next example.

T.H.E. Electric Co.

Electric utility billing provides an example of an important part of an organizational data processing and information system. Figure 19.2 presents a simplified schematic of the monthly billing cycle, starting with the meter reader holding a handful of service cards. These cards were prepared for the meter reader ahead of time by the data processing system. On each card has been punched the date, an identifying number for the card, and information to identify the meter (sometimes the address). To one side of the card are a number of columns, each with 10 digits (0–9) in them. The meter reader's job is to mark the digit in each column corresponding to the meter reading with a special pencil. These are called "mark sensed" cards. When the meter reader turns in the monthly service cards at the end of the day they are input to a special optical scanner and punch which "reads" the marks and punches the cards according to the meter reading indicated.

On occasion, a card will be missing or blank because the meter reader lost that

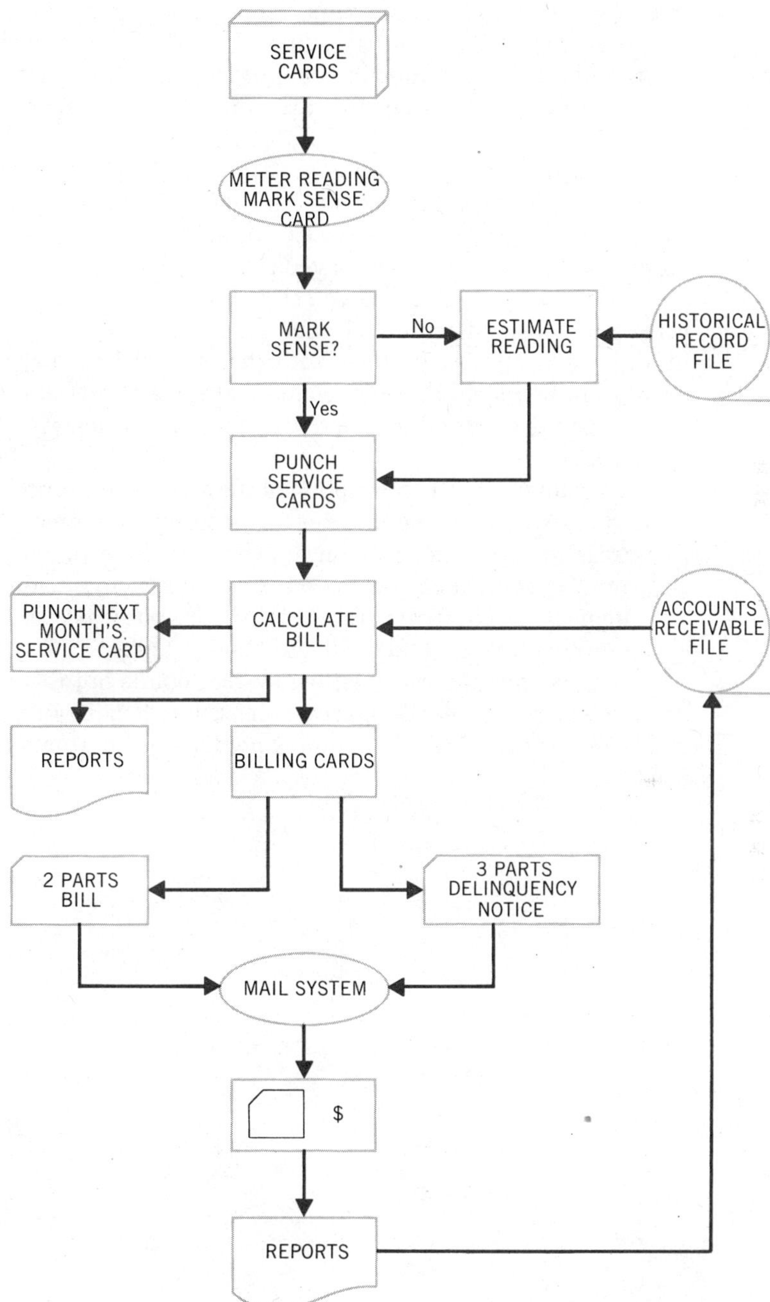

Figure 19.2 Electric billing system.

card or was unable to get a reading, for any number of reasons (e.g., "dog"). In that case, the computer *estimates* a reading for the month based on historical usage stored in a record file. If the computer *underestimates* the bill then the following month's reading will automatically correct the mistake by the appropriate overcharge, and vice versa.

The next step is a strategic one. Based on the punched service card and an accounts receivable (A/R) file, the monthly bill is calculated, including any overdue amounts, the next month's service cards are punched, billing and usage reports are printed, and three-part pre-perforated cards are punched for mailing to the customer.

For normal billing, only two parts of the billing card are mailed, the third part being torn off and discarded. The customer then tears off one section of the card for his or her own files, and returns the other part with the payment. If the account is overdue, however, all three parts are sent, the last part being a delinquency notice. Upon return of the third part, and payment, income reports are printed and the A/R file updated.

Not included in this description of the system are control procedures to process an account even if payment is not forthcoming, to correct the A/R file if a check "bounces," to ensure meter readings are not estimated for too many months in a row, and a number of other ancillary, but important system functions.

Originally an effective manual system, this one was updated through EAM to an electromechanical one, and finally, to a computerized EDP system. This description of a relatively simple utility billing system points out the complexity of just one function of a service firm's information system. In addition to the billing/collection cycle there is the relatively complex production-information side of the business itself.

TOOLS AND APPLICATIONS

19.3 THE DATA PROCESSING SYSTEM

Earlier we discussed the concept of information. More often than not the two terms "data" and "information" are considered to be synonyms for one another. This misinterpretation leads to poor communication about information systems and often results in confused systems design. To avoid misuse of the two terms we will define both as used herein.

Data and Information

Data as raw facts.

Data are raw facts, or simply, the recorded measurements of activities, objects, and events. Data are used to represent the following items, for example: 260 assembly hours, six milling machines, and four new car sales. Data is constantly being generated within and outside the organization and this data is only a small fraction of what might be produced. Events and activities are constantly taking place which could, at the desire of the organization, be measured and recorded, thus creating data.

Information as processed data with meaning.

The only reason for the collection of data within an organization is to produce *information.* **Information** is simply data that has been processed so as to be meaningful to the person who receives it. Clearly, what is "information" to some may well be simply meaningless "data" to another. For example, a radio announcement of the Sunday football game scores of "17 to 6, 33 to 0, and 10 to 7" would only be "data" to football fans. However, the announcement "the Jets over the Rams, 17 to 6; the Cowboys shut out the Vikings by 33 points; and the Oilers edged the Dolphins 10 to 7" would be highly informative to the fans, although perhaps still just meaningless data to many other people.

A more operational definition has been given by Davis [4]: "Information is data that has been processed in a form meaningful to the recipient and is of real or perceived value in current or prospective decisions." In short, information is processed data—processed in a way that makes it useful to some end user within or outside the organization. This idea guides the entire design of any information system. Only data that can be processed to provide information meaningful to and valuable for decisions made by a given end user should be collected. There is a clear analogy between an information system and a manufacturing system. Data is the raw material of the information system. The procedures for compiling, sorting, summarizing, and reporting are equivalent to the manufacturing process. And information is the finished output of the process.

Basic Data Processing Functions

Data is converted to information through the use of a data "processing" system. While this system can be made up of various combinations of people, paper, and equipment, the same basic functions must exist within any system (see Reference 2, pp. 26–27). These basic functions are

1. **Capturing**—measuring and recording the original event, activity, or object in some form that can be subjected to further processing (e.g., recording receipt of a shipment on an invoice, recording hours worked on a particular job on a time card).
2. **Verifying**—checking and validating the data to be sure that it was originally captured correctly.
3. **Classifying**—placing the captured data into categories to increase the usefulness of the data (e.g., a purchase of $36.12 in materials can be categorized as cash or credit, by inventory type of the items purchased, by department, and by date).
4. **Arranging**—otherwise called sorting, this operation puts data into some prespecified sequence so that it can be processed further [e.g., an invoice file might be sorted in customer number order so that it can be matched against the accounts receivable (A/R) file for A/R updating].
5. **Summarizing**—reducing data by either mathematically aggregating it (e.g., finding the average output of all machinists) or by logically reducing it (e.g., finding all workers whose output exceeds 90 units a day).
6. **Calculating**—performing mathematical and/or logical operations on data (e.g., computing gross pay; net pay; state, local, and federal income tax; unemployment compensation tax; and other deductions from an employee's time card).
7. **Storing**—placing data onto some medium so that it can later be recalled (e.g., typing a list of employee names and social security numbers, writing a tape file of the current finished goods inventory).
8. **Retrieving**—searching and accessing specific data from locations where it was previously stored (e.g., randomly accessing a customer record from a computer disk file, going to the file cabinet and pulling the grade lists for the POM 350 class, Spring 1978).
9. **Reproducing**—duplicating data from one location to another (e.g., copying a letter on a Xerox copier, copying the contents of a large file to a disk file on a computer).
10. **Communicating**—transmitting data from one location to another (e.g., sending a memo through the campus mail, telecommunicating data from a remote data collection terminal to a host computer in a large scale data processing network).

All data processing systems make use of these 10 functions, although not every function is required in the production of a particular information output.

Data Processing Methods

In most modern organizations the information system (or data processing system) is composed of elements representative of three distinct methods of data processing activity. These methods are

1. Manual processing.
2. Electromechanical processing.
3. Electronic processing.

Manual

The **manual** method combines people with other simple elements (pencils, forms, typewriters, etc.) to form a data processing system. Although simple in basis, the system may be mechanized or automated to varying degrees. The mechanical elements might include an adding machine, typewriter, checkwriter, cash register, calculator, duplicating machine, and so forth.

Integrated data processing (**IDP**) procedures may be utilized also. IDP refers to the reduction of duplication in the processing of data. This is accomplished in a manual system through the use of carbon paper, window envelopes, credit cards, and other such techniques which minimize the chance for errors in duplicating information. Of course, since the original recording of the information is reused so frequently it is crucial that it be correct.

Electromechanical

Although electrically driven machines may have been used in the manual data processing method, the term **electromechanical** is reserved for methods that utilize a *machine-readable* input, such as punched paper tape or, more commonly, punched cards. Since these systems are all generally oriented to punched cards these days, the electromechanical method is also referred to as the "punched-card method." Other names for this method are the **unit record** method, the **tabulating** method, and the "electric accounting machine" (**EAM**) method.

In this method, people do not enter raw data directly into the system but instead through punched cards prepared on a **keypunch** machine (Figure 19.3) which, in turn, are read by the system. These systems do *not* convert data into electronic form, as a computer does, but mechanically manipulate the punched cards instead, according to the punches in them which are read electrically. The system consists of a number of separate machines which can punch and sort cards, add, subtract, multiply, divide, and print and convert data. They are best used for strict accounting purposes.

Electronic

Here is where the computer is used to transform and manipulate data in magnetic and electronic impulse form. There is so much to be said about computers and **electronic data processing** that we will devote the next section exclusively to this topic.

Figure 19.3 IBM 029 card read/punch.

The growth of minicomputers.

Relatively few organizations use only one method of data processing. Typical systems within medium and large scale organizations consist of elements from each of the three classes of data processing methods. Only relatively small organizations rely solely on manual systems and, with the recent advent of very low cost ($5–$15,000) mini- and microcomputers, even fewer will be relying on manual systems in the near future.

19.4 COMPUTERS AND ELECTRONIC DATA PROCESSING

EDP.

Electronic data processing (**EDP**) systems, or computer systems, in organizations are made up of three major elements.

1. Hardware.
2. Software.
3. People.

Hardware

The term EDP **hardware** refers to the equipment that is necessary to process data electronically. This equipment is further subdivided by major function as

1. The central processing unit (**CPU**).
2. Input devices.
3. Output devices.

Central processing unit

The crucial CPU.

General purpose objective.

This is the computer in the system. A computer, as the term is generally used here, refers to a *general purpose, electronic machine* which is capable of receiving and *internally storing* a set of *instructions* as well as *input data* and, *without human intervention, executing* the instructions by performing *mathematical and logical operations* in a *digital* fashion, and finally producing an *output.* This definition eliminates such devices (which are also correctly referred to as computers) as special energy management systems for buildings (Figure 19.4), ignition (carburetor timing) devices for automobiles, and process control computers used in steel mills and petroleum refineries. While all of these devices receive input, execute instructions without human intervention, and produce some signal as output, they are special purpose rather than general and in many cases are **analog**, not **digital** systems (i.e., they measure flows rather than impulses).

Digital versus analog.

Figure 19.5 illustrates the relationships between the CPU and input and output devices. The CPU is generally made up of

Primary storage

Control unit

Arithmetic/logic unit

As can be seen in the figure, data and instructions are transmitted from input devices to primary storage. All data and results of processing (such as computed amounts, etc.) are stored temporarily in the **primary storage**.

The workings of the CPU.

The **control unit** literally sends messages to all other elements of the system to tell the input devices when to transmit data and instructions, the primary storage where to store data and instructions, the **arithmetic/logic** unit what operations to perform, where to store the results back in primary storage, and when and where to send any output.

The arithmetic/logic unit performs addition, subtraction, multiplication, division, and logical operations (such as comparisons of two numbers to determine the largest). The unit performs one operation at a time and in the order specified in the stored instructions, returning all intermediate results to primary storage.

Input devices

Input devices are equipment that provide one or both of the following functions:

1. Convert original data from human readable to machine readable form.
2. Convert machine readable data into signals to be transmitted electronically to the CPU.

The major input devices (some of which also serve as **secondary storage** devices) are

1. Console typewriter.
2. **Card reader.**

Honeywell can help you achieve energy savings far greater than you got by adjusting thermostats and reducing lighting levels during your initial energy conservation efforts. In fact, we can probably cut energy waste by 20-30% . . . and you won't even feel it—except on the bottom line.

We do it with our Delta energy management system. As a management tool, Delta puts real teeth into energy accountability. It gives you the necessary information and control capability to analyze, monitor and reduce your building's energy consumption.

The Delta energy management computer ties together all of your primary energy-using systems—boilers, chillers, motors, pumps, ventilating systems, lighting, the whole works—into a single system. It centrally collects building operating information on a constant, real time basis, processes the information into meaningful data, and automatically "closes the loop" by taking corrective action. Net result: drastically reduced total energy expense—electricity, oil, gas, coal and steam.

The Delta computer and its related hardware do the energy saving functions for you—automatically—without the constant attention of an operator. The only time you want your operator involved is when something goes wrong . . . or when he wants to manually turn down a temperature set-point, or override the automatic program, for example.

Then, we make it easy for him. The Delta console was engineered to give the operator all the information he needs in a simple, uncomplicated and uncluttered way. Coupled with schematic projections, the operator can receive information, send data signals and analyze every mechanical and electrical system in your building.

Depending on building needs and your requirements, other peripheral units can be added to assist your building operations personnel.

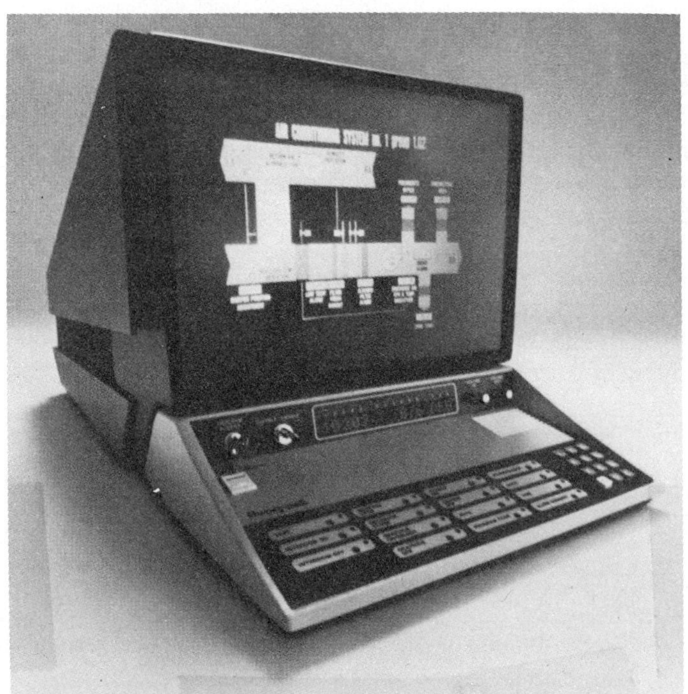

Figure 19.4 The Delta energy management system. (*Source.* Company brochure. Reprinted courtesy of Honeywell. Delta 1000 is copyrighted.)

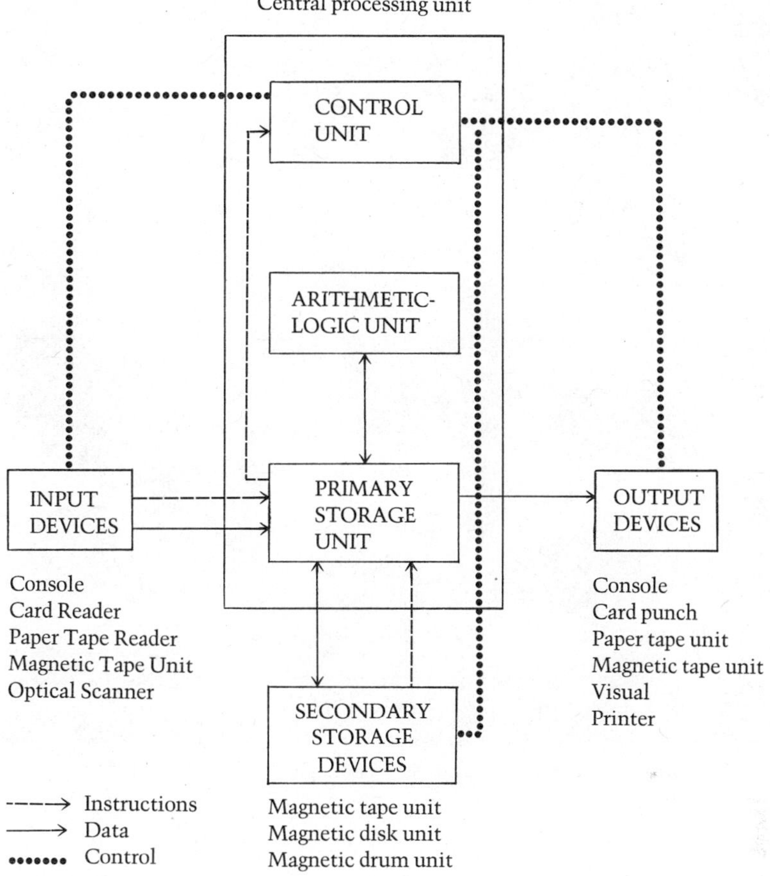

Figure 19.5 Computer system schematic.

3. Magnetic **tape drive**.
4. Magnetic **disk drive**.

CRT. 5. Cathode ray tube (**CRT**) terminal (Figure 19.6).

OCR. MICR. POS. In addition to these there are special devices such as optical character recognition machines (**OCR**), magnetic ink character recognition machines (**MICR**), paper tape punches and readers, keyboard-to-tape systems, and point of sale (**POS**) systems.*

Output devices

Output devices are machines that accept the results of computer processing in either human readable form or in a form that can be further processed by machine. The major output devices are

* Detailed discussion of each of the input and output devices listed in this chapter is beyond the scope of this text. For more information the student is directed to References 1 or 2.

Figure 19.6 A CRT terminal. *Source.* Reprinted courtesy of Sylvania Commercial Electronics Corporation.

1. **Card punch.**
2. **Printer.**
3. Magnetic tape drive.
4. Magnetic disk drive.
5. **Paper tape punch.**
6. CRT terminal.

In addition to these devices, special audio response systems, microfilm printers, and line plotters can also receive and transmit output from the CPU. Figures 19.4 and 19.6 illustrate some of these output devices.

Software

Software: the program instructions.

The term **software** refers to the computer programs necessary for the operation of any computer system. Without software, computers cannot perform even the simplest function of addition or subtraction, cannot read even a single card, or print one line of output. Software is usually either **system software** or **applications software.**

System software

OS.

Control by supervisory programs.

This consists of **supervisory** or *executive* programs (typically called the **operating system, OS**) which act to control the allocation of computer resources and the operation of peripheral equipment, and compilers which convert user programs into machine language instructions.

Supervisory programs serve several functions which include

1. Allocating storage space and maintaining locations of data and user programs.
2. Allocating computer operating time to specific tasks.
3. Input/output scheduling and execution.
4. Monitoring the status of peripheral input and output devices.

Translation by the compiler.

Compilers translate programs written in high level computer programming languages such as **BASIC, FORTRAN, PL1,** and **COBOL** into programs in **machine language**. Since the computer can only understand instructions coded in **binary** (0 and 1) form, all instructions must either be originally programmed in machine language or be converted. System software is typically provided by the computer vendor although there are some firms that specialize in developing advanced computer operating software.

Applications software

Programs for specific applications.

This software is made up of the various programs designed for specific data processing functions. For example, the set of programs required to produce monthly inventory reports and to maintain the accounts receivable file for a hardware wholesaler is called an applications system or package. Applications programs are generally developed and programmed by the user in user-oriented languages such as BASIC or PL1 although there is a distinct trend toward the use of "packaged" systems. Software packages are developed by "software houses" to serve a general function in an organization. Copies of the package are sold or leased to numerous users, generally at a cost that is significantly less than "in house" development of the same system.

People

Four EDP personnel functions.

Data processing personnel are the third major component of any EDP system. Since the computer requires special knowledge to program and operate, various computer personnel are required. At least four functions are routinely fulfilled by people in an EDP system.

- **Systems analyst**—analyzes information needs of the end user and communicates these needs to the programmer as system design specifications.
- **Programmer**—converts the design specifications into a set of computer programs and operating instructions that will accomplish the user's needs.
- **Data entry** operator—converts input data in human readable (source document) form into machine readable form (i.e., computer cards, punched paper tape, magnetic tape, etc.).

- **Operator**—follows operating instructions in running applications system on the computer, loads and unloads data, programs, and files.

Types of EDP Systems

Batch versus real time systems.

Electronic data processing systems in organizations are either **batch** or **real time** systems. In both cases, organizational data processing is typified by high volumes of input and output, with relatively simple and repetitive computations and logic. Typical business data processing applications include payroll processing, billing and collection, inventory management, and accounts payable processing.

File maintenance.

Many data processing applications, particularly the routine accounting applications, consist of maintaining up-to-date data files. That is, files are updated with new information as organizational transactions take place. It is common for input documents, which contain the information from each transaction, to be accumulated in batches that, at specified intervals, are used to update the necessary files. Batch proc-

"Good news, Miss Morgan . . . your keypunch machine will be here tomorrow."

essing applications are those that do not require a constantly up-to-date file. For example, a general ledger system that is used to produce a monthly income statement and balance sheet for a company such as that shown in Figure 19.7 does not have to be constantly up-to-date. Journal entries to this system can be batched until the end of the month whereupon they are keypunched and processed as one batch as in Figure 19.7.

On the other hand, many operations data processing systems must be real time systems. That is, data files (such as inventory or job status) must be constantly up-to-

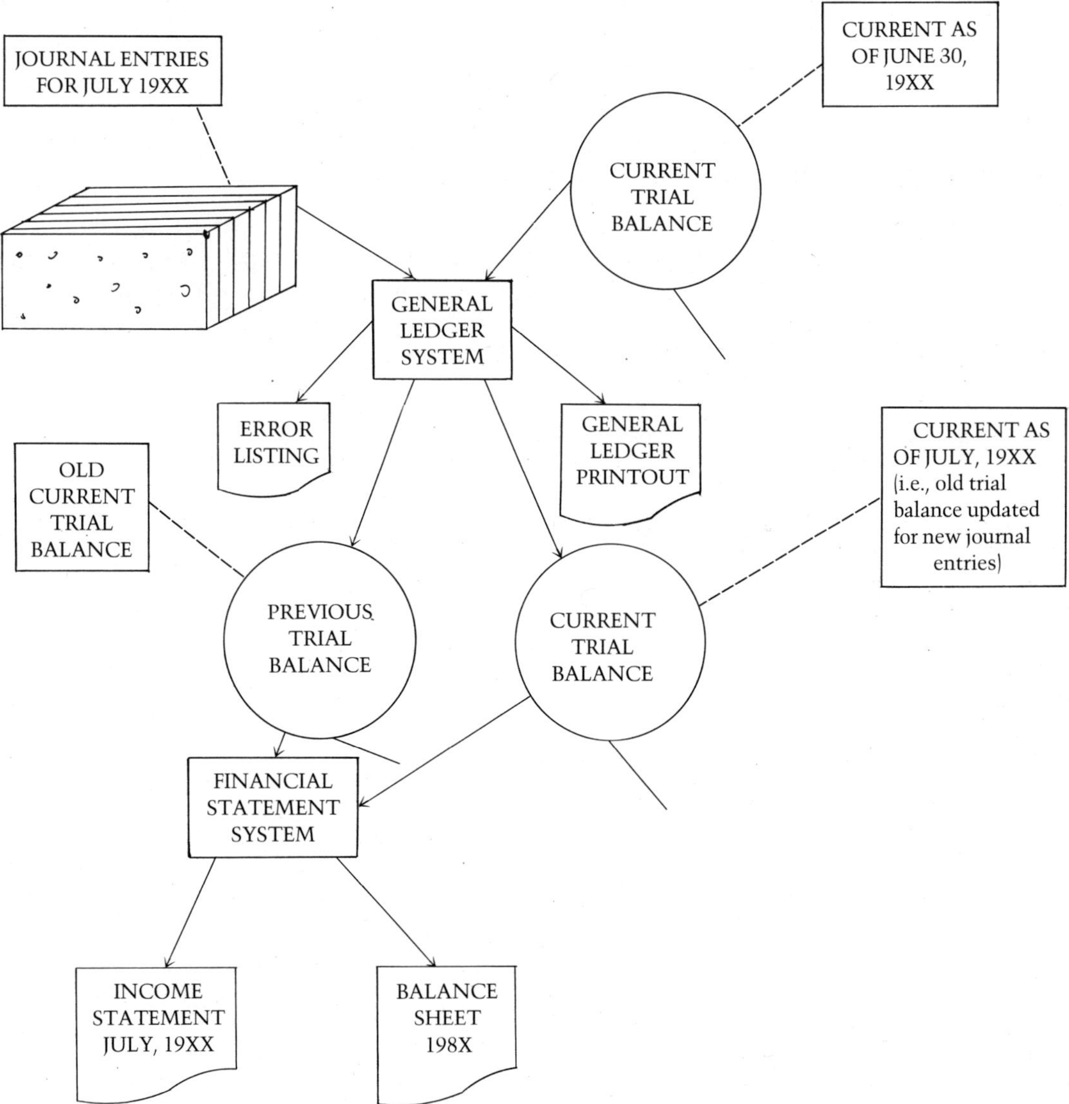

Figure 19.7 Typical accounting system.

date as a result of inquiries regarding that data. Rather than batching transactions for subsequent processing, real time systems process transaction data and update files as the transactions take place. Data files must be maintained **on line** to the computer at all times in order to allow constant interaction between the file and those desiring to update or inquire into the status of a particular record.

On-line systems.

Real time systems for reservations.

The most widely recognized of the real time systems are the airlines and hotel reservations systems similar to that shown in Figure 19.8. These systems constantly maintain the status of, for example, all flights and passengers so that a reservationist at any location can inquire into the availability of a seat and can update the file to indicate the "sale" of a seat. Typically, real time processing systems are most often justified in terms of providing better service to customers or for day-to-day organizational decisions which require a high degree of "currency" in the information used.

Minis and Micros

The general-purpose minicomputer.

No, we are not referring to 1960s skirt fashions (sadly). Instead, we are concerned with a 1970s trend toward even smaller computers (see Figure 19.9). A **minicomputer** is simply a lower cost, physically small, general purpose computer. While there is no standard price, commercial minicomputers range in price from $10,000 to $100,000 with an average installed price of approximately $35,000. They are physically smaller

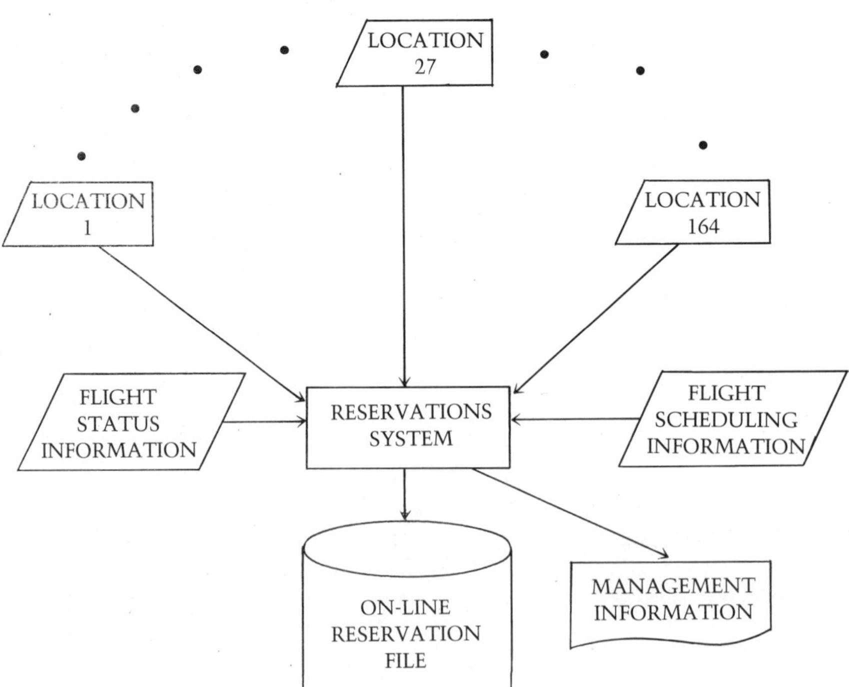

Figure 19.8 A real time reservation system.

and more adaptable than their larger counterparts. Minicomputers typically require no special environmental conditions such as raised floors, temperature/humidity control, and so forth. But, the minicomputer has its limitations. A minicomputer's primary memory is usually smaller, accessing and processing times are slower, and the CPU can usually process one or only a few programs at one time.

The special purpose microcomputer.

A **microcomputer** is literally "a computer on a chip." The silicon chip, which is an integrated circuit produced in microminiature size, was first used in the early 1970s. Originally intended as the brain of modern "pocket" calculators, the silicon chip has allowed computerization of numerous pieces of equipment. Among the most widely recognized uses are manufacturing process control, numerical control of machine tools, automotive ignition and fuel injection timing, and energy control. The microcomputer, unlike the minicomputer, is typically developed for a specific

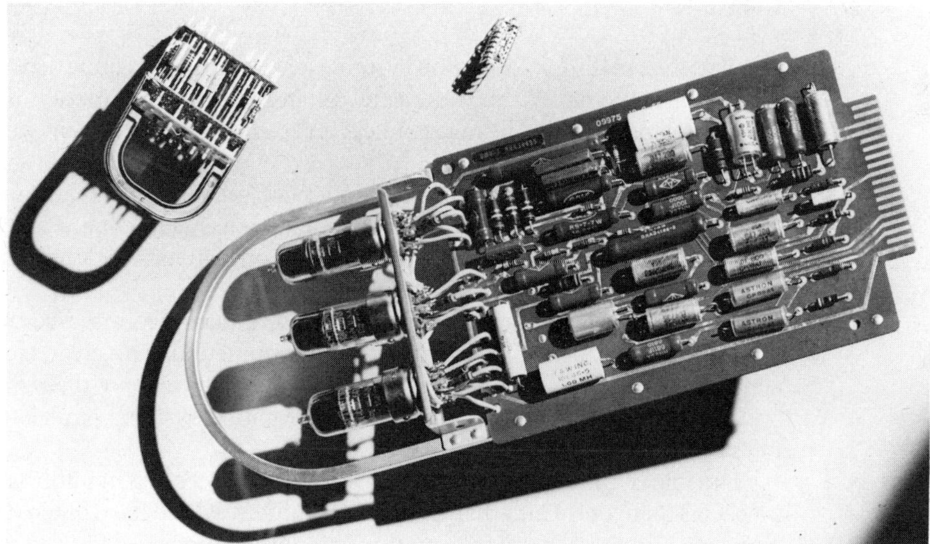

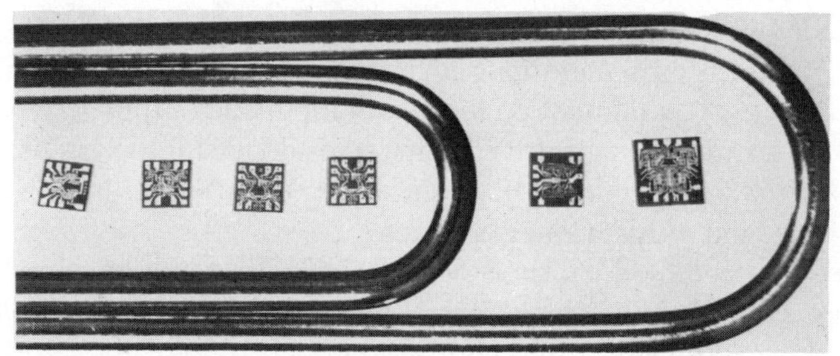

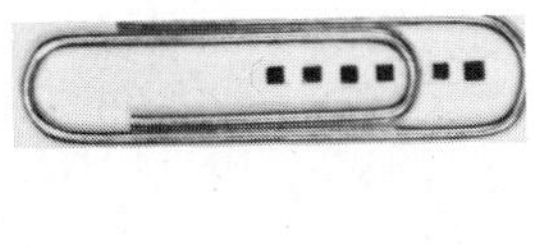

Figure 19.9 Four generations of computer circuitry. (Courtesy of Burroughs Corporation.)

function. The mini, on the other hand, is intended to be a general-purpose data processing system.

The continuing growth of small computers.

From an operations standpoint, both minis and micros have and will continue to revolutionize the operations environment. Further applications in production process control and materials management will be found for microcomputers. The minicomputer will continue to bring more and more data processing power to even lower levels in the organization. As computer costs drop, availability will increase. Such methods of inventory/production control as MRP are simply impossible to apply without the aid of the high speed computers. Minis are bringing these methods to smaller organizations and are giving departments of larger organizations access to the computer which was heretofore unavailable.

19.5 SUMMARY

Organizations require information systems just as humans require sensing and communication systems. Without the external and internal information that organizations use, plans could not be made or kept and goals could not be achieved (or, for that matter, even established).

Information is said to have several functions, including scorekeeping, attention-directing, and problem-solving. Information also has real value. This value can be measured in an economic sense, but information also has model value and action-effectiveness value.

An organizational information system can be classified into five categories—financial, logistical, personnel, marketing, environmental. Any given fact or data element can usually be categorized as belonging to one or more of these classes. Taken together in various combinations, these information systems provide the organization's reports.

The role of the computer and electronic data processing in information systems has been a large one. Data that, prior to computers, would have taken days or weeks to process into meaningful information can now be processed in time to aid in management's decisions. The decision to use manual, electromechanical, or electronic data processing methods depends upon the volume of data and time requirements of the information to be produced.

EDP systems are made up of hardware (equipment), software (programs), and people. Hardware is categorized as either an input device, processing equipment, or an output device. Several pieces of equipment perform both input and output activities (e.g., a cathode ray tube terminal, a tape drive). Software is divided into systems software and applications software. Primary EDP personnel are the systems analyst, the programmer, the operator, and the data entry operator.

EDP systems can be either batch or real time systems. Mini- and microcomputers are currently creating entirely new markets for EDP technology. Many small businesses that were unable to afford EDP equipment are now able to bring the same processing capability to bear on their information system functions as large firms.

19.6 READINGS

Scrambled Readout

Cities' Computer Financial Controls Often Are a Mixed Bag, Detroit's System Shows.

BY BYRON KLAPPER
Staff Reporter of THE WALL STREET JOURNAL

DETROIT—In 1974, Detroit had high hopes that a new computer system would solve the problems of its outmoded financial controls.

The Financial Information and Control System it purchased from Arthur Andersen & Co., the big accounting firm, was expected to help Detroit in many ways. The FICS would set up budgetary controls by matching each dollar spent against each dollar of income, eliminate the need for duplicate bookkeeping by city departments, and give managers fast, accurate financial data to use in making decisions. The system seemed so promising that it won for Detroit a 1976 achievement award from the Municipal Finance Officers Association, a professional group.

These days, though, FICS isn't winning any plaudits. Instead, it is underused and under fire, with critics complaining that the Motor City may have bought itself a $1.5 million lemon. After city officials recently asked Peat, Marwick, Mitchell & Co. to review the system as part of its city audit, the accounting firm concluded that FICS helps the finance director keep track of the budget but is of little value to many departments in managing finances or keeping track of costs.

OTHER CITIES' PROBLEMS

For its part, Arthur Andersen says that its system is working as it was designed to and that the criticisms aren't justified. Whatever the case, Detroit's experience may be instructive for cities like New York, Boston and Washington as they try to adopt computer management systems.

There are some who believe that the complexity of city financial structures defies the effective use of computer management systems. In January of last year, the federal Department of Housing and Urban Development scrapped a $26 million program called USAC after eight years of trying to develop computer programs that could be used from city to city. Its failure was reported in a study, "Requiem for USAC," by Kenneth L. Kramer, professor of administration at the University of California. "The scope and complexity of building a total municipal information system is greater than originally thought," he concluded.

THE LURE OF THE COMPUTER

In 1974, however, the idea of a centralized accounting and information system had a lot of appeal for Detroit officials. It was a time of recession, and the city's fiscal situation was a mess. Slowdowns in the auto industry and municipal layoffs pushed local unemployment to almost 25%. The city budget that fiscal year had a $35.6 million deficit, and Detroit's credit rating was declining.

As the situation worsened, the Detroit city council came up with a recovery plan that required tighter controls of budget, accounting and reporting than the city's antiquated manual ledgers could provide. The answer seemed to lie in a management system Arthur Andersen had designed previously for the state of Louisiana that would be adapted for use on Detroit's existing Burroughs computers.

HOSTILITY OF WORKERS

But a lot went wrong from the outset with Detroit's system. City department heads who weren't asked to participate in its planning felt snubbed and resisted the change. Many city workers were also hostile; they often referred to the matte-black computer terminals as "boob tubes." A number of managers simply ignored the monthly computer printouts of financial material in deciding how to spend the tax dollars. Coding errors, such as one that billed $30,000 to the transportation department for horsemeat delivered to the city zoo, damaged the system's credibility.

Things didn't get any better as time went on. Early last year, the city's 29-year-old auditor general, Marie D. Farrell-Donaldson, reported that nine out of 11 city departments checked weren't using the FICS system as it was intended. Their failure to do so, she said, was "completely destroying the worth of this system."

Among city departments, the word was that FICS wasn't adaptable to their needs. Stephen T. Kish, chief accountant for transportation, says, for example, that the system can't handle 90% of the transportation department's paper work, such as profit-and-loss statements and reports to federal and state agencies.

KEEPING IN THE BLACK

Though FICS hasn't lived up to expectations in Detroit, it can't be rated as a failure, either. In at least one instance, it has been credited with helping to keep this year's city budget from slipping into the red.

Last July, data printouts from FICS started showing a $100,000-a-month loss in bus and trolley fares. Coupled with a 25% increase in diesel-fuel costs and higher pension costs, the loss in fares put the transportation department's budget in the red and threatened the overall city budget, because a 1973 court ruling made the city responsible for transit operations. "By June we expected to be $4.8 million behind the eight ball and unable to meet payrolls," says Mr. Kish of the transportation department.

With the computer's early warning, however, the city budget director was able to move quickly to offset the deficit. He pushed an ordinance through the city council that raised transit fares to 50 cents, a 10-cent increase, and raised student fares a nickel, to 30 cents. The council passed the ordinance in January.

Source. The Wall-Street Journal, May 24, 1978. Reprinted by permission of *The Wall Street Journal,*

19.7 KEY TERMS

Concepts

external information (p. 628)
scorekeeping (p. 630)
internal information (p. 629)
attention-directing (p. 630)
problem-solving (p. 630)
MIS (p. 631)
economic value (p. 632)
model value (p. 632)
action-effectiveness value (p. 632)
integrated information system (p. 635)
informal information system (p. 631)
exception reports (p. 633)

Tools and Applications

data (p. 641)
information (p. 641)
capturing (p. 642)
verifying (p. 642)
classifying (p. 642)
arranging (p. 642)
summarizing (p. 642)
calculating (p. 642)
retrieving (p. 642)
reproducing (p. 642)
communicating (p. 642)
manual processing (p. 643)
electromechanical processing (p. 643)
electronic processing (p. 643)
hardware (p. 644)
software (p. 648)
primary storage (p. 645)
digital (p. 645)
analog (p. 645)
control unit (p. 645)
arithmetic/logic unit (p. 645)
secondary storage (p. 645)
POS (p. 647)
MICR (p. 647)
OCR (p. 647)
supervisory programs (p. 649)
operating systems (OS) (p. 649)
compiler (p. 649)
BASIC (p. 649)
FORTRAN (p. 649)
CPU (p. 644)
tabulating (p. 643)
unit record (p. 643)
EAM (p. 643)
EDP (p. 644)
IDP (p. 643)
keypunch (p. 643)
card reader (p. 645)
disk drive (p. 647)
tape drive (p. 647)
CRT (p. 647)
card punch (p. 648)
printer (p. 648)
paper tape punch (p. 648)
system software (p. 648)
applications software (p. 648)
systems analyst (p. 649)
programmer (p. 649)
data entry (p. 649)
batch (p. 650)
real time (p. 650)
minicomputer (p. 652)
microcomputer (p. 653)
PL1 (p. 649)
COBOL (p. 649)
binary (p. 649)
machine language (p. 649)
on line (p. 652)

19.8 REVIEW TEST

Concepts

1. Scorekeeping information is used to identify impending problems. (p. 630)
   a. True b. False
2. The "grapevine" is an important part of the informal information system. (p. 631)
   a. True b. False
3. Exception reporting has been instituted to minimize the excessive amount of data reported to managers. (p. 633)
   a. True b. False
4. Systems should *never* be computerized unless a successful manual system exists first. (p. 633)
   a. True b. False

Tools and Applications

5. What is information to some is simply data to others. (p. 641)
   a. True b. False
6. Integrated data processing combines the departmental data processing needs into one system. (p. 643)
   a. True b. False
7. Electromechanical data processing sometimes uses punched IBM cards. (p. 643)
   a. True b. False
8. The CPU is the control unit in the computer. (p. 645)
   a. True b. False

9. Software refers to the printed output of computers. (p. 648)
   a. True b. False

10. Compilers act as translators between the human and the computer. (p. 649)
    a. True b. False

11. The "binary" digits are 1 and 2. (p. 649)
    a. True b. False

12. The programmer is a higher level job than the systems analyst. (p. 649)
    a. True b. False

13. Batch processing does not require an up-to-date file. (p. 650)
    a. True b. False

14. A microcomputer is an especially small minicomputer. (p. 653)
    a. True b. False

19.9 DISCUSSION QUESTIONS

1. What reasons could you give for some managers ignoring the elaborate MIS systems in their company?
2. Can the typical portable handheld electronic calculator be classified as a computer? What are the input, output, and processing hardware in these devices?
3. What type of information systems would you expect to find in a government agency such as the Census Bureau?
4. Why is it important that managers have access to the informal organizational information system in a company?
5. What objectives could you establish for an EDP system to enhance the probability of its successful implementation in a company?
6. Which of the three functions of information do you feel is most critical in aiding operations managers?
7. How should one determine if data should be stored for later use; and how long should historical data be kept in the files of various organizations?
8. What problems can you see with banks and savings and loans using the electronic funds transfer systems so prevalent today in the area of customer relations?
9. How much data should be reported to managers to avoid "overreporting?"
10. Does not the fact that "what is *information* depends on the receiver" make the idea of an *organizational* information system ridiculous?
11. Why are special-purpose digital electronic devices not considered computers?
12. Does the systems analyst's task sound very difficult?
13. What is the primary motivating force behind the explosive adoption of new technology (such as minicomputers)?

19.10 PROBLEMS

Concepts

1. John, the production foreman, has normal capacity to produce 100 parts per month. His schedule is made up two months in advance. John has been requesting for six months that the marketing department prepare a report each month of all orders due to be shipped two months in the future. John wants this because 30 percent of the time he requires more than a 100 part capacity. When this happens he must run an entire overtime shift to produce the necessary parts. This costs John $2000.

   John knows that he can buy production time from a small job shop which can produce his excess capacity requirements at the cost of $500. But, the job shop must be scheduled two months in advance in order to get the work out. John knows that he can buy the necessary time each month (at a cost of $500) and use it only when necessary, but he is sure that the report would help him.

a. Should John buy the job shop time at $500 per month instead of running an entire shift when needed?
b. What expected value would John assign to a perfect report from the marketing department?
c. Write a one paragraph justification to the marketing department in support of the shipping report.

19.11 CASE BUCKEYE FOOD STORES

Buckeye Food Stores began operation in Dayton, Ohio, in 1947. Buckeye was initially formed as a cooperative venture between five local independent grocery stores as a means of reaping the economies of scale typical of the newer chain supermarkets. The idea worked well until 1951 at which time there were nine stores as members of the cooperative. Management problems and differences of opinion eventually resulted in the cooperative being disbanded and the food distributorship was sold to Joe Marcelle and Bill Pownell, owners of two of the original cooperative stores. Bill and Joe reorganized the distributorship keeping all but one of the stores as customers.

Buckeye Food Stores grew rapidly during the 1950s and early 1960s. But with the heavy competition in the 1960s and 1970s from major chain stores, Buckeye's growth leveled off for several years and then continued to increase at approximately 6½ percent per year. Sales in 1974 were 12.5 million dollars. The company leases 200,000 square feet of warehouse space and is currently (1978) planning the addition of 50,000 additional square feet.

In 1974, Bill and Joe attended an industry trade show and spent several hours watching the demonstration of a wholesaler's inventory control and billing system being demonstrated by a major computer vendor. The system maintained a perpetual inventory of every item in a several thousand item inventory. The system processed customer orders and produced order picking documents for the warehouse employees, shipping documents for order shipping, and invoices to the customer. In addition, inventory records were perpetually updated to show the balance available for sale as of the last order entered. The system also automatically calculated the reorder points and economic order quantities for the wholesaler, provided sales analysis by customer and product type, produced low stock reports for the purchasing agents, and slow moving stock reports for the salesmen. Added features of the system included a truck loading algorithm, which optimized truck routes and loaded the truck according to the optimal route, and an individual store profitability analysis system, which could be provided to store owners as a service. The store analysis system produced reports of profitability per dollar of inventory purchased and profitability by inventory volume. This information was used to assist the store owner/manager in determining the proper amount of space to be allocated to each product.

Bill and Joe felt that some parts of the system were very much needed to improve the efficiency of their own operations. The recent growth in several rural markets and the decline in volume in some of the urban markets was causing Buckeye to work for progressively smaller gross profits. A computer system would allow them to continue growing without the necessity of adding new order takers and other clerical personnel as the growth continued. But when the vendor announced that the price for the hardware and software to implement the system was in excess of $750,000, Bill and Joe lost their enthusiasm.

Bill and Joe recently returned from the 1979 trade association meeting. The same vendor was demonstrating a similar wholesale distribution computer system at that meeting. But, the system was now being operated on a minicomputer with a price tag under $100,000. Both of the owners felt that without such a system, any continued growth would be nearly impossible.

QUESTIONS FOR DISCUSSION

1. What is the appropriate justification for the purchase of a computer system and the necessary computer software?
2. What manual and automated alternatives to an in-house computer exist?
3. Presume that the computer's software is priced according to the functions desired. If Buckeye wishes to minimize its software costs, what systems components or features should be purchased? Try to rank the functions in descending order of information content or value.
4. To provide the functions you feel necessary, what information will be required in the inventory record of each product?

19.12 REFERENCES AND BIBLIOGRAPHY

1. Awad, E. M., *Business Data Processing,* 4th ed., Englewood Cliffs, N.J.: Prentice-Hall, 1975.
2. Burch, J. G., and F. R. Strater, *Information Systems: Theory and Practice,* Santa Barbara, Calif.: Wiley/Hamilton, 1974.
3. Cushing, B. E., *Accounting Information Systems and Business Organizations,* 2nd ed., Reading, Mass.: Addison-Wesley, 1978.
4. Davis, G. B., *Management Information Systems,* New York: McGraw-Hill, 1974.
5. Gordon, J. R. M., *Perspectives,* (Academy of Management) 5:19 (Fall, 1977).
6. Mock, T. J., "Concepts of Information Value and Accounting," *The Accounting Review,* 46:765–778 (1971).
7. Simon, H. A., *Administrative Behavior,* 2nd ed., New York: Macmillan, 1961.
8. Turban, E., and J. R. Meredith, *Fundamentals of Management Science,* Dallas: Business Publications, Inc., 1977.

EPILOGUE: THE FUTURE OF OPERATIONS MANAGEMENT

The future of operations management will be characterized by activities concerned with a number of challenges. Some of these challenges are taking shape today and can be foreseen while others will appear unexpectedly.

SERVICES

Challenge: service productivity.

The growth of services in our economy appears to be gaining strength and importance, showing no sign of letup. As discussed in Chapters 1 and 3, the need to improve the productivity of these services will pose a major challenge to operations management in the future. Techniques and approaches will have to be developed to handle scheduling problems, quality control, cost constraints, and the myriad of other issues typically faced by operations management. In some cases, adaptations of manufacturing techniques will suffice; in other situations totally new approaches must be conceived.

INFORMATION

Challenge: reacting quickly to recent events.

The world has grown considerably "smaller" in the last 30 years with the advent of jet travel, television, satellite relayed telephones, computerized monitoring and information systems, and so forth. The net effect of this "future shock" on operations management is an increased need for fast responses, on the one hand, and an accelerated rate of impact of distant events on the other. Due to modern technology, as illustrated above, word of increased prices for energy, Supreme Court decisions on hiring, embargoing of scarce materials, increases in the prime interest rate, passage of bills in Congress, or a fall of the dollar against the franc is instantly relayed to operations managers and requires immediate decisions to find alternate sources of supplies, to divert shipments, sell off inventories, and to change product mixes.

The result will be a greater need for contingency planning in operations, and an increased importance on operations flexibility as compared with efficiency, effectiveness, and capacity. Flexibility will also be an aid in offering output variety to consumers and recipients as the public becomes more educated and selective in the satisfaction of its needs. Undoubtedly, an even greater emphasis will be placed on the *quality* of each person's life, from the general environment to custom services.

INFLATION

Challenge: continuing inflation.

It appears that inflation has become permanently built into our economic system. This will pose a continuing challenge to operations managers to reduce costs as the prices for labor, materials, equipment, and everything else escalates. Some economic theories hold that it is impossible for a government to maintain a fixed level of inflation without encouraging a recession and, to maintain growth and a stable economy, must continue to increase the *rate* of inflation. Some responses by operations managers to high inflation rates and unstable currencies has been to purchase resources and dispose of output through barter arrangements, using brokers when required.

COMPUTERS

Computers for rote, massive, and complex tasks.

It is clear that the use of computers will continue to permeate all areas of the organization, especially with the much lower cost of mini-and microcomputers. In general, the computer will continue to take over the rote, clerical tasks; the massive information tasks (for accounting, or MRP, purposes); and the complex mathematical-statistical tasks which were formerly done poorly, by intuition, or not at all.

SYSTEMS

Challenge: coordination of large systems.

In spite of the certain growth of minicomputers in organizations for the planning, monitoring, and control of operations within departments, the use of large-scale computers with integrated information systems is also expected to increase. The challenge of coordinated planning of outputs by tying together output rates, mixes, quality, costs, materials requirements, manpower needs, and so on demands a *systems* view of the entire organization. Only large-scale computers tying together multiple data bases within and external to the organization can provide such an all-encompassing systems view.

The continuing role of management.

Such systems would then allow the organization-wide coordination of purchasing, marketing, finance, operations, and personnel, and handling of the repetitive, clerical tasks and the massive data manipulation tasks (such as MRP and accounting). This facilitates coordination, thereby increasing efficiency but makes little provision for effectiveness. That is, the *management* tasks of goal setting, assessing returns to the organization, evaluating information, and making decisions will not be solved simply through better coordination and more timely information. These will always remain the challenge to management.

APPENDIX A

TABLES

TABLE A1 PRESENT VALUE OF $1

Period	1%	2%	3%	4%	5%	6%	7%	8%	9%	10%	12%	14%	15%	16%	18%	20%	24%	28%	30%	32%	36%	40%	50%	60%	70%	80%	90%
1	0.990	0.980	0.971	0.962	0.952	0.943	0.935	0.926	0.917	0.909	0.893	0.877	0.870	0.862	0.847	0.833	0.806	0.781	0.769	0.758	0.735	0.714	0.667	0.625	0.588	0.556	0.526
2	0.980	0.961	0.943	0.925	0.907	0.890	0.873	0.857	0.842	0.826	0.797	0.769	0.756	0.743	0.718	0.694	0.650	0.610	0.592	0.574	0.541	0.510	0.444	0.391	0.346	0.309	0.277
3	0.971	0.942	0.915	0.889	0.864	0.840	0.816	0.794	0.772	0.751	0.712	0.675	0.658	0.641	0.609	0.579	0.524	0.477	0.455	0.435	0.398	0.364	0.296	0.244	0.204	0.171	0.146
4	0.961	0.924	0.889	0.855	0.823	0.792	0.763	0.735	0.708	0.683	0.636	0.592	0.572	0.552	0.516	0.482	0.423	0.373	0.350	0.329	0.292	0.260	0.198	0.153	0.120	0.095	0.077
5	0.951	0.906	0.863	0.822	0.784	0.747	0.713	0.681	0.650	0.621	0.567	0.519	0.497	0.476	0.437	0.402	0.341	0.291	0.269	0.250	0.215	0.186	0.132	0.095	0.070	0.053	0.040
6	0.942	0.888	0.838	0.790	0.746	0.705	0.666	0.630	0.596	0.564	0.507	0.456	0.432	0.410	0.370	0.335	0.275	0.227	0.207	0.189	0.158	0.133	0.088	0.060	0.041	0.029	0.021
7	0.933	0.871	0.813	0.760	0.711	0.665	0.623	0.583	0.547	0.513	0.452	0.400	0.376	0.354	0.314	0.279	0.222	0.178	0.159	0.143	0.116	0.095	0.059	0.037	0.024	0.016	0.011
8	0.923	0.853	0.789	0.731	0.677	0.627	0.582	0.540	0.502	0.467	0.404	0.351	0.327	0.305	0.266	0.233	0.179	0.139	0.123	0.108	0.085	0.068	0.039	0.023	0.014	0.009	0.006
9	0.914	0.837	0.766	0.703	0.645	0.592	0.544	0.500	0.460	0.424	0.361	0.308	0.284	0.263	0.226	0.194	0.144	0.108	0.094	0.082	0.063	0.048	0.026	0.015	0.008	0.005	0.003
10	0.905	0.820	0.744	0.676	0.614	0.558	0.508	0.463	0.422	0.386	0.322	0.270	0.247	0.227	0.191	0.162	0.116	0.085	0.073	0.062	0.046	0.035	0.017	0.009	0.005	0.003	0.002
11	0.896	0.804	0.722	0.650	0.585	0.527	0.475	0.429	0.388	0.350	0.287	0.237	0.215	0.195	0.162	0.135	0.094	0.066	0.056	0.047	0.034	0.025	0.012	0.006	0.003	0.002	0.001
12	0.887	0.788	0.701	0.625	0.557	0.497	0.444	0.397	0.356	0.319	0.257	0.208	0.187	0.168	0.137	0.112	0.076	0.052	0.043	0.036	0.025	0.018	0.008	0.004	0.002	0.001	0.001
13	0.879	0.773	0.681	0.601	0.530	0.469	0.415	0.368	0.326	0.290	0.229	0.182	0.163	0.145	0.116	0.093	0.061	0.040	0.033	0.027	0.018	0.013	0.005	0.002	0.001	0.001	0.000
14	0.870	0.758	0.661	0.577	0.505	0.442	0.388	0.340	0.299	0.263	0.205	0.160	0.141	0.125	0.099	0.078	0.049	0.032	0.025	0.021	0.014	0.009	0.003	0.001	0.001	0.000	0.000
15	0.861	0.743	0.642	0.555	0.481	0.417	0.362	0.315	0.275	0.239	0.183	0.140	0.123	0.108	0.084	0.065	0.040	0.025	0.020	0.016	0.010	0.006	0.002	0.001	0.000	0.000	0.000
16	0.853	0.728	0.623	0.534	0.458	0.394	0.339	0.292	0.252	0.218	0.163	0.123	0.107	0.093	0.071	0.054	0.032	0.019	0.015	0.012	0.007	0.005	0.002	0.001	0.000	0.000	
17	0.844	0.714	0.605	0.513	0.436	0.371	0.317	0.270	0.231	0.198	0.146	0.108	0.093	0.080	0.060	0.045	0.026	0.015	0.012	0.009	0.005	0.003	0.001	0.000	0.000		
18	0.836	0.700	0.587	0.494	0.416	0.350	0.296	0.250	0.212	0.180	0.130	0.095	0.081	0.069	0.051	0.038	0.021	0.012	0.009	0.007	0.004	0.002	0.001	0.000	0.000		
19	0.828	0.686	0.570	0.475	0.396	0.331	0.276	0.232	0.194	0.164	0.116	0.083	0.070	0.060	0.043	0.031	0.017	0.009	0.007	0.005	0.003	0.002	0.000	0.000			
20	0.820	0.673	0.554	0.456	0.377	0.312	0.258	0.215	0.178	0.149	0.104	0.073	0.061	0.051	0.037	0.026	0.014	0.007	0.005	0.004	0.002	0.001	0.000	0.000			
25	0.780	0.610	0.478	0.375	0.295	0.233	0.184	0.146	0.116	0.092	0.059	0.038	0.030	0.024	0.016	0.010	0.005	0.002	0.001	0.001	0.000	0.000					
30	0.742	0.552	0.412	0.308	0.231	0.174	0.131	0.099	0.075	0.057	0.033	0.020	0.015	0.012	0.007	0.004	0.002	0.001	0.000	0.000	0.000						
40	0.672	0.453	0.307	0.208	0.142	0.097	0.067	0.046	0.032	0.022	0.011	0.005	0.004	0.003	0.001	0.001	0.000										
50	0.608	0.372	0.228	0.141	0.087	0.054	0.034	0.021	0.013	0.009	0.003	0.001	0.001	0.001	0.000												

TABLE A2 PRESENT VALUE OF AN ANNUITY OF $1

Period	1%	2%	3%	4%	5%	6%	8%	10%	12%	14%	15%	16%	18%	20%	24%	30%	40%	50%
1	0.990	0.980	0.971	0.962	0.952	0.943	0.926	0.909	0.893	0.877	0.870	0.862	0.847	0.833	0.806	0.769	0.714	0.667
2	1.970	1.942	1.914	1.886	1.859	1.833	1.783	1.736	1.690	1.647	1.626	1.605	1.566	1.528	1.457	1.361	1.224	1.111
3	2.941	2.884	2.829	2.775	2.723	2.673	2.577	2.487	2.402	2.322	2.283	2.246	2.174	2.106	1.981	1.816	1.589	1.407
4	3.902	3.808	3.717	3.630	3.546	3.465	3.312	3.170	3.037	2.914	2.855	2.798	2.690	2.589	2.404	2.166	1.849	1.605
5	4.853	4.713	4.580	4.452	4.330	4.212	3.993	3.791	3.605	3.433	3.352	3.274	3.127	2.991	2.745	2.436	2.035	1.737
6	5.795	5.601	5.417	5.242	5.076	4.917	4.623	4.355	4.111	3.889	3.784	3.685	3.498	3.326	3.020	2.643	2.168	1.824
7	6.728	6.472	6.230	6.002	5.786	5.582	5.206	4.868	4.564	4.288	4.160	4.039	3.812	3.605	3.242	2.802	2.263	1.883
8	7.652	7.325	7.020	6.733	6.463	6.210	5.747	5.335	4.968	4.639	4.487	4.344	4.078	3.837	3.421	2.925	2.331	1.922
9	8.566	8.162	7.786	7.435	7.108	6.802	6.247	5.759	5.328	4.946	4.772	4.607	4.303	4.031	3.566	3.019	2.379	1.948
10	9.741	8.983	8.530	8.111	7.722	7.360	6.710	6.145	5.650	5.216	5.019	4.833	4.494	4.192	3.682	3.092	2.414	1.965
11	10.368	9.787	9.253	8.760	8.306	7.887	7.139	6.495	5.938	5.453	5.234	5.029	4.656	4.327	3.776	3.147	2.438	1.977
12	11.255	10.575	9.954	9.385	8.863	8.384	7.536	6.814	6.194	5.660	5.421	5.197	4.793	4.439	3.851	3.190	2.456	1.985
13	12.134	11.348	10.635	9.986	9.394	8.853	7.904	7.103	6.424	5.842	5.583	5.342	4.910	4.533	3.912	3.223	2.468	1.990
14	13.004	12.106	11.296	10.563	9.899	9.295	8.244	7.367	6.628	6.002	5.724	5.468	5.008	4.611	3.962	3.249	2.478	1.993
15	13.865	12.849	11.938	11.118	10.380	9.712	8.559	7.606	6.811	6.142	5.847	5.576	5.092	4.676	4.001	3.268	2.484	1.995
16	14.718	13.578	12.561	11.652	10.838	10.106	8.851	7.824	6.974	6.265	5.954	5.668	5.162	4.730	4.033	3.283	2.488	1.997
17	15.562	14.292	13.166	12.166	11.274	10.477	9.122	8.022	7.120	6.373	6.047	5.749	5.222	4.775	4.059	3.295	2.492	1.998
18	16.398	14.992	13.754	12.659	11.690	10.828	9.372	8.201	7.250	6.467	6.128	5.818	5.273	4.812	4.080	3.304	2.494	1.999
19	17.226	15.678	14.324	13.134	12.085	11.158	9.604	8.365	7.366	6.550	6.198	5.878	5.316	4.844	4.097	3.311	2.496	1.999
20	18.046	16.351	14.877	13.590	12.462	11.470	9.818	8.514	7.469	6.623	6.259	5.929	5.353	4.870	4.110	3.316	2.497	1.999
21	18.857	17.011	15.415	14.029	12.821	11.764	10.017	8.649	7.562	6.687	6.312	5.973	5.384	4.891	4.121	3.320	2.498	2.000
22	19.660	17.658	15.937	14.451	13.163	12.042	10.201	8.772	7.645	6.743	6.359	6.011	5.410	4.909	4.130	3.323	2.498	2.000
23	20.456	18.292	16.444	14.857	13.489	12.303	10.371	8.883	7.718	6.792	6.399	6.044	5.432	4.924	4.137	3.325	2.499	2.000
24	21.213	18.914	16.936	15.247	13.799	12.550	10.529	8.985	7.784	6.835	6.434	6.073	5.451	4.937	4.143	3.327	2.499	2.000
25	22.023	19.523	17.413	15.622	14.094	12.783	10.675	9.077	7.843	6.873	6.464	6.097	5.467	4.918	4.147	3.329	2.499	2.000
26	22.795	20.121	17.877	15.933	14.375	13.003	10.810	9.161	7.896	6.906	6.491	6.118	5.480	4.956	4.151	3.330	2.500	2.000
27	23.560	20.707	18.327	16.330	14.643	13.211	10.935	9.237	7.943	6.935	6.514	6.136	5.492	4.964	4.154	3.331	2.500	2.000
28	24.316	21.281	18.764	16.663	14.898	13.406	11.051	9.307	7.984	6.961	6.534	6.152	5.502	4.970	4.157	3.331	2.500	2.000
29	25.066	21.814	19.188	16.984	15.141	13.591	11.158	9.370	8.022	6.983	6.551	6.166	5.510	4.975	4.159	3.332	2.500	2.000
30	25.808	22.396	19.600	17.292	15.372	13.765	11.258	9.427	8.055	7.003	6.566	6.177	5.517	4.979	4.160	3.332	2.500	2.000
40	32.835	27.355	23.115	19.793	17.159	15.046	11.925	9.779	8.244	7.105	6.642	6.234	5.548	4.997	4.166	3.333	2.500	2.000
50	39.196	31.424	25.730	21.482	18.256	15.762	12.233	9.915	8.304	7.133	6.660	6.246	5.554	4.999	4.167	3.333	2.500	2.000

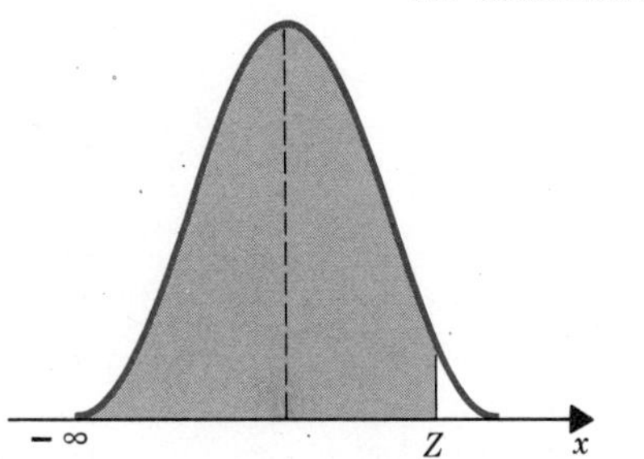

TABLE A3 AREA UNDER THE NORMAL DISTRIBUTION

Z	0.00	0.01	0.02	0.03	0.04	0.05	0.06	0.07	0.08	0.09
0.0	0.5000	0.5040	0.5080	0.5120	0.5160	0.5199	0.5239	0.5279	0.5319	0.5359
0.1	0.5398	0.5438	0.5478	0.5517	0.5557	0.5596	0.5636	0.5675	0.5714	0.5753
0.2	0.5793	0.5832	0.5871	0.5910	0.5948	0.5987	0.6026	0.6064	0.6103	0.6141
0.3	0.6179	0.6217	0.6255	0.6293	0.6331	0.6368	0.6406	0.6443	0.6480	0.6517
0.4	0.6554	0.6591	0.6628	0.6664	0.6700	0.6736	0.6772	0.6808	0.6844	0.6879
0.5	0.6915	0.6950	0.6985	0.7019	0.7054	0.7088	0.7123	0.7157	0.7190	0.7224
0.6	0.7257	0.7291	0.7324	0.7357	0.7389	0.7422	0.7454	0.7486	0.7517	0.7549
0.7	0.7580	0.7611	0.7642	0.7673	0.7704	0.7734	0.7764	0.7794	0.7823	0.7852
0.8	0.7881	0.7910	0.7939	0.7967	0.7995	0.8023	0.8051	0.8078	0.8106	0.8133
0.9	0.8159	0.8186	0.8212	0.8238	0.8264	0.8289	0.8315	0.8340	0.8365	0.8389
1.0	0.8413	0.8438	0.8461	0.8485	0.8508	0.8531	0.8554	0.8577	0.8599	0.8621
1.1	0.8643	0.8665	0.8686	0.8708	0.8729	0.8749	0.8770	0.8790	0.8810	0.8830
1.2	0.8849	0.8869	0.8888	0.8907	0.8925	0.8944	0.8962	0.8980	0.8997	0.9015
1.3	0.9032	0.9049	0.9066	0.9082	0.9099	0.9115	0.9131	0.9147	0.9162	0.9177
1.4	0.9192	0.9207	0.9222	0.9236	0.9251	0.9265	0.9279	0.9292	0.9306	0.9319
1.5	0.9332	0.9345	0.9357	0.9370	0.9382	0.9394	0.9406	0.9418	0.9429	0.9441
1.6	0.9452	0.9463	0.9474	0.9484	0.9495	0.9505	0.9515	0.9525	0.9535	0.9545
1.7	0.9554	0.9564	0.9573	0.9582	0.9591	0.9599	0.9608	0.9616	0.9625	0.9633
1.8	0.9641	0.9649	0.9656	0.9664	0.9671	0.9678	0.9686	0.9693	0.9699	0.9706
1.9	0.9713	0.9719	0.9726	0.9732	0.9738	0.9744	0.9750	0.9756	0.9761	0.9767
2.0	0.9772	0.9778	0.9783	0.9788	0.9793	0.9798	0.9803	0.9808	0.9812	0.9817
2.1	0.9821	0.9826	0.9830	0.9834	0.9838	0.9842	0.9846	0.9850	0.9854	0.9857
2.2	0.9861	0.9864	0.9868	0.9871	0.9875	0.9878	0.9881	0.9884	0.9887	0.9890
2.3	0.9893	0.9896	0.9898	0.9901	0.9904	0.9906	0.9909	0.9911	0.9913	0.9916
2.4	0.9918	0.9920	0.9922	0.9925	0.9927	0.9929	0.9931	0.9932	0.9934	0.9936
2.5	0.9938	0.9940	0.9941	0.9943	0.9945	0.9946	0.9948	0.9949	0.9951	0.9952
2.6	0.9953	0.9955	0.9956	0.9957	0.9959	0.9960	0.9961	0.9962	0.9963	0.9964
2.7	0.9965	0.9966	0.9967	0.9968	0.9969	0.9970	0.9971	0.9972	0.9973	0.9974
2.8	0.9974	0.9975	0.9976	0.9977	0.9977	0.9978	0.9979	0.9979	0.9980	0.9981
2.9	0.9981	0.9982	0.9982	0.9983	0.9984	0.9984	0.9985	0.9985	0.9986	0.9986
3.0	0.9987	0.9987	0.9987	0.9988	0.9988	0.9989	0.9989	0.9989	0.9990	0.9990
3.1	0.9990	0.9991	0.9991	0.9991	0.9992	0.9992	0.9992	0.9992	0.9993	0.9993
3.2	0.9993	0.9993	0.9994	0.9994	0.9994	0.9994	0.9994	0.9995	0.9995	0.9995
3.3	0.9995	0.9995	0.9995	0.9996	0.9996	0.9996	0.9996	0.9996	0.9996	0.9997
3.4	0.9997	0.9997	0.9997	0.9997	0.9997	0.9997	0.9997	0.9997	0.9997	0.9998

TABLE A4 RANDOM NUMBERS

39	73	72	75	37	02	87	98	10	47	93	21	95	97	69	41	91	80	67	59	34	18	04	52	35
79	57	92	36	59	89	74	39	82	15	08	58	94	34	74	21	89	11	47	99	11	20	99	45	18
22	45	44	84	11	87	80	61	65	31	09	71	91	74	25	95	18	94	06	97	27	37	83	28	71
80	45	67	93	82	59	73	19	85	23	53	33	65	97	21	97	08	31	55	73	10	65	81	92	59
53	58	47	70	93	66	56	45	65	79	45	56	20	19	47	69	26	88	86	13	59	71	74	17	32
26	72	39	27	67	53	77	57	68	93	60	61	97	22	61	41	47	10	25	03	87	63	93	95	17
43	00	65	98	50	45	60	33	01	07	98	99	46	50	47	91	94	14	63	62	08	61	74	51	69
52	70	05	48	34	56	65	05	61	86	90	92	10	70	80	80	06	54	18	47	08	52	85	08	40
15	33	59	05	28	22	87	26	07	47	86	96	98	29	06	67	72	77	63	99	89	85	84	46	06
85	13	99	24	44	49	18	09	79	49	74	16	32	23	02	59	40	24	13	75	42	29	72	23	19
87	03	04	79	88	08	13	13	85	51	55	34	57	72	69	02	89	08	16	94	85	53	83	29	95
52	06	79	79	45	82	63	18	27	44	69	66	92	19	09	87	18	15	70	07	37	79	49	12	38
46	72	60	18	77	55	66	12	62	11	08	99	55	64	57	98	83	71	70	15	89	09	39	59	24
47	21	61	88	32	27	80	30	21	60	10	92	35	36	12	10	08	58	07	04	76	62	16	48	68
12	73	73	99	12	49	99	57	94	82	96	88	57	17	91	47	90	56	37	31	71	82	13	50	41
63	62	06	34	41	79	53	36	02	95	20	26	36	31	62	58	24	97	14	97	95	06	70	99	00
78	47	23	53	90	79	93	96	38	63	31	56	34	19	19	47	83	75	51	33	30	62	38	20	46
87	68	62	15	43	97	48	72	66	48	98	40	07	17	66	23	05	09	51	80	59	78	11	52	49
47	60	92	10	77	26	97	05	73	51	24	33	45	77	48	69	81	84	09	29	93	22	70	45	80
56	88	87	59	41	06	87	37	78	48	01	31	60	10	27	35	07	79	71	53	28	99	52	01	41
22	17	68	65	84	87	02	22	57	51	56	27	09	24	43	21	78	55	09	82	72	61	88	73	61
19	36	27	59	46	39	77	32	77	09	48	13	93	55	96	41	92	45	71	51	09	18	25	58	94
16	77	23	02	77	28	06	24	25	93	00	06	41	41	20	14	36	59	25	47	54	45	17	24	89
78	43	76	71	61	97	67	63	99	61	58	76	17	14	86	59	53	11	52	21	66	04	18	72	87
03	28	28	26	08	69	30	16	09	05	27	55	10	24	92	28	04	67	53	44	95	23	00	84	47
04	31	17	21	56	33	73	99	19	87	74	13	39	35	22	68	95	23	92	35	36	63	70	35	33
61	06	98	03	91	87	14	77	43	96	76	51	94	84	86	13	79	93	37	55	98	16	04	41	67
23	68	35	26	00	99	53	93	61	28	79	57	95	13	91	09	61	87	25	21	56	20	11	32	44
15	39	25	70	99	93	86	52	77	65	77	31	61	95	46	20	44	90	32	64	26	99	76	75	63
58	71	96	30	24	18	46	23	34	27	48	38	75	93	29	73	37	32	04	05	60	82	29	20	25
93	22	53	64	39	07	10	63	76	35	81	83	83	04	49	77	45	85	50	51	79	88	01	97	30
78	76	58	54	74	92	38	70	96	92	92	79	43	89	79	29	18	94	51	23	14	85	11	47	23
61	81	31	96	82	00	57	25	60	59	48	40	35	94	22	72	65	71	08	86	50	03	42	99	36
42	88	07	10	05	24	98	65	63	21	64	71	06	21	66	89	37	20	70	01	61	65	70	22	12
77	94	30	05	39	28	10	99	00	27	06	94	76	10	08	81	30	15	39	14	81	83	17	16	33
39	65	76	45	45	19	90	69	64	61	94	61	09	43	62	20	21	14	68	86	84	95	48	46	45
73	71	23	70	90	65	97	60	12	11	34	85	52	05	09	21	43	01	72	73	14	93	87	81	40
72	20	47	33	84	51	67	47	97	19	53	16	71	13	81	59	97	50	99	52	24	62	20	42	31
75	17	25	69	17	17	95	21	78	58	88	46	38	03	58	72	68	49	29	31	75	70	16	08	24
37	48	79	88	74	63	52	06	34	30	65	88	69	58	39	07	29	73	72	38	51	28	84	89	47

TABLE A5 ACCEPTANCE SAMPLING TABLE*

AQL \ LTPD	4.51 to 5.60	5.61 to 7.10	7.11 to 9.00	9.01 to 11.2	11.3 to 14.0	14.1 to 18.0	18.1 to 22.4
0.451 to 0.560	80 1	60 1	60 1	50 1	15 0	15 0	10 0
0.561 to 0.710	100 2	80 1	50 1	50 1	40 1	10 0	10 0
0.711 to 0.900	100 2	80 2	50 1	40 1	40 1	30 1	7 0
0.901 to 1.12	120 3	80 2	60 2	40 1	30 1	30 1	25 1
1.13 to 1.40	150 4	100 3	60 2	50 2	30 1	25 1	25 1
1.41 to 1.80	200 6	120 4	80 3	50 2	40 1	25 1	20 1
1.81 to 2.24	300 10	150 6	100 4	60 3	40 2	30 2	20 1
2.25 to 2.80	n c	250 10	120 6	70 4	50 3	30 2	25 2
2.81 to 3.55	n c	n c	200 10	100 6	60 4	40 3	25 2
3.56 to 4.50	n c	n c	n c	150 10	80 6	50 4	30 3
4.51 to 5.60	n c	n c	n c	n c	120 10	60 6	40 4

* Entries are $\frac{n}{c}$ and assume $\alpha = 0.05$ and $\beta = 0.10$. (*Source:* J. L. Riggs, *Production Systems: Planning, Analysis, and Control*, Second Edition, John Wiley and Sons, Inc., 1976. Reproduced by permission.)

Appendix B:

Probability And Statistics

This appendix is intended to serve as a brief review of the probability and statistics concepts which are used in this text. Students who require more review than is available in this appendix should consult one of the texts listed in the bibliography.

PROBABILITY

Uncertainty in organizational decision making is a fact of life. Demand for an organization's output is uncertain. The number of employees who will be absent from work on any given day is uncertain. The price of a stock tomorrow is uncertain. Whether it will snow or not tomorrow is uncertain. Each of the *events* described above are more or less uncertain. We do not know exactly whether the event will occur or not, nor do we know the value that a particular *random variable* (e.g., price of stock, demand for output, number of absent employees) will assume.

In common terminology we reflect our uncertainty with such phrases as "not very likely," "not a chance," "for sure," "hasn't got a snowball's chance in hell." But, while these descriptive terms communicate one's feeling regarding the chances of a particular event's occurrence, they simply are not precise enough to allow analysis of chances and odds.

Simply put, *probability* is a number on a scale used to measure uncertainty. The range of the probability scale is from 0 to 1, with a 0 probability indicating that an event has no chance of occurring and a probability of 1 indiciating that an event is absolutely sure to occur. The more likely an event is to occur, the closer its probability is to 1. This probability definition, which is general, needs to be further augmented to illustrate the various types of probability which decision makers can assess. There are three types of probability that the operations manager should be aware of. These are

- Subjective probability.
- Logical probability
- Experimental probability.

Subjective Probability

Subjective probability is based upon individual information and belief. Different individuals will assess the chances of a particular event in different ways and the same individual may assess different probabilities for the same event at different points in time. For example, one need only watch the blackjack players in Las Vegas to see that different people assess probabilities in different ways. Also, daily trading in the stock market is the result of different probability assessments by those trading. The sellers sell because it is their belief that the probability of appreciation is low and the buyers buy because they believe that the probability of appreciation is high. Clearly, these different probability assessments are about the same events.

Logical Probability

Logical probability is based upon physical phenomena and upon symmetry of events. For example, the probability of drawing a three of hearts from a standard 52-card playing deck is 1/52. Each card has an equal likelihood of being drawn. In flipping a coin, the chance of "heads" is .50. That is, since there are only two possible outcomes from one flip of a coin, each event has one-half the total probability, or .50. A final example is the roll of a single die. Since each of the six sides are identical, the chance of any one event (i.e., a 6, a 3, etc.) is 1/6.

Experimental Probability

Experimental probability is based upon frequency of occurrence of events in trial situations. For example, in determining the appropriate inventory level to maintain in the raw material inventory, we might measure and record the demand each day from that inventory. If, in 100 days, demand was 20 units on 16 days, the probability of demand equalling 20 units is said to be .16 (i.e., 16/100). In general, experimental probability of an event is given by

$$\text{probability of event} = \frac{\text{number of times event occurred}}{\text{total number of trials}}$$

Both logical and experimental probability are referred to as *objective* probability in contrast to the individually assessed subjective probability. Each of these are based upon, and directly *computed* from, hard facts.

EVENT RELATIONSHIPS AND PROBABILITY LAWS

Events are classified in a number of ways which allow us to further state rules for probability computations. Some of these classifications and definitions follow.

1. Independent events—events are independent if the occurrence of one does not affect the probability of occurrence of the others.
2. Dependent events—events are termed dependent if the occurrence of one does affect the probability of occurrence of others.
3. Mutually exclusive events—two events are termed mutually exclusive if the occurrence of one precludes the occurrence of the other. For example, in the birth of a child, the events "It's a boy!" and "It's a girl!" are mutually exclusive.
4. Collectively exhaustive events—a set of events is termed collectively exhaustive if on any one trial at least one of them must occur. For example, in rolling a die, one of the events 1, 2, 3, 4, 5, or 6 must occur and therefore these six events are collectively exhaustive.

We can also define the union and intersection of two events. Consider two events A and B. The *union* of A and B includes all outcomes in A or B or in both A and B. For example, in a card game you will win if you draw a diamond or a jack. The union of these two events includes all diamonds (including the jack of diamonds) and the remaining three jacks (hearts, clubs, spades). The *or* in the union is the inclusive or. That is, in our example you will win with a jack or a diamond or a jack of diamonds (i.e., both events).

The *intersection* of two events includes all outcomes that are members of *both* events. For example, in our previous example of jacks and diamonds, the jack of diamonds is the only outcome contained in both events and is therefore the only member of the intersection of the two events.

Let us now consider the relevant probability laws based upon our understanding of the above definitions and concepts. For ease of exposition let us define the following notation:

$P(A)$ = probability that event A will occur
$P(B)$ = probability that event B will occur

If two events are mutually exclusive, then their joint occurrence is impossible. Hence, $P(A \text{ and } B) = 0$ for mutually exclusive events. If the events are not mutually exclusive $P(A \text{ and } B)$ can be computed (as we will see in the next section) and this probability is termed the *joint* probability of A and B. Also, if A and B are not mutually exclusive, then we can also define the *conditional* probability of A *given that* B has already occurred or the conditional probability of B given that A has already occurred. These probabilities are written as $P(A \mid B)$ and $P(B \mid A)$, respectively.

THE MULTIPLICATION RULE

The joint probability of two events that are not mutually exclusive is found by using the multiplication rule. If the events are dependent events the joint probability is given by

$$P(A \text{ and } B) = P(A) \times P(B \mid A) \quad \text{or} \quad P(B) \times P(A \mid B)$$

If the events are independent, the $P(B \mid A)$ and $P(A \mid B)$ are equal to $P(B)$ and $P(A)$, respectively, and therefore the joint probability is given by

$$P(A \text{ and } B) = P(A) \times P(B)$$

From these two relationships we can find the conditional probability for two dependent events from

$$P(A \mid B) = \frac{P(A \text{ and } B)}{P(B)}$$

and

$$P(B \mid A) = \frac{P(A \text{ and } B)}{P(A)}$$

Also, the $P(A)$ and $P(B)$ can be computed if the events are independent, as

$$P(A) = \frac{P(A \text{ and } B)}{P(B)}$$

and

$$P(B) = \frac{P(A \text{ and } B)}{P(A)}$$

THE ADDITION RULE

The addition rule is used to compute the probability of the union of two events. If two events are mutually exclusive then $P(A \text{ and } B) = 0$ as we indicated above. Therefore, the probability of either A or B or both is simply the probability of A or B. This is given by

$$P(A \text{ or } B) = P(A) + P(B)$$

But, if the events are not mutually exclusive, then the probability of A or B is given by

$$P(A \text{ or } B) = P(A) + P(B) - P(A \text{ and } B)$$

We can denote the reasonableness of the above expression by looking at the following Venn diagram.

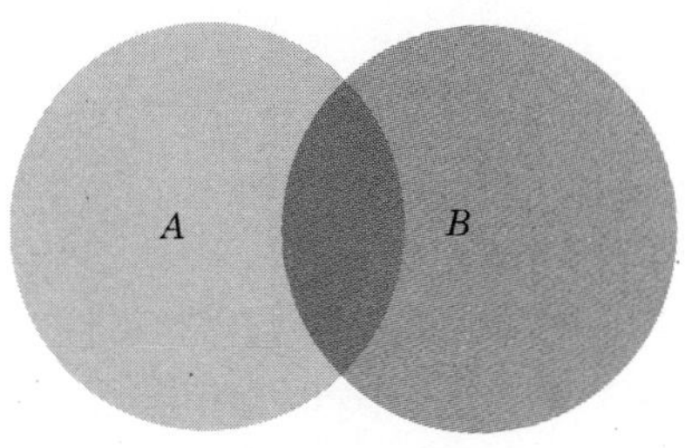

The two circles represent the probabilities of the events A and B, respectively. The shaded area represents the overlap in the events; that is, the intersection of A and B. If we add the area of A and the area of B, we have included the shaded area twice and therefore, to get the total area of A or B we must subtract one of the areas of the intersection that we have added.

If two events are collectively exhaustive, then the probability of A or B is equal to 1. That is, for two collectively exhaustive events, one or the other or both must occur and therefore the probability of A or B must be 1.

STATISTICS

Because events are uncertain we must employ special analyses in organizations to assure that our decisions take recognition of the chance nature of outcomes. We employ statistics and statistical analysis to

1. Concisely express the tendency and the relative uncertainty of a particular situation.
2. Develop inferences or understanding about a situation.

"Statistics" is an elusive and often misused term. Batting averages, birth weights, student grade points are all statistics. They are *descriptive* statistics. That is, they are quantitative measures of some entity and, for our purposes, can be considered as data about the entity. The second use of the term "statistics" is in relation to the body of theory and methodology used to analyze available evidence (typically quantitative) and to develop inferences from the evidence.

Two descriptive statistics that are often used in presenting information about a population of items (and consequently in inferring some conclusions about the population) are the *mean* and the *variance*. The mean of a population (denoted as μ) can be computed in two ways, each of which gives identical results.

$$\mu = \sum_{j=1}^{k} X_j P(X_j)$$

where

k = the number of discrete values that the random variable X_j may assume
X_j = the value of the random variable
$P(X_j)$ is the probability (or relative frequency) of X_j in the population

Also the mean can be computed as

$$\mu = \sum_{i=1}^{N} X_i/N$$

where

N = the size of the population (the number of different items in the population)
X_i = the value of the ith item in the population

The mean is also termed the *expected value* of the population and is written as $E(X)$.

The variance of the items in the population measures the dispersion of the items about their mean. It is computed in one of the following two ways.

$$\sigma^2 = \sum_{j=1}^{k} (X_j - \mu)^2 P(X_j)$$

or

$$\sigma^2 = \sum_{i=1}^{N} \frac{(X_i - \mu)^2}{N}$$

The standard deviation, another measure of dispersion, is simply the square root of the variance or

$$\sigma = \sqrt{\sigma^2}$$

DESCRIPTIVE VERSUS INFERENTIAL STATISTICS

Organizations are typically faced with decisions for which a large portion of the relevant information is uncertain. In hiring graduates of your university, the "best" prospective employee is unknown to the organization. Also, in introducing a new product, proposing a tax law change to boost employment, drilling an oil well, and so on, the outcomes are always uncertain.

Statistics can often aid management in reducing this uncertainty. This is accomplished through the use of one or the other, or both, of the purposes of statistics. That is, statistics is divided according to its two major purposes: *describing* the major characteristics of a large mass of data and *inferring* something about a large mass of data from a smaller sample drawn from that mass. One methodology summarizes all of the data; the other reasons from a small set of the data to the larger total.

Descriptive statistics uses such measures as the mean, median, mode, range, variance, standard deviation, and such graphical devices as the bar chart and the histogram. When an entire population (a complete set of objects or entities with a common characteristic of interest) of data is summarized by computing such measures as the mean and the variance of a single characteristic, the measure is referred to as a *parameter* of that population. For example, if the population of interest is all female freshmen at your university and all of their ages were used to compute an arithmetic average of 19.2 years, this measure is called a parameter of that population.

Inferential statistics also uses means and variances, but in a different manner. The objective of inferential statistics is to infer the value of a population parameter through the study of a small sample (a portion of a population) from that population. For example, a random sample of 30 freshmen females could produce the information that there is 90 percent certainty that the average age of all freshmen women is between 18.9 and 19.3 years. We do not have as much information as if we had used the entire population, but then we did not have to spend the time to find and determine the age of each member of the population either.

Before considering the logic behind inferential statistics, let us define the primary measures of central tendency and dispersion used in both descriptive and inferential statistics.

MEASURES OF CENTRAL TENDENCY

The central tendency of a group of data represents the average, middle, or "normal" value of the data. The most frequently used measures of central tendency are the *mean*, the *median*, and the *mode*.

The mean of a population of values was given earlier as

$$\mu = \sum_{i=1}^{N} \frac{X_i}{N}$$

where

μ = the mean (μ pronounced mu)
X_i = the value of the ith data item
N = the number of data items in the population

The mean of a *sample* of items from a population is given by

$$\overline{X} = \sum_{i=1}^{n} \frac{X_i}{n}$$

where

X = the sample mean (pronounced $\overline{X}$ bar)
X_i = the value of the ith data item in the sample
n = the number of data items selected in the sample

The *median* is the middle value of a population of data (or sample) where the data is ordered by value. That is, in the following data set

3, 2, 9, 6, 1, 5, 7, 3, 4

4 is the median since (as you can see when we order the data)

1, 2, 3, 3, 4, 5, 6, 7, 9

50 percent of the data values are above 4 and 50 percent below 4. If there are an even number of data items, then the mean of the middle two is the median. For example, if there had also been an 8 in the above data set, the median would be 4.5 [(4+5)/2].

The *mode* of a population (or sample) of data items is the value that most frequently occurs. In the above data set, 3 is the mode of the set. A distribution can have more than one mode if there are two or more values that appear with equal frequency.

MEASURES OF DISPERSION

Dispersion refers to the scatter around the mean of a distribution of values. Three measures of dispersion are the range, the variance, and the standard deviation.

The *range* is the difference between the highest and the lowest value in the data set, that is, $X_{\text{high}} - X_{\text{low}}$.

The *variance of a population* of items is given by

$$\sigma^2 = \sum_{i=1}^{N} \frac{(X_i - \mu)^2}{N}$$

where

σ^2 = the population variance (pronounced sigma squared)

The *variance of a sample* of items is given by

$$S^2 = \sum_{i=1}^{n} \frac{(X_i - \overline{X})^2}{n}$$

where

S^2 = the sample variance.

The *standard deviation* is simply the square root of the variance. That is,

$$\sigma = \sqrt{\sum_{i=1}^{N} \frac{(X_i - \mu)^2}{N}}$$

and

$$S = \sqrt{\sum_{i=1}^{n} \frac{(X_i - \overline{X})^2}{n}}$$

σ and S are the population and sample standard deviations, respectively.

INFERENTIAL STATISTICS

A basis of inferential statistics is the *interval estimate.* Whenever we infer from partial data to an entire population, we are doing so with some uncertainty in our inference. Specifying an interval estimate (e.g., the average weight is between 10 and 12 pounds) rather than a *point estimate* (e.g., the average weight is 11.3 pounds) simply helps to relate that uncertainty. The interval estimate is not as *precise* as the point estimate.

Inferential statistics uses probability samples where the chance of selection of each item is known. A random sample is one in which each item in the population has an equal chance of selection.

The procedure used to estimate a population mean from a sample is to

1. Select a sample of size n from the population.
2. Compute $\overline{X}$ the mean and S the standard deviation.
3. Compute the precision of the estimate (i.e., the $\pm$ limits around $\overline{X}$ within which the mean μ is believed to exist).

Steps 1 and 2 are straightforward, relying on the equations we have presented in earlier sections. Step 3 deserves elaboration.

The precision of an estimate for a population parameter depends on two things: the standard deviation of the *sampling distribution,* and the confidence you desire to have in the final estimate. Two statistical laws provide the logic behind step 3.

First, the law of large numbers states that as the size of a sample increases toward infinity, the difference between the estimate of the mean and the true population mean tends toward zero. For practical purposes, a sample of size 30 is assumed to be "large enough" for the sample estimate to be a good estimate of the population mean.

Second, the central limit theorem states that if all possible samples of size n were taken from a population with any distribution, the distribution of the means of those samples would be normally distributed with a mean equal to the population mean and a standard deviation equal to the standard deviation of the population divided by the square root of the sample size. That is, if we took all of the samples of size 100 from the population shown in Figure B1, the sampling distribution would be as shown in Figure B2. The logic behind step 3 is that

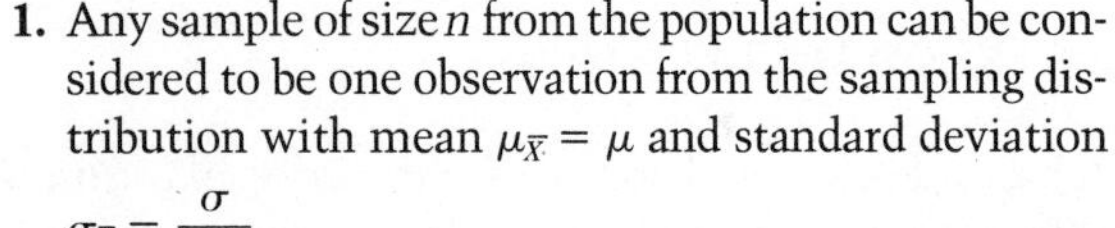

1. Any sample of size n from the population can be considered to be one observation from the sampling distribution with mean $\mu_{\bar{X}} = \mu$ and standard deviation $\sigma_{\bar{X}} = \dfrac{\sigma}{\sqrt{n}}$.

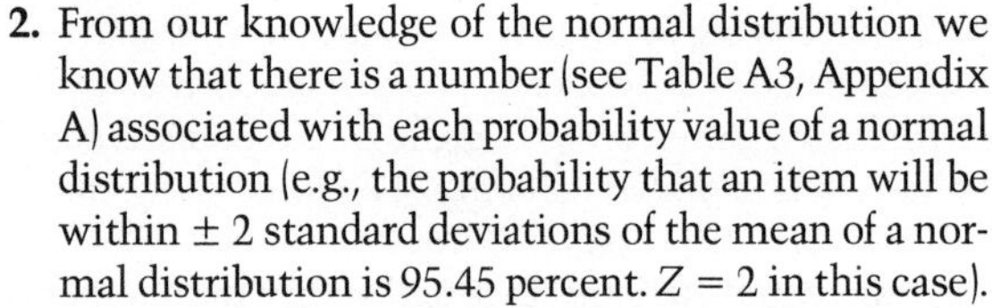

2. From our knowledge of the normal distribution we know that there is a number (see Table A3, Appendix A) associated with each probability value of a normal distribution (e.g., the probability that an item will be within ± 2 standard deviations of the mean of a normal distribution is 95.45 percent. $Z = 2$ in this case).

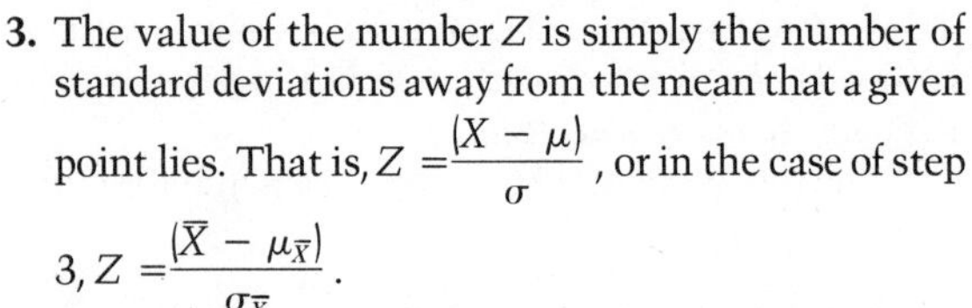

3. The value of the number Z is simply the number of standard deviations away from the mean that a given point lies. That is, $Z = \dfrac{(X - \mu)}{\sigma}$, or in the case of step 3, $Z = \dfrac{(\bar{X} - \mu_{\bar{X}})}{\sigma_{\bar{X}}}$.
4. The precision of a sample estimate is given by $Z\sigma_{\bar{X}}$.
5. The interval estimate is given by the point estimate $\bar{X}$ plus or minus the precision, or $\bar{X} \pm Z\sigma_X$.

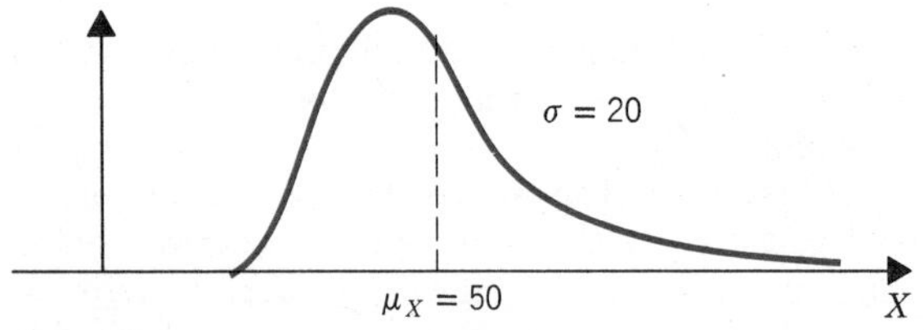

Figure B1 Population distribution.

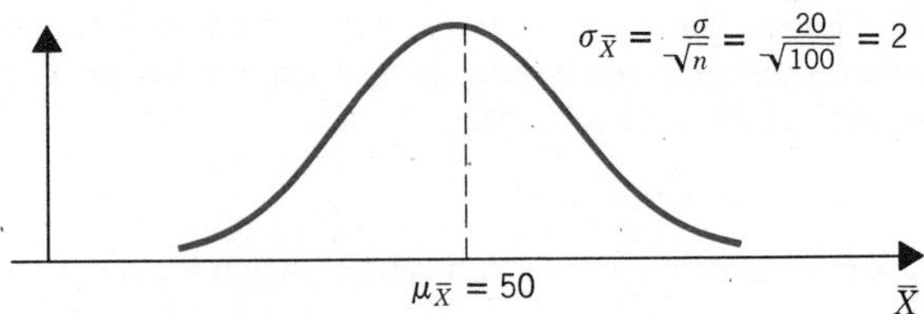

Figure B2 Sampling distribution.

In the previous example shown in Figures B1 and B2, suppose that the sample estimate $\bar{X}$ was 306 and the population standard deviation σ was 20. Also, suppose that the desired confidence was 90 percent. Since the associated Z value is 1.645, the interval estimate for μ is

$$306 \pm 1.645\left(\frac{20}{\sqrt{100}}\right)$$

or

$$306 \pm 3.29 \quad \text{or} \quad 302.71 \text{ to } 309.29$$

This interval estimate of the population mean is based solely upon information derived from a sample and states that the estimator is 90 percent confident that the true mean is between 302.71 and 309.29. There are numerous other sampling methods and other parameters that can be estimated; the student is referred to one of the references for further discussion.

REFERENCES

Boot, John C. G., and Edwin B. Cox, *Statistical Analysis for Managerial Decisions,* New York: McGraw Hill, 1974.

Dixon, W. J., and F. J. Massey, Jr., *Introduction to Statistical Analysis,* 3rd ed., New York: McGraw Hill, 1969.

Parsons, Robert, *Statistical Analysis: A Decision-Making Approach,* New York: Harper & Row, 1974.

Schlaifer, R., *Introduction to Statistics for Business Decisions,* New York: McGraw Hill, 1961.

Appendix C

Review Test Answers

	Chapter																		
Question	**1**	**2**	**3**	**4**	**5**	**6**	**7**	**8**	**9**	**10**	**11**	**12**	**13**	**14**	**15**	**16**	**17**	**18**	**19**
1	T	F	F	T	F	F	T	T	T	T	T	F	F	T	F	F	F	T	F
2	T	F	T	F	F	c	F	F	F	T	T	F	T	F	F	F	T	T	T
3	T	T	F	F	F	F	T	F	T	T	F	F	F	F	T	F	F	T	T
4	F	F	F	T	F	T	F	F	F	T	F	F	F	F	T	F	T	T	F
5	F	F	F	T	T	T	F	F	F	F	T	T	F	F	T	F	T	F	T
6	T	F	T	F	T	F	F	T	F	T	F	F	F	T	T	F	T	F	F
7	F	F	F	T	T	T	T	F	T	T	T	T	F	T	T	T	T	T	T
8	T	F	F	c	T	T	T	F	F	T	F	T	F	T	F	T	T	F	T
9	T	F	F	F	T	T	F	T	F		F	T	F	T	T	T	T	T	F
10	F	T	F	T	F	F	F	T	T			F	T	T	F	T	T	T	T
11	F	T	F	T	T	T	T	T	F			T	T	F	F	T	F	T	F
12	T		T	T	F	T	T	F	T			T	F	T	F	T	T	F	F
13	F		F	b		T	F	T	F			T	T	F	T	F	T	F	T
14	F		F	T		F	F	F	T			F		T		T	F		F
15	F			T			F	T	T			T				F	F		
16	T						T	T	T			F				F	T		
17							F	F	F			F							
18							T	T	F			F							
19							T	T	F			T							
20							T	F	F			F							
21							T	F	F										
22							F	T	T										
23							T	F	F										
24							T		T										
25							T		T										
26							F		T										
27							F		F										
28							T		T										

Appendix D

Glossary

ABC (80-20) categorization of elements into three levels of importance.
Acceptable Quality Level (AQL) that percent defective that corresponds to the producer's risk.
Activity Chart a time-scaled chart showing the activity of an operator and his or her equipment.
Aggregate combined into one measure.
ALDEP automated layout design. Program for layout planning.
Algorithm a set of logical steps that lead to a solution.
Allowance a proportion of normal time allowed for fatigue, maintenance, etc.
Analogue simulation through another system or process.
Annuity a fixed sum of payments over a set of years.
Anthropometric human body measurements.
Assembly Chart a chart showing how parts go together and in what order.
Assignment Method a specialized type of linear program particulary suitable for allocation on a one-to-one basis.
A/R accounts receivable.
Attributes nonmeasurable characteristics such as number of defects.
Automation replacing human sensing with machines.

Backordering ordering an item for a customer when a shortage has occurred.
Balance Delay 1.0-efficiency.
Balanced Line a production line whose task times in each station conform to the overall cycle time.
Balking not joining the queue.
BASIC a computer language.
Bill of Materials the list of materials.
Binary the 0, 1 number system used by a computer.
Block Control a control system for batch production.
Brainstorming a process for improving creativity by building new ideas on previous thoughts without evaluation.
Breakeven the point of no profit nor loss beyond which a profit will accrue.
Buffer safety amount.

Canned existing, available.
Capital Intensive large investment in machinery and equipment as opposed to labor.
Causal identifying events which cause other events.
Chain of Command the line of authority.
Challenger a new item that can do a task economically.

Chase Demand a policy of producing only the amount demanded in each period.
Chronocyclegraph time exposure of hand motions.
COBOL a computer language.
Comfort Zone a temperature-humidity zone comfortable to humans.
Comparator an element that compares actual performance to expected.
Compile convert into computer code
COMSOAL a computerized technique for line balancing.
Constraint limitation or restriction on actions.
Consumer's Risk the chance that a bad lot will be accepted.
Containerization use of standard-sized containers for ease in transporting.
Contingency Theory a management theory that relates the situation to the proper decision.
Control Limit the boundary on a control chart beyond which variation is considered to be assignable.
CORELAP computerized relationship layout planning.
Corrective Maintenance repairing an item when it fails.
Correlation the amount of relationship between two variables.
COVERT *C* over *T* priority rule.
CPM critical path method for project scheduling and control.
CPU central processing unit.
CRAFT computerized relative allocation of facilities technique for layout planning.
Crashing expediting a project activity.
Criteria measures of performance.
Critical if delayed, it will delay the project.
Critical Ratio a method to determine what item to next run on a facility.
CRP capacity requirements planning; also, cash requirements planning.
CRT cathode ray tube.
Cycle Time the uniform time that output comes out of the facility.
Cyclic a long term variation about the trend.
Cycling returning to the queue after service.

dB decibels of noise.
Dead Load File the file of jobs to be done that are not yet dispatched.
Decentralization delegation of authority.
Decision Tree a set of nodes and branches representing a decision or chance situation.
Decouple disengage, isolate.
Defender an old item that does a task.
Delphi a special form of nominal group analysis.
Design Freezing that point in the design process where the production process is decided upon.
Deviation a difference between two points.
Dispatching releasing work orders.
Division of Labor specialization to increase efficiency.
DOLT demand over lead time.
Double-Declining Balance a depreciation method.
DS Dynamic Slack Priority rule.
Dummy not real but shows precedence.
Duty Tours extra long work shifts.

EAM Electric Accounting Machine.
Econometric a quantitative approach used in Economics.
Economies of Scale the reduction in unit cost with increasing size.
EDP Electronic Data Processing.
Effectiveness ratio of actual to potential or desired attainment.
Effector an element that takes action to modify a system.
Efficiency output per unit input.
ELS economic lot size for least cost production runs.
EOQ economic order quantity for least cost purchases.
Ergonomics the study of work.
Expectancy Theory a motivation theory based on the worker's anticipated results.
Expected Value the average or mean.
Expediting rushing a job through operations.
Exploding detailing each part of a system so its relationship to the other parts can be seen.
Exponential Smoothing weighting a set of data with exponentially decreasing coefficients.

FCFS first come, first served priority rule.
Feedback information returned to an effector for control purposes.
Firm Order an actual customer order.
Fixed Position large production operations that are usually treated as projects.
Flow Process Chart (see **Operations Process Chart**).
Flow Shop a continuous production operation.
FORTRAN a computer language.

Gantt Chart a chart with time along the horizontal axis used to display the status of multiple jobs, machines, etc.
Generic generalizable to all such functions.
Grapevine the informal communication channel.

Heuristic a logically or experimentally derived procedure or rule of thumb.
Hierarchy consisting of a set of ordered levels.
Holistic considering all of the effects of each part on the whole.
Hot Jobs rush jobs.
Hygiene Factor (see **Two-factor Theory**).

IDP Integrated Data Processing.
Incremental Analysis making small changes in each direction to ascertain the effect.
Index Method an approach for allocating jobs to work centers.
Infant Mortality early, premature failures.
Infinite Loading adding work to a resource without regard for its capacity.
Interface the region where two elements or functions meet.
Intermittent in a stop and go fashion as with customized work.
Internal Rate of Return the rate of interest that makes a future or past return worth the present value.
Iterative repetitive, with an improvement each cycle.

Job Enlargement the addition of task variety to a job to reduce boredom.
Job Enrichment the addition of responsibility to a job to reduce boredom.

Job Shop an intermittent production operation.
Jockeying moving to another queue.
Johnson's Rule a technique for sequencing jobs.

Key Job a job that sets the pay for other jobs.

Lead Time the delay in obtaining something.
Lessee one who leases.
Level Production a policy of producing the same amount.
Level Zero final products.
Life Cycle a generalized, four-stage life model.
Line the workers who produce the output.
Linear straight line.
Linear Decision Rule (LDR) a solution approach to the aggregate scheduling problem that approximates costs with quadratic functions.
Load Control a control system for careful scheduling of bottleneck resources to maximize their utilization.
Load Matrix a matrix showing the work between elements.
Logistics supplying and maintaining material resources.
Lot Sizing determining production lot size.
Lot Tolerance Percentage Defective (LTPD) that percent defective corresponding to the consumer's risk.

MTM methods time measurement for constructing time standards for jobs.
MAD the mean absolute deviation equal to $\Sigma \mid x - \overline{x} \mid /n$.
Maintainability designing equipment to be easily kept in operating condition.
Maintenance Factors (see **Two-factor Theory**).
MALB a computerized technique for line balancing.
Management Coefficients an aggregate scheduling approach that imitates manager's behavior.
Man-Machine Chart (see **Activity Chart**).
Margin the increase or decrease from one more unit.
Master Schedule the actual production schedule for items.
Matrix Organization an organization structure with two superiors per worker.
Mechanization replacing human labor with machines.
Memomotion use of a slow speed camera akin to "time lapse" photography.
MICR magnetic ink character recognition.
Microchronometer a high speed clock.
MIS management information system.
Mode common method; most common value.
Modularization using standardized components in different combinations to achieve variety in outputs.
Monitor sample or tap performance.
Monte Carlo a simulation process using random numbers.
Mortality Curve a curve on a graph showing the number still alive or the number dead.
Motion Study analyzing the motions involved in a job in order to simplify and improve it.
MRP material requirements planning for dependent demand inventory.

Multiple Sampling using more than a single sample in order to reduce sampling costs.
Murphy's Law "What can go wrong, will go wrong."

Need Hierarchy Maslow's theory of need levels.
Net Change calculating only the effect of changes on the master schedule.
Net Requirement gross requirement less-on hand stock.
Nominal Group a group in name only, which may not meet face to face.
Normal Time the time an average worker takes when performing normally.
Numerical Control (NC) machine processing by coded numerical instructions.

Objective Function the criterion in a programming problem.
OCR optical character recognition.
On-Line connected directly to the computer.
Open-Loop no feedback control is used.
Operating Characteristic the relationship between percent defective and probability of acceptance.
Operations Process Chart a chart showing part specifications and production requirements and times.
Organizational Fit the matching against the characteristics of the organization.
OSHA Occupational Safety and Health Act.
Output Mix the proportion of items output in each category.

Paced Line a production line where every item must be completed in the same amount of time.
Pallet a platform for stacking materials.
Parent Item (see **Level Zero**).
Part-Period Balancing a method for lot sizing which attempts to balance holding and setup costs.
Payback a method of evaluating projects.
Performance Rating a factor in work measurement indicating how fast the worker performed in comparison to an average worker.
PERT program evaluation review technique for project scheduling and control.
PICS IBM's Production-Inventory Control System.
Piggyback truckload trailers hauled on railroad flatcars.
Pipelining sending materials through a pipe.
PL1 a computer language.
POS point of sale terminal.
PPBS program planning budgeting system.
Precedence the order in which tasks must be completed.
Present Value the worth today of something in the future or past.
Preventive Control controlling by anticipation rather than by feedback.
Preventive Maintenance repairing an item before it fails.
Priority Rules policies designed to give good sequences.
Producer's Risk the chance that a good lot will be rejected.
Product Tree the detailing of assemblies and subassemblies for parent items.
Productivity output per worker-hour.
Programming formulating and/or solving a problem by use of an algorithm.

Quadratic of second degree.
Qualitative not defined by numbers (frequently subjective).
Queue waiting line.

R & D research and development.
RAND random priority rule.
Random unpredictable, occurring by chance.
Random Number a number occurring purely by chance.
Random Sample a sample in which every element has an equal chance of being selected.
Regeneration recalculating the entire master schedule on a regular basis.
Regression a mathematical equation fit to a set of data.
Reliability the chance that an item will work over a given period of time.
Reneging leaving the queue.
Representative Number a number corresponding to a point in a distribution.
Route Sheet a chart describing each operation, the responsible department, the equipment needed, and the setup and running times.
Routing finding a best route between stops.

Safety Stock inventory stock to protect against a shortage.
Satisfice choosing a satisfactory action rather than an optimum one.
Scanlon Plan a group incentive plan.
Seasonal a regular variation during the period.
Self-Actualization fulfillment.
Sequencing determining the best sequence for work orders.
Service Level fraction of time demand can be filled from stock.
Setup the process of preparing for an action.
Shrink Wrap a plastic film for holding and protecting pallet loads.
Simplification attempting to eliminate portions of elements.
Simulation an imitation of reality with a model.
Simo Chart a time-scaled chart showing the simultaneous activities of each of a worker's hands.
Slack unutilized.
Slurry a liquified mixture.
Smoothing Constant alpha, a value between 0 and 1 which weights the importance of the last datum in exponential smoothing.
Snap-Back Timing resetting the stopwatch to zero after each work element is measured.
Software computer programs.
Sole Source using only one supplier.
SOT shortest operation time priority rule.
Span of Control the number of workers supervised.
SS static slack priority rule.
Staff the workers who support the line workers.
Staging Areas places for accumulating materials and resources around a fixed position project.
Standard Time normal time plus allowances.
Standardization making every output or element the same so as to improve efficiency and reduce costs.

Stockout running out of material, a shortage.
Stretched-S (see **Life Cycle**).
Suboptimize to optimize one part of a system but not, perhaps, the entire system.
Sum-of-Year's Digits a depreciation method.
Sunk Cost a past cost that cannot be recovered.
Surrogate an element used in place of another.
SYMAP a computer printed symbol map.
Synergism parts working together to form more than their independent sum.
Synthesis putting together or combining.

Tactical midlevel operations, not strategic or global which is typically a policy level.
Therblig a small element of time.
Throughput Time the amount of time to go through an operation.
Time-Phasing listing the actions to be taken at the times that are required when considering their lead times.
Time Study analyzing a job to determine performance standards for it.
TMU time measurement units of .00001 hours.
TPOP time phased order points for statistical inventory control.
Transient not yet in steady state motion.
Transportation Method a special type of linear program particularly useful in analyzing distribution problems.
Trend the average long run change.
Two-Bin a simple perceptual inventory system based on TPOP.
Two-Factor Theory Herzberg's concept of dissatisfying ("maintenance" or "hygiene") job factors.

Unit Load combining items into one standard size.
Unitization applying the unit load principle.
UPC Universal Product Code to identify the producer and product.

Value Analysis analyzing an output's function to find a less expensive alternative.
Variance deviation from standard.
Venn Diagram a pictorial schematic of event probabilities.
VOPI value of perfect information.

Weighted Average the average of a set of data where some elements are treated as more important than other elements.
Work Sampling a random sampling approach to time study.

ZBB Zero Base Budgeting.

Index